T0215840

Lecture Notes in Computer Science 10958

Commenced Publication in 1973
Founding and Former Series Editors:
Gerhard Goos, Juris Hartmanis, and Jan van Leeuwen

More information about this series at http://www.springer.com/series/7410

Aviv Zohar · Ittay Eyal
Vanessa Teague · Jeremy Clark
Andrea Bracciali · Federico Pintore
Massimiliano Sala (Eds.)

Financial Cryptography and Data Security

FC 2018 International Workshops
BITCOIN, VOTING, and WTSC
Nieuwpoort, Curaçao, March 2, 2018
Revised Selected Papers

 Springer

Editors
Aviv Zohar
Hebrew University
Jerusalem, Israel

Ittay Eyal
Technion – Israel Institute of Technology
Haifa, Israel

Vanessa Teague (iD)
University of Melbourne
Parkville, VIC, Australia

Jeremy Clark
Concordia University
Beaconsfield, QC, Canada

Andrea Bracciali (iD)
Computer Science and Mathematics
Stirling University
Stirling, UK

Federico Pintore (iD)
Mathematical Institute
University of Oxford
Oxford, UK

Massimiliano Sala (iD)
Department of Mathematics
University of Trento
Trento, Italy

ISSN 0302-9743   ISSN 1611-3349 (electronic)
Lecture Notes in Computer Science
ISBN 978-3-662-58819-2   ISBN 978-3-662-58820-8 (eBook)
https://doi.org/10.1007/978-3-662-58820-8

Library of Congress Control Number: 2019932182

LNCS Sublibrary: SL4 – Security and Cryptology

This Springer imprint is published by the registered company Springer-Verlag GmbH, DE
part of Springer Nature
The registered company address is: Heidelberger Platz 3, 14197 Berlin, Germany

BITCOIN 2018: 5th Workshop on Bitcoin and Blockchain Research

The year leading to the Bitcoin 2018 workshop witnessed a continuing increase in research on the Bitcoin protocols and on many related blockchain systems. The workshop, along with its parent conference FC, continued its tradition of providing a venue for some of the leading results in the field. Even as many alternative workshops and conferences have begun to accept and attract research on blockchains, the Bitcoin workshop remains the prominent venue for such work. The workshop received a large number of submissions: A total of 27 papers were submitted for review. Of these, a selection of 11 papers (nine full papers and two short papers) were accepted after review by the Program Committee and ten chose to be included in the proceedings. A single paper deferred from BITCOIN 2017 is also included in these proceedings.

Topics covered in the workshop provide a wide coverage of both theoretical and practical aspects of cryptocurrencies and included: economically driven attacks on cryptocurrencies, as well as non-economic extrinsically motivated attacks, an analysis of the Ponzi scheme ecosystem, approaches to cryptocurrency fee systems, topology inference in the Bitcoin network, a protocol for securely setting the public parameters of zk-SNARKs, discussions of cryptocurrency governance, analysis of the UTxO set, mechanisms to upgrade the rules of blockchains, and the use of blockchains for transparent certificate signing and revocation.

The workshop included a keynote talk By Dahlia Malkhi of VMWare Research that discussed blockchain protocols through the lens of classic research on distributed computing, and concluded with a joint panel session organized by the Workshop on Trusted Smart Contracts (WTSC 2018) and the Workshop on Advances in Secure Electronic Schemes (VOTING 2018).

We would like to thank the members of the Program Committee, whose work and remarks contributed greatly to the high quality of the workshop, as well as the chairs of WTSC 2018 and VOTING 2018 for their cooperation in organizing joint sessions during the workshops. We are also grateful for support by the FC chairs and BITCOIN 2017 co-chairs for their support and assistance during the organization of the workshop.

The Bitcoin Workshop is a victim of its own success: For next year, IFCA's governing board decided to merge the workshop with the main conference, a true sign that the topic of bitcoin and blockchain research has entered the mainstream, evidenced by the large number of submissions in the area sent to the conference and to the workshop together.

September 2018

Ittay Eyal
Aviv Zohar

Program Committee

Elli Androulaki	IBM Zürich, Switzerland
Foteini Baldimtsi	George Mason University, USA
Iddo Bentov	Cornell, USA
Alex Biryukov	University of Luxembourg, Luxembourg
Rainer Böhme	University of Innsbruck, Austria
Christian Cachin	IBM Research – Zurich, Switzerland
Srdjan Capkun	ETH Zürich, Switzerland
Melissa Chase	Microsoft Research, USA
Nicolas Christin	Carnegie Mellon University, USA
Jeremy Clark	Concordia University, Canada
Phil Daian	Cornell, USA
Christian Decker	Blockstream, USA
Tadge Dryja	MIT DCI, USA
Stefan Dziembowski	University of Warsaw, Poland
Juan Garay	Texas A&M University, USA
Christina Garman	Johns Hopkins University, USA
Arthur Gervais	ETH Zürich, Switzerland
Sharon Goldberg	Boston University, USA
Jens Grossklags	Technical University of Munich, Germany
Ethan Heilman	Boston University, USA
Garrick Hileman	University of Cambridge, UK
Aquinas Hobor	National University of Singapore, Singapore
Philipp Jovanovic	EPFL, Switzerland
Aniket Kate	Purdue University, USA
Aggelos Kiayias	University of Edinburgh, UK
Yoad Lewenberg	The Hebrew University, Israel
Joshua Lind	Imperial College London, UK
Patrick McCorry	University College London, UK
Ian Miers	Johns Hopkins University, USA
Tyler Moore	University of Tulsa, USA
Malte Möser	Princeton University, USA
Olaoluwa Osuntokun	Lightning Labs, USA
Michael Riabzev	Technion, Israel
Peter Rizun	Bitcoin Unlimited, Canada
Abhi Shelat	Northeastern University, USA
Yonatan Sompolinsky	The Hebrew University, Israel
Eran Tromer	Tel Aviv University, Israel
Luke Valenta	University of Pennsylvania, USA
Peter Van Valkenburgh	Coin Center, USA
Marco Vucolic	IBM Research – Zurich, Switzerland
Roger Wattenhofer	ETH Zürich, Switzerland
Nathan Wilcox	Zcash, USA
Fan Zhang	Cornell, USA

VOTING 2018: Third Workshop on Advances in Secure Electronic Voting Schemes

This year's Voting workshop covered a variety of different themes, all related to voting security and privacy.

Mebane and Bernhard presented the first careful analysis of investigations into recount methods and vote anomalies in Wisconsin and Michigan from the 2016 presidential election. They found a collection of fascinating results, noting severe problems in Detroit and the basic uselessness of machine recounts for detecting errors in the initial count.

Several authors presented advances in cryptographic techniques relevant to voting, including Strand's verifiable shuffle for a post-quantum cryptosystem (which also included an engaging explanation of why other attempts were invalid), Maini and Haenni's examination of efficient outsourcing of modular exponentiation, and Grontas and colleagues' new protocol that works, "Towards everlasting privacy and efficient coercion resistance in remote electronic voting."

Two papers presented careful formal models and analysis of existing components and protocols. Hauser and Haenni modeled a bulletin board based on broadcast channels with memory, while Smyth contributed a new analysis of the verifiability of the Helios Mixnet.

Although some have advocated the use of blockchains for remote Internet voting in government elections, the far more interesting questions concerned the use of cryptographic election verification to decision-making within online communities such as Etherium and other blockchains. We joined with the Bitcoin Workshop for a paper by Asouvi, Maller, and Meiklejohn entitled, "Egalitarian Society or Benevolent Dictatorship: The State of Cryptocurrency Governance," in which the authors explained that many cryptocurrencies are much less decentralized and democratic than they are assumed to be. Joseph Bonneau then followed up by quantifying the cost of "Hostile Blockchain Takeovers," which are surprisingly (and frighteningly) cheap.

We would like to thank all the authors, Program Committee members, external reviewers, and participants for their valuable contributions. We are also grateful to the FC chairs for their support and assistance during the organization of the workshop.

January 2019

Jeremy Clark
Vanessa Teague

Program Committee

Roberto Araujo	Universidade Federal do Pará, Brazil
Chris Culnane	The University of Melbourne, Australia
Jeremy Epstein	SRI International, USA
Aleksander Essex	Western University, Canada
David Galindo	University of Birmingham, UK
Kristian Gjøsteen	Norwegian University of Science and Technology, Norway
Rajeev Goré	The Australian National University, Australia
Reto Koenig	Berne University of Applied Sciences, Switzerland
Steve Kremer	Inria, France
Robert Krimmer	Tallinn University of Technology, Estonia
Olivier Pereira	Université catholique de Louvain, Belgium
Peter Roenne	University of Luxembourg, Luxembourg
Peter Y. A. Ryan	University of Luxembourg, Luxembourg
Steve Schneider	University of Surrey, USA
Carsten Schuermann	IT University of Copenhagen, Denmark
Philip Stark	University of California, Berkeley, USA
Poorvi Vora	The George Washington University, USA

External Reviewers

Vincenzo Iovino	University of Luxembourg
Marie-Laure Zollinger	University of Luxembourg

WTSC 2018: Second Workshop on Trusted Smart Contracts

These proceedings collect the papers accepted at the Second Workshop on Trusted Smart Contracts (WTSC 2018, http://fc18.ifca.ai/wtsc/) associated with the Financial Cryptography and Data Security 2018 (FC 2018) conference held in Curaçao in 2018 (February 26 to March 2, 2018).

WTSC 2018 focused on *smart contracts*, i.e., self-enforcing agreements in the form of executable programs, and other decentralized applications that are deployed to and run on top of (specialized) blockchains. These technologies introduce a novel programming framework and execution environment, which, together with the supporting blockchain technologies, carry unanswered and challenging research questions. Multidisciplinary and multifactorial aspects affect correctness, safety, privacy, authentication, efficiency, sustainability, resilience, and trust in smart contracts and decentralized applications.

WTSC 2018 aimed to address the scientific foundations of trusted smart contract engineering, i.e., the development of contracts that enjoy some verifiable "correctness" properties, and to discuss open problems, proposed solutions, and the vision on future developments among a research community that is growing around these themes and brings together users, practitioners, industry, institutions, and academia. This was reflected in the multidisciplinary Program Committee of this second edition of WTSC, comprising members from companies, universities, and research institutions from several countries worldwide, who kindly accepted to support the event. The association with FC 2018 provided an ideal context for our workshop to be run in. WTSC 2018 was partially supported by the University of Stirling, UK, the University of Trento, Italy, and FC 2018 IFCA-ICRA.

This second edition of WTSC 2018 received 13 submissions by about 30 authors, of which eight were accepted after peer review as full papers, and are collected in the present volume. These works analyzed the current state of the art and legal implications of smart contracts; addressed aspects of security and scalability; proposed protocols for sealed-bid auctions, for lending cryptocurrencies, for distribution and managements of digital certificates; and introduced logging schemes, models, and theorem-proving-based verification for smart contracts.

WTSC 2018 enjoyed Arthur Breitman (Tezos Founder) and Bud Mishra (NYU, USA) as keynote speakers. Arthur gave a talk on present and future perspectives in models for smart contracts, while Bud presented a model for decentralized drug development. WTSC 2018 also enjoyed collaboration with the other FC workshops, including a keynote talk by Dahlia Malkhi of VMWare Research on blockchain protocols from BITCOIN 2017, and a joint panel session organized together with VOTING 2018 on voting, governance, and decentralized democracy on blockchain.

The WTSC 2018 chairs would like to thank all those who supported the workshop for their valuable contributions: authors, Program Committee members and reviewers, and participants. WTSC 2018 also enjoyed the support of IFCA, FC 2018, and Ray Hirschfeld in the organization of the event.

January 2019

Andrea Bracciali
Federico Pintore
Massimiliano Sala

Program Committee

Marcella Atzori	UCL, UK/IFIN, Italy
Daniel Augot	Inria, France
Massimo Bartoletti	University of Cagliari, Italy
Devraj Basu	Strathclyde University, UK
Alex Biryukov	University of Luxembourg, Luxembourg
Stefano Bistarelli	University of Perugia, Italy
Andrea Bracciali	University of Stirling, UK
Daniel Broby	Strathclyde University, UK
Bill Buchanan	Napier University, UK
Martin Chapman	King's College London, UK
Tiziana Cimoli	University of Cagliari, Italy
Nicola Dimitri	University of Siena, Italy
Stuart Fraser	Wallet.Services, UK
Neil Ghani	Strathclyde University, UK
Davide Grossi	Utrecht University, The Netherlands
Oliver Giudice	Banca d'Italia, Italy
Yoichi Hirai	Ethereum DEV UG, Germany
Ioannis Kounelis	Joint Research Centre, European Commission
Victoria Lemieux	The University of British Columbia, Canada
Loi Luu	National University of Singapore, Singapore
Carsten Maple	Warwick University, UK
Michele Marchesi	University of Cagliari, Italy
Fabio Martinelli	IIT-CNR, Italy
Peter McBurney	King's College London, UK
Neil McLaren	Avaloq, UK
Philippe Meyer	Avaloq, UK
Bud Mishra	NYU, USA
Carlos Molina-Jimenez	University of Cambridge, UK
Federico Pintore	University of Trento, Italy
Massimiliano Sala	University of Trento, Italy
Ilya Sergey	UCL, UK
Thomas Sibut-Pinote	Inria, France
Jason Teutsch	TrueBit Establishment, Liechtenstein
Roberto Tonelli	University of Cagliari, Italy
Luca Viganò	University of Verona, Italy
Philip Wadler	University of Edinburgh, UK
Santiago Zanella-Beguelin	Microsoft, UK

Contents

Advances in Secure Electronic Voting Schemes

Trusted Smart Contracts

Bitcoin and Blockchain Research

Smart Contracts for Bribing Miners

Patrick McCorry, Alexander Hicks$^{(\boxtimes)}$, and Sarah Meiklejohn

University College London, London, UK
{p.mccorry,alexander.hicks,s.meiklejohn}@ucl.ac.uk

Abstract. We present three smart contracts that allow a briber to fairly exchange bribes to miners who pursue a mining strategy benefiting the briber. The first contract, `CensorshipCon`, highlights that Ethereum's uncle block reward policy can directly subsidise the cost of bribing miners. The second contract, `HistoryRevisionCon`, rewards miners via an in-band payment for reversing transactions or enforcing a new state of another contract. The third contract, `GoldfingerCon`, rewards miners in one cryptocurrency for reducing the utility of another cryptocurrency. This work is motivated by the need to understand the extent to which smart contracts can impact the incentive mechanisms involved in Nakamoto-style consensus protocols.

1 Introduction

Cryptocurrencies such as Bitcoin and Ethereum have collectively achieved a market capitalisation of over \$600 bn in January 2018. The success of cryptocurrencies relies on an append-only public ledger called the blockchain, and on Nakamoto consensus, a mechanism to reward honest participants (miners) for updating the blockchain. The consensus protocol is designed with the idea of "one-cpu-one-vote" as miners compete to solve a computationally difficult cryptographic puzzle. The first miner to present a valid solution wins the authority to append his block containing a list of recent transactions to the blockchain. Thus, the security and reliability of the blockchain is dependent on the assumption that a majority of the network's computational power is honest. If not, an adversary is able to control the content of the blockchain.

Since the introduction of Bitcoin in 2009, the mining process has changed drastically, with advances in graphic processing units (GPUs), field-programmable gate arrays (FPGAs) and application-specific integrated circuits (ASICs) offering much greater performance than a single CPU. Thus, today's miners must invest in expensive hardware before competing meaningfully in the consensus protocol. Similarly, pooled mining allows a single appointed pool master to decide which transactions to include in a block and how to distribute any earned block rewards amongst a co-operative group of miners. Solutions such as P2Pool [28] and SmartPool [14] allow an algorithm to play the role of the pool master, but have not yet gained widespread use. The combination of these two factors has undeniably led to a decrease in the number of participants in the consensus protocol underlying Bitcoin. In fact, a panel session at Scaling

© International Financial Cryptography Association 2019
A. Zohar et al. (Eds.): FC 2018 Workshops, LNCS 10958, pp. 3–18, 2019.
https://doi.org/10.1007/978-3-662-58820-8_1

Bitcoin 2015 was made up of eight participants who together controlled 80% of the Bitcoin network's computational power [20].

Whilst it is assumed that miners will honestly follow the consensus protocol, the assumption that the honest mining strategy is the most rewarding has been criticised. Eyal and Sirer [9] proposed selfish-mining strategies that can be deployed by rational miners with at least 25% of the network's computational power to gain more rewards than they deserve. This work was extended by Sapirshtein et al. [22] and Nayak et al. [18]. Although selfish-mining strategies theoretically weaken the 51% honest mining assumption, there is no evidence that any miners are engaging in them in major deployed cryptocurrencies. This suggests that miners are indeed honest and will not deviate from the honest mining strategy. Yet mining is not always profitable[1] in the short-term [6] and in August 2017 miners have exhibited rational behaviour in order to boot short-term profit. For example some mining pools including ViaBTC mined either Bitcoin or Bitcoin cash depending on which cryptocurrency was more profitable in the short-term. On the other hand influential members of the Bitcoin community have also suggested that miners may be accepting out-of-band bribes to mine Bitcoin Cash [24].

This type of mining behaviour reflects a tragedy of the commons first identified by Bonneau [3]. Individually rational miners have an incentive to maximise their profit (i.e., accept bribes to mine an alternative fork), but collectively share a concern for the network's long-term health. Liao and Katz [13] extend the work of Bonneau by proposing "whale" transactions, which use anomalously large fees to bribe miners. A new whale transaction is authorised for every new block in the alternative fork in order to reward the bribed miners for their continuous support. While Bonneau concludes that bribery attacks should be considered when attempting to prove that a Nakamoto-style consensus protocol is incentive compatibility, so far bribery attacks have not been seen as practical by the wider community. Although the question of how to attack or disrupt a minority chain in the event of new Bitcoin forks is increasingly an active area of discussion [1,5,30]. In fact, the founder of the mining pool BTC.TOP (which held 13% of the network's computational power as of October 2017) stated in an interview:

> "We have prepared $100 million USD to kill the small fork of CoreCoin, no matter what proof of work algorithm, sha256 or scrypt or X11 or any other GPU algorithm. Show me your money. We very much welcome a CoreCoin change to POS." [19]

Looking beyond Bitcoin, it is important to consider whether the additional functionality provided by alternative cryptocurrencies can be used to enable new forms of bribery, and in particular whether a platform like Ethereum that supports smart contracts enables the automated (and thus fair) payment of bribes to miners who change their mining strategy. For pooled mining, Velner et al. [27] demonstrate a smart contract that rewards miners in a pool who

---

[1] A surge in the Bitcoin price this year made mining profitable in the short-term for "hobbyist miners" [21].

perform so-called block withholding attacks[2] and later provide the contract with a proof-of-stale-work. Teutsch et al. [25] show that a briber can set up a script puzzle that diverts the network's mining power, thus removing competition for the briber's mining power. They demonstrate that a briber with at least 38.2% of the network's hashrate can achieve a positive pay-off that also covers the cost of each script puzzle.

This paper proposes three new contracts that reward miners who provide evidence that their mining strategy has changed according to a briber's intention. Our bribery attacks differ to previously proposed contracts, in that they do not focus on disrupting mining pool protocols or attempt to divert miners from solving the network's puzzle. Instead, our contracts facilitate renting hardware by rewarding miners using an in-band bribe (i.e. coins within the cryptocurrency) or an out-of-band bribes (i.e. coins from another cryptocurrency).

Our three smart contracts are as follows:

- In Sect. 3, we propose `CensorshipCon`, which relies on Ethereum's block reward policy to subsidise a briber wanting full control over the blockchain's content. We provide an analysis to show that a briber with at least 25% of the network's computational power can maximise the subsidy while also earning a small profit.
- In Sect. 4, we propose `HistoryRevisionCon`, which rewards miners that reverse transactions and computations in the blockchain by mining an alternative fork. It is also the first history-revision bribery attack where the briber and bribee trust only the contract (and not each other).
- In Sect. 5, we propose and implement `GoldfingerCon`, which rewards miners who can prove their mining strategy has reduced the utility of another cryptocurrency. We provide a proof-of-concept implementation to evaluate the feasibility of our attack and demonstrate that accepting a bribe costs approximately $0.46.

2   Background

In this section we provide an overview of Bitcoin and Ethereum with a focus on the expressiveness of Bitcoin Script, Ethereum smart contracts, and the reward policies in each consensus protocol.

2.1   Bitcoin

Bitcoin [17] is a global public ledger, maintained by a distributed set of miners, that facilitates trading a single asset (bitcoins) in a publicly verifiable manner. All coins are exchanged using transactions that have a list of inputs (the source

---

[2] In such an attack, a miner sends only partial proofs-of-work to the pool master, discarding all full proofs-of-work. The miner is rewarded by the master for attempting to find a new block but does not contribute to the pool's income as new blocks are discarded.

of the coins) and outputs (the destination of the coins). A mechanism called Bitcoin Script is used to specify conditions that must be satisfied before the coins associated with a transaction output can be spent. The most popular script, *pay-to-pubkey-hash*, requires a digital signature from the corresponding Bitcoin address (i.e., the hash of a public key). Another example of a script is *pay-to-pubkey*, which requires a digital signature from the public key's corresponding private key.

All transactions are recorded on the ledger, also called a blockchain, which is replicated by the peer-to-peer network. In order to update the ledger with a list of recent transactions contained in a block, miners compete to solve a computationally difficult puzzle. The first miner to present a solution wins the right to append his block to the blockchain, and receives 12.5 bitcoins in addition to all transaction fees collected in the block. A block is expected to be found approximately every 10 min.

A Bitcoin block is made up of two components. The first component is the block header, which contains the previous block hash, a Merkle tree root committing to all transactions in this block, a nonce to support the proof-of-work puzzle, and a timestamp. The second component is a list of transactions, the first of which is called the coinbase and is used to distribute the block reward. If the block contains no new transactions, the Merkle tree root is replaced with the hash of the coinbase transaction.

2.2 Ethereum

Ethereum [29] was proposed to facilitate users writing, storing and executing expressive, but bounded programs (i.e. smart contracts) within the Ethereum Virtual Machine (EVM). This EVM alongside all storage and computation is replicated across the peer-to-peer network and the blockchain is responsible for storing transactions that authorise state transitions. If all transactions are re-executed by a new peer joining the network, then the peer will eventually discover the contract's most recent state. All computation and storage is measured in units of gas and this is purchased using Ethereum's native currency (i.e. ether) by the user when they are authorising a transaction. As of January 2018, the vast majority of contracts are written in Solidity and like Bitcoin, all users have an Ethereum account which is the hash of a public key (and the corresponding private key is used to sign transactions).

Ethereum has a Nakamoto-style consensus protocol that relies on a distributed set of miners and its blockchain is a variation of GHOST [23], which is a tree-based blockchain. GHOST introduced the concept of an uncle block, which is a competing block that failed to make it into the blockchain but has its block header included in a future block; we call this future block the *publisher block*. For example, consider the case in which there are two competing blocks at height i, b_A^i and b_B^i. If b_A^i is accepted into the blockchain, the block header for b_B^i can still be included in a future block $b_{publ}^{i+\delta}$, at which point we can call it an uncle block $b_{B,uncle}^i$. This new block type was proposed in GHOST to allow stale blocks to contribute towards the blockchain's overall weight, although uncle blocks in Ethereum did not contribute towards the blockchain's weight until the Byzantium upgrade in October 2017 [4]. This consensus rule was changed in response to an uncle block mining strategy proposed by Lerner [12] that could reward miners more coins than they deserve by exclusively mining uncle blocks.

The notable difference between GHOST and Ethereum's implementation is the uncle block reward policy. In Ethereum, a miner can include a maximum of two uncle blocks in a newly mined block and the miner receives a publisher reward of $c_{pub} = \frac{1}{32}c_{block}$ for each uncle block included, where c_{block} is the normal block reward. Once included in the blockchain, the uncle block's miner is sent an uncle block reward of $c_{uncle} = (1 - \frac{\delta}{8})c_{block}$, where δ is the distance (number of blocks) between the competing main block $b^i_{A,main}$ and the publisher block $b^{i+\delta}_{publ}$. As of January 2018, the full block reward is 3 ETH and the maximum distance permitted for an uncle block to be included in the blockchain is 6.

Finally, an Ethereum block header can be split into four sections. This includes the previous block hash, gas statistics to highlight the computations involved in this block, a solution to the memory-hard proof-of-work Ethash, and a list of Patricia trie roots for the uncle block headers, transactions, and the global state transaction. This is reflected in the size of an Ethereum block header, which is 480 bytes compared to Bitcoin's 80 bytes.

3   Subsidised Bribery

To set the scene, we consider the case of a briber, Alice, with less than a majority of Ethereum's computational power. Her goal is to control which transactions are accepted into the blockchain. Rather than purchasing or renting new hardware to achieve a majority, she decides to rent hashing power from other miners (which we collectively name Bob) by bribing them. An existing approach for miners to accept in-band bribes without trusting the briber involves whale transactions [13], but this requires Alice to pay the full cost.

Instead, we propose a smart contract that rewards Bob for intentionally mining uncle blocks. As a result, Ethereum's uncle block reward policy is used to directly subsidise bribes paid by Alice. In the best case, Bob is rewarded $\frac{7}{8}$ of the block reward c_{block} for mining an uncle block. If Bob can prove to Alice's smart contract that he mined an uncle block, then this contract will automatically send Bob an additional payout c_{payout}. This second payment covers the remaining fraction of the block reward c_{block} and includes an additional bonus c_{bribe} for accepting the bribe. As a result Bob will always earn more coins than mining honestly, and the uncle block reward subsidises bribes paid by Alice.

3.1   Censorship Contract

The contract CensorshipCon[3] rewards Bob for performing an uncle block mining strategy. Bob must withhold a new block until a competing block by Alice is accepted into the blockchain, only then publishing his block for inclusion as

---

[3] A partial implementation is available at [15].

an uncle block. He must then prove to `CensorshipCon` that his uncle block was included in the blockchain for the contract to send him the bribe. In the following we highlight how to initialise the contract and how to allow bribed miners to accept their subsidised bribe. Afterwards we provide an overview of Appendix A to highlight that the briber requires at least 25% of the network's computational power in order to maximise the subsidy.

Briber Assumption. For this contract we assume Alice includes all uncle blocks and transactions that pay Bob his bribe into the blockchain. We consider this a reasonable assumption as accepting these blocks/transactions maximises her subsidy and encourages Bob to pursue the uncle block mining strategy. Finally we assume that Alice has bribed a sufficient portion of miners for the attack to succeed such that all blocks in the blockchain are mined by her.

Contract Setup. Alice must set the network's block reward c_{block}, the bribe amount c_{bribe} and also deposit d coins into the deployed contract `CensorshipCon` before publicly advertising the bribe. This contract has a single function called `AcceptSubsidisedBribe()` that we describe below.

Accepting the Subsidised Bribe. Bob must perform the uncle block mining strategy in order to be eligible for the bribe. If he has mined a new block b_B^i, then he must withhold this block until Alice publishes a competing b_A^i and her block is accepted into the blockchain. Afterwards he can publish his block b_B^i to the network, which allows Alice to include it as an uncle block in one of her future blocks; this future block is the publisher block $b_{publ}^{i+\delta}$. Once his uncle block is accepted into the blockchain he must prove that he is entitled to the payout c_{payout}.

To prove this, Bob creates a transaction that invokes `AcceptSubsidisedBribe`. This function requires as input Bob's uncle block header $b_{B,uncle}^i$, Alice's competing block header $b_{A,main}^i$ and the publisher block $b_{publ}^{i+\delta}$.

Once invoked, the function verifies if Alice's competing block $b_{A,main}^i$ and the publisher block $b_{publ}^{i+\delta}$ are in the blockchain. This involves retrieving the most recent 256 block hashes B_{256},[4] hashing both block headers and checking if $H(b_{A,main}^i) \in B_{256}$ and $H(b_{publ}^{i+\delta}) \in B_{256}$. Next the contract checks if the publisher block $b_{publ}^{i+\delta}$ has indeed included Bob's uncle block $b_{B,uncle}^i$ and if the two competing blocks $b_{A,main}^i$ and $b_{B,uncle}^i$ extend the same block b^{i-1}.[5]

If the above verification is satisfied and Bob has not already received a bribe for $b_{B,uncle}^i$, the contract calculates his payout. To do this it first computes the number of blocks δ between $b_{A,main}^i$ and $b_{publ}^{i+\delta}$, as this is used to calculate Bob's

---

[4] The contract environment provides access via `block.blockhash(uint)` for the latest 256 blocks (except the current block).

[5] This is similar to how a proof-of-stale block is verified by Velner et al. [27].

uncle block reward $c_{uncle} = (1 - \frac{\delta}{8})c_{block}$. His uncle block reward is the subsidy provided by the network for the briber, and his final payout is calculated as $c_{payout} = c_{bribe} + c_{block} - c_{uncle}$. The contract then sends these coins to the miner's Ethereum account, as stored in $b^i_{B,uncle}$.

3.2   Lower-Bound on Briber's Hashrate

Appendix A contains an analysis of the computational power required by Alice to maximise the network's subsidy and an overview is presented here. Briefly, we begin by denoting m_A, m_B, and m_H as the network's hashrate shares controlled by Alice, Bob and remaining honest miners. Only Alice and the honest miners compete to create new blocks once Bob has decided to pursue an uncle block mining strategy. His computational power is considered in the network's difficulty calculation [4], but Alice only needs to control more computational power than the honest miners such that $m_A > m_H$ to control the blockchain. To maximise the subsidy she must also ensure that for every new block mined by her, Bob only has the computational power to mine up to two uncle blocks. This final requirement means she must have at least half of Bob's hash rate such that $m_A \geq \frac{1}{2}m_B$. If we combine both requirements then Alice's hashrate must be $m_A > \frac{1}{4}$ to ensure she can out-compete the honest miners and also include all blocks mined by Bob as uncle blocks.

We highlight that there is an issue with the lower bound of $m_A > \frac{1}{4}$ as the briber can potentially exclude all blocks mined by honest miners. As a result it is reasonable to assume that honest miners may defect and also pursue the uncle block mining strategy in order to accept her bribe. If this happens, then the requirement $m_A \geq \frac{1}{2}m_B$ may no longer hold as the bribed miners account for more than half of the network's hashrate such that $m_B > \frac{1}{2}$. As a result it is possible that three uncle blocks are created for every new block by Alice and unfortunately one block must be discarded due to the uncle block limit. In order to satisfy the goal of maximising the briber's subsidy we consider the scenario where miners will only accept the bribe if it is guaranteed that no uncle blocks are discard. This requires Alice's computational power to be $m_A \geq \frac{1}{2}(1 - m_A)$ and leads to a new lower bound of $m_A > \frac{1}{3}$, allowing any value $m_B \in [\frac{1}{3}, \frac{2}{3})$.

4   History Revision Bribery

The contract `HistoryRevisionCon`[6] extends the work of Bonneau [3] and Liao et al. [13], and allows Alice to reward miners for mining on a fork other than the current longest chain. She can also retroactively dictate the starting block for a new fork and also enforce an expressive forking condition. In the following example we use a double-spend transaction to change the balance of two accounts, A_2 and A_3, but in a manner similar to the "hard-fork oracle" outlined by McCorry et al. [16], the forking condition could also depend on other events such as a reversal of the infamous TheDAO theft [10].

---

[6] A partial implementation is available at [15].

Briber Assumptions. The briber is no longer involved in the attack after setting up the contract. For the subsidised bribe we also assume that all bribed miners will include the transactions from other miners. This is reasonable as the bribed miners are collectively working together to ensure the alternative fork becomes the longest (and heaviest) chain.

Contract Setup. Alice creates three accounts A_1, A_2, A_3, the first account A_1 creates the bribery contract, A_2 spends coins in the longest chain and A_3 receives the double-spent coins from A_2 in the alternative fork. She then publishes the transaction $T_{A_2,spend}$ that spends her coins from A_2; we denote the block that includes this transaction as b^i. Alice waits until the receiver considers $T_{A_2,spend}$ as confirmed in the blockchain.

Afterwards she publishes the double-spend transaction $T_{A_2,double}$ that sends all coins from A_2 to A_3 and the transaction $T_{A_1,fork}$ which will create the `HistoryRevisionContract` contract. Both transactions must be included in the first bribed block at height i by Bob before he can be rewarded a bribe. Of course the contract will check the balance of A_2, A_3 and that it was created in block i before rewarding any bribes.

Accepting the Bribe. An accept bribe transaction must be included in every new block and it calls the `AcceptBribe()` function. The `AcceptBribe()` function requires no inputs and invokes the contract to check that a bribe has not already been paid for this block before sending the full bribe c_{bribe} to the miner's Ethereum account.[7] If his block fails to be included in the blockchain, then he must wait until this block is included as an uncle block.

Accepting the Subsidised Bribe. Similarly to the mechanism presented in Sect. 3.1, Bob can call `AcceptSubsidisedBribe()` and be rewarded for mining an uncle block. If the number of uncle blocks remains low (e.g., two or fewer uncle blocks for every block in the blockchain), then the briber can maximise the subsidy and ensure all stale blocks mined are also rewarded.

5   Goldfinger Bribery

As proposed by Kroll et al. [11], a "Goldfinger attack" can be modeled as a game between an adversary who receives external utility from devaluing (or destroying) a currency and the network that aims to run/maintain the value of a currency. One approach for devaluing a cryptocurrency is to effectively reduce its usefulness such that there is no guarantee a transaction will be accepted (or remain confirmed) in the blockchain. This can be accomplished by performing significant blockchain re-organisations (such as reversing 10 or more blocks in the blockchain) [1] or mining consecutive empty blocks. We propose that a briber can use a smart contract-enabled blockchain to fairly reward miners for mining empty blocks in another cryptocurrency.

---

[7] This can be accessed in the contract environment as `block.coinbase`.

5.1   Goldfinger Contract

We present `GoldfingerCon`, the first contract to realise a Goldfinger-style attack. This contract rewards miners in a smart contract-enabled blockchain for reducing the utility of another cryptocurrency by mining empty blocks.[8] In the following we discuss how to set up the Goldfinger contract, how Bob can prove he mined an empty block to the contract, the technical hurdles for this attack and our proof of concept implementation.

Contract Setup. Alice creates `GoldfingerCon`, deposits d coins and must set the payout for each empty block as c_{bribe}. In order to activate the contract she must set the identification hash of the initial block $H(b_B^i)$ and all miners should begin mining empty blocks from $H(b_B^i)$ onwards. This contract is publicly announced to all miners in the victim cryptocurrency.

Accepting the Bribe. Bob must audit the code for `GoldfingerCon` to verify that the contract will reward him for mining empty blocks in the victim cryptocurrency. Once he has decided to pursue the Goldfinger attack, then every new block $b_{B,btc}^i$ he mines should only contain the coinbase transaction and he must wait for the block to achieve a sufficient depth in the blockchain. Next he must publish an accept bribe transaction $T_{B,accept}$ that includes the block header $b_{B,btc}^{i,*}$ and the corresponding coinbase transaction $T_{B,coinbase}^i$ in its payload.

This transaction calls the `AcceptBribe` function in `GoldfingerCon` and as a result the contract will verify whether $H(b_B^i)$ is an empty block before sending Bob his bribe. In order to verify that it is indeed an empty block, the contract checks that the identification hash of the coinbase transaction $H(T_{B,coinbase}^i)$ is stored in the block header's Merkle root field. Once the verification is complete, the contract extracts the public key PK_B from the coinbase transaction's output (assuming it is a *pay-to-pubkey* script), computes an Ethereum account B from PK_B and sends B the bribe c_{bribe}.

Validating and Propagating Empty Blocks. In order to verify that the chain of empty blocks represents the most computational weight it is important that `GoldfingerCon` has access to all known forks in the victim cryptocurrency. We recommend that block headers follow a strict pre-defined format to ensure they are valid for both the contract and the victim cryptocurrency. Finally it is also important for Alice to remain online and ensure all empty blocks are propagated throughout the victim cryptocurrency's network. Otherwise a cartel of miners could mine headers for the contract, but they are not used (or potentially be invalid) in the victim cryptocurrency network. Another option is to build an escape hatch into the contract which allows her to terminate the bribe if cheating is detected, but this may also undermine the contract's credibility.

---

[8] It is also possible to bribe miners for building an alternative fork by dictating that a block hash $H(b_B^i)$ cannot be in the blockchain.

Table 1. A breakdown of the gas and financial cost for submitting several existing Bitcoin blocks and accepting a bribe from `GoldfingerCon`.

Step	Purpose	Gas Cost	US$ Cost
1.	Create contract	3,505,654	4.21
2.	Submit block header 49,996 (checkpoint)	316,799	0.38
3.	Submit block header 50,000 (out of order)	276,663	0.33
4.	Submit block header 49,999 (out of order)	261,727	0.31
5.	Submit block header 49,998 (out of order)	261,727	0.31
6.	Submit block header 49,997 (in order)	314,017	0.38
7.	Organise orphan blocks	284,206	0.34
8.	Accept bribe for block 50,000	152,579	0.18

5.2   Proof-of-Concept Implementation

We have implemented `GoldfingerCon` [15] in Solidity (0.4.10) and performed experiments on an Ethereum private network in October 2017 (before the Byzantium update). Our implementation demonstrates the cost of maintaining the longest chain of block headers and parsing Bitcoin block headers and coinbase transactions. It does not, however, rigorously validate block headers or coinbase transactions according to the network's consensus rules as discussed in Sect. 5.1. In the following we present the cost of creating the contract, publishing five blocks in the reverse order, computing the current longest fork (i.e. a blockchain re-organisation within the contract) and accepting a single bribe.

Table 1 presents the gas and financial breakdown for each transaction, assuming 1 ETH is worth $300 (a reasonable estimate as of October 2017 [8]) and the gas price is 4 Gwei.[9] The first step involved creating the `GoldfingerCon` contract alongside setting the payout for each bribe and the contract's owner as the briber. The second step required the owner to set the starting block (i.e. the checkpoint) as Bitcoin block 49,996 and thus the contract will only send bribes for new empty blocks that extend this checkpoint.

The next series of steps (i.e. 2–6) involved an ad-hoc Ethereum account sending the contract four Bitcoin blocks 50,000 to 49,997 in the reverse order. This resulted in the contract recognising block 49,997 as the latest block in the blockchain. Step 7 notified the contract to evaluate the orphan blocks (i.e. blocks 49,998 to 50,000) and this resulted in the contract setting block 50,000 as the latest block in the blockchain. This demonstrates that handling small block re-organisations within an Ethereum contract can be gas-efficient.

Finally step 8 involves simulating a miner publishing the coinbase transaction for block 50,000 to accept their bribe. The contract verified that the identification hash of the coinbase transaction was stored in the Merkle tree root of block

---

[9] 1 gwei = 10^{-18} ether.

50, 000. The public key from the coinbase transaction output is then extracted[10] to construct an Ethereum address. The miner's bribe is sent to the constructed Ethereum address and the bribe for block 50, 000 is marked as claimed.

6   Discussion

Countering Goldfinger Attacks. Bonneau [3] identified that the intended victims of a Goldfinger attack could counter-bribe the miners in order to protect the blockchain's integrity, but he went further to argue that it is not desirable to rely on wealthy members of the community to protect Nakamoto-style consensus. Another counter-measure that is often suggested by the Bitcoin community is to change the proof-of-work algorithm in response to an attack [7] and effectively punish the miners for participating in the attack by making their mining hardware redundant. We highlight that this is only a viable option if there is not an another cryptocurrency with significant value that also relies on the same proof of work algorithm. Also, it is only a one-shot approach as the briber could then rent the next viable hardware (e.g., GPUs). In terms of a new proof-of-work algorithm it may be useful to select one that is not easily verified within a smart contract environment to hinder our smart contracts. As demonstrated by Luu et al. [14], however, this defence can be overcome.

Removing Asymmetrical Trust Assumption for History-Revision Bribery Attacks. The closest mechanism to our history-revision contract is whale transactions, where Alice includes large fees to entice miners to include her transactions, but these have asymmetrical trust assumptions. Briefly, if the bribed miners do not trust the briber, then the briber must sign a list of transactions in advance with incrementing time-locks (to ensure that only a single bribe accepted is included per block). On the other hand, if the briber does not trust the bribed miners, then to ensure that they do not collude and mine a fork without the briber's desired revision, the briber can publish a new whale transaction after every new block [13]. HistoryRevisionCon removes this asymmetry, as both the briber and bribed miners can trust only the contract.

Towards a 51% Collusion. All bribery attacks require a strategy that persuades the network's computational power to join the attack and accept this bribe. In CensorshipCon and GoldfingerCon, miners are rewarded for every uncle/empty block mined, whereas in HistoryRevisionCon miners are paid only if the attack is successful. One approach for persuading miners to accept this bribe is to provide a greater reward for miners that join the attack early, and a list of deadlines can be set to ensure that there is a proportional increase in bribed blocks over time. For example, GoldfingerCon may require 10% of all blocks to be empty by time t_1 and 20% by time t_2. The contract can terminate if a

---

[10] All early coinbase transactions (including block 50,000) used pay-to-pubkey bitcoin scripts.

deadline is missed. So far our contracts have assumed that a sufficient share of miners have joined the attack. We leave it as future work to devise reliable strategies for ramping up support amongst miners.

In-Band vs Out-of-Band Payments. Out-of-band payment for bribery attacks such as `GoldfingerCon`, script puzzles [25] and proof-of-stale blocks [27] are viable as the utility received by miners is external to the cryptocurrency which is being attacked. Bribery attacks that rely on in-band payments like whale transactions [13], `CensorshipCon`, `HistoryRevisionCon` can potentially be viewed as not practical due to their public nature undermining the bribed miner's reward. There have been a few circumstances such as TheDAO fork [10] where in-band bribery could potentially have been used to reward miners for mining an alternative fork. We do not claim that in-band bribery attacks are immediately feasible today, but this may change in the future as the political climate surrounding cryptocurrencies continues to evolve.

Impact on Nakamoto Consensus. Our contract `CensorshipCon` demonstrates how subtle changes to Ethereum's implementation of GHOST has directly enabled a subsidy for bribery attacks, whereas `GoldfingerCon` highlights that miners do not need to trust the briber when attacking the consensus protocol of another cryptocurrency. Bonneau [3] argued that bribery attacks are not recognised as a viable attack due to their public (and sometimes trusted) nature and this is reflected in the community as no new Nakamoto-style consensus protocol has considered bribery attacks in their threat model. We argue that with rise of smart contract-enabled blockchains, centralisation of mining hardware [26], politically motivated actors [19,24] and wealthy pseudonymous thieves [2,10], it appears that bribery-style attacks are indeed becoming increasingly viable. We thus also argue that new Nakamoto-style consensus protocols should consider bribery attacks when evaluating whether the protocol is incentive-compatible.

7   Conclusion

In this paper, we proposed three contracts to evaluate whether a smart contract-enabled blockchain can have an impact on Nakamoto consensus. Our contracts highlight that Ethereum's uncle block reward policy can be used to directly subsidise a bribery attack, that a briber can dictate the conditions that must be satisfied (i.e. reverse theft) when bribed miners mine an alternative fork and the feasibility of Goldfinger-style attacks that reward miners for reducing the utility of another cryptocurrency. Our contracts (including the work in [3,13,25,27]) are the first steps towards realising practical bribery strategies that overcome the inherent trust issue between a briber and bribee. This is achieved as all contracts self-enforce the bribery agreement and the fair exchange of coins.

Acknowledgements. Patrick McCorry and Sarah Meiklejohn are supported in part by EPSRC grant EP/N028104/1, and Alexander Hicks is supported in part by OneSpan (https://www.onespan.com/) and UCL through an EPSRC Research Studentship. We would like to thank Joseph Bonneau for discussions around bribery attacks, Ilya Sergey, Changyu Dong, and Abhiram Kothapalli for comments on early drafts of this paper, and Sergio Lerner and Adrian Eidelman for bringing to our attention that Ethereum's Byzantium upgrade changed the network's difficulty calculation.

A   Subsidy Analysis

This section is concerned with determining lower bounds on Alice's hash rate in order to both maximise the subsidy from Ethereum's uncle block reward policy and to provide her with full control over the blockchain. We find the lowest bound she requires is more than $\frac{1}{4}$ of the network's hashrate, but this does not allow all other miners to pursue the uncle block mining strategy and accept the bribe. This can be overcome if she has more than $\frac{1}{3}$ of the network's hashrate as this will allow all other miners to mine uncle blocks and for her to include every uncle block in the blockchain. In the following we present our assumptions for the subsidy analysis before presenting the subsidy value, whether a profit is possible for the briber and how to derive the two lower bounds.

Assumptions. We assume that miners do not perform selfish mining strategies and that Alice has control of the minimum hashrate required to execute the attack.

Lower Bounds on Hashrate. Keeping the same model, we denote m_A, m_B and m_H the portion of network's hashrate controlled by Alice, Bob and the remaining honest miners respectively. Alice's hashrate must satisfy two requirements before she out compete the honest miners and maintain the longest chain with only her blocks:

- Alice's hashrate must be at least half of the bribed miner's computational power such that $m_A \geq \frac{1}{2} m_B$.
- Alice's hashrate must be greater than the remaining honest miners on the network such that $m_A > m_H$.

The first requirement ensures Alice can include all new blocks published by Bob as uncle blocks. Recall she can only include up to two uncle blocks per block she published. The second requirement allows Alice to win against the remaining honest miners in creating blocks for the blockchain as she controls a majority portion of the effective hashrate (i.e. the network's hashrate attempting to mine main blocks which excludes the bribed miners). Putting these together gives a lower bound of $m_A > \frac{1}{4}$ on Alice's portion of the hashrate. This is enough for her to support Bob controlling $m_B = \frac{1}{2}$ of the hashrate, which ensures $m_A > m_H$.

The case above assumes that honest miners are not willing to accept the bribe which may be not be realistic as miners are economically motivation. In particular, honest miners may find themselves competing against Alice and if she controls a majority of the effective hashrate then all their blocks will be excluded. It is then necessary to revise our first requirement such that it now takes the form $m_A \geq \frac{1}{2}(1 - m_A)$. This allows Alice to support the inclusion of withheld blocks from all other miners (i.e. the remaining network's hashrate) as uncle blocks. Alice can then bribe the necessary portion of miners $m_B \geq \frac{1}{3}$ which satisfies the requirement $m_A \geq \frac{1}{2}m_B$ and allows $m_A > m_H$ to hold.

Subsidy and Expectation Values. Alice can maximise her subsidy by minimising the number of blocks δ it takes until a bribed block is included in the blockchain as an uncle block. Ideally, she should include uncle blocks in her next block. otherwise δ may range between 1 and 6 if an uncle is delayed entry.

Before highlighting the impact of this subsidy for Alice, recall that she also receives an additional publisher reward $c_{pub} = \frac{1}{32}c_{block}$ for each uncle block she includes. Hence for one uncle, Alice only has to pay Bob $c_{payout} > \frac{4\delta - 1}{32}c_{block}$ to guarantee him a higher payout than if he had won the full block reward. If she includes two uncle blocks, she has to pay $c_{payout} > \frac{4\delta - 1}{16}c_{block}$ to ensure both blocks have a higher payout.

As Alice receives a block reward for every block she mines, she can still profit from the reward while ensuring Bob receives a higher payout. If her payout to Bob is less than the block reward (i.e. $c_{payout} < c_{block}$), she will have earned more than she spent. The values of δ required for her to make a profit are then easily found by solving the inequality with the expressions for c_{payout} previously given. For example, if she only includes a single uncle in her block, then she is guaranteed a profit for any δ as the reward is sufficient to ensure Bob receives the full block reward c_{block} alongside an additional c_{bribe}. If she includes two uncle blocks, then she must be efficient as the δ for both blocks must be less than 4 on average in order to satisfy the condition. Of course this analysis is only concerned with the potential mining profit, and does not take into account the preliminary costs of gaining the required hashrate.

As previously mentioned, the payout c_{payout} should be sufficient for Bob to be guaranteed a higher reward than the block reward and giving him a clear incentive to accept bribes. If the attack is successful, Alice will control the effective majority of the network's hashrate and honest miners will see their expectation value decrease as their blocks are excluded from the blockchain. They will then be further incentivized to accept bribes.

References

1. Andresen, G.: Ways to enhance Post-fork withering of Core chain. RedditBTC, March 2017
2. Bloomberg: Ethereum Bandits Stole $225 Million This Year. Fortune, August 2017
3. Bonneau, J.: Why buy when you can rent? In: Clark, J., Meiklejohn, S., Ryan, P.Y.A., Wallach, D., Brenner, M., Rohloff, K. (eds.) FC 2016. LNCS, vol. 9604, pp. 19–26. Springer, Heidelberg (2016). https://doi.org/10.1007/978-3-662-53357-4_2
4. Buterin, V.: Change difficulty adjustment to target mean block time including uncles. Ethereum EIP Github Repository, October 2017
5. Dinkins, D.: If Hard Fork Happens, Chain Backed By Majority of Miners Will Likely Win. Cointelegraph, October 2017
6. Donnelly, J.: Winter is Coming: Bitcoin Mining for Heat (And Profit). CoinDesk, September 2016
7. Dorier, N.: Proof-of-Work update is not a threat to miners, it is a necessity for users. Medium, March 2017
8. ETHGasStation: Bribery Contracts. ETH Gas Station, October 2016
9. Eyal, I., Sirer, E.G.: Majority is not enough: bitcoin mining is vulnerable. In: Christin, N., Safavi-Naini, R. (eds.) FC 2014. LNCS, vol. 8437, pp. 436–454. Springer, Heidelberg (2014). https://doi.org/10.1007/978-3-662-45472-5_28
10. Hanson, R.: A $50 Million Hack Just Showed That the DAO Was All Too Human. Wired, June 2016
11. Kroll, J.A., Davey, I.C., Felten, E.W.: The economics of Bitcoin mining, or Bitcoin in the presence of adversaries. In: WEIS 2013 (2013)
12. Lerner, S.D.: Uncle Mining, an Ethereum Consensus Protocol Flaw. Bitslog blog, April 2016
13. Liao, K., Katz, J.: Incentivizing blockchain forks via whale transactions. In: Brenner, M., et al. (eds.) FC 2017. LNCS, vol. 10323, pp. 264–279. Springer, Cham (2017). https://doi.org/10.1007/978-3-319-70278-0_17
14. Luu, L., Velner, Y., Teutsch, J., Saxena, P.: Smart pool: practical decentralized pooled mining. IACR Cryptology ePrint Archive, 2017:19 (2017)
15. McCorry, P.: Bribery Contracts. GitHub, January 2017
16. McCorry, P., Heilman, E., Miller, A.: Atomically trading with Roger: gambling on the success of a hardfork. In: Garcia-Alfaro, J., Navarro-Arribas, G., Hartenstein, H., Herrera-Joancomartí, J. (eds.) ESORICS/DPM/CBT -2017. LNCS, vol. 10436, pp. 334–353. Springer, Cham (2017). https://doi.org/10.1007/978-3-319-67816-0_19
17. Nakamoto, S.: Bitcoin: a peer-to-peer electronic cash system (2008)
18. Nayak, K., Kumar, S., Miller, A., Shi, E.: Stubborn mining: generalizing selfish mining and combining with an eclipse attack. In: IEEE European Symposium on Security and Privacy (EuroS&P), pp. 305–320. IEEE (2016)
19. Quentson, A.: Bitcoin Market Needs Big Blocks. Says Founder of BTC.TOP Mining Pool, Cryptocoinsnews, February 2017
20. Redman, J.: The Scaling Bitcoin Workshop Hong Kong Wrap-Up. BitcoinCom-News, December 2015
21. Reutzel, B.: Bitcoin's Price Surge is Making Hobby Mining Profitable Again. Coin-Desk, July 2017
22. Sapirshtein, A., Sompolinsky, Y., Zohar, A.: Optimal selfish mining strategies in Bitcoin. In: Grossklags, J., Preneel, B. (eds.) FC 2016. LNCS, vol. 9603, pp. 515–532. Springer, Heidelberg (2017). https://doi.org/10.1007/978-3-662-54970-4_30

23. Sompolinsky, Y., Zohar, A.: Secure high-rate transaction processing in Bitcoin. In: Böhme, R., Okamoto, T. (eds.) FC 2015. LNCS, vol. 8975, pp. 507–527. Springer, Heidelberg (2015). https://doi.org/10.1007/978-3-662-47854-7_32

24. Song, J.: Why Miners Are Mining Bitcoin Cash - and Losing Money Doing It. CoinDesk, August 2017

25. Teutsch, J., Jain, S., Saxena, P.: When cryptocurrencies mine their own business. In: Grossklags, J., Preneel, B. (eds.) FC 2016. LNCS, vol. 9603, pp. 499–514. Springer, Heidelberg (2017). https://doi.org/10.1007/978-3-662-54970-4_29

26. Tuwiner, J.: Bitcoin Mining in China. Buy Bitcoin Worldwide, March 2017

27. Velner, Y., Teutsch, J., Luu, L.: Smart contracts make Bitcoin mining pools vulnerable. IACR Cryptology ePrint Archive, 2017:230 (2017)

28. Voight, F.: Wiki on P2Pool. Bitcoin Wiki, June 2011

29. Wood, G.: Ethereum: a secure decentralised generalised transaction ledger. Ethereum Project Yellow Paper, 151 (2014)

30. Zhuo'er, J.: [Ending the Soft/Hard Fork Debate] – A Safe Hard Fork is the same as a Soft Fork. Medium, October 2016

A Systematic Approach
to Cryptocurrency Fees

Alexander Chepurnoy[1,2]([envelope]), Vasily Kharin[3], and Dmitry Meshkov[1,2]

[1] Ergo Platform, Sestroretsk, Russia
[2] IOHK Research, Sestroretsk, Russia
{alex.chepurnoy,dmitry.meshkov}@iohk.io
[3] Helmholtz Institute Jena, Froebelstieg 3, 07743 Jena, Germany
v.kharin@protonmail.com

Abstract. This paper is devoted to the study of transaction fees in massively replicated open blockchain systems. In such systems, like Bitcoin, a snapshot of current state required for the validation of transactions is being held in the memory, which eventually becomes a scarce resource. Uncontrolled state growth can lead to security issues. We propose a modification of a transaction fee scheme based on how much additional space will be needed for the objects created as a result of transaction processing and for how long will they live in the state. We also work out the way to combine fees charged for different resources spent (bandwidth, random-access state memory, processor cycles) in a composite fee and demonstrate consistency of the approach by analyzing the statistics from Ethereum network. We show a possible implementation for state-related fee in a form of regular payments to miners.

1 Introduction

Bitcoin [16] was introduced in 2008 by Satoshi Nakamoto as a purely peer-to-peer version of electronic cash with a ledger written into blockchain data structure securely replicated by each network node. Security of the cryptocurrency relies on its mining process. If majority of miners are honest, then Bitcoin meets its security goals as formal analysis [10] shows. For the work done a miner is claiming a reward which consists of two parts. First, some constant number of bitcoins are created out of thin air according to a predefined and hard-coded token emission schedule. Second, a miner claims fees for all the transactions included into the block.

As shown in [7], constant block rewards are an important part of the Bitcoin protocol. Once a predetermined number of coins will enter the circulation and miners will be rewarded by transaction fees only, their rational behavior could be different from the default mining strategy. It is still an open question whether Bitcoin will meet its security goals in such circumstances, but at least number of orphaned blocks will increase making Bitcoin less friendly for regular users.

© International Financial Cryptography Association 2019
A. Zohar et al. (Eds.): FC 2018 Workshops, LNCS 10958, pp. 19–30, 2019.
https://doi.org/10.1007/978-3-662-58820-8_2

A transaction fee, which is set by a user during transaction creation, is useful to limit miners resource usage and prevent spam. In most cases a user pays a fee proportional to transaction size, limiting miners *network* utilization. A rational miner does not include all the valid transactions into blocks as, due to the increased chances of orphaning a block, the cost of adding transactions to a block could not be ignored [3,18]. As shown in [18], even in the absence of block size limit Bitcoin fee market is healthy and the miner's surplus is maximized at a finite size of a block. Thus miners are incentivized to produce blocks of a limited size, so only transactions providing enough value to a miner will be included in a block. The paper [18] provides a procedure to estimate transaction fee based on block propagation time.

Besides network utilization, transaction processing requires a miner to spend some *computational* resources. In Bitcoin the transactional language [4] is very limited, and a number of CPU cycles needed to process a transaction is strictly bounded, and corresponding computational costs are not included in the fee. In contrast, in cryptocurrencies supporting smart contract languages, such as Solidity [1] and Michelson [13], transaction processing may require a lot of computations, and corresponding costs are included in the transaction fee. Analysis of this fee component is done for concrete systems in [8,14], and is out of scope of this paper.

In this work we address the problem of miners *storage* resources utilization. A regular transaction in Bitcoin fully spends outputs from previous transactions, and also creates new outputs of user-defined values and protecting scripts. A node checks a transaction in Bitcoin by using a set of unspent outputs (UTXO). In other cryptocurrencies a representation of a *state* needed to validate and process an arbitrary transaction could be different (for example, in Ethereum [22] such structure is called the *world state* and fixed by the protocol). To process a transaction quickly, the state (or most accessed part of it) should reside in expensive random-access memory (RAM). Once it becomes too big to fit into RAM an attacker can perform denial-of-service attacks against cryptocurrency nodes. For example, during attacks on Ethereum in Autumn, 2016, an attacker added about 18 million accounts to the state (whose size was less than 1 million accounts before the attack) and then performed successful denial-of-service attacks against the nodes [20]. Similarly, in 2013 a denial-of-service attack against serialized transactions residing in a secondary storage (HDD or SSD) was discovered in Bitcoin [19].

In all the cryptocurrencies we are aware of, an element of the state once created lives potentially forever without paying anything for that. This leads to perpetually increasing state (e.g. the Bitcoin UTXO size [6]). Moreover, state may grow fast during spam attacks, for example, 15 million outputs were quickly put into the UTXO set during spam attacks against Bitcoin in July, 2015 [5], and most of these outputs are not spent yet. The paper [17] is proposing a technical solution for non-mining nodes where only miners hold the full state (assuming that they can invest money in random-access memory of sufficiently large capacity), while other nodes are checking proofs of state transformations generated by miners, and a size of a proof (in average and also in a worst case) is about $\log(|s|)$, where $|s|$ is a state size. Nevertheless, big state could lead to centralization of mining or SPV mining [2], and these concerns should be addressed. The question of internalizing the costs of state load was raised in [15], but to the best of our knowledge there has not been any practical solution proposed yet. Also, there is an increasing demand to use a blockchain as a data provider, and permanently storing objects in the state without a cleaning procedure in such a case is not a viable option.

1.1 Our Contribution

In this paper we propose an economic solution to the problem of unreasonable state growth (such as spam attacks or objects not being used anymore but still living in the validation state). It consists in introducing a new mandatory fee component. A user should pay a fee based on both the additional space needed to store objects created by a transaction, and the lifetime of the new bytes. Such an approach is typical for the cloud storage services where users pay for gigabytes of data per month.

We also consider a method of combining fees for various resources consumed by a transaction: bandwidth, random-access memory to hold state, and processor cycles to process computations prescribed by the transaction. The option being analyzed is to charge only for a resource which is consumed most of all, so we can talk about storage-oriented, network-oriented or computation-oriented transactions. The evaluation is conducted for Ethereum usage data, and it shows that it is both possible and meaningful for this cryptocurrency to determine transaction type.

A way to charge for state memory consumption (with the output lifetime taken into account) is proposed as well. Our scheme of "scheduled payments" is convenient for users not knowing the duration of their outputs' storage in advance.

1.2 Structure of the Paper

The paper is organized as follows. The model assumptions and their analysis are in Sect. 2. An algorithm for a composite fee assignment is in Sect. 3. A possible approach to charging for state memory consumption is in Sect. 4. The results of Ethereum data evaluation are in Sect. 5. Section 6 contains the conclusions.

2 Preliminaries

We shape our model with the following assumptions:

- a transaction creates new objects called outputs and spends outputs from previous transactions. Thus the state needed for transaction validation consists of an unspent outputs. The size of the state then is the sum of sizes of all the unspent outputs.

– single transaction does not change size of the state significantly
– it is always profitable for a miner to collect fees from unspent outputs.
– we are considering minimal mandatory fees in the paper. All the nodes are checking that a fee paid by a transaction is not less than a minimum and rejecting the whole block if it contains a transaction violating fee rules. Thus a fee regime is considered as a part of consensus protocol in our work. A user can pay more than the minimum to have a higher priority for a transaction of interest to be included into a block.

3   An Algorithm for the Fee Assignment

As mentioned in the introduction, we develop a fee regime with two goals in mind, namely incentivization of miners and spam prevention. In this chapter we reason about the guiding principles for the fee assignment and end up with an example of a practically useful fee assignment rule.

The evolution of blockchain networks has demonstrated the main resources being used. First and the most important so far, the memory of network nodes is limited resource. Blocks in the blockchain after processing are stored in a secondary storage, where a cost of a storage unit is low. In contrast, to validate a transaction, some state is needed (for example, unspent outputs set in Bitcoin is used to validate a transaction), and this state should reside in expensive random-access memory.

Second, it is obvious, especially with the development of smart contracts, that a cost to process a transaction can be more than just a storage cost: transactions can contain relatively complicated scripts which are meant to be executed by all the nodes in the network. The most famous example is the Ethereum network implementing the concept of a "world computer" [22].

Third, there is the network load created by every transaction. If an output is created in one block and spent right in the next one, it provides almost zero overhead in terms of validation state size, but creates the network load needed for synchronization.

A transaction fee should incorporate all the three components stated above. As shown in [8], assigning the fee to the storage as if it was execution of some code can lead to significant disbalance for rich enough scripting language (for example, for the data being written with an opcode other than the conventional storage one). Thus, we propose to charge for a component which demands more resources. That is, storage-oriented transactions should be charged for state memory consumption, the computation-oriented transactions should be charged for script execution, and all the others by the network load. This can be formalized as follows:

$$\text{Fee}(tx) = \max\left(\alpha \cdot N_b(tx), \beta \cdot N_c(tx), S(state) \cdot \sum_i (B_i \cdot L_i)\right). \quad (1)$$

Here α and β are the pricing coefficients, $N_b(tx)$ is transaction size which defines the network load, $N_c(tx)$ is the estimate of the computational cost of transaction,

$S(state)$ is the cost of the storing one byte in the state for the unit of time (a block), L_i is the time for which the output i is being stored in the state, and B_i is its size in bytes.

Since the time for the data to reside in the state is usually unknown, the third argument of max() in Eq. (1) cannot be deduced directly at transaction submission time. For this purpose we introduce a notion of scheduled payments later in Sect. 4. The third argument in Eq. (1) becomes dominant over time. Starting from the moment sT since the transaction happened, the fee is increasing at a constant rate (see Fig. 1a). The possible implementation of this algorithm is described in Sect. 4.

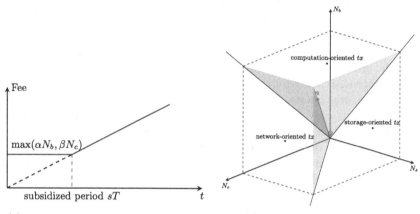

(a) Transaction cost as a function of the output existence time.

(b) Space of transactions split by Eq. (1) into the subregions of the dominant fees.

Fig. 1. Fee differentiation by resource consumption

The remaining questions here are the following. First, what are guiding principles for choosing α, β and $S(\cdot)$? Second, how can one estimate $N_c(tx)$? For Turing–complete languages second can only be solved by executing script in general case. The problem is known as the worst case execution time [21], and is left beyond the scope of the paper. The first question is answered below.

3.1 Choice of the Relative Values of α, β, $S(state)$

Assume for now that for every transaction we know for how long its outputs will be stored in the state. We will overcome this difficulty later. Based on Eq. (1), one can introduce the space of transactions, which is three–dimensional in our case — every transaction is defined by three numbers: $N_b(tx)$, $N_c(tx)$, $N_s(state, tx) = \sum_i (B_i \cdot L_i)$. Equation (1) divides this space into three regions: network–oriented transactions, space–oriented transactions, and computation–oriented transactions (see Fig. 1b). The splitting is governed by the direction of vector n which defines the line $\alpha N_b = \beta N_c = S(state)N_s$. Varying the coefficients α and β, one can change the direction of n adjusting the formal fee prescription to the sensible values.

3.2 Choice of $S(state)$

The simplest way of assigning the $S(state)$ value is by making it constant. However, this does not fully solve the problem of limiting the state size. What is being controlled in this case, that is the rate at which the data is being submitted, but not the state size itself. One could also manually define the maximal size of the state for the network. This solution, in turn, has its own caveats. For example, once the state is kept (almost) full by the participants, it can be (almost) impossible to submit the transaction increasing the state size. The time till it becomes possible is hardly predictable.

The desired properties of the current state size could be formulated as follows: it should be predictable, stable, and below some externally given value (an upper bound on state size, being unique for the whole network).

Another natural question arising is whether the rigid state size restriction is necessary? It is easy to imagine the situation where the formal possibility of exceeding the state size upper bound is still present, but hardly ever being used. For example, if one wants to constrain the state size to 10MB, the possible solution is to set normal price for submitting data to store if the state size after submission is below 10MB, but some astronomical price for the luxury of storage above 10MB. So, formally it will be possible, but in fact, hardly ever used, with every usage bringing significant profit to the miners. The generalization of this idea is to form the explicit dependence of price on the state load (it will referred to as "pricing curve"). A good pricing curve should provide at least one stable equilibrium of the state size; the minimal dependence on initial conditions (if possible), and high rewards for miners. The latter could serve as good optimization parameter. Extreme cases are zero price with huge data submission and miners get nothing; and infinite price with zero data submission and miners get nothing. As usual, the maximal outcome is in between. The pricing policies described above are two particular cases of pricing curve (see Fig. 2). That is, we assume that the price of data storage in the state $S(state)$ varies with the current state load $x = |s|$.

Note that the pricing curve is defined by a small number of parameters and to be the same for all the network. To impose an upper bound on the state size, one can choose the pricing curve formally going to infinity at some finite state size. The rigid boundary can be provided by divergence higher than $1/(x_{max}-x)$. One can also try to estimate the optimal state size for a given differentiable pricing curve. The data submission rate $N(S(x))$ is fully defined by the current storage price $S(x)$. Rewards rate obtained by the miners for stable state size at price S per unit time is given by $y = S \cdot N(S)$. An example is provided in Fig. 3. First, it provides a possible method of measuring explicit form of the function $N(S)$ in the model: one has to set up the price, and observe the static rewards. Second, one may wonder about the price S^*, optimal for the miners in terms of rewards.

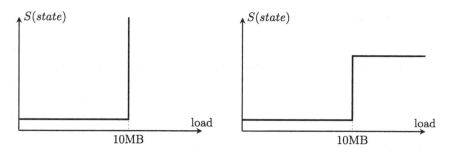

Fig. 2. Examples of pricing curves: rigid state size restriction (left) and overflow fees (right, see text). The value of 10MB is taken arbitrarily.

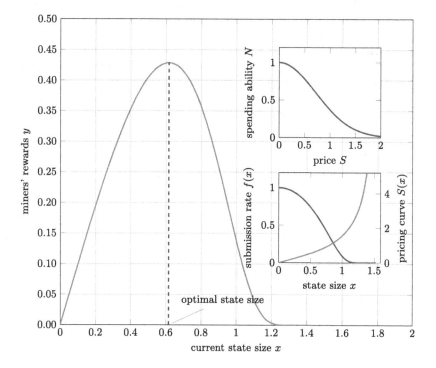

Fig. 3. Example of the rewards curve.

Obviously, it satisfies $N(S^*) + S^* \cdot N'(S^*) = 0$, where prime is derivative with respect to price. As usual, the optimal price here does not depend on the pricing policy, but rather the implicit property of the network. Having the price varying freely can be considered beneficial both for miners and for network as a whole, since it allows the first ones to optimize signing strategy, and herewith the state size is automatically adjusted to the relatively predictable level $S^{-1}(S^*)$.

4   Scheduled Payments

In this section we propose a concrete method to charge for state bytes consumed (or released). There is a couple of possible options for that. A user, for example, may specify lifetime for a coin during its creation and pay for it in advance, this is not very convenient for him though. Another option is to charge when coin is spent, or allow to spend a coin (by anyone, presumably, a miner) when its value is overweighted by the state fee. As a drawback, if coin is associated with a big value, it could live for very long time, maybe without a reason.

We propose more convenient method of charging; we name it *scheduled payments*. In this scheme a user must set special predefined script for a coin (otherwise a transaction and also a block containing it are invalid), which contains a user-specific logic (we call it a *regular script*) and a spending condition which allows anyone (presumably, a miner) to create a transaction claiming this output, necessarily creating a coin with the same guarding condition and a value not less than original minus a state fee. These two parts (regular script and a fee charging condition) are connected by using the $\vee$ conjecture. We assume that α and β are fixed. We also assume that subsidized period sT is to be stored along with the coin by each validating node. Then a guarding script for the coin would be like:

$$
\begin{aligned}
&(regular\_script)\vee \\
&(height > (out.height + sT) \wedge (out.value \le S_c \cdot B \cdot sT \vee \\
&\quad tx.has\_output(value = out.value - S_c \cdot B \cdot sT, script = out.script))),
\end{aligned} \tag{2}
$$

where *height* is a height of a block which contains a spending transaction; *out.height* is a height when the output was created; *out.height* and *out.script* contain value and spending script of the output, respectively; *tx.has_output()* checks whether a spending transaction has an output with conditions given as the predicate arguments, and S_c is the value of $S(state)$ when the coin was created. As in the Sect. 3, the B constant is the output size.

5   Evaluation

In this section we experimentally study what could be the real-world ratio between the pricing coefficients $\alpha, \beta, S(state)$. To extract the realistic values, and to verify the validity of the described transaction classification, the data from the Ethereum network is taken. We consider Ethereum a good example, since all the three fee components are present in this cryptocurrency. The network load parameter $N_b(tx)$ is simply a transaction size; the state load $\Delta(tx)$ can be deduced from the blockchain by extracting SSTORE and CREATE operations from the transaction tx[1]. To determine the computational load $N_c(tx)$, we count Ethereum gas consumed by the transaction processing minus its storage cost and the so-called base cost, which is proportional to the transaction size.

---

[1] Information on these operations can be found in the Ethereum Yellow Paper [22].

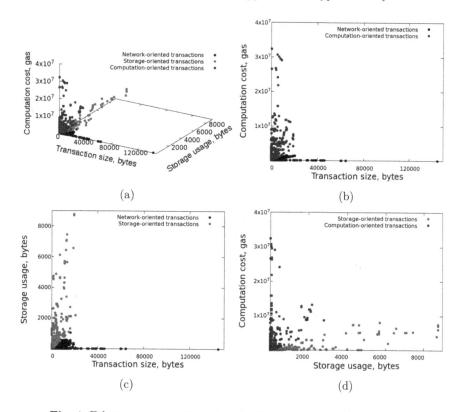

Fig. 4. Ethereum transactions classification by resource consumption

The results of processing first $2 \cdot 10^6$ blocks in Ethereum network are presented in Fig. 4. Each point corresponds to a transaction. One can notice that parts of the distribution in Fig. 4 extend along the coordinate axis; these are the transactions which can be unambiguously distinguished by their type of the resource consumption. Their presence confirms our expectations on the nature of resource consumption, and serves as a justification of the proposed classification scheme. The space of transactions is split into three parts by the aforementioned vector **n** with the endpoint at the first momentum of the transactions with at least 2 non-zero components.

Another parameter of interest is a storage object lifetime. Associating it directly with smart contract data lifetime is weakly relevant to our scheme as the users are not incentivized to remove data from the state earlier rather than later. Thus we consider the delay between the data submission and a first request to be the reliable parameter reflecting the needs of the users. Analysis of Ethereum blockchain shows that in a lot of cases data stored in the world state is touched by other transactions in the same block or few blocks after creation. We filter out such cases as they do not show using blockchain as a storage. Excluding such short-lived data from our analysis we estimate that average lifetime of a data object in Ethereum is 23,731 blocks (or about 4 days considering $15\,\mathrm{s}$ average delay between blocks).

This gives the following estimation on the ratio between the pricing coefficients for the expected state size:

$$
\begin{aligned}
\frac{\beta}{\alpha} &\approx 7.7 \cdot 10^{-3} \text{bytes/gas}, \\
\frac{S}{\alpha} &\approx 6.7 \cdot 10^{-4} \text{blocks}^{-1},
\end{aligned}
\tag{3}
$$

where S is the cost of the storage of byte of output in the state for one block, which does not depend on state size in Ethereum. The estimations are quite approximate, while changing them does not affect fees for most of transactions unambiguously attributed by a concrete type of the resource consumption.

6   Concluding Remarks

Blockchain technology relies on miners, that safeguard the integrity of the blockchain in exchange for a revenue, that usually consist of two parts: block reward and transaction fees. Transaction fees are useful to limit miners resource usage and prevent spam.

While in most of cryptocurrencies a transaction fee is addressed as an atomic concept, in this paper we have shown that it is reasonable to introduce the components of a fee associated with resources utilized: network, computation or storage. The analysis of Ethereum blockchain shows that transactions in such a three-dimensional space are distributed close to one of the axes, allowing us to unambiguously classify transactions by consumed resource.

Storage part of the fee has already been discussed in literature as a necessary tool to limit miners storage consumption [15,17]. This fee component is required to make the state size more predictable, but its implementation is challenging since the output lifetime is not known at the time when the transaction is created. In current paper we have described the concrete method to charge for state bytes consumed that can be fully implemented on the script level.

Besides limiting the size of the state, storage fee provides valuable side effects. In particular, it provides a way to return coins with lost keys into circulation. Although necessity of coin recirculation is still an open question, it has been widely discussed in literature (e.g. [11,12]) in connection with the prevention of the deflation, which may eventually occur in cryptocurrencies with fixed supply. Enforced coin recirculation has been implemented in some cryptocurrencies [9].

Another important side effect of the storage fee is that it provides additional rewards for miners. Even when all coins are emitted and fixed block reward goes to zero, storage fee will provide stable rewards for miners, which do not depend on user transactions included into block. This will make destructive mining strategies described in [7] less profitable.

With these factors taken into account, the ready-to-implement system is provided, which is believed to solve the problem of uncontrollable state growth. It bears some valuable side effects by the same means, while preserving currently existing methods for transaction fees and code execution costs.

References

1. Solidity language. https://solidity.readthedocs.io
2. SPV mining. https://bitcoin.org/en/alert/2015-07-04-spv-mining
3. Andresen, G.: Back-of-the-envelope calculations for marginal cost of transactions (2013). https://gist.github.com/gavinandresen/5044482
4. Bitcoin Wiki: Bitcoin script. https://en.bitcoin.it/wiki/Script
5. Bitcoin Wiki: July 2015 flood attack. https://en.bitcoin.it/wiki/July_2015_flood_attack
6. Blockchain.info: Number of unspent transaction outputs. https://blockchain.info/charts/utxo-count?timespan=all
7. Carlsten, M., Kalodner, H., Weinberg, S.M., Narayanan, A.: On the instability of Bitcoin without the block reward. In: Proceedings of the 2016 ACM SIGSAC Conference on Computer and Communications Security, pp. 154–167. ACM (2016)
8. Earls, J.: The Economics of Gas Models. Conference talk. In: CESC 2017 – Crypto Economics Security Conference, Berkeley, USA (2017). http://earlz.net/view/2017/10/02/1550/economics-of-fees-and-gas
9. Friedenbach, M.: Freicoin. http://freico.in
10. Garay, J., Kiayias, A., Leonardos, N.: The Bitcoin backbone protocol: analysis and applications. In: Oswald, E., Fischlin, M. (eds.) EUROCRYPT 2015, Part II. LNCS, vol. 9057, pp. 281–310. Springer, Heidelberg (2015). https://doi.org/10.1007/978-3-662-46803-6_10
11. Gjermundrød, H., Chalkias, K., Dionysiou, I.: Going beyond the coinbase transaction fee: alternative reward schemes for miners in blockchain systems. In: Proceedings of the 20th Pan-Hellenic Conference on Informatics, p. 35. ACM (2016)
12. Gjermundrød, H., Dionysiou, I.: Recirculating *Lost* coins in cryptocurrency systems. In: Abramowicz, W., Kokkinaki, A. (eds.) BIS 2014. LNBIP, vol. 183, pp. 229–240. Springer, Cham (2014). https://doi.org/10.1007/978-3-319-11460-6_20
13. Goodmani, L.: Michelson: the language of smart contracts in tezos. https://www.tezos.com/static/papers/language.pdf
14. Luu, L., Teutsch, J., Kulkarni, R., Saxena, P.: Demystifying incentives in the consensus computer. In: Proceedings of the 22nd ACM SIGSAC Conference on Computer and Communications Security, pp. 706–719. ACM (2015)
15. Möser, M., Böhme, R.: Trends, tips, tolls: a longitudinal study of bitcoin transaction fees. In: Brenner, M., Christin, N., Johnson, B., Rohloff, K. (eds.) FC 2015. LNCS, vol. 8976, pp. 19–33. Springer, Heidelberg (2015). https://doi.org/10.1007/978-3-662-48051-9_2
16. Nakamoto, S.: Bitcoin: a peer-to-peer electronic cash system (2008)
17. Reyzin, L., Meshkov, D., Chepurnoy, A., Ivanov, S.: Improving authenticated dynamic dictionaries, with applications to cryptocurrencies. In: International Conference on Financial Cryptography and Data Security (2017)
18. Rizun, P.R.: A transaction fee market exists without a block size limit (2015)

19. Vasek, M., Thornton, M., Moore, T.: Empirical analysis of denial-of-service attacks in the Bitcoin ecosystem. In: Böhme, R., Brenner, M., Moore, T., Smith, M. (eds.) FC 2014. LNCS, vol. 8438, pp. 57–71. Springer, Heidelberg (2014). https://doi.org/10.1007/978-3-662-44774-1_5
20. Wilcke, J.: The Ethereum network is currently undergoing a DoS attack. https://blog.ethereum.org/2016/09/22/ethereum-network-currently-undergoing-dos-attack/
21. Wilhelm, R., et al.: The worst-case execution-time problem—overview of methods and survey of tools. ACM Trans. Embed. Comput. Syst. **7**(3), 36:1–36:53 (2008). https://doi.org/10.1145/1347375.1347389
22. Wood, G.: Ethereum: A secure decentralised generalised transaction ledger. Ethereum Project Yellow Paper (2014). https://ethereum.github.io/yellowpaper/paper.pdf

A Wild Velvet Fork Appears! Inclusive Blockchain Protocol Changes in Practice
(Short Paper)

A. Zamyatin[1,2(✉)], N. Stifter[2], A. Judmayer[2], P. Schindler[2], E. Weippl[2], and W. J. Knottenbelt[1]

[1] Imperial College London, London, UK
{a.zamyatin,w.knottenbelt}@imperial.ac.uk
[2] SBA Research, Vienna, Austria
{nstifter,ajudmayer,pschindler,eweippl}@sba-research.org

Abstract. The loosely defined terms *hard fork* and *soft fork* have established themselves as descriptors of different classes of upgrade mechanisms for the underlying consensus rules of (proof-of-work) blockchains. Recently, a novel approach termed *velvet fork*, which expands upon the concept of a soft fork, was outlined in [22]. Specifically, velvet forks intend to avoid the possibility of disagreement by a change of rules through rendering modifications to the protocol backward compatible *and* inclusive to legacy blocks. We present an overview and definitions of these different upgrade mechanisms and outline their relationships. Hereby, we expose examples where velvet forks or similar constructions are already actively employed in Bitcoin and other cryptocurrencies. Furthermore, we expand upon the concept of velvet forks by proposing possible applications and discuss potentially arising security implications.

1 Introduction

Nakamoto consensus, the underlying agreement protocol of permissionless blockchains, enables eventual consensus on the state updates to a distributed ledger if certain majority assumptions on the hashrate of honest mining participants are upheld [16,27]. A substantial amount of research has focused on correctly assessing the provided security guarantees, such as the ability for an adversary to succeed in double spending transactions [5,21,31]. Despite these remarkable efforts, there still remain open questions and gaps in our understanding of this agreement mechanism. One such topic is approaches for securely changing consensus rules of *permissionless* blockchain protocols [35], such as Bitcoin and Ethereum, which is currently topic of ongoing debate. Reaching agreement on a common set of protocol rules in a decentralized manner could prove to be a problem as difficult as the double-spending problem Bitcoin originally set out to solve.

A. Zamyatin and N. Stifter—Contributed equally to this work.

© International Financial Cryptography Association 2019
A. Zohar et al. (Eds.): FC 2018 Workshops, LNCS 10958, pp. 31–42, 2019.
https://doi.org/10.1007/978-3-662-58820-8_3

In this paper we first provide a brief background on core concepts related to this topic after which we discuss and define current protocol upgrade mechanisms considered in permissionless blockchain systems, such as *hard forks* and *soft forks*. In particular, we focus on the recently proposed concept of *velvet forks* by Kiayias et al. [22], which seeks to render protocol upgrades via soft forks more inclusive. We then provide real-world examples where velvet forks or similar concepts are, or have already been, employed. Furthermore, possible negative impacts of such an approach are outlined. In particular with regards to the underlying (game-theoretic) incentive model, such changes may lead to negative side effects in permissionless blockchains. Finally, we suggest the applicability of velvet forks to a number of existing protocol improvement proposals and outline interesting directions for future work.

2 Background

The fundamental mechanism by which Bitcoin and similar *permissionless* blockchain-based systems reach agreement depends, among other, upon consensus participants extending a proof-of-work weighted hash chain, i.e., a *blockchain*. Specifically, it is assumed that a sufficient honest majority of these participants, so called *miners*, will only build upon the branch with the most cumulative proof-of-work, where each element, e.g., *block*, adheres to some pre-agreed set of protocol rules $\mathcal{P}$ under which it is considered valid. The non-deterministic nature of the hash-based proof-of-work employed in such systems, as well as the relatively weak synchrony assumptions of the underlying peer-to-peer network, can lead to situations, where multiple branches are created and extended in parallel. However, the probability of such a blockchain *fork* prevailing for prolonged periods decreases exponentially in its length, if a sufficient majority of miners adhere to protocol rules $\mathcal{P}$ and, in particular, only extend the heaviest chain (known to them) [16,26]. We use $b \in \mathcal{V}$ to denote a block b is contained in the validity set $\mathcal{V}$ defined by $\mathcal{P}$, i.e., in the set of all blocks considered valid under the protocol rules $\mathcal{P}$.

This brings us to the question how a change $\mathcal{P} \rightarrow \mathcal{P}'$ to the underlying protocol rules may affect this consensus mechanism. *Disagreement* on the validity of a block b under different rules, i.e., $b \in \mathcal{V}$ but $b \notin \mathcal{V}'$, can lead to a *permanent* fork in the blockchain, where a subset of participants will always reject branches building on a, to them invalid, block, regardless of the cumulative proof-of-work these branches accumulate. The requirement for agreement on the block validity also extends to participants not actively involved in the consensus process by mining, such as *fully validating* and *simple payment verification* (SPV) [26] nodes. The former generally adhere to the same full set of rules $\mathcal{P}$ as miners, while the latter only consider a subset $\mathcal{P}_{spv} \subset \mathcal{P}$. For simplification we shall refer to such non-mining participants as *clients*.

3   Mechanisms for Consensus Rule Changes

The term *hard fork* has established itself [8,18] as a descriptor for protocol changes which can incur a permanent split of the blockchain, as they permit or even enforce the creation of blocks considered invalid under previous protocol rules. As an alternative, *soft forks* intend to retain some level of compatibility to older protocol versions, specifically towards *clients* adhering to previous protocol rules. The concepts of both hard- and soft forks are described in the Bitcoin developer guide [13], as well as the Bitcoin-Wiki [6]. In scientific literature, some of the principal differences between these two types of consensus rule upgrades have been covered in [8,12,18]. McCorry et al. furthermore provide a history of forking events in both Bitcoin and Ethereum as part of their work on how parties can bindingly perform atomic cross-chain trades in case of a permanent blockchain fork [25]. A closer description of different protocol forking mechanisms and their relation to each other was also presented in a blog post by Buterin in [9].

Differentiating Between Hard and Soft Forks. If we consider the possibility of a permanent blockchain split as the defining characteristic of hard forks, most protocol changes would fall into this category. For example reducing the validity set of rules in a protocol update, which is generally considered to be a *soft fork*, can lead to a permanent split in case the majority of consensus participants is not upgraded. Conversely, if an expanding protocol change, i.e. a *hard fork*, does not reach a majority among consensus participants, no permanent fork is actually incurred as upgraded clients will continue to follow the chain with the most cumulative proof-of-work.

This dichotomy helps outline the difficulties in presenting a clear distinction between hard and soft forks.

To provide a finer distinction between possible impacts of protocol upgrades and their potential for permanent blockchain forks we present the following classes of protocol changes:

- **Expanding.** The new protocol rules $\mathcal{P}'$ increase the set of blocks V' considered valid with respect to the previous protocol rules $\mathcal{P}$, i.e., $V' \supset V$. Expanding protocol changes can cause a permanent split in the blockchain if the consensus participants adhering to $\mathcal{P}'$ form a majority. However, if a majority retains protocol rules $\mathcal{P}$ no permanent fork occurs as clients adhering to $\mathcal{P}'$ also consider any block under protocol rules $\mathcal{P}$ as valid. Examples include blocksize increase and defining previously unused values as new opcodes.
- **Reducing.** The new protocol rules $\mathcal{P}'$ reduce the set of blocks considered valid with respect to the previous protocol rules. Specifically, the new set of valid blocks V' is a proper subset of the valid blocks of the previous protocol, i.e., $V' \subset V$. Reducing protocol changes represent a soft fork as long as the majority of consensus participants adheres to the new rules $\mathcal{P}'$. If, however, $\mathcal{P}$ retains a majority, a permanent fork is incurred as updated clients and

miners will consider some blocks valid under old protocol rules $\mathcal{P}$ as invalid. Examples could be: blocksize decrease, introduction of SegWit (BIP 141 [24]) and removal of an opcode.

- **Conflicting (Bilateral).** We refer to updates introducing mutual incompatibilities as *conflicting* or *bilateral* protocol changes. Here, the goal is to intentionally cause a permanent fork of the blockchain and prevent potential interactions between the resulting chains, such as the chain ID introduced in Ethereum for replay protection.

- **Conditionally Reducing (Velvet).** Velvet protocol changes are a special form of update where the new set of *reducing* protocol rules $\mathcal{P}'$ is *conditionally* applied only when the considered elements, such as blocks or transactions, are *valid* under the new rules. Otherwise, the new rules are ignored and previous protocol rules $\mathcal{P}$ are relied upon to determine validity. Since the new rules in $\mathcal{P}'$ are reducing, velvet protocol changes in fact never incur a (permanent) protocol fork as any element considered valid under $\mathcal{P}'$ is also considered valid under $\mathcal{P}$, therefore $V' = V$. Examples, such as P2Pool [3] and overlay protocols, are discussed in Sect. 4.

Table 1. Overview of classes of protocol updates $\mathcal{P} \to \mathcal{P}'$. $\mathcal{V}$ and $\mathcal{V}'$ denote the validity sets of old ($\mathcal{P}$) and new ($\mathcal{P}'$) protocol rules, respectively. $\mathcal{N}$ denotes the validity set changes introduced by the protocol update.

Type	Validity set		Incurred fork		Examples
	New	Relation to old	Soft	Permanent/Hard	
Expanding	$\mathcal{V}' = \mathcal{V} \cup \mathcal{N}$, $\exists n \in \mathcal{N} :$ $n \notin \mathcal{V}$	$\mathcal{V}' \supset \mathcal{V}$	Never	$\mathcal{V}'$ is majority	Blocksize increase, new opcode
Reducing	$\mathcal{V}' = \mathcal{V} \setminus \mathcal{N}$, $\mathcal{N} \subset \mathcal{V}$	$\mathcal{V}' \subset \mathcal{V}$	$\mathcal{V}'$ is majority	$\mathcal{V}$ is majority	Blocksize decrease, opcode removal, SegWit
Conflicting (Bilateral)	$\mathcal{V}' = (\mathcal{V} \cup \mathcal{N}) \setminus (\mathcal{V} \cap \mathcal{N}) = V \triangle N$	$(\mathcal{V}' \not\subseteq \mathcal{V})$, $(\mathcal{V} \not\subseteq \mathcal{V}')$, $V' \cap V \neq \emptyset$	Never	Always	Opcode redefinition, chain ID for replay protection
Conditionally reducing (Velvet)	$\mathcal{V}' = \mathcal{V}$	$\mathcal{V}' = \mathcal{V}$	Never	Never	P2Pool, merged mining, colored coins

Adhering to convention and previous definitions, i.e., [8,9,12], both expanding and bilateral protocol changes are generally considered to be hard forks while reducing protocol changes are referred to as soft forks. In this context the so called *velvet fork* considered in this work would also fall into the latter category of soft forks (Table 1).

Velvet Forks. The velvet fork, as described in [22], does not require support of a majority of participants *and* can potentially avoid rule disagreement forks from happening altogether. In a velvet fork, the new protocol rules $\mathcal{P}'$ are not enforced by upgraded consensus participants and any valid block adhering to the new rules is also a valid block in terms of the old rules. Effectively, velvet forks leverage on the consensus mechanism of protocol $\mathcal{P}$ to bootstrap their own consensus rules $\mathcal{P}'$ which, as part of their rules, produce forward-compatible blocks to $\mathcal{P}$. In principle, protocol updates introduced as velvet forks are always successful, as legacy nodes remain unaware of the changes. However, some protocol updates may not be applicable as a velvet fork, in particular if they require non-upgraded participants to also adhere to the new rules, or the new rules must hold over the span of multiple, possibly arbitrarily many, mined blocks[1].

Other Protocol Update Mechanisms

User Activated Forks. The concept of *user activated soft forks* (UASF) was recently proposed as a mechanism, whereby non-mining participants of the system attempt to take influence on the consensus and protocol upgrade process [4,9]. We note that user activated forks generally apply to all types of protocol update mechanisms. Specifically, user activated forks aim to incentivize mining participants to perform a consensus protocol upgrade $\mathcal{P} \rightarrow \mathcal{P}'$: users and *economic* actors of the system present pledges stating they will strictly enforce the new consensus rules $\mathcal{P}'$ at a certain activation date by their *client software*, regardless of the amount of support of active consensus participants, i.e. miners.

Emergent Consensus. Emergent consensus (EC) is a concept that was proposed as an improvement proposal in the Bitcoin Unlimited client (BUIP001 [34]). Its goal is specifically geared towards reaching dynamic agreement upon the permissible size of Bitcoin blocks, which is currently part of the consensus rules of the Bitcoin protocol. However, the mechanism in principle could also be applied to other protocol rules. EC assumes that a consensus participant will nevertheless accept a, to them invalid, block if sufficient other proof-of-work blocks build upon it. In theory, forks caused by disagreement on the protocol rules could hereby be resolved. However, the resulting impact on security properties is still subject of ongoing discussion and in particular Zhang et al. were able to show models of EC are not incentive compatible, even if all miners fully comply with the protocol [36].

4   Observation of Velvet Forks in Practice

In this section we identify blockchain protocol extensions closely related to velvet forks, which either already have been deployed or whose design follows the same approach.

---

[1] For example, repurposing anyone-can-spend outputs as is the case with SegWit (BIP 141).

P2Pool. P2Pool [3] is a protocol for implementing decentralized mining pools presented in 2011. In contrast to conventional mining pools, attestation of each miner's contribution to solving the next block's PoW puzzle and the distribution of rewards are accomplished without a trusted operator. P2Pool uses an additional, length-bounded blockchain, the *sharechain*, consisting of otherwise valid blocks which fail to meet the mining difficulty target d but exceed a minimal target d_{share}, agreed upon and determined by the protocol[2], sometimes referred to as *near* or *weak blocks*. These blocks are used to attest each miner's contribution, while the reward distribution is in turn achieved by introducing the following rule: "*Each time a miner finds a block exceeding the target d, she can claim 0.5% of the block reward, while the rest must be distributed among all participating miners according to their portion of the last N sharechain blocks*".

While this additional axiom is an extension to the mined blockchain's rule set, it generates fully backward compatible blocks, and hence remains oblivious to all but P2Pool miners. As a result, any valid block generated by P2Pool miners will be accepted by non-P2Pool miners. In turn, P2Pool miners accept any valid blocks produced by non-P2Pool miners, i.e., even blocks that do not adhere to the above mentioned rule. Since the set of accepted blocks by both parties is exactly the same, P2Pool can be considered a velvet fork.

Sub-chains with Weak Blocks. The concept of *sub-chains* was initially proposed by TierNolan (pseudonymous) in 2013 [28] and has been extended, for instance, by Rizun [29]. It builds upon the idea of exchanging *weak blocks* between miners to form sub-chains between consecutive full blocks, by referencing the previous' weak blocks header in an additional pointer.

The required subchain pointer can be readily included in a miner-definable data field, such as the coinbase transaction in the case of Bitcoin. Miners that have adopted sub-chain rules will also accept blocks containing invalid, or no pointer data to sub-blocks. As a result, the set of accepted blocks remains identical for both miners using sub-chains and as those following legacy rules, rendering this proposed protocol extension a form of velvet fork.

Merged Mining. Merged mining refers to the process of reusing (partial) PoW solutions from a *parent* blockchain as valid proofs-of-work for one or more *child* block-chains [20]. It was first introduced in Namecoin [7] both as a bootstrapping technique and to mitigate the fragmentation of computational power among competing cryptocurrencies sharing the same PoW. While a *child* cryptocurrency may require a hard fork to implement merged mining, *parent* blockchains only need to allow for miners to include additional arbitrary data in its blocks. This arbitrary field is then used to link to blocks to the merge mined child cryptocurrency.

Merged mining can be considered closely related to velvet forks, as new consensus rules, namely those of the merge mined children, are incorporated in the parent blockchain in a fully backward compatible way. If either invalid or no

---

[2] The target d_{share} is adjusted such that the sharechain maintains an average block interval of 30 s.

links to child blocks are included in a block, the data will be ignored by participants of merged mining and the block is nevertheless accepted. Merged mining and P2Pool make use of the same principle mechanisms, with the marked difference being that in merged mining additional rewards are received in the child cryptocurrency, whereas P2Pool sharechain blocks represent claims to portions of the next valid block's reward on the main chain.

Overlay Protocols and Colored Coins. Another concept closely related to the idea of velvet forks is that of overlay protocols and colored coins, inter alia described in [30]. The term colored coin refer to cryptocurrency transactions where the outputs are additionally "colored" to represent some assets or tokens, allowing to use such outputs in transactions to transfer their ownership. We consider colored coins to be part of the class of overlay protocols and herein focus on the latter, more general concept.

Overlay protocols leverage on an underlying property of Bitcoin and similar block-chain systems, namely providing eventual consensus on the ordering of transactions. This primitive, termed *total order broadcast* or *atomic broadcast* has been shown to be equivalent to consensus [11] and can, for instance, be used to readily implement state machine replication. As such, encoding messages in regular valid transactions allows overlay protocols to utilize Bitcoin or similar systems as if they were a (eventual) total order broadcast protocol. While this approach may provide overlay protocols with a mechanism for reaching agreement on the ordering of messages, it does not extend any guarantees towards their *correctness*. In particular, miners may remain completely oblivious to the consensus rules $\mathcal{O}$ of the overlay protocol and only adhere to the underlying base protocol $\mathcal{P}$. Hence, transactions encoding invalid messages of the overlay protocol $\mathcal{O}$, which have to be ignored by the participants of the overlay system, may be included in blocks [8]. However, if participants in the overlay system agree to both the same set of rules $\mathcal{O}$ and the (eventual) ordering of both valid and invalid messages, then ignoring messages considered invalid under $\mathcal{O}$ by all (honest) participants leads to the same (eventually) consistent system state.

Overlay protocols are comparable to velvet forks in that they impose no restrictions and apply new protocol rules $\mathcal{O}$ only if the input is considered valid[3]. The primary difference is that velvet forks additionally assume an active participation in the underlying consensus protocol of $\mathcal{P}$, whereas overlay protocols only take on the role of *clients*. Practical examples of overlay protocols are Omni-Layer (previously Mastercoin) [2] and Counterparty [1].

5   Considering Security Implications

As outlined in Sect. 4, velvet forks can be utilized to introduce consensus rule changes in a backward compatible way. However, non-upgraded miners may be unaware of these changes and the potential alterations to the incentives of

---

[3] We point out that the agreement problem on the overlay protocol rules themselves is hereby of course not solved, and an upgrade $\mathcal{O} \rightarrow \mathcal{O}'$ may cause a logical fork with similar problems to those of the underlying consensus protocol, discussed previously.

upgraded *velvet miners* that they entail. As such, blocks produced in accordance with the old rules $\mathcal{P}$ may no longer have the same (economic) utility for velvet miners, as blocks generated under $\mathcal{P}'$, i.e., velvet miners may be biased towards accepting upgraded over legacy blocks. This in turn can have an unclear impact on the security assumptions of such systems, as current attack models mostly do not assume a variable utility of blocks. The following examples outline commonly described attack strategies and how they may relate to velvet forks.

Double Spending. The double spending problem was one of the first studied threats in Bitcoin [5,21,31]. As miners are required to invest significant amounts of computational power into solving the proof-of-work puzzles, attacks on transactions with sufficient number of confirmations are generally considered economically infeasible. However, long waiting times are often impracticable, while a trade-off between security and usability may be inevitable and must be considered carefully [33]. The necessary thresholds for transaction security assumptions can be shifted in blockchains experiencing a velvet fork, as some blocks may be attributed a higher utility than others by a subset of miners in the system, and must be re-evaluated.

Selfish Mining. Selfish mining [15,32] is known to allow adversaries to increase their expected revenue by deviating from the correct protocol rules. Thereby, selfish miners intentionally withhold blocks and attempt to create a longer secret chain. Determined by the respective strategy, the selfish miner will only publish a select number of blocks from her secret chain, overriding progress in the public chain and forcing honest miners into reorganization. The success rate of the attack is, among other, dependent on the network connectivity of the adversary and the acceptance probability of the blocks in the attacking parallel chain.

However, a velvet fork may significantly impact the success rate of an attacker if some blocks attain a higher probability of acceptance than others, based on the protocol rules they adhere to. In the latter case, an attacker potentially has a higher chance of overriding the public chain, as upgraded miners may prefer her blocks over those of honest (legacy) miners. It is conceivable that the disparity in rewards may even incentivize miners to behave against protocol rules and discard more than one block, i.e., intentionally disregard the heaviest chain rule. Carlsten et al. have shown that selfish mining performs better in Bitcoin under a block reward free model, i.e., when blocks have different economic value and adversaries can utilize this information to better time their attacks [10], and these insights may similarly apply to velvet forks.

Insidious Soft Forks. A velvet fork could potentially be abused to enforce a regular soft fork in a hostile manner. Assume a new protocol update $\mathcal{P} \rightarrow \mathcal{P}'$, favored by some portion of the community, does not reach a majority among miners. Hence, it could be deployed as a velvet fork at first. However, if it at some point gains sufficient, i.e, >50% adoption, miners adhering to these rules could start to enforce them on the remaining unupgraded participants, i.e., by unilaterally declaring old blocks as invalid and triggering a soft fork. As the velvet miners had sufficient time to accumulate a wider range of support, the fork now has better chances of success due to economic asymmetry, i.e., the unupgraded may conform out of economic interest.

6 Applicability to Existing Proposals

We now move on to provide a non-exhaustive list of consensus extension proposals which could potentially be implemented as velvet forks.

Bitcoin-NG. In [14] Eyal et al. present Bitcoin-NG, which aims at improving latency and bandwidth consumption compared to Bitcoin, while maintaining similar security properties. Bitcoin-NG distinguishes between normally mined *key* blocks and so called *microblocks*, which are generated at a significantly lower interval by a *leader*, i.e., the miner of the previous key block. Fees earned from transactions included in microblocks are split in a 40:60 ratio between miners of consecutive key blocks. To disincentivize double spending by malicious leaders, honest leaders can submit *proof of fraud* transactions to the blockchain if they detect attacks, invalidating the funds paid to the adversary.

Velvet Fork Applicability. Bitcoin-NG adds three rules to the Bitcoin consensus layer, two of which are compatible as a velvet fork. Similar to sub-chains, unupgraded miners would remain agnostic to microblocks, if microblock transactions are included in the subsequent key block[4]. By adding a pointer to the previous Bitcoin-NG key block[5], the new reward scheme can be implemented, despite the presence of legacy blocks. However, the invalidation of funds paid to a malicious leader by a *proof of fraud* transaction must also be accepted by unupgraded miners, which remains an open problem.

Aspen. Aspen [17] is an extension to the Bitcoin-NG concept that allows consensus participants to fully validate the correct functionality of blockchain services in a trustless manner, while only keeping track of a, to them, relevant subset of blocks. Service specific data is stored in chains of key and microblocks, thereby, there can exist multiple independent layers of microblock chains used by different services.

Velvet Fork Applicability. Apart from the rules required to implement Bitcoin-NG, the Aspen protocol requires the annotation of outputs with so called service numbers, which determine on which microblock chains the referenced funds can be spent. In Bitcoin, this could be achievable for instance through using the OP_RETURN script opcode. We note that Aspen in its current form could possibly also be implemented using the previously described concept of sub-chains, thereby evading potentially incompatible requirements introduced by Bitcoin-NG.

---

[4] And do not exceed Bitcoin's block size limitations.
[5] In the data used as input to the proof-of-work of the block.

Extension Blocks. The Extension block proposal was introduced by Lau [23] and further expanded upon by Jeffrey et al. [19]. It aims at increasing the transaction throughput by introducing an additional layer of (potentially larger) blocks atop the Bitcoin blockchain. While each extension blocks are linked to Bitcoin blocks via the coinbase transaction in a 1-to-1 mapping, they maintain their own independent set of transactions, creating a parallel accounting system.

Velvet Fork Applicability. To allow users to transfer funds between normal and extension blocks, the proposal re-purposes the OP_TRUE opcode, which in turn would render such funds spendable by anyone in the eyes of legacy miners. While the presented approach necessitates a soft fork, alternative constructions possibly allowing for a velvet fork deployment (e.g., multisig locks) may be conceivable.

7   Future Work and Conclusion

Herein, we outlined and extended upon the previously described concept of *velvet forks* and contextualize it to other blockchain consensus rule change mechanisms such as hard- and soft forks. Furthermore we show that variants of this new upgrade mechanism have already been employed in real-world scenarios. Velvet forks present a possible new upgrade path to blockchain consensus rules that could help avoid long-lasting scaling debates and discord in the community. New protocol extensions could be actively deployed without necessitating at least majority agreement by all consensus participants. On the other hand, velvet forks could introduce new possible attacks and threats and fundamentally impact the game-theoretic incentives of the underlying blockchain. In any case, this interesting new concept deserves further research attention.

Acknowledgments. This research was funded by Blockchain (GB) Ltd., FFG-Austrian Research Promotion Agency Bridge Early Stage 846573 A2Bit, Bridge 1 858561 SESC, and COMET K1.

References

1. Counterparty. https://counterparty.io/. Accessed 11 Apr 2017
2. Omni layer. http://www.omnilayer.org/. Accessed 11 Apr 2017
3. P2Pool. http://p2pool.org/. Accessed 10 May 2017
4. UASF. https://github.com/OPUASF/UASF. Accessed 11 Apr 2017
5. Androulaki, E., Capkun, S., Karame, G.O.: Two bitcoins at the price of one? Double-spending attacks on fast payments in bitcoin. In: CCS (2012)
6. Bitcoin Community: Bitcoin wiki. https://bitcoin.it/. Accessed 30 June 2015
7. Bitcoin Wiki: Merged mining specification. https://en.bitcoin.it/wiki/Merged_mining_specification. Accessed 10 May 2017
8. Bonneau, J., Miller, A., Clark, J., Narayanan, A., Kroll, J.A., Felten, E.W.: SoK: research perspectives and challenges for bitcoin and cryptocurrencies. In: IEEE Symposium on Security and Privacy (2015)

9. Buterin, V.: Hard forks, soft forks, defaults and coercion (2017). http://vitalik.ca/general/2017/03/14/forks_and_markets.html. Accessed 11 Apr 2017

10. Carlsten, M., Kalodner, H., Weinberg, S.M., Narayanan, A.: On the instability of bitcoin without the block reward. In: Proceedings of the 2016 ACM SIGSAC Conference on Computer and Communications Security, pp. 154–167. ACM (2016)

11. Chandra, T.D., Toueg, S.: Unreliable failure detectors for reliable distributed systems. J. ACM (JACM) **43**, 225–267 (1996)

12. Duong, T., Chepurnoy, A., Fan, L., Zhou, H.-S.: TwinsCoin: a cryptocurrency via proof-of-work and proof-of-stake. In: Proceedings of the 2Nd ACM Workshop on Blockchains, Cryptocurrencies, and Contracts, BCC 2018, Incheon, Republic of Korea, pp. 1–13. ACM, New York (2018). ISBN 978-1-4503-5758-6. https://doi.org/10.1145/3205230.3205233

13. Bitcoin Community: Bitcoin developer guide-transaction data. https://bitcoin.org/en/developer-guide#transaction-data. Accessed 11 Apr 2017

14. Eyal, I., Gencer, A.E., Sirer, E.G., van Renesse, R.: Bitcoin-NG: a scalable blockchain protocol. In: 13th USENIX Security Symposium on Networked Systems Design and Implementation (NSDI 2016). USENIX Association, March 2016

15. Eyal, I., Sirer, E.G.: Majority is not enough: bitcoin mining is vulnerable. In: Christin, N., Safavi-Naini, R. (eds.) FC 2014. LNCS, vol. 8437, pp. 436–454. Springer, Heidelberg (2014). https://doi.org/10.1007/978-3-662-45472-5_28

16. Garay, J., Kiayias, A., Leonardos, N.: The bitcoin backbone protocol: analysis and applications. In: Oswald, E., Fischlin, M. (eds.) EUROCRYPT 2015. LNCS, vol. 9057, pp. 281–310. Springer, Heidelberg (2015). https://doi.org/10.1007/978-3-662-46803-6_10

17. Gencer, A.E., van Renesse, R., Sirer, E.G.: Short paper: service-oriented sharding for blockchains. In: Kiayias, A. (ed.) FC 2017. LNCS, vol. 10322, pp. 393–401. Springer, Cham (2017). https://doi.org/10.1007/978-3-319-70972-7_22

18. Giechaskiel, I., Cremers, C., Rasmussen, K.B.: On bitcoin security in the presence of broken cryptographic primitives. In: Askoxylakis, I., Ioannidis, S., Katsikas, S., Meadows, C. (eds.) ESORICS 2016. LNCS, vol. 9879, pp. 201–222. Springer, Cham (2016). https://doi.org/10.1007/978-3-319-45741-3_11

19. Jeffrey, C., Poon, J., Indutny, F., Pair, S.: Extension blocks (draft) (2017). https://github.com/tothemoon-org/extension-blocks/blob/master/spec.md. Accessed 11 Apr 2017

20. Judmayer, A., Zamyatin, A., Stifter, N., Voyiatzis, A.G., Weippl, E.: Merged mining: curse or cure? In: Garcia-Alfaro, J., Navarro-Arribas, G., Hartenstein, H., Herrera-Joancomartí, J. (eds.) ESORICS/DPM/CBT -2017. LNCS, vol. 10436, pp. 316–333. Springer, Cham (2017). https://doi.org/10.1007/978-3-319-67816-0_18

21. Karame, G.O., Androulaki, E., Roeschlin, M., Gervais, A., Čapkun, S.: Misbehavior in bitcoin: a study of double-spending and accountability. ACM Trans. Inf. Syst. Secur. (TISSEC) **18**, 2 (2015)

22. Kiayias, A., Miller, A., Zindros, D.: Non-interactive proofs of proof-of-work. Cryptology ePrint Archive, Report 2017/963 (2017). https://eprint.iacr.org/2017/963.pdf. Accessed 03 Oct 2017

23. Lau, J.: [bitcoin-dev] Extension block softfork proposal (2017). https://lists.linuxfoundation.org/pipermail/bitcoin-dev/2017-January/013490.html. Accessed 11 Apr 2017

24. Lombrozo, E., Lau, J., Wuille, P.: BIP141: segregated witness (consensus layer) (2012). https://github.com/bitcoin/bips/blob/master/bip-0141.mediawiki. Accessed 10 May 2017

25. McCorry, P., Heilman, E., Miller, A.: Atomically trading with Roger: gambling on the success of a hardfork. In: Garcia-Alfaro, J., Navarro-Arribas, G., Hartenstein, H., Herrera-Joancomartí, J. (eds.) ESORICS/DPM/CBT -2017. LNCS, vol. 10436, pp. 334–353. Springer, Cham (2017). https://doi.org/10.1007/978-3-319-67816-0_19

26. Nakamoto, S.: Bitcoin: a peer-to-peer electronic cash system (2008). https://bitcoin.org/bitcoin.pdf. Accessed 01 July 2015

27. Pass, R., Seeman, L., Shelat, A.: Analysis of the blockchain protocol in asynchronous networks. In: Coron, J.-S., Nielsen, J.B. (eds.) EUROCRYPT 2017. LNCS, vol. 10211, pp. 643–673. Springer, Cham (2017). https://doi.org/10.1007/978-3-319-56614-6_22

28. Pseudonymous ("TierNolan"): Decoupling transactions and POW (2013). https://bitcointalk.org/index.php?topic=179598.0. Accessed 10 May 2017

29. Rizun, P.R.: Subchains: a technique to scale bitcoin and improve the user experience. Ledger **1**, 38–52 (2016)

30. Rosenfeld, M.: Overview of colored coins (2012). https://bitcoil.co.il/BitcoinX.pdf. Accessed 09 Mar 2016

31. Rosenfeld, M.: Analysis of hashrate-based double spending (2014). http://arxiv.org/abs/1402.2009. Accessed 09 Mar 2016

32. Sapirshtein, A., Sompolinsky, Y., Zohar, A.: Optimal selfish mining strategies in bitcoin. In: Grossklags, J., Preneel, B. (eds.) FC 2016. LNCS, vol. 9603, pp. 515–532. Springer, Heidelberg (2017). https://doi.org/10.1007/978-3-662-54970-4_30

33. Sompolinsky, Y., Zohar, A.: Bitcoin's security model revisited (2016). http://arxiv.org/pdf/1605.09193. Accessed 04 July 2016

34. Stone, A.: Bip152: compact block relay (2015). https://github.com/BitcoinUnlimited/BUIP/blob/master/001.mediawiki. Accessed 01 Dec 2018

35. Swanson, T.: Consensus-as-a-service: a brief report on the emergence of permissioned, distributed ledger systems (2015). http://www.ofnumbers.com/wp-content/uploads/2015/04/Permissioned-distributed-ledgers.pdf. Accessed 03 Oct 2017

36. Zhang, R., Preneel, B.: On the necessity of a prescribed block validity consensus: analyzing bitcoin unlimited mining protocol. In: International Conference on Emerging Networking EXperiments and Technologies-CoNEXT 2017. ACM (2017)

Confidential Assets

Andrew Poelstra$^{(\boxtimes)}$, Adam Back, Mark Friedenbach, Gregory Maxwell,
and Pieter Wuille

Blockstream, Mountain View, CA, USA
{apoelstra,adam,mark,gmaxwell,pwuille}@blockstream.com

Abstract. Bitcoin is an online distributed ledger in which coins are distributed according to the *unspent transaction output (UTXO)* set, and transactions describe changes to this set. Every UTXO has associated to it an amount and signature verification key, representing the quantity that can be spent and the entity authorized to do so, respectively.

Because the ledger is distributed and publicly verifiable, every UTXO (and the history of all changes) is publicly available and may be used for analysis of all users' payment history. Although this history is not directly linked to users in any way, it exposes enough structure that even small amounts of personally identifiable information may completely break users' privacy. Further, the ability to trace coin history creates a market for "clean" coins, harming the fungibility of the underlying asset.

In this paper we describe a scheme, *confidential transactions*, which blinds the amounts of all UTXOs, while preserving public verifiability that no transaction creates or destroys coins. This removes a significant amount of information from the transaction graph, improving privacy and fungibility without a trusted setup or exotic cryptographic assumptions.

We further extend this to *confidential assets*, a scheme in which a single blockchain-based ledger may track multiple asset types. We extend confidential transactions to blind not only output amounts, but also their asset type, improving the privacy and fungibility of all assets.

1 Introduction

Deployed in 2009, Bitcoin [16] is an online currency with no trusted issuer or transaction processor, which works by means of a publicly verifiable distributed ledger called a *blockchain*. The blockchain contains every transaction since its inception, resulting in a final state, the *unspent transaction output set (UTXO set)*, which describes the amounts and owners of all coins.

Each UTXO contains an amount and a verification key; transactions destroy UTXOs and create new ones of equal or lesser total amount, and must be signed with the keys associated to each destroyed UTXO. This model allows all users to verify transaction correctness without trusting any payment processor to be honest or reliable. However, this model has a serious cost to user privacy, since every transaction is preserved forever, exposing significant amounts of information directly and indirectly [10].

© International Financial Cryptography Association 2019
A. Zohar et al. (Eds.): FC 2018 Workshops, LNCS 10958, pp. 43–63, 2019.
https://doi.org/10.1007/978-3-662-58820-8_4

One suggestion to obscure transaction structure is CoinJoin [13], which allows users to interactively combine transactions, obscuring which inputs map to which outputs. However, because transaction amounts are exposed, it is difficult to use CoinJoin in such a way that these mappings cannot be recovered, at least in a statistical sense [20]. In particular, unless all output amounts are the same, they are distinguishable and may be grouped.

We propose a partial solution to the exposure of transaction data, which blinds the amounts of all outputs, while preserving public verifiability of the fact that the total output amount is equal to the total input amount. This solution, termed *confidential transactions*, has been described informally by Maxwell [14] and deployed on the Elements Alpha sidechain [2] for over a year. In brief, each explicit UTXO amount is replaced by a homomorphic commitment to the amount. Since these amounts are homomorphic over a finite ring rather than the set of integers, we also attach a rangeproof to each output to prevent attacks related to overflow.

First, we formalize and improve confidential transactions, describing a space optimization of the underlying ring signature used in Elements Alpha. Then we extend confidential transactions to a new scheme, *confidential assets*, which further supports multiple asset types within single transactions. We retain public verifiability that no assets are created or destroyed, while hiding both the output amount(s) and the output asset type(s).

Related Work. Multi-asset blockchains were described in 2013 in Friedenbach and Timón's Freimarkets [8], though the supported assets were not confidential; that is, the amounts and asset tags of all inputs and outputs of transactions are publicly visible.

Support for asset issuance on top of Bitcoin has been proposed by means of *colored coins* [12], a scheme in which individual coins are marked in such a way that they are identifiable as representing distinct asset types. In effect, it works by exploiting Bitcoin's imperfect fungibility.

Ethereum [22] directly supports asset issuance using its smart contracting language, and has a standard means to do so which ensures interoperability with supporting software [18]. Like the above schemes, no attempt is made to obfuscating either the asset types or their amounts.

ZCash [21] is a recently announced cryptocurrency project which supports blinding of amounts, as well as any other identifying information about transaction inputs and outputs. It does not support multiple assets, though its use of zk-SNARKs [3], which are general-purpose zero-knowledge arguments, mean that asset support would not be a difficult extension.

However, ZCash's privacy comes at a significant cost: the underlying SNARKs use a trusted setup, meaning it is initialized by multiple parties who are able to collude to silently inflate the currency; it relies on novel cryptographic assumptions; its zero-knowledge proofs are very slow to compute. To contrast, the scheme described in this paper relies only on elliptic curve discrete logarithm (ECDL) being hard and the random oracle model, and all computations involve few and standard elliptic curve operations (e.g. no pairings).

2   Preliminaries

Definition 1. *We define a* Bitcoin transaction *as the following data:*

- *A list of* outputs, *containing a verification key and an amount.*
- *A list of* inputs, *which are unambiguous references to the outputs of other transactions. These also have signatures using the verification keys of their respective outputs.*
- *A* fee, *which is computed as the total input amount minus the total output amount, and is captured by the network.*

(To bootstrap the system, we also need *coinbase transactions*, which have outputs but no inputs; for the purpose of this paper they can be considered as transactions with negative fee.)

In Bitcoin, all amounts are explicit, and for a (non-coinbase) transaction to be valid, it must have a non-negative fee as well as valid signatures of the transaction with all inputs' verification keys.

We will replace these explicit amounts with homomorphic commitments, for which we need the following definitions.

Definition 2. *Given a message space* $\mathcal{M} = \mathbb{Z}_q$, *commitment space* $\mathcal{C} \simeq \mathcal{M}$ *and public parameters space* $\mathcal{PP}$, *we define a homomorphic commitment scheme as a triple of algorithms:*

- Setup: $\cdot \to \mathcal{PP}$
- Commit: $\mathcal{PP} \times \mathcal{M} \times \mathcal{M} \to \mathcal{C}$,
- Open: $\mathcal{PP} \times \mathcal{M} \times \mathcal{M} \times \mathcal{C} \to \{\text{true}, \text{false}\}$

satisfying, for pp $\leftarrow$ Setup,

- *for all* $(m, r) \in \mathcal{M} \times \mathcal{M}$, Open(pp, m, r, Commit(pp, m, r)) *accepts; and*
- *if*

$$\text{Open(pp}, m_1, r_1, C_1) \text{ and Open(pp}, m_2, r_2, C_2)$$

both accept, then

$$\text{Open(pp}, m_1 + m_2, r_1 + r_2, C_1 + C_2)$$

also accepts.

We will often leave pp *implicit and not mention it as an input to* Commit *or* Open. *Unless otherwise specified, all theorems are understood to hold for all* pp $\in \mathcal{PP}$.

We further require our commitments be binding and hiding, by which we mean the following.

Definition 3. *A commitment is* perfectly binding *if for all* $m \neq m' \in \mathcal{M}$, *all* $r, r' \in \mathcal{M}$, Open(m, r, Commit(m', r')) *rejects.*

It is computationally binding *if for all p.p.t. adversaries* $\mathcal{A}$, *the probability of* $\mathcal{A}$ *producing* (m', r') *with* $m' \neq m$ *such that* Open(m, r, Commit(m', r')) *accepts is negligible.*

Definition 4. *A commitment scheme is (perfectly, statistically, computationally) hiding if given* pp *and* $m_1 \neq m_2$, *the distributions*

$$U_1 = \{C : C \leftarrow \text{Commit}(\text{pp}, m_1, r), r \xleftarrow{\$} \mathcal{M}\}$$

$$U_2 = \{C : C \leftarrow \text{Commit}(\text{pp}, m_2, r), r \xleftarrow{\$} \mathcal{M}\}$$

are (equal, statistically indistinguishable, computationally indistinguishable).

For the purposes of this paper, we will use Pedersen commitments, which are computationally binding, perfectly hiding homomorphic commitments [17]. They are defined as follows.

Definition 5. *The* Pedersen commitment scheme *is the following triple of algorithms. We take* $\mathcal{M} = \mathbb{Z}_q$ *and* $\mathcal{C}$ *to be an isomorphic elliptic curve group; further* $\mathcal{H}$ *is a point-valued hash function modeled as a random oracle.*

- Setup *takes a cyclic group with distinguished generator* $(\mathcal{G}, G)$ *as well as auxiliary input* α. *It computes* $H = \mathcal{H}(\alpha)$ *and outputs* pp $= \{\mathcal{G}, G, H\}$.
- Commit(m, r) *outputs* $mH + rG$.
- Open(m, r, C) *accepts iff* $C = mH + rG$.

(The original Pedersen scheme uses uniformly random generators G, H, rather than taking H as the output of a hash function. In the random oracle model, these are equivalent.)

In order to commit to transaction amounts, which are integers, we will need to represent them as elements of $\mathcal{M} = \mathbb{Z}_q$, which will complicate matters since every multiple of q will be indistinguishable from zero. To avoid problems, we will need one more primitive.

Definition 6. *Given a homomorphic commitment scheme as above, and* $0 \leq A \leq B \leq q$, *we define a* rangeproof *of the range* $[A, B]$ *as a pair of randomized algorithms*

- Prove$_{[A,B]} : \mathcal{PP} \times \mathcal{M} \rightarrow \mathcal{C} \times \mathcal{M} \times \mathcal{S}$ *takes a value and generates a commitment to that value with opening information and an associated rangeproof.*
- Verify$_{[A,B]} : \mathcal{PP} \times \mathcal{C} \times \mathcal{S} \rightarrow \{\text{true}, \text{false}\}$ *takes a commitment and rangeproof and either accepts or rejects it.*

where $\mathcal{S}$ *represents the space of possible rangeproofs. We require that for all* $v \in [A, B]$, $(C, r, \pi) \leftarrow \text{Prove}_{[A,B]}(v)$ *that both*

$$\text{Verify}_{[A,B]}(C, \pi) \text{ and } \text{Open}(v, r, C)$$

accept.

We require the following security properties of rangeproofs:

Definition 7 *(Proving).* *Let* $0 \leq A \leq B \leq q$. *Then a rangeproof scheme is* proving *an amount in the range* $[A, B]$ *if for any p.p.t. algorithm* $\mathcal{A}$ *that outputs* $(C, \pi) \in \mathcal{C} \times \mathcal{S}$ *such that* Verify(C, π) *accepts, a simulator* $\mathcal{B}$ *exists which given oracle access to* $\mathcal{A}$ *can produce* (v, r) *such that* $v \in [A, B]$ *and* Open(v, r, C) *accepts.*

We observe that since the commitment scheme is binding, an opening to an amount in $[A, B]$ precludes an opening to any amount outside of $[A, B]$.

In light of Definition 7, given a commitment C with valid rangeproof π, we can talk about "the opening information (v, r) of C" unambiguously in simulation-based proofs, even without knowledge of it (since this knowledge can in principle be obtained by the simulator). In particular, any security proof which requires an adversary to produce opening information of commitments will continue to hold if the opening information is replaced by rangeproofs.

Definition 8 *(Statistical zero-knowledge). Given* pp $\in \mathcal{PP}$ *and two values* $v_1, v_2 \in [A, B]$, *the following distributions are identical:*

$$\{(C, \pi) : (C, \cdot, \pi) \leftarrow \text{Prove}\,(\text{pp}, v_1)\}$$

$$\{(C, \pi) : (C, \cdot, \pi) \leftarrow \text{Prove}\,(\text{pp}, v_2)\}$$

3   Confidential Transactions

3.1   Rangeproofs

We begin by describing an efficient rangeproof for Pedersen commitments over the interval $[0, m^n - 1]$, which has total size proportional to $1 + nm$, using a variant of a folklore bit-decomposition based rangeproof, in which numbers are expressed in base m and each digit is proven to lie in $[0, m - 1]$ using a ring signature.

We use a variant of Borromean Ring Signatures [15], which itself is a variant of the Abe-Ohkubo-Suzuki ring signature [1], tweaked to exploit the fact that many small rings of related keys are used.

Unlike some other rangeproofs in the literature [6], ours does not require a trusted setup[1]. In fact, the only cryptographic assumption it relies on is the hardness of discrete logarithm in the random oracle model. Nor is it interactive, as is the scheme described in [5]. Despite these improvements, our scheme still produces smaller proofs than these papers for the ranges (30–80 bits) that we are interested in.

Schoenmakers [19] described a simple rangeproof of base-b digits using the conjuction of zero-knowledge OR proofs of each digit. Our work is based on this rangeproof with the following changes: our OR proofs are based on Borromean Ring Signatures, which allow sharing a random challenge across every digit's proof, and we remove one scalar from each proof by a novel trick in which we may change the commitment to each digit (without changing the digit itself) while we produce the proof.

---

[1] While our rangeproof does require setup, the only generated parameters are uniformly random curvepoints, which can be generated with no possibility of trapdoor information, e.g. by the algorithm by Fouque and Tibouchi [7].

Definition 9 *(Back-Maxwell Rangeproof). Consider a Pedersen commitment scheme with generators G, H, and let $\mathcal{H} : \mathcal{C} \to \mathcal{M}$ be a random oracle hash.*

- Verify $\left(C, \pi = \left\{e_0, \left(C^0, s_1^0, s_2^0, \ldots, s_{m-1}^0\right), \ldots \left(C^{n-1}, s_1^{n-1}, s_2^{n-1}, \ldots, s_{m-1}^{n-1}\right)\right\}\right)$
  works as follows:
  1. *For each $i \in \{0, \ldots, n-1\}$,*
     (a) *Define $e_0^i = e_0$ for consistency of the following equations.*
     (b) *For each $j \in \{1, \ldots, m-1\}$, compute*

     $$e_j^i \leftarrow \mathcal{H}\left(s_j^i G - e_{j-1}^i \left[C^i - jm^i H\right]\right) \tag{1}$$

     (c) *Compute $R^i \leftarrow e_{m-1}^i C^i$.*
  2. *Compute $\hat{e}_0 \leftarrow \mathcal{H}(R^0 \| \cdots \| R^{n-1})$.*
  3. *Accept iff:*
     - *$\hat{e}_0 = e_0$; and*
     - *$C = \sum_i C^i$.*
- Prove(v, r). *Proving works as follows.*
  1. *Write v in base m as $v^0 + v^1 m + \cdots + v^{n-1} m^{n-1}$. (Note that superscripts on m are exponents while superscripts on v are just superscripts.)*
  2. *For each $i \in \{0, \ldots, n-1\}$,*

     (a) *If $v^i = 0$, choose $k_0^i \xleftarrow{\$} \mathbb{Z}_q$ and set $R^i \leftarrow k_0^i G$.*
     (b) *Otherwise,*
        i. *Choose r^i uniformly randomly and compute $C^i \leftarrow$ Commit $(m^i v^i, r^i)$.*
        ii. *Choose $k^i \xleftarrow{\$} \mathbb{Z}_q$ and compute $e_{v^i}^i \leftarrow \mathcal{H}(k^i G)$.*
        iii. *For each $j \in \{v^i + 1, \ldots, m-1\}$, choose $s_j^i \xleftarrow{\$} \mathbb{Z}_q$, and compute e_j^i directly from Eq. (1). (If $v^i = m - 1$, this step is a no-op.)*
        iv. *Compute $R^i \leftarrow e_{m-1}^i C^i$.*
  3. *Set $e_0 \leftarrow \mathcal{H}(R^0 \| \cdots \| R^{n-1})$.*
  4. *For each $i \in \{0, \ldots, n-1\}$,*
     (a) *If $v^i = 0$,*
        i. *For each $j \in \{1, \ldots, m-1\}$, choose*

        $$k_j^i \xleftarrow{\$} \mathbb{Z}_q$$
        $$e_j^i \leftarrow \mathcal{H}(k_j^i + e_{j-1}^i m^i j H)$$

        taking $e_0^i = e_0$.
        ii. *Set $C^i \leftarrow R^i / e_{m-1}^i = \frac{k_0^i}{e_{m-1}^i} G$.*
        iii. *For each $j \in \{1, \ldots, m-1\}$, set $s_j^i \leftarrow k_j^i + \frac{k_0^i e_{j-1}^i}{e_{m-1}^i}$.*
     (b) *Otherwise,*
        i. *For each $j \in \{1, \ldots, v^i - 1\}$, choose $s_j^i \xleftarrow{\$} \mathbb{Z}_q$, and compute e_j^i directly from Eq. (1), taking $e_0^i = e_0$. (If $v_i = 1$ this is a no-op.)*
        ii. *Set $s_{v^i}^i = k^i + e_{v^i-1}^i r^i$.*

5. *Set $C \leftarrow \sum_{i=0}^{n-1} C^i$. Output*

$$\pi = \left\{ e_0, \left(C^0, s_1^0, s_2^0, \ldots, s_{m-1}^0 \right), \ldots \left(C^{n-1}, s_1^{n-1}, s_2^{n-1}, \ldots, s_{m-1}^{n-1} \right) \right\}.$$

We observe that this is nearly the same construction as Borromean Ring Signatures except for the following two differences:

- There are no s_0^i values, which were used in the calculation of $\hat{e}_0$ in the Borromean Ring Signature construction, saving i scalars in the total proof.
- The commitments C^i are no longer included in any hashes (which is necessary when computing sub-commitments to the digit $(m-1)$, as seen in step 4(a)ii of the Prove algorithm).

    Unfortunately, the resulting construction is no longer a secure ring signature in general; the proof of security depends on all keys being binding commitments rather than arbitrary public keys.

It is immediate that the above construction is a correct rangeproof. We argue security in the next two theorems.

Theorem 1. *If the underlying commitment scheme is binding in the sense of Definition 3, then the above construction is a proving rangeproof in the sense of Definition 7.*

Proof. Let (C, π) be generated by some p.p.t. algorithm $\mathcal{A}$, such that Verify(C, π) accepts. Write

$$\pi = \left\{ e_0, \left(C^0, s_1^0, s_2^0, \ldots, s_{m-1}^0 \right), \ldots \left(C^{n-1}, s_1^{n-1}, s_2^{n-1}, \ldots, s_{m-1}^{n-1} \right) \right\}.$$

By Theorem 8 in Appendix A, with nonnegligible probability $\mathcal{A}$ can be used to obtain openings (v^i, r^i) of each C^i with $v^i \in \{0, m^i, 2m^i, \ldots, (m-1)m^i\}$. By summing these we obtain an opening (v, r) of C with $v \in [0, m^n]$.

Theorem 2. *The above construction is zero-knowledge in the sense of Definition 8.*

Proof. This is nearly immediate. Observe that all values output by the Prove algorithm are selected independently uniformly at random, except where they are forced by the verification equations (which are independent of the committed values).

3.2   Confidential Transactions

We now modify the definition of Bitcoin transaction (Definition 1).

Definition 10. *We define a* confidential transaction *as the following data:*

- *A list of* outputs, *containing a verification key, Pedersen commitment to an amount, and Back-Maxwell rangeproof that it lies in a range $[0, 2^n - 1]$ with n significantly smaller than the bit-length of size of the committed-value group.*

- *A list of* inputs, *which are unambiguous references to the outputs of other transactions, with signatures using the verification keys of those outputs.*
- *A fee f, which is listed explicitly.*

Our validity condition is changed as follows: the fee must be non-negative (except for coinbase transactions), the sum of all input commitments minus all output conditions must equal fH, and there must be valid signatures with all inputs' verification keys. This equation is important enough to give it a name.

Definition 11. *The* verification equation *is: input amounts minus output amounts equals fee (times H, when these amounts are considered as commitments).*

To summarize, the differences between confidential transactions and Bitcoin transactions are:

- Explicit amounts are replaced by homomorphically committed ones.
- Rather than computing the fee, it is given explicitly and checked that the inputs minus outputs commit to it.

Payment authorization is achieved by means of the input signatures, which are unchanged from Bitcoin and not discussed in this paper. However, we need to argue that this change does not allow coins to be created invalidly.

Theorem 3. *Consider a valid confidential transaction with fee f, inputs committing to amounts $\{I_i\}_{i=0}^k$, and outputs committing to amounts $\{O_i\}_{i=0}^\ell$. Suppose also that $k + \ell + 1 < |\mathcal{C}|/R$, where the output rangeproofs are to the range $[0, R-1]$ and $f \in [0, R-1]$[2]. If the rangeproofs are proving and the commitments are binding, then no subset of $\{O_i\}$ commits to more than $\sum_{i=0}^k I_i - f$.*

We observe that simply arguing that $\sum_{i=0}^k I_i - f = \sum_{i=0}^\ell O_i$ is insufficient: for example, with zero inputs and fee, an attacker could commit to two output amounts $\{1, -1\}$, and have created a coin from nowhere even though the total equation balances.

Proof. Since all rangeproofs are valid and commitments are binding, for each i we have $0 \le O_i \le R$. Similarly for the inputs, which are outputs of previous (valid) transactions.

Next, since the input commitments minus output commitments equal fH, we have $\sum_{i=0}^k I_i - f - \sum_{i=0}^\ell O_i \equiv 0 \pmod{|\mathcal{C}|}$, or

$$\sum_{i=0}^k I_i - f - \sum_{i=0}^\ell O_i = m|\mathcal{C}|$$

---

[2] Typically the group order $\mathcal{C} \approx 2^{256}$ and $R \approx 2^{64}$ so this requirement is physically impossible to violate in practice.

for some integer m. Now, since $k + \ell + 1 < |\mathcal{C}|/R$, and by our bounds on the individual terms, we can bound the left side of this equation as

$$-|\mathcal{C}| < \sum_{i=0}^{k} I_i - f - \sum_{i=0}^{\ell} O_i < |\mathcal{C}|.$$

But this implies that $m = 0$, i.e. that the input amounts add to the output amounts (plus fee).

Finally, since all output amounts are positive, every subset of outputs must sum to less than or equal to $\sum_{i=0}^{k} I_i - f$, as desired.

3.3 Performance

Consider a group $\mathcal{G}$ where both scalars and group elements are encoded in 1 unit of space (in practice, 32 bytes or 256 bits). We contrast three schemes: a naive folklore rangeproof using separate AOS ring signatures for each digit; one using Borromean Ring Signatures [15] as implemented in Elements Alpha [2]; and our scheme described above. We compare asymptotic and also look at the specific case $2^{38} \approx 3^{24}$. While the naive and Alpha schemes are space-optimal in base 4, our scheme is space-optimal in base 3^3.

Scheme	Base	Digits	Range	Total Size
Naive	m	n	m^n	$(m+2)n$
Alpha	m	n	m^n	$1 + (m+1)n$
Ours	m	n	m^n	$1 + mn$
Naive	4	19	2^{38}	114
Alpha	4	19	2^{38}	96
Ours	3	24	3^{24}	73

For this range we observe a 24% reduction from the Alpha rangeproof and 36% reduction from the naive rangeproof at a slightly larger range.

4 Confidential Assets

4.1 Asset Commitments and Surjection Proofs

Before moving on, we need a few more primitives.

Definition 12. *Given some asset description A (whose precise form is given in Sect. 4.4), the associated* asset tag *is an element $H_A \in \mathcal{G}$ obtained by execution of the Pedersen commitment* Setup *using A as auxiliary input.*

When using multiple Pedersen commitment schemes, we distinguish them by adding their second generator as a subscript to their algorithms, like Open_{H_A} *or* Commit_{H_A}.

---

[3] The optimality of one base over another comes from the fact that numbers in higher bases have fewer digits, reducing the size of each OR proof, while increasing the size of the individual OR proofs. Since in base b, the Alpha rangeproof requires b scalars and a commitment, while our optimization requires only $b - 1$ scalars and a commitment, the optimum has shifted.

In particular, in the random oracle model an asset tag is a uniformly random curve point whose discrete logarithm is not known with respect to G or any other asset tag.

Definition 13. *Given an asset tag H_A, an (ephemeral) asset commitment is a point of the form $H = H_A + rG$, for uniformly random r. We sometimes abuse terminology to say that H is a commitment to the asset H_A.*

In the next section, we are going to use these asset commitments in place of the generator H in our Pedersen commitments. The following theorems justify this.

Theorem 4. *Let H be an asset commitment to asset tag H_A, and C a Pedersen commitment such that $\mathrm{Open}_H(v, r, C)$ accepts. Then if $H_A = H + sG$, $\mathrm{Open}_{H_A}(v, r - sv, C)$ accepts.*

This theorem is immediate, and implies that Pedersen commitments to an amount with some asset commitment as generator are also Pedersen commitments to the same amount with the underlying asset tag as generator. Further, anyone who knows the blinding factor s and the opening information with respect to one generator can determine the opening information with respect to the other generator.

Such Pedersen commitments commit not only to the committed amount, but also to the underlying asset tag, in the following sense.

Theorem 5. *If a p.p.t. algorithm $\mathcal{A}$ exists which can win with nonnegligible probability in the following game, then a simulator $\mathcal{B}$ exists which can solve the discrete logarithm problem for $\mathcal{G}$ with nonnegligible probability.*

1. *$\mathcal{A}$ calls Setup_i to produce asset tags H_i for $i = 0, 1, \ldots, n$.*
2. *$\mathcal{A}$ produces commitments C_i and openings (v_i, r_i) such that $\mathrm{Open}_i(v_i, r_i, C_i)$ accepts for $i = 1, \ldots, n$.*
3. *$\mathcal{A}$ produces an opening (v, r) such that $v \neq 0$ and $\mathrm{Open}_0(v, r, \sum_{i=1}^n C_i)$ accepts.*

The proof of this theorem is given in the Appendix.

By the comment following Definition 7, the same theorem holds if the adversary is required to produce rangeproofs rather than opening information.

We will attach fresh random asset commitments to all transaction outputs, and we need a way to link inputs and outputs without revealing the mapping. The following tool will be essential.

Definition 14. *An* asset surjection proof *(ASP) scheme consists of the following algorithms.*

- Prove *takes a collection $\{H_i\}_{i=1}^n$ of "input" asset commitments, an "output" commitment $H = H_{i^*} + rG$ for some $1 \le i^* \le n$, and r. It outputs a proof π.*
- Verify *takes a collection $\{H_i\}_{i=1}^n$, H, and a proof π and either accepts or rejects.*

We often say that an ASP is *from* the set $\{H_i\}$ of input commitments *to* the output commitment H.

Definition 15. *An ASP is secure if a proof π produced by the* Prove *algorithm is a zero-knowledge proof of knowledge (zkPoK) of the blinding factor r.*

This is easy to construct from a ring signature which is a zkPoK of one of its secret keys, for example the AOS ring signatures described in [1].

Definition 16. *The* AOS ASP *is the following:*

- Prove *computes the n differences $H - H_i$ for $i = 1, \ldots, n$ (one of which will be r) and computes a ring signature of an empty message with these differences. The proof π is the signature.*
- Verify *computes the same differences and verifies the ring signature.*

It is immediate that the AOS ASP is secure if the underlying AOS ring signature scheme is a zkPoK.

4.2   Confidential Assets

Up to now, we have considered a single asset (for example Bitcoin) and transactions which move this asset from one holder to another. Consider an extension of this scheme which supports multiple non-interchangeable *asset types* (for example, BTC and a USD proxy) within single transactions. This increases the value of the chain by allowing it to serve more users, and also enables new functionality, such as atomic trades of different assets.

We could accomplish this by attaching to each output an *asset tag* identifying the type of that asset, and having verifiers check that the verification equation holds for subsets of the transaction which have only a single asset type. (Basically, treating the transaction as multiple single-asset transactions, except that each input signs the entire aggregate transaction.)

This requires verification of multiple equations, increases complexity, and more importantly, gives chain analysts an additional data point to consider, reducing the privacy of the users of the chain. This also could lead to censorship of transactions involving specific asset types, since all asset types are visible.

We instead propose a scheme for which all asset tags are blinded, so that no relationship between output asset types can be inferred. This avoids the privacy loss and greatly *improves* privacy by hiding the specific assets used by individual transactions. This is especially important for assets with low transaction volume where use of the asset alone is sufficient to identify users.

Definition 17. *A* confidential asset transaction *is the following data:*

- *A list of* inputs, *which are one of two forms:*
    - *an unambiguous reference to an output of another transaction, with a signature using that output's verification key*

- an asset issuance input, *which has an explicit amount and asset tag; the precise validity rules for these are defined outside of this paper, but they are discussed further in Sect. 4.4.*
- A list of outputs, *containing*
  - *a verification key,*
  - *an asset commitment H_o with a ASP from all input asset commitments to H_o;*
  - *Pedersen commitment to an amount using generator H_o in place of H, with Back-Maxwell rangeproof (also using H_o in place of H) that it lies in a range $[0, 2^n - 1]$ with n significantly smaller than the bit-length of size of the committed-value group.*
- A fee $\{(f_i, H_i)\}_{i=1}^n$, *which is listed explicitly. Here the f_i's are scalar amounts denominated in the assets whose tags are the respective H_i. We require all H_i's to be distinct for simplicity. (Note that the asset types used to pay fees must be revealed. In practice we expect a working system to use fees denominated in only one asset, say, Bitcoin, so privacy is not lost.)*

  Each f_i must always be nonnegative; assets originate in asset-issuance inputs, which take the place of coinbase transactions in confidential transactions.

The validity equation is identical to that for confidential transactions, except that the fee commitment is calculated as $\sum_{i=1}^n f_i H_i$ instead of simply fH.

Again, payment authorization is achieved by means of the input signatures, so we do not argue this, only that no assets are created. We first prove a theorem to argue that the construction is sensible.

Theorem 6. *Consider a valid confidential asset transaction and let H be any fixed asset tag. Then the transaction is valid for H, in the following sense. Restrict the transaction to those inputs and outputs whose asset commitments are to H, and take $f = f_i$ if $H_i = H$ for any i and zero otherwise.*

Then if the discrete logarithm problem is hard in the underlying group, the sum of input commitments minus the sum of output commitments of this restricted transaction cannot be opened to any amount except f.

Proof. Consider the algorithm $\mathcal{A}$ which produced the transaction, and the transactions whose outputs are used as inputs, and so on. (In practice $\mathcal{A}$ will be the conjunction of many different transacting parties, but this does not affect our argument.)

Since every output has a rangeproof and ASP associated to it, which are proofs of knowledge of the opening information and asset commitment blinding factor, respectively, of every output, there exists a simulator $\mathcal{B}$ which extracts this information from $\mathcal{A}$. Using the blinding factors and Theorem 4, we can consider every rangeproof as being with respect to the underlying asset tag, rather than the asset commitment.

Now, consider the sum of the outputs minus inputs minus fH of the restricted transaction is some commitment C. This commits to some amount of H. But since the non-restricted transaction is valid, we have that the remaining outputs minus inputs, minus remaining fees, equals $-C$. Since the remaining inputs, outputs, and fees are commitments to non-H asset tags, by Theorem 5, C must commit to 0, completing the proof.

Theorem 7. *Consider a valid confidential asset transaction and let H be any fixed asset tag. Suppose the transaction has fee f $\{(f_i, H_i)\}_{i=1}^{n}$, inputs committing to amounts $\{I_i\}_{i=0}^{k}$, and outputs committing to amounts $\{O_i\}_{i=0}^{\ell}$. Suppose also that $k + \ell < |\mathcal{C}|/R$, where the rangeproofs prove to the range $[0, R - 1]$. If the rangeproofs are proving and the commitments are binding, then no subset of $\{O_i\}$ commits to more than $\sum_{i=0}^{k} I_i - f$.*

Proof. By the above theorem, the transaction restricted to only inputs and outputs with asset tag H is a valid confidential transaction, except that the output commitments minus input commitments minus fee sum to a commitment to 0, rather than the 0 point itself. The proof of Theorem 3, which does not make use of this distinction, therefore goes through without change on the restricted transaction.

4.3   Performance

In Sect. 3.3 we described the size of our rangeproofs, which are attached to every transaction output. This is unchanged for confidential assets, but we also require two additional pieces of data: an asset commitment and an ASP showing that this commitment is legitimate.

In the units of Sect. 3.3, the asset commitment has size 1 and the ASP has size $n + 1$, where n is the number of inputs that a given output may have come from.

For any entire transaction with m outputs and n inputs, the additional data therefore has size $m(n + 2)$. We can improve this at the cost of privacy by using a weaker form of an ASP which proves an asset commitment is the same as one of 3 inputs, rather than being the same as any of them. The additional data would then have cost only $5m$, which is asymptotically better.

4.4   Issuance

As discussed in Sect. 4.1, the *asset tag* is an element $H_A \in \mathcal{G}$ obtained by execution of the Pedersen commitment Setup using an auxiliary input A. In the context of a blockchain, we want to ensure that any input A is used only once to ensure assets cannot be inflated by means of multiple independent issuances. Associating an issuance with the spend of a UTXO, and a maximum of one issuance per specific UTXO achieves this uniqueness property. The unambiguous reference to the UTXO being spent is hashed together with a issuer-specified value, the *Ricardian contract hash* [9], to generate the auxiliary input A to the Pedersen commitment.

Definition 18. *Given an input being spent I, itself an unambiguous reference to an output of another transaction, and the issuer-specified Ricardian contract C, the asset entropy E is defined as $Hash(Hash(I) \| Hash(C))$.*

The *Ricardian contract* is a machine parseable legal document specifying the conditions for use, and especially redemption of the asset being issued [9]. The details of how such a contract might be designed or enforced is outside the scope of this paper. All that matters for the purposes here is that such a document exists and that its hash is irrevocably committed to in the issuance of the asset.

Definition 19. *Given an* asset entropy E, *the* asset tag *is the element* $H_A \in \mathcal{G}$ *obtained by execution of the Pedersen commitment* Setup *using* $Hash(E\|0)$ *as the auxiliary input.*

Every non-coinbase transaction input can have associated with it up to one new asset issuance:

Definition 20. *An* asset issuance input *consists of an UTXO spend I (interpreted as a non-issuance input of the same transaction); a* Ricardian contract C; *an initial issuance explicit value v_0, or Pedersen commitment H and Back-Maxwell rangeproof P_0; and a Boolean field indicating whether reissuance is allowed.*

Reissuance will be explained in Sect. 4.5.

4.5   Reissuance and Capability Tokens

Assets may be either of fixed issuance or, optionally, enable later reissuance using a *asset reissuance capability*. This capability is a token providing its owner with the ability to change the amount of asset in circulation at any point after the initial issuance. When a reissuable asset is created, both the initial asset issuance and the reissuance capability token are generated at the same time.

Definition 21. *Given an* asset entropy E, *the* asset reissuance capability *is the element* $H_A \in \mathcal{G}$ *obtained by execution of the Pedersen commitment* Setup *using* $Hash(E\|1)$ *as the auxiliary input.*

An asset which supports reissuance indicates this in its asset issuance input, and the transaction contains an additional output of amount 1 which commits to asset tag H_A.

Note the parallel to the definition of the *asset tag* given in Sect. 4.4, but with the concatenation of a different constant before hashing. In this way an asset tag is linked to its corresponding reissuance capability, and the holder of such a capability is able to assert their reissuance right simply by revealing the blinding factor for the capability along with the original asset entropy.

Definition 22. *An* asset reissuance input *consists of a spend of a UTXO containing an asset reissuance capability; the original asset entropy E; the blinding factor for the asset commitment of the UTXO being spent; and either an explicit reissuance amount v_i, or Pedersen commitment H and Back-Maxwell rangeproof P_i.*

We call attention to the fact that this reissuance mechanism is a specific instance of a general capability-based authentication scheme. It is possible to use the same scheme to define capabilities that gate access to other restricted operations. In the authors' implementation there exists separate capabilities for increasing and decreasing issuance, and explicit vs committed reissuance amounts. In general the right being protected could even be made extensible by making the commitment generator the hash of a script that validates the spending transaction.

4.6   Performance

In contrast to Confidential Transactions, in which every output has an attached rangeproof, each Confidential Assets output must also have an asset tag and asset surjection proof. As in Sect. 3.3, we consider curvepoints and scalars to have the same size,

For an output whose amount is in the range $[0, m^n)$ and whose asset references A assets, the total size of the rangeproof and ASP is therefore $(1+mn)+(2+A)$ where the first term is the contribution of the rangeproof and the second the contribution of the asset tag and ASP. For a prototypical example of a $[0, 3^{24})$ rangeproof and three inputs, the total is 78 scalars, or 19968 bits.

4.7   "Small Assets" and "Big Assets"

To prove that the asset commitments associated to outputs commit to legitimately issued asset tags, we have used asset surjection proofs which show that they commit to the same asset tag as some input (if those inputs are outputs of previous transactions, they have ASP's showing the same thing, and so on until the process terminates at an asset issuance input which has an explicit asset tag).

This allows confidential assets to work on a blockchain which supports indefinitely many asset types, which may be added after the chain has been defined.

An alternate scheme, which works for a small fixed set of asset tags, is to define the asset tags at the start of the chain, and to have each output include an ASP to the global list of asset tags. We refer to this scheme as "small assets" and the more general scheme as "big assets".

It is also possible to do an intermediate scheme, by having a global dynamic list of assets with each transaction selecting a subset of asset tags which its outputs have an ASP to. In general, there is room to adapt this scheme for optimal tradeoff between ASP size and privacy for specific use cases.

We observe that small assets is compatible with Mimblewimble [11], a new extension to confidential transactions which improves privacy and scaling by removing information from the transaction graph, while big assets is not.

5   Future Research

The authors describe some research directions they would like to see.

Rangeproof Efficiency. While this paper describes the most efficient rangeproof construction without trusted setup that the authors are aware of, in practice for a blockchain-based currency, rangeproofs are still the bulk of the transaction data. Further improvements, especially asymptotic ones, would help.

ASP Efficiency. Similarly, the ASP construction scales with both the number of inputs and the number of outputs; by restricting the set of inputs it uses we improve this at cost of user privacy, but it is desirable to avoid this tradeoff.

Aggregate Rangeproofs. If it were possible to aggregate rangeproofs (*e.g.* to combine proofs that C_1 and C_2 commit to values in $[0, 2^n - 1]$ into a single proof that $C_1 + C_2$ commits to a value in $[0, 2^{n+1} - 1]$), this would also improve the efficiency of a blockchain-based system, since proofs could be placed in a Merkle-sum tree whose nodes contained an aggregate rangeproof of the rangeproofs of their children. Then validators could check only the root to ensure an entire tree did not cause any inflation, delaying checking the proofs on individual outputs until those outputs are spent.

Quantum Resistance. The primitives described in this paper all depend on the elliptic-curve discrete logarithm assumption, which is known to be insecure against a quantum adversary. A quantum-hard analogue would require a replacement for Pedersen commitments (perhaps [4]), for the ring signatures used by ASP's, and for rangeproofs.

Acknowledgements. We thank Ben Gorlick for his input on the practical requirements of a confidential assets-based system, and his technical review, and feedback on the systems design.

A   Appendix: Proofs

Theorem 8. *Fix integers $i \geq 0$, $m > 0$. Consider an algorithm $\mathcal{A}$ which can produce the tuple*

$$\pi = (\alpha, e_0, C, s_1, \ldots, s_{m-1})$$

such that one can define, for $j \in \{1, \ldots, m-1\}$,

$$e_j \leftarrow \mathcal{H}\left(s_j G - e_{j-1}\left[C - jm^i H\right]\right),$$

$$R \leftarrow e_{m-1} C,$$

and it holds that $e_0 = \mathcal{H}(R\|\alpha)$. (Observe that the formula for e_j is the same as (1) from Definition 9; this represents the verification equation of a single ring. Here α is auxiliary data that $\mathcal{A}$ chooses, but in the full algorithm it consists of the R values from the other rings.)

Then a simulator $\mathcal{B}$ exists, which given oracle access to $\mathcal{A}$, can extract an opening (v, r) such that $\text{Open}(v, r, C)$ accepts and $v \in \{0, m^i, \ldots, (m-1)m^i\}$.

Proof. Suppose that $\mathcal{A}$ makes at most q random oracle queries. $\mathcal{B}$ acts as follows. For each random oracle query it chooses a uniformly random scalar and responds with this.

It chooses $i^* \in \{1, \ldots, q\}$ uniformly at random, and on the i^*th query, $\mathcal{B}$ forks $\mathcal{A}$ into $\mathcal{A}$ and $\mathcal{A}'$. It gives e_{i^*} to $\mathcal{A}$, e'_{i^*} to $\mathcal{A}'$, and answers further queries from other algorithms with uniformly random values.

Let the final output of the two algorithms be

$$\pi = (\alpha, e_0, C, s_1, \ldots, s_{m-1})$$

$$\pi' = (\alpha', e'_0, C', s'_1, \ldots, s'_{m-1})$$

and similarly e_j and e'_j are defined as in the hypothesis.

With probability $1/q - negl$, we have $e_j = e'_j$ for all j except one, j^*. (This is the probability that the i^*th query was the last e_j that $\mathcal{A}$ needed, and that it obtained every e_j by querying the random oracle rather than guessing.) Abort otherwise.

We consider four cases.

1. If $j^* = m - 1$, then

$$e_0 = \mathcal{H}(e_{m-1}C\|\alpha) = \mathcal{H}(e'_{m-1}C'\|\alpha') = e'_0$$

so that except with negligible probability, $\alpha = \alpha'$ and $C = \frac{e'_{m-1}}{e_{m-1}}C'$. Now,

$$e_{m-1} = \mathcal{H}\left(s_{m-1}G - e_{m-2}\left[C - (m-1)m^iH\right]\right)$$

$$e'_{m-1} = \mathcal{H}'\left(s'_{m-1}G - e_{m-2}\left[C' - (m-1)m^iH\right]\right)$$

where $\mathcal{H}$, $\mathcal{H}'$ are used to emphasize which side of the fork received these random oracle responses. But by hypothesis, the input to these queries is the same, that is,

$$s_{m-1}G - e_{m-2}\left[C - (m-1)m^iH\right] = s'_{m-1}G - e_{m-2}\left[C' - (m-1)m^iH\right]$$

which is sufficient to solve for the discrete logarithms r, r' of $C - (m-1)m^iH$ and $C' - (m-1)m^iH$, giving us openings $(m-1, r)$ and $(m-1, r')$ for the commitments of the two forks.

2. If $j^* \neq m - 1$ and $C = C'$, then

$$e_{j^*+1} = \mathcal{H}\left(s_{j^*+1}G - e_{j^*}\left[C - j^*m^iH\right]\right)$$
$$= \mathcal{H}\left(s'_{j^*+1}G - e'_{j^*}\left[C - j^*m^iH\right]\right)$$
$$= e'_{j^*+1}$$

and we can solve for the discrete logarithm r of $C - j^*m^iH$, and our desired opening for C (the output of both forks) is (j^*m^i, r).

3. If $j^* = 0$ and $C \neq C'$, we have that the inputs to

$$e_0 = \mathcal{H}(e_{m-1}C\|\alpha)$$

$$e_0' = \mathcal{H}(e_{m-1}'C'\|\alpha')$$

are the same, and $e_{m-1} = e_{m-1}'$ by hypothesis. This implies $C = C'$, a contradiction.

4. If $0 < j^* < m - 1$ and $C \neq C'$, observe that

$$e_{j^*} = \mathcal{H}\left(s_{j^*}G - e_{j^*}\left[C - j^*m^iH\right]\right)$$

$$e_{j^*}' = \mathcal{H}'\left(s_{j^*}'G - e_{j^*}'\left[C' - j^*m^iH\right]\right)$$

and as in case 1, by hypothesis

$$s_{j^*}G - e_{j^*}\left[C - j^*m^iH\right] = s_{j^*}'G - e_{j^*}'\left[C' - j^*m^iH\right] \tag{2}$$

Similarly,

$$\begin{aligned}
e_{m-1} &= \mathcal{H}\left(s_{m-1}G - e_{m-2}\left[C - (m-1)m^iH\right]\right) \\
&= \mathcal{H}\left(s_{m-1}'G - e_{m-2}'\left[C' - (m-1)m^iH\right]\right) \\
&= e_{m-1}'
\end{aligned}$$

so

$$s_{m-1}G - e_{m-1}\left[C - (m-1)m^iH\right] = s_{m-1}'G - e_{m-1}'\left[C' - (m-1)m^iH\right] \tag{3}$$

Now, after rearranging, (2) is

$$\frac{1}{j^*m^i(e_{j^*}' - e_{j^*})}\left[(s_{j^*} - s_{j^*}')G + e_{j^*}'C' - e_{j^*}C\right] = H$$

and (3) is

$$\frac{1}{(m-1)m^i(e_{m-1}' - e_{m-1})}\left[(s_{m-1} - s_{m-1}')G + e_{m-1}'C' - e_{m-1}C\right] = H$$

which combine to determine the discrete logarithms r, r' of C and C', so that $(0, r)$ and $(0, r')$ are the desired openings.

A.1   Proof of Theorem 3

Proof. Recall that G is a fixed random generator of $\mathcal{G}$. Let (G, X) be $\mathcal{B}$'s discrete logarithm challenge, *i.e.* $\mathcal{B}$ succeeds if it outputs x such that $X = xG$. We consider two types of adversary: a type I adversary's output satisfies $\sum_{i=1}^n r_i \neq r$, while a type II has equality. We assume that $\mathcal{A}$ makes at most q random oracle queries.

For a Type I adversary, $\mathcal{B}$ acts as follows.

First, $\mathcal{B}$ responds to random oracle queries by choosing random scalars r and replying with rX. Then from $\mathcal{A}$'s perspective, Setup_i outputs uniformly a random generators H_i; however $\mathcal{B}$ knows scalars s_i such that $H_i = s_i X$.

Now, let (C_i, v_i, r_i, v, r) for $i = 1, \ldots, n$ be the output of $\mathcal{A}$. Write $C = \sum_{i=1}^{n} C_i$. We have

$$0 = C - \sum_{i=1}^{n} C_i$$

$$= vH_0 + rG - \sum_{i=1}^{n} [v_i H_i + r_i G]$$

$$= vs_0 X + rG - \sum_{i=1}^{n} [v_i s_i X + r_i G]$$

$$= \left[vs_0 - \sum_{i=1}^{n} v_i s_i \right] X + \left[r - \sum_{i=1}^{n} r_i \right] G$$

Since the sum in the right term is nonzero for a type I adversary, so must be the sum in the left term, so we have

$$x = \frac{r - \sum_{i=1}^{n} r_i}{vs_0 - \sum_{i=1}^{n} v_i s_i}$$

which satisfies $X = xG$.

For a Type II adversary, $\mathcal{B}$ acts as follows. It responds for the Type I simulator, except for one random oracle queries it replies with sG rather than sX. Then with probability $1/q$ we have $H_0 = s_0 G$, and if not we abort. We also abort if $s_0 = 0$, which occurs with negligible probability.

The above equation then becomes

$$0 = \left[\sum_{i=1}^{n} v_i s_i \right] X + \left[vs_0 + r - \sum_{i=1}^{n} r_i \right] G$$

where the right term is equal to $vs_0 \neq 0$, so the left term must also be nonzero, and

$$x = \frac{vs_0}{\sum_{i=1}^{n} v_i s_i}$$

satisfies $X = xG$.

References

1. Abe, M., Ohkubo, M., Suzuki, K.: 1-out-of-n signatures from a variety of keys. In: Zheng, Y. (ed.) ASIACRYPT 2002. LNCS, vol. 2501, pp. 415–432. Springer, Heidelberg (2002). https://doi.org/10.1007/3-540-36178-2_26
2. Back, A.: Announcing sidechain elements: open source code and developer sidechains for advancing bitcoin. Blockstream blog post (2015). https://blockstream.com/2015/06/08/714/
3. Ben-Sasson, E., Chiesa, A., Genkin, D., Tromer, E., Virza, M.: SNARKs for C: verifying program executions succinctly and in zero knowledge. Cryptology ePrint Archive, Report 2013/507 (2013). http://eprint.iacr.org/2013/507
4. Cabarcas, D., Demirel, D., Göpfert, F., Lancrenon, J., Wunderer, T.: An unconditionally hiding and long-term binding post-quantum commitment scheme. Cryptology ePrint Archive, Report 2015/628 (2015). http://eprint.iacr.org/2015/628
5. Camenisch, J., Chaabouni, R., Shelat, A.: Efficient protocols for set membership and range proofs. In: Pieprzyk, J. (ed.) ASIACRYPT 2008. LNCS, vol. 5350, pp. 234–252. Springer, Heidelberg (2008). https://doi.org/10.1007/978-3-540-89255-7_15
6. Chaabouni, R., Lipmaa, H., Zhang, B.: A non-interactive range proof with constant communication. In: Keromytis, A.D. (ed.) FC 2012. LNCS, vol. 7397, pp. 179–199. Springer, Heidelberg (2012). https://doi.org/10.1007/978-3-642-32946-3_14
7. Fouque, P.-A., Tibouchi, M.: Indifferentiable hashing to Barreto–Naehrig curves. In: Hevia, A., Neven, G. (eds.) LATINCRYPT 2012. LNCS, vol. 7533, pp. 1–17. Springer, Heidelberg (2012). https://doi.org/10.1007/978-3-642-33481-8_1
8. Friedenbach, M., Timón, J.: Freimarkets: extending bitcoin protocol with user-specified bearer instruments, peer-to-peer exchange, off-chain accounting, auctions, derivatives and transitive transactions (2013). http://freico.in/docs/freimarkets-v0.0.1.pdf
9. Grigg, I.: The ricardian contract. In: First IEEE International Workshop on Electronic Contracting. IEEE (2004)
10. Hearn, M.: Merge avoidance: privacy enhancing techniques in the bitcoin protocol (2013). http://www.coindesk.com/merge-avoidance-privacy-bitcoin/
11. Jedusor, T.: Mimblewimble. Defunct hidden service (2016). http://5pdcbgndmprm4wud.onion/mimblewimble.txt. Reddit discussion at https://www.reddit.com/r/Bitcoin/comments/4vub3y/mimblewimble_noninteractive_coinjoin_and_better/
12. jl2012: OP_CHECKCOLORVERIFY: soft-fork for native color coin support. BitcoinTalk post (2013). https://bitcointalk.org/index.php?topic=253385.0
13. Maxwell, G.: CoinJoin: bitcoin privacy for the real world. BitcoinTalk post (2013). https://bitcointalk.org/index.php?topic=279249.0
14. Maxwell, G.: Confidential transactions. Plain text (2015). https://people.xiph.org/~greg/confidential_values.txt
15. Maxwell, G., Poelstra, A.: Borromean Ring Signatures (2015). http://diyhpl.us/~bryan/papers2/bitcoin/Borromean%20ring%20signatures.pdf
16. Nakamoto, S.: Bitcoin: a peer-to-peer electronic cash system (2009). https://www.bitcoin.org/bitcoin.pdf
17. Pedersen, T.P.: Non-interactive and information-theoretic secure verifiable secret sharing. In: Feigenbaum, J. (ed.) CRYPTO 1991. LNCS, vol. 576, pp. 129–140. Springer, Heidelberg (1992). https://doi.org/10.1007/3-540-46766-1_9

18. Project Ethereum: Create your own crypto-currency with Ethereum (2016). https://www.ethereum.org/token. Accessed 31 Oct 2016
19. Schoenmakers, B.: Interval proofs revisited. In: Slides Presented at International Workshop on Frontiers in Electronic Elections (2005)
20. Southurst, J.: Blockchain's sharedcoin users can be identified, says security expert (2014). http://www.coindesk.com/blockchains-sharedcoin-users-can-identified-says-security-expert/
21. Wilcox-O'Hearn, Z.: Zcash begins. ZCash Blog Post (2016). https://z.cash/blog/zcash-begins.html. Accessed 31 Oct 2016
22. Wood, G.: Ethereum: a secure decentralised generalised transaction ledger (2014). http://gavwood.com/paper.pdf

A Multi-party Protocol for Constructing the Public Parameters of the Pinocchio zk-SNARK

Sean Bowe[1], Ariel Gabizon[1(✉)], and Matthew D. Green[1,2]

[1] Zcash, Boulder, USA
{info,ariel}@z.cash, ariel.gabizon@gmail.com
[2] Johns Hopkins University, Baltimore, USA

Abstract. Recent efficient constructions of zero-knowledge Succinct Non-interactive Arguments of Knowledge (zk-SNARKs), require a setup phase in which a common-reference string (CRS) with a certain structure is generated. This CRS is sometimes referred to as the *public parameters of the system*, and is used for constructing and verifying proofs. A drawback of these constructions is that whomever runs the setup phase subsequently possesses trapdoor information enabling them to produce fraudulent pseudoproofs.

Building on a work of Ben-Sasson, Chiesa, Green, Tromer and Virza [BCG+15], we construct a multi-party protocol for generating the CRS of the Pinocchio zk-SNARK [PHGR16], such that as long as at least one participating party is not malicious, no party can later construct fraudulent proofs except with negligible probability. The protocol also provides a strong zero-knowledge guarantee *even in the case that all participants are malicious.*

This method has been used in practice to generate the required CRS for the Zcash cryptocurrency blockchain.

1 Introduction

The recently deployed Zcash cryptocurrency supports shielded (private) transactions where sender, receiver and amount are not revealed; and yet, an outside observer can still distinguish between a valid and non-valid transaction. The "cryptographic engine" that enables these shielded transactions is a zero-knowledge Succinct Non-interactive Argument of Knowledge (zk-SNARK); currently, Zcash uses the Pinocchio zk-SNARK [PHGR16], or more precisely, the variant of it described in [BCTV14] as implemented in libsnark [lib].

A potential weakness of Zcash, is that if anybody obtained the trapdoor information corresponding to the Common Reference String (CRS) used for constructing and verifying the SNARKs, they could forge unlimited amounts of the currency, potentially without anyone detecting they are doing so.

Motivated by this, Zcash generated the required CRS in an elaborate "ceremony" [Wil] to reduce the chance of this happening. The purpose of this technical

© International Financial Cryptography Association 2019
A. Zohar et al. (Eds.): FC 2018 Workshops, LNCS 10958, pp. 64–77, 2019.
https://doi.org/10.1007/978-3-662-58820-8_5

report is to give a detailed description of the multi-party protocol that was used in the ceremony.

Our Results: Ben-Sasson, Chiesa, Green, Tromer and Virza [BCG+15] presented a generic method for computing CRSs of zk-SNARKs in a multi-party protocol, with the property that only if all players collude together they can reconstruct the trapdoor, or, more generally, deduce any other useful information beyond the resultant CRS.

Based on [BCG+15], we devise an arguably simpler method for generating the CRS of the Pinocchio zk-SNARK [PHGR16] with a similar security guarantee: Namely, given that the CRS generated by the protocol is later used to verify proofs; a party controlling all but one of the players will not be able to construct fraudulent proofs except with negligible probability. See full version for details.

Moreover, we show that even if a malicious party controls *all* players, statistical zero-knowledge holds when constructing proofs according to the resultant parameters. Interestingly, this means the protocol is useful also when *run by one player*; as the transcript will provide proof to the prover that sending her proof will not leak additional information[1].

This property has been recently called *subversion Zero-Knowledge* [BFS16]. As opposed to the soundness guarantee, zero-knowledge only requires the random oracle model; and in particular, no knowledge assumptions in contrast to some recent works on subversion-ZK [Fuc17, ABLZ17]. On the other hand, our proof only obtains statistical-ZK with polynomially small error (with simulator polynomial running time depending on the desired polynomial error), as opposed to the mentioned recent works that can obtain negligible error (again, using knowledge assumptions). See full version for details.

Comparison to [BCG+15]: Our protocol is not significantly different from that of [BCG+15] for duplex-pairing groups, described in Sect. 5 of that paper. The main purpose here is to give full details for the case of the Pinocchio CRS. Nonetheless, some advantages of this writeup compared to [BCG+15] are:

1. Eliminating the need for NIZK proofs for the relation R_{aux} described in Sect. 5 there; this is since in Sect. 3.1 we do not commit directly to secret values s, but only to "random s-pairs".
2. Reducing the memory per player and simplifying the protocol description, by not using [BCG+15]'s generic "sampling to evaluation" procedure, but rather, explicitly presenting the protocol for our use case. In particular, individual players only need to store the messages of the player preceding them, and not the whole transcript as in a straightforward implementation of [BCG+15]. This simplified approach was later generalized [BGM17] for circuits with a certain layered structure.

---

[1] Thanks to Eran Tromer for pointing this out, and more generally the connection to subversion zero-knowledge. We note that if one wishes to run the protocol with one player, transcript verification can stay the same, but the player should be altered to take advantage of field rather than group operations when possible for better efficiency.

3. Reducing transcript verification complexity, by taking advantage of bi-
linearity of pairings and randomized checking (see Corollary 1). In particular,
the number of pairing operations to verify the transcript is constant, while
in [BCG+15] it grows linearly with the size of the circuit for which we are
constructing SNARK parameters.
4. Giving a full proof of both soundness and subversion zero-knowledge. In
[BCG+15] the soundness proof is only sketched, and the subversion zero-
knowledge property is not described (though it holds for their protocol).

Organization of Paper: Section 2 introduces some terminology and auxiliary
methods that will be used in the protocol. Section 3 describe the protocol in
detail. The full version of the paper describes the security proof of the protocol.

2   Definitions, Notation and Auxiliary Methods

Terminology: We always assume we are working with a field $\mathbb{F}_r$ for prime r chosen
according to a desired security parameter (more details on this in full version).
We assume together with $\mathbb{F}_r$ we have generated groups $\mathbb{G}_1, \mathbb{G}_2, \mathbb{G}_t$, all cyclic of
order r; where we write $\mathbb{G}_1$ and $\mathbb{G}_2$ in additive notation and $\mathbb{G}_t$ in multiplicative
notation. Furthermore, we have access to generators $g_1 \in \mathbb{G}_1, g_2 \in \mathbb{G}_2$, and an
efficiently computable pairing $e : \mathbb{G}_1 \times \mathbb{G}_2 \to \mathbb{G}_t$, i.e., a non-trivial map such
that for any $a, b \in \mathbb{F}_r$

$$e(a \cdot g_1, b \cdot g_2) = g_T^{a \cdot b},$$

for a fixed generator $g_T \in \mathbb{G}_t$. We use the notations $g := (g_1, g_2)$ and $G^* :=
\mathbb{G}_1 \setminus \{0\} \times \mathbb{G}_2 \setminus \{0\}$.

We think of the field size r as a parameter against which we measure efficiency. In particular, we say a circuit A is *efficient* if its size is polynomial in
$\log r$. More precisely, when we refer in the security analysis to an efficient adversary or efficient algorithm, we mean it is a (non-uniform) sequence of circuits
indexed by r, of size $\text{poly} \log r$. When we say "with probability p", we mean
"with probability at least p".

We assume we have at our disposal a function COMMIT taking as input
strings of arbitrary length; that, intuitively speaking, behaves like a commitment
scheme. That is, it is infeasible to deduce COMMIT's input from seeing its output,
and it is infeasible to find two inputs that COMMIT maps to the same output.
In our implementation we use the BLAKE-2 hash function as COMMIT. For the
actual security proof, we need to assume that COMMIT's outputs are chosen by
a random oracle.

Symmetric Definitions: In the following sections we introduce several methods
that receive as parameters elements of both $\mathbb{G}_1$ and $\mathbb{G}_2$. We assume implicitly
that whenever such a definition is made, we also have the symmetric definition
where the roles are reversed between what parameters come from $\mathbb{G}_1$ and $\mathbb{G}_2$. For
example, if we define a method receiving as input a vector of $\mathbb{G}_1$ elements and
a pair of $\mathbb{G}_2$ elements. We assume thereafter that we also have the symmetric
method receiving as input a vector of $\mathbb{G}_2$ elements and a pair of $\mathbb{G}_1$ elements.

2.1   Comparing Ratios of Pairs Using Pairings

Definition 2.1. *Given $s \in \mathbb{F}_r^*$, an s-pair is a pair (p, q) such that $p, q \in \mathbb{G}_1 \backslash \{0\}$, or $p, q \in \mathbb{G}_2 \backslash \{0\}$; and $s \cdot p = q$. When not clear from the context whether p, q are in $\mathbb{G}_1$ or $\mathbb{G}_2$, we use the terms $\mathbb{G}_1$-s-pair and $\mathbb{G}_2$-s-pair.*

A recurring theme in the protocol will be to check that two pairs of elements in $\mathbb{G}_1$ and $\mathbb{G}_2$ respectively, "have the same ratio", i.e., are s-pairs for the same $s \in \mathbb{F}_r^*$.

SameRatio$((p, q), (f, H))$:

1. If one of the elements p, q, f, H is zero; return rej.
2. Return acc if $e(p, H) = e(q, f)$; return rej otherwise.

Claim. Given $p, q \in \mathbb{G}_1$ and $f, H \in \mathbb{G}_2$, SameRatio$((p, q), (f, H)) = $ acc if and only if there exists $s \in \mathbb{F}_r^*$ such that (p, q) is a $\mathbb{G}_1$-s-pair and (f, H) is a $\mathbb{G}_2$-s-pair.

Proof. Suppose that $s \cdot p = q$ and $s' \cdot f = H$. Write $p = a \cdot g_1, f = b \cdot g_2$ for some $a, b \in \mathbb{F}_r$. Note that if one of $\{a, b, s, s'\}$ is 0, we return rej in the first step.

Otherwise, we have

$$e(p, H) = (a \cdot g_1, bs' \cdot g_2) = g_T^{abs'},$$

and

$$e(q, f) = (as \cdot g_1, b \cdot g_2) = g_T^{abs},$$

and thus SameRatio$((p, q), (f, H)) = 1$ if and only if $s = s' \pmod{r}$.

Let $V = ((p_i, q_i))_{i \in [d]}$, be a vector of pairs in $\mathbb{G}_1$. We say V is an s-*vector* in $\mathbb{G}_1$ if for each $i \in [d]$, (p_i, q_i) is a $\mathbb{G}_1$-s-pair, or is equal to $(0, 0)$. We make the analogous definition for $\mathbb{G}_2$, and similarly to above, sometimes omit the group name when it is clear from the context what group the elements are in, simply using the term s-vector. In our protocol we often want to check if a long vector $((p_i, q_i))_{i \in [d]}$ is an s-vector for some $s \in \mathbb{F}_r^*$. The next claim enables us to do so with just one pairing.

Claim. Suppose that $((p_i, q_i))_{i \in [d]}$ is a vector of elements in $\mathbb{G}_1 \backslash \{0\}$ that is not an s-vector. Choose random $c_1, \ldots, c_d \in \mathbb{F}_r$ and define

$$p \triangleq \sum_{i \in [d]} c_i \cdot p_i, \quad q \triangleq \sum_{i \in [d]} c_i \cdot q_i.$$

Then, with probability at least $1 - 2/r$, both $(p, q) \neq (0, 0)$ and (p, q) is not an s-pair.

Proof. Write $p_i = a_i \cdot g_1$ for $a_i \in \mathbb{F}_r$, and $q_i = s_i \cdot p_i$ for some $s_i \in \mathbb{F}_r$. Thus, we have $p = a \cdot g_1$ for $a \triangleq \sum_{i \in [d]} c_i a_i$ and $q = b \cdot g_1$ for $b \triangleq \sum_{i \in [d]} \alpha_i a_i s_i$. Let us assume $a \neq 0$. This happens with probability $1 - 1/r$. Write $[d]$ as a disjoint union

$S \cup T$ where S is the set of indices of the s-pairs. That is $S \triangleq \{i \in [d] | s_i = s\}$. We have

$$b/a = \frac{\sum_{i \in [d]} c_i a_i s_i}{\sum_{i \in [d]} c_i a_i} = s + \frac{\sum_{i \in T} c_i \cdot (s - s_i)}{\sum_{i \in [d]} c_i a_i} = s + \frac{\sum_{i \in T} c_i \cdot (s - s_i)}{a}.$$

Thus, $b/a = s$ if and only if the fraction in the right hand side is zero. As the numerator is a random combination of non-zero elements, this happens with probability $1/r$.

We conclude that with probability at least $1 - 2/r$, (p, q) is not an s-pair.

Claim 2.1 implies the correctness of sameRatio$(V, (f, H))$ that given an s-pair (f, H) in $\mathbb{G}_2$, checks whether V is an s-vector in $\mathbb{G}_1$.

sameRatio$(V = ((p_i, q_i))_{i \in [d]}, (f, H))$:

1. If there exists a pair of the form $(0, a)$ or $(a, 0)$ for some $a \neq 0$ in V; return rej.
2. "Put aside" all elements of the form $(0, 0)$, and from now on assume all pairs in V are in $\mathbb{G}_1 \setminus \{0\}$. (If all pairs are of the form $(0, 0)$ then return acc).
3. Choose random $c_1, \ldots, c_d \in \mathbb{F}_r$.
4. Define $p \triangleq \sum_{i \in [d]} c_i \cdot p_i$, and $q \triangleq \sum_{i \in [d]} c_i \cdot q_i$.
5. If $p = q = 0$, return acc.
6. Otherwise, return SameRatio$((p, q), (f, H))$.

Corollary 1. *Suppose* rp_s *in a* $\mathbb{G}_2$-s-pair, *and* V *is a vector of pairs of* $\mathbb{G}_1$ *elements. If* V *is an* s-vector, sameRatio(V, rp_s) *accepts with probability one. If* V *is not an* s-vector, sameRatio(V, rp_s) *accepts with probability at most* $2/r$.

Let V be a vector of $\mathbb{G}_1$-elements and rp_s be a pair of $\mathbb{G}_2$-elements. We also use a method sameRatioSeq(V, rp_s) that given an s-pair rp_s, checks that each two consecutive elements of V are an s-pair. It does so by calling sameRatio(V', rp_s) with $V' = ((V_0, V_1), (V_1, V_2), \ldots, (V_{d-1}, V_d))$.

2.2 Schnorr NIZKs for Knowledge of Discrete Log

We review and define notation for using the well-known Schnorr protocol [Sch89]. Given an s-pair $\mathsf{rp}_s = (f, H = s \cdot f)$, and a string h, we define the (randomized) string NIZK(rp_s, h) that can be interpreted as a proof that the generator of the string knows s.

NIZK(rp_s, h):

1. Choose random $a \in \mathbb{F}_r^*$ and let $R := a \cdot f$.
2. Let $c := \mathsf{COMMIT}(R \circ h)$ and interpret c as an element of $\mathbb{F}_r$, e.g. by taking it's first $\log r$ bits.
3. Let $u := a + cs$.
4. Define NIZK$(\mathsf{rp}_s, h) := (R, u)$.

Let us denote by π a string that is supposedly of the form $\mathrm{NIZK}(\mathsf{rp}_s, h)$, for some string h.

VERIFY-NIZK(rp_s, π, h) is a boolean predicate that verifies that π is indeed of this form for the same given h.

VERIFY-NIZK$((f, H), \pi, h)$:

1. Let R, u be as in the description above.
2. Compute $c := \mathsf{COMMIT}(R \circ h)$.
3. Return acc when $u \cdot f = R + c \cdot H$; and rej otherwise.

2.3   The Random-Coefficient Subprotocol

A large part of the protocol will consist of invocations of the *random-coefficient subprotocol*. In this subprotocol, we multiply a vector of $\mathbb{G}_1$ elements coordinate-wise by the same scalar $\alpha \in \mathbb{F}_r^*$. α here is a product of secret elements $\{\alpha_i\}_{i \in [n]}$, that we refer to later as *comitted elements*. By this we mean, that before the subprotocol is invoked, for each $i \in [n]$, P_i has broadcasted a $\mathbb{G}_2$-α_i-pair, denoted rp_{α_i}, that is accessible to the protocol verifier. (This will become clearer in the context of Sect. 3).

RCPC(V, α):

Common Input: vector $V \in \mathbb{G}_1^d$.

Individual Inputs: element $\alpha_i \in \mathbb{F}_r^*$ for each $i \in [n]$.

Output: vector $\alpha \cdot V \in \mathbb{G}_1^d$, where $\alpha = \prod_{i=1}^n \alpha_i$.

1. P_1 computes broadcasts $V_1 := \alpha_1 \cdot V$.
2. For $i = 2, \ldots, n$, P_i broadcasts $V_i := \alpha_i \cdot V_{i-1}$.
3. Players output V_n (which should equal $\alpha \cdot V$).

Before discussing the transcript verification we define one more useful notation. For vectors $S, T \in \mathbb{G}_1^d$ and a $\mathbb{G}_2$-α-pair rp_α, $\mathsf{sameRatio}((S, T), \mathsf{rp}_\alpha)$ returns $\mathsf{sameRatio}(V, \mathsf{rp}_\alpha)$, where $V_i := (S_i, T_i)$. The transcript verification procedure receives as input $V, V_1, \ldots, V_n$, and for each $i \in [n]$, the $\mathbb{G}_2$-α_i-pair, rp_{α_i}.

verifyRCPC(V, α):

Input: V, protocol transcript $V_1, \ldots, V_n \in \mathbb{G}_1^d$, for each $i \in [n]$ a $\mathbb{G}_2$-α_i-pair rp_{α_i}.

Output: acc or rej.

1. Run $\mathsf{sameRatio}((V, V_1), \mathsf{rp}_{\alpha_1})$.
2. For $i = 2, \ldots, n$, run $\mathsf{sameRatio}((V_{i-1}, V_i), \mathsf{rp}_{\alpha_i})$.
3. Return acc if all invocations returned acc; and return rej otherwise.

From the correctness of the $\mathsf{sameRatio}(,)$ method (Corollary 1) we have that

Claim. If the players follow the protocol correctly, the output is $\alpha \cdot V$, and transcript verification outputs acc with probability one. Otherwise, transcript verification outputs acc with probability at most $2/r$.

3 Protocol Description

The Participants: The protocol is conducted by n players, a coordinator, and a protocol verifier. In the implementation the role of the coordinator and protocol verifier can be played by the same server. We find it useful to separate these roles, though, as the actions of the protocol verifier may be executed only after the protocol has terminated, if one wishes to reduce the time the players have to be engaged. Moreover, any party wishing to check the validity of the transcript and generated parameters can do so solely with access to the protocol transcript. On the other hand, this has the disadvantage that non-valid messages will be detected only in hindsight, and the whole process will have to be restarted if one wishes to generate valid SNARK parameters.

Similarly, the role of the coordinator is not strictly necessary if one assumes a blackboard model where each player sees all messages broadcasted. (In our actual implementation the coordinator passes messages between the players). Our security analysis holds when all messages are seen by all players. However, even in such a blackboard model there is an advantage of having of a coordinator role: At the beginning of Round 3 a heavy computation needs to performed (Subsect. 3.3) that in theory could be performed by the first player before he sends his message for that round. However, as this heavy computation does not require access to any secrets of the players, having the coordinator perform it can save much time, if the coordinator is run on a strong server, and the players have weaker machines.

The protocol consists of four "round-robin" rounds, where for each $i \in [n]$, player P_i can send his message after receiving the message of P_{i-1}. P_1 can send his message after receiving an "initializer message" from the coordinator, which is empty in some of the rounds. An exception of this is the first round, where all players may send their message to the coordinator in parallel. However, security is not harmed if a player sees other players' messages before sending his in that round. Round 2 is divided into several parts for clarity, however the messages of a player P_i in all parts of that round can be sent in parallel. Similarly, Round 3 and 4 consist of several one round round-robin subprotocols; however, the messages of a player P_i in all these subprotocols can be sent in parallel.

3.1 Round 1: Commitments

For each $i \in [n]$, P_i does the following.

1. Generate a set of uniform elements in $\mathbb{F}_r^*$

$$\text{secrets}_i := \{\tau_i, \rho_{A,i}, \rho_{B,i}, \alpha_{A,i}, \alpha_{B,i}, \alpha_{C,i}, \beta_i, \gamma_i\}.$$

Omitting the index i for readability from now on, let

$$\text{elements}_i := \{\tau, \rho_A, \rho_B, \alpha_A, \alpha_B, \alpha_C, \beta, \gamma, \rho_A\alpha_A, \rho_B\alpha_B,$$

$$\rho_A\rho_B, \rho_A\rho_B\alpha_C, \beta\gamma\}$$

2. Now P_i generates the set of group elements[2]

$$\mathsf{e}_i := (\tau, \rho_A, \rho_A\rho_B, \rho_A\alpha_A, \rho_A\rho_B\alpha_B, \rho_A\rho_B\alpha_C, \gamma, \beta\gamma) \cdot g.$$

3. P_i computes $h_i := \mathsf{COMMIT}(\mathsf{e}_i)$ and broadcasts h_i.

3.2   Round 2

Part 1: Revealing commitments: For each $i \in [n]$

1. P_i broadcasts e_i.
2. The protocol verifier checks that indeed $h_i = \mathsf{COMMIT}(\mathsf{e}_i)$.

Committed Elements: From the end of Round 2, part 1 of the protocol, we refer to the elements of $\mathsf{elements}_i$ for some $i \in [n]$ as *committed elements*. The reason is that by this stage of the protocol, for each $s \in \mathsf{elements}_i$, P_i has sent an s-pair in both $\mathbb{G}_1$ and $\mathbb{G}_2$, effectively committing him to the value of s. For each such element s, we refer to the s-pair in $\mathbb{G}_1$ by rp_s and the s-pair in $\mathbb{G}_2$ by rp_s^2. We list the corresponding elements and s-pairs, omitting the i subscript for readability:

- τ: $(\mathsf{rp}_\tau^1, \mathsf{rp}_\tau^2) = (g, \tau \cdot g)$.
- ρ_A: $(\mathsf{rp}_{\rho_A}^1, \mathsf{rp}_{\rho_A}^2) = (g, \rho_A \cdot g)$.
- ρ_B: $(\mathsf{rp}_{\rho_B}^1, \mathsf{rp}_{\rho_B}^2) = (g, \rho_B \cdot g)$.
- α_A: $(\mathsf{rp}_{\alpha_A}^1, \mathsf{rp}_{\alpha_A}^2) = (\rho_A \cdot g, \rho_A\alpha_A \cdot g)$.
- α_B: $(\mathsf{rp}_{\alpha_B}^1, \mathsf{rp}_{\alpha_B}^2) = (\rho_A\rho_B \cdot g, \rho_A\rho_B\alpha_B \cdot g)$.
- α_C: $(\mathsf{rp}_{\alpha_C}^1, \mathsf{rp}_{\alpha_C}^2) = (\rho_A\rho_B \cdot g, \rho_A\rho_B\alpha_C \cdot g)$.
- β: $(\mathsf{rp}_\beta^1, \mathsf{rp}_\beta^2) = (\gamma \cdot g, \beta\gamma \cdot g)$.
- γ: $(\mathsf{rp}_\gamma^1, \mathsf{rp}_\gamma^2) = (g, \gamma \cdot g)$.
- $\rho_A\alpha_A$: $(\mathsf{rp}_{\rho_A\alpha_A}^1, \mathsf{rp}_{\rho_A\alpha_A}^2) = (g, \rho_A\alpha_A \cdot g)$.
- $\rho_B\alpha_B$: $(\mathsf{rp}_{\rho_B\alpha_B}^1, \mathsf{rp}_{\rho_B\alpha_B}^2) = (\rho_A \cdot g, \rho_A\rho_B\alpha_B \cdot g)$.
- $\rho_A\rho_B$: $(\mathsf{rp}_{\rho_A\rho_B}^1, \mathsf{rp}_{\rho_A\rho_B}^2) = (g, \rho_A\rho_B \cdot g)$.
- $\rho_A\rho_B\alpha_C$: $(\mathsf{rp}_{\rho_A\rho_B\alpha_C}^1, \mathsf{rp}_{\rho_A\rho_B\alpha_C}^2) = (g, \rho_A\rho_B\alpha_C \cdot g)$.
- $\beta\gamma$: $(\mathsf{rp}_{\beta\gamma}^1, \mathsf{rp}_{\beta\gamma}^2) = (g, \beta\gamma \cdot g)$.

Of course, we need to check that P_i has committed to the *same* element $s \in \mathbb{F}_r^*$ by rp_s and rp_s^2. This is done by the protocol verifier in the next stage.

Part 2: Checking Commitment Consistency Between both Groups: For each $i \in [n]$, and $s \in \mathsf{elements}_i$, the protocol verifier runs $\mathsf{SameRatio}(\mathsf{rp}_s, \mathsf{rp}_s^2)$, and outputs rej if any invocation returned rej.

---

[2] In the actual code a more complex set of elements is used that can be efficiently derived from $\mathsf{elements}_i$, as described in the full version. The reason we use the more complex set is that it potentially provides more security as it contains less information about $\mathsf{secrets}_i$. However, the proof works as well with this definition of e_i and it provides a significantly simpler presentation. We explain in the full version the slight modification for protocol and proof for using the more complex element set.

Part 3: Proving and Verifying Knowledge of Discrete Logs: Let $h :=$ COMMIT$(h_1 \circ \ldots \circ h_n)$ be the hash of the transcript of Round 1. P_1 computes and broadcasts h.

For each $i \in [n]$

1. For $s \in \mathsf{secrets}_i$, let $h_{i,s} := h \circ \mathsf{rp}_s^1$. Note that both P_i and the protocol verifier, seeing the transcript up to this point, can efficiently compute the elements $\{h_{i,s}\}$.
2. For each $s \in \mathsf{secrets}_i$, P_i broadcasts $\pi_{i,s} := \mathrm{NIZK}(\mathsf{rp}_s^1, h_{i,s})$.
3. The protocol verifier checks for each $s \in \mathsf{secrets}_i$ that $\mathrm{VERIFY\text{-}NIZK}(\mathsf{rp}_s^1, \pi_{i,s}, h_{i,s}) = \mathsf{acc}$.

Part 4: The Random Powers Subprotocol: The purpose of the subprotocol is to output the vector

$$\mathrm{POWERS}_\tau := \left((1, \tau, \tau^2, \ldots, \tau^d) \cdot g_1, (1, \tau, \tau^2, \ldots, \tau^d) \cdot g_2\right),$$

where $\tau := \tau_1 \cdots \tau_n$. Recall that $\tau_1, \ldots, \tau_n$ are committed values from Round 1.

For a vector $V \in \mathbb{G}_1^{d+1}$, and $a \in \mathbb{F}_r$, we use below the notation $\mathsf{powerMult}(V, a) \in \mathbb{G}_1^{d+1}$, defined as

$$\mathsf{powerMult}(V, a)_i \triangleq a^i \cdot V,$$

for $i \in \{0, \ldots, d\}$. We use the analogous notation for a vector $V \in \mathbb{G}_2^{d+1}$.

Phase 1: Computing Power Vectors

1. P_1 does the following.
   (a) Computes $V_1 = (1, \tau_1, \tau_1^2, \ldots, \tau_1^d) \cdot g_1$ and $V_1' = (1, \tau_1, \tau_1^2, \ldots, \tau_1^d) \cdot g_2$.
   (b) Broadcasts (V_1, V_1').
2. For $i = 2, \ldots, n$, P_i does the following:
   (a) Compute $V_i \triangleq \mathsf{powerMult}(V_{i-1}, \tau_i)$ and $V_i' \triangleq \mathsf{powerMult}(V_{i-1}', \tau_{i-1})$.
   (b) Broadcasts (V_i, V_i').

Phase 2: Checking Power Vectors are Valid: The protocol verifier performs the following checks[3] on the broadcasted data from Phase 1:

1. Check that
$$\mathsf{sameRatioSeq}(V_1, \mathsf{rp}_{\tau_1}^2),$$
and
$$\mathsf{sameRatioSeq}(V_1', (V_{1,0}, V_{1,1}))$$

---

[3] The checks below could be simplified if we had also used $\mathsf{rp}_{\tau_i}^1$. We do not use it as in the actual code, as explained in the full version, we do not have a $\mathbb{G}_1$-τ_i-pair.

2. For each $i \in [n] \setminus \{1\}$ check that

$$\mathsf{sameRatioSeq}(V_i, (V'_{i,0}, V'_{i,1})),$$

$$\mathsf{sameRatioSeq}(V'_i, (V_{i,0}, V_{i,1})),$$

and

$$\mathsf{SameRatio}((V_{i-1,1}, V_{i,1}), \mathsf{rp}^2_{\tau_1})$$

The protocol verifier rejects the transcript if one of the checks failed; otherwise, the coordinator defines $(PK_H \triangleq V_n, PK'_H \triangleq V'_n)$ is taken as the subprotocol output.

Phase 3: Checking we didn't Land in the Zeros of Z: The zero-knowledge property of the SNARK requires we weren't unlucky and τ landed in the zeroes of $Z(X) := X^d - 1$.

– Protocol verifier and all players check that $Z(\tau) \cdot g_1 = (\tau^d - 1) \cdot g_1 = V_{n,d} - V_{n,0} \neq 0$. If the check fails the protocol is aborted and restarted.

3.3 Coordinator After Round 2: Computing Lagrange Basis Using FFT, and Preparing the Vectors A, B and C

To avoid a quadratic proving time the polynomials in the QAP must be evaluated in a Lagrange basis. There seems to be no way of directly computing a Lagrange basis at τ in a 1-round MPC in a similar way we did for the standard basis in the Random-Powers subprotocol. Thus we will do 'FFT in the coefficient' to compute the Lagrange basis on the output of the random-powers subprotocol. Details and definitions follow. Let $\omega \in \mathbb{F}_r$ be a primitive root of unity of order $d = 2^\ell$, in code d is typically the first power of two larger or equal to the circuit size.

For $i = 1, \ldots, d$, we define L_i to be the i'th Lagrange polynomial over the points $\{\omega^i\}_{i \in [d]}$. That is, L_i is the unique polynomial of degree smaller than d, such that $L_i(\omega^i) = 1$ and $L_i(\omega^j) = 0$, for $j \in [d] \setminus \{i\}$.

Claim. For $i \in [d]$ we have

$$L_i(X) := c_d \cdot \sum_{j=0}^{d-1} (X/\omega^i)^j,$$

for $c_d := \frac{1}{d}$.

Proof. Substituting $X = \omega^{i'}$ for $i' \neq i$ we have a sum over all roots of unity of order d which is 0. Substituting $X = \omega^i$ we have a sum of d ones divided by d which is one.

For $\tau \in \mathbb{F}_r^*$, denote by we denote by $\mathrm{LAG}_\tau \in \mathbb{G}_1^d \times \mathbb{G}_2^d$ the vector

$$\mathrm{LAG}_\tau := \left((L_i(\tau) \cdot g_1)_{i \in [d]}, (L_i(\tau) \cdot g_2)_{i \in [d]} \right).$$

The purpose of the FFT-protocol is to compute LAG_τ from POWERS_τ. Let us focus for simplicity how to compute the first half containing the $\mathbb{G}_1$ elements. Computing the second half is completely analogous. We define the polynomial $P(Y)(= P_\tau(Y))$ by

$$P(Y) := \sum_{j=0}^{<d} (\tau \cdot Y)^j.$$

It is easy to check that

Claim. For $i \in [d]$
$$L_i(\tau) = P(\omega^{-i}) = P(\omega^{d-i}),$$

and thus

$$\mathrm{LAG}_\tau = (P(\omega^{-i}))_{i \in [d]} \cdot g$$

Thus our task reduces to computing the vector $(P(\omega^i))_{i \in [d]} \cdot g_1$ (and then reordering accordingly). We describe an algorithm to compute the vector $(P(\omega^i))_{i \in [d]}$ using the vector $(1, \tau, \tau^2, \dots, \tau^d)$ as input and only linear combination gates. This suffices as these linear combinations can be simulated by scalar multiplication and addition in $\mathbb{G}_1$, when operating on POWERS_τ. We proceed to review standard FFT tricks that will be used.

For a polynomial $P(Y) = \sum_{i=0}^{<d} a_i \cdot Y^i$ of degree smaller than d, where d is even, we define the polynomials

$$P_{\mathrm{EVEN}}(Y) := \sum_{i=0}^{<d/2} a_{2i} \cdot Y^i,$$

and

$$P_{\mathrm{ODD}}(Y) := \sum_{i=0}^{<d/2} a_{2i+1} \cdot Y^i.$$

It is easy to see that

$$P(Y) = P_{\mathrm{EVEN}}(Y^2) + Y \cdot P_{\mathrm{ODD}}(Y^2).$$

In particular, for $i \in [d]$

$$P(\omega^i) = P_{\mathrm{EVEN}}(\omega^{2i}) + \omega^i \cdot P_{\mathrm{ODD}}(\omega^{2i})$$

For $j = 0, \dots, \ell - 1$ denote $\omega_j \triangleq \omega^{2^j}$. Note further that $\{\omega^{2i}\}_{i \in [d]}$ is a subgroup if size $d/2$ generated by ω_1. More generally, for $j = 1, \dots, \ell - 1$ $\{\omega_{j-1}^{2i}\}_{i \in [d]}$ is a subgroup of size 2^{d-j} generated by ω_j. The above discussion suggests the following (well-known FFT) recursive algorithm.

FFT

input: Polynomial P, given as list of coefficients, element $\omega \in \mathbb{F}_r$ generating a group of size $d = 2^\ell$.

output: The vector $V = (P(\omega^i))_{i \in [d]}$.

1. If $d = 2$ compute V directly.
2. Otherwise,
   (a) Call the method recursively twice; first with P_{EVEN} and ω^2 to obtain output $E := (P_{\text{EVEN}}(\omega^{2i}))_{i \in [d/2]}$, and then with P_{ODD} and ω^2 to obtain the vector $O := (P_{\text{ODD}}(\omega^{2i}))_{i \in [d/2]}$.
   (b) Compute the vector V using E, O and the equality mentioned above. More specifically, each element V_i of V is computed as

$$V_i = P(\omega^i) = P_{\text{EVEN}}(\omega^{2i}) + \omega^i \cdot P_{\text{ODD}}(\omega^{2i}) = E_i + \omega^i \cdot O_i,$$

   (where we subtract $d/2$ from indices of E and O when they are larger than $d/2$).

In summary, we obtain LAG_τ by applying the FFT and the polynomial P described above, with coefficients $1, \tau, \ldots, \tau^{d-1}$ and an ω of order d - which should be the same ω used in the QAP construction. After getting the result from the FFT, we reverse the order of the vector and multiply each element by the scalar $1/d$.

Preparing the vectors $\boldsymbol{A}, \boldsymbol{B}$ and $\boldsymbol{C}$: We need to compute the vectors $\boldsymbol{A} := (A_i(\tau))_{i \in [0..m+1]} \cdot g_1$, $\boldsymbol{B} := (B_i(\tau))_{i \in [0..m+1]} \cdot g_1$, $\boldsymbol{B_2} := (B_i(\tau))_{i \in [0..m+1]} \cdot g_2$, and $\boldsymbol{C} := (C_i(\tau))_{i \in [0..m+1]} \cdot g_1$. We remark that [BCTV14] use the same notation for vectors of polynomials, while we are looking at the vector of these polynomials evaluated at τ.

Note that[4] $A_{m+1} = B_{m+1} = C_{m+1} := Z[\tau] \cdot g_1 = (\tau^d - 1) \cdot g_1$. After the FFT, we have obtained LAG_τ, so each such element is a linear combination of elements of LAG_τ; except $Z(\tau) \cdot g$, that can be computed using the elements $\tau^d \cdot g$ in POWERS_τ.

3.4   Round 3

After the random-powers subprotocol and the FFT, the MPC consists of a few invocations of the random-coefficient subprotocol. These invocations add a total of two rounds to the MPC, as sometimes and random-coefficient subprotocol will need the output of a previous random-coefficient subprotocol as input.

---

[4] A technicality is that in the protocol description in [BCTV14] $Z(\tau) \cdot g_2$ is appended with index $m + 2$ in $\boldsymbol{B_2}$, and $Z(\tau) \cdot g_1$ is appended in index $m + 3$ in C. However in the actual libsnark code, they are appended in index $m + 1$, and the prover algorithm is slightly modified to take this into account. But for the security proof we assume later on as in [BCTV14] that $A_{m+1} = C_{m+3} = Z(\tau) \cdot g_1$, $B_{m+2} = Z(\tau) \cdot g_2$, $A_{m+2}, A_{m+3}, B_{m+1}, B_{m+3}, C_{m+1}, C_{m+2} = 0$.

Part 1: Broadcasting Result of FFT: The coordinator broadcasts the vectors $\boldsymbol{A}, \boldsymbol{B}, \boldsymbol{C}, \boldsymbol{B_2}$.

Part 2: Random Coefficient Subprotocol Invocations: We apply the random-coefficient subprotocol numerous times to obtain the different key elements. For an element $\alpha_i \in$ elements$_i$, we abuse notation here and denote $\alpha := \alpha_1 \cdots \alpha_n$ (as opposed to ommitting the index i and writing α for α_i which we did when describing Round 1).

1. $PK_A = \text{RCPC}(\boldsymbol{A}, \rho_A)$.
2. $PK_B = \text{RCPC}(\boldsymbol{B_2}, \rho_B)$.
3. $PK_C = \text{RCPC}(\boldsymbol{C}, \rho_A \rho_B)$.
4. $PK'_A = \text{RCPC}(\boldsymbol{A}, \rho_A \alpha_A)$
5. $PK'_B = \text{RCPC}(\boldsymbol{B}, \rho_B \alpha_B)$.
6. $PK'_C = \text{RCPC}(\boldsymbol{C}, \rho_A \rho_B \alpha_C)$
7. $temp_B = \text{RCPC}(\boldsymbol{B}, \rho_B)$
8. $VK_Z = \text{RCPC}(g_2 \cdot Z(\tau), \rho_A \rho_B)$. We use that $g_2 \cdot Z(\tau) = g_2 \cdot (\tau^d - 1)$ can be computed from PK'_H that was computed in Round 2, part 2, as described in Sect. 3.2.
9. $VK_A = \text{RCPC}(g_2, \alpha_A)$.
10. $VK_B = \text{RCPC}(g_1, \alpha_B)$.
11. $VK_C = \text{RCPC}(g_2, \alpha_C)$.

3.5   Round 4: Computing Key Elements Involving β, Especially PK_K

Each player (or just the coordinator) computes $V := PK_A + temp_B + PK_C$. The players compute

1. $PK_K = \text{RCPC}(V, \beta)$
2. $VK_\gamma = \text{RCPC}(g_2, \gamma)$
3. $VK^1_{\beta\gamma} = \text{RCPC}(g_1, \beta\gamma)$.
4. $VK^2_{\beta\gamma} = \text{RCPC}(g_2, \beta\gamma)$.

Finally, the protocol verifier will run verifyRCPC(,) on the input and transcript of each subprotocol executed in Round 3 or 4; and output acc if and only if all invocations of verifyRCPC(,) returned acc.

The proof of security for the protocol is given in the appendix.

Acknowledgements. We thank Eli Ben-Sasson, Alessandro Chiesa, Jens Groth, Daira Hopwood, Hovav Shacham, Eran Tromer, Madars Virza, Nathan Wilcox and Zooko Wilcox for helpful discussions. We thank Daira Hopwood for pointing out some technical inaccuracies. We thank Eran Tromer for bringing to our attention the work of [CGGN17], and the relevance of our protocol to that work, and the connection to subversion zero-knowledge in general. We thank the anonymous reviewers of the 5th Workshop on Bitcoin and Blockchain Research for their comments.

References

[ABLZ17] Abdolmaleki, B., Baghery, K., Lipmaa, H., Zając, M.: A subversion-resistant SNARK. In: Takagi, T., Peyrin, T. (eds.) ASIACRYPT 2017. LNCS, vol. 10626, pp. 3–33. Springer, Cham (2017). https://doi.org/10.1007/978-3-319-70700-6_1

[BCG+15] Ben-Sasson, E., Chiesa, A., Green, M., Tromer, E., Virza, M.: Secure sampling of public parameters for succinct zero knowledge proofs. In: 2015 IEEE Symposium on Security and Privacy, SP 2015, San Jose, CA, USA, 17–21 May 2015, pp. 287–304 (2015)

[BCTV14] Ben-Sasson, E., Chiesa, A., Tromer, E., Virza, M.: Succinct non-interactive zero knowledge for a von neumann architecture. In: Proceedings of the 23rd USENIX Security Symposium, San Diego, CA, USA, 20–22 Aug 2014, pp. 781–796 (2014)

[BFS16] Bellare, M., Fuchsbauer, G., Scafuro, A.: Nizks with an untrusted CRS: security in the face of parameter subversion. IACR Cryptology ePrint Archive 2016:372 (2016)

[BGM17] Bowe, S., Gabizon, A., Miers, I.: Scalable multi-party computation for zk-SNARK parameters in the random beacon model (2017)

[CGGN17] Campanelli, M., Gennaro, R., Goldfeder, S., Nizzardo, L.: Zero-knowledge contingent payments revisited: attacks and payments for services. In: ACM Communications (2017)

[Fuc17] Fuchsbauer, G.: Subversion-zero-knowledge SNARKs. In: Abdalla, M., Dahab, R. (eds.) PKC 2018. LNCS, vol. 10769, pp. 315–347. Springer, Cham (2018). https://doi.org/10.1007/978-3-319-76578-5_11

[lib] https://github.com/scipr-lab/libsnark, https://github.com/zcash/libsnark

[PHGR16] Parno, B., Howell, J., Gentry, C., Raykova, M.: Pinocchio: nearly practical verifiable computation. Commun. ACM 59(2), 103–112 (2016)

[Sch89] Schnorr, C.P.: Efficient identification and signatures for smart cards. In: Brassard, G. (ed.) CRYPTO 1989. LNCS, vol. 435, pp. 239–252. Springer, New York (1990). https://doi.org/10.1007/0-387-34805-0_22

[Wil] Wilcox, Z.: https://z.cash/blog/the-design-of-the-ceremony.html

Analysis of the Bitcoin UTXO Set

Sergi Delgado-Segura$^{(\boxtimes)}$, Cristina Pérez-Solà, Guillermo Navarro-Arribas, and Jordi Herrera-Joancomartí

Department of Information Engineering and Communications, Universitat Autònoma de Barcelona, CYBERCAT-Center for Cybersecurity Research of Catalonia, Barcelona, Spain
{sdelgado,cperez,gnavarro,jherrera}@deic.uab.cat

Abstract. Bitcoin relies on the Unspent Transaction Outputs (UTXO) set to efficiently verify new generated transactions. Every unspent output, no matter its type, age, value or length is stored in every full node. In this paper we introduce a tool to study and analyze the UTXO set, along with a detailed description of the set format and functionality. Our analysis includes a general view of the set and quantifies the difference between the two existing formats up to the date. We also provide an accurate analysis of the volume of dust and unprofitable outputs included in the set, the distribution of the block height in which the outputs where included, and the use of non-standard outputs.

1 Introduction

Bitcoin makes use of the Unspent Transaction Output (UTXO) set in order to keep track of output transactions that have not been yet spent and thus can be used as inputs to new transactions. Bitcoin full nodes keep a copy of the UTXO set in order to validate transactions and produce new ones without having to check the whole blockchain. This allows, for instance, the use of so called pruned nodes (introduced in Bitcoin Core v0.11 [1]), which can operate without having to persistently store the full blockchain.

The UTXO set is thus a key component of Bitcoin. The format, content, and operation of this set has an important impact on Bitcoin nodes' operations. The size of the UTXO set directly impacts on the storage requirements of a Bitcoin node, and its efficiency directly determines the node validation speed.

We believe that a deep understanding of the Bitcoin UTXO set is needed to clearly understand the operation of Bitcoin, helping to find potential scalability and efficiency problems. To that end, we present STATUS (STatistical Analysis Tool for UTXO Set), a tool to analyze the UTXO set of Bitcoin. To the best of our knowledge there is no clear description in the literature of the UTXO set, its format, and how to actually analyze it. We provide such description along with a deep analysis of the set, and the tools needed to perform it.

© International Financial Cryptography Association 2019
A. Zohar et al. (Eds.): FC 2018 Workshops, LNCS 10958, pp. 78–91, 2019.
https://doi.org/10.1007/978-3-662-58820-8_6

The paper is organized as follows. Section 2 describes the UTXO set, its format, and introduces the STATUS analytical tool. Section 3 provides the actual analysis, including a general overview, the analysis of dust and unprofitable UTXOs, the distribution of the block height in which the outputs were included and the use of non-standard outputs. Finally, Sect. 4 concludes the paper.

2   The UTXO Set

The Unspent Transaction Output (UTXO) set is the subset of Bitcoin transaction outputs that have not been spent at a given moment. Whenever a new transaction is created, UTXOs are used to claim the funds they are holding, and new UTXOs are created. Basically, transactions consume UTXOs (in their inputs) and generate new ones (in their outputs). Therefore, transactions produce changes in the UTXO set.

Since the UTXO set contains all unspent outputs, it stores all the required information to validate a new transaction without having to inspect the full blockchain. As the name already suggests, UTXOs are indeed Bitcoin outputs, and, as such, they consist of two parts: the amount transferred to the output and the locking script (scriptPubKey) that specifies the conditions to be met in order to spend the output.

The UTXO set is stored in the chainstate, a LevelDB database that provides persistent key-value storage. LevelDB [2] is used to store the chainstate database since Bitcoin v0.8. Apart from the UTXO set, the chainstate database stores two additional values: the block height at which the set is updated and an obfuscation key that is used to mask UTXO data [3,4]. Such an obfuscation key is used to obtain a different file signature of the UTXO set file for every different wallet in order to avoid false-positives with antivirus software.

The format of the chainstate database changed in version v0.15 of the Bitcoin Core. We will refer to the previous format as 0.14, although it has been used in versions from 0.8 to 0.14.

2.1   The UTXO Bitcoin Core 0.14 Format

The chainstate database of Bitcoin Core v0.14 uses a per-transaction model: there exists a record in the database (i.e., a key-value pair) for each transaction that has at least one unspent output. Multiple UTXOs belonging to the same transaction are thus stored under the same key. The key of the record is the 32-byte transaction hash, preceded by the prefix "c". This prefix is needed to distinguish transactions from other data that are also stored in the database, and is also used to discriminate v0.14 format from the recently released v0.15[1].

The value of the record stores metadata about the transaction (version, height and whether it is coinbase or not) and a compressed representation of the UTXOs of the transaction [5].

---

[1] Bitcoin Core v0.15.0 was released on 14th of September 2017.

Regarding the UTXOs, the encoding first identifies the indexes of the outputs of the transaction that are unspent and then includes information about those outputs. The encoding is optimized to favor the first two outputs. UTXOs are then encoded taking into account their type. Six different types are specially established, that allow to efficiently store P2PKH, P2SH and four different cases of P2PK scripts. For these types, only the required data are stored since there is no need to store the full script (the type uniquely determines it). For instance, for P2PKH outputs only the address is stored. For scripts other than these specific types, the full output script is stored. Additionally, for each output regardless of its type, a compact representation of the amount of bitcoins is also stored.

2.2   The UTXO Bitcoin Core 0.15 Format

One of the main changes from the last Bitcoin Core's major release (v0.15) has been a change of the internal representation of the chainstate in favor of a better performance both in reading time and memory usage [6,7].

This new format uses a per-output model in contrast to the previously defined per-transaction model, that is, every entry in the chainstate now represents a single UTXO, instead of a collection of all the UTXOs available for a given transaction. To achieve this, the key-value (known as *outpoint-coin* in the source code) structure has been modified. Keys encode both the 32-byte transaction hash and the index of the unspent output, preceded by the prefix "C". Regarding *coins*, each one encodes a code, that contains metadata about the block height and whether the transaction is coinbase or not (notice that the transaction version has been dropped), a compressed amount of bitcoins, and the output type and script encoded in the same way as the version v0.14.

Storing unspent outputs one by one instead of aggregated in a same transaction greatly simplifies the structure of the *coin* and reduces the UTXOs accessing time. By using the previous structure when a transaction with more than one unspent output was accessed all data needs to be decoded, and all the non used outputs encoded and written back into the database. However, this new format has the downside of increasing the total size of the database [7].

2.3   *STATUS*: The UTXO Analytic Tool

We have created *STATUS (STatistical Analysis Tool for Utxo Set)*, an open source code tool that provides an easy way to access, decode, and analyze data from the Bitcoin's UTXO set[2] STATUS is coded in Python 2 and works for both the existing versions of Bitcoin Core's UTXO set, that is, the first defined format (versions 0.8−0.14) and the recently defined one (version 0.15). STATUS reads from a given chainstate folder and parses all the UTXO entries into a file. From the parsed file STATUS allows you to perform two types of analysis: a UTXO based one, and a transaction based one, by decoding all the parsed information from the chainstate.

---

[2] It can be found under a bigger Bitcoin Tools library at https://github.com/sr-gi/ bitcoin_tools/tree/v0.1/bitcoin_tools/analysis/status.

In the UTXO based analysis, apart from the data mentioned in Sects. 2.1 and 2.2 that STATUS directly decodes, it also creates additional meta-data about each parsed entry, such as dust and unprofitable fee rate limit, that will be deeply analyzed in Sect. 3. Regarding transaction based analysis, STATUS aggregates all the parsed UTXOs that belong to the same transaction, providing additional meta-data such as total number of UTXOs from a given transaction, total unspent value of the transaction, etc. Finally, STATUS uses *numpy* and *matplotlib* Python's libraries to provide several statistical data analyses and charts for all the analyzed data.

3   UTXO Set Analysis

In this section we analyze the UTXO set of the blockchain state at block 491,868, corresponding to the 26th of October 2017 at 13:13:38 using the STATUS tool. First, we provide a general view of the data included, regarding the total number of outputs and their size depending on the Bitcoin Core UTXO set format. We also analyze different output subsets within the UTXO set that could be interesting to measure in order to provide some hints whether a more efficient UTXO set codification could be used.

3.1   General View

Using STATUS, we can retrieve details related to the general numbers behind the UTXO set. Table 1 presents a summary of such basic facts of the analyzed UTXO set. There are 52 and a half million UTXOs in the set, belonging to more than 23 million different transactions. Although this gives an average of 2.26 UTXOs per transaction, the distribution is very skewed, with most of the transactions having just one unspent output.

Table 1. Summary

	v0.14	v0.15
Num. of tx	23,241,914	
Num. of UTXOS	52,543,649	
Avg. num. of UTXOS per tx	2.26	
Std. dev. num. of UTXOS per tx	18.27	
Median num. of UTXOS per tx	1	
Size of the (serialized) UTXO set	2.02 GB	3.00 GB
Avg. size per register	93.45 B	61.46 B
Std. dev. size per register	443.20	7.65 B
Median size per register	62	61

Figure 1a shows a cumulative distribution function (cdf) of the number of UTXOs per transaction.[3] Note that 87.9% of the transactions have only 1 UTXO[4] and 94.97% have less than 3. The maximum number of UTXOs per transaction is 3,452 [8] which originally had 5,419 outputs.

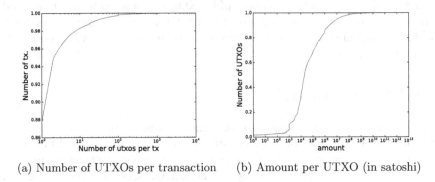

(a) Number of UTXOs per transaction   (b) Amount per UTXO (in satoshi)

Fig. 1. (a) Number of UTXOs per transaction, (b) Amount per UTXO (in satoshi)

Differences between both data formats (v0.14 and v0.15) are clear regarding the serialized UTXO set size (see Table 1). While the v0.14 format uses 2.02 GB with an average size per record of 93.45 bytes (a total of 23,241,914 records), the 0.15 format expands the information to 3.00 GB which represents an average size per record of 61.46 bytes (with 52,543,649 records). Such a difference is due to the way outputs are stored in both formats, as detailed in Sect. 2. However, the median size per register of both versions is very similar, with most registers occupying between 59 and 64 bytes. Such measurement is sound since both versions store the 32-byte transaction id and some identifier of the output, so the size difference for every register is only significant when the transaction has more than a single UTXO. Whereas the number of registers with less than 59 bytes is negligible (just 30 of them for v0.14 and 222 for v0.15), 83.25% of them in v0.14 and 99.0% in v0.15 are ≤63-byte long.

As a matter of fact, the smallest stored register in v0.14 is just 41-byte long [9] and contains a single non-standard UTXO with a 1-byte length script containing an invalid opcode. This UTXO is also one of the smallest registers in v0.15, with 40 bytes (12 additional registers have also the same size in v0.15). Section 3.4 provides an exploration of non-standard transactions in the UTXO set.

---

[3] All the analysis plots included in this section show cumulative distribution functions. Therefore, a point (x, y) in the plot shows the probability y that a given variable (depicted in the x axis label) will take a value less than or equal to x.

[4] Notice that such measure indicates that, although the average number of outputs in regular Bitcoin transactions is higher, the number of outputs that remain unspent is, mostly, only one.

Another interesting information of the UTXO set that can be retrieved with STATUS is the amount of UTXOs of each type, as detailed in Table 2. Notice that UTXOs are classified between the different standard types also providing a distinction between compressed and uncompressed keys for the P2PK type. As data show, more than 99% of the UTXO set are P2PKH and P2SH outputs, being P2PKH the vast majority of stored outputs. In Sect. 3.4 we provide detailed information regarding the 0.8% of UTXOs classified as others.

Table 2. UTXO types

Num. of utxos	52,543,649	100%
Pay-to-PubkeyHash (P2PKH)	43,079,604	81.99%
Pay-to-ScriptHash (P2SH)	8,987,799	17.11%
Pay-to-Pubkey (P2PK)	66,759	0.12%
Compressed	29,977	0.06% (44.90%)
Uncompressed	36,782	0.07% (55.10%)
Others	409,487	0.8%

Figure 1b provides information about the amount of satoshi deposited in each UTXO, showing that 98.46% of the UTXOs store less than one Bitcoin, with an average of 0.32Ƀ per UTXO.

3.2   Dust and Unprofitable UTXOs

An interesting type of outputs included into the UTXO set are those whose economical value is small enough to represent a problem when they have to be spent. One well identified type of these UTXOs is tagged as dust. According to the Bitcoin Core reference implementation [10], **a dust output** is the output of a transaction in which the fee to redeem it is greater than 1/3 of its value. Besides this well known definition we also define **an unprofitable output** as the output of a transaction that holds less value than the fee necessary to be spent, resulting in financial loses when used in a transaction.

In order to identify both types of outputs, it is important to recall that the amount of fees a transaction has to pay to be included in a new block depends on two factors: the fee-per-byte rate that the network is expecting at the time of creating the transaction and the size of the transaction. The fee-per-byte rate, measured in satoshi, is a highly variable factor that depends on the transaction backlog (i.e. how many transactions are pending to be included in new blocks).

Since fees depend on the transaction size, in order to label the outputs in the UTXO set as a dust or unprofitable, we need an estimation of the size of data needed to spend such output. In order to identify the minimum information needed, we can consider an already standard transaction with its inputs and its outputs and enough fees to be relayed. Then, we define the **minimum-input of a UTXO** as the smallest size input that spends such UTXO. The size of such minimum-input, together with the value held in the output and the fee rate, will determine whether a UTXO may be included into the dust or unprofitable categories.

In order to measure the size of such minimum-input, we need to review the structure of a Bitcoin transaction. As depicted in Fig. 2, all transactions follow a standard structure containing some fixed length parameters that determine a minimum transaction size, and some variable length parameters, depending on the transaction type. When a transaction is created, inputs are defined referring to some UTXOs. Such inputs have different size depending on the output type they are related to. On the other hand, new outputs are generated for every new transaction, and thereby some additional size, which will depend on the new output type, will be added to the transaction.

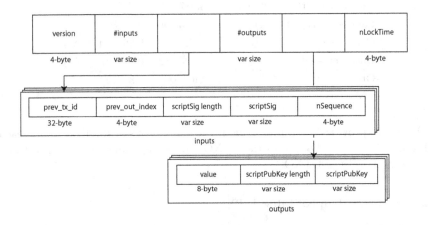

Fig. 2. Generic transaction structure

Depending on the UTXO type, its minimum-input size will be different. Such measure can be split in two parts: fixed size and variable size. Regarding the fixed size, as depicted in Fig. 2 (taking into account only the input box), we can identify three fields: prev_tx_id, pev_out_index and nSequence. Therefore, for every UTXO, its minimum-input will be at least 40-byte long independently of its type. On the other hand, the content and length of the fields scriptSig and scriptSig length depend on the UTXO type, specified in the field scriptPubKey of the UTXO.

The different types of outputs, with their corresponding size, can be classified as follows:

Pay-to-PubKey (P2PK) Outputs: The minimum-input of this type of UTXO specifies just a digital signature to redeem the output and the scriptSig includes the following data:

```
PUSH  sig (1 byte) + sig (71 bytes)
```

Bitcoin uses DER encoded ECDSA signatures in the scripts of its transactions, which can be between 71 and 73 bytes long depending on their r and s components. Such variability comes from the randomness of the r parameter, so by iterating the signature generation it is possible to craft an specific signature within 71 bytes.[5] Hence, minimum-input size for a P2PK UTXO will be 71-bytes long and scriptSig len field will be 1-byte long, so a total of 72 bytes.

Pay-to-PubkeyHash (P2PKH) Outputs: For this UTXO to be redeemed, both a signature (*sig*) and a public key (*pk*) are needed in the scriptSig, as shown below:

PUSH sig (1 byte) + sig (71 bytes) + PUSH pk (1 byte) +
pk (33–65 bytes)

Regarding the signatures, the same assumptions as for P2PK outputs applies, that is, 71-byte length can be considered. Regarding public keys used by Bitcoin, they can either be compressed or uncompressed, which will significantly vary their size:

– Uncompressed keys: Such keys were used, by default, in the first versions of the Bitcoin core client, and they are 65-byte long.
– Compressed keys: By 30th March 2012 (around block height 173480) Bitcoin core started using this more efficient type of keys, which are almost half size of the previous ones (33 bytes), and therefore make smaller scripts.

So, the size for the scriptSig varies from 106 to 138 and then the scriptSig length field will be 1-byte long, resulting in a total minimum-input size between 107 and 139 bytes.

Pay-to-Multisig (P2MS) Outputs: The size of the minimum-input to redeem such a script highly varies depending on the number of signatures required, which ranges up to 20 (20-of-20 multisig)[6], so the scriptSig for redeeming such output is as follows:

OP_0 (1 byte) + (PUSH sig (1 byte) + sig (71 bytes)) *
required_signatures (1–20)

Thus, the size of the scriptSig field will range between 73 and 1441 bytes, making the scriptSig len field range between 1 and 2 bytes, so the total minimum-input size will be between 74 and 1443.

---

[5] Notice that this procedure assumes, in contrast to the normal behaviour of standard wallets, that the ECDSA implementation does not use a deterministic function to compute r.

[6] Although the standard considers a maximum number of 3 signatures in a P2MS output, up to 20 are valid regarding the consensus rule [11] so they could potentially be found in the UTXO set.

Pay-to-ScriptHash (P2SH) Outputs: Unlike any previous output type, input size created from P2SH outputs can not be straightforwardly defined in advance. P2SH outputs hide the actual input script behind a hash, in order to make smarter outputs, by making them smaller and thus, allowing the payer to pay lower fees. However, the scripts held by those UTXOs give us no clue about how the minimum-input should be build.

Table 3 summarizes the sizes of the minimum-input for each UTXO type.

Table 3. Minimum-input size summary

| UTXO type | Fixed size | scriptSig length | scriptSig | | Push data | Total size |
			sig	pk		
P2PK	40	1	71	-	1	113
P2PKH	40	1	71	33−65	2	147−179
P2MS	40	1−2	71−1420	-	2-21	114−1483
P2SH	40	var	var	var	var	40-var

Notice that the previous analysis does not take into account the new SegWit transaction format [12]. The minimum-input size for such type of outputs needs an extended analysis. However, at present time, the total outputs in the UTXO set that correspond to a SegWit output is upper bounded by a 2.26% (see Sects. 3.1 and 3.4) so, giving such small amount of data, the results presented here will not significantly change, we leave such analysis for further research.

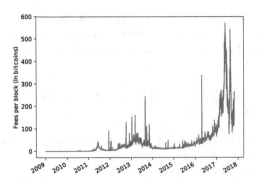

Fig. 3. Evolution of fees (Source: Blockchain (https://www.blockchain.info).

Once we determined the amount of data of the minimum-input for each type of UTXO, based on a defined fee-per-byte rate, we can identify those outputs form the UTXO set that fall into both the dust and the unprofitable categories.

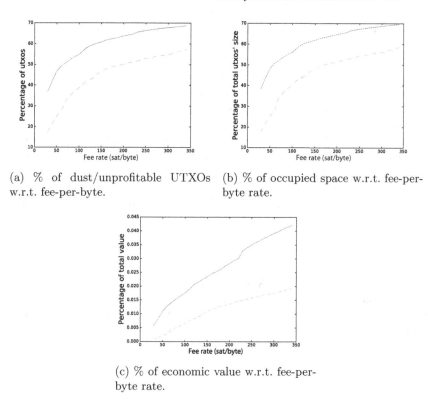

(a) % of dust/unprofitable UTXOs w.r.t. fee-per-byte.

(b) % of occupied space w.r.t. fee-per-byte rate.

(c) % of economic value w.r.t. fee-per-byte rate.

Fig. 4. Dust and unprofitable analysis (blue and green lines respectively). (Color figure online)

To obtain the data, the following considerations have been taken. The minimum-input size for P2PK and P2MS outputs have been precisely computed since the information to determine the exact size of the minimum-input can be derived from the output data itself. However, it is not possible to exactly determine such value for the P2PKH neither for the P2SH. In the first case, we have taken the following approach. For those outputs up to block 173480 we have considered uncompressed addressed and for the newer ones we have take the of most conservative approach, assuming that all public keys from that point onward are in compressed form (33 bytes) so reducing the number of UTXO that fall into both categories. For the P2SH, being not able to set a proper lower bound for the variable part, we have performed the analysis assuming only the fixed 40 bytes.

Finally, the last parameter to set is the fee-per-byte rate. As depicted in Fig. 3, such rate is far from fixed and has high variability. Thus, in order to measure different possible scenarios, we have considered a wide fee-per-byte spectrum, ranging from 30 to for 340 satoshi/byte.

The volume of both dust outputs and unprofitable outputs (blue and dotted green lines respectively) in the UTXO set are depicted in Fig. 4.

Figure 4a shows the relative size of dust and unprofitable output sets within the total UTXO set. Notice that for a fee-per-byte as small as 80 satoshi/byte onwards, more than the 50% of UTXOs (26.29 million outputs) from the set can be considered dust, whereas the same 50% size for the unprofitable set is reached for 240 satoshi/byte onward. Regarding the size that such data, Fig. 4b shows how those UTXOs represent a relevant part of the total size from the set (more than the 50% for around 70 satoshi/byte onward), while the same can be seen for unprofitable UTXO for a rate of 200 satoshi/byte onward. Finally, from an economic point of view, Fig. 4c shows, as expected, how those dust and unprofitable UTXOs represent a negligible amount from the total value of the UTXO set, that is the total number of bitcoins in circulation.

3.3 Height

Another interesting type of UTXO outputs are those that were created a long time ago. Although it is difficult to determine the average time in which a UTXO will be spent, some old UTXOs may belong to keys that are lost, so such old UTXOs may will never be spent.

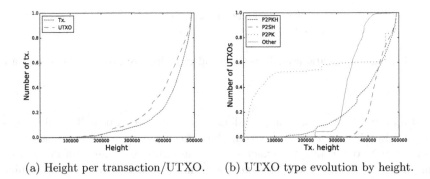

(a) Height per transaction/UTXO.   (b) UTXO type evolution by height.

Fig. 5. Output age-based analysis (Color figure online)

Figure 5a depicts the height of the block where the transaction is included in a per transaction (v0.14 register, blue line) and per UTXO (v0.15 register green line) fashion. Half of the stored UTXOs are older than January 2017 (block 449,896 corresponds to the median), whereas the other half are younger. This means that almost half of the current UTXO set is used by UTXOs created in the current year (2017). On the other hand, there are still very old UTXOs: 2% of them are older than August 2012 (block height 194,635).

In Fig. 5b we can see the evolution in time of the different types of outputs in the UTXO set. Notice that P2PKH and P2SH show a stable distribution in time. On the other hand, outputs labelled as "others" are mainly from old transactions since 95% of them are older than March 2016 (block height 403,052). Finally, the graphic also shows that P2PK outputs have an irregular behaviour. 50% of them were created before block 91,542 which is an expected result since P2PKH were developed afterwards as an improvement of P2PK. However, it is interesting to see that, after a long time with very few outputs of this type, around March 2017 and during 324 blocks, 15% of the actual P2PK outputs included in the UTXO set were created.

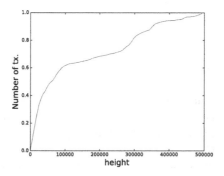

Fig. 6. Coinbase evolution by height.

Figure 6 shows an already known fact that indicates that most of the bit-coins created at the beginning of the cryptocurrency are still pending to redeem. More precisely, 75% of the coinbase outputs in the UTXO set were created before block 274,946 (December 2013). In contrast, just 6% of the current UTXOs were created before that block (see Fig. 5a).

3.4   Non-standard

As shown in Table 2, we have labelled as "others" 409,487 UTXOs from the UTXO set since they do not fall into the main categories P2PK, P2PKH and P2SH. A detailed analysis of such UTXOs, provided in Table 4, shows that almost all UTXOs correspond to a Pay-to-Multisig (P2MS) outputs being the configu-ration of 1–2 and 1–3 the most popular cases. Notice that, the UTXOs included are those with configuration up to three public keys, which is sound according to the fact that this is the upper bound for a multisignature output to be con-sidered standard by the Bitcoin network transaction relaying policies. Finally, it is worth to mention that there exist 828 UTXOs with 1−1 configuration, a fact that does not make much sense since it is an output with functionality equivalent to a P2PK but with a larger script size and so highers fees may be needed to spent it.

Regarding the 1,169 outputs labeled as others in Table 4, 34.05% of them (398) are new native SegWit type outputs. More precisely, Pay-to-Witness-Public-Key-Hash (P2WPKH) account for 40 outputs and Pay-to-Witness-Script-Hash (P2WSH) accounts a total of 358.

Table 4. Multisig analysis.

1–1	828	0.20%
1–2	199,904	48.81%
2–2	1,353	0.33%
1–3	206,096	50.33%
2–3	117	0.02%
3–3	20	0.005%
Others	1,169	0.28%

4   Conclusions and Further Research

In this paper we have introduced STATUS, a tool to analyze the UTXO set of Bitcoin (based on the Bitcoin Core implementation), and we have provided an analysis of such set, paying special attention to dust and unprofitable transactions. We have also provided a detailed description of the UTXO set format, including the new format introduced in Bitcoin Core v0.15. The use of this format as compared to the previous one does not have an impact on the analysis we have presented in this paper. The new version provides more efficient access to the UTXO information at the expense of slightly higher storage requirements. Additionally, we provide interesting data that shows the high percentage of "static information" (in the sense that is not going to be spent -dust and unprofitable-) included in the UTXO set that reduces the efficiency of the database in terms of space. Finally, it is interesting to notice that currently there is a very low percentage of SegWit UTXO, upper bounded by a 2.26% of the total outputs stored in the UTXO set. As this will possibly increase in the future, the analysis of dust and unprofitable transactions will need to be revisited in further research in order to update the results with these new types of outputs.

Acknowledgements. This work is partially supported by the Spanish ministry under grant number TIN2014–55243-P and the Catalan *Agència de Gestió d'Ajuts Universitaris i de Recerca* (AGAUR) grant 2014SGR-691.

References

1. Bitcoin Core. Bitcoin core 0.11.0 release notes, July 2015. https://github.com/bitcoin/bitcoin/blob/v0.11.0/doc/release-notes.md
2. Ghemawat, S., Dean, J.: Leveldb (2014). https://github.com/google/leveldb. Accessed Oct 2017
3. Bitcoin Core. Bitcoin core 0.12.0 release notes, February 2016. https://bitcoin.org/en/release/v0.12.0
4. Bitcoin Core. Obfuscate database files. Bitcoin Core Github Issue 6613, July 2015. https://github.com/bitcoin/bitcoin/issues/6613
5. The Bitcoin Core developers. Bitcoin core 0.14 source code: `coins.h` (2017). Github: https://github.com/bitcoin/bitcoin/blob/0.14/src/coins.h

6. Bitcoin Core. Bitcoin core 0.15.0 release notes, September 2017. https://bitcoin.org/en/release/v0.15.0

7. Greg Maxwell. A deep dive into bitcoin core 0.15. SF Bitcoin Developers Meetup, September 2017. http://diyhpl.us/wiki/transcripts/gmaxwell-2017-08-28-deep-dive-bitcoin-core-v0.15/

8. Blockcypher. Bitcoin transaction. https://live.blockcypher.com/btc/tx/d8505b78a4cddbd058372443bbce9ea74a313c27c586b7bbe8bc3825b7c7cbd7/. Accessed Oct 2017

9. Blockcypher. Bitcoin transaction. https://live.blockcypher.com/btc/tx/8a68c461a2473653fe0add786f0ca6ebb99b257286166dfb00707be24716af3a/. Accessed Oct 2017

10. Bitcoin Core developers. Bitcoin core 0.10.0rc3 source code: transaction.h, line 137, December 2014. Github: https://github.com/bitcoin/bitcoin/blob/v0.10.0rc3/src/primitives/transaction.h#L137

11. Wuille, P.: Answer to: What are the limits of m and n in m-of-n multisig addresses? Bitcoin StackExchange (2014). https://bitcoin.stackexchange.com/a/28092/30668

12. Lombrozo, E., Lau, J., Wuille, P.: Segregated witness (consensus layer). Technical Report BIP-141, Bitcoin Improvement Proposal (2015). https://github.com/bitcoin/bips/blob/master/bip-0141.mediawiki

Hostile Blockchain Takeovers
(Short Paper)

Joseph Bonneau[✉]

New York University, New York, USA
jbonneau@gmail.com

Abstract. Most research modelling Bitcoin-style decentralised consensus protocols has assumed profit-motivated participants. Complementary to this analysis, we revisit the notion of attackers with an extrinsic motivation to disrupt the consensus process (Goldfinger attacks). We outline several routes for obtaining a majority of decision-making power in the consensus protocol (a hostile takeover). Our analysis suggests several fundamental differences between proof-of-work and proof-of-stake systems in the face of such an adversary.

1 Introduction

Bitcoin [15] has achieved significant popularity since its 2009 launch, with a monetary base nominally worth over US$100 billion at the time of this writing. Perhaps Bitcoin's most important innovation is its decentralised consensus protocol. Bitcoin-style consensus (or "Nakamoto consensus") uses computational (proof-of-work) puzzles to maintain consensus on the blockchain, a public append-only ledger storing all transactions to prevent double-spending. The computational puzzles are intended to make disrupting the consensus protocol expensive, as an attacker must obtain a large fraction of all computational power in the system to deviate from the default protocol. This basic design has been adapted in dozens of follow-up cryptocurrencies with similar consensus protocols, notably Ethereum [21] which is itself worth close to US$30 billion.

It was known from the start that an attacker with a majority of computational power can easily cause arbitrarily deep forks in the blockchain [15]. It has subsequently been shown that an attacker with substantially less power can, at the very least, undermine the fair distribution of rewards in the system [4,16,18]. These attack strategies are profitable in a fixed exchange-rate model (in which an attacker's utility is solely measured in currency units within the system itself). A similar modelling approach has been used in many papers [6–8,10,11,17] analyzing Bitcoin-style protocols with the goal of proving positive results about *incentive-compatibility*; that is, that given a specific utility model for miners intended properties of the system will emerge such as an ever-growing longest chain (stability) and proportional distribution of mining rewards (fairness).

An inherent limitation to this approach is that real-world attacks may negatively affect systems' value (and exchange rate with external currencies), making some mining strategies which deviate from the standard protocol to increase

© International Financial Cryptography Association 2019
A. Zohar et al. (Eds.): FC 2018 Workshops, LNCS 10958, pp. 92–100, 2019.
https://doi.org/10.1007/978-3-662-58820-8_7

nominal miner revenue actually yield less utility. A more realistic utility function is revenue denominated in a stable external currency (such as US dollars). Because accurately modeling the impact of miner behavior on exchange rates is difficult, analysis along these lines is usually qualitative. Thus, our ability to compare the stability of competing protocol flavours like proof-of-work and proof-of-stake remains limited.

In this work, we analyse the stability of consensus protocols from a different viewpoint. Rather than considering the risk of an attacker undermining desired properties to maximise utility, we consider an attacker whose explicit goal is to undermine and destabilise the consensus protocol. Kroll et al. [11] first considered such an attacker, which they called a Goldfinger attacker after the James Bond villain who attempted to irradiate US Treasury reserves. This attack model has received relatively little research attention since its proposal. Yet if the cost of undermining a currency system is low relative to the total value of currency in the system, the system may not be stable even if there were no motivation to mount such an attack.

Revisiting the dynamics of Goldfinger-style attacks is useful for two reasons. First, the potential motivations for a Goldfinger attack have become more plausible. Kroll et al. [11] hypothesised a government-sponsored attack, a social protest movement, or an attacker with a significant short position on the target currency's exchange rate. In the 4 years since, Bitcoin has received increased attention (often negative) from governments as well as social movements (particularly due to environmental concerns). Shorting a cryptocurrency is also more realistic as cryptocurrency option markets mature. Additionally, the plethora of cryptocurrencies in existence today provide a new motivation: under the simplifying assumption that various cryptocurrencies are competing for adoption from a fixed pool of cryptocurrency users and investors, eliminating a competing system might increase the value of a surviving system. For example, an investor with significant Bitcoin holdings might profit from undermining Ethereum, or undermining a fork of Bitcoin such as Bitcoin Cash.

Second, many variants of Nakamoto consensus are now deployed. In particular, there are now ASIC-mined blockchains (e.g. Bitcoin), GPU-mined blockchains (e.g. Ethereum) as well as many proposals for proof-of-stake and other variants. Goldfinger attacks provide an interesting comparison of these competing designs.

In the remainder of this work we analyze the difficulty of mounting a Goldfinger-style attack. We focus specifically on attacks in which an attacker obtains significant decision-making power (which we call *capacity*) and uses it to introduce forks in the system to cause significant damage, calling such an attack a *hostile takeover*. For simplicity, we focus on an attacker obtaining a majority, though of course significant damage may be done with less capacity. Other avenues for a Goldfinger attack exist which we do not consider, for example, denial-of-service attacks on the transaction relay network [9,20]. Our primary contribution is categorising the avenues for a hostile takeover and providing some basic analysis. We also posit several hypotheses about the difference in difficulty of mounting a hostile takeover against different variants of Nakamoto consensus.

Table 1. Four basic strategies for gaining capacity in a Nakamoto consensus protocol.

		duration of control	
		temporary	**permanent**
source	**new**	Rent	Build
	existing	Bribe	Buy out

2   Methods of Obtaining Capacity

An attacker aiming to take over a Nakamoto consensus protocol needs to obtain *capacity*, the details of which vary for different protocol designs. For a proof-of-work blockchain, they must obtain control of a large amount of computational capacity (similarly, a large amount of storage capacity for proof-of-space systems, and so forth). For a proof-of-stake blockchain, they must obtain control of a large amount of stake (currency) in the system.[1]

We consider two primary axes to compare methods of obtaining capacity:

- **New vs. existing capacity:** Is the attacker introducing new capacity into the system which was not previously used for the consensus protocol, or obtaining control of capacity already in use? Note that for proof-of-stake systems, the amount of capacity is fixed so it is not possible to introduce new capacity into the system.
- **Permanent vs. temporary control:** Is the attacker obtaining permanent control of the capacity, or only temporary control?

We can consider whether the attacker is obtaining mining capacity permanently or temporarily, and whether they are introducing new capacity into the system or capturing existing mining capacity. This yields four basic attack strategies, as shown in Table 1. We now consider each of these in turn.

2.1   Rental Attacks

In a rental attack, the attacker temporarily obtains control of capacity external to the system. For example, an attacker might rent computational power or storage space from a cloud computing service or rent control of a large botnet. A key advantage of this approach is that the attacker has low up-front costs and no long-term liability. We note that this attack is impossible for proof-of-stake systems (as there is no external capacity to obtain).

---

[1] There are other potential attacks on proof-of-stake systems, such as purchasing keys from former stakeholders to induce a long fork (the "nothing-at-stake problem"). In this paper, we assume some solution exists for this problem and that a takeover requires obtaining a majority of the *current* stake in the system.

Furthermore, rental is generally feasible only for blockchains in which the capacity is a commodity with external applications. Ethereum fits this description today as mining is dominated by graphics cards (GPUs).[2] Proof-of-storage [14,19], proof-of-space [5] or proof-of-elapsed-time [3] are also candidates for rental. However, for ASIC-dominated proof-of-work blockchains, such as Bitcoin, the rent strategy is likely not possible because there is a negligible amount of Bitcoin mining hardware that is not already dedicated to Bitcoin mining.

Case Study: Rental Attacks on Ethereum. As a representative example we consider[3] the cost of renting GPU capacity from Amazon's Elastic Compute Cloud (EC2). Currently, Amazon rents machines with Nvidia K80 GPUs for about $1 per hour at spot prices, with bulk discounts available. These units are estimated to perform 50–100 MH/s. Therefore it might require renting about 1 million GPUs for a price of about $1 million/hr to perform a temporary takeover of the Ethereum blockchain. Even a few hours of disruptive attacks could be sufficient to cause a major loss in value to the system, which has a market cap of almost $30 billion. As a sanity check, Ethereum miners currently earn roughly $250,000/hr in mining revenue (from block rewards and gas fees), so renting capacity would not be profitable on its own, even with a considerable bulk discount.

2.2 Building Attacks

In a building attack, the attacker permanently obtains new capacity. For example, the attacker might building a new mining farm. Again, this approach is not applicable to proof-of-stake, but is possible for all types of proof-of-work system.

Case Study: Building Attacks on Bitcoin. We consider the AntMiner S9, a state-of-the-art ASIC miner built with 16 nm features. It retails for about $2,000 and can perform about 14 TH/s (consuming over 1 kW of electricity). Given the Bitcoin network's current hash rate of roughly 10^{18} H/s, an upfront capital cost of roughly $1.5 billion would build enough capacity to take over the Bitcoin blockchain. Of course, this figure is approximate. It would be far cheaper to buy this hardware in bulk, however there would also be additional infrastructure and cooling costs when building a large mining farm.

Case Study: Building Attacks on Ethereum. For Ethereum, we consider the Radeon Rx Vega 56 GPU as an example mining card offering among the best performance for cost. Each card can perform about 36 MH/s and costs around $550. Although less powerful than the Nvidia units available for rent, lower unit costs mean the Radeon cards are more cost-effective. Given Ethereum's current hash rate of approximately 10^{11} H/s, this means an attacker must spend roughly $1.5 billion to build enough capacity to take over the Ethereum blockchain.

---

[2] In addition to rendering graphics, GPUs are now commonly used for a variety of tasks including scientific computing and machine learning.

[3] Our case studies are based on market data as of November 2017. We leave all values approximate to two significant figures. All values are in US dollars.

Comparison. Interestingly, we obtain similar figures for a building attack against both Bitcoin and Ethereum—about $1.5 billion. This indicates there has been higher investment in Ethereum hardware relative to the system's total market value. There are two simple explanations: first, while Ethereum overall has a lower total value by a factor of more than three, the rate of revenue earned by Ethereum miners is relatively higher, about half that of Bitcoin. Second, nearly all current Bitcoin mining hardware was built specifically for mining Bitcoin, whereas Ethereum hardware may be acquired used or rented. Similarly, Ethereum miners may be more willing to invest in hardware knowing that they can sell if the system declines in value.

From either figure, we see a roughly thousand-fold increase between the cost of a building attack and the cost (per hour) of a rental attack against Ethereum. A building attack is also much slower and more logistically complex to execute. This is an argument in favor of ASIC-friendly mining puzzles as a defense against rental attacks.

2.3   Bribery Attacks

In a bribery attack, the attacker offers payments to existing miners to deviate from the default protocol and mine on the attacker's branch. Note that we do not use the term "bribery" to indicate illegal or unethical behavior, simply that a side payment is being made. Several mechanisms for bribery have been proposed with various trust and risk properties [1,12]. For an example, an attacker might pay miners outside the protocol directly or through a negative-fee mining pool, or within the system by broadcasting anybody-can-spend transactions or transactions with abnormally high fees which are redeemable only on the attacker's branch. We suggest that it is also feasible for an attacker to create a smart contract to autonomously bribe miners working on another blockchain by checking that they have found blocks building on a designated starting point (similar techniques have been developed for implementing a mining pool in Ethereum [13]).

Previous analysis considered bribes motivated by executing a fork-and-double-spend attack (a "Finney attack"). In the simplest model, the attacker only needs to ensure that mining on the attack chain is more profitable than mining on the longest chain. Unlike renting or building attacks, the miner only needs to bribe half of the current capacity (rather than duplicating all of it), meaning about $125,000/hr for Ethereum or $250,000/hr for Bitcoin.[4] Of course, successfully executing a bribery attack may require paying a premium to override miner loyalty and convince miners to work on a fork that would be highly detrimental to the system. Though as argued previously [1] refusing to accept bribes representing a significant increase in revenue would be a tragedy of the commons. Presumably, similar dynamics would apply to proof-of-stake systems.

---

[4] Note that we only consider bitcoin-denominated revenue. Many Bitcoin miners earn a small amount of additional revenue through merge-mining other currencies.

We note that bribery appears cheaper than even rental attacks and thus could be a significant threat to distributed consensus protocols. The cost is directly proportional to the rate of miner revenue, implying that even in a proof-of-stake system stability may require paying a non-trivial portion of the system's total value in fees. It has previously been argued [2] that Bitcoin may be unstable without the fixed block reward as rewards become time-varying. It also may be unstable simply because fees are too small relative to the value of the system.

2.4   Buy-Out Attacks

A buy-out attack would involve purchasing the majority of existing capacity from current owners. For proof-of-stake systems, the cost is half of the current monetary base, for example about $15 billion for Ethereum or $50 billion for Bitcoin. For proof-of-work systems, the cost should be about half of the net present value of all future mining rewards. It appears that proof-of-stake systems are much more secure here, as the attacker must buy half of all value of the system, whereas with proof-of-work the attacker must only buy half of the future mining rewards (which should be less than the entire market cap).

Traditionally, external buyers hoping to obtain a majority stake in a firm (in a hostile corporate takeover) must pay a premium over the current market price. This may not be true in a cryptocurrency buyout; in fact the opposite may hold due to the interesting possibility of a *race to the door* among current capacity owners. If an attacker can credibly commit to buying out half of all capacity and using it to destroy the system, current owners will have a strong incentive to sell to avoid being left in the 49% which does not sell and ends up holding worthless capacity. As the attacker gains more capacity (which is easy to authentically signal by including messages in block headers), the perceived likelihood of a successful attack increases. In response more owners may sell, potentially leading to a vicious cycle as owners race to avoid missing their chance to sell. This scenario does not occur in hostile corporate takeover because current shareholders retain (sometimes increased) value if they refuse to sell. The purchased firm will usually rise in market cap; if the firm's management do not believe the takeover will increase market value they can employ a wide variety of anti-takeover manoeuvres, none of which apply in a cryptocurrency takeover.

We observe that an attacker might credibly commit to a buy-out attack using a smart contract programmed to buy a large amount of stake through a reverse-price auction. This is similar to the suggested use of a smart contract above to implement bribery. Note, of course, that this is only feasible against a substantially smaller system, as the smart contract must be able to hold significantly more funds than the value of the target system.

Proof-of-stake systems are the most vulnerable to a race-to-the-door, since the stake has no value if the system crashes. ASIC-resistant proof-of-work systems appear less likely to suffer from a race-to-the-door, since capacity owners who do not sell to the attacker can still sell their hardware even if the attack succeeds. With ASIC-friendly proof-of-work, miners may retain some salvage value in unsold hardware, but this amount is likely small enough to ignore.

2.5 Countermeasures

For all of the above attack models, there is the possibility of countermeasures by current capacity owners in the face of an attack. In theory, current owners can deploy any of the applicable attack strategies themselves as a counter-measure, though it likely makes the most sense to respond in kind. In all cases, there is a collective action problem as all current owners would like to see the system continue, though there is no mechanism to compel them to contribute equally to defensive action.

The collective action problem is particularly acute for temporary (bribing or renting) attacks, as the temporary counter-measure yields no long-term benefit to those participating. In contrast, those responding to an attack by buying out or building will can benefit from the increased capacity for the future. Against a buy out, this may be a particularly lucrative (if the attack fails) a defensive buyer may profit as the currency gains value in light of a thwarted attack.

Proof-of-stake systems have one distinct disadvantage, which is that a successful buy-out attack will be permanent. In contrast, it is possible for proof-of-work protocols to recover from a successful attack by increasing total capacity, though significant damage may have already been done.

3 Discussion and Open Questions

The difficulty of hostile takeovers provides an interesting new lens for comparing decentralised consensus protocols. Our hope is that this manuscript is a starting point for further modeling and discussion.

Among proof-of-work systems, our analysis indicates a clear security advantage for ASIC-dominated mining, as rental attacks are not possible and existing miners should have more incentive to resist bribery attacks. However, the ability to rent capacity may be an advantage for ASIC-friendly mining in some cases.

Our model of ASIC-friendly proof-of-work is also simplistic, in that for Bitcoin there are now multiple competing systems (e.g. Bitcoin Cash) which use the same proof-of-work. These systems may effectively provide a pool of rentable mining capacity. It is also possible that rentable capacity exists from older mining hardware which is no longer profitable to operate, but may be operated at a loss by an attacker. This may be particularly dangerous as this capacity is essentially free to rent (or buy) as it has little other value.

At first glance, proof-of-stake systems appear less vulnerable to hostile takeovers than proof-of-work. They are not vulnerable to rental or building attacks. Bribery attacks appear similar, while buy-out attacks appear strictly more costly. However, proof-of-stake may be more fragile due to its vulnerability to an attacker inspiring a race-to-the-door. Additionally, renting or building new capacity is not available as a countermeasure.

Consistent with previous work, our analysis suggests bribery is a particularly troubling avenue of attack. Previous work suggested the problem that miner revenue is low relative to the potential profits to be had from double spending.

We further suggest here that miner revenue is inherently low compared to the total value of the system and hence feasible for a Goldfinger attacker to match with relatively small bribes. It remains unclear what rate of miner revenue is required to ensure stability in practice.

References

1. Bonneau, J.: Why buy when you can rent? In: Clark, J., Meiklejohn, S., Ryan, P.Y.A., Wallach, D., Brenner, M., Rohloff, K. (eds.) FC 2016. LNCS, vol. 9604, pp. 19–26. Springer, Heidelberg (2016). https://doi.org/10.1007/978-3-662-53357-4_2

2. Carlsten, M., Kalodner, H., Weinberg, S.M., Narayanan, A.: On the instability of bitcoin without the block reward. In: Proceedings of the 2016 ACM SIGSAC Conference on Computer and Communications Security, pp. 154–167. ACM (2016)

3. Chen, L., Xu, L., Shah, N., Gao, Z., Lu, Y., Shi, W.: On security analysis of proof-of-elapsed-time (PoET). In: Spirakis, P., Tsigas, P. (eds.) SSS 2017. LNCS, vol. 10616, pp. 282–297. Springer, Cham (2017). https://doi.org/10.1007/978-3-319-69084-1_19

4. Eyal, I., Sirer, E.G.: Majority is not enough: bitcoin mining is vulnerable. In: Christin, N., Safavi-Naini, R. (eds.) FC 2014. LNCS, vol. 8437, pp. 436–454. Springer, Heidelberg (2014). https://doi.org/10.1007/978-3-662-45472-5_28

5. Fuchsbauer, G., Park, S., Kwon, A., Pietrzak, K., Alwen, J., Gazi, P.: Spacemint

6. Garay, J., Kiayias, A., Leonardos, N.: The bitcoin backbone protocol with chains of variable difficulty. In: Katz, J., Shacham, H. (eds.) CRYPTO 2017, Part I. LNCS, vol. 10401, pp. 291–323. Springer, Cham (2017). https://doi.org/10.1007/978-3-319-63688-7_10

7. Garay, J., Kiayias, A., Leonardos, N.: The bitcoin backbone protocol: analysis and applications. In: Oswald, E., Fischlin, M. (eds.) EUROCRYPT 2015, Part II. LNCS, vol. 9057, pp. 281–310. Springer, Heidelberg (2015). https://doi.org/10.1007/978-3-662-46803-6_10

8. Gervais, A., Karame, G.O., Wüst, K., Glykantzis, V., Ritzdorf, H., Capkun, S.: On the security and performance of proof of work blockchains. In: Proceedings of the 2016 ACM SIGSAC Conference on Computer and Communications Security, pp. 3–16. ACM (2016)

9. Johnson, B., Laszka, A., Grossklags, J., Vasek, M., Moore, T.: Game-theoretic analysis of DDoS attacks against bitcoin mining pools. In: Böhme, R., Brenner, M., Moore, T., Smith, M. (eds.) FC 2014. LNCS, vol. 8438, pp. 72–86. Springer, Heidelberg (2014). https://doi.org/10.1007/978-3-662-44774-1_6

10. Kiayias, A., Koutsoupias, E., Kyropoulou, M., Tselekounis, Y.: Blockchain mining games. In: Proceedings of the 2016 ACM Conference on Economics and Computation

11. Kroll, J.A., Davey, I.C., Felten, E.W.: The economics of bitcoin mining, or bitcoin in the presence of adversaries. In: WEIS, June 2013

12. Liao, K., Katz, J.: Incentivizing double-spend collusion in bitcoin. In: Financial Cryptography Bitcoin Workshop (2017)

13. Luu, L., Velner, Y., Teutsch, J., Saxena, P.: Smart pool: practical decentralized pooled mining. IACR Cryptology ePrint Archive 2017, 19 (2017)

14. Miller, A., Juels, A., Shi, E., Parno, B., Katz, J.: Permacoin: repurposing bitcoin work for data preservation. In: IEEE Security & Privacy (2014)

15. Nakamoto, S.: Bitcoin: a peer-to-peer electronic cash system (2008)
16. Nayak, K., Kumar, S., Miller, A., Shi, E.: Stubborn mining: generalizing selfish mining and combining with an eclipse attack. In: IEEE EuroS&P (2016)
17. Pass, R., Shi, E.: Fruitchains: a fair blockchain. In: Proceedings of the ACM Symposium on Principles of Distributed Computing, pp. 315–324. ACM (2017)
18. Sapirshtein, A., Sompolinsky, Y., Zohar, A.: Optimal selfish mining strategies in bitcoin. In: Grossklags, J., Preneel, B. (eds.) FC 2016. LNCS, vol. 9603, pp. 515–532. Springer, Heidelberg (2017). https://doi.org/10.1007/978-3-662-54970-4_30
19. Sengupta, B., Bag, S., Ruj, S., Sakurai, K.: Retricoin: bitcoin based on compact proofs of retrievability. In: Proceedings of the 17th International Conference on Distributed Computing and Networking, p. 14. ACM (2016)
20. Vasek, M., Thornton, M., Moore, T.: Empirical analysis of denial-of-service attacks in the bitcoin ecosystem. In: Böhme, R., Brenner, M., Moore, T., Smith, M. (eds.) FC 2014. LNCS, vol. 8438, pp. 57–71. Springer, Heidelberg (2014). https://doi.org/10.1007/978-3-662-44774-1_5
21. Wood, G.: Ethereum: a secure decentralised generalised transaction ledger. Ethereum Project Yellow Paper 151 (2014)

Analyzing the Bitcoin Ponzi Scheme Ecosystem

Marie Vasek[1(✉)] and Tyler Moore[2]

[1] Computer Science, University of New Mexico, Albuquerque, USA
vasek@cs.unm.edu
[2] Tandy School of Computer Science, The University of Tulsa, Tulsa, USA
tyler-moore@utulsa.edu

Abstract. This paper analyzes the supply and demand for Bitcoin-based Ponzi schemes. There are a variety of these types of scams: from long cons such as Bitcoin Savings & Trust to overnight doubling schemes that do not take off. We investigate what makes some Ponzi schemes successful and others less so. By scouring 11 424 threads on bitcointalk.org, we identify 1 780 distinct scams. Of these, half lasted a week or less. Using survival analysis, we identify factors that affect scam persistence. One approach that appears to elongate the life of the scam is when the scammer interacts a lot with their victims, such as by posting more than a quarter of the comments in the related thread. By contrast, we also find that scams are shorter-lived when the scammers register their account on the same day that they post about their scam. Surprisingly, more daily posts by victims is associated with the scam ending sooner.

Keywords: Bitcoin · Cybercrime measurement

1 Introduction

Bitcoin draws out risk-seeking individuals. The exchange rate is volatile; many businesses built on top of it are speculative in nature; the currency is pseudo-anonymous and distributed. Consequently, it is perhaps unsurprising that many Bitcoin users have taken to Ponzi schemes (and Ponzi scheme runners to Bitcoin).

In this paper, we look at the ecosystem around Ponzi schemes advertised to Bitcoin users. Previous work of ours has established a lower bound for the amount of money earned by criminals through Bitcoin scams [12]. Here we more comprehensively study the scams by gathering data where they are promoted. As well as shedding light on the "supply" side of Ponzi schemes, we also look at the "demand" side by gathering data on victim interactions with the scams. People keep falling for Bitcoin scams, but why? Bitcoin users like to purport themselves as particularly technologically savvy, but does that help or hinder their susceptibility to scams? How do the steps taken by scammers, such as engaging shills to promote their products, affect their success? Ultimately, our goal is to shed light on why criminals are able to prosper in this ecosystem.

© International Financial Cryptography Association 2019
A. Zohar et al. (Eds.): FC 2018 Workshops, LNCS 10958, pp. 101–112, 2019.
https://doi.org/10.1007/978-3-662-58820-8_8

Even with the improved coverage relative to previous work, our results are necessarily incomplete. There are inevitably scams which use Bitcoin and we do not measure. There are also scammers which create multiple accounts to talk about their scam and we only are able to extricate the obvious cases of this behavior. Despite these limitations, we provide a large-scale analysis of this online Ponzi scheme ecosystem.

The research contributions for this paper are both in the data collection methodology and in the analysis of the gathered data.

- Section 2 outlines our data collection contributions: gathering candidate scam data directly from scammer advertising venues, automatically confirming scams by inspecting payout mechanisms, and, for confirmed scams, collecting usage, performance and demographic indicators from forum posts. This yields a richer dataset on Ponzi schemes than has been collected before in prior work.
- Our data analysis contributions (found in Sect. 3) leverage this novel dataset to describe supply-side characteristics of scams and scammers as well as describe demand-side characteristics of victims.

2   Methodology

We aim to measure scams by collecting data from the places they are advertised. This helps us generate a comprehensive list of advertised scams. For the purposes of this study, we elect to focus on Ponzi schemes exclusively. Of course, there are many different types of scams affecting Bitcoin, as shown by Vasek and Moore [12]. We focus on Ponzi schemes due to their reliance on public advertising and the consistency of locations for such advertising. Since Ponzi schemes must advertise to stay in business, we are relatively confident in the comprehensiveness of our approach.

We collect our data from the forum bitcointalk.org. This forum was created in the same year as Bitcoin and by the same pseudonymous entity[1]. This forum is the top place where Bitcoin community members go to discuss Bitcoin and is currently one of the 1 000 most popular websites in the world, according to Alexa. We chose this as our sole source for this work based both on its popularity in the Bitcoin ecosystem and its popularity within the subsection of Ponzi scheme investors within the Bitcoin ecosystem, as we found in our previous work in this space [12].

In order to collect information about the scams, we crawl the entire history of three subforums of bitcointalk.org: Scam accusations, Gambling: Games and Rounds, and Gambling: Investment Games. Investment games is a subforum where users submit Ponzi schemes or moderators move threads on Ponzi schemes. We can find a number of Ponzi schemes advertised in other subforums of bitcointalk. However, we choose the two most popular subforums for Ponzi schemes that had the highest signal to noise ratio: scam accusations and games

---

[1] https://bitcointalk.org/index.php?topic=5.

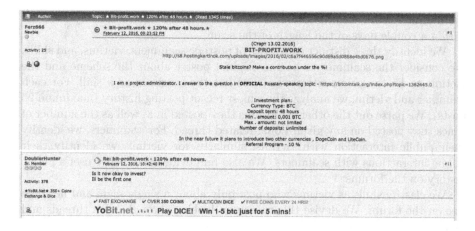

Fig. 1. Screenshots of the initial posting for the Ponzi scheme and an example victim response.

and rounds. In total, we crawl 11 424 threads on these three subforums from June 2011 through November 2016. We consider all the subforums of bitcointalk where we found any posts advertising a Ponzi scheme. We then look at the forums, particularly for Ponzi schemes. We omit subforums like the gambling subforum which predominantly contained posts about online card games and other non-Ponzi scheme activity.

Since threads on these forums cover other topics than just promoting Ponzi schemes, we refine this further to threads that referenced "ponzi" or "hyip" in the first 10 comments. We then process these further to only consider threads which contained a URL or bitcoin address for the scam. This left us with 1 810 scams advertised through 1 804 Ponzi-registered domains, as well as 1 448 Bitcoin addresses collated from 2 617 threads. We merge threads containing the same domain or Bitcoin address, since many scams were advertised multiple times or in different places. Note that we throw out threads containing a whitelist of legitimate gambling domains[2]. We also do not consider popular domains, removing from consideration any URLs in the Alexa top 10 000 domains such as google.com and wikipedia.org.

Our objective is to extract as much information about reflecting supply and demand for scams by examining threads discussing the schemes. In particular, we are interested in measuring the lifetime of the scam, the profiles of the scammers and their victims, and how interactive the threads on scams are. We considered the opening time a scheme was operational to be the first time it was advertised on bitcointalk and the closing time to be the last comment time on threads relating to the scheme. The difference between these times is the lifetime of the scam. We closely analyzed 10 different scams for which we had ground truth on

---

[2] This list was curated by bitcointalk user **mem** here: https://bitcointalk.org/index.php?topic=75883.0.

the lifetime of the scam, and found that this method was reasonably accurate within a couple days of the length of the scam.

We identify three distinct categories of posters: scammers, victims, and shills. We consider the scammer to be the original poster about the scheme and the victims to be the commenters who were not the scammer or a shill. For each scammer and victim, we analyze their most recent posting history (maximum 20 posts). We parse out the other subforums they posted in as well as the number of times they posted on any given Ponzi-related thread. For scammers, we identify their public interaction with victims; similarly, for victims, we identify their public interactions with scammers. We also find evidence of every user's public history on the forums.

We classify shills as victims who post only about a single scam and nowhere else on the forum. We devise this rule upon looking through scam threads and finding users who were extremely positive. Some of these users posted about multiple threads, seemingly different content, and largely had corroborating evidence, such as transaction information. Others only posted about one or a few scams with similar content. We attempt to identify these posters automatically, and the most straightforward way is by number of threads posted on. While not all shills only post about one particular scam and not all posters with history on only one scammer thread are shills, we have concluded from manual inspection that this simple approach provides an effective approach to identify many shills without miscategorizing legitimate users.

Finally, we sought a way to measure the effort the scammer made to imbue trust in his scheme from the Bitcoin forum. The markers of trust and reputation that we use include the time between registration and posting about a scam (with shorter gaps seemingly less trustworthy) and the overall posting history of the scammer including frequency and topics.

3   Results

We find 1 780 scams from 1 956 scammers on 2 625 forum posts. Scams with multiple scammers have multiple threads about the scam originating from different usernames. By randomly inspecting 20 such instances of this, we find that in most cases, both usernames appear to be the same scammer or at least operating the same scam. We identify 11 990 users who posted in response to these posts.

Figure 2 shows the lifetimes of the scams, where lifetime is measured as the length of time between the first post about a given scam and the last. About a quarter of the attempted scams did not last a day and half only lasted a week. However, some scams lasted a long time, with the longest lasting scam lasting over three years. From manual inspection, many of the scams lasting a day were shut down by the moderators or other entities. The rest of this section will break down this vast difference in lifetimes between these scams and quantify the differences both in attacker strategies and in victimology.

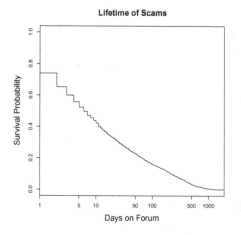

Fig. 2. Survival analysis of the lifetime of scams.

3.1 Scammer Interaction and Scam Lifetime

Figure 3 shows the difference in lifetime based on the amount of scammer interaction. Out of the 344 threads that only had one post by the scammer on them, less than 50% lasted longer than a day – 19 of them only consisted of one post total. We find that more scammer posting helped enliven the scam – whereas an average scam lasted about a week, the average scam where the scammer posted at least half of the posts lasted about three weeks. Scammers interacting with their victims seem to prop up their scam, at least in the short term.

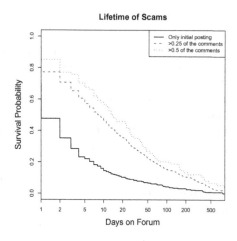

Fig. 3. Lifetime of the scam based on the fraction of the comments about the scam from the scammer.

The difference in these curves, measured by running the survival curve difference test, is statistically significant at the p = 0.01 level.

We can see if we can see the same effect for shills as well as scammers, since most of the postings by scammers seems rather overt. Figure 4 shows the average lifetime of a scam based on the percentage of posts by shills. Scams where more than 10% of the posts are from shills last longer than those where more than 10% of the posts are from scammers. Furthermore, more shill posts seems to be more effective than the combined strategy, considering both shill posts and scam posts to contribute to the lifetime. Running a survival curve differences test, the effect of the differing shill interaction percentages on the lifetime of a scam are statistically significantly different at the p = 0.1 level.

We indirectly measure scammer reputation in two ways: by examining where scammers post and by measuring the time between registration and scam posting. Figure 5 shows the breakdown in the efficacy of the scam by the reputation of the scammer. On the left we look at the other posts/comments made by the user who first posted the scam. We distinguish between only posting on one scam, only posting on (multiple) scam posts, and those scammers who post in other parts of bitcointalk. We notice that scammers that only post on one scam have a lower lifetime compared to scammers that post outside of just one scam. The difference in these survival lifetimes are significant at the p = 0.01 level. Figure 5b shows the lifetime based on if the scammer account was created on the same day as the scam or not. 39% of scammer accounts were created within a day as the corresponding bitcointalk post. We discover that scams advertised by scammer with newly created accounts die quicker than those with older accounts. Half of scams that have been created at least a day prior to posting end within 26 days compared to only 4 days for those created the same day. The difference in these survival plots is statistically significant at the p = 0.01 level.

3.2   Victim Behavior

We measure the responses from 11 902 victims from 89 439 comments on 2 629 threads on 1 779 scams. In this section, we examine characteristics of the user accounts that post in threads about Ponzi schemes.

In Fig. 4 we separate out shills from the victims and the scammers. We can see that shill and scammer activity are associated with longer lifetimes. Active shills do appear to survive slightly longer than active scammers for the first couple of months, but the overall effect is indistinguishable between shills and scammers.

Table 1 shows how Ponzi scheme victims' post history compares to that of other users active on bitcointalk. For this, we scrape bitcointalk's aggregated posts statistics for ground truth and categorize each post using bitcointalk's categories. The Ponzi victims' post history is statistically significantly different (at the p = 0.01 level) than the general post history, both aggregating by thread and by overall topic. Ponzi victims are overrepresented in the "economy" section, which is unsurprising since this is the section where Ponzi scheme advertisements are located. Ponzi victims are also overrepresented in the "other" section.

Table 1. Bitcointalk forum categories and where scam victims post. Categories are marked as under or overrepresented according to a chi-squared test with 97.5% confidence. Categories with at least 50 000 posts are included.

Category	# Victim posts	# Other posts	
Altcoins (all)	32 536	5 429 022	(−)
Alternative Clients	106	54 159	(−)
Bitcoin Discussion	8 872	998 246	(+)
Development & Technical Discussion	683	162 405	(−)
Group Buys	498	84 734	
Hardware	2 730	518 728	(−)
Mining	427	1 044 148	(−)
Mining software (miners)	274	67 561	(−)
Mining speculation	616	63 071	(+)
Pools	885	177 985	(−)
Press	696	74 437	(+)
Project Development	1 526	137 245	(+)
Technical Support	586	58 952	(+)
Auctions	1 865	108 048	(+)
Collectibles	1 063	60 745	(+)
Computer hardware	1 462	118 584	(+)
Currency exchange	3 124	138 264	(+)
Digital goods	7 303	277 903	(+)
Economics	3 692	1 204 450	(−)
Gambling	12 070	1 297 038	(+)
Gambling discussion	5 677	340 593	(+)
Games and rounds	23 331	388 689	(+)
Goods	1 251	587 681	(−)
Investor-based games	15 402	115 454	(+)
Lending	3 230	138 108	(+)
Marketplace	517	5 372 844	(−)
Micro Earnings	3 694	144 797	(+)
Scam Accusations	4 643	116 151	(+)
Securities	1 338	202 813	
Service Announcements	2 338	288 993	(+)
Service Discussion	3 692	330 535	(+)
Services	8 528	407 342	(+)
Speculation	5 058	883 584	(−)
Trading Discussion	1 678	257 930	
Local (all)	14 932	4 454 405	(−)
Archival	1 026	147 836	
Beginners & Help	3 923	564 720	
Meta	1 960	134 319	(+)
Off-topic	8 309	563 710	(+)
Politics & Society	2 181	290 782	

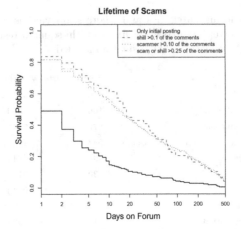

Fig. 4. Lifetime of the scam by interaction by "shill" commenters.

When we look further into this forum category, we find that Ponzi victims are overrepresented in the "Off Topic" and "meta" board commenters and under represented in "Politics & Society" and "Beginners". We also see Ponzi victims underrepresented in many technical boards, like "Development & Technical Discussion" and "Mining" but are overrepresented in "Mining Speculation".

We can also observe what time these victims posted on threads about the scheme. The median time for victims to comment on a thread is about 5 days after the initial post. Figure 6 analyzes this effect further. While most victims post within a week, there is quite a long tail of victim posts. We discover new victims posting over half a year after the start of the initial scam posting.

3.3   Proportional Hazards Model

To distill the varying effects on the lifetime of a Ponzi scheme, we run a Cox proportional hazards model. Our dependent variable is the lifetime of the scam, measured in days. For independent variables, we use the following:

daily # victim comments. This measures the number of *victim* comments over the lifetime of the scam. We use a daily count, since the overall count is, unsurprisingly, highly correlated with the lifetime of the scam.

daily # scammer comments. This measures the number of *scammer* comments over the lifetime of the scam. Again, we use a daily count to control for the correlation between this variable and the lifetime of the scam.

shill has posted? This is true if a "shill" (described more thoroughly in Sect. 3.1) has posted anywhere in the thread. This accounts for their presence, since the number of comments by these users is so low.

same day account. This is true if the scammers' bitcointalk account was registered the same day as the original post for the scam.

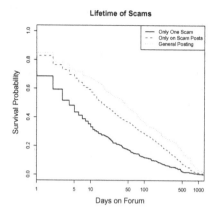

(a) Lifetime of scams, distinguishing between post history.

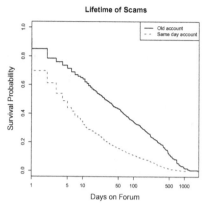

(b) Lifetime of scams, distinguishing between newly created accounts and older accounts.

Fig. 5. Measuring lifetimes of scams based on attacker accounts.

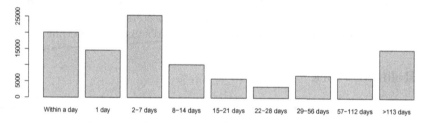

Fig. 6. Number of victim posts after a thread starts.

Table 2 shows the results of running this regression. We note that all the variables are statistically significant to at least the $p = 0.05$ level, with three of the variables highly significant. The best way to interpret the table is to focus on the exp(coef) column. Values greater than one correspond to an increase in the hazard rate, while those less than one correspond to a decrease. The hazard

Table 2. Cox proportional hazards model: measuring scammer and victim effects on the lifetime of the scam.

	coef	exp(coef)	95% CI	p value
Daily # victim comments	0.028	1.029	(1.022 , 1.036)	≪0.0001
Daily # scammer comments	0.022	1.022	(1.002 , 1.043)	0.034
Shill has posted?	−0.846	0.429	(0.385 , 0.479)	≪0.0001
Same day account	0.374	1.453	(1.320 , 1.599)	≪0.0001
Log-rank test: $Q = 489.2$, $p \ll 0.0001$, $R^2 = 0.218$.				

rate captures the instantaneous probability that a scam will shut down, so an increased hazard rate means a greater risk of shutdown.

Each additional daily comment by a victim correlates to a 2.9% increase in the hazard rate. The effect is similar, though slightly weaker, for additional posts by the scammer. The result is somewhat counterintuitive; one might have expected scams with more active participation to be longer-lived, yet the opposite is true. One possible explanation is that victims are more likely to post when there are problems, and so are scammers.

By contrast, a shill posting on a thread is correlated with a massive 57% decrease in the hazard rate. This indicates that shills may play a significant role in prolonging the lives of scams, helping to draw in more victims and settle the nerves of existing investors.

Unsurprisingly, a scammer creating an account on the same day as the initial post correlates with a shorter scam lifetime. This confirms the intuition from Fig. 5, which suggests that no post history shortens the lifetime of the scam. The Cox model shows that scams created by newly registered posters face a 45% increase in the hazard rate.

Reflecting on the overall model, we conclude that posts by shills may prolong a scam's lifetime dramatically, whereas posts made by victims and scammers have the opposite effect. Finally, the reputation of posters as indicated by posting history also appears to significantly affect the scam's expected lifetime.

4   Related Work

This paper fits into the greater literature of reputation mechanisms. Resnick et al. provide a general overview for reputation systems as well as drawbacks in them [9]. Shen et al. provide analysis of reviewers posting about products on online retailers [10]. They found that popular reviewers post about popular products that have few reviews and also tend to provide similar reviews to the existing ones about the product.

This paper also fits into greater literature about Bitcoin. Bitcoin has a small community of actors [2]. Maurer et al. associated the distributed network of Bitcoin nodes with the distributed network of conversations, like those found on the Bitcoin forums [6]. We agree that the "sociality of trust" that Bitcoin offers seems to be both ingrained in the code and the community. We use this small network of trust ingrained in code and in people to more easily measure communications.

To this end, other researchers have mined Bitcoin forum posts to infer activity in the Bitcoin ecosystem. Vasek et al. searched for reports of DDoS attacks to infer after the fact when they occurred [13]. Fleder et al. searched for Bitcoin addresses to categorize them [4]. Using this information, they were able to tie bitcointalk users to Silk Road transactions. Similarly, Vasek and Moore use bitcointalk to identify addresses for potential Bitcoin scams [12] and Liao et al. use the Bitcoin subreddit to seed their ransomware address finder [5]. Most similarly to this paper's methodology, Xie et al. analyze how, among other things, the social network in the Bitcoin forums leads to price swings in Bitcoin [14]. They found that bitcointalk users that invite long discussions are more likely to share relevant information. When looking at the connectedness of bitcointalk users, they found that the more connected the users are at a given time, the more intense the trading frequency is.

Our work also falls in the literature on online Ponzi schemes, also known as high yield investment programs (HYIPs). Moore et al. overviewed the ecosystem using HYIP aggregator websites [7]. They found that the lifetime of any given HYIP could be predicted by interest payments and the mandatory investment term. Neisius and Clayton followed up on this work, concentrating on the incentives promoting this criminal behaviors [8]. They found that HYIP operators paid to be listed on aggregator websites and also received a referral bonus for users directed to HYIPs. They also crawled the criminal forums behind people that run HYIPs and HYIP aggregator websites, and found that the majority of these criminals are based in the US. Drew and Moore found clusters of replicated HYIP websites, pointing to the high use of HYIP kits in creating Ponzi scheme websites [3]. Vasek and Moore carried out the first analysis of Bitcoin-based Ponzi schemes [12]. They directly measured the profits of 32 Ponzi schemes and found that these scammers were bringing in over $7 million. Bartoletti et al. analyzed Ponzi schemes using the cryptocurrency Ethereum and found similar results as Vasek and Moore found with Bitcoin-based Ponzi scams [1,12]. Soska and Christin looked at online black marketplaces and found that some would "exit scam" or run the marketplace legitimately for a time and then take all the money deposited in it and leave [11]. They found that this behavior lowered users' confidences in these marketplaces for a couple months, but long term, the online drug market was resilient to these scams.

5   Conclusion

Bitcoin Ponzi schemes are alluring. The victims of these scams enjoy the thrill of the risk and the opportunity to earn a windfall. The scammers are seduced by the opportunity to earn hard-to-trace money with seemingly little effort.

To measure this, we crawl 11 424 threads on three subforums of the Bitcoin forums from June 2011 through November 2016 to find 1 780 scams from 1 956 scammers on 2 625 forum posts targeting 11 990 users. We find that more daily scammer and victim interaction shortens the life of the scam. Furthermore, we analyze that shill interaction, or users that only post in one thread, and discover that it lengthens the life of the scam. We demonstrate that having a reputation on the Bitcoin forum matters: posting a scam the same day as an account was created is associated with a quicker demise.

In addition to investigating perpetrators of these frauds, we also analyze the users who fall victim to them. We compare the post history of scam victims to overall Bitcoin forum statistics and find that scam victims disproportionately post in other forums like "Off-Topic" and "Mining Speculation". We find that most victims post within the first five days of a scam post, with a long tail that post even over a year after the initial posting.

References

1. Bartoletti, M., Carta, S., Cimoli, T., Saia, R.: Dissecting Ponzi schemes on Ethereum: identification, analysis, and impact. arXiv preprint arXiv:1703.03779 (2017)
2. Bohr, J., Bashir, M.: Who uses Bitcoin? an exploration of the Bitcoin community. In: Twelfth Annual International Conference on Privacy, Security and Trust, pp. 94–101. IEEE (2014)
3. Drew, J., Moore, T.: Automatic identification of replicated criminal websites using combined clustering. In: International Workshop on Cyber Crime, pp. 116–123. IEEE (2014)
4. Fleder, M., Kester, M.S., Pillai, S.: Bitcoin transaction graph analysis. arXiv preprint arXiv:1502.01657 (2015)
5. Liao, K., Zhao, Z., Doupé, A., Ahn, G.-J.: Behind closed doors: measurement and analysis of a CryptoLocker ransoms in Bitcoin. In: Eleventh APWG eCrime Researcher's Summit, June 2016
6. Maurer, B., Nelms, T.C., Swartz, L.: "When perhaps the real problem is money itself!": the practical materiality of Bitcoin. Soc. Semiot. **23**(2), 261–277 (2013)
7. Moore, T., Han, J., Clayton, R.: The postmodern ponzi scheme: empirical analysis of high-yield investment programs. In: Keromytis, A.D. (ed.) FC 2012. LNCS, vol. 7397, pp. 41–56. Springer, Heidelberg (2012). https://doi.org/10.1007/978-3-642-32946-3_4
8. Neisius, J., Clayton, R.: Orchestrated crime: the high yield investment fraud ecosystem. In: Proceedings of the Eighth APWG eCrime Researcher's Summit, Birmingham, AL, September 2014
9. Resnick, P., Kuwabara, K., Zeckhauser, R., Friedman, E.: Reputation systems. Commun. ACM **43**(12), 45–48 (2000)
10. Shen, W., Hu, Y.J., Ulmer, J.R.: Competing for attention: an empirical study of online reviewers' strategic behavior. MIS Quart. **39**(3), 683–696 (2015)
11. Soska, K., Christin, N.: Measuring the longitudinal evolution of the online anonymous marketplace ecosystem. In: USENIX Security Symposium, pp. 33–48 (2015)
12. Vasek, M., Moore, T.: There's no free lunch, even using bitcoin: tracking the popularity and profits of virtual currency scams. In: Böhme, R., Okamoto, T. (eds.) FC 2015. LNCS, vol. 8975, pp. 44–61. Springer, Heidelberg (2015). https://doi.org/10.1007/978-3-662-47854-7_4
13. Vasek, M., Thornton, M., Moore, T.: Empirical analysis of denial-of-service attacks in the bitcoin ecosystem. In: Böhme, R., Brenner, M., Moore, T., Smith, M. (eds.) FC 2014. LNCS, vol. 8438, pp. 57–71. Springer, Heidelberg (2014). https://doi.org/10.1007/978-3-662-44774-1_5
14. Xie, P., Chen, H., Hu, Y.J.: Network structure and predictive power of social media for the Bitcoin market (2017). https://papers.ssrn.com/sol3/papers.cfm?abstract_id=2894089

Exploiting Transaction Accumulation and Double Spends for Topology Inference in Bitcoin

Matthias Grundmann[✉], Till Neudecker, and Hannes Hartenstein

Institute of Telematics, Karlsruhe Institute of Technology, Karlsruhe, Germany
{matthias.grundmann,till.neudecker,hannes.hartenstein}@kit.edu

Abstract. Bitcoin relies on a peer-to-peer network for communication between participants. Knowledge of the network topology is of scientific interest but can also facilitate attacks on the users' anonymity and the system's availability. We present two approaches for inferring the network topology and evaluate them in simulations and in real-world experiments in the Bitcoin testnet. The first approach exploits the accumulation of multiple transactions before their announcement to other peers. Despite the general feasibility of the approach, simulation and experimental results indicate a low inference quality. The second approach exploits the fact that double spending transactions are dropped by clients. Experimental results show that inferring the neighbors of a specific peer is possible with a precision of 71% and a recall of 87% at low cost.

1 Introduction

Bitcoin [9] is a digital currency system that stores transactions in a blockchain. Participants are connected via a peer-to-peer (P2P) network in order to exchange transactions and blocks. The topology of the P2P network is an important aspect in ensuring anonymity of users and robustness against denial of service attacks [5], double spending attacks [6], and attacks on mining [3,10]. For instance, knowledge of the network topology can enable network based attacks on anonymity [1,4,7].

In this work we present and analyze two approaches that aim at inferring the topology of the publicly reachable Bitcoin network. Peers that are not reachable (e.g., peers that do not accept incoming connections) as well as *private* networks such as FIBRE[1] or mining pool networks are not covered by our work. Neither of the presented approaches rely on the existence of side channels (e.g., peer discovery), because they exploit properties of the implementation of the flooding protocol used for transaction propagation.

---

[1] http://bitcoinfibre.org/.

© International Financial Cryptography Association 2019
A. Zohar et al. (Eds.): FC 2018 Workshops, LNCS 10958, pp. 113–126, 2019.
https://doi.org/10.1007/978-3-662-58820-8_9

2   Related Work

Topology inference in Bitcoin has been the subject of several previous works. Peer discovery in Bitcoin allows clients to query their neighbors for IP addresses of other peers in order to establish connections to them. The queried neighbor then sends a list with IP addresses along with a `lastseen` timestamp. Until March 2015 the timestamp was not randomized sufficiently and allowed Miller et al. [8] to exploit this mechanism and infer the network topology. Peer discovery can also be exploited for topology inference by sending marker IP addresses to remote peers [1].

Neudecker et al. [11] performed a timing analysis of the propagation of transactions in order to infer the network topology. By connecting to all reachable peers of the network and observing the timestamps of receptions of certain transactions, the path of the transaction and thereby the connections between peers can be inferred. This approach requires connections to all reachable peers and requires the adversary to actively create transactions if he is unable to determine the creator of a transaction. Furthermore, changes made to the propagation mechanism of the reference client Bitcoin Core[2] in 2015 render this method much more difficult nowadays.

3   Fundamentals

For this work the networking code and especially the forwarding of transactions is relevant. After a peer creates or receives a transaction, it sends an `INV` message containing the hash of the transaction to each of its neighbors. A peer receiving an `INV` message checks whether it has already received the transaction, and, if the transaction is new, sends a `GETDATA` message to the peer it received the `INV` message from. This peer then replies with a `TX` message containing the actual transaction.

When a peer receives a transaction, it validates the correctness of the transaction. This includes checking the correct format, checking whether the sum of input values is at least as large as the sum of output values, and checking whether the inputs of the transaction are actually spendable. Because every transaction output can only be spent once, a transaction with an input that was already spent by a transaction received earlier is regarded invalid and dropped silently. We will demonstrate how to exploit this behavior regarding *double spends* for topology inference in Sect. 6.

In order to enhance privacy by impeding timing analysis, `INV` messages are not sent out immediately after receiving and validating a transaction, but are delayed according to a non-deterministic function. Bitcoin Core maintains one outgoing queue for each connected peer. When a new transaction is received or created, this transaction is added to all queues. Therefore, each queue contains all transactions that are to be announced to that peer. At certain times all

---

[2] https://github.com/bitcoin/bitcoin.

messages in a queue are announced to the neighbor via a single INV message.[3] These times are chosen according to an exponential distribution[4] to model a Poisson process. Every time the elements of the queue are sent to the neighbor, a new sending time is determined. This mechanism has the property that all transactions received between two sending timestamps are sent in one single INV message. We will demonstrate how to exploit this *transaction accumulation* for topology inference in Sect. 5.

4   Problem Statement and Assumptions

Let $G = (V, E)$ be the undirected graph modeling the peers (V) and connections (E) of the Bitcoin network. Given a subset $R \subseteq V$ of the reachable peers of the network, the adversary tries to infer all connections between all peers in R. The inference can lead to false positives (i.e., inferring a connection although no connection exists) and false negatives (i.e., not inferring a connection although a connection exists). We will use precision (i.e., the share of inferred connections that are true positives) and recall (the share of existing connections that were inferred) as metrics to describe the success of the inference.

We assume that the adversary can run a small number of peers, which can connect to as many other peers as possible. This number is limited by the number of reachable peers and the network capabilities of the adversary.[5] We also assume that the adversary is able to precisely estimate the latency between its own peers and remote peers, e.g., based on the observation of Bitcoin ping messages or ICMP ping messages. Furthermore, we assume that the adversary is able to create a large number of transactions. These transactions can transfer funds between addresses controlled by the adversary, however, transaction fees still have to be paid. The adversary is not assumed to have information that an ISP or state actor organization might have about connections and traffic of other peers. We do not consider stronger adversary models (e.g., ISPs), as these adversaries could simply monitor the network traffic in order to infer the network topology.

5   Exploiting Transaction Accumulation

We will now describe how the transaction accumulation mechanism implemented in Bitcoin Core (cf. Sect. 3) can be used for topology inference.

---

[3] If there are more than 35 transactions in the queue (which occurs only infrequently), only 35 transactions are announced at once.

[4] The next time is calculated as: $current\_time$ + $\ln\left(1 + X \cdot \frac{-1}{2^{48}}\right)$ · $average\_interval\_seconds$ · -1000000 + 0.5 (all timestamps are in microseconds, $X \in \mathcal{U}[0 : 2^{48} - 1]$, $average\_interval\_seconds$ is 5 s for incoming connections and 2 s for outgoing connections).

[5] Our measurements show that maintaining connections to $\approx$10,000 peers consumes about 20 Mbit/s.

5.1 Description

Assume for now that the adversarial monitor peer v_M is connected to all peers $v_I \in V$ of the network. The adversary creates one transaction $t_I \in \mathcal{T}$ for each connected peer v_I. All transactions are independent and not conflicting in any way (i.e., they are spending different outputs). All transactions are sent to the peer they were created for (i.e., t_I to v_I) so that they arrive at all peers at the same time. Afterwards the adversary monitors the first INV messages that will be received by v_M from all connected peers, and infers information about the topology by using the following inference rules:

1. If the first INV message that peer v_A sends to v_M contains only t_B (i.e., the transaction sent to v_B) and no other transaction from the set of created transactions $\mathcal{T}$, then v_A and v_B are connected.
2. If the first INV message that peer v_A sends to v_M contains more than one transaction from the set of created transactions $\mathcal{T}$, at least one the peers associated with the announced transactions is connected to v_A.

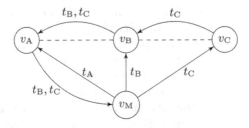

Fig. 1. Exploiting transaction accumulation for topology inference. Dashed lines indicate existing connections. Solid lines indicate the transmission of transactions.

Let us consider the scenario depicted in Fig. 1 to demonstrate the correctness of the rules. v_M is connected to v_A, v_B, and v_C. v_A is connected to v_B, v_B is connected to v_C. After the transactions were sent by the adversary, each peer has only the transaction designated for itself (and transactions created by other participants, which can be ignored). Statement 1 is equal to *If v_A and v_C are* **not** *directly connected, then v_A will* **not** *send an INV message that contains only t_C and no other transaction from the set of created transactions $\mathcal{T}$*.

Because v_A and v_C are not connected, t_C has to be relayed by another peer (v_B) to v_A. As we assumed that the adversary is connected to all peers, the adversary is also connected to v_B and has sent a transaction t_B to v_B. Because of the queuing mechanism described in Sect. 3, v_B's queue for v_A already contains t_B. Therefore, t_B and t_C will be announced together to v_A, which announces them together to v_M. It is also possible that t_B will be sent earlier than t_C, because the queue at v_B is sent between the reception of t_B and t_C by v_B. However, it is not possible that t_C arrives earlier than t_B at v_A.

This scenario also explains the second statement: If v_A sends an INV message that contains t_B and t_C, the adversary does not know whether v_B, v_C, or both are directly connected to v_A. The transactions initially sent to all peers serve as identifiable flags that the remote peers attach to the first group of transactions they forward after receiving their transaction. This allows the adversary to reconstruct the path of transactions and thereby infer connections between peers.

5.2   Discussion and Variants

While this topology inference approach is possible under perfect conditions, there are several issues that can arise when not all assumptions are met.

If there are peers on the network that the adversary is not connected to, false positives can occur. Consider again the scenario depicted in Fig. 1, but let us assume that v_M is not connected to v_B. Then, v_B would not have received a transaction t_B, and the INV message sent by v_A would only include t_C, which would lead to the wrong conclusion that v_A and v_C were directly connected.

False positives can also occur when the adversary cannot guarantee that all transactions arrive at all peers at the same time. While the latency measurement might be precise in general, temporal changes, e.g., due to bandwidth peaks, are possible and hard to foresee by the adversary. Furthermore, sending several thousand transactions within a few hundred milliseconds in a coordinated way can require much bandwidth and computational effort.

Even when all assumptions are met, the success of the approach depends on the order in which the remote peers forward transactions to their neighbors. This order is determined by the sending times of the respective queues and is unknown to the adversary. Therefore, repeating the approach many times is required in order to infer a large number of connections.

Another issue with the approach is that it is not possible to explicitly target a specific remote peer in order to infer the connections of that peer only. Instead, the inferred connections are a mostly random subset of all existing connections, which cannot be influenced by the adversary.

Variant *DS*: We will now present a variant of the discussed approach that reduces the cost by reducing the incurring transaction fees. Assuming 10,000 peers on the network and transaction fees of \$1 per transaction, the cost for one run of the approach is \$10,000.[6] A possibility to reduce this cost is to still create one transaction per peer, but to create these transactions so that they are all double spends of only a few different outputs. The number of different inputs among all transactions is a parameter freely chosen by the adversary (e.g., DS_3 denotes variant *DS* with three different inputs). Each transaction is still unique (e.g., by having different outputs), which enables the mapping of one transaction to one remote peer. That way, the adversary has to pay only for those transactions that get included in the blockchain. However, this approach

---

[6] Due to extreme fluctuations in transaction fees and exchange rates, this calculation is just an example.

can cause transactions to be dropped, which can cause false positives. We will evaluate the effect of double spendings on this approach in the next subsection.

5.3 Simulation Results

We will now briefly describe the used simulation setup before the results of the simulation are presented and discussed. Simulations were performed using a discrete event simulation. The network topology was generated by creating eight outbound connections to uniformly chosen peers for each simulated peer. This results on average in eight incoming and 16 total connections per peer. The adversary was modeled as a specific peer that establishes a large number of connections (depending on scenario) and sends and receives the transactions according to the presented inference strategy.

While the simulation matches the general behavior of the Bitcoin client, several simplifications were made. First, we model the three-step transaction propagation process (INV - GETDATA - TX) as one single event. Secondly, the latencies between peers are chosen according to a normal distribution ($\mu = 100\,\text{ms}$, $\sigma = 50\,\text{ms}$, truncated to $[1\,\text{ms}, 6000\,\text{ms}]$). Thirdly, when peers forward transactions and have more than 35 transactions in their queue, they choose the transactions to forward uniformly at random, but prefer transactions created by the adversary[7]. Therefore, our simulation is not a precise model of the Bitcoin network or testnet and the results should be seen as a proof of concept.

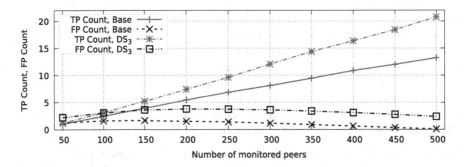

Fig. 2. Number of true positives and false positives per run for the base approach and the variant DS with three different inputs.

Figure 2 shows the true positive (TP) and false positive (FP) count depending on the number of connected peers for the base variant and variant DS with three different inputs for one run of the approach. The total number of peers on the network is 500. If the adversary is connected to all remote peers, one run of the approach results in about 21 correctly detected connections for variant DS, and

---

[7] This models the scenario that the adversary pays higher transaction fees than the fees for the other transactions.

in about 13 correctly detected connections for the base variant. Reduction of the share of connected peers leads to a decline in the true positive count. While we expected the false positive count of variant DS to be higher than that of the base variant, variant DS also results in a higher true positive count compared to the base variant. Double spends limit the propagation of individual transactions, because they are dropped at all peers that already received another transaction with the same input. This limitation of propagation is actually beneficial for the approach, because only single-hop propagation of each transaction (i.e., from one remote peer to another and back to v_M) is required and leads to the correct detection of a connection.

Simulations of larger network sizes showed a linear relationship between the number of peers and the TP and FP counts, i.e., a network with twice the number of peers results in about twice the number of true positives and false positives (cf. Appendix Fig. 7).

5.4   Experimental Results

In order to perform a ground truth validation of our simulation results, we set up several peers on the Bitcoin testnet: Two peers perform the role of the adversarial peers and connect to all reachable public peers (around 520 connections during the experiments in November 2017[8]). Another five peers running Bitcoin Core (0.15.0.1) serve as validation targets. These peers establish eight outgoing connections and are reachable to the adversarial peers via IPv4 and IPv6. In this setup the adversarial peers are connected to all neighbors of the validation targets, which is a best-case scenario for inference.

During the experiments one of the adversarial peers sends transactions to other peers so that they arrive at the same time. The latency to remote peers was measured using ICMP ping, TCP SYN packets, and Bitcoin ping messages.

We performed 50 runs of variant *DS* of the described inference approach using transactions with three different inputs. A total of 632 unique connections were detected, which roughly conforms to our simulation results. Out of these 632 connections, only 9 connections were connections from or to one of our validation peers. From these 9 detected connections, only 6 actually existed, which corresponds to an observed precision of 67%.[9] Roughly estimating the total number of connections on the testnet to be 4,160[10], and assuming a precision of 67% results in a recall (with respect to all connections of the network) of about 10% after 50 runs for a total cost of $50 * 3 = 150$ transaction fees.

Although the small sample size only allows very rough estimates of the real quality to be expected, and a more extensive ground truth validation could result in more precise estimations of the expected precision and recall, the results still help in assessing the topology inference approach. While the discussed approach

---

[8] Peers were found using https://github.com/ayeowch/bitnodes/.

[9] Because of the small sample size, the real precision can strongly deviate from the observed precision.

[10] 520 peers with 8 connections each.

is in fact possible to perform, we believe its execution to be hardly practical. For scientific purposes the approach is too invasive and lacks validation possibilities. For adversarial purposes the lack of influence on which connections are inferred prevents targeted attacks, especially taking into account that topology inference is only an intermediate goal for further attacks.

6   Exploiting Double Spends

One major drawback of the approach presented in Sect. 5 is that it is not possible to infer the connections of a specific peer only, rather than inferring random connections of the network. This is not only problematic for adversaries, but also makes validation a challenge. We will now describe and analyze an approach that allows inferring the connections of a specific peer v_T by exploiting the fact that clients drop transactions that double spend bitcoins.

6.1   Description

Again, assume for now that the adversarial monitor peer v_M is connected to all peers $v_I \in V$ of the network. One of the connected peers is the target peer v_T, the connections of which the adversary wants to infer. The adversary creates one transaction $t_I \in T$ for each connected peer v_I, except for the target peer v_T. All transactions have the same input, i.e., they are double spends, but all transactions are unique, e.g., by specifying different output addresses. Again, all transactions are sent to the peer they were created for (i.e., t_I to v_I) so that they arrive at all peers at the same time. Then the adversary monitors which transaction the target peer v_T forwards to the monitor peer v_M and can conclude that the peer associated with the forwarded transaction is directly connected to the target peer v_T.

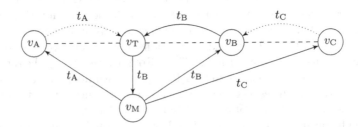

Fig. 3. Exploiting double spends for topology inference. Dashed lines indicate existing connections. Solid lines indicate the transmission of transactions. Dotted lines indicate dropping of transactions by the receiver because of an earlier reception of a conflicting transaction.

Let us consider the scenario depicted in Fig. 3 to demonstrate the correctness of the strategy. The monitor peer v_M is connected to v_A, v_T, v_B, and v_C.

The target peer v_T is connected to v_A and v_B, while v_B is also connected to v_C. After the transactions were sent by the adversary, every peer only has the transaction designated for itself, and v_T has no transaction received yet. Every peer will only accept and forward *exactly one* of the created transactions, because they are all double spends of the same output. Therefore, if v_C forwards t_C to v_B (dotted line), v_B will drop t_C because of the earlier reception of the conflicting transaction t_B. Because the target peer v_T has not yet received any of the conflicting transactions, it will accept exactly one transaction forwarded by one of its neighbors (transaction t_B in Fig. 3). This transaction gets forwarded to the monitor peer v_M and indicates a neighbor of the target peer v_T.

6.2 Discussion and Variants

If the adversary is not connected to all peers of the network, or if the transactions are not received by all peers at the same time, false positives can occur. The reason is basically the same as for the approach exploiting transaction accumulation discussed in Sect. 5.2: A neighbor of v_T that did not receive its double spending transaction from v_M will accept another double spending transaction t_I from its neighbor v_I and forward that transaction to v_T, which may forward t_I to the adversary causing the false inference of a connection between v_T and v_I. Obviously, if the adversary cannot establish a connection to v_T, the connections of v_T cannot be inferred using the discussed approach. We will now discuss three variants of the presented approach that aim at optimizing the inference even when not all assumptions are met.

Variant *Count*: When repeating the approach several times, one would expect the transactions associated with real neighbors (true positives) to be sent to the adversary by v_T more often than those of peers that are not connected to v_T (false positives), because those transactions have to be relayed by another peer and should be slower. In order to reduce false positives, the approach can be repeated and connections are only identified, if the number of transactions indicating a specific peer as a neighbor of v_T is larger than a certain threshold.

Variant *Ignore*: Assume that t_A is forwarded by v_T to v_M. If the adversary was unable to synchronize the reception of all transactions at all remote peers (e.g., due to bad latency estimation or bandwidth limitation), it is possible that t_A is *also* forwarded to v_M by another peer, say, v_B. As such a reception indicates the violation of a key assumption and v_T might have received t_A from v_B rather than directly from v_A, the adversary can opt to ignore the result without concluding a connection between v_T and v_A.

Variant *Suppress*: The cost for a single run of the approach is one transaction fee. However, one single run reveals at most one connection of the target peer. In order to infer more connections, additional runs are necessary, which each come at the cost of one transaction fee. Which connection can be inferred depends on which transaction arrives first at v_T, which is determined by the sending times of the remote peers and the latencies between peers. With bad luck (or single clients being very fast), multiple runs of the approach can all result in inference of the same, already known, connection. Variant *Suppress* slightly modifies the approach to eliminate the repeated inference of the same connection. Consider again the example depicted in Fig. 3 and assume that the adversary inferred the connection between v_T and v_B in the first run of the approach. For the next run, we (1) want the transaction t_B to be dropped at v_T and (2) we do not want v_B to forward any other transaction t_I. While simply not sending any transaction to v_B would satisfy the first requirement, it would make v_B a hidden node and violate the second requirement. Therefore, we modify the way the double spending transactions are created. Assume there are two unspent outputs o_1 and o_2 that will be used as inputs to the transactions in the following way:

- All peers v_I, except for v_T and v_B, receive transactions t_I spending o_1 only.
- v_T receives a transaction t_T spending o_2 only.
- v_B receives a transaction t_B spending o_1 and o_2.

This approach satisfies both requirements: v_T will drop t_B because it is a double spend of o_2. Any transaction t_I will be dropped by v_B because they are double spending o_1. Yet, any transaction t_I will be accepted by v_T because they are spending a different output than t_T (o_1 and o_2).

6.3   Simulation Results

We simulated the approach exploiting double spends with the same simulation setup as described in Sect. 5.3. Figure 4 shows how recall and precision develop depending on the number of runs for the base version of the approach. If the monitor peer v_M is connected to all peers of the network, the recall reaches 95% after 100 runs while the precision decreases slowly. The precision decreases because once all neighbors of the target are detected, the precision can only fall by detecting more false positives. Detecting the same neighbor multiple times is used in the variant *Count*. While variant *Count* can maintain a high precision, the recall is worse than for other variants (cf. Appendix Fig. 8).

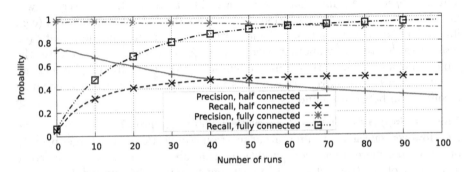

Fig. 4. Precision and recall depending on the number of runs with v_M being connected to 250 (half connected) and 500 (fully connected) of 500 peers.

If the adversary is connected to only half of the peers of the network, the maximum possible recall is 50%, because the adversary is on average only connected to half of the neighbors of v_T. As described above, the target's neighbors being not connected to the adversary cause false positives and thus the precision is lower than for the fully connected scenario.

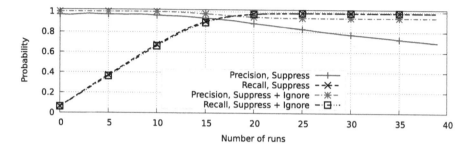

Fig. 5. Precision and recall depending on the number of runs for variants *Suppress* and *Suppress + Ignore* with v_M being connected to 500 of 500 peers (fully connected).

Figure 5 shows precision and recall of the approach when using the variant *Suppress* with v_M being connected to all peers. Using only this variant results in the recall growing faster, because this variant prevents neighbors from being detected multiple times. However, not only true neighbors are detected faster, but also false positives, which results in a faster declining precision. If v_M is not connected to all peers, the precision falls even faster, because the likelihood that a detection is a false positive is higher.

The precision can be improved by combining the variants *Suppress* and *Ignore*, for which precision and recall are also shown in Fig. 5. Combining both variants results in a recall of 96% after 25 runs with a precision of about 94% if the monitor is connected to all peers.

6.4   Experimental Results

We validated the approach in the testnet with the setup described in Sect. 5.4 with the exception that the adversarial peers did not send any transactions to the IPv6 addresses of the validation targets. The reason for this exception is that otherwise the presented approach infers connections between the IPv4 and IPv6 addresses of the validation target. While this might also be an interesting application for the approach, it would impair our validation.

We ran the approach six times against each of the five validation targets with 50 runs each using the combination of the variants *Suppress* and *Ignore*. Analyzing the data generated during the experiments in different ways results in various combinations of precision and recall. Two of them using *Suppress* and *Ignore* are shown in Fig. 6. The combination of the variants *Suppress* and *Ignore* results in a recall of 60% and a precision of 97%. The recall can be improved though by relaxing the restrictions imposed by *Ignore* by using only the variant *Suppress*. This combination results in a recall of 87% and a precision of 71% (also shown in Fig. 6) for a total cost of 99 transaction fees.

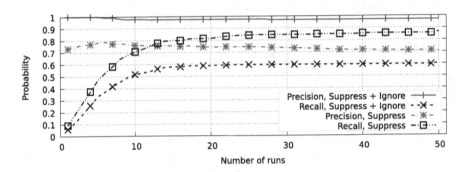

Fig. 6. Experimental Result: Precision and recall depending on the number of runs using variant *Suppress* and *Suppress+Ignore*.

While these results indicate a high inference quality, we emphasize again that the adversarial peer was connected to all neighbors of the validation peers in our experiments and hidden neighbors could impair the inference quality.

Because not only our validation peers were dual-stacked (i.e., connected via IPv4 and IPv6 to the network) but also other peers on the network are, it is possible that a peer v_N is connected via IPv4 to one of our validation targets and via IPv6 to the adversary peer. In this situation the approach might infer a connection between v_N's IPv6 address and the validation target's IPv4 address. While this is technically a false positive, it is still correct that both peers are connected. As this situation might have occurred several times, some connections that were categorized as false positives might actually be correctly inferred.

7   Conclusion

While the presented approach exploiting transaction accumulation is likely not suitable for topology inference, the approach exploiting double spends showed sufficient detection quality at reasonable cost. We emphasize that transaction accumulation still leaks information that might be exploited in more advanced approaches. A simple countermeasure that prevents these kinds of attacks would be to mix the order of transactions, e.g., by regularly sending only a subset of the transactions in the outgoing queues.

An obvious countermeasure against the approach exploiting double spends would be to forward double spends, which, however, would create the potential for DoS attacks. Another countermeasure could be to not always forward the transaction that was received first, but to decide randomly which double spending transaction will be forwarded, which could affect security against double spending attacks in fast payments [2,6]. Furthermore, individual peer operators may choose to deny incoming connections, which prevents the discussed approaches from working, but is not desirable from an overall network's perspective. On the other hand, operating a reachable peer with a large number of incoming connections from unreachable peers also impedes the presented inference approaches. Finally, because of the large number of transactions created, such attacks can be observed by monitoring large parts of the network.

While we presented some optimizations and variants of the approaches, many more variants and combinations (e.g., including timing information, making use of more than one adversarial peer, continuous sending of transactions, further combination of double spending inputs) are possible and might result in better inference quality. Although the validation in the Bitcoin testnet gives an idea of the general feasibility, a validation in the real Bitcoin network promises more insights, but is currently not feasible for the presented approaches due to high transaction fees. Finally, while our approaches aimed at topology inference, similar approaches exploiting the same mechanisms might be used against the anonymity of users.

Acknowledgements. This work was supported by the German Federal Ministry of Education and Research (BMBF) within the project *KASTEL_IoE* in the Competence Center for Applied Security Technology (*KASTEL*). The authors would like to thank the anonymous reviewers for their valuable comments and suggestions.

Appendix

Figure 7 shows that the approach exploiting the accumulation of transactions scales linearly with the network size.

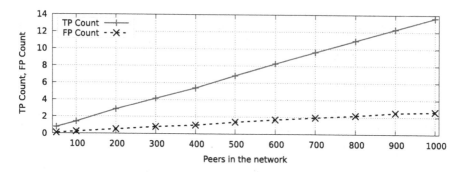

Fig. 7. Exploiting transaction accumulation: Number of true positives and false positives depending on the network size for v_M being connected to half of the peers.

Figure 8 shows precision and recall for the variant *Count* of the approach exploiting double spends. As can be seen, the recall increases in steps. These steps are caused by adjusting the threshold for the required number of receptions.

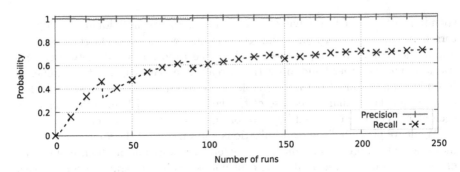

Fig. 8. Precision and recall depending on the number of runs for variant *Count* and v_M being connected to 375 of 500 peers.

While this variant can be used to reach high precision, the recall is limited even after more than 200 runs.

References

1. Biryukov, A., Khovratovich, D., Pustogarov, I.: Deanonymisation of clients in Bitcoin P2P network. In: Proceedings of the 2014 ACM SIGSAC Conference on Computer and Communications Security. ACM (2014)
2. Decker, C., Wattenhofer, R.: Information propagation in the Bitcoin network. In: 2013 IEEE Thirteenth International Conference on Peer-to-Peer Computing (P2P), pp. 1–10. IEEE (2013)
3. Eyal, I., Sirer, E.G.: Majority is not enough: Bitcoin mining is vulnerable. In: Christin, N., Safavi-Naini, R. (eds.) FC 2014. LNCS, vol. 8437, pp. 436–454. Springer, Heidelberg (2014). https://doi.org/10.1007/978-3-662-45472-5_28
4. Fanti, G., Viswanath, P.: Anonymity properties of the Bitcoin P2P network. arXiv preprint arXiv:1703.08761 (2017)
5. Heilman, E., Kendler, A., Zohar, A., Goldberg, S.: Eclipse attacks on Bitcoin's peer-to-peer network. In: 24th USENIX Security Symposium (USENIX Security 15), pp. 129–144 (2015)
6. Karame, G.O., Androulaki, E., Capkun, S.: Double-spending fast payments in Bitcoin. In: Proceedings of the 2012 ACM conference on Computer and communications security, pp. 906–917. ACM (2012)
7. Koshy, P., Koshy, D., McDaniel, P.: An analysis of anonymity in bitcoin using P2P network traffic. In: Christin, N., Safavi-Naini, R. (eds.) FC 2014. LNCS, vol. 8437, pp. 469–485. Springer, Heidelberg (2014). https://doi.org/10.1007/978-3-662-45472-5_30
8. Miller, A., et al.: Discovering Bitcoin's public topology and influential nodes (2015)
9. Nakamoto, S.: Bitcoin: A Peer-to-Peer Electronic Cash System (2008)
10. Nayak, K., Kumar, S., Miller, A., Shi, E.: Stubborn mining: generalizing selfish mining and combining with an eclipse attack. In: 2016 IEEE European Symposium on Security and Privacy (EuroS&P), pp. 305–320. IEEE (2016)
11. Neudecker, T., Andelfinger, P., Hartenstein, H.: Timing analysis for inferring the topology of the Bitcoin peer-to-peer network. In: 2016 International IEEE Conference on Advanced and Trusted Computing (ATC), pp. 358–367, July 2016

Egalitarian Society or Benevolent Dictatorship: The State of Cryptocurrency Governance

Sarah Azouvi[✉], Mary Maller, and Sarah Meiklejohn

University College London, London, UK
{sarah.azouvi.13,mary.maller.15,s.meiklejohn}@ucl.ac.uk

Abstract. In this paper we initiate a quantitative study of the decentralization of the governance structures of Bitcoin and Ethereum. In particular, we scraped the open-source repositories associated with their respective codebases and improvement proposals to find the number of people contributing to the code itself and to the overall discussion. We then present different metrics to quantify decentralization, both in each of the cryptocurrencies and, for comparison, in two popular open-source programming languages: Clojure and Rust. We find that for both cryptocurrencies and programming languages, there is usually a handful of people that accounts for most of the discussion. We also look into the effect of forks in Bitcoin and Ethereum, and find that there is little intersection between the communities of the original currencies and those of the forks.

1 Introduction

Cryptocurrencies are an alternative to fiat currencies that aim to replace traditional institutions with a digital platform (or *blockchain*) whose rules are enforced largely by consensus, with anyone able to participate (a property typically called *decentralization*) and check that they are being followed (*transparency*). Whereas fiat currencies inherently rely on some degree of trust in central entities such as banks, blockchains thus promise a radical shift away from trusted parties.

In a decentralized system, no one entity can act to censor transactions or prevent individuals from joining the network (as is possible with traditional institutions [17]). Instead, there is a network of peers that is collectively responsible for entering information into the ledger. In theory, each peer in the network has a "vote" proportional to their computational power, which is used to seal transactions into the ledger. Provided the peers controlling the majority of the network's computational power are honest, only valid information enters the ledger, which — if the ledger is made globally visible — can be checked by anyone. It is unclear, however, to what extent this theoretical promise of decentralization and transparency has been achieved in practice. Indeed, previous research has

© International Financial Cryptography Association 2019
A. Zohar et al. (Eds.): FC 2018 Workshops, LNCS 10958, pp. 127–143, 2019.
https://doi.org/10.1007/978-3-662-58820-8_10

demonstrated that even the enforcement of the rules is not as decentralized and transparent as originally intended [12,16].

Beyond enforcement, we must also consider how the rules governing a cryptocurrency are set in the first place, and who gets to set them. The founders of a cryptocurrency necessarily make numerous decisions regarding both its design and its implementation. For example, they decide on the interval between the generation of blocks, the reward for generating a block, and the size of the blocks. Thus there is a governance structure underlying all blockchains, and these governance structures have a seemingly inherent degree of centralization. Many cryptocurrencies address this by open-sourcing their code and opening their protocols to so-called "improvement proposals," in which anyone can propose changes to the high-level protocol. These improvement proposals serve not only to reduce the degree of centralization in the maintenance of the platform, but also can provide a significant degree of transparency into the decision-making process. As these rules impact the functioning of a cryptocurrency just as much as the actual enforcement of the consensus protocol, it is important to consider not only the decentralization and transparency of the blockchain itself, but also of its underlying governance structure.

Our Contributions. In this paper, we study the centralization in the existing governance structures of Bitcoin and Ethereum, which as of this writing are the top two cryptocurrencies by market capitalization [4]. In order to determine whether or not our results should be expected for any open-source software, we also conduct our study on two popular open-source programming languages: Clojure and Rust.

For each platform, we measured two different properties: the number of developers contributing to each file in the codebase, and the number of people contributing to the discussion around the platform by making comments in the relevant part of its GitHub repository. In terms of contributions to the codebase, we found that the distributions amongst the contributors were all different. In terms of the discussion, we found that for all the systems we studied, at any given time at most eighteen contributors accounted for a majority of all comments.

To evaluate the decision-making infrastructure in Bitcoin and Ethereum, we looked into who creates and comments on improvement proposals. Ethereum appears more centralized than Bitcoin in terms of improvement proposals, but is more decentralized in terms of the discussion around its codebase, according to our metrics. Finally, we compared the communities behind Bitcoin and its fork Bitcoin Cash, and Ethereum and its fork Ethereum Classic, to see whether these forks bring in new people or split the initial community. In both cases, the fork seems to bring in a new community.

2   Related Work

Much of the previous research examining decentralization on blockchains focuses specifically on Bitcoin, or on the general governance issues associated with blockchains. In terms of centralization within Bitcoin, Gervais et al. observe that some of the key operations in Bitcoin, in particular the mining process and the maintenance of the protocol, are not decentralized [16]. Moore and Christin find a high degree of centralization in popular Bitcoin exchanges [22], and observe that popular exchanges are more likely to suffer security breaches. Böhme et al. look at the various centralized intermediaries within the broader Bitcoin ecosystem, such as currency exchanges, wallet providers, mixers, and mining pools [12]. They also evaluate the decisions that the designers make regarding how much money there should be in the system, and de Filippi and Loveluck examine the overall decision-making process of the Bitcoin developers [13]. In particular, they discuss the "block size" debate and the difficulty in deciding whether or not to fork Bitcoin in order to increase the block size.

In terms of other cryptocurrencies, Reyes et al. examine the theft of 3.6 million ether from The DAO in June 2016, and discuss the lessons learned and the potential strengths and weaknesses of decentralized organizations [26]. Gandal and Halaburda analyze how network effects affect competition in the cryptocurrency market [15]. In particular they look at competition between different currencies and competition between cryptocurrency exchanges and observe that there was a "winner takes all" effect in early markets, but not today.

More generally, Atzori gives a critical evaluation of whether blockchains are suitable as political tools [11], and examines to which extent they can mitigate coercion, centralization, and hierarchical structures. Reijers et al. study the question of governance from the perspective of social contract theory and finds that it fails to incorporate aspects of distributive justice [25]. Similarly, Lehdonvirta poses the "blockchain paradox," in which he argues that once you solve the problem of decentralized governance, you no longer need blockchains [20].

Finally, Srinivasan and Lee [30] introduce a metric for measuring the decentralization in cryptocurrencies that they call the Nakamoto coefficient. We use this metric, in addition to several others, in order to compare and contrast the level of decentralization in Bitcoin and Ethereum.

3   Background

3.1   Bitcoin

Bitcoin [23] was created by the pseudonymous Satoshi Nakamoto, who deployed the currency on January 3 2009. In September 2012, some prominent members of the community created the Bitcoin Foundation, a non-profit organization based on the model of the Linux Foundation, but today there is also a significant development effort by Blockstream [3], which is a for-profit company run by the core developers. We refer the reader to the Bitcoin textbook [24] for a more technical presentation of the Bitcoin protocol.

3.2   Ethereum

Ethereum [6] was created by Vitalik Buterin, and launched on July 30 2015. Its initial development was done by the Ethereum Foundation, a Swiss non-profit, but today there is also a significant development effort by Parity [8], which is a for-profit company developing one of the main Ethereum clients. Ethereum is designed to support a broader functionality beyond atomic transfers of money from one set of parties to another.

3.3 Improvement Proposals

No system is perfect, and cryptocurrency protocols sometimes need updating due to flaws or vulnerabilities. These changes can be fundamental and affect all users. To keep the improvement decision process open and fair, most cryptocurrencies have an *Improvement Proposal* system, where anyone can propose changes to the protocol and discuss existing proposals. If support exists for a proposal, it may be incorporated into the codebase. There is no formal definition of how to agree upon an improvement proposal [1]. The Improvement Proposals process happens mainly on GitHub, but there are many other places for discussion, such as mailing lists, forums and IRC channels.

3.4 Forks

When disagreements occur in cryptocurrency communities, the only way to resolve them might be for the communities to split. Anyone disagreeing with the current core developers can fork the code and create their own currency. This has happened in both Ethereum and Bitcoin. For example, in June 2016 more than 50M USD of ether was stolen due to a code vulnerability in a smart contract [19]. The Ethereum Foundation decided to "roll back time" in order to take the stolen ether back from the hacker. Arguing that this contradicts the fundamental immutability property of blockchains, some members of the community forked Ethereum and Ethereum Classic was born [7]. In Bitcoin, the "block size" debate has been ongoing for years. Arguing that one of the main limitations of the Bitcoin protocol is scalability and that this problem could be solved with larger block sizes, some members of the community forked Bitcoin, resulting in Bitcoin Cash in August 2017 [2].

4   Methodology

4.1   Comparison with Programming Languages

To determine whether the governance structures of Bitcoin and Ethereum are as decentralized as should be expected, we compare them against those of open-source, general-purpose programming languages. We chose programming languages as, similarly to cryptocurrencies, they tend to have a large amount of participation from their user communities. For an even closer comparison, we sought out programming languages that: (1) have existed for a similar length of time to the cryptocurrency; (2) have a similar number of users (which we measured according to the number of watchers and stars on the GitHub codebase [18]); and (3) are decentralized in the sense that they are maintained by an online community rather than a private company or government. We could not find programming languages that fully satisfied each of these properties, but we decided that a relatively fair comparison was between Bitcoin and Clojure, and Ethereum and Rust.

Bitcoin and Clojure were both proposed by individuals (or a set of individuals) and were both released in 2009 (Bitcoin in January, and Clojure in May). While Bitcoin has a much larger userbase than Clojure (close to 2000 watchers and 18k stars, as opposed to roughly 700 watchers and 7k stars), we ultimately decided to stick with this comparison rather than use a programming language like Go, which does have a larger userbase, as Go is closely tied to Google.

Ethereum and Rust were both released in 2015 (Ethereum in July, and Rust in May), and are both tied to not-for-profit foundations (Ethereum with the Ethereum Foundation, and Rust with Mozilla). Rust has a larger, but not incomparable, userbase than Ethereum: roughly 1500 vs. 900 watchers, and 24k vs. 8k stars.

4.2   Data Collection

To quantitatively measure the level of centralization in the maintenance of Bitcoin and Ethereum, we analyzed their codebases, and the extent to which these codebases are produced and maintained in a decentralized fashion. We obtained copies of the open-source repositories for Bitcoin, Bitcoin Cash, Ethereum, Ethereum Classic, Rust and Clojure. A summary of the locations of these repositories is in Table 1.

Table 1. The open-source repositories for the various cryptocurrencies we consider. For Ethereum and Ethereum Classic, the listed repositories contain the code for the Go, C++, and Python versions of the client. Parity is compatible with both Ethereum and Ethereum Classic.

Name	Repository URL
Bitcoin	https://github.com/bitcoin/bitcoin
Bitcoin Cash (ABC)	https://github.com/Bitcoin-ABC/bitcoin-abc
Clojure	https://github.com/clojure/clojure
Ethereum	https://github.com/ethereum/
Parity	https://github.com/paritytech/parity
Ethereum JS	https://github.com/ethereumjs/ethereumjs-lib
Ethereum Ruby	https://github.com/cryptape/ruby-ethereum
Ethereum Classic	https://github.com/ethereumproject
Rust	https://github.com/rust-lang/rust

One notable property of these platforms is that Bitcoin has only one reference client, whereas the others tend to have many. For Ethereum, we collected the repositories for all the clients as listed in the Ethereum documentation.[1] For Ethereum Classic, we considered the Go, C++ and Python clients, as the ones for JavaScript, Java, and Ruby were not listed. The Parity client supports both Ethereum and Ethereum Classic. For Bitcoin Cash, we picked the most popular one in terms of watchers and stars, which was Bitcoin ABC.

Since contribution to the protocol is also captured through discussions in addition to lines of codes written, we also scraped all the discussion threads for pull requests and issues (both open and closed). The discussions of Improvement Proposals were not included in the Bitcoin and Ethereum repositories themselves, so we also scraped the main pages, pull requests, and issues on the respective GitHub repositories for Bitcoin (BIPS) [1] and Ethereum (EIPS) [5].

4.3 Centrality Metrics

Table 2 lists some of the centrality metrics used in this paper. In addition to these, we also use the mean and the median. The interquartile range (IQR) represents where the bulk of values lie and is computed as the difference between the 75% and the 25%, and the interquartile mean (IQMean) is the mean of the data in the IQR. The benefit of using the IQMean (as compared to the regular mean) is that, as with the median, it is not affected by outliers.

To confirm the statistical significance of our findings, we use a two-sample Kolmogorov-Smirnov test [21, 28], which determines whether or not two vectors of values have the same probability distribution. More specifically, it quantifies the distance between the empirical distribution functions of the two samples. The p-value, used to determine the statistical significance of the test, must be under 0.05 in order to reject the null hypothesis (i.e., in order to show that the two vectors have a different distribution). We used the Bootstrap version of the Kolmogorov-Smirnov test [27], which is designed to work on discrete distributions.

The Nakamoto index, introduced by Srinivasan and Lee [30], represents the minimum number of contributors to a dataset needed to get 51% of the data. We refer to the normalized version of this index as the Satoshi index, which

Table 2. Centrality metrics used in this paper.

Centrality metric	Usage
Interquartile range (IQR)	Measure of spread
Interquartile mean (IQMean)	Mean of the data in the IQR
Kolmogorov-Smirnov test	See if two vectors have same probability distribution
Nakamoto index	Minimum # of contributors making 51% of the data
Satoshi index	Minimum % of contributors making 51% of the data
Sørensen-Dice index	Measure of similarity of two sets

---

[1] http://ethdocs.org/en/latest/ethereum-clients/choosing-a-client.html#why-are-there-multiple-ethereum-clients.

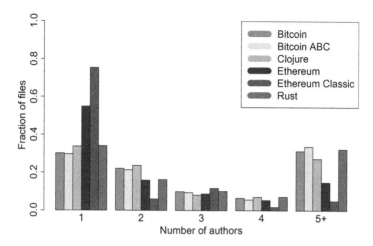

Fig. 1. The coverage of each file in a given repository, as determined by the number of authors that have contributed to that file. Different clients are grouped according to the cryptocurrency they support.

represents the minimum percentage of all contributors needed to get 51% of the data. Finally, the Sørensen-Dice index [14, 29] captures the similarity of two sets. It is defined as $SD(X, Y) = \frac{2|X \cap Y|}{|X|+|Y|}$, so in particular has a value of 1 for sets that are equal and 0 for sets that are disjoint.

5   Data Analysis

5.1   Contributors to the Main Codebase

For each repository, we collected all non-hidden files and measured how many distinct authors had contributed to that file throughout its lifetime (in terms of Git commits). The results of this measurement can be seen in Fig. 1. While the number of contributors to the Bitcoin and Bitcoin Cash codebases follow a fairly similar pattern, the number of contributors to the Ethereum Classic codebase follows a different distribution to that of the Ethereum codebase, even though Ethereum Classic is a fork of Ethereum. Both Clojure and Rust seem to follow a fairly similar pattern to that of Bitcoin.

For Bitcoin, 30% of all files were written by a single author, and 24% of these files were written by the same author, Wladimir van der Laan. This means that one author wrote 7% of the files. In Ethereum, 55% of all files were written by a single author, and 36% of these files were written by the same author, Tomasz Drwiega. This means that one author wrote 20% of the files.

Table 3 contains the mean, median, IQR, and IQMean for each of the repositories. We see relatively similar metrics for Bitcoin (and Bitcoin Cash) and both of the programming languages, and see that Ethereum and Ethereum Classic are both lower for all metrics.

Table 3. Centrality metrics for the number of contributors per file and the number of comments per author in the pull requests and issues.

Repository	# Authors per file				# Comments per author			
	Mean	Median	IQR	IQMean	Mean	Median	IQR	IQMean
Bitcoin	5.56	2	5	2.78	27.2	2	4	2.4
Bitcoin Cash	5.48	2	6	2.94	3.8	2	2	1.8
Ethereum	2.58	1	2	1.49	17.0	2	3	1.9
Ethereum Classic	1.69	1	0	1.00	11.1	2	3	1.8
Clojure	4.03	2	4	2.41	1.9	1	1	1.3
Rust	5.17	2	5	2.79	69.8	3	8	3.5

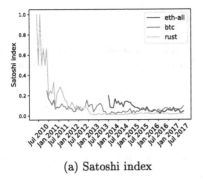

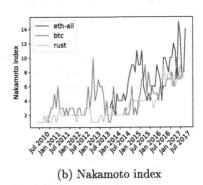

(a) Satoshi index   (b) Nakamoto index

Fig. 2. The evolution of the Satoshi and Nakamoto indexes over time. The values for Ethereum are in blue, for Bitcoin in red, and for Rust in green. (Color figure online)

We performed a Kolmogorov-Smirnov test to confirm the statistical significance of our findings; the resulting p-values are in Table 7. We see that the results are statistically significant for all the comparisons except for Bitcoin and Bitcoin Cash, indicating that the respective numbers of codebase authors are drawn from different distributions, except for Bitcoin and Bitcoin Cash. This is expected as Bitcoin Cash is a very recent fork of Bitcoin.

We acknowledge, however, that measuring levels of centralization by looking at the codebase is limited in some respects, as it is not practical — or even necessarily important for accountability — to have many people contributing to the same files, and there are likely people looking over and discussing files in ways that are not reflected in Git commits. This is why we look next at the discussion around the code.

5.2 Commenters on the Main Code Base

To get a feeling for the evolution of the distribution of comments over the life of a cryptocurrency, we compute the Nakamoto and Satoshi indexes over time in Fig. 2, using the discussion threads in the pull requests and issues of the GitHub

Table 4. Minimal number of commenters that contribute to $x\%$ of all the comments.

	10	20	30	40	50	60	70	80	90	100
Bitcoin	1	1	3	5	8	13	21	41	239	2443
Clojure	2	5	9	15	23	33	45	65	85	104
Ethereum	2	5	8	12	18	29	49	127	467	3139
Rust	1	1	1	2	4	10	21	43	181	3882

repository. These graphs exclude Clojure, as ultimately we believed the dataset was too small to get any real insights. For example, there were only 72 pull requests, as compared to 11,604 for Bitcoin. Similarly, since Bitcoin Cash and Ethereum Classic are relatively recent forks, and thus have a far smaller level of discussion so far, we also exclude them from this analysis.

In Fig. 2, we see that in all the repositories there is a strong tendency towards centralization in the number of commenters, with a handful of people contributing to most of the comments. The Nakamoto indexes for the codebases of Bitcoin, Rust, and Ethereum are consistently relatively low, as every month there are no more than 10 authors contributing to half of the comments for Bitcoin and Rust and 15 for Ethereum. When normalized by the total number of commenters per month, for Bitcoin and Ethereum this is less than a quarter of the commenters each month (as seen in Fig. 2a).

To see whether it was the same people making most of the comments each month or different people every time, we plotted in Fig. 3 the number of comments per author every month. For Bitcoin and Rust, we see that there is one commenter that accounts for most of the comments each month (for Bitcoin, Wladimir van der Laan is the top commenter with 13,923 comments in total, followed by Jonas Schnelli with 4,409 comments), and for Ethereum there is a small handful of commenters who stand out from the rest (the top three are Gavin Wood with 3,352 total, Péter Szilágyi with 2,242, and Jeffrey Wilcke with 2,230). Overall for Bitcoin there are only eight people contributing to half of all the comments, which represents 0.3% of all commenters. For Ethereum there are 18 people (or 0.6% of all commenters), and for Rust there are four (or 0.1%). These results are summarized in Table 4.

This centralized trend is confirmed by the values in Table 3, as we see that the mean is much greater than the IQMean or median, which are values that typically ignore outliers. The mean is one order of magnitude higher than the IQMean for Bitcoin, Ethereum, and Rust. This means that the tails of the distribution (i.e., the top 25% of the distribution) differ a lot from the value in the main range. This can also be confirmed by looking at the number of comments for the top commenters, compared to the average number of comments per author. Generally this confirms that a handful of people (less than 10) contribute to most of the comments. As this is true for all the repositories, we conclude that this is potentially a common (and somewhat natural) feature in open-source systems.

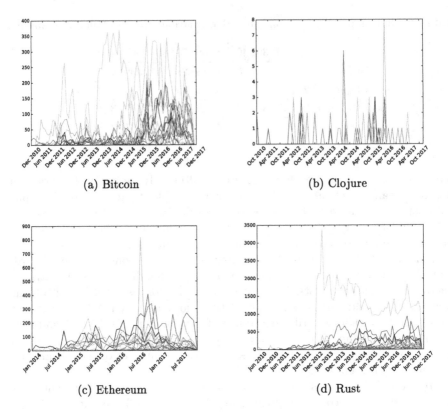

(a) Bitcoin   (b) Clojure

(c) Ethereum   (d) Rust

Fig. 3. Number of comments per commenters per month.

We also computed, in Table 8, a Kolmogorov-Smirnov test on the total number of comments per author. We see that the number of comments per author from Bitcoin, Ethereum, and Rust are drawn from different distributions. In the next two sections, we will focus on Bitcoin and Ethereum, looking more closely at the improvement proposals process in Sect. 5.3 and comparing the communities behind the main codebases, the improvement proposals, and forks in Sect. 5.4.

5.3 Improvement Proposals for Bitcoin and Ethereum

In this section, we looked at the improvement proposal (IP) process. Together with pull requests, this is the main road to contributing to the design and development of the currency. For each author we counted how many improvement proposals they made to Ethereum and Bitcoin, and what states these proposals were in (i.e., if they were accepted, rejected, or under review). In Fig. 4, we notice that only a handful of people are contributing to Bitcoin improvement proposals (BIPS). In Fig. 5, there is mostly just one person, Vitalik Buterin, that is contributing to Ethereum improvement proposals (EIPS).

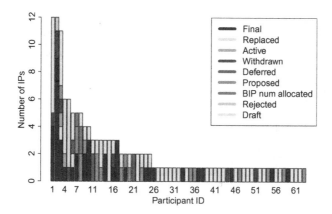

Fig. 4. The authors of BIPs, identified by a unique numeric value, along with the number of proposals they have created and the respective status of those proposals. The top five contributors are Gavin Andresen (with 12 proposals and 9 accepted) and Pieter Wuille (12 proposals, 4 accepted), Luke Dashjr (11 proposals), Eric Lombrozo (6 proposals), and Johnson Lau (6 proposals).

Table 5. Centrality metrics for the number of comments per author.

	Mean	Median	IQR	IQMean
BIPS	11.41	2.0	6.5	2.95
EIPS	9.16	2.0	5.0	2.56

There are usually many people contributing to the discussion for every proposal, so we measured the level of centrality in terms of the number of comments in pull requests for each user in the BIPS and EIPS repositories. The results are in Table 5. The trend here is similar to the one observed in the previous section: the datasets contain many outliers, corresponding to the top 25% of commenters who comment significantly more than the rest.

5.4   Diversity of Communities

In this section, we look at whether or not the same people contribute to the discussion in the main codebase and in the improvement proposals, and whether or not there is any similarity between the community behind a cryptocurrency and its fork; i.e., any resemblance between Bitcoin and Bitcoin Cash and between Ethereum and Ethereum Classic. Because Ethereum Classic does not have a separate implementation for every client, we focus in this section only on the Go client for each platform, as it is the most popular.

To do this, we first computed the Sørensen-Dice index on the set of the 30 top commenters, which account for roughly 75% of all the comments in the relevant repositories (see Table 4 in the Appendix). As we see in Table 6, the set of main commenters in the main Bitcoin repository and in the BIPS repository

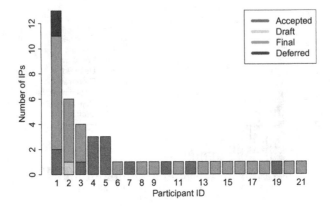

Fig. 5. The authors of EIPs, identified by a unique numeric value, along with the number of proposals they have created and, if in the main set of EIPs, the status of those proposals. The top three contributors are (1) Vitalik Buterin, with 13 proposals, 11 of which were accepted or finalized; (2) Alex Beregszaszi, with 6 proposals; and (3) Nick Johnson, with 4 proposals.

overlap, with a Sørensen-Dice index of 0.5. This means that out of the 30 main commenters of Bitcoin and BIPS, 15 are in both communities. This is much more than for Ethereum compared to EIPs, with 7 commenters in both sets.

To include all commenters, we use a weighted version of the whole set of commenters. To do so, we weighted commenters by their number of comments and then computed the Sørensen-Dice index on these augmented sets. The results are in Table 6. Taking the weight (and all the commenters) into account, the similarity between Ethereum and EIPS is still meaningful, with an index of 0.108. The value for Bitcoin vs BIPS, however, drops to 0.069. Therefore, although half of the main commenters for Bitcoin also comment on BIPS, they do not write as many comments in the BIPS repository.

Table 6. Sørensen-Dice index for the top 30 commenters, and weighted Sørensen-Dice index for all the commenters.

Repositories	Sørensen-Dice index	
	Top 30	All (weighted)
Bitcoin/BIPS	0.50	0.0686
Ethereum/EIPS	0.23	0.1077
Bitcoin/Bitcoin Cash	0.03	0.0050
Ethereum/Ethereum Classic	0.03	0.0030

The overlap in the communities of Bitcoin and Bitcoin Cash, and Ethereum and Ethereum Classic, is small. The Sørensen-Dice index was 0.033 for both. Hence only one of the top commenters of the main repository is also a commenter in the forked one. This low value shows that the forked currency is really the formation of a new community rather than a separation of the initial one.

6   Discussion

According to our metrics on the number of contributors per file in the codebases, we found that Bitcoin, Rust, and Clojure were all more decentralized than Ethereum, even given the fact that Ethereum has many more reference clients. The distributions of the number of authors for all the codebases was different except for Bitcoin and Bitcoin Cash, which is not surprising given that Bitcoin Cash is a recent fork of Bitcoin and thus their codebases are very similar. Interestingly, while Ethereum Classic is a fork of Ethereum, the number of authors on these two codebases is still quite different. However, this fork happened a longer ago and there have been numerous changes to the Ethereum Classic codebase since the fork occurred. Our data implies that one cannot necessarily assume a natural pattern for the number of authors on an open source code base.

There was a greater number of participants in the Bitcoin improvement proposals than in those of Ethereum. Although the distribution of the number of comments on the Bitcoin codebase was different from the one on the BIPS, the distribution from Ethereum was similar to EIPS (Table 8). The intersection between the main commenters on Bitcoin's main codebase and the commenters on the BIPS was greater than the intersection between the commenters on Ethereum's main code base and the commenters on the EIPS. However, when considering the weighted intersection, we found the opposite applied. Generally there are very few people that account for most of the comments for Bitcoin, where for Ethereum this number is higher.

Finally, both the Bitcoin and Ethereum communities seem relatively unaffected by the hard forks. The number of people commenting was not significantly different before and after the forks, and there was little intersection between the people participating in the original codebases and the forked codebases. This implies that the forks did not split the communities, and that a large proportion of the community decided to stay with the original codebases. However in our discussion we only considered Bitcoin ABC, the most popular client for Bitcoin Cash, which could limit our results. We leave for future work the study of all the Bitcoin Cash clients. Our data implies that there could feasibly be a natural pattern in the number of comments per author in cryptocurrencies.

7   Conclusions

Measuring levels of centralization by looking at the codebase or by looking at specific sources is inherently limited. While our measurements captured the number of people writing code changes and commenting on the GitHub files, they do not capture the number of people voting on whether or not changes should be accepted. We also did not capture conversations appearing in other places such as on Reddit, the main forums, or the mailing lists. We considered only two main cryptocurrencies, but there are a multitude of other ones, and it would be interesting to see whether similar patterns appear in these other cryptocurrencies, or indeed in other open-source projects in general.

We are aware of two projects that aim to tackle the centralization in governance structures of cryptocurrencies: Tezos [10], a decentralized system that incorporates governance into the consensus protocol, and Steemit [9], a decentralized social media platform in which users are incentivized to post and curate content by receiving a reward in the native cryptocurrency. However, we are not aware of any studies that analyze these solutions. Mostly we hope this work will encourage other work that proposes metrics for centrality, or other empirical studies on the governance structures of decentralized platforms.

Acknowledgments. All authors are supported in part by EPSRC Grant EP/N028104/1. Mary Maller is supported by a scholarship from Microsoft Research. The authors would like to thank Sebastian Meiser and Tristan Caulfield for helpful discussions.

A   Statistical Tables and Figures

See (Fig. 6).

Table 7. p-values for the Kolmogorov-Smirnov test on the number of authors per file.

	Bitcoin Cash	Clojure	Ethereum	Ethereum Classic	Rust
Bitcoin	0.4749	0.001	$<10^{-16}$	$<10^{-16}$	0.001
Bitcoin Cash		0.003	$<10^{-16}$	$<10^{-16}$	0.002
Clojure			$<10^{-16}$	$<10^{-16}$	0.028
Ethereum				$<10^{-16}$	$<10^{-16}$
Ethereum Classic					$<10^{-16}$

Table 8. p-values for the number of comments per author

	Bitcoin ABC	BIPS	Clojure	Ethereum	Ethereum Classic	EIPS	Rust
Bitcoin	0.045	0.04	0.113	0.029	0.583	0.414	$<10^{-16}$
Bitcoin ABC		0.008	0.142	0.027	0.12	0.041	$<10^{-16}$
BIPS			0.015	0.434	0.958	0.285	0.712
Clojure				0.033	0.043	0.07	0.021
Ethereum					0.857	0.536	$<10^{-16}$
Ethereum classic						0.854	0.873
EIPS							0.044

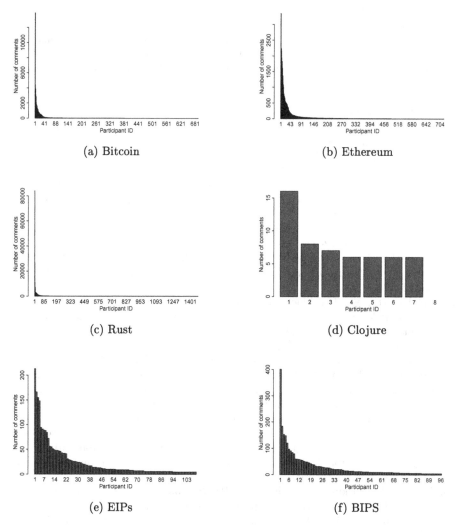

(a) Bitcoin

(b) Ethereum

(c) Rust

(d) Clojure

(e) EIPs

(f) BIPS

Fig. 6. The number of commenters for each repository, ranked from most to fewest comments, ignoring commenters with less than 5 comments.

References

1. BIPS GitHub. github.com/bitcoin/bips
2. Bitcoin Cash. https://www.bitcoincash.org/
3. Blockstream. https://blockstream.com/
4. Cryptocurrency market capitalizations. https://coinmarketcap.com/. Accessed 3 Nov 2017
5. EIPs GitHub. github.com/ethereum/EIPs
6. Ethereum. https://ethereum.org/
7. Ethereum Classic. https://ethereumclassic.github.io/
8. Parity. https://parity.io/
9. Steemit. steemit.com
10. Tezos. tezos.com
11. Atzori, M.: Blockchain technology and decentralized governance: is the state still necessary? (2015)
12. Böhme, R., Christin, N., Edelman, B., Moore, T.: Bitcoin: economics, technology, and governance. J. Econ. Perspect. **29**(2), 213–238 (2015)
13. De Filippi, P., Loveluck, B.: The invisible politics of bitcoin: governance crisis of a decentralised infrastructure. Internet Policy Rev. **5**, 1–28 (2016)
14. Dice, L.R.: Measures of the amount of ecologic association between species. Ecology **26**(3), 297–302 (1945)
15. Gandal, N., Halaburda, H.: Can we predict the winner in a market with network effects? Competition in cryptocurrency market. Games **7**(3), 1–21 (2016)
16. Gervais, A., Karame, G., Capkun, S., Capkun, V.: Is bitcoin a decentralized currency? In: IEEE Security and Privacy (2014)
17. Greenberg, A.: Visa, Mastercard move to choke WikiLeaks, December 2010. http://www.forbes.com/sites/andygreenberg/2010/12/07/visa-mastercard-move-to-choke-wikileaks/
18. Hu, Y., Zhang, J., Bai, X., Yu, S., Yang, Z.: Influence analysis of GitHub repositories. SpringerPlus **5**(1), 1268 (2016)
19. Jesus, C.D.: The DAO heist undone: 97% of eth holders vote for the hard fork, July 2016. https://futurism.com/the-dao-heist-undone-97-of-eth-holders-vote-for-the-hard-fork/
20. Lehdonvirta, V.: The blockchain paradox: why distributed ledger technologies may do little to transform the economy (2016). www.oii.ox.ac.uk/the-blockchain-paradox-why-distributed-ledger-technologies-may-do-little-to-transform-the-economy/
21. Mehta, S.: Statistics Topics. Createspace Independent Pub. (2014)
22. Moore, T., Christin, N.: Beware the middleman: empirical analysis of bitcoin-exchange risk. In: Sadeghi, A.-R. (ed.) FC 2013. LNCS, vol. 7859, pp. 25–33. Springer, Heidelberg (2013). https://doi.org/10.1007/978-3-642-39884-1_3
23. Nakamoto, S.: Bitcoin: a peer-to-peer electronic cash system (2008)
24. Narayanan, A., Bonneau, J., Felten, E., Miller, A., Goldfeder, S.: Bitcoin and Cryptocurrency Technologies. Princeton University Press, Princeton (2016)
25. Reijers, W., O'Brolcháin, F., Haynes, P.: Governance in blockchain technologies and social contract theories. Ledger **1**, 134–151 (2016)
26. Reyes, C.L., Packin, N.G., Edwards, B.P.: Distributed governance (2016)
27. Sekhon, J.S.: Multivariate and propensity score matching software with automated balance optimization: the matching package for R. J. Stat. Softw. **42**(7), 1–52 (2011)

28. Simard, R., LÉcuyer, P., et al.: Computing the two-sided Kolmogorov-Smirnov distribution. J. Stat. Softw. **39**(11), 1–18 (2011)
29. Sørensen, T.: A method of establishing groups of equal amplitude in plant sociology based on similarity of species and its application to analyses of the vegetation on Danish commons. Biol. Skr. K. Dan. Vidensk. Selsk. **5**, 1–34 (1948)
30. Srinivasan, B., Lee, L.: Quantifying decentralization (2017). https://news.earn.com/quantifying-decentralization-e39db233c28e

Blockchain-Based Certificate Transparency and Revocation Transparency

Ze Wang[1,2,3], Jingqiang Lin[1,2,3(✉)], Quanwei Cai[1,2], Qiongxiao Wang[1,2,3], Jiwu Jing[1,2,3], and Daren Zha[1,2]

[1] State Key Laboratory of Information Security, Institute of Information Engineering, Chinese Academy of Sciences, Beijing 100093, China
{wangze,linjingqiang,caiquanwei,wangqiongxiao}@iie.ac.cn
[2] Data Assurance and Communication Security Research Center, Chinese Academy of Sciences, Beijing 100093, China
[3] School of Cyber Security, University of Chinese Academy of Sciences, Beijing 100049, China

Abstract. Traditional X.509 public key infrastructures (PKIs) depend on certification authorities (CAs) to sign certificates, used in SSL/TLS to authenticate web servers and establish secure channels. However, recent security incidents indicate that CAs may (be compromised to) sign fraudulent certificates. In this paper, we propose blockchain-based certificate transparency and revocation transparency. Our scheme is compatible with X.509 PKIs but significantly reinforces the security guarantees of a certificate. The CA-signed certificates and their revocation status information of an SSL/TLS web server are published by the subject (i.e., the web server) as a transaction, and miners of the community append it to the global certificate blockchain after verifying the transaction and mining a block. The certificate blockchain acts as append-only public logs to monitor CAs' certificate signing and revocation operations, and an SSL/TLS web server is granted with the cooperative control on its certificates to balance the absolute authority of CAs in traditional PKIs. We implement the prototype system with Firefox and Nginx, and the experimental results show that it introduces reasonable overheads.

Keywords: PKI · SSL · TLS · Blockchain · Transparency · Trust

1 Introduction

In X.509 public key infrastructures (PKIs), a certification authority (CA) signs certificates to bind the public key of a server to its identity (typically a DNS

This work was partially supported by National Basic Research 973 Program of China (Award No. 2014CB340603), National Natural Science Foundation of China (Award No. 61772518), and Cyber Security Program (Award No. 2017YFB0802100) of National Key RD Plan of China.

A. Zohar et al. (Eds.): FC 2018 Workshops, LNCS 10958, pp. 144–162, 2019.
https://doi.org/10.1007/978-3-662-58820-8_11

name). Then, these certificates are used in SSL/TLS [14,21] to authenticate the web servers. Trusting the CAs, browsers obtain the servers' public keys from CA-signed certificates in SSL/TLS negotiations, to establish secure channels.

However, recent security incidents indicate that CAs are not so trustworthy as they are assumed to be. CAs may sign fraudulent certificates due to intrusions [11,24,46,58], reckless identity validations [44,54,55,61], misoperations [33,45,62], flawed cryptographic algorithms [53,60], or government compulsions [15,52]. Typical fraudulent certificates bind a DNS name to key pairs held by counterfeit web servers [5,11,15]. Then, the counterfeit servers will launch man-in-the-middle (MITM) attacks, even when a browser follows the strict steps of certificate validation [12] to establish SSL/TLS sessions.

Certificate transparency [35] was proposed to enhance the accountability of CA operations, using *append-only* public logs. A CA-signed certificate is publicly recorded in log servers; otherwise, a browser rejects it in SSL/TLS negotiations. Therefore, a fraudulent certificate will be observed by monitors or interested parties, especially the owner of the DNS name (or the SSL/TLS web server). The certificates in log servers are organized as a Merkle hash tree, and auditors periodically verify the integrity of logs to ensure that they are append-only, i.e., a (fraudulent) certificate will never be deleted or modified after being appended.

Certificate transparency follows a reactive philosophy. It depends on the monitors to observe fraudulent certificates after they have been signed and recorded in the log servers. So a fraudulent certificate may be accepted by browsers before it is observed by any interested party. Moreover, to ensure append-only records, and the detection of deleted or modified (fraudulent) certificate relies on the periodical detection of auditors. Considering the huge number and increment of current certificates, it is a high burden to monitor or audit the public logs.

In this paper, we proposes a blockchain-based scheme to construct append-only logs for certificate transparency. In our scheme, CA-signed X.509 certificates are published by their subjects (i.e., the corresponding web servers) in *certificate transactions* in a *global certificate blockchain*. The global certificate blockchain acts as an inherently append-only public log to monitor CAs' operations. To publish its certificates, each web server has a *publishing key pair* to sign its certificate transactions, which is different from the key pair bound in the certificate. This design of subject-controlled certificate publication allows an web server to manage its certificates cooperatively with CAs. It shares the same spirit with trust assertions for certificate keys (TACK) [39] and PoliCert [56] that a web server is involved in the validation of its certificates.

SSL/TLS web servers compose an interdependent community, to balance the absolute authority of CAs in traditional PKIs. Particularly, the publishing key of a web server is initially certified by a certain number of these interdependent web servers explicitly and also a CA implicitly. So CAs are unable to publish a certificate in the certificate blockchain, without the consent of the community of web servers. The certified publishing key of each web server is also publicly recorded in the blockchain. It means that the publication of a certificate is also publicly accountable.

Each certificate transaction has a period of validity, shorter than those of the published certificates. It enforces a web server to publish its certificates and update revocation status periodically. When an unexpired certificate is revoked, it will be absent from the next transaction, and the corresponding certificate revocation list (CRL) file or online certificate status protocol (OCSP) response will be included in the transaction instead. Therefore CAs' revocation operations are also recorded and revocation transparency [34,51] is achieved in the certificate blockchain.

The proposed scheme protects browsers against the impersonation attacks using fraudulent certificates. Browsers utilize the certificate blockchain to validate the certificates received in SSL/TLS negotiations. A certificate is accepted only if it is published in an unexpired transaction, therefore a fraudulent certificate signed by compromised CAs but not published in the blockchain will be rejected by browsers.

We implemented the prototype system with Nginx and Firefox. The Nginx server sends its certificate transactions to browsers as SSL/TLS extensions, and the browser validates the received certificates with the help of the certificate blockchain. The analysis based on the real-world statistics and the experimental results show that our scheme introduces reasonable overheads, in terms of storage, certificate validation delay, communication, and incentive cost.

The remainder is organized as follows. In Sect. 2, we introduce the security model, and the system details are described in Sect. 3. Then, the proposed scheme is analyzed in Sect. 4, and the prototype system is evaluated in Sect. 5. Section 6 is related work, and Sect. 7 concludes this paper.

2   Threat Model and Design Goal

Attackers attempt to impersonate an SSL/TLS web server using fraudulent certificates, and a successful attack means that browsers accept the fraudulent certificates in SSL/TLS negotiations. We assume that the attackers could compromise some trusted CAs, to sign fraudulent certificates binding the target web server's DNS name to any key pair. The attackers may also compromise the target server's publishing key to generate fraudulent messages. However, we assume that they could not compromise more than a threshold of certifiers of the target server and certify a fraudulent publishing key. That is, the worst scenario our scheme considers is that the publishing key pair is held or known by attackers and fraudulent certificates are signed by compromised CAs at the same time.

The attackers do not hold computation resource which exceeds 30% of all computation power in the community, and all cryptographic primitives are secure. The attackers cannot block the network for a long enough time to take attack actions; that is, honest entities communicate with each other in a loosely synchronized manner.

We aims to protect browsers against the impersonation attacks using fraudulent certificates. If a browser follows our scheme to validate certificates in SSL/TLS negotiations, the authenticated peer is ensured to be the legitimate server of the visited DNS name. Even in the extreme case that a fraudulent certificate has been published in the blockchain by a compromised publishing key pair, the browsers are most likely to reject this fraudulent certificate and it will be recovered soon by countermeasure transactions in the certificate blockchain.

3   System Architecture

3.1   Overview

Web servers publish their certificate transactions in an unique, global certificate blockchain. Like Bitcoin, each block in the certificate blockchain consists of a block header and multiple transactions, which are organized as a Merkle hash tree. A block header is composed of: (a) the time when the miner starts to mine this block, (b) the digest of the last block header in the blockchain, (c) the Merkle hash tree root of the included transactions, (d) a list of (Type, DNS_Name) tuples of the included transactions, sorted in lexicographic order, and (e) a PoW nonce computed by brute force, so that the hash value of this block is less than the PoW target. The list of (Type, DNS_Name) tuples is included, so browsers or web servers find a transaction conveniently without iterating through all included transactions.

In the certificate blockchain, there are overall two types of certificate transactions. A *Type-I transaction* is signed by a web server using its publishing key pair, to periodically publish certificates. When a certificate expires and is updated, the new one will be included in the next transaction. If a certificate is revoked, it will be excluded from the next transaction; at the same time, the corresponding CRL file or OCSP response will be included instead. *Type-II transactions* are used to initialize or reset publishing key pairs. When a DNS name (or web server) is initially introduced into this community, its publishing key is signed by a number of other web servers (called *certifiers*) using their publishing key pairs. This publishing key may be reset by another Type-II transaction, if it is compromised or lost.

All certificate transactions labeled with the same DNS name, either Type-I or Type-II, are chained together chronologically, as shown in Fig. 1. For every web server, its continuous history of certificates and publishing keys is then archived publicly in the blockchain. If a fraudulent certificate or publishing key appears, it will be observed soon. We design a series of regulations that enable the honest web servers to take countermeasures and recover their certificates or publishing keys.

A miner collects, verifies certificate transactions from others and mines the block for them, according to the regulations of certificate transaction stated as below. It also collects mined blocks from other miners, verifies the blocks, and appends valid ones to its local copy to make it be longer. Incentive mechanism like Bitcoin can be introduced to our scheme to encourage mining. Namely, the miner who mines a particular block will be awarded by some coins, and the coins are purchased and consumed by the web servers when they publish certificate transactions.

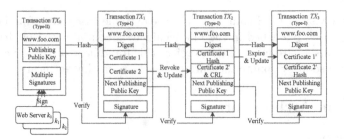

Fig. 1. The history of certificates and publishing keys.

In every block, a web server is allowed to publish at most one transaction. If the miners of the blockchain receive both a Type-I and a Type-II transaction with a same DNS name, the Type-II transaction has priority. If there are multiple transactions of the same DNS name and type, a miner selects one of them based on its own implementation.

A browser communicates with the P2P network of web servers/miners to download the updated blockchain, to keep a local copy. When the browser is establishing SSL/TLS sessions with a web server, it validates the web server's certificate with the help of its local copy of the certificate blockchain. We will explain this procedure in further details in the following subsections.

3.2   Subject-Controlled Certificate Publication

A certificate is signed and published by its subject, in Type-I certificate transactions. Only the web sever who holds the publishing key pair, is able to sign Type-I transactions labelled with its DNS name. Therefore, a (compromised) CA cannot publish certificates without the consent of the subject. Each Type-I transaction includes:

1. DNS_Name, the DNS name of the web server.
2. Prev_TX_Hash, the hash value of the previous transaction with the same DNS name, either Type-I or Type-II.
3. Type, marked as Type I.
4. Validity, the validity period of this certificate publication.
5. List_of_Cert_Chain, a list of published certificate chains. The web server may hold multiple, currently valid certificates.
6. Next_Publishing_Key, the publishing public key. The corresponding private key is used to sign the *next* Type-I transaction with this DNS name.
7. Sig, the signature of this transaction using the *current* publishing key pair (i.e., the one bound in the most recent transaction with this DNS name, either Type-I or Type-II).

For each certificate chain in List_of_Cert_Chain, if the web server's certificate is published for the first time, the whole chain from the self-signed root

CA certificate to the end-entity certificate is provided. It facilitates the miners to validate the certificate. Otherwise, when the chain is published in the subsequent periodical Type-I transactions, only a simplified entry is provided, including the hash value of the web server's certificate and the information to check its "dynamic" validity status. Such information includes the validity of certificate, the CRL distribution point or OCSP location, and the identifier to check its revocation status via CRL or OCSP (e.g., the serial number). Such design of simplified entries enables the miners to verify the consistency of these transactions and check the certificate's dynamic revocation status, but greatly reduces the overheads of storage and communication.

Certificate transparency is achieved since certificates are publicly visible as transactions in the append-only blockchain. For Type-I transactions, their period of validity is required to be comparable with that of certificate status refresh in current PKI. Therefore, a certificate is usually published for several times during its lifecycle, and its updated revocation status is also reflected in certificate transactions. When a certificate is revoked, the web server replaces this certificate with related revocation information in the next transaction, and publish it immediately or until the next period. So CA's revocation operations are also recorded in the blockchain, which enables *revocation transparency*.

3.3   Initialization and Reset of Publishing Keys

Type-II transactions are used to (a) initialize the publishing key of a web server and (b) reset it if compromised. A Type-II transaction includes the following fields:

1. DNS_Name, the DNS name of the web server.
2. Prev_TX_Hash, the hash value of the previous transaction with the same DNS name, either Type-I or Type-II.
3. Type, marked as Type II.
4. Publishing_Key, the public key of the certified publishing key pair.
5. Certifier_Group, a list of certifiers' DNS names. The corresponding web servers are authorized to control the publishing key of this DNS name.
6. List_of_Cert_Chain, a list of web server's certificate information, *optional*. It is used to remove fraudulent certificates falsely appeared in previous Type-I transactions in emergency.
7. Sig_by_Owner, some signatures by the certified web server. They are verified using corresponding some CA-signed certificates binding the DNS name, which are also included in this field.
8. List_of_Sig, a list of signatures signed by certifier web servers using their current publishing key pairs. The signers' DNS names are also in this field.

Each Type-II transaction is signed by at least G certifier web servers. To sign its *initial* Type-II transaction (i.e., the first transaction labeled with the DNS name), a web server contacts at least G servers it trusted whose publishing keys have been certified in the blockchain, as its certifiers. The *initial* Type-II transaction is signed by *all* certifiers. Then, any following *non-initial* Type-II transaction must be signed by at least G certifiers specified in `Certifier_Group` of the previous Type-II transaction. The certifier group can be modified in *non-initial* Type-II transactions, while the number of the certifiers in `Certifier_Group` must be not less than G. Besides, Type-II transactions are also signed by the web server itself in `Sig_by_Owner`, which indirectly certified by one or more CAs.

An initial Type-II transaction is set with a "frozen" period before the certified publishing key becomes valid. It allows interested parties (not only the web server) to observe impersonation attack attempts. During the frozen period, another initial Type-II transaction with the same DNS name whose certificates in `Sig_by_Owner` are signed by more publicly-trusted CAs invalidates this Type-II transaction. If such dispute case happens, the frozen period is automatically extended to provide the target web server more time to contact CAs and out-of-band actions may be taken. The publishing key becomes valid, after the frozen period without disputes.

The field of `List_of_Cert_Chain` is used in the extreme attack case that fraudulent certificates are published by a compromised publishing key pair, so the target web server recovers its control on publishing keys and delete fraudulent certificates by only one transaction. No revocation information is needed in this field of Type-II transactions. Note that, `List_of_Cert_Chain` is not allowed to include any newly appeared certificate; otherwise, it provides a fast track for attackers to publish fraudulent certificates.

To reduce the storage requirement of miners, each web server publishes its Type-II transactions *periodically*, even when it is unnecessary to reset the publishing key pair or modify its certifier group. In these "shadow" Type-II transactions, `Publishing_Key` and `Certifier_Group` must be identical with those in the previous transaction, while `List_of_Cert_Chain` and the certificates in `Sig_of_Owner` must be absent. A shadow Type-II transaction is signed only by the web server itself, and no signatures by certifiers are required. So, a miner only stores (a) the recent block headers and (b) the latest transactions of both types of each DNS name, within a certain period.

In the *genesis* block of the certificate blockchain, $G + 1$ or more special Type-II transactions are included to certify at least $G + 1$ web servers' publishing keys. Each of these transactions, is signed by other G web servers. The publishing keys in the genesis block are self-certified by these web servers cooperatively (and some CAs indirectly). Then, these web servers will publish their certificates.

An initial period shall be needed for the founder servers to invite highly-ranked web servers (assumed to be honest) to join, i.e., initially certify other web servers' publishing keys. During the initial period, the certificate blockchain is publicly visible but the community is not open to join. After a certain number of honest web servers are introduced into the community, so that any new participants will not introduces overwhelmed computation power, it is open to the public and the non-founder web servers as well operate as certifiers after their publishing keys have been certified and published in the certificate blockchain.

3.4   Certificate Validation by Browsers

A browser validates the certificates received in SSL/TLS negotiations, with the help of the certificate blockchain. First, a browser communicates with (the P2P network of) web servers/miners to incrementally download the up-to-date block headers. The browser verifies whether the downloaded headers are chained correctly and each header contains a valid PoW nonce, and updates its local copy if a longer chain is received. Browsers download and store only block headers but no transactions, to reduce the overhead of communication and storage. This synchronization may be performed when there is no SSL/TLS negotiation.

The certificate transactions to validate a certificate are sent by the visited web server during the SSL/TLS negotiation via SSL/TLS message extensions. The identifier of block and the Merkle audit path for the transaction (i.e., the shortest list of additional nodes to compute the Merkle hash tree root [35]) are also sent to enable browsers to verify the certificate transaction.

A certificate chain received in SSL/TLS negotiations is valid, if (a) the certificate (or its hash value) is published in List_of_Cert_Chain of an *unexpired* transaction, which is sent by the visited web server, (b) it is signed by a *trusted* root CA of the browser, (c) the transaction is included in a *fully-confirmed* block, not in the latest N ones of the blockchain, to ensure that the certificate transaction has been accepted by enough miners [8] and the published certificates have been monitored by interested parties, and (d) in the blocks subsequent to this fully-confirmed block, including the N non-fully-confirmed ones, if there are any transactions with the visited DNS name, then the received certificate shall also appear in these transactions. Note that browsers are immune to downgrading attacks, since they will determine whether a web server has published transaction in the blockchain according to their local copies of block headers, and perform standard certificate validation for those servers who has not.

Because the certificate chain has been validated by the majority of honest miners, the browser only needs to check whether the root CA certificate is trusted by itself or not. Other processing [12] such as CA signatures, periods of validity, and certificate extensions, is unnecessary. That is, the certificate validation of browsers is delegated to the community of miners, and the delegated certificate validation is also transparent (i.e, publicly visible).

Since the validity period of Type-I transactions may be greater than the general CRL/OCSP update period, a browser with high security concerns may take extra actions to check the revocation status of the received certificates.

4   Security Analysis

In this section, we analyze the proposed scheme under various attack scenarios. We present the countermeasures and evaluate the impacts, when some entities except the target web server were compromised. The network attacks on the certificate blockchain are also analyzed.

4.1   Security with Compromised Key Pairs

In order to impersonate a web server, the attackers could compromise a CA, and/or compromise some web servers' publishing key pairs. Note that, an attack is considered as successful only if a fraudulent certificate is accepted by browsers.

We do not assume that the attackers could compromise at least G certifiers of the target web server, considering the certifiers are carefully selected by the target server, and G can be set large enough. We neither consider the situation that the key pair bound in the target web server's certificate is compromised by attackers, in which the attackers could launch MITM attacks without a fraudulent certificate. Such attacks should be prevented or mitigated by the approaches other than certificate management, which are out of the scope of this paper.

Compromised CAs. When only CAs are compromised, our scheme ensures that no fraudulent certificate is accepted by browsers, because the target web server will not publish such certificates in the blockchain. Note that in traditional PKIs compromising a CA is sufficient to launch MITM attacks, while in our scheme attackers need to concurrently compromise the target server's publishing key, which is more difficult.

Compromised Publishing Key Pairs. An attacker fails to impersonate the target web server, if it only compromises its publishing key pair. The attacker may modify List_of_Cert_Chain in a Type-I transaction, by including an expired or revoked one, or excluding a currently-valid certificate. But the verification of such a transaction will fail, because miners will validate all included certificates and only expired or revoked certificates shall be excluded compared with the previous transaction.

The attacker may modify Next_Publishing_Key with another key pair through Type-I transactions, to prevent the web server from updating its Type-I transactions. This case will be further discussed in the following paragraphs.

Compromised CAs and Publishing Key Pairs. The attackers might compromise a CA to sign fraudulent certificates and also compromise the target web server's publishing key pair. Then, the attacker could publish fraudulent certificates in a Type-I transaction, while simultaneously modify Next_Publishing_Key with another key pair held by itself. This transaction will be considered as correct by miners, and finally included into a mined block.

Once the fraudulent Type-I transaction is observed by the target web server (or any other interested parties), the web server will immediately contact its certifiers to sign a countermeasure Type-II transaction, to exclude the fraudulent certificates by properly setting List_of_Cert_Chain and to simultaneously reset its publishing key in Publishing_Key. As shown in Fig. 2, if the countermeasure Type-II transaction appears in time (i.e, in any of the N subsequent blocks after the fraudulent transaction), browsers will detect the conflict and reject the fraudulent certificates (see Sect. 3.4). Such a Type-II transaction thoroughly counters the impact of the fraudulent Type-I transaction. If the countermeasure transaction is not signed in time, the fraudulent certificates might be accepted temporarily but rejected after the countermeasure transaction.

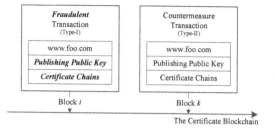

Fig. 2. A fraudulent Type-I transaction in Block i, and the countermeasure Type-II transaction in Block k. If $i < k \leq i + N$, the fraudulent certificate is never accepted; if $k > i + N$, it may be accepted before the countermeasure transaction.

In all above scenarios, there is no attack impact if target web servers observe attacks and take countermeasures in time (i.e. $k \leq i + N$). Since attackers can not compromise G certifiers, a web server can always counters the impact by a Type-II transaction.

4.2   Attacks on the Certificate Blockchain

The attackers may attempt to prevent browsers from accessing the recent blocks of the certificate blockchain. First, it is extremely difficult and expensive to isolate a browser from a great number of P2P nodes, while allow it to access (counterfeit) web servers. Even if such an attack could be performed, the victim browser is aware of it when subsequent blocks take far more time than average block interval, since the mining time is contained in block headers.

Powerful attackers might publish a fraudulent certificate and include it in a branch of the blockchain. Then, subsequent blocks are mined on the branch by attackers, while countermeasure transactions are elaborately excluded. It requires the attackers to control 33% of computation resources [20], which breaks our security assumption on attackers' computation power [48].

5   Implementation and Evaluation

This section presents the prototype of the proposed scheme, and evaluates its performance.

5.1   Implementation and Setting

The prototype system is comprised of, (a) a browser that validates certificates in SSL/TLS negotiations, based on its local copy of the certificate blockchain, (b) a web server that delivers its certificates transactions in SSL/TLS negotiations as extensions, and (c) an instance of the certificate blockchain.

The browser is implemented on Firefox Nightly (version 54.0a1). The function VerifySSLServerCert() is modified as described in Sect. 3.4 to validate the received certificate. The web server is implemented on Nginx (version 1.10.3). Extensions of ClientHello and ServerHello are defined and implemented in the handshake of SSL/TLS, to request and respond the certificate transactions and the corresponding Merkle audit paths. The browser and the visited web server are connected directly. The browser runs on a desktop (Intel i7-4770s/3.10GHz CPU, 8 GB RAM, and ST-1000DM003 hard disk) with Windows 7 Professional, and the web server is on another desktop of the same hardware configuration with Ubuntu 16.04 LTS (32-bit).

Table 1 summarizes the values of all related parameters in the prototype. The reasons why we choose these values are explained in the appendix in detail.

Table 1. The values of parameters in the prototype blockchain.

Mark	Value	Note
T_B	2 h	Average block interval
T_I	10 days	Type-I transaction validity
T_{II}	100 days	The period of shadow Type-II transactions
G	5/10	The threshold of signed certifier in a Type-II transaction
N	6	Number of blocks after a block to fully confirm the block

There are currently about 54.35M valid SSL/TLS certificates according to Censys.io [43], and on average each website has 1.34 certificates [57]. Nearly 70% of these certificates are issued for free (e.g. by Let's Encrypt). We think these certificates' owners are sensitive to price, and would not participate in the incentive mechanism in our scheme. Thus, we mainly focus on the non-free certificates (approximately 13.88M, corresponding to about 10.36M websites). Note that we do not require all certificates to participate since our scheme is immune to downgrading attack. We include all these certificates basically for performance estimation.

We generate a prototype blockchain using 10.36M random DNS names, and average-size certificates by testing CAs. The prototype blockchain contains 1200 blocks (within about T_{II}) and transactions for all 10.36M web servers. In the prototype, each server periodically publishes a Type-I transaction every 114 blocks, to ensure that a transaction does not expire until the next one is fully-confirmed. So on average each block contains 10.36M /114 $\approx$ 93.06K Type-I transactions and 10.36M/1200 $\approx$ 8.84K Type-II transactions. On average each web site has 1.34 certificate chains and each chain is composed of three certificates. We use OpenSSL-1.0.1g to generate the prototype certificate blockchain. Besides, DNS names are randomly generated in the prototype blockchain with the average length of 14 bytes, according to the average domain name length of Alexa top 1M websites [2].

OCSP responses (1.60 KB on average) are included as the revocation status information, because of OCSP is widely deployed [37] and smaller than CRL

(51 KB on average [37]). According to the real-world statistics, the revocation rate is normally 1% and may increase to 11% when an emergency happens [37].

5.2   Evaluation

Storage. Table 2 lists the average size of each element. A browser keeps the block headers within T_I for certificate validation, so the storage overhead is about $120 \times 1.40\,\text{MB} \approx 168.00\,\text{MB}$.

Table 2. The size of data elements in the blockchain.

Item	Average size
Type-I transaction	
With 1/2/3 certificate chain(s)	4.65/8.71/12.77 KB
With 1/2/3 partial certificate(s)	0.83/1.07/1.30 KB
Type-II certificate transaction	
Without certifier signature (shadow)	1.02 KB
With 5/10 certifier's signatures	5.10/5.36 KB
Block header	559.18 KB
Block, including the header and transactions	
No certificate revoked	95.05 MB
1% certificates revoked (by OCSP/CRL) and 1% new certificates	101.05/162.62 MB
11% certificates revoked (by OCSP/CRL) and 11% new certificates	161.13/838.42 MB

A miner keeps the latest Type-I and Type-II transactions of each DNS name, and all block headers within T_{II}, which is about $10.36\text{M} \times (0.91\,\text{KB} + 1.02\,\text{KB}) + 1200 \times 4 \times 1.40\,\text{MB} \approx 26.64\,\text{GB}$. Here, 0.91 KB is the estimated size of Type-I transaction with 1.34 certificate chains. Besides, all transactions in the N non-fully-confirmed blocks shall be kept always, to ensure the verification of blocks in multiple concurrent non-fully-confirmed branches; and the size is about $6 \times (93.06\text{K} \times 0.91\,\text{KB} + 8.84\text{K} \times 1.02\,\text{KB}) \approx 0.55\,\text{GB}$. That is, a miner stores at least 27.19 GB data. If 1% certificates are revoked by OCSP, the storage overhead increases to 27.36 GB (we consider it as a "typical" size); if 11% are revoked by CRL, the overhead is 109.62 GB. Even when all valid certificates are included in the blockchain, the typical storage overhead of a miner will not exceed 150 GB. As a comparison, each miner in Bitcoin stores over 150 GB data.

Delay. A browser validates the received certificate as follows: (*a*) checks whether the root CA is trusted, (*b*) reads a block header from the hard drive, (*c*) checks if a block header contains a transaction of the visited DNS name, and (*d*) checks whether the received transaction is in the found block and the certificate is in the transaction. Operations (*b*), (*c*) and (*d*) are performed repeatedly, until it confirms that the certificate is in an unexpired transaction in the recent fully-confirmed blocks (and also all of its subsequent transactions in non-fully-confirmed blocks, if appear).

The browser validates certificates when the target transaction is in the middle/end of the blockchain (each for 1000 times). The average time of these operations is listed in Table 3.

Table 3. The time of certificate validation in browsers.

Operation	Average time
Standard certificate validation	9.86 ms
Basic operation	
(a) Check trust anchors	<0.01 ms
(b) Read a block header from hard drive	1.11 ms
(c) Search the DNS name in a block header	0.01 ms
(d) Verify a transaction and the certificate	0.25 ms
Validate a certificate with the blockchain	
Operation $(a)+(b)+(c)+(d)$, target locates in the middle/end	71.87/135.38 ms
Operation $(a)+(c)+(d)$, target locates in the middle/end	0.98/1.65 ms

The time cost is greatly reduced if a browser loads all block headers (about 168.00 MB) into memory when it starts up. In such case, Operation (b) is unnecessary and the average delay is 0.98 ms. This number will increase to 3.20 ms when all valid certificates are included in the blockchain.

The browser takes about 9.86 ms to validate a certificate using the standard method except checking revocation. Adopting our method may significantly accelerate the validation process.

Communication. In an SSL/TLS negotiation, the introduced communication overhead is typically one certificate transaction, and will not exceeds $N + 1$ transactions. It is about 1.53 KB, and not larger than 10.71 KB ($N = 6$).

Besides, a browser periodically updates its local copy of block headers, about 16.80 MB every day. The number can be decreased to about 5~8 MB daily via common commercial compress software. Compared to traditional methods who need extra links to download CRLs/OCSPs during SSL/TLS negotiations, which degrades performance even they are small, our scheme enable browsers to download block headers when they are idle.

6   Related Work

Several **public-accountable-log-based services**, such as CIRT [51], RT [34], ARPKI [7], and CONIKS [41], have been introduced to achieved certificate transparency and/or revocation transparency, by recording certificates in Merkle hash trees. These schemes do not involve subject control on certificate publication so that a fraudulent certificate (or public key) might be accepted before it is observed by interested parties, while our blockchain-based scheme supports subject-controlled certificate publication. AKI [31] and Policert [56] enable the certificate subject to define its own certificate parameters (e.g., trusted CAs and log servers). The subject certificate policy, can as well listed in Type-II transactions, to enhance the subject's control. All above append-only logs depend on extra auditors which are not needed in our scheme. On the contrary, our scheme is based on the append-only blockchain maintained by web servers and miners.

Other **subject-controlled certificate services**, like DANE [27], CAA [26], Sovereign Key [16] were also proposed to balance the absolute authority of CAs. In these enhancements, a browser communicates with extra components (a DNSSEC server [4,6] or a timestamp server) when validating a certificate or public key, so privacy information about the secure session is leaked; however, in our scheme, all browsers download uniform block headers and no such information is exchanged.

Public key pinning requires browsers to locally store a public key (or certificate) for a certain domain [19,32,39,50]. These schemes follow the assumption of trust on first use, so the first visit shall be established without attacks. Moreover, existing pinning mechanisms do not consider certificate revocation or update, while these events are handled as transactions in our scheme.

Notary-based approaches allow clients to compare certificates from the SSL/TLS sessions and other sources, such as Perspectives [59], Convergence [38], ICSI Notary [29], and EFF SSL Observatory [17]. Crossbear [28] localises the SSL/TLS MITM attacks based on such records. Doublecheck [3,18] and Laribus [42] allow clients compares certificates received from different network paths. Some notary-based approaches [17,29,38,42,59] leak the privacy information about secure sessions, while the others [3,18,42] only work for localized attacks.

Browsers may enforce **enhanced security policies** when validating a certificate [1]. CA-TMS [9], Certlock [52] and Cage [30] separately evaluate the trustworthiness of CAs based on the client's local experiences or the CA's domain name scope. DVCert [13] delivers a certificate list to browsers, protected by previously-established user credentials, to validate certificates in the SSL/TLS negotiations. Such enhancements may be integrated into our scheme as additional rules to validate certificates. The surveys [10,25] comprehensively discussed the vulnerabilities of the SSL/TLS ecosystem and the countermeasures.

Some **blockchain-based alternatives** allow subjects to publish keys or credentials in blockchain [22,23,36,49]. In these DNS systems [22,23,49], the key pairs are controlled entirely by the owner of the DNS name. So the private key can not be recovered ever since it is compromised. Our solution distributes the control among CAs and the community of web servers, so an attacker cannot bind an arbitrary key pair to the DNS name after breaking a single entity. An IKP reaction policy signed by issuers and a domain certificate policy signed by domains construct a smart contract in the Ethereum blockchain [40], intending to be triggered by fraudulent certificates. Blockstack [47] improves Namecoin by separating controls and data. This separation design can be integrated with our solution, making the storage of certificate transactions outsourced.

7   Conclusion

We propose to record certificates and revocation status information in the global certificate blockchain, which is inherently append-only, to achieve certificate transparency and limited-grained revocation transparency. Our scheme balances the absolute authority of CAs, and provides a continuous history of certificates for each SSL/TLS web server. The publishing key pairs used to sign transactions, are controlled cooperatively by CAs and the community of web servers, and recorded in the blockchain. The proposed scheme is compatible with X.509 PKIs but significantly reinforces the security guarantees of certificates. Our scheme also provides transparent and delegated certificate validation services for browsers. Since each certificate chain is validated by a majority of miners before included in the certificate blockchain. The analysis and the experimental results show that, our scheme introduces reasonable overheads in terms of storage, certificate validation delay, communication, and incentive cost.

A Parameters Selection

The time interval between two adjacent blocks (denoted as T_B) determines how soon a certificate will be accepted by browsers after it has been included in the blockchain. It is reasonable for a web server to require its published certificates to be accepted within 24 h, i.e., $N \times T_B < 1,440$ min. On the other hand, a smaller T_B enforces the web server to watch for fraudulent certificates in the blockchain more frequently, and take countermeasures more quickly. Accordingly, we set $T_B = 120$ min as a typical value and let $N = 6$ (the same as the requirement in Bitcoin). In order to keep the block mining stable, the community adjusts the PoW target of the blockchain periodically.

The validity period of Type-I transactions (denote as T_I) is chosen to provide moderate revocation transparency. First, only when a transaction has been included in a fully-confirmed block (not in the latest N ones of the blockchain), the contained certificates are considered as valid by browsers. So, $T_I \gg (N+1) \times T_B$; otherwise, it is never accepted by browsers before it expires. Meanwhile, T_I shall be not significantly greater than the general revocation status update period, to enforce the web servers to update their transactions in a timely manner. So we require that $T_I \leq 10 \times T_{Revoke}$, where T_{Revoke} is the revocation status update period. For more than 95% of CRL files, T_{Revoke} is not larger than 1 day. OCSP provides timely revocation status services, but the validity period of OCSP responses is typically 4 or 7 days.[1] Thus, we set $T_I = 14,400$ min (or 10 days) in the prototype.

T_{II} determines the frequency of shadow Type-II transactions. We set $T_{II} = 10 \times T_I$ (i.e., 100 days).

---

[1] We visited the Alexa top-50 websites, and observed 29 unique certificate chains for these websites (averagely 4.05 KB), each of which is composed of three certificates. We collected OCSP responses (averagely 1.60 KB) for these certificates, and the distribution of the validity periods is: 17 are 7-day, 9 are 4-day, 2 are 1.5-day, and 1 is 5-day.

References

1. Abadi, M., Birrell, A., Mironov, I., Wobber, T., Xie, Y.: Global authentication in an untrustworthy world. In: 14th USENIX Conference on Hot Topics in Operating Systems (HotOS) (2013)
2. Alexa: Alexa Top 1M Websites (2017). http://s3.amazonaws.com/alexa-static/top-1m.csv.zip
3. Alicherry, M., Keromytis, A.: Doublecheck: multi-path verification against man-in-the-middle attacks. In: 14th IEEE Symposium on Computers and Communications (ISCC), pp. 557–563 (2009)
4. Arends, R., Austein, R., Larson, M., Massey, D., Rose, S.: DNS Security Introduction and Requirements. Technical report, IETF RFC 4033 (2005)
5. Arthur, C.: Rogue Web Certificate Could Have Been Used to Attack Iran Dissidents, August 2011. https://iranian.com/main/news/2011/08/30/rogue-web-certificate-could-have-been-used-attack-iran-dissidents.html
6. Ateniese, G., Mangard, S.: A new approach to DNS security (DNSSEC). In: 8th ACM Conference on Computer and Communications Security (CCS), pp. 86–95 (2001)
7. Basin, D., Cremers, C., Kim, H., Perrig, A., Sasse, R., Szalachowski, P.: ARPKI: attack resilient public-key infrastructure. In: 21st ACM Conference on Computer and Communications Security (CCS), pp. 382–393 (2014)
8. bitcoin.org: Bitcoin Developer Guide (2016). https://bitcoin.org/en/developer-guide
9. Braun, J., Volk, F., Classen, J., Buchmann, J., Mühlhäuser, M.: CA trust management for the web PKI. J. Comput. Secur. **22**(6), 913–959 (2014)
10. Clark, J., van Oorschot, P.: SoK: SSL and HTTPS: revisiting past challenges and evaluating certificate trust model enhancements. In: 34th IEEE Symposium on Security and Privacy (S&P), pp. 511–525 (2013)
11. Comodo Group Inc.: Comodo Report of Incident, March 2011. https://www.comodo.com/Comodo-Fraud-Incident-2011-03-23.html
12. Cooper, D., Santesson, S., Farrell, S., Boeyen, S., Housley, R., Polk, W.: Internet X.509 Public Key Infrastructure Certificate and Certificate Revocation List (CRL) Profile. Technical report, IETF RFC 5280 (2008)
13. Dacosta, I., Ahamad, M., Traynor, P.: Trust no one else: detecting MITM attacks against SSL/TLS without third-parties. In: Foresti, S., Yung, M., Martinelli, F. (eds.) ESORICS 2012. LNCS, vol. 7459, pp. 199–216. Springer, Heidelberg (2012). https://doi.org/10.1007/978-3-642-33167-1_12
14. Dierks, T., Rescorla, E.: The Transport Layer Security (TLS) Protocol. Technical report, IETF RFC 5246 (2008)
15. Eckersley, P.: A Syrian Man-in-the-Middle Attack against Facebook, May 2011. https://www.eff.org/deeplinks/2011/05/syrian-man-middle-against-facebook
16. Eckersley, P.: Sovereign Key Cryptography for Internet Domains. Technical report, IETF Internet-draft (2012)
17. Eckersley, P., Burns, J.: Is the SSLiverse a Safe Place, December 2010. https://events.ccc.de/congress/2010/Fahrplan/events/4121.en.html
18. Engert, K.: DetecTor, September 2013. http://www.detector.io/DetecTor.pdf
19. Evans, C., Palmer, C., Sleevi, R.: Public Key Pinning Extension for HTTP. Technical report, IETF RFC 7469 (2015)
20. Eyal, I., Sirer, E.G.: Majority Is Not Enough: Bitcoin Mining Is Vulnerable, pp. 436–454 (2013)

21. Freier, A., Karlton, P., Kocher, P.: The Secure Sockets Layer (SSL) Protocol Version 3.0 (2011)
22. Fromknecht, C., Velicanu, D., Yakoubov, S.: A Decentralized Public Key Infrastructure with Identity Retention (2014). https://eprint.iacr.org/2014/803.pdf
23. Fromknecht, C., Velicanu, D., Yakoubov, S.: CertCoin: A NameCoin Based Decentralized Authentication System, Massachusetts Institute of Technology, MA, USA (2014). http://courses.csail.mit.edu/6.857/2014/files/19-fromknecht-velicann-yakoubov-certcoin.pdf
24. GlobalSign: Security Incident Report (2011). https://www.globalsign.com/resources/globalsign-security-incident-report.pdf
25. Grant, A.: Search for Trust: An Analysis and Comparison of CA System Alternatives and Enhancements. Technical report, Dartmouth Computer Science, Technical Report TR2012-716 (2012)
26. Hallam-Baker, P., Stradling, R.: DNS Certification Authority Authorization (CAA) Resource Record. Technical report, IETF RFC 6844 (2013)
27. Hoffman, P., Schlyter, J.: The DNS-Based Authentication of Named Entities (DANE) Transport Layer Security (TLS) Protocol: TLSA. Technical report, IETF RFC 6698 (2012)
28. Holz, R., Riedmaier, T., Kammenhuber, N., Carle, G.: X.509 forensics: detecting and localising the SSL/TLS men-in-the-middle. In: Foresti, S., Yung, M., Martinelli, F. (eds.) ESORICS 2012. LNCS, vol. 7459, pp. 217–234. Springer, Heidelberg (2012). https://doi.org/10.1007/978-3-642-33167-1_13
29. ICSI: The ICSI Certificate Notary (2011). https://notary.icsi.berkeley.edu/
30. Kasten, J., Wustrow, E., Halderman, J.A.: CAge: taming certificate authorities by inferring restricted scopes. In: Sadeghi, A.-R. (ed.) FC 2013. LNCS, vol. 7859, pp. 329–337. Springer, Heidelberg (2013). https://doi.org/10.1007/978-3-642-39884-1_28
31. Kim, T., Huang, L., Perrig, A., Jackson, C., Gligor, V.: Accountable key infrastructure (AKI): a proposal for a public-key validation infrastructure. In: 22nd International Conference on World Wide Web (WWW), pp. 679–690 (2013)
32. Langley, A.: Public Key Pinning, May 2011. https://www.imperialviolet.org/2011/05/04/pinning.html
33. Langley, A.: Further Improving Digital Certificate Security, December 2013. https://security.googleblog.com/2013/12/further-improving-digital-certificate.html
34. Laurie, B., Kasper, E.: Revocation Transparency (2012). http://sump2.links.org/files/RevocationTransparency.pdf
35. Laurie, B., Langley, A., Kasper, E., Google: Certificate Transparency. Technical report, IETF RFC 6962 (2014)
36. Lewison, K., Coralla, F.: Backing Rich Credentials with a Blockchain PKI (2016). http://pomcor.com/techreports/BlockchainPKI.pdf
37. Liu, Y., Tome, W., Zhang, L., Choffnes, D., et al.: An end-to-end measurement of certificate revocation in the web's PKI. In: 15th Internet Measurement Conference (IMC), pp. 183–196 (2015)
38. Marlinspike, M.: Convergence, September 2011. https://github.com/moxie0/Convergence
39. Marlinspike, M.: Trust Assertions for Certificate Keys. Technical report, IETF Internet-draft (2013)
40. Matsumoto, S., Reischuk, R.: IKP: turning a PKI around with decentralized automated incentives. In: 38th IEEE Symposium on Security and Privacy (S&P) (2017)

41. Melara, M., Blankstein, A., Bonneau, J., Felten, E., Freedman, M.: CONIKS: bringing key transparency to end users. In: 24th USENIX Conference on Security Symposium, pp. 383–398 (2015)
42. Micheloni, A., Fuchs, K., Herrmann, D., Federrath, H.: Laribus: privacy-preserving detection of fake SSL certificates with a social P2P notary network. In: 8th International Conference on Availability, Reliability and Security (ARES), pp. 1–10 (2013)
43. University of Michigan. Censys, April 2016. https://censys.io/
44. Microsoft: MS01-017: Erroneous VeriSign-Issued Digital Certificates Pose Spoofing Hazard, March 2001. https://technet.microsoft.com/library/security/ms01-017
45. Morton, B.: Public Announcements Concerning the Security Advisory, January 2013. https://www.entrust.com/turktrust-unauthorized-ca-certificates
46. Morton, B.: More Google Fraudulent Certificates, July 2014. https://www.entrust.com/google-fraudulent-certificates/
47. Muneeb, A., Jude, N., Ryan, S., Michael, J.: Blockstack: a global naming and storage system secured by blockchains. In: 2016 USENIX Annual Technical Conference, pp. 181–194 (2016)
48. Nakamoto, S.: Bitcoin: A Peer-to-Peer Electronic Cash System (2008). https://bitcoin.org/bitcoin.pdf
49. Namecoin Team: Namecoin (2011). https://www.namecoin.org/
50. PSYC: Certificate Patrol (2014). http://patrol.psyced.org/
51. Ryan, M.: Enhanced certificate transparency and end-to-end encrypted mail. In: 21st ISOC Network and Distributed System Security Symposium (NDSS) (2014)
52. Soghoian, C., Stamm, S.: Certified lies: detecting and defeating government interception attacks against SSL (Short Paper). In: Danezis, G. (ed.) FC 2011. LNCS, vol. 7035, pp. 250–259. Springer, Heidelberg (2012). https://doi.org/10.1007/978-3-642-27576-0_20
53. Sotirov, A., Stevens, M.: MD5 Considered Harmful Today, December 2008. http://www.win.tue.nl/hashclash/rogue-ca/
54. SSL Shopper: SSL Certificate for Mozilla.com Issued Without Validation, December 2008. https://www.sslshopper.com/article-ssl-certificate-for-mozilla.com-issued-without-validation.html
55. Start Commercial (StartCom) Limited: Critical Event Report, December 2008. https://blog.startcom.org/wp-content/uploads/2009/01/ciritical-event-report-12-20-2008.pdf
56. Szalachowski, P., Matsumoto, S., Perrig, A.: PoliCert: secure and flexible TLS certificate management. In: 21st ACM Conference on Computer and Communications Security (CCS), pp. 406–417 (2014)
57. Vandersloot, B., Amann, J., Bernhard, M., Durumeric, Z., et al.: Towards a complete view of the certificate ecosystem. In: 16th Internet Measurement Conference (IMC), pp. 543–549 (2016)
58. VASCO Data Security International Inc.: DigiNotar Reports Security Incident, August 2011. https://www.vasco.com/about-vasco/press/2011/news_diginotar_reports_security_incident.html
59. Wendlandt, D., Andersen, D., Perrig, A.: Perspectives: improving SSH-style host authentication with multi-path probing. In: 2008 USENIX Annual Technical Conference, pp. 321–334 (2008)
60. Wikipedia: Flame(malware), March 2017. https://en.wikipedia.org/wiki/Flame_(malware)

61. Wilson, K.: Distrusting New CNNIC Certificates, April 2015. https://blog.mozilla. org/security/2015/04/02/distrusting-new-cnnic-certificates/
62. Zusman, M.: Criminal Charges Are Not Pursued: Hacking PKI (2009). https:// defcon.org/images/defcon-17/dc-17-presentations/defcon-17-zusman-hacking_ pki.pdf

Advances in Secure Electronic Voting Schemes

A Verifiable Shuffle for the GSW Cryptosystem

Martin Strand$^{(\boxtimes)}$

Norwegian University of Science and Technology, Trondheim, Norway
martin.strand@gmail.com

Abstract. We provide the first verifiable shuffle specifically for fully homomorphic schemes. A verifiable shuffle is a way to ensure that if a node receives and sends encrypted lists, the content will be the same, even though no adversary can trace individual list items through the node. Shuffles are useful in e-voting, traffic routing and other applications.

We build our shuffle on the ideas and techniques of Groth's 2010 shuffle, but make necessary modifications for a less ideal setting where the randomness and ciphertexts admit no group structure.

The protocol relies heavily on the properties of the so-called gadget matrices, so we have included a detailed introduction to these.

Keywords: Verifiable shuffle · Fully homomorphic encryption · Post-quantum

1 Introduction

A verifiable shuffle is used to prove that two sets of ciphertexts will decrypt to the same values, but without revealing how the sets relate. Such shuffles are well-known for group homomorphic schemes, and are still being developed and improved. Today, shuffles are particularly useful in e-voting and mixnets, in order to make it hard to correlate the input and the output of a node.

Fully homomorphic encryption has also been suggested as a useful primitive for both e-voting [10] and private network routing. Complex voting systems in particular can take advantage of the features of fully homomorphic encryption, but the FHE toolbox is still missing a number of useful protocols. Recent development have brought shuffling for FHE within reach.

Our result starts from Groth's 2010 shuffle [11], which uses an idea from Neff [15]. A polynomial $(X-x_1)(X-x_2)\cdots(X-x_n)$ is obviously unchanged when the roots are permuted. One can then ask the prover to evaluate the polynomial at random points. The probability of two nonidentical polynomials evaluating to the same value at a random point is negligible. While later development have resulted in even more efficient protocols, Groth's 2010 approach has the advantage of simplicity and that there are few compromises: the protocol satisfies a standard soundness condition and it is honest-verifier zero knowledge. We return to the details in Sect. 2.

© International Financial Cryptography Association 2019
A. Zohar et al. (Eds.): FC 2018 Workshops, LNCS 10958, pp. 165–180, 2019.
https://doi.org/10.1007/978-3-662-58820-8_12

The polynomial mentioned above is hidden in a subprotocol which is used to prove correctness of a shuffle of known content. The subprotocol is completely independent of the encryption scheme, and uses only a homomorphic commitment scheme. It is important to note that the commitment scheme need only be homomorphic with respect to a single operation. We return to the selection of such schemes. The protocol is then completed by binding the secret data – which we want to prove the claim for – to the known content for which one can prove the relation.

Groth's protocol depends crucially on the fact that some group homomorphic schemes are homomorphic both with respect to the message and the randomness. For instance, the product of two ElGamal ciphertexts with messages m_1 and m_2 and randomness r_1 and r_2, will be a new ciphertext encrypting m_1m_2 using r_1+r_2 as randomness. Generally, a necessary requirement for the original shuffle is that the equation $\mathsf{Enc}(m_0 \oplus_\mathcal{M} m_1; r_0 \oplus_\mathcal{R} r_1) = \mathsf{Enc}(m_0; r_0) \oplus_\mathcal{C} \mathsf{Enc}(m_1; r_1)$. holds, where $\oplus_\mathcal{M}$, $\oplus_\mathcal{R}$ and $\oplus_\mathcal{C}$ are the algebraic operations used in the message, randomness and ciphertext groups respectively. Note that $r_1 \oplus r_2$ is an equally likely randomness as either r_1 or r_2.

The noise-based homomorphic schemes do not satisfy the above requirements, since the ciphertext spaces usually are far from being groups at all. The reason is the noise management; even sufficiently many additions will eventually make the ciphertext decrypt to the wrong value, there need not be an identity element, and associativity may not hold, especially for multiplication in combination with noise management techniques. In fact, the Gentry-Sahai-Waters scheme even exploits this property to minimise the noise growth [9].

Furthermore, the homomorphic property does in general not hold concurrently for the messages and the randomisers. It can, however, be possible to compute the noise after an operation for certain simple cases. We show that the abelian group requirement is not necessary, so that a variant of the original protocol is secure also for a noise-based homomorphic scheme.

The final issue is to take advantage of the quantum security of the lattice based encryption schemes, and then make the protocol future-proof. The secrecy requirements for verifiable shuffles is long-term, while soundness is only short-term. This allows us to achieve security against a potential future quantum adversary using a perfectly hiding commitment scheme, since the computational binding property is only necessary until the proof has been verified.

However, using a lattice based commitment scheme by Baum et al. [3], we can also clear the protocol completely of classic cryptography.

A Naive Approach. Recall the polynomial $(X - x_1)(X - x_2) \cdots (X - x_n)$, where the roots $x_1, x_2, \ldots, x_n$ are the secret data to be shuffled. Assume we have two sets of ciphertexts, say $\{E_i\}$ and $\{e_i\}$, and some secret permutation π

such that $\mathsf{Dec}(E_i) = \mathsf{Dec}(e_{\pi(i)})$. The straightforward approach to shuffling using fully homomorphic encryption is to compare the two polynomials

$$P_1(X) = (X - e_1)(X - e_2)\cdots(X - e_n)$$
$$P_2(X) = (X - E_1)(X - E_2)\cdots(X - E_n)$$

by requiring the prover to demonstrate that the ciphertext $P_2(e_i)$ for one or more i given by the verifier decrypts to 0. Such proofs exist [3,5], given that the prover has decryption capabilities. Also, it would be straightforward to verify this protocol using multilinear maps [7] with their zero-test abilities. However, at the time of writing, all multilinear map candidates are broken for this application [1]. Additionally, this computation would require a very *deep* circuit, i.e. high degree polynomials, which with today's FHE techniques is forbiddingly expensive.

Related Work. Independently, Costa, Martínez and Morillo [6] have published a shuffle for lattice based schemes. Their shuffle is based on an idea of Wikström using *permutation matrices*. Unfortunately, one cannot guarantee the secrecy of the shuffle due to lack of circuit privacy for their re-encryption procedure. They observe that the RLWE scheme is additively homomorphic, and suggest to re-encrypt by adding an encryption of 0. This idea is sound for group homomorphic schemes since the randomness is near-uniformly distributed over the group. With noise-based schemes, the randomness is typically a Gaussian, so decryption and a following analysis of the noise term can reveal extra information about the ciphertext. As a consequence, the permutation can leak from the ciphertexts regardless of the properties of the zero-knowledge protocol for which the authors provide a proof.

Our Contribution. Our main contribution is the first adaptation of a verifiable shuffle specifically for a FHE cryptosystem under the assumption of equal noise levels in the input ciphertexts. The efficiency is mostly affected by the inherent limitations of the cryptosystem. The assumption can if necessary be met using bootstrapping.

A second contribution is a detailed exposition of the properties of the gadget matrix, and it is our hope that it can be useful for others who need to work with the details of the GSW ciphertexts.

Outline. We have introduced the main ideas here in Sect. 1. The upcoming section will in turn describe the concepts we need to build our protocol, such as *gadget matrices*, the GSW cryptosystem, commitment schemes, zero-knowledge protocols, and Groth's original shuffle. Then, in Sect. 3, we describe our modifications and present the shuffle in full, including a proof of it being a zero-knowledge argument.

2   Preliminaries

This section introduces the concepts and technical terms needed in this paper to successfully use the Groth shuffle on GSW ciphertexts. Before we discuss the cryptosystem, we look at gadget matrices in detail.

Following the description of GSW, we will discuss commitment schemes, zero-knowledge proofs and Groth's verifiable shuffle protocol.

2.1   Gadget Matrices

Much of the notation will follow Alperin-Sheriff and Peikert [2]. Assume we work in a field $\mathbb{Z}_q = \mathbb{Z}/q\mathbb{Z}$, and let $\ell = \lceil \log_2 q \rceil$. One can then define the gadget vector $\boldsymbol{g} \in \mathbb{Z}_q^\ell$ as

$$\begin{pmatrix} 1 \\ 2 \\ 4 \\ \vdots \\ 2^{\ell-1} \end{pmatrix}$$

For any $a \in \mathbb{Z}_q$, it is clear that there exist many vectors $\boldsymbol{x} \in \mathbb{Z}_q^\ell$ such that $\langle \boldsymbol{g}, \boldsymbol{x} \rangle = a$. In particular, the vector $\boldsymbol{x}$ can be the binary decomposition of a, with all entries 0 or 1. The binary decomposition is the output of the function or algorithm denoted $\boldsymbol{g}_{\text{det}}^{-1}$.

Sometimes, we want a random preimage of $\boldsymbol{g}$ rather than the binary decomposition. Let $X = \{\boldsymbol{x} \mid \langle \boldsymbol{x}, \boldsymbol{g} \rangle = 0\}$, the set of all preimages of 0. Let $\boldsymbol{g}_{\text{rand}}^{-1}$ denote an algorithm that computes $\boldsymbol{g}_{\text{det}}^{-1}$ and samples a value $\boldsymbol{x}$ from X, typically from a Gaussian distribution with a prescribed radius, and outputs the sum $\boldsymbol{g}_{\text{det}}^{-1} + \boldsymbol{x}$.

From now on, we will use subscripts when it is necessary to distinguish between the two variants of the algorithm. If no subscript is given, then the discussion applies equally to both.

Next, we can expand the whole process to handle an n-dimensional vector $\boldsymbol{a}$ rather than a single value. Define the sparse matrix

$$G = \begin{pmatrix} 1 \dots 2^{\ell-1} & & & \\ & 1 \dots 2^{\ell-1} & & \\ & & \ddots & \\ & & & 1 \dots 2^{\ell-1} \end{pmatrix} \in \mathbb{Z}_q^{n \times n\ell}.$$

The matrix G is known as the *gadget matrix*, and the literature often express it in shorthand as $\boldsymbol{g}^T \otimes I_n$.

The map from $\mathbb{Z}_q^{n\ell}$ to $\mathbb{Z}_q^n$ induced by the matrix G is not invertible, but it is easy to find preimages. As with g, the binary decomposition of each coordinate is a preimage. In line with the literature, let G_{det}^{-1} denote this function. It is not linear, since the sum of two binary decompositions need not be all binary again. The output of G^{-1} is a right-inverse for the map G, and we can extend it to

$\mathbb{Z}_q^{n \times m}$ by applying G^{-1} column-wise to some $n \times m$ matrix A. As with $\boldsymbol{g}^{-1}$, we sometimes want random samples, and denote the resulting sampling algorithm by G_{rand}^{-1}. We use the notation $X \leftarrow G_{\text{rand}}^{-1}(A)$ when we want to indicate that we sample from some distribution imposed on the algorithm.

The following properties are straightforward to derive from the above construction.

Lemma 1. *Assume all operations are modulo some q, and let $A \in \mathbb{Z}_q^{n \times m}$ and $\lambda \in \mathbb{Z}_q$ be some scalar. Then,*

1. $G \cdot G^{-1}(I) = I = I_n \in \mathbb{Z}_q^{n \times n}$
2. $G \cdot G^{-1}(A) = A \in \mathbb{Z}_q^{n \times m}$
3. *In particular, $G \cdot G^{-1}(\lambda G) = \lambda G$*

We get a particularly nice structure when applying the G^{-1} algorithm on multiples of G.

Lemma 2. *Assume all operations are modulo some q, and let $\lambda \in \mathbb{Z}_q$ be some scalar with binary decomposition $\sum_{i=0}^{\ell-1} \lambda_i 2^i$. Then*

$$
G_{\text{det}}^{-1}(\lambda G) = \begin{pmatrix} \Lambda & & & \\ & \Lambda & & \\ & & \ddots & \\ & & & \Lambda \end{pmatrix} \in \mathbb{Z}_q^{n\ell \times n\ell}
$$

where

$$
\Lambda = \begin{pmatrix} \lambda_0 & \lambda_{\ell-1} & \cdots & \lambda_1 \\ \lambda_1 & \lambda_0 & \cdots & \lambda_2 \\ \vdots & \vdots & \ddots & \vdots \\ \lambda_{\ell-1} & \lambda_{\ell-2} & \cdots & \lambda_0 \end{pmatrix} \in \mathbb{Z}_q^{\ell \times \ell}
$$

In particular, $G_{\text{det}}^{-1}(G)$ is the $n\ell \times n\ell$ identity matrix.

The pattern comes from the fact that multiplying by 2 corresponds with one-step shifts in the binary expression of a number.

One can view $G_{\text{det}}^{-1}(\lambda G)$ as a representation of λ, and consider all representations as equivalent (modulo the kernel of G). Then the G^{-1} algorithm is homomorphic on equivalence classes, which is crucial for the GSW cryptosystem. Recall that linear mappings can be represented by matrices. Consider the mapping $G : \mathbb{Z}_q^{n\ell} \to \mathbb{Z}_q^n$ given by $\boldsymbol{x} \mapsto G\boldsymbol{x}$. This mapping have several right-inverses $H : \mathbb{Z}_q^n \to \mathbb{Z}_q^{n\ell}$ such that

$$
(G \circ H)(\boldsymbol{x}) = GH\boldsymbol{x} = \boldsymbol{x},
$$

so $G \circ H = \text{id}_{\mathbb{Z}_q^n}$. Fix G^{-1} as one specific such right-inverse. Then, for all H,

$$
G^{-1}(\boldsymbol{x}) - H(\boldsymbol{x}) \in \ker G.
$$

As explained above, we can expand the map G to $\mathbb{Z}_q^{n\ell \times m} \to \mathbb{Z}_q^{n \times m}$, and we can expand the right-inverses as well. By the above relation, for each H we then get

$$G^{-1}(A) = HA + B_A, \qquad G(B_A) = 0,$$

and so for scalars $a, b \in \mathbb{Z}_q$, we have

$$
\begin{aligned}
G^{-1}(aG)G^{-1}(bG) &= (aHG + B_a)(bHG + B_b) \\
&= ab(HGHG + b^{-1}HGB_b + a^{-1}B_aHG + (ab)^{-1}B_aB_b) \\
&= ab(HIG + b^{-1}H \cdot 0 + a^{-1}B_aHG + (ab)^{-1}B_aB_b) \\
&= abHG + B' \qquad \text{(with } GB' = 0\text{)} \\
&= G^{-1}(abG) + B' - B_{ab}.
\end{aligned}
$$

As a consequence, $G^{-1}(aG)G^{-1}(bG)$ and $G^{-1}(abG)$ can be said to encode the same scalar ab, but with a difference which lies in the kernel of G. A similar computation holds for the sum $G^{-1}(aG) + G^{-1}(bG)$.

We can illustrate this with a toy example. Let $q = 7, \ell = 3$ and $n = 3$. Then

$$
G = \begin{pmatrix} 1\,2\,4\,0\,0\,0\,0\,0\,0 \\ 0\,0\,0\,1\,2\,4\,0\,0\,0 \\ 0\,0\,0\,0\,0\,0\,1\,2\,4 \end{pmatrix}.
$$

Consider $G_{\det}^{-1}(5G)$ and $G_{\det}^{-1}(3G)$, which will have blocks $\left[\begin{smallmatrix} 1&1&0 \\ 0&1&1 \\ 1&0&1 \end{smallmatrix}\right]$ and $\left[\begin{smallmatrix} 1&0&1 \\ 1&1&0 \\ 0&1&1 \end{smallmatrix}\right]$. Both their sum and product will be $\left[\begin{smallmatrix} 2&1&1 \\ 1&2&1 \\ 1&1&2 \end{smallmatrix}\right]$ which contains a 2, something we cannot avoid since we are computing modulo 7. However, a new encoding of $5 \cdot 3 \equiv 5 + 3 \equiv 1 \pmod 7$ is just the identity matrix.

This is an effect one has to take into account when computing. Still, it is certainly so that the different matrices represent the same value. In particular,

$$
\begin{pmatrix} 2\,1\,1 \\ 1\,2\,1 \\ 1\,1\,2 \end{pmatrix} = \begin{pmatrix} 1\,0\,0 \\ 0\,1\,0 \\ 0\,0\,1 \end{pmatrix} + \begin{pmatrix} 1\,1\,1 \\ 1\,1\,1 \\ 1\,1\,1 \end{pmatrix},
$$

and note that

$$
(1\,2\,4) \cdot \begin{pmatrix} 1\,1\,1 \\ 1\,1\,1 \\ 1\,1\,1 \end{pmatrix} \equiv (0\,0\,0) \pmod 7.
$$

In other words, $(1, 1, 1)$ is in the kernel of G.

2.2 The GSW Cryptosystem and Circuit Privacy

The 2013 cryptosystem by Gentry, Sahai and Waters (GSW) [9] is based on hiding the message as an eigenvalue of the ciphertext. The private key is an *approximate eigenvector*. For simplicity, we will use the symmetric formulation by Alperin-Sheriff and Peikert [2], and at the end explain how to make the scheme public key. Let n be an integer, let q be a modulus and $\ell = \lceil \log_2 q \rceil$. Finally, let χ be a subgaussian distribution (Gaussian with very small tails) over $\mathbb{Z}$.

Key generation Let $\bar{s} \leftarrow \chi^{n-1}$ coordinate-wise, and output $s = (\bar{s}, 1)$ as the private key.

Encryption To encrypt a message $\mu \in \{0, 1\}$, choose a random matrix $\bar{C}$ from $\mathbb{Z}_q^{(n-1) \times m}$, where $m = n\ell$, an error vector $e \leftarrow \chi^m$ and set $b^T = e^T - \bar{s}^T \bar{C}$ (mod q). Let

$$C = \begin{pmatrix} \bar{C} \\ b^T \end{pmatrix} + \mu G.$$

Decryption Given s and C, let c be the penultimate column of C, and output 0 if $\langle s, c \rangle$ (mod q) is closer to 0 than 2^{l-2}. Otherwise, output 1[1].

Addition Add the matrices C_1 and C_2.

Multiplication Define $C_1 \odot C_2$ as $C_1 \cdot G^{-1}(C_2)$.

The cryptosystem is usually only defined for a binary plaintext space, but the definition can be modified even up to the large space $\mathbb{Z}_q$ by modifying the decryption algorithm to extract bits from more columns than the penultimate, and then building the message from the bits. However, this has a strong negative impact on the noise behaviour. When two ciphertexts encrypting binary messages are multiplied, the noise grows far less than with previous FHE cryptosystems. The growth is a function of the encrypted value of the first ciphertext, so larger plaintext spaces can potentially also give worse noise problems. Nonetheless, we will have to assume a large message space for our application, in the order of 160–180 bits, in order to facilitate the scalar multiplications we will perform. This fact is the main drawback of our work.

The original GSW scheme does not achieve *circuit privacy*. Informally, this property guarantees that nobody are able to deduce which circuit output a given ciphertext. Gentry [8] defined the notion by requiring that an encryption of an evaluation of a circuit should be indistinguishable from an encryption of evaluation of the circuit on encrypted data. In other words, evaluate-then-encrypt should be the same as encrypt-then-evaluate. Bourse et al. [4] provide a simulation based definition – capturing mostly the same intuition – and prove that the GSW cryptosystem is circuit private if the multiplication algorithm is slightly modified and all input ciphertexts have low noise from the same distribution. The definitions only differ in that Bourse et al. allow the length of the circuit to leak.

Alperin-Sheriff and Peikert [2] proposed to use the G_{rand}^{-1} algorithm instead of G_{det}^{-1} for performance reasons. Bourse et al. go one step further, and also add a matrix which is 0 everywhere except for the bottom row, which constitutes *gaussian shift* on the ciphertext,

$$C_1 \odot C_2 = C_1 G_{\text{rand}}^{-1}(C_2) + \begin{pmatrix} 0 \\ y^T \end{pmatrix},$$

---

[1] See Alperin-Sheriff and Peikert [2] for a justification of this algorithm.

where C_1 and C_2 are ciphertexts and y is a vector drawn from χ^m. In particular, one can scale C_1 by α by letting $C_2 = \alpha G$. Also note that $\begin{pmatrix} 0 \\ y^T \end{pmatrix}$ is a valid encryption of 0. We will use this fact in the upcoming protocol.

Finally, we note that the GSW scheme can be made public-key by publishing the above $\begin{pmatrix} \bar{C} \\ b^T \end{pmatrix}$ as, say, $\hat{A}$ and define encryption as

$$C \leftarrow \hat{A}R + \mu G,$$

where R is a random matrix with entries in $\{-1, 0, 1\}$.

2.3   Commitment Schemes

A commitment scheme is an important tool in protocols. The concept allows a player to make a binding promise to use certain values, but without revealing them at the time of the promise. The commitment can later be verified when the committer reveals the opening information. Formally, a commitment scheme consists of three algorithms:

KeyGen On input 1^ℓ, output a public key pk
Commit On input (pk, m, r), return c.
Verify On input (pk, m, r, c), return accept if c is a valid commitment to m, otherwise reject.

We say that (m, r) is an opening of c. The key material will normally be omitted to simplify notation.

Any public key cryptosystem can be turned into a commitment scheme which is unconditionally binding. Pedersen commitments [16] is an example of a scheme that is unconditionally hiding and where binding depends on the discrete logarithm problem being hard. A particularly nice property about the Pedersen scheme is that it is homomorphic; we have $\mathsf{Commit}(m_1, r_1) \cdot \mathsf{Commit}(m_2, r_2) = \mathsf{Commit}(m_1 + m_2, r_1 + r_2)$.

A commitment scheme must satisfy two security properties. The scheme must be *hiding*, which means that a commitment to some message m_1 is indistinguishable from a commitment to some other message m_2. Next, it must be *binding*, which means that it is hard to find two openings for distinct messages for a single commitment. At most one of these properties may hold unconditionally, but both may hold only computationally.

Lately, Baum et al. [3] proposed a new additively homomorphic commitment scheme based on the Ring-SIS problem. This is conjectured to be safe also against quantum computers. Recall from the introduction that also classical commitment schemes that are unconditionally hiding and computationally binding will remain secure and usable until the adversary has quantum computers readily available, since the binding property is only needed during the protocol execution to provide soundness.

2.4   Zero-Knowledge Protocols

Zero-knowledge protocols capture the intuition of being able to convince someone else about the validity of some claim, but without revealing any other information.

Definition 1. *Let R be a relation, and let $(x, w) \in R$. An* honest-verifier zero-knowledge *protocol $(\mathcal{P}, \mathcal{V})$ for R is a two-party game between a prover $\mathcal{P}$ on input (x, w) and a verifier $\mathcal{V}$ on input x, satisfying*

Completeness *Whenever $(x, w) \in R$, $\mathcal{V}$ accepts.*
Soundness *If $(x, w) \notin R$, then for any $\mathcal{P}^*$, $\mathcal{V}$ will only accept with negligible probability.*
Honest-verifier zero knowledge (HVZK) *There exists a simulator $\mathcal{M}$ running in expected polynomial time on input x such that the output is indistinguishable from the transcripts of $(\mathcal{P}, \mathcal{V})$ run with (x, w) as input to $\mathcal{P}$.*

The w is called a witness *for the relation.*

If the prover is only given bounded computationally resources, the protocol is usually called an *argument*, otherwise we call it a *proof*. The zero-knowledge property can be varied by requiring the indistinguishability to hold computationally, statistically or unconditionally.

The simulator can choose all messages arbitrarily. A proof or argument is *special* honest-verifier zero knowledge (SHVZK) if the output of the simulator is indistinguishable from a real transcript if it has to use truly random messages as simulated challenges from the verifier (as opposed to being able to choose such challenges arbitrarily).

To guarantee that a zero-knowledge protocol can be used as a subprotocol in a larger context, Lindell [12] introduced the notion of witness-extended emulation, which loosely speaking requires that there exists a machine that on basis of sufficiently many rounds of the protocol (reusing the prover's commitments) is able to both output a valid witness for the relation as well as a valid simulated transcript. Our use of this property is limited to noting that the shuffle of known content satisfies it in order for us to be able to use it for our protocol, so we refer to the original source for details.

2.5   Groth's Shuffle

In 2010, following up on Neff's idea [15] of proving the validity of a shuffle by using the fact that a polynomial $\prod(X - x_i)$ is stable under permutation of the roots x_i, Groth presented an efficient, yet conceptually simple shuffle [11]. The idea is two-fold. First, one uses the polynomial idea to prove that some c is a commitment to a permutation of messages $m_1, \ldots, m_n$. The values are known by the verifier, but the permutation remains hidden. Next, one binds the secret data to the known data, and proves that the same permutation is still used.

It is important to note that the shuffle of known content is independent of the encryption scheme employed in the main protocol, and only requires a group homomorphic commitment scheme. Later, we can therefore reuse the shuffle of known content completely, and rely on the following properties [11, Theorem 1].

- The shuffle satisfies special honest-verifier zero knowledge with witness-extended emulation.
- If the commitment scheme is statistically hiding we get statistical HVZK.
- If the commitment scheme is unconditionally binding we get unconditional soundness.

Recall that the property of witness-extended emulation guarantees that we can use the SKC protocol as a building block of the full shuffle.

While the SKC protocol only uses the commitment scheme, the outer protocol depends heavily on the encryption scheme, in particular rerandomisation and cancellation of original randomness. Both of these features are less straightforward in FHE schemes than in classical group homomorphic schemes, and call for some modifications to the original protocol.

Remark 1. Groth introduces two security parameters, ℓ_e and ℓ_s, subject to the conditions that

- ℓ_e must be sufficiently large to make it hard to break soundness, i.e. it must be hard to predict a challenge of length ℓ_e,
- For any a sampled from the uniform distribution on $[0, 2^{\ell_e}] \cap \mathbb{Z}$, d and $a + d$, must be statistically indistinguishable whenever d is sampled from the uniform distribution on $[0, 2^{\ell_e + \ell_s}] \cap \mathbb{Z}$, and
- If the commitment space has message space $\mathbb{Z}_q^n$, then $2^{\ell_e + \ell_s} \leq q$.

The second bullet point is to avoid leakage of information whenever $a + d < 2^{\ell_e}$ or $2^{\ell_e + \ell_s} \leq a + d$. Notice that we can achieve the same result with smaller parameters if we employ rejection sampling [13,14]. The probability of $2^{\ell_e} \leq a + d \leq 2^{\ell_e + \ell_s}$ is approximately $1 - \frac{1}{2^{\ell_s}} - \frac{1}{2^{\ell_s + \ell_e}}$.

The third bullet point is to avoid overflow that would require modular reductions. However, Groth notes that "[w]hen the cryptosystem has a message space where $m^q = 1$ for all messages, this requirement can be waived".

Concretely, Groth suggests $\ell_e = \ell_s = 80$ for the interactive variant, and $\ell_e = 160$ and $\ell_s = 20$ if the protocol is made non-interactive using the Fiat-Shamir heuristic and rejection sampling. We will keep the same parameters for our protocol.

3   Verifiable Shuffle for GSW

Now we can combine the tools and ideas above to get a verifiable shuffle for GSW ciphertexts. Let n denote the number of ciphertexts, and recall that ℓ_e and ℓ_s denote security parameters for the zero-knowledge protocol. We now briefly describe the changes that must be made to Groth's shuffle.

The first part of a shuffle is to permute and rerandomise the ciphertexts. Given an ElGamal ciphertext $(a = g^r, b = \mu h^r)$, a new ciphertext will typically look like $(ag^{r'}, bh^{r'})$, and one can easily prove that it is hard to find the correct correspondence between the old and new set as long as r' is random. The fundamental reason is that the randomness of ElGamal forms a group, and that any rerandomisation is indistinguishable from a fresh encryption.

This is not the case for FHE in general and GSW in particular. The randomness is not bounded, and the Eval algorithm will result in a new ciphertext with randomness being a function of both the messages and the randomness of the inputs. We need to employ Bourse et al.'s technique for circuit privacy. Let the old and new ciphertexts be denoted by $\{e_i\}$ and $\{E_i\}$, and the permutation by π.

Ideally, the shuffling circuit should have all old ciphertexts and the permutation as input, such that all old ciphertexts contribute to each new ciphertext,

$$E_i = \sum_{j=1}^{n} e_{\pi(i)} G_{\text{rand}}^{-1}(\delta_{\pi(i),j}G) + \begin{pmatrix} 0 \\ y_i^T \end{pmatrix}$$

where $\delta_{a,b}$ is 1 if $a = b$ and 0 otherwise, and y is some vector chosen by the circuit privacy algorithm [4].

However, this is causing problems for achieving the completeness property of the protocol, so we have opted for a simpler version. For each i, sample $X_i \leftarrow G_{\text{rand}}^{-1}(G)$, and let

$$E_i = e_{\pi(i)} X_i + \begin{pmatrix} 0 \\ y_i^T \end{pmatrix}$$

which is sufficient under the condition that all $\{e_i\}$ have the same noise level and equal-length decryptions. Note that one can only measure the noise by using the decryption key.[2] The order is not coincidental. The shuffling circuit is essentially included in X_i, and this order of multiplication hides it [4]. If necessary, enforce the noise-level condition by bootstrapping the ciphertexts before shuffling them. Bootstrapping is an deterministic operation which only requires the public key.

The original protocol was expressed using multiplications. Since we are using the additive structure of the GSW scheme, we switch from multiplications and exponentiations to additions and scalar multiplications. This is in itself a favourable move, as the efficiency of the original protocol was measured in exponentiations, while additions and scalar multiplications are almost for free in FHE schemes.

Finally, one of the verifications step in the original protocol involved creating a ciphertext using randomness provided by the prover. Since we lack the nice structure on the randomness in the GSW cryptosystem, we need to provide complete ciphertexts instead of just randomness. This requires us to convince the verifier that the ciphertext is "innocent", in the sense that it doesn't encrypt a value that allows the prover to cheat. Fortunately, we can observe that the

---

[2] An anonymous reviewer pointed out that it is important to ensure that a malicious mix server cannot mark the ciphertexts, typically by using randomness of different size, resulting in more noise. This may lead to a DoS attack unless one employ bootstrapping, but should not compromise secrecy since only the decryption service can measure noise.

ciphertext in question will be all zeros except for the bottom row, which guarantees that it can only encrypt 0.

The complete protocol follows.

Precomputation. Start with fresh ciphertexts $\{e_i\}$ with equal noise levels. Bootstrap each ciphertext to achieve near-freshness if necessary. Shuffle using a random permutation π and re-encrypt to get new ciphertexts $\{E_i\}$.

Common Input. Fresh ciphertexts $\{e_i\}$ and shuffled ciphertexts $\{E_i\}$.

Private input to $\mathcal{P}$. Permutation π, matrices $X_i \leftarrow G_{\text{rand}}^{-1}(G)$ and vectors $\boldsymbol{y}$ such that for each i,

$$E_i = e_{\pi(i)}X_i + \begin{pmatrix} 0 \\ \boldsymbol{y}_i^T \end{pmatrix}$$

Protocol

$\mathcal{P}1$ Select randomness r and r_d for the commitment scheme, and select n random values d_i of length $\ell_e + \ell_s$.
Let

$$c \leftarrow \mathsf{Commit}(\pi(1), \ldots, \pi(n); r)$$
$$c_d \leftarrow \mathsf{Commit}(-d_1, \ldots, -d_n; r_d).$$

Set $D_i \leftarrow G_{\text{rand}}^{-1}(d_iG)$, $\boldsymbol{y}_d \leftarrow \chi_{\mathbb{Z}^m}$ and $E_d \leftarrow \sum_{i=1}^{n} E_i D_i + \begin{pmatrix} 0 \\ \boldsymbol{y}_d^T \end{pmatrix}$
Send c, c_d and E_d to the verifier.
$\mathcal{V}1$ Return a set of random numbers $\{t_i\}$ of length ℓ_e.
$\mathcal{P}2$ Set $f_i \leftarrow t_{\pi(i)} + d_i$, compute X_i' such that

$$X_{\pi(i)}' = G_{\det}^{-1}(t_{\pi(i)}G) - X_iG_{\det}^{-1}(f_iG) + X_iD_i,$$

and set $Z = \sum_{i=1}^{n} \left(\begin{pmatrix} 0 \\ \boldsymbol{y}_i^T \end{pmatrix} G_{\det}^{-1}(f_iG) - \begin{pmatrix} 0 \\ \boldsymbol{y}_i^T \end{pmatrix} D_i \right) - \begin{pmatrix} 0 \\ \boldsymbol{y}_d^T \end{pmatrix}$. Cancel if not $2^{\ell_e} \leq f_i \leq 2^{\ell_e + \ell_s}$ for all i.
Send $\{f_i\}, \{X_i'\}, Z$ to the verifier.
$\mathcal{P}-\mathcal{V}$ Run the shuffle of known content to prove that

$$c^\lambda c_d \mathsf{Commit}(f_1, \ldots, f_n) = \mathsf{Commit}(\lambda\pi(1) + t_{\pi(1)}, \ldots, \lambda\pi(n) + t_{\pi(n)}),$$

where λ is a challenge from the verifier.
$\mathcal{V}2$ Verify the following
  - The elements c and c_d are in the commitment space
  - For all i, $2^{\ell_e} \leq f_i \leq 2^{\ell_e + \ell_s}$
  - $GX_i' = 0$ for all i
  - The shuffle of known content
  - The matrix Z is of the form $\begin{pmatrix} 0 \\ \boldsymbol{y}^T \end{pmatrix}$
  - $\sum_{i=1}^{n} E_iG_{\det}^{-1}(f_iG) - \sum_{i=1}^{n} e_i(G_{\det}^{-1}(t_i) - X_i') - E_d = Z$

Theorem 1. *Assume that $\{e_i\}$ is a set of fresh ciphertexts. Then the above protocol is a special honest-verifier zero-knowledge argument for correctness of a shuffle of fully homomorphic ciphertexts. If the commitment scheme is statistically binding, then the scheme is an SHVZK proof of a shuffle.*

Proof. Completeness

Recall from Remark 1 that the probability of $\mathcal{P}$ aborting is $\frac{1}{2^{\ell_s}} + \frac{1}{2^{\ell_e + \ell_s}}$, which can be made arbitrarily small with a suitable choice of ℓ_s.

We need to check two of the verification equations, the rest is straightforward. Note that X_i comes from the G^{-1} algorithm and encodes a 1. By the discussion in Sect. 2.1, one can see that $X'_{\pi(i)}$ must encode $-f_i + t_{\pi(i)} + d_i = 0$ for all i, hence $GX'_i = 0$, all i.

Next, we verify that $\sum_{i=1}^{n} E_i G_{\det}^{-1}(f_i G) - \sum_{i=1}^{n} e_i (G_{\det}^{-1}(t_i) - X'_i) - E_d = Z$. This is a tedious, but uncomplicated computation.

Soundness

We need to prove that there exists a permutation π, such that $\mathsf{Dec}(e_{\pi(i)}) = \mathsf{Dec}(E_i)$ for all $1 \leq i \leq n$. We can extract the permutation using rewinding, but we will not extract the matrices X_i used to rerandomise the ciphertexts (although we can prove that they must exist, and have been generated in an honest way).

Run the protocol $(\mathcal{P}^*, \mathcal{V})$ until the prover outputs a transcript. Due to the rejection sampling, the prover may try several times. If the verifier would reject the transcript, we output $\bot$. Following the exact same argument as in Groth's original proof, we can extract π and $\{-d_i\}$ using two valid transcripts [11, p. 562].

Because of the commitment we now know that $f_i = t_{\pi(i)} + d_i$, and since $GX'_i = 0$, we know that $\mathsf{Dec}(X'_i) = 0$. Also, we know that $\mathsf{Dec}(Z) = 0$. Recall that we scale a ciphertext C by computing $CG^{-1}(\lambda G)$, hence if we apply the decryption function to

$$\sum_{i=1}^{n} E_i G_{\det}^{-1}(f_i G) - \sum_{i=1}^{n} e_i (G_{\det}^{-1}(t_i) - X'_i) - E_d = Z,$$

we get

$$\sum_{i=1}^{n} f_i \mathsf{Dec}(E_i) - \sum_{i=1}^{n} (t_i + 0)\mathsf{Dec}(e_i) - \mathsf{Dec}(E_d)$$

$$= \sum_{i=1}^{n} t_i \mathsf{Dec}(E_{\pi^{-1}(i)}) + \sum_{i=1}^{n} d_i \mathsf{Dec}(E_i) - \sum_{i=1}^{n} t_i \mathsf{Dec}(e_i) - \mathsf{Dec}(E_d)$$

$$= \sum_{i=1}^{n} t_i (\mathsf{Dec}(E_{\pi^{-1}(i)}) - \mathsf{Dec}(e_i)) + \sum_{i=1}^{n} d_i \mathsf{Dec}(E_i) - \mathsf{Dec}(E_d)$$

$$= \mathsf{Dec}(Z) = 0.$$

Since only one sum depends on $\{t_i\}$, both sums must be 0 individually. Furthermore, since each t_i is unpredictable, each summand must be 0. Hence, $\mathsf{Dec}(E_{\pi^{-1}(i)}) = \mathsf{Dec}(e_i)$, which we wanted to prove.

Note that we can apply the decryption function without actually being able to compute it for unknown ciphertexts.

Special Honest-Verifier Zero Knowledge

Let π_0 and π_1 be two permutations, and let C_0 and C_1 be the corresponding shuffle circuits. By circuit privacy, the adversary cannot decide whether C_0 or C_1 was used to generate $\{E_i\}$ from $\{e_i\}$. Hence, the precomputation step does not leak any information.

To prove that the shuffle itself is HVZK given the challenges, we construct a simulator whose output will be indistinguishable from a real protocol transcript. We provide the simulator through a hybrid argument.

Sim I Simulate the shuffle of known content, and select c and c_d as random commitments.

It follows from the properties of the shuffle of known content that Sim I is indistinguishable from a real transcript.

Sim II Construct a random Z from the same distribution as the original. The distribution is hard to give explicitly, but does not depend on secret data, so it can be simulated by choosing the fundamental terms of the sum independently, and adding. Likewise, choose $\{X_i'\}$ by choosing $\{(\bar{X}_i, \bar{d}_i)\}$ under the same distributions as the prover would, and some permutation $\bar{\pi}$. Compute $\{X_i'\}$ by the equation in $\mathcal{P}2$, such that $GX_i' = 0$ for all i. Choose $\{f_i\}$ from the sum of the uniform distributions over $[0, 2^{\ell_e}] \cap \mathbb{Z}$ and $[0, 2^{\ell_e+\ell_s}] \cap \mathbb{Z}$ under the constraint that $2^{\ell_e} \leq f_i \leq 2^{\ell_e+\ell_s}$. Then choose E_d to fit.

The simulated values for Z, $\{X_i'\}$ and $\{f_i\}$ have the same distribution since they are computed from the same formulas as the original, but using new (but identically distributed) random values instead of X_i and π. Then E_d becomes a valid ciphertext by the homomorphic property of GSW. Circuit privacy makes a simulated E_d indistinguishable from a real E_d, and the IND-CPA property of the cryptosystem will finally provide computational SHVZK.

4 Further Work

We have presented a verifiable shuffle for fully homomorphic schemes. Shuffling techniques have evolved further since the protocol we have chosen to forge from, and we believe it would be interesting to see adaptions of newer shuffles.

Furthermore, Groth's original shuffle can be used with a large family of group homomorphic encryption schemes. The result in this paper can only use the GSW scheme, due to the existence of the efficient and computationally simple circuit privacy technique. However, one should pick one's scheme based on what the application needs, so the shuffling primitive should be available for more schemes. This requires more research on techniques for circuit privacy.

Finally, it would be interesting to see an implementation of verifiable shuffling for FHE schemes, coupled with a real-life application. Only then will one be able to see if the parameters and the runtime of the proof will be acceptable. For instance, we predict that the scheme will be unsuitable for applications with many shuffles, such as onion routing. However, for elections, where one can spend minutes or even hours on the process, this protocol may already be mature.

Acknowledgements. The author wishes to thank Jens Groth for his useful comments to an early version of this manuscript, as well as to the anonymous reviewers.

References

1. Albrecht, M., Davidson, A.: Are graded encoding scheme broken yet? (2017). http://malb.io/are-graded-encoding-schemes-broken-yet.html. Accessed 30 Aug 2017
2. Alperin-Sheriff, J., Peikert, C.: Faster bootstrapping with polynomial error. In: Garay, J.A., Gennaro, R. (eds.) CRYPTO 2014. LNCS, vol. 8616, pp. 297–314. Springer, Heidelberg (2014). https://doi.org/10.1007/978-3-662-44371-2_17
3. Baum, C., Damgård, I., Oechsner, S., Peikert, C.: Efficient commitments and zero-knowledge protocols from ring-SIS with applications to lattice-based threshold cryptosystems. Cryptology ePrint Archive, Report 2016/997 (2016). http://eprint.iacr.org/2016/997
4. Bourse, F., Del Pino, R., Minelli, M., Wee, H.: FHE circuit privacy almost for free. In: Robshaw, M., Katz, J. (eds.) CRYPTO 2016. LNCS, vol. 9815, pp. 62–89. Springer, Heidelberg (2016). https://doi.org/10.1007/978-3-662-53008-5_3
5. Carr, C., Costache, A., Davies, G.T., Gjøsteen, K., Strand, M.: Zero-knowledge proof of decryption for FHE ciphertexts (2017). Manuscript
6. Costa, N., Martínez, R., Morillo, P.: Proof of a shuffle for lattice-based cryptography (full version). Cryptology ePrint Archive, Report 2017/900, 2017. http://eprint.iacr.org/2017/900
7. Garg, S., Gentry, C., Halevi, S.: Candidate multilinear maps from ideal lattices. In: Johansson, T., Nguyen, P.Q. (eds.) EUROCRYPT 2013. LNCS, vol. 7881, pp. 1–17. Springer, Heidelberg (2013). https://doi.org/10.1007/978-3-642-38348-9_1
8. Gentry, C.: A fully homomorphic encryption scheme. Ph.D. thesis, Stanford University (2009). crypto.stanford.edu/craig
9. Gentry, C., Sahai, A., Waters, B.: Homomorphic encryption from learning with errors: conceptually-simpler, asymptotically-faster, attribute-based. In: Canetti, R., Garay, J.A. (eds.) CRYPTO 2013. LNCS, vol. 8042, pp. 75–92. Springer, Heidelberg (2013). https://doi.org/10.1007/978-3-642-40041-4_5
10. Gjøsteen, K., Strand, M.: A roadmap to fully homomorphic elections: stronger security, better verifiability. In: Brenner, M., et al. (eds.) FC 2017. LNCS, vol. 10323, pp. 404–418. Springer, Cham (2017). https://doi.org/10.1007/978-3-319-70278-0_25
11. Groth, J.: A verifiable secret shuffle of homomorphic encryptions. J. Cryptology **23**(4), 546–579 (2010)
12. Lindell, Y.: Parallel coin-tossing and constant-round secure two-party computation. J. Cryptology **16**(3), 143–184 (2003)

13. Lyubashevsky, V.: Lattice-based identification schemes secure under active attacks. In: Cramer, R. (ed.) PKC 2008. LNCS, vol. 4939, pp. 162–179. Springer, Heidelberg (2008). https://doi.org/10.1007/978-3-540-78440-1_10

14. Lyubashevsky, V.: Fiat-Shamir with aborts: applications to lattice and factoring-based signatures. In: Matsui, M. (ed.) ASIACRYPT 2009. LNCS, vol. 5912, pp. 598–616. Springer, Heidelberg (2009). https://doi.org/10.1007/978-3-642-10366-7_35

15. Neff, C.A.: A verifiable secret shuffle and its application to e-voting. In: Reiter, M.K., Samarati, P., (eds.) CCS 2001, Proceedings of the 8th ACM Conference on Computer and Communications Security, pp. 116–125. ACM (2001)

16. Pedersen, T.P.: Non-interactive and information-theoretic secure verifiable secret sharing. In: Feigenbaum, J. (ed.) CRYPTO 1991. LNCS, vol. 576, pp. 129–140. Springer, Heidelberg (1992). https://doi.org/10.1007/3-540-46766-1_9

Outsourcing Modular Exponentiation in Cryptographic Web Applications

Pascal Mainini and Rolf Haenni$^{(\boxtimes)}$

Bern University of Applied Sciences, 2501 Biel/Bienne, Switzerland
{pascal.mainini,rolf.haenni}@bfh.ch

Abstract. Modern web applications using advanced cryptographic methods may need to calculate a large number of modular exponentiations. Performing such calculations in the web browser efficiently is a known problem. We propose a solution to this problem based on outsourcing the computational effort to untrusted exponentiation servers. We present several efficient outsourcing protocols for different settings and a practical implementation consisting of a JavaScript client library and a server application. Compared to browser-only computation, our solution improves the overall computation time by an order of magnitude.

1 Introduction

Due to the limited performance of interpreted JavaScript code, web browsers are relatively slow computational environments compared to high-performance servers running compiled native or pre-compiled VM code. With recent performance improvements of the most common JavaScript engines, this is no longer a real limitation for most modern web applications. However, exceptionally expensive client-side computations are required in applications of public-key cryptography. Usually, the most critical operation in such applications is modular exponentiation (modexp), i.e., the computation of $z = x^y \bmod n$ for given integer inputs x, y, and n of length 2048 bits or higher. While web browsers compute modexps efficiently to establish TLS connections to servers, JavaScript developers have no built-in access to such a primitive, not even using the recently standardized Web Cryptography API.[1] To allow the development of cryptographic code in JavaScript, several libraries provide an API for dealing with large integers and an implementation of the most important arithmetic operations. With the best libraries available today, computing a small number of modexps is possible in a modern web browser, but the performance is more than one order of magnitude inferior compared to native code.[2]

---

[1] The Web Cryptography API offers operations for Diffie-Hellman key exchanges and DSA signatures, but currently only elliptic curves are supported. Therefore, we do not see a way of exploiting this interface for computing modular exponentiations.

[2] We expect significant performance improvements in libraries making use of the recently introduced WebAssembly technology for web browsers.

© International Financial Cryptography Association 2019
A. Zohar et al. (Eds.): FC 2018 Workshops, LNCS 10958, pp. 181–195, 2019.
https://doi.org/10.1007/978-3-662-58820-8_13

If a large number of modexps needs to be computed in a cryptographic application, the limited performance of JavaScript leads to major usability problems. In such cases, calculating the modexps may take several minutes, which is not tolerated by most users. Examples of such applications exist in the context of cryptographic voting protocols. In [5,6], for example, the web client used for vote casting requires up to $2k$ modexps in a k-out-of-n election. In parliamentary elections, where k represents the number of seats and n the number of candidates, it can happen that several hundred modexps need to be computed in the web browser for these protocols. The problem gets even worse in advanced voting protocols with extended security properties. For instance, in the protocol presented in [9], depending on the size of the electorate and the chosen security parameters, several thousand modexps may be required for ensuring everlasting privacy while casting a vote. Cases like this cannot be handled in reasonable time by JavaScript engines in current web browsers.

To solve this problem, we propose to outsource modexp computations to external *exponentiation servers*. Note that modexp computations in cryptographic applications often involve secret values such as private keys or encryption randomizations. Therefore, the main challenge of this approach is to ensure that the input parameters—the base x, the exponent y, or both x and y—and the output parameter z remain secret, even if exponentiation servers are not fully trustworthy (the modulus n is usually a public parameter). Secret parameters must therefore be cryptographically blinded before sending them out. Another challenge is to ensure the correctness of the results in the presence of servers that may act maliciously, or at least to detect such attacks with adequate probability. Client-side algorithms for dealing with these challenges must do so without falling back on expensive operations.

A very different, but more common approach to speed up expensive cryptographic computations on limited devices is working with elliptic curves. For providing equivalent security, point multiplications on such curves are significantly faster than exponentiations in modular groups. The main problem with elliptic curves in voting protocols such as the ones mentioned above is the difficulty of encoding complex voting options as curve points (while preserving the encryption homomorphism). In [5,6], for example, voting options are encoded as a product of prime numbers. Using modular groups, such products can be efficiently aggregated under encryption and decoded after decryption. We are not aware of an equivalent encoding for elliptic curves.

1.1 Related Work

There is a large amount of literature about outsourcing modular exponentiations. The approaches can be classified along two lines. The first is the number of required exponentiation servers. There are approaches for one, two, or four servers. In the two-server and four-server cases, it is assumed that the servers do not collude and that they can be reached over confidential channels. No such assumptions exist in the one-server case. Server-side authentication is a requirement in all cases to ensure the origin of the server responses. The second classification criterion is the adversary model attributed to the exponentiation servers. The main differentiation is between semi-honest and malicious servers. In the semi-honest model, no particular measures need to be taken to ensure the correctness of the responses.

A comprehensive analysis and compilation of one-server protocols for semi-honest adversaries can be found in [3]. This document also contains proven optimality results for certain protocols in form of lower bounds for the total number of necessary modular multiplications. The main drawback of most one-server protocols is the assumption that random pairs $(r, g^r \bmod n)$ can be generated efficiently by the client, where g is a fixed value. This may be difficult to achieve in a web application. Some protocols also require a large number of modular multiplications on the client, which reduces the potential performance gain of the outsourcing process. Similar remarks hold for the protocols presented in [1,8], which consider the one-server case in the presence of malicious adversaries.

The main reference in the literature on two-server outsourcing protocols is the paper by Hohenberger and Lysyanskaya [7]. They introduced a property called β-checkability, which means that deviations from the protocol by malicious servers are detected by the client with probability β or greater. Some other authors proposed similar protocols with improved efficiency [2,12]. A very different two-server approach based on the subset-sum-problem has been proposed in [10]. For a more detailed overview of the available references and methods, we refer to the summary given in [11].

1.2   Contribution and Paper Overview

The contribution of this paper consist of three parts. In Sect. 2, we present outsourcing protocols for some of the most important settings. Except for the number of involved servers, our protocols are the most efficient ones in the literature, with only up to two client-side modular multiplications during the execution of the protocols. A detailed performance comparison is shown in Table 1.

The second contribution is the implementation of the outsourcing protocols from Sect. 2. To the best of our knowledge, such an implementation has not yet existed before. To enable the embedding of our implementation in a practical system, we provide a client library in JavaScript, which handles the secure communication with the servers and executes the outsourcing algorithms. The flexible architecture of this library enables the inclusion of further outsourcing algorithms from the literature. We also provide a server application in Java, which can be deployed on ordinary server infrastructure. Details of our implementation are given in Sect. 3.

The third contribution of this paper is the experimental performance analysis of our implementation in Sect. 4. Compared to browser-only computation, the analysis shows that our implementation improves the overall computation time by an order of magnitude. In the two use cases mentioned in the introduction, in which a large number of modexps need to be computed for casting a vote in the web browser, this solves the aforementioned usability problem. In Sect. 5, we summarize our findings and mention some remaining open problems.

Table 1. Performance comparison of different outsourcing protocols. Each row of the table shows the number of servers involved in the corresponding protocol, the number of modexps computed by each server, the number of modular multiplications computed by the client, the number of multiplicative inverses computed by the client, the number of random pairs $(r, g^r \bmod n)$ generated by the client, and the checkability factor β. Some one-server protocols from [3] are omitted, for example the ones that are limited to a fixed base or the ones that are special cases of others.

Paper	Protocol name	Secret		Number of					β
		Base	Exp.	Servers	ModExps	Mult.	Inv.	Rand.	
[3]	Protocol 7	yes	no	1	2	3	1	3	0
	Protocol 5	no	yes	1	$s \geq 1$	$\frac{\log p}{s+1}$	–	–	0
	Protocol 6	yes	yes	1	$s \geq 2$	$\frac{\log p}{s}$	–	2	0
[7]	*Exp*	yes	yes	2	4	9	5	6	1/2
[2]	**Exp**	yes	yes	2	3	7	3	5	2/3
This	Algorithm 1	yes	no	2	1	2	–	–	0
	Algorithm 2	no	yes	2	1	1	–	–	0
	Algorithm 3	yes	no	2	2	2	–	–	1/2
	Algorithm 4	no	yes	2	2	1	–	–	1/2
	Algorithms 1 and 2 combined [11]	yes	yes	4	1	4	–	–	0
	Algorithms 3 and 4 combined [11]	yes	yes	4	2	4	–	–	1/2

2   Outsourcing Protocols

Most outsourcing algorithms in the literature are based on the same basic principles. Privacy is achieved by blinding x and y based on the homomorphic property of the exponentiation function, which comes in two flavors, depending on whether x or y is fixed:

$$\exp(x, y_1 + y_2) = x^{y_1 + y_2} = x^{y_1} x^{y_2} = \exp(x, y_1) \exp(x, y_2),$$
$$\exp(x_1 x_2, y) = (x_1 x_2)^y = x_1^y x_2^y = \exp(x_1, y) \exp(x_2, y).$$

These properties also hold if all multiplications are performed modulo n and all additions modulo $\phi(n)$, where ϕ denotes the Euler function. Since $\phi(n)$ cannot be computed efficiently without knowledge of the prime factors of n, we restrict ourselves to the particular case where n is prime and $\phi(n) = n - 1$. We emphasize this point by writing $x^y \bmod p$ instead of $x^y \bmod n$.

From a group theory perspective, we perform exponentiations in the multiplicative group $\mathbb{Z}_p^* = \{1, \ldots, p - 1\}$ of integers modulo p, or in corresponding subgroups $\langle x \rangle \subseteq \mathbb{Z}_p^*$ generated by x. We denote such a subgroup by $\mathbb{G}_q = \langle x \rangle$ and assume that its order q (which divides $p - 1$) is known in the given context. Operations in the exponent can then be computed in the additive group $\mathbb{Z}_q = \{0, \ldots, q - 1\}$ of integers modulo q. Note that $\mathbb{Z}_p^*$ (and large subgroups $\mathbb{G}_q \subseteq \mathbb{Z}_p^*$) are by far the most widely used groups in cryptographic applications based on the discrete logarithm (DL), computational Diffie-Hellman (CDH), or decisional Diffie-Hellman (DDH) assumption. Other popular groups such as elliptic curves are not treated explicitly in this paper. However, all algorithms presented in this section generalize naturally to arbitrary groups.

In the next subsection, we introduce two of the most basic outsourcing protocols for semi-honest servers. The first protocol protects the secrecy of x and the second the secrecy of y (both protocols protect the secrecy of $z = x^y \bmod p$). In Sect. 2.2, we show that each protocol of Sect. 2.1 can be extended easily to reach $1/2$-checkability in the presence of malicious servers. We present each two-server protocol by an algorithm $\mathsf{ModExp}(x, y, p, q, S_1, S_2)$ executed by the client. These algorithms contain calls to $S_i.\mathsf{ModExp}(x_i, y_i, p)$, which invoke the transmission of x_i, y_i, and p to server $i \in \{1, 2\}$, and the receipt of the server's response over a secure channel. In every protocol, we assume that the servers are non-colluding.[3]

2.1 Semi-Honest Servers

In the semi-honest adversary model, it is assumed that every server involved in the outsourcing protocol executes $S_i.\mathsf{ModExp}(x_i, y_i, p)$ faithfully, i.e., the server always returns the correct result of computing $x_i^{y_i} \bmod p$ to the client.

Secret Base. If the base $x \in \mathbb{G}_q$ is secret and the exponent $y \in \mathbb{Z}_q$ is public, only y can be sent in cleartext to the involved servers. However, by decomposing x into values $x_1 \in_R \mathbb{G}_q$ (picked uniformly at random from $\mathbb{G}_q$) and $x_2 = x\, x_1^{-1} \bmod p$, which implies $x = x_1 x_2 \bmod p$, we can apply the homomorphic property of the exponentiation function,

$$x^y \equiv (x_1 x_2)^y \equiv x_1^y x_2^y \pmod{p},$$

to split the computation of $x^y \bmod p$ into $x_1^y \bmod p$ for the first server and $x_2^y \bmod p$ for the second server. Since x_1 is a random value and x_2 is derived from a random value, x remains entirely hidden from both servers. A disadvantage of this simple approach is that the client needs to compute the multiplicative inverse $x^{-1} \bmod p$, which is a relatively expensive operation.

A slightly different approach consists in selecting values $x_1 \in_R \mathbb{G}_q$ and $x_2 = x\, x_1 \bmod p$, which implies $x = x_1^{-1} x_2 \bmod p$. By applying again the homomorphic property of the exponentiation function, we obtain

$$x^y \equiv (x_1^{-1} x_2)^y \equiv (x_1^{-1})^y x_2^y \equiv x_1^{-y} x_2^y \pmod{p},$$

which implies that $x_1^{-y} \bmod p$ can be given to the first server and $x_2^y \bmod p$ to the second server. For the same reasons as above, x remains entirely hidden from both servers. The details of this procedure are depicted in Algorithm 1. Note that the main computational work for the client consists of two modular multiplications in $\mathbb{G}_q$ (we assume that operations in $\mathbb{Z}_q$ are negligible).

---

[3] Requiring two non-colluding servers is admittedly a strong assumption. We believe that this assumption can be justified, if adequate organizational measures are put in place. Otherwise, we suggest extending our protocols to three or more servers or considering the one-server protocols from [3].

Secret Exponent. In the opposite case of a public base $x \in \mathbb{G}_q$ and a secret exponent $y \in \mathbb{Z}_q$, only x can be sent in cleartext to the involved servers. Here, a viable solution results directly from applying the homomorphic property of the exponentiation function to $y = y_1 + y_2 \bmod q$ for values $y_1 \in_R \mathbb{Z}_q$ and $y_2 = y - y_1 \bmod q$:

$$x^y \equiv x^{y_1 + y_2} \equiv x^{y_1} x^{y_2} \pmod{p}.$$

Algorithm 2 shows the procedure of outsourcing $x^{y_1} \bmod p$ to the first server and $x^{y_2} \bmod p$ to the second server. Since y_1 is a random value and y_2 is derived from a random value, y remains entirely hidden from both servers. Here the workload for the client is a single modular multiplication in $\mathbb{G}_q$.

Algorithm: $\mathsf{ModExp}(x, y, p, q, S_1, S_2)$
Input: Secret base $x \in \mathbb{G}_q$
Public exponent $y \in \mathbb{Z}_q$
Prime modulus p
Group order q
Semi-honest servers S_1, S_2
$x_1 \in_R \mathbb{G}_q,\ x_2 \leftarrow x\,x_1 \bmod p$
$z_1 \leftarrow S_1.\mathsf{ModExp}(x_1, -y \bmod q, p)$
$z_2 \leftarrow S_2.\mathsf{ModExp}(x_2, y, p)$
return $z_1 z_2 \bmod p$

Algorithm 1: Two-server outsourcing protocol for secret base and public exponent.

Algorithm: $\mathsf{ModExp}(x, y, p, q, S_1, S_2)$
Input: Public base $x \in \mathbb{G}_q$
Secret exponent $y \in \mathbb{Z}_q$
Prime modulus p
Group order q
Semi-honest servers S_1, S_2
$y_1 \in_R \mathbb{Z}_q,\ y_2 \leftarrow y - y_1 \bmod q$
$z_1 \leftarrow S_1.\mathsf{ModExp}(x, y_1, p)$
$z_2 \leftarrow S_2.\mathsf{ModExp}(x, y_2, p)$
return $z_1 z_2 \bmod p$

Algorithm 2: Two-server outsourcing protocol for public base and secret exponent.

Secret Base and Exponent. If both the base $x \in \mathbb{G}_q$ and the exponent $y \in \mathbb{Z}_q$ are secret, we can combine the two protocols from above to hide both secret values from the servers. The resulting protocol is almost equally efficient for the client (four multiplications in $\mathbb{G}_q$, see Table 1), but it requires four non-colluding servers, i.e., any pair of colluding servers can reconstruct at least one of the two secret values. This is a very strong trust assumption for the protocol to be implemented in a real-world application. Therefore, we do not discuss this setting and the resulting protocol in more detail.

2.2   Malicious Servers

In the literature on outsourcing modular exponentiation in the presence of malicious servers, various authors have applied a similar technique to detect a cheating server [1,2,7]. The idea consists in challenging each involved server with at least one additional modexp computation, but without letting the server know which one is the real task and which one the challenge. If x_i and y_i are the real parameters and x_i' and y_i' the challenges for server S_i, then this is achieved by randomizing the order of the calls $S_i.\mathsf{ModExp}(x_i, y_i, p)$ and $S_i.\mathsf{ModExp}(x_i', y_i', p)$. In the simplest possible case, the same random challenge is sent to multiple servers. The client then checks the consistency of the servers' responses and aborts the protocol in case of a mismatch. This general approach can be applied to both protocols from the previous subsection in slightly different forms.

To pass the above consistency check, a cheating server must respond correctly to the challenge, but if the challenge and the real task are indistinguishable for the server, the chance of identifying the challenge is $1/2$. If two servers are cheating simultaneously, the chance of guessing both challenges is $1/4$, and if four servers are cheating, the chance is $1/16$. Therefore, the chance that an attack by malicious servers remains undetected is always at most $1/2$, which implies that a protocol equipped with this technique offers $1/2$-checkability. Note that a higher value for β can be achieved by sending multiple challenges in random order to each server. Generally, we obtain $\beta = \frac{c}{c+1}$ for sending $c \geq 0$ challenges in random order to each server.

Secret Base. If $x \in \mathbb{G}_q$ is secret and $y \in \mathbb{Z}_q$ is public, the parameters of the challenges sent to the servers must be indistinguishable from those of Algorithm 1. Therefore, while choosing the base $x' \in_R \mathbb{G}_q$ at random for making it indistinguishable from the random values x_1 and x_2, the same public exponents must be used, i.e., $-y \bmod q$ for S_1 and y for S_2. If we extend Algorithm 1 with corresponding calls $S_1.\mathsf{ModExp}(x', -y \bmod q, p)$ and $S_2.\mathsf{ModExp}(x', y, p)$, and randomize the order of the calls using a random bit $r \in_R \{0, 1\}$, the client obtains values $z_1' = (x')^{-y} \bmod p$ and $z_2' = (x')^y \bmod p$. Their consistency can be checked by $z_1' z_2' \bmod p = 1$ using a single additional multiplication. This whole procedure is shown in Algorithm 3.

Secret Exponent. If $x \in \mathbb{G}_q$ is public and $y \in \mathbb{Z}_q$ is secret, the situation is reversed. For making the challenge parameters indistinguishable, we must pick a random exponent $y' \in_R \mathbb{Z}_q$ while using the same public base x. This means that exactly the same challenge $S_i.\mathsf{ModExp}(x, y', p)$ is sent to both servers and that the consistency of their responses, $z_i' = x^{y'} \bmod p$, can be tested by verifying if they are identical. In Algorithm 4, we show the resulting protocol obtained as an extension of Algorithm 2.

3   Practical Implementation

Despite the large amount of literature on the subject of outsourcing modular exponentiation, we were not able to find practical and implemented solutions. However, for validating the use cases in cryptographic voting protocols from Sect. 1, we require such a practical implementation and we thus provide it as part of our contribution. We have defined two main objectives for the implementation:

- Providing a robust API for integration into cryptographic web applications.
- Supporting performance measurements and comparisons of different protocols.

Algorithm: $\mathsf{ModExp}(x, y, p, q, S_1, S_2)$

Input: Secret base $x \in \mathbb{G}_q$
  Public exponent $y \in \mathbb{Z}_q$
  Prime modulus p
  Group order q
  Malicious servers S_1, S_2

$x_1 \in_R \mathbb{G}_q$, $x_2 \leftarrow x\,x_1 \bmod p$, $x' \in_R \mathbb{G}_q$
$r \in_R \{0, 1\}$
if $r = 0$ **then**
  $z_1 \leftarrow S_1.\mathsf{ModExp}(x_1, -y \bmod q, p)$
  $z_1' \leftarrow S_1.\mathsf{ModExp}(x', -y \bmod q, p)$
  $z_2 \leftarrow S_2.\mathsf{ModExp}(x_2, y, p)$
  $z_2' \leftarrow S_2.\mathsf{ModExp}(x', y, p)$
else
  $z_1' \leftarrow S_1.\mathsf{ModExp}(x', -y \bmod q, p)$
  $z_1 \leftarrow S_1.\mathsf{ModExp}(x_1, -y \bmod q, p)$
  $z_2' \leftarrow S_2.\mathsf{ModExp}(x', y, p)$
  $z_2 \leftarrow S_2.\mathsf{ModExp}(x_2, y, p)$
if $z_1' z_2' \bmod p = 1$ **then**
  return $z_1 z_2 \bmod p$
else
  return $\bot$

Algorithm 3: Two-server outsourcing protocol for secret base and public exponent with $\beta = 1/2$.

Algorithm: $\mathsf{ModExp}(x, y, p, q, S_1, S_2)$

Input: Public base $x \in \mathbb{G}_q$
  Secret exponent $y \in \mathbb{Z}_q$
  Prime modulus p
  Group order q
  Malicious servers S_1, S_2

$y_1 \in_R \mathbb{Z}_q$, $y_2 \leftarrow y - y_1 \bmod q$, $y' \in_R \mathbb{Z}_q$
$r \in_R \{0, 1\}$
if $r = 0$ **then**
  $z_1 \leftarrow S_1.\mathsf{ModExp}(x, y_1, p)$
  $z_1' \leftarrow S_1.\mathsf{ModExp}(x, y', p)$
  $z_2 \leftarrow S_2.\mathsf{ModExp}(x, y_2, p)$
  $z_2' \leftarrow S_2.\mathsf{ModExp}(x, y', p)$
else
  $z_1' \leftarrow S_1.\mathsf{ModExp}(x, y', p)$
  $z_1 \leftarrow S_1.\mathsf{ModExp}(x, y_1, p)$
  $z_2' \leftarrow S_2.\mathsf{ModExp}(x, y', p)$
  $z_2 \leftarrow S_2.\mathsf{ModExp}(x, y_2, p)$
if $z_1' = z_2'$ **then**
  return $z_1 z_2 \bmod p$
else
  return $\bot$

Algorithm 4: Two-server outsourcing protocol for public base and secret exponent with $\beta = 1/2$.

Our solution, which we call *famodulus*[4], fulfills both objectives. It consists of the following three logically distinct components:[5]

- *famodulus-client*, a JavaScript library for outsourcing modexp calculations to *famodulus-server* (in the current version, only Algorithms 2 and 4 are implemented),
- *famodulus-server*, an implementation of the exponentiation server,
- *famodulus-demo*, a comprehensive demonstrator application using *famodulus-client* and *famodulus-server*.

In Sects. 3.1 and 3.2, we further describe the *famodulus-server* and *famodulus-client* components. *famodulus-demo*, which is a simple HTML5 web application used for testing and demos, consists of a user interface for outsourcing single or multiple modular exponentiations using *famodulus-client* to the servers,

---

[4] *famodulus* is a combination of the Latin words *famulus* (servant) and *modulus* (measure), i.e., *famodulus* is a servant for modular exponentiation calculations.
[5] All three components have been released as open-source software under the MIT license, see https://github.com/mainini/famodulus.

and provides support for parameter generation and execution time measurements. Communication between the client and the servers takes place over a minimal RESTful interface, which is also described in Sect. 3.2.

3.1 Client Library

In order to provide an API for cryptographic web applications to outsource modexp calculations, client code for the web browser currently has to be written in JavaScript. Our library focuses on clean and robust implementation as well as on performance and extensibility. Even if a considerable amount of deployed web browsers are still not supporting the full JavaScript ES6 specification, our library makes use of some of its advanced functionalities.[6] We expect an even broader adoption for ES6 soon. Where browser upgrades are not easily possible, so-called *polyfills* may be loaded by the application to support the missing language features.

Client-Side Technologies. Recently, JavaScript has also gained importance on the server side with the rise of *Node.js* in the last few years.[7] *Node.js* brings a widely adopted module system, which simplifies development and supports modularity of JavaScript code. For this reason, *famodulus-client* has been developed as a *Node.js* module, which gets transformed into a single file for the browser using *browserify*.[8] A side effect of this development model is the simplification of unit tests, which do not necessarily require a browser for execution. In principle, *famodulus-client* could thus also be used for outsourcing modexp calculations from a server running in JavaScript, even though calculating modexps through native bindings instead of sending them over the network would probably be a more sensible choice.

Outsourcing protocols require client-side calculations with big integers in JavaScript, which, as opposed to Java, has no built-in support for such types. We have thus conducted a small benchmark of libraries for big integer operations in JavaScript before starting development, focusing on performance for the required arithmetic operations. Based on the results, two libraries where considered for *famodulus-client*, the *BigInt* library by B. Leemon[9] and the *Verificatum JavaScript Cryptographic Library* (VJSC)[10] by D. Wikström, with the latter being slightly faster. We finally decided to use Leemon's library, mostly due to licensing concerns. While working with this library, we encountered critical efficiency problems with the bigInt2str and str2bigInt functions for converting big integers into strings and vice versa. By rewriting these functions, we improved their performance by an order of magnitude.

---

[6] See http://www.ecma-international.org/ecma-262/6.0/.
[7] See https://nodejs.org.
[8] See http://browserify.org.
[9] See https://www.npmjs.com/package/BigInt.
[10] See http://www.verificatum.com/html/product_vjsc.html.

```
const servers = ['server_1', 'server_2'];
const checked = true;

let fam = new FamodulusClient(servers, checked);
fam.decExponent([{b: '2', e: '4', m: '5'},{b: '4', e:'2', m
    :'5'}]).then(result => {
  // do something with result
});
```

Listing 1. Outsourcing two simultaneous modexps to two servers using *famodulus-client* and Algorithm 4.

Modexp Computations. In an application of *famodulus-client* in the web browser, a global FamodulusClient object is exported, which is initialized with a list of exponentiation servers and additional configuration values. After initialization, functions for outsourcing modexps according to the different protocols can be invoked. A code example of using *famodulus-client* for outsourcing a batch of two modexps, 2^4 mod 5 and 4^2 mod 5, is shown in Listing 1. The flag checked in the constructor of the FamodulusClient object indicates that servers are possibly malicious and that their responses need to be checked using the techniques from Sect. 2.2. The function decExponent performs a decomposition of the exponent in order to protect its secrecy. This setting corresponds to the outsourcing protocol of Algorithm 4. Switching the checked flag to false leads to invocation of the unchecked version of the protocol in Algorithm 2.

3.2   Exponentiation Server

The main objective of an exponentiation server according to our definition is to provide efficient modular exponentiation calculations. It should also provide a convenient interface for submitting calculation tasks and a secure channel for the transmission of the parameters and the responses. *famodulus-server* fulfills these requirements.

Server-Side Technologies. For ease of integration with current electronic voting projects at our institute, we decided to implement the exponentiation server in Java. This choice of platform has no influence on the functionality, and we consider porting the exponentiation server to another platform or programming language to be straightforward. While Java provides a reasonably efficient modexp implementation, we have decided to rely upon the native *GNU Multiple Precision Arithmetic Library* (GMPLib) for all server-side calculations.[11] A short series of benchmarks conducted during an initial evaluation phase indicates a performance gain of roughly a factor of four compared to Java's built-in BigInteger. modPow() method. We conducted our measurements using OpenJDK 1.8 on the Linux platform.

---

[11] See https://gmplib.org.

As of today, RESTful interfaces as defined by R. T. Fielding can be considered state-of-the-art for interaction between web applications and back-end services on the server side [4]. *famodulus-server* offers a very simple, yet flexible RESTful interface to submit modexp calculations and obtain corresponding results. Its implementation is based on JAX-RS, which specifies an API for RESTful services in Java. While multiple implementations for JAX-RS exist, we have chosen *Jersey*, the reference implementation.[12] Jersey applications offer greatest flexibility with support for deployment to various containers. By expecting that *famodulus-server* will almost always be deployed standalone on a server for optimal performance, we provide a configuration using the modern *Grizzly* standalone HTTP server.[13]

Modexp Computations. Modular exponentiations are submitted to *famodulus-server* over a secure HTTPS connection. Note that using TLS on top of HTTP is a critical precondition for protecting the secrecy of the parameters in outsourcing algorithms with multiple servers. The parameters (base, exponent, modulus) are encoded as JSON data enclosed in the body of the HTTP POST request. The JSON data format is widely used in RESTful interfaces. A single modexp is encoded as follows:

{"b": String , "e": String , "m": String}

The three attributes `"b"` (base), `"e"` (exponent), and `"m"` (base) are encoded as hexadecimal strings. The reason for this encoding is the missing data type for big integers in JavaScript, which makes parsing the JSON data impossible on the client side when the numbers exceed $2^{53} - 1$.

Each request submitted to the server must contain at least one single modexp in the JSON data format given above, it can however also contain many modexps at the same time. In practical applications, multiple modexps often share common parameters, for instance the prime modulus. For efficiency reasons, our JSON data format allows the definition of a common base, a common exponent, a common modulus, or a combination of common base, exponent, or modulus. These are the default values for modexps which do not provide the corresponding parameter. The complete message sent in a single HTTP Post request to the server then looks as follows:

{"b": String , "e": String , "m": String ,
 "modexps": [modexp_1 , ... , modexp_n] ,
 "brief": Boolean}

The first three lines are the default parameters, as described above, and may be omitted individually. The `"modexps"` attribute is a list of one or multiple modexps declarations, possibly with missing parameters. If parameters are missing, they are substituted in the calculations by the default values. The final

---

[12] See https://jersey.java.net.
[13] See https://grizzly.java.net.

attribute instructs the server to either return the results together with the full query ("brief": false) or the results only ("brief": true), depending on the client's needs.

4   Performance Analysis

This section describes the experimental performance analysis of *famodulus* that we have conducted. All test runs were conducted on a single machine with a Core i7 CPU (eight cores), running at 1.73 GHz with 8 GB of RAM, and with an installation of Debian GNU/Linux from the current testing branch. During the experiments, two *famodulus-server* instances were started by assigning corresponding processes to different CPU cores. Adherence to this setting was monitored. Processes which were not required for the experiments, for monitoring, or for the operating system itself have been stopped. Memory consumption during the experiments was monitored throughout. The experiments themselves were conducted with an off-the-shelf Firefox 50.1.0 web browser, with no specific configuration and with network communication taking place over the loop-back device. Conducting performance tests locally is a reasonable choice for our setting, given the fact that typical Internet network delays are several orders of magnitude smaller than the effective computing times spent on the servers. The Firefox process has been pinned to a separate CPU core.

4.1   Server-Only and Browser-Only Computations

The first series of experiments have been conducted on server-only and browser-only configurations in batches of 50, 100, 500, and 1000 modexps for modulus bit lengths of 1024, 2048, and 3072 bits.[14] The goal was to obtain an estimation of the performance difference of computing modular exponentiations using the native GMPLib and the JavaScript engine of the Firefox web browser. We selected the VJSC library for this purpose to obtain the best possible browser-only results. On the server side, we conducted the measurements using *famodulus-server*. Currently, no performance optimizations other than using GMPLib have been implemented, i.e., modexp computations are computed sequentially on a single CPU core upon receiving a batch of such tasks.

The results of our experiments are depicted in Table 2. They show that—depending on the bit lengths of the parameters—executing native code on the server is up to 18 times faster than corresponding JavaScript calculations in the web browser. The results also show that the browser-only running times become problematical from a user perspective for batch sizes of 100 modexps or more and bit lengths of 2048 bits or more. We get approximately 20 s for the 100/2048-setting and more than 10 min for the 1000/3072-setting. Batches of that size are necessary in the use cases mentioned in Sect. 1. In the server-only

---

[14] In all our experiments, we selected the smallest prime modulus p of the corresponding bit length. Base and exponent were picked at random from $\mathbb{Z}_p^*$ and $\mathbb{Z}_{p-1}$, respectively.

Table 2. Performance measurements of server-only (GMPLib) and browser-only (VJSC Library) modexp computations for different bit lengths. The last three columns show the relative advantage of server-only over browser-only computations.

ModExps	Server-Only			Browser-Only			Server Adv.		
	1024	2048	3072	1024	2048	3072	1024	2048	3072
50	0.09 s	0.73 s	2.26 s	1.63 s	11.02 s	31.38 s	18.45	15.19	13.87
100	0.18 s	1.47 s	4.48 s	3.32 s	22.14 s	62.69 s	18.89	15.02	13.98
500	0.88 s	7.09 s	22.57 s	16.48 s	103.19 s	310.78 s	18.71	14.55	13.77
1000	1.77 s	14.26 s	44.90 s	33.04 s	205.38 s	626.62 s	18.65	14.40	13.96

columns of Table 2, the 1000/3072-setting seems to be the only critical case with a running time of approximately 45 s. However, with better server hardware and by parallelizing the tasks onto different cores or multiple CPUs, the speed of the server computations can be increased arbitrarily.

4.2   Outsourcing Protocols

To evaluate the performance of the outsourcing protocols implemented in *famodulus*, we repeated the experiments from the previous subsection using the same batch sizes and bit lengths. We did the analysis for Algorithms 2 and 4, the two most efficient protocols from Table 1 with a single client-side modular multiplication each. All other algorithms of this paper require only an additional modular multiplication and are therefore not expected to perform much worse. Since Algorithm 4 requires each server to compute two modular exponentiations—the real one and the challenge—for each task in the batch, we expect a performance loss of up to 50% for each server running on a single core. This expectation gets confirmed by the measurement results shown in Table 3, especially for the batch size of 1000 modexps, where the relative overhead of both the client-side computations and the communication costs gets minimal in comparison with the costs of the necessary server-side computations. In all such cases, Algorithm 2 runs roughly 1.7 times faster than Algorithm 4.

The most interesting result of our experimental analysis is the performance of the outsourcing algorithms implemented in *famodulus* compared to browser-only computations. Relative values for 3072-bit parameters are shown in Table 3 (column 5 and 9). In case of Algorithm 2, the outsourcing protocol is approximately 13 times faster than browser-only computations. In comparison with the factor 14 obtained in the server-only setting for 3072 bits, we conclude that the overhead for the client and the communication is less than 8% of the total running time. In case of Algorithm 4, the outsourcing protocol is still between 7 and 8 times faster than client-only computations.

The absolute running times shown in Table 3 only get problematical for batch sizes of 500 modexps or more with 3072-bit parameters, for example approximately 80 s in the 1000/3072-setting of Algorithm 4. To obtain more acceptable running times in such extreme use cases, optimizations on the server side are

Table 3. Performance measurements of outsourcing modexp computations using Algorithms 2 and 4 for different bit lengths. Columns 5 and 9 show the relative advantage of the outsourcing protocols over browser-only computations for 3072-bit parameters.

ModExps	Algorithm 2			Adv.	Algorithm 4			Adv.
	1024	2048	3072	3072	1024	2048	3072	3072
50	0.16 s	0.88 s	2.49 s	12.58	0.23 s	1.40 s	4.09 s	7.68
100	0.29 s	2.01 s	4.86 s	12.89	0.46 s	2.78 s	8.11 s	7.73
500	1.36 s	8.11 s	24.30 s	12.79	2.17 s	13.32 s	40.70 s	7.64
1000	2.70 s	16.21 s	48.21 s	13.00	4.27 s	26.59 s	80.54 s	7.78

mandatory. Such optimizations are also required to serve multiple users simultaneously. Nevertheless, we conclude from our experiments that even without such optimizations on the server side, the outsourcing protocols implemented in *famodulus* increase the overall computation time by approximately one order of magnitude.

5   Conclusion

In this paper, we presented our results from studying and implementing secure outsourcing protocols for modular exponentiations in the context of cryptographic web applications. The first conclusion is derived from the theoretical performance analysis of our protocols compared to existing protocols in the literature. In Table 1, by giving a summary of the relevant client-side operations, we have demonstrated that our protocols are much more efficient than comparable two-server protocols from the literature. Similar conclusions can be drawn by comparing the client-side workload of our protocols with the one-server protocols from [3]. Their advantage, however, are the weaker underlying trust assumptions, which result from the public nature of the parameters sent to the server. Implementing these protocols, measuring corresponding running times, and comparing them to the results from this paper is left for future work.

The second conclusion of this paper results from the experimental performance analysis of our protocols in Sect. 4. In Sect. 1 we mentioned two use cases in the context of cryptographic voting protocols, in which a large amount of modexps need to be computed in the web browser. With our outsourcing protocols, we managed to reduce unacceptable in-browser running times by an order of magnitude. By optimizing or upgrading the server performance, further improvements of the overall running times are possible. We see at least three different approaches for server-side optimizations. The first is to execute the computations on high-performance server hardware, the second is to distribute the workload to all CPU cores or to a CPU cluster, and the third is to perform server-side precomputations for fixed-base or fixed-exponent modexps. The possibility of conducting modexp computations in parallel makes our whole approach highly scalable. Especially in scenarios with limited battery power (e.g., mobile devices), we consider this an important property. High scalability remains an important advantage even if client-side performance is further improved with new technologies such as WebAssembly. Setting up corresponding server infrastructure and conducting an experimental performance analysis for such a configuration is another topic left for future work.

Acknowledgment. We thank the anonymous reviewers for their thorough reviews. We appreciated their valuable comments and suggestions.

References

1. Cavallo, B., Di Crescenzo, G., Kahrobaei, D., Shpilrain, V.: Efficient and secure delegation of group exponentiation to a single server. In: Mangard, S., Schaumont, P. (eds.) RFIDSec 2015. LNCS, vol. 9440, pp. 156–173. Springer, Cham (2015). https://doi.org/10.1007/978-3-319-24837-0_10
2. Chen, X., Li, J., Ma, J., Tang, Q., Lou, W.: New algorithms for secure outsourcing of modular exponentiations. IEEE Trans. Parallel Distrib. Syst. **25**(9), 2386–2396 (2014)
3. Chevalier, C., Laguillaumie, F., Vergnaud, D.: Privately outsourcing exponentiation to a single server: cryptanalysis and optimal constructions. In: Askoxylakis, I., Ioannidis, S., Katsikas, S., Meadows, C. (eds.) ESORICS 2016, Part I. LNCS, vol. 9878, pp. 261–278. Springer, Cham (2016). https://doi.org/10.1007/978-3-319-45744-4_13
4. Fielding, R.T.: Architectural Styles and the Design of Network-Based Software Architectures. Ph.D. thesis, University of California, Irvine, USA (2000)
5. Galindo, D., Guasch, S., Puiggalí, J.: 2015 Neuchâtel's cast-as-intended verification mechanism. In: Haenni, R., Koenig, R.E., Wikström, D. (eds.) VOTELID 2015. LNCS, vol. 9269, pp. 3–18. Springer, Cham (2015). https://doi.org/10.1007/978-3-319-22270-7_1
6. Haenni, R., Koenig, R.E., Dubuis, E.: Cast-as-intended verification in electronic elections based on oblivious transfer. In: Krimmer, R., et al. (eds.) E-Vote-ID 2016. LNCS, vol. 10141, pp. 73–91. Springer, Cham (2017). https://doi.org/10.1007/978-3-319-52240-1_5
7. Hohenberger, S., Lysyanskaya, A.: How to securely outsource cryptographic computations. In: Kilian, J. (ed.) TCC 2005. LNCS, vol. 3378, pp. 264–282. Springer, Heidelberg (2005). https://doi.org/10.1007/978-3-540-30576-7_15
8. Kiraz, M.S., Uzunkol, O.: Efficient and verifiable algorithms for secure outsourcing of cryptographic computations. Int. J. Inf. Secur. **15**(5), 519–537 (2016)
9. Locher, P., Haenni, R.: Verifiable internet elections with everlasting privacy and minimal trust. In: Haenni, R., Koenig, R.E., Wikström, D. (eds.) VOTELID 2015. LNCS, vol. 9269, pp. 74–91. Springer, Cham (2015). https://doi.org/10.1007/978-3-319-22270-7_5
10. Ma, X., Li, J., Zhang, F.: Outsourcing computation of modular exponentiations in cloud computing. Cluster Comput. **16**(4), 787–796 (2013)
11. Mainini, P.: Efficient and Secure Outsourcing of Modular Exponentiation. Bachelor thesis, Bern University of Applied Sciences, Biel, Switzerland (2017)
12. Ye, J., Chen, X., Ma, J.: An improved algorithm for secure outsourcing of modular exponentiations. In: 29th International Conference on Advanced Information Networking and Applications Workshops, AINA 2015, Gwangju, Korea, pp. 73–76 (2015)

Voting Technologies, Recount Methods and Votes in Wisconsin and Michigan in 2016

Walter R. Mebane Jr.[1] and Matthew Bernhard[2(✉)]

[1] Department of Political Science and Department of Statistics,
University of Michigan, Haven Hall, Ann Arbor, MI 48109-1045, USA
wmebane@umich.edu
[2] Department of Computer Science and Engineering, University of Michigan,
Bob and Betty Beyster Building, 2260 Hayward Street,
Ann Arbor, MI 48109-2121, USA
matber@umich.edu

Abstract. We present data from the 2016 presidential election recounts done in Wisconsin and Michigan and information about the voting technologies that were used there to explain why it is challenging to show that the voting technologies treated candidates Trump and Clinton symmetrically. Lack of clarity about which type of technology was used to record vote counts, a mix of mostly small but sparse large counted differences between original and recounted vote totals, features that relate to voters, technologies and recount methods, and selectivity concerns are among the obstacles.

1 Introduction

Were the outcomes in Wisconsin and Michigan in the 2016 presidential election correct? Candidate Trump won both states—by margins over Clinton of 22,748[1] and 10,702[2], respectively—but the results are controversial. One concern is whether the vote tabulation technologies were hacked, as much of the equipment used to tabulate votes in 2016 has been shown to be particularly vulnerable.[3] Russian hacking had already taken place during the campaign, as acknowledged by [24], and it seems reasonable that in their efforts to influence the election vote manipulation may have been attempted. Recounts were prompted in both states by the Stein campaign [10,13,14].

Prepared for presentation at the 3rd Workshop on Advances in Secure Electronic Voting at Financial Cryptography and Data Security 2018. Thanks to Preston Due, Joseph Hansel and Barry Snyder for assistance. Thanks to Philip Stark for suggestions and to Alex Halderman and Dan Wallach for discussions.

[1] Wisconsin margin computed using recounted vote values in [29].
[2] Michigan margin computed using official values in [16].
[3] See California's Top-to-Bottom review [5] and Ohio's Project EVEREST [20].

A. Zohar et al. (Eds.): FC 2018 Workshops, LNCS 10958, pp. 196–209, 2019.
https://doi.org/10.1007/978-3-662-58820-8_14

We describe data from the recounts about the distribution of voting technologies and the ways votes changed during the recount. These data might be used as evidence about whether the voting technology treated candidates Trump and Clinton symmetrically in places in these states that had votes recounted. Presumably, a hack intended to benefit or harm one candidate more than the other would cause asymmetric treatment.

2   Recount Data

It is useful to look at raw numbers from the recounts both to show one of the difficulties in the way of estimating the number of affected votes. The following issues with the numerical distributions are by no means the most serious challenge to performing an analysis in terms of exact vote counts, but it's not clear how to resolve them.

The problem with the exact vote counts is that they are mostly small but there are a few relatively large values. We focus on the differences between the recounted vote counts for each candidate and the original vote counts: the original vote count in each ward (Wisconsin) or precinct (Michigan) is subtracted from the recounted vote count. Tables 1 and 2 enumerate the distribution of differences by major party candidate in Wisconsin, separately for each recount method, and Tables 3 and 4 enumerate the distribution of differences by candidate in Michigan, separately for each vote-casting method.[4] In all four cases the most frequent difference is zero, meaning the count of votes for the candidate did not change in the recount from the original count. The next most frequent differences are small decreases or increases.

Table 1. Trump: recounted votes minus original votes, Wisconsin

	−25	−18	−16	−11	−10	−9	−7	−6	−5	−4	−3	−2	−1	0	1	2	3	4	5	6	7	8	9	10
Hand	1	1	0	0	1	1	2	2	5	9	15	43	167	1457	199	57	39	11	7	4	3	2	1	1
Machine	0	0	1	1	0	0	2	1	2	4	9	18	58	810	100	27	7	7	3	2	2	0	1	2
Mixed	0	0	0	0	0	0	0	0	0	2	3	3	21	199	31	8	3	1	2	0	0	1	0	0
	11	14	23	29	31	32	39	50	65	246														
Hand	1	2	1	2	0	1	1	1	1	0														
Machine	0	1	0	0	1	0	0	0	0	1														
Mixed	0	0	0	0	0	0	0	0	0	0														

The problem is the sporadic double-digit and even a few triple-digit differences: in Wisconsin Trump gains 246 votes in one machine-recounted ward; in Michigan Trump loses 209 votes and Clinton loses 287 votes in absentee (AV) precincts. The large differences are probably produced by different processes than the smaller differences, but it is not obvious how to distinguish the processes. Simply declaring the larger values "outliers" [21,25] seems incurious about what

---

[4] All recounting in Michigan was manual.

Table 2. Clinton: recounted votes minus original votes, Wisconsin

	−30	−18	−17	−14	−12	−10	−8	−7	−6	−5	−4	−3	−2	−1	0	1	2	3	4	5	6	7	8	9
Hand	1	0	1	0	1	0	0	1	0	5	6	17	52	161	1457	187	79	22	10	9	5	8	4	0
Machine	0	1	0	1	0	1	2	2	1	4	6	8	15	82	734	126	31	18	6	4	6	5	2	1
Mixed	0	0	0	0	0	0	0	0	1	0	1	4	6	25	199	23	6	1	3	3	1	0	0	1

	10	11	13	14	15	17	19	22	24	33	68	79
Hand	2	1	1	1	1	1	1	1	1	0	1	1
Machine	0	0	0	1	0	1	1	0	0	1	0	0
Mixed	0	0	0	0	0	0	0	0	0	0	0	0

Table 3. Trump: recounted votes minus original votes, Michigan

	−209	−25	−19	−10	−8	−7	−6	−5	−4	−3	−2	−1	0	1	2	3	4	5	6	7	8	10	11	15	16	24	26
PCT	0	1	2	1	1	1	2	1	4	12	25	119	1306	370	111	34	11	4	2	2	0	1	1	1	1	1	1
AV	1	0	0	1	0	0	0	0	0	2	10	45	810	123	29	8	2	0	2	0	1	2	0	0	0	0	0

Table 4. Clinton: recounted votes minus original votes, Michigan

	−287	−41	−29	−24	−20	−8	−7	−6	−5	−4	−3	−2	−1	0	1	2	3	4	5	6	7	10	16	20	23	25	26
PCT	0	1	1	1	1	0	1	1	4	2	8	35	139	1182	418	121	58	23	6	5	1	2	1	1	1	1	1
AV	1	0	0	0	0	1	0	1	1	4	6	13	78	757	119	41	9	0	3	0	2	0	0	0	0	0	0

produced them; specifying a mixture model is challenging given the complexities of technologies and procedures in the states, which we do not elaborate here.[5]

At least in Wisconsin we observe that larger differences tend to be associated with particular reasons cited to explain recount changes in official "minutes" documents [31, 36]. As Table 5 shows, in Wisconsin the largest average differences (in magnitude) occur when the reasons cited are "nonstandard pens or ballots" (mentioned four times) or "voting machine/tabulator error" (mentioned 13 times).[6] Both of these reasons concern features of the voting technologies

---

[5] But see the discussion of DRE usage on page 5.

[6] In Table 1 the biggest increase (from CITY OF MILWAUKEE Ward 34) is not explained but the recounted vote count in [29] matches the count reported in minutes [22, 17–18], the second biggest (from CITY OF MARINETTE Wards 1,3,5) is explained by "nonstandard pens or ballots" and "voting machine/tabulator error," and the third biggest (from CITY OF MARINETTE Wards 2,4,6) is explained by "nonstandard pens or ballots," "ballots found during recount" and "ballots rejected during recount." In Table 2 the biggest increase (from CITY OF MARINETTE Wards 1,3,5) is explained by "nonstandard pens or ballots" and "voting machine/tabulator error," and the second biggest (from CITY OF MARINETTE Wards 2,4,6) is explained by "nonstandard pens or ballots," "ballots found during recount" and "ballots rejected during recount." The Marinette wards used Eagle opscan machines (vendor Command Central), and minutes mention problems with "improper pens," "Problems with the voting machine rejecting ballots on election night" and "Machine parts were obtained [...] and installed per instructions from Command Central, voting equipment vendor" [19, 43–44].

Table 5. Recounted votes minus original votes, mean by reason, Wisconsin

Reason	N^a	Trump	Clinton
Ballots rejected during recount	316	−.199	.0158
Ballots found during recount	72	1.38	3.38
Nonstandard pens or ballots	4	13.8	16.9
Ballots marked incorrectly	296	.993	1.17
Lost ballots	23	−1.43	−1.17
Human counting error	37	.0213	−1.23
Paper jam	21	−.870	−.696
Ballots wrongfully rejected	73	1.09	1.82
Voting machine error	13	7.56	7.83
No explanation	759	.680	.389

Note: mean of nonzero differences between the recounted and original vote count in Wisconsin wards. ^{a} Number of occurrences of each reason. Multiple reasons are cited for some wards

and so may be worrisome. Many nonzero changes occur ($N = 759$) that lack explanation.

3 Technologies and Covariates

Another challenge in the way of determining whether technologies treated the candidates symmetrically is that neither voters nor technologies are randomly assigned to votes, so that many unknown attributes may relate to both and different kinds of voters used each type of technology. Some voters and some technologies make or induce more mistakes than others, even if there is no malfeasance [15]. Whether voters or technologies act independently of one another is also unknown, although given conditioning on appropriate manifest covariates independence may be plausible as a null hypothesis. Observationally we also face a problem in that it is not clear what technology was used to produce each vote: in some cases the original voting technology is unknown and sometimes the recounting method is unclear. We detail some of these complications for each state.

3.1 Wisconsin

Figure 1 shows the different voting technologies in Wisconsin municipalities. The number of recounted votes across all presidential candidates is positive for $n = 3,500$ Wisconsin wards.[7] Table 6 shows the frequency distribution of voting technology and recount method types across all Wisconsin wards for which

---

[7] Recount methods distribution: hand, 2,126; machine, 1.066; mixed, 286; other, 22.

Voting Technology

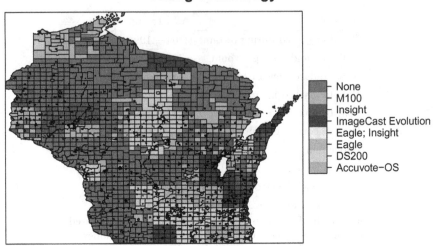

Fig. 1. Wisconsin technologies by municipality

Accessibility Technology

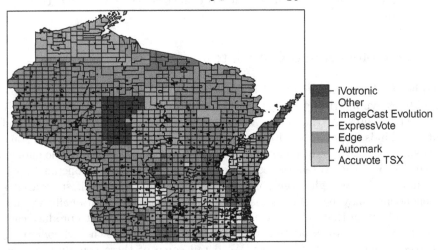

Fig. 2. Wisconsin accessibility technologies by municipality

the total number of recounted votes across all presidential candidates is positive $(n = 3,500)$. Each municipality has its own technology.[8]

---

[8] Category "Other" in Fig. 2 contains the technologies Populex 2.3, Vote-Pad and "Edge; Automark." "None" indicates that votes are tabulated by hand or technology is not reported.

Table 6. Wisconsin ward voting technologies and recount methods

Voting Technology		Recount Method	
None	850	Hand	2126
Accuvote-OS	154	Machine	1066
DS200	1475	Mixed	286
Eagle	294	other	22
Eagle; Insight	4		
ImageCast Evolution	287		
Insight	229		
M100	205		

Note: number of wards using each type of Voting Technology or recount method. Voting technology taken from [35]. Recount methods gleaned from [30] and from county minutes at [32]

In addition to the types of systems listed as Voting Technology all wards also have "accessibility technology" [33], shown in Fig. 2 . Table 7 shows the pattern in which Voting Technology overlaps in wards with Accessibility Technology. Voters can choose which mode to use to vote. While all the voting technologies except "None" are opscan systems, several of the accessibility systems are Direct Record Electronic (DRE) systems (Accuvote TSX, Edge and iVotronic; Automark and ExpressVote are ballot marking devices, ImageCast Evolution and Populex 2.3 are accessible ballot marking and scanning devices).[9] As Table 8 shows many wards have some votes cast using DRE systems.

---

[9] Problems that required "programmer" or vendor Command Central help to resolve or that may suggest there was some kind of software error are reported for the Edge machine in several county minute files. In at least seven wards a programmer or Command Central had to help to retrieve ballots (TOWN OF ARLAND Ward 1 and TOWN OF CUMBERLAND Ward 1 [1, 11–12]; TOWN OF GILMANTON Ward 1 [8, 14]; TOWN OF RUSK Ward 1 and VILLAGE OF WEBSTER Wards 1–2 [4, 15, 27]; TOWN OF HARRISON Ward 1 [11, 22]; TOWN OF OCONTO FALLS Ward 1–2 [23, 46]). in at least nine wards the machine count was wrong (TOWN OF RED CEDAR Ward 1–3, TOWN OF WILSON Ward 1 and CITY OF MENOMONIE Wards 5,7 [9, 13, 23, 34]; TOWN OF BEETOWN Ward 1, TOWN OF BLOOMINGTON Ward 1, TOWN OF BOSCOBEL Wards 1–2 [11, 10, 12–13]; TOWN OF CHASE Wards 1–5 [23, 22]; TOWN OF HELVETIA Wards 1–2 [26, 8]; TOWN OF WAUTOMA Ward 1–3 [27, 20]). In at least four wards ballots did not print out or needed to be reprinted (TOWN OF STANFOLD Ward 1 [1, 22]; TOWN OF COLBURN Ward 1 and TOWN OF GOETZ Wards 1–2 [7, 13, 20]; CITY OF BERLIN Ward 1–6 [12, 2]). Overall the minutes report 41 wards with explicitly described problems with their Edge machines, and 1270 wards with Edge machines but nothing reported regarding them. Problem reports are not always associated with nonzero changes in votes counts.

Table 7. Wisconsin ward voting and accessibility technologies

Voting Technology	Accessibility Technology								
	Accuvote TSX	Auto-mark	Edge	Edge; Automark	Express-Vote	ImageCast Evolution	Populex 2.3	Vote Pad	iVotronic
None	1	64	727	0	0	0	2	9	47
Accuvote-OS	120	0	34	0	0	0	0	0	0
DS200	0	1141	0	0	333	0	0	0	1
Eagle	0	8	286	0	0	0	0	0	0
Eagle; Insight	0	0	4	0	0	0	0	0	0
ImageCast Evolution	0	0	0	0	0	287	0	0	0
Insight	0	0	229	0	0	0	0	0	0
M100	0	183	1	1	0	0	0	0	20

Note: number of wards using each type of Voting Technology and Accessibility Technology by Vendor. Technologies taken from [35]

Vendor

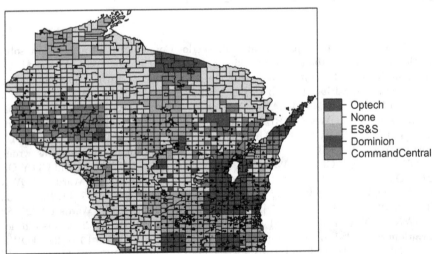

Fig. 3. Wisconsin vendors by municipality

Accessibility Vendor

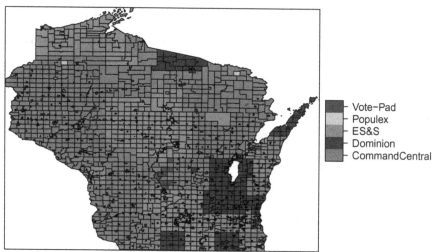

Fig. 4. Wisconsin accessibility vendors by municipality

A challenge to estimating the association between Voting Technology and votes is that we rarely know precisely which mode was used to record each vote. Votes cast using DRE systems were not changed in the recount, but only rarely are all ballots reported as having been cast using DREs.[10] This is especially important to note because if DRE machines were corrupted, the paper audit trail generated by the machines would likely reflect the manipulated votes. If voters fail to verify that their vote has been correctly recorded by the machine (which may occur, see [6]), then neither the paper trail nor analysis of recount data would detect manipulation. If a sufficient fraction of voters successfully verify their vote as recorded on the paper, this is in principle enough to detect manipulation—but we have no data regarding such verifications, and prior work suggests that voters don't verify their votes [6]. However, no incidences of incorrect votes recorded on the paper audit trail were reported in Wisconsin; while this does not rule out DRE tampering, it does narrow the likelihood that it occurred. Some ballots in each case may be produced using accessibility technology.

Several variables relate to Voting Technology and Recount Method: Clinton (HRC) vote proportion, a ratio of two different estimates of the number of registered voters,[11] the proportion of DRE votes, the absentee proportion,[12]

---

[10] In [28] only 21 wards report a positive number of DRE votes and zero votes cast using other modes, which are **Paper Ballots**, **Optical Scan Ballots**, and **Auto-Mark**.

[11] The ratio is the number of registered voters from [34], over the number of registered voters from [28].

[12] The "proportion" is the ratio of **Absentee Issued** to **Total Voters**, both from [28]. In one ward the ratio is greater than 1: in "VILLAGE OF FOOTVILLE Ward 1" the ratio is 556/410.

Table 8. Wisconsin ward voting technologies by vendor

Voting Technology	Some DRE Votes?		Vendor				
	No	Yes	Command None	Central	Dominion	ES&S	Optech
None	83	765	850	0	0	0	0
Accuvote-OS	119	35	0	33	121	0	0
DS200	1458	16	0	0	0	1475	0
Eagle	87	205	0	281	0	0	13
Eagle; Insight	4	0	0	4	0	0	0
ImageCast Evolution	282	5	0	0	287	0	0
Insight	21	208	0	218	11	0	0
M100	186	19	0	0	0	205	0

Accessibility Technology	Vendor				
	Command None	Central	Dominion	ES&S	Optech
Accuvote TSX	1	0	120	0	0
Automark	64	2	0	1324	6
Edge	727	534	12	1	7
Edge; Automark	0	0	0	1	0
ExpressVote	0	0	0	333	0
ImageCast Evolution	0	0	287	0	0
Populex 2.3	2	0	0	0	0
Vote Pad	9	0	0	0	0
iVotronic	47	0	0	21	0

Note: number of wards using each type of Voting Technology or Accessibility Technology by Vendor. Technologies and Vendors taken from [35].

turnout[13] and county total votes. Different types of voters use different types of technologies and cast ballots that were subject to varying kinds of vetting.

A specific suspicion in the election is that some vendors may have corrupted votes using the software they installed in voting technology. Figures 3 and 4 shows how the vendors are distributed across municipalities. As the top part of Table 8 shows, several opscan system vendors provided several different types of voting technology. As the bottom part of the table shows, various kinds of accessibility technology are collocated in wards with the vendors' opscan systems.

3.2 Michigan

The number of recounted votes across all presidential candidates is positive in $n = 3,051$ Michigan precincts. Each city or township has its own technology. Figure 5 shows how the technologies are distributed across townships. Table 9

---

[13] Turnout is computed using the ratio of the recounted **Total Votes** from [29] over the number of registered voters from [34].

Voting Technology

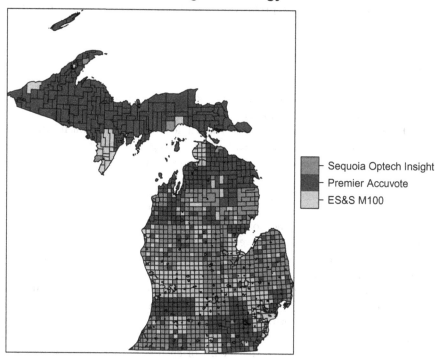

Fig. 5. Michigan technologies by City and Township

Table 9. Michigan precinct voting technologies

Precincts				
All			Recounted	
Technology	PCT	AV	PCT	AV
ES&S M100	2490	2021	1362	768
Premier Accuvote	579	492	348	132
Sequoia Optech Insight	323	151	298	126

shows the frequency distribution of types of voting technology both across all Michigan precincts and across the precincts that were recounted.

Several variables relate to Voting Technology: Clinton (HRC) vote proportion,[14] turnout,[15] active voter proportion[16] and county vote population. Different types of voters use different types of technologies.

4   Conclusion

Analysis of these data can address only Wisconsin wards and Michigan precincts for which recounts occurred and for which we have data from official sources. While the recount in Wisconsin covered the whole state, the recount in Michigan did not. We would have nothing to say about Michigan precincts that were not recounted, apart from noting that severe problems have been documented in Detroit [17].

Likewise analysis might depend on assuming that hand recounted ballots that were originally cast manually on paper provide "true" tabulations, but in Wisconsin about half of the votes were recounted by machine. If the same machines—or different machines—were used to recount as to originally tabulate votes, and these machines were corrupted, then the recount data provides no veneration of those results.

For both states we think the prospects are not good for using the kinds of data we have assembled to produce exact statistical estimates—using the exact vote counts—of the effects voting technologies (and recount methodologies) may have had. In Wisconsin the profound problem is that we cannot be sure which technology was used to produce the record of each vote, and cases of machine recounting do not meet sufficiently rigorous standards to establish the correct outcome. In Michigan the decision to recount in each county were based on vastly more information than we have as analysts, and there is no reason to believe these decisions are unrelated to features associated with both voting technologies and potential distortions in votes. In fact, such a self-selection concern affects all the data we have, given that someone chose which voting technologies to implement in each jurisdiction and then someone chose which modality to use to cast, count and record each vote: self-selections qualify as well any analysis we might do.

The best way to get evidence about whether the vote counts are correct is to perform either a risk-limiting audit [18] or a full manual retabulation. Such evidence about the accuracy of the vote counts would still leave the problem of determining whether voting technologies—or something else—distorted votes. Forensic analysis might also provide significant insight into the correctness of the election, but given advanced intrusion such analysis may not provide useful evidence.

---

[14] HRC vote proportion is computed using recounted vote counts in [2].

[15] Turnout is the ratio of the precinct total of votes cast for president in the recount data [2] over the total number of registered voters in the town the precinct is in [3].

[16] The active voter proportion is the ratio of ActiveVoters over RegisteredVoters, both town-level variables from [3].

References

1. Barron County Board of Canvass. Minutes (2016). http://elections.wi.gov/
   sites/default/files/recount_2016/barron_county_unapproved_recount_minutes_pdf_
   15035.pdf
2. Bureau of Elections. file `by precinct.xlsx`, obtained via Freedom of Information
   Act request from Melissa Malerman (MDOS), MI Bureau of Elections, 31 March
   31 2017
3. Bureau of Elections. 2016 bienniel precinct report. file Biennial-
   Precinct2016_531265_7.pdf, http://www.michigan.gov/documents/sos/Biennial
   Precinct2016_531265_7.pdf, Michigan Department of State, 31 March 2017
4. Burnett County Board of Canvassers. Recount minutes (2016). http://elections.wi.
   gov/sites/default/files/recount_2016/burnett_county_recount_minutes_pdf_11690.
   pdf
5. California Secretary of State's Office. Top-to-bottom review of electronic voting systems (2007). http://wwws.os.ca.gov/elections/voting-systems/oversight/
   top-bottom-review/
6. Campbell, B.A., Byrne, M.D.: Now do voters notice review screen anomalies? a
   look at voting system usability. In: EVT/WOTE (2009)
7. Chippewa County Board of Canvass. Board of canvass minutes (2016). http://
   elections.wi.gov/sites/default/files/recount_2016/chippewa_county_recount_
   minutes_pdf_11482.pdf
8. County of Buffalo. Date of recount: 12/1/2016 (2016). http://elections.wi.gov/
   sites/default/files/recount_2016/buffalo_county_recount_minutes_pdf_15905.pdf
9. Dunn County. Recount minutes (2016). http://elections.wi.gov/sites/default/files/
   recount_2016/dunn_county_recount_minutes_pdf_10781.pdf
10. Friess, S.: Inside the Recount. The New Republic, February 2017. https://
    newrepublic.com/article/140254/inside-story-trump-clinton-stein-presidential-
    election-recount
11. Grant County. Recount minutes (2016). http://elections.wi.gov/sites/default/files/
    recount_2016/grant_county_recount_minutes_pdf_17421.pdf
12. Green Lake County Board of Canvassers. Recount minutes (2016). http://elections.
    wi.gov/sites/default/files/recount_2016/green_lake_county_recount_minutes_pdf_
    60039.pdf
13. Gupta, P.: Jill Stein on What's Next With the Recount Effort in Wisconsin,
    Michigan, and Pennsylvania. Cosmopolitan Magazine, December 2016. http://
    www.cosmopolitan.com/politics/a8467128/jill-stein-voter-recount-wisconsin-
    michigan-pennsylvania/
14. Halderman, J.A., Bernhard, M.: Recount 2016: An Uninvited Security Audit of
    the U.S. Presidential Election. Chaos Communications Congress, December 2016.
    https://www.youtube.com/watch?v=E7Wo55F08-Y
15. Herrnson, P.S., Niemi, R.G., Hanmer, M.J., Bederson, B.B., Conrad, F.G., Trau-
    gott, M.W.: Voting Technology: The Not-So-Simple Act of Casting a Ballot, Brook-
    ings, Washington, D.C. (2008)
16. Johnson, R.: Election precinct results search. file 2016GEN.zip, http://miboecfr.
    nictusa.com/cgi-bin/cfr/precinct_srch.cgi?elect_year_type=2016GEN&county_
    code=00&Submit=Search, Secretary of State, downloaded 28 March 2017
17. Johnson, R.: Executive Summary of Audits Conducted in Detroit and Statewide
    in Relation to the 8 November 2016 General Election. http://www.michigan.gov/
    documents/sos/Combined_Detroit_Audit_Exec_summary_551188_7.pdf, 9 Febru-
    ary 2017, Secretary of State

18. Lindeman, M., Stark, P.B.: A gentle introduction to risk-limiting audits. IEEE Secur. Priv. **10**, 42–49 (2012)
19. Marinette County. Date of recount: 1 December 2016 - agenda exhibit a (2016). http://elections.wi.gov/sites/default/files/recount_2016/marinette_county_unapproved_recount_minutes_pdf_85823.pdf
20. McDaniel, P., et al.: EVEREST: evaluation and validation of election-related equipment, standards and testing, December 2007. http://www.patrickmcdaniel.org/pubs/everest.pdf
21. Mebane Jr., W.R., Sekhon, J.S.: Robust estimation and outlier detection for overdispersed multinomial models of count data. Am. J. Polit. Sci. **48**, 392–411 (2004)
22. Milwaukee County. Milwaukee county city of milwaukee canvass statement, recount election (2016). http://elections.wi.gov/sites/default/files/recount_2016/city_of_milwaukee_wards_26_50_minutes_pdf_18183.pdf
23. Oconto County Board of Canvass. Recount minutes (2016). http://elections.wi.gov/sites/default/files/recount_2016/oconto_county_recount_minutes_pdf_86884.pdf
24. ODNI. Assessing Russian Activities and Intentions in Recent US Elections. Office of the Director of National Intelligence, January 2017. https://www.dni.gov/files/documents/ICA_2017_01.pdf
25. Wand, J., Shotts, K., Sekhon, J.S., Mebane Jr., W.R., Herron, M., Brady, H.E.: The butterfly did it: the aberrant vote for buchanan in palm beach county, Florida. Am. Polit. Sci. Rev. **95**, 793–810 (2001)
26. Waupaca County. Waupaca county recount minutes part 2 (2016) http://elections.wi.gov/sites/default/files/recount_2016/waupaca_county_recount_minutes_part_2_pdf_16707.pdf
27. Waushara County Board of Canvassers. Recount of presidential race (2016). http://elections.wi.gov/sites/default/files/recount_2016/waushara_county_recount_minutes_pdf_60143.pdf
28. Wisconsin Elections Commission. 2016 general election el-190f: Election voting and registration statistics report. file 2016_presidential_and_general_election_el_190_2017_18402.xlsx, http://elections.wi.gov/node/4952, downloaded 10 May 2017
29. Wisconsin Elections Commission. 2016 presidential recount. file **Ward by Ward Original and Recount President of the United States**.xlsx, http://elections.wi.gov/elections-voting/recount/2016-presidential, downloaded 4 February 2017
30. Wisconsin Elections Commission. 2016 presidential recount county cost estimates and counting methods. http://elections.wi.gov/sites/default/files/story/presidential_recount_county_cost_estimate_and_reco_16238.pdf, as of 19 May 2017
31. Wisconsin Elections Commission. 2016 presidential recount results, county by county. http://elections.wi.gov/elections-voting/recount/2016-presidential/county-by-county, as of 19 May 2017
32. Wisconsin Elections Commission. 2016 presidential recount results, county by county. files downloaded from URL http://elections.wi.gov/elections-voting/recount/2016-presidential/county-by-county, on 3 February 2017
33. Wisconsin Elections Commission. Accessible voting equipment. http://elections.wi.gov/voters/accessibility/accessible-voting-equipment, as of 24 May 2017
34. Wisconsin Elections Commission. 1 February 2017 voter registration statistics. file registeredvotersbywards_xlsx_48154.csv, http://elections.wi.gov/publications/statistics/registered-voters-2017-february-1, downloaded 4 February 2017

35. Wisconsin Elections Commission. Voting equipment use by Wisconsin municipalities. file voting_equipment_by_municipality_09_2016_xlsx_78114.xlsx, http:// elections.wi.gov/elections-voting/voting-equipment/voting-equipment-use, downloaded 25 November 2016

36. Wisconsin Elections Commission. Wisconsin recount results update - day 11. file explanation_of_changes_per_reporting_unit_12_11_16_10043.pdf, http://elections. wi.gov/publications/statistics/recount/2016/12-11-spreadsheet, downloaded on 10 May 2017

Towards Everlasting Privacy and Efficient Coercion Resistance in Remote Electronic Voting

Panagiotis Grontas[1](✉), Aris Pagourtzis[1], Alexandros Zacharakis[1], and Bingsheng Zhang[2]

[1] School of Electrical and Computer Engineering,
National Technical University of Athens, Athens, Greece
{pgrontas,azach}@corelab.ntua.gr, pagour@cs.ntua.gr
[2] School of Computing and Communications, Lancaster University, Bailrigg, UK
b.zhang2@lancaster.ac.uk

Abstract. In this work, we propose a first version of an e-voting scheme that achieves end-to-end verifiability, everlasting privacy and efficient coercion resistance in the JCJ setting. Everlasting privacy is achieved assuming an anonymous channel, without resorting to dedicated channels between the election authorities to exchange private data. In addition, the proposed scheme achieves coercion resistance under standard JCJ assumptions. As a core building block of our scheme, we also propose a new primitive called *publicly auditable conditional blind signature* (PACBS), where a client receives a token from the signing server after interaction; the token is a valid signature only if a certain condition holds and the validity of the signature can only be checked by a designated verifier. We utilize this primitive to blindly mark votes under coercion in an auditable manner.

Keywords: Electronic voting · End-to-end verifiability ·
Coercion resistance · Everlasting privacy ·
Publicly auditable conditional blind signatures

1 Introduction

The cryptographic research on electronic voting spans almost four decades. Despite the proliferation of proposed schemes, few have been implemented and used in actual elections. This can be attributed to the fact, that e-voting systems must reconcile conflicting properties with *integrity* and *privacy* being the most important ones. Integrity is usually achieved through verifiability, which can be individual, universal or administrative, allowing the voter, the public

---

This is work in progress; some properties rely on assumptions which should be lifted in order to lead to a fully functional practical solution.
B. Zhang was partially supported by EPSRC grant EP/P034578/1 and Petras PRF.

© International Financial Cryptography Association 2019
A. Zohar et al. (Eds.): FC 2018 Workshops, LNCS 10958, pp. 210–231, 2019.
https://doi.org/10.1007/978-3-662-58820-8_15

or some trusted authorities, respectively, to check that all participants followed the protocol. Privacy protection comes in many layers: At the most basic level the secrecy of the vote is protected from the talliers. *Everlasting privacy* aims to protect against future and more powerful adversaries modelling the fact that theoretical and practical advances (e.g. quantum computing) might render obsolete the cryptographic assumptions upon which privacy rests. *Receipt Freeness* protects from a dishonest voter wanting to sell her vote to a passive adversary. *Coercion Resistance* is the essential property that will enable remote electronic voting, where the lack of a controlled environment for vote casting, leaves the voters vulnerable to active adversaries that can 'look over their shoulder' and dictate their behavior.

Juels, Catalano and Jakobsson proposed in [12] a framework to defend against coercion attacks, which was implemented in Civitas [19]. Their main idea was, that in order to achieve coercion resistance, the aspiring coercer must not be able to tell whether his attempt succeeded or not. This can be done by allowing the voter, to cast many ballots accompanied by anonymous credentials. Specifically, she obtains a valid credential through a one-time use of an untappable channel. Moreover she is assumed to have the capability to generate many different but indistinguishable ones. Under coercion, she uses fake (unregistered) credentials, indistinguishable from the valid one, which is employed when the voter has a moment of privacy, a necessary condition for coercion resistance. To correctly count the votes, however, the system must filter out the ballots that correspond to false credentials. This is done by comparing (in encrypted form) the supplied credentials with the valid ones that are published in a master list - the voter roll - after registration ends. Moreover, since the JCJ scheme allows for multiple votes per voter, duplicate ballots must be removed before counting. In principle, these operations are of quadratic complexity with respect to the number of ballots cast, which is typically quite larger than the number of voters, making the scheme impractical for large scale elections.

The motivation for this work stems from the reasonable assumption, first stated in [15], that the importance of integrity peaks during and immediately after the voting process, but diminishes as more parties are convinced about the result and concede. On the other hand, privacy is important during both voting and counting but retains its importance long after the announcement of the results, since the votes serve as evidence of one's political beliefs. Verifiability implies that such evidence is available to many third parties, making it in effect undeletable. This can have dire consequences in the case of a future oppressive regime. Therefore, our focus is a voting protocol that enhances privacy, both during and after voting without sacrificing verifiability.

Our Contribution. We propose a first version of a voting protocol based on the architecture of FOO [4], one of the most privacy aware voting schemes in the literature, augmented with an efficient implementetation of the coercion resistance properties of JCJ [12]. In particular, we take advantage of the fact that in FOO, voting occurs in two phases, namely authorization and counting, and use it to overcome the performance bottleneck of JCJ. We achieve this by using the idea of [38], i.e. marking the fake credentials during the authorization phase where voter identification is available. By using the voter ID the correct credential can be efficiently retrieved and compared to the supplied one with no need to check all credentials. Of course, during this phase the ballot contents must be blinded, as they can be correlated with the voter ID. The fact that the credential is invalid is conveyed to the counting phase by applying a publicly auditable variation of a novel cryptographic primitive, *Conditional Blind Signatures* (CBS) [41]. The counter receives the ballot and an authorization in the form of a blind signature, that contains a bit that specifies if the vote is valid or under coercion. The perfect blindness property of the CBS scheme combined with an anonymous channel enable us to achieve the everlasting privacy property, without residing to dedicated channels between the authorities. Our protocol achieves verifiability, coercion resistance and everlasting privacy with minimal assumptions.

Related Work. Various efforts in the literature have tried to overcome the performance bottleneck of the JCJ scheme. In [13,17] linear complexity is achieved, by blinding the credentials and then stripping off the encryption randomization. As a result, they could be efficiently compared through a hashtable. Both schemes, however, were later found by [16] not to be coercion resistant by using a classic tagging attack. In the same paper, a new approach improves the quadratic complexity of identifying invalid credentials, by representing them as tuples with an underlying mathematical structure and not as mere random group elements. Hashing could then be used on part of the credential, without affecting the coercion resistance property. This approach was improved in [20,29,34] by utilizing different forms of credential structure and renewal methods, in order to enable use in multiple elections and minimize reliance on the untappable channel. In a different line of work, in [26] it is pointed out that the tagging attack is irrelevant in the duplicate removal subphase. As a result, the blind hashtables can be used there, thus achieving the goal of linearity in the number of votes. For linear fake removal the voter retrieves through the untappable channel, during registration, the index where her real credential is stored in the voter roll. Through this index, coerced credentials are identified. In an alternate approach, [23] and [27] employ the idea of anonymity sets. During vote casting the voter presents the real credential mixed with reencryptions of some other credentials from the voter roll. Finally, [37] with the Selene system and [32] with coercion evidence less strict definitions of coercion resistance are offered which might prove easier to reconcile with the other conflicting properties of voting systems. Our work utilizes ideas from all these works and integrates them in an efficient manner via a new cryptographic primitive, conditional blind signatures.

The term everlasting privacy was introduced by [15]. In [21], a protocol that uses perfectly hiding commitments and homomorphic encryption was proposed. Their main idea was that the public votes are protected perfectly using the commitment scheme, while the openings are computationally protected but are exchanged through private channels. As a result they are not publicly available. This idea is presented as a primitive that can be integrated in any homomorphic tallying scheme in [31], while in [30] it is applied to mixnets providing everlasting privacy towards the public. This is further expanded and formalized as practical everlasting privacy in [28] by noting that such a future adversary might be more powerful in terms of computing power, but will have less information to operate on, since ephemeral data generated by the protocol will be unavailable in the long run. More recently, in [40], the authors implement the commitments with verifiable secret sharing and present a scheme that provides privacy and integrity against unbounded adversaries. However they assume untappable channels between the authorities and deny voters the ability to individually verify their votes. Our scheme differs from this line of work, since we do not assume or use specific channels between the authorities. All information is exchanged through the public Bulletin Board. This mode of communication is more realistic since a future regime with advanced cryptographic capabilities will have access to information exchanged by former governmental agencies in a private manner. Moreover our scheme also provides coercion resistance.

Coercion resistance combined with everlasting privacy seems to be an important desideratum in recent works. However this has not yet been possible in the JCJ framework, which is what our scheme accomplishes. In [39], a version of Selene enhanced for JCJ coercion resistance is equipped with everlasting privacy towards the public with the use of pseudonyms. However the creation process of pseudonyms and their relationship to real voter IDs and credentials requires trust assumptions and private channels between the members of the registration authority. Our work requires only the use of an anonymous channel and provides the same guarantees to both insiders and outsiders. In [36], everlasting privacy is achieved by using perfectly hiding commitments to registered identity credentials along with an anonymous channel. To achieve coercion resistance, votes can be overwritten and only the last one counts. As a result a voter under coercion can save her real vote for the end. This is a much stronger assumption than a simple moment of privacy required by our scheme and the JCJ framework; for example, an adversary who is able to cast a last minute vote achieves coercion.

2 Preliminaries

We begin by describing the agents, the functional components and the cryptographic primitives that make up our scheme.

- The main participants are naturally the *n voters*. In our protocol, like in [23], we assume that there exist pro democratic organizations that cast extra votes for registered voters in an effort to increase the size of the anonymity set.
- The *registration authority RA* registers the identities of the voters and provides credentials. We assume this occurs offline using an untappable channel.
- The *tallying authority TA* authorizes which ballots are accepted for counting by using a blind signature with an implicit validity bit. Later in the tallying phase it counts the valid ballots and announces the result.

In our scheme the registration authority and the tallying authority can be the same physical election authority *EA*. In reality they both consist of many members with conflicting interests for the election outcome. For clarity, however, we shall refer to them henceforth as if they consist only of a single member.

Bulletin Board (BB). A standard component of most electronic voting schemes. It is an authenticated broadcast channel with memory. It is meant to be implemented with Byzantine agreement algorithms. We do not provide implementation details here, following the vast majority of the electronic voting literature. We assume that whenever the voters use the BB, they are doing so through an *anonymous* channel that reveals no information about the identity of the sender of a message and that all the messages (requests, votes, proofs etc.) produced by our protocol can be found on the BB.

Homomorphic Encryption Scheme. We assume all cryptographic operations are performed by a JCJ compatible cryptosystem, i.e. one that supports reencryption and verifiable threshold decryption. In order to prove coercion resistance for our scheme we will use the Modified El Gamal (M-El Gamal) cryptosystem as presented in JCJ. It operates in a group $\mathbb{G}$ of prime order q where the DDH Problem is hard. Two generators g_1, g_2 are chosen randomly. The secret key is an element $x \in \mathbb{Z}_q$ and the public key is $h = g_1^x$. Encryption[1] is performed as: $E_h(m, r) = (g_1^r, g_2^r, mh^r)$ while decryption as: $D_x(a, b, c) = c \cdot a^{-x}$.

Proofs of Knowledge. We make extensive use of non-interactive zero knowledge (NIZK) proofs of knowledge. For instance a (M-El Gamal) ciphertext (a, b, c) is accompanied by proof that a, b have the same secret discrete logarithm relative to g_1, g_2. This can be implemented with the Chaum - Pedersen protocol [6] and made non interactive with the Fiat - Shamir heuristic [2]. We denote this by the functionality NIZK in the following way: $\mathsf{NIZK}\{(g_1, g_2, a, b), (x) : a = g_1^x \wedge b = g_2^x\}$. We also use proofs that a value is a member of a set. We achieve this by using OR compositions of Chaum - Pedersen proofs as described in [7]. We also use proofs of knowledge of a discrete logarithm [3]. Finally designated verifier proofs [8], denoted as DVP, convince the voter but not the coercer that his credential was correctly encrypted, as in JCJ.

Verifiable Shuffles. We assume a functionality Shuffle, like the one proposed in [25], that takes as input a list of encrypted values and outputs a random permutation and reencryption of these values along with NIZK proofs that these operations were correctly performed. We use shuffles in tallying as in JCJ.

---

[1] For compactness we omit the encryption randomness, except when it is absolutely necessary for the operation of our scheme. We also use the plain ElGamal to describe the protocol and refer to M-El Gamal only in the coercion resistance analysis.

Blind Signatures. They allow a signer to sign messages without having access to their contents [1]. To this end the user *blinds* the message and the signer signs it in this blinded form. The user subsequently *unblinds* the signature, and retrieves a valid signature for the plain message. Their security properties [9,24] are *blindness* or *unlinkability* which states that the signer cannot retrieve the signed message or associate signatures with protocol executions. *Unforgeability* states that the user cannot generate more message-signature pairs than those obtained by the signer. In the proposed protocol we use a variation of blind signatures, Conditional Blind Signatures, to enable everlasting privacy and move the marking of coerced votes from the tallying to the authorization phase.

Plaintext Equivalence Test. The functionality PET is a primitive introduced in [11] to convince a distributed set of entities, who share a decryption key that two ciphertexts indeed encrypt the same plaintext. It works by first having the participants blind the ciphertexts and then employing the homomorphic properties of the underlying cryptosystem to compute a function on them, such that a joint decryption of the result indicates if the two initial ciphertexts encrypt the same message or not. We use PET to mark duplicate votes and also embed them in the signatures that mark coerced votes in the authorisation phase.

3   Publicly Auditable Conditional Blind Signatures

Our voting scheme is built on a variation of Conditional Blind Signatures (CBS) [41]. This primitive allows a signer S to blindly generate signatures on messages submitted by the user U. These signatures however are verifiable only by a designated verifier V, like in [8]. Furthermore, their validity depends on a secret information bit 'injected' into the signature along with the possession of a secret key by the designated verifier. In this way the signer can 'instruct' the verifier to accept the signature or not. The secret bit cannot be learned by the user however, since both cases are indistinguishable to her. Note that the roles of S and V can be played by the same entity, thus allowing the signer to send information regarding attributes of blinded messages to herself in the future.

The security of CBS extends the standard security properties of blind signatures such as blindness and protection against One More Forgery to account for the secret bit b. Additionally, to formally express the idea that b controls the validity of the signature an extra property, *Conditional Verifiability*, is defined in [41]. We must observe here that the user cannot validate the signature she receives, since she does not have knowledge of b. Although this seems counter-intuitive with respect to traditional signatures, in our setting it is essentially the exact property we need to achieve coercion resistance.

In [41] an instantiation of CBS is given by extending the well known three-round Okamoto-Schnorr blind signatures [5] (Appendix B). This instantiation is proved to have perfect blindness, computational resistance to *Strong* One More Forgery under the Computational Diffie Hellman assumption and Conditional Verifiability under the Decisional Diffie Hellman assumption.

In practice, the scheme's round complexity can be reduced by randomly generating the initial commitment in a preagreed manner. Moreover it can also be combined with a multiplicatively homomorphic encryption scheme as the one we assume in our voting protocol. We present this modified version in Appendix C, where the signer and verifier are the same entity.

Public Auditability. The purpose of the CBS in the proposed voting scheme is to "mark" a ballot as valid if it is accompanied by an encryption of the same credential σ that was generated during registration. If any other credential σ' is used, the ballot is marked as invalid, indicating that the voter is under coercion. The CBS scheme can be used to convey this bit of information to the verifier, but by design it hides it from the user. As a result we cannot apply it as-is, since this will lead to loss of verifiability. We overcome this by introducing *Publicly Auditable* CBS, which adds auditability using NIZK proofs of correctness during signing and verifiaction. In particular the CBS conditional bit is implicitly

---

Common input: $\mathrm{params}_{\mathrm{CBS}}$, $\mathrm{pk}_{\mathrm{CBS}}$, $C_1, C_2 \in \mathbb{G}^2$, $\mathcal{H}_1 : \mathbb{G}^4 \to \mathbb{G}$, $\mathcal{H}_2 : \mathcal{M} \times \mathbb{G} \to \mathbb{Z}_q$
$\mathcal{U}$'s private input: $m \in \mathcal{M}$
$\mathcal{S}$'s private input: $s \in \mathbb{Z}_q$ s.t. $k = g_1^s$

$\mathcal{U}$ executes the Blind Algorithm:

  – Compute $x := \mathcal{H}_1(C_1, C_2)$;
  – Pick random $u_1, u_2, d \leftarrow_R \mathbb{Z}_q$ and compute $x^* := xg_1^{u_1}g_2^{u_2}v^d$, $e^* := \mathcal{H}_2(m, x^*)$
    and $e := e^* - d$;
  – Send e to $\mathcal{S}$.

$\mathcal{S}$ executes the Sign Algorithm:

  – Compute $x := \mathcal{H}_1(C_1, C_2)$;
  – Pick random $y_2 \leftarrow_R \mathbb{Z}_q$ as the second part of the CBS;
  – Compute $\nu := xg_2^{-y_2}v^{-e}$;
  – Pick random $t \in \mathbb{Z}_q$ and compute $N := \mathrm{E}_h(\nu; t)$;
  – Pick random blinding factor $\alpha \in \mathbb{Z}_q$ and compute $W := (C_2/C_1)^\alpha$ and apply
    signing key to compute $B := (N \cdot W)^s$ with:

$$\pi_1 \leftarrow \mathsf{NIZK}\{(h_1, h, \nu, N), (t) : N = \mathrm{E}_h(\nu; t)\}$$
$$\pi_2 \leftarrow \mathsf{NIZK}\{(C_1, C_2, W), (\alpha) : W = (C_2/C_1)^\alpha\}$$
$$\pi_3 \leftarrow \mathsf{NIZK}\{(h, k, N, W, B), (s) : B = (N \cdot W)^s \wedge k = g^s\}$$

  – Set $\mathtt{bsig} := (B, N, W, y_2, \pi_1, \pi_2, \pi_3)$ and send $\mathtt{bsig}$ to the $\mathcal{U}$.

$\mathcal{U}$ executes the Unblind Algorithm:

  – Verify π_1, π_2, π_3;
  – Unblind by computing $sig_1 := B \cdot \mathrm{E}_h(k^{u_1})$ and $sig_2 := y_2 + u_2$.
  – Set $\mathtt{sig} := (x^*, e^*, sig_1, sig_2)$ and output $(m, \mathtt{sig})$.

Fig. 1. The publicly auditable CBS sign protocol PACBS Sign

computed and embedded in the signature by applying the PET functionality on the registered and voting credentials.

The PACBS scheme operates in a group $\mathbb{G}$ of prime order q, where the DDH is hard. During the parameter generation phase random group elements (g_1, g_2, v, h_1) are selected. These elements are the public parameters of the protocol and are denoted as $\texttt{params}_{\text{CBS}}$. A signing key $s \in \mathbb{Z}_q$ and an encryption key $z \in \mathbb{Z}_q$ are also selected. These secret keys are collectively denoted as $\texttt{sk}_{\text{CBS}}$. The corresponding public keys are $k := g_1^s$ and $h := h_1^z$, denoted as $\texttt{pk}_{\text{CBS}}$.

The PACBS signing protocol in Fig. 1 assumes two random oracles $\mathcal{H}_1, \mathcal{H}_2$.

The signer obtains after registration an encryption of the valid credential $C_1 := \texttt{E}(\sigma)$. During voting the voter provides an encryption of the voting credential $C_2 := \texttt{E}(\sigma')$ along with a blinded version e of the message being signed (the vote). The value (C_2/C_1) is blinded with a random $\alpha \in \mathbb{Z}_q$ and multiplied with the signature. The essence of this procedure is that (C_2/C_1) is an encryption of a random element unless $\sigma = \sigma'$ in which case it is an encryption of 1. In the former case the random element will 'corrupt' the signature. In the latter case the signature will be valid, since it is homomorphically multiplied by 1. Every interested entity can verify that the signer did not deviate from the protocol by checking the transcript and the proofs. Thus, an honest voter who knows the input and in particular whether C_1, C_2 are encryptions of the same plaintext knows that his output corresponds to a valid signature.

The PACBS verification algorithm is given in Fig. 2. The verifier $\mathcal{V}$, given a message a signature and key pair, outputs whether the signature is valid or not

---

Public input: $\texttt{params}_{\text{CBS}}, \texttt{pk}_{\text{CBS}}, m \in \mathcal{M}, \texttt{sig}_{\text{CBS}}$ and $\mathcal{H}_2 : \mathcal{M} \times \mathbb{G} \to \mathbb{Z}_q$
Signer's Private input: $\texttt{sk}_{\text{CBS}}$

- If $\mathcal{H}_2(m, x^*) \neq e^*$ then $\mathcal{S}$ sends $\perp$.
- Otherwise $\mathcal{S}$ picks a random $\beta \in \mathbb{Z}_q$ and computes

$$\text{validity} := x^* \cdot g_2^{-s i g_2} \cdot v^{-e^*}; \quad M := \texttt{E}_h(\text{validity}; r_1); \quad V := M^s;$$

$$R := \left(\frac{V}{sig_1}\right)^\beta \quad \text{and} \quad \text{result} := \texttt{D}_z(R)$$

$$\pi_1 \leftarrow \texttt{NIZK}\{(h_1, h, \text{validity}), (r_1) : M = \texttt{E}_h(\text{validity}; r_1)\}$$

$$\pi_2 \leftarrow \texttt{NIZK}\{(k, g_1, V, M), (s) : V = M^s\}$$

$$\pi_3 \leftarrow \texttt{NIZK}\{(V, sig_1, R), (\beta) : R = \left(\frac{V}{sig_1}\right)^\beta\}$$

$$\pi_4 \leftarrow \texttt{NIZK}\{(h_1, h, \text{result}, R), (z) : \text{result} = \texttt{D}_z(R)\}$$

- $\mathcal{S}$ sends $M, V, R, \text{result}, \pi_1, \pi_2, \pi_3, \pi_4$ to $\mathcal{V}$
- If a proof is not correct $\mathcal{V}$ outputs $\perp$.
- Otherwise $\mathcal{V}$ outputs 1 (valid) iff $\text{result} = 1$.

Fig. 2. The publicly auditable CBS verify protocol PACBS Verify

in a way that every other entity can be convinced about it. In reality, $\mathcal{V}$ embeds the PET functionality inside the signature verification equation, which will again hold only if the credentials supplied are the same.

4   The Voting Protocol

Our scheme builds on the variation of FOO presented in [10] that is based on public key encryption instead of commitments, thus reducing the number of communication rounds. We use an extra authorization phase, where the issued credentials are secretly marked as valid or invalid using PACBS. Our main idea is that the validity checks for the credentials are (implicitly) done during vote authorization and not during tallying. The protocol has a one-time *Registration* phase and in each election there are three phases, namely *Authorization*, *Voting* and *Tallying*. To achieve the security properties we take advantage of the separation between Authorization and Voting phases. We stress that each phase starts only after the previous one has ended. A simplified view of the workflow of our protocol is depicted in Fig. 3. In the Authorization phase the *EA* checks for the validity of the supplied voter credentials. This can be done in constant time as the voter identity is known (but not the vote) and the *EA* has access to the voter roll. As a result, it compares the voter supplied credential $E_h(\sigma')$ with the voter roll version $E_h(\sigma)$ and finds out if the voter is under coercion. Since the identity of the voter is known at this point, the *EA* can use it to check eligibility by inspecting if there is a corresponding credential in the voter roll. Moreover it can be used to group all the ID and credential pairs so that only one is kept,

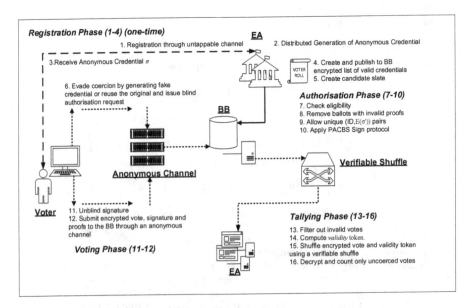

Fig. 3. Framework architecture and workflow

according to some predefined rule (e.g. last credential counts). Finally the voter and the EA interact according to the PACBS Sign protocol and obtain a validity token on the blinded ballot. While the honest voter knows that $\sigma = \sigma'$ and can be sure that the signature will be valid, a coercer without this information cannot know if the ballot will be counted.

In the Voting phase, the voter casts the (unblinded) signature and the ballot to the BB. In the Tallying phase the EA must act as the verifier in PACBS and counts the votes only if the signature is valid. However, the ballot and result pairs must also be shuffled, so that the coercer loses track. Only then can they be decrypted to yield the final tally. This cannot be achieved directly by the PACBS Verify algorithm in Fig. 2 because shuffling must occur before decryption. Consequently the EA, actually uses a slight variation of PACBS Verify, which does not decrypt the final result nor create the proof of correct decryption, since these take place "outside" of the algorithm. We denote this alternate verification procedure EncVerify. In this stage neither the ID nor any credential information is present so the ballot cannot be linked to a voter.

A detailed description is given in Fig. 4. Correctness follows by inspecting Figs. 1, 2 and 4. We assume that honest voters intentionally issue invalid votes during authorization to thwart forced abstention attacks.

Distributed EA. The EA can be modeled as a set of mutually distrustful parties executing secure protocols. In particular, the parameters for the protocol can be securely generated using standard techniques. The keys can be computed using a verifiable secret sharing scheme. The credentials can be generated as in [19]. Apart from the PACBS Sign and PACBS Verify all other actions performed by the EA (Decryption, Shuffle) are also standard and the checking for doubly issued credentials can be performed using PETs. The PACBS Sign and PACBS Verify can easily be extended by essentially performing the same protocols with each key share and combining the results.

Performance. Our analysis closely resembles [22]. Excluding the elimination of double votes all computations are linear in the number of votes. If $|ID_i|$ denotes the number of votes cast with ID_i and $m = \max_i |ID_i|$ then the number of computations is $\mathcal{O}(m^2 n)$. This can be further reduced to $\mathcal{O}(mn)$ using a method like the blind hashtables of [17], since the tagging attack is not applicable in this phase. In any case, assuming that the number of duplicates per voter will be constant in practice - i.e. $m = \mathcal{O}(1)$ - then the number of computations becomes linear in the number of voters n.

5 Security Analysis

Threat Model. Since our work is an extension of [12], our assumptions follow theirs closely. Firstly we require trusted implementation in software and hardware. While the amount of trust required can be decreased by using techniques

Common input: params$_{\text{CBS}}$
EA's private input: sk$_{\text{CBS}}$
EA's public keys: pk$_{\text{CBS}}$
Voter's private input: $v \in \mathbf{C}$

One Time Registration Phase:

- The EA generates the voter credential $\sigma \leftarrow_R \mathbb{G}$ and computes: $C_1 := \mathsf{E}_h(\sigma)$ along with $\delta \leftarrow \mathsf{DVP}\{C_1 = \mathsf{E}_h(\sigma)\}$.
- The EA publishes the encrypted credential $\mathsf{BB} \Leftarrow (\mathsf{ID}, C_1)$ and sends σ, δ to the voter using an untappable channel.

Election Setup Phase:

- The EA publishes the candidate slate $\mathbf{C} \subset \mathbb{G}$ by assigning a random group element to each candidate and a list of IDs denoted $\mathcal{I}$ corresponding to the voters with a right to vote in the election.

Authorization Phase:

- The voter computes a new credential $\sigma' \leftarrow_R \mathbb{G}$ and $C_2 := \mathsf{E}_h(\sigma'; r_1)$ along with:

$$\pi_1 \leftarrow \mathsf{NIZK}\{(g_1, h, C_2), (\sigma', r_1) : C_2 = \mathsf{E}_h(\sigma'; r_1)\}$$

- The voter encrypts his vote as $C := \mathsf{E}_h(v; r_v)$ along with:

$$\pi_2 \leftarrow \mathsf{NIZK}\{(g_1, h, \mathbf{C}, C), (v, r_v) : v \in \mathbf{C} \wedge C = \mathsf{E}_h(v; r_v)\}$$

- The voter invokes Blind (Figure 1) for $m := C$ to get:

$$e := \mathsf{Blind}(\text{params}_{\text{CBS}}, \text{pk}_{\text{CBS}}, C, C_1, C_2)$$

- The voter posts (ID, C_2, e, π_1) to the BB.
- The EA checks the validity of the proof and that $\mathsf{ID} \in \mathcal{I}$.
- The EA checks that no other request C_2' with the same supplied credential σ' is submitted for ID. If some condition fails the request is ignored as double and the EA publishes

$$\pi_{C_2} \leftarrow \mathsf{NIZK}\{(h_1, h, C_2, C_2')(z) : \mathsf{D}_z(C_2/C_2') = 1\}$$

- Otherwise the EA publishes $\mathsf{BB} \Leftarrow \mathsf{bsig}$ where:

$$\mathsf{bsig} := \mathsf{Sign}_{\text{CBS}}(\text{params}_{\text{CBS}}, \text{sk}_{\text{CBS}}, e, C_1, C_2)$$

- The voter computes:

$$\mathsf{sig} := \mathsf{Unblind}(\text{params}_{\text{CBS}}, \text{pk}_{\text{CBS}}, \mathsf{bsig})$$

Voting Phase:

- The voter appends to the BB the vote tuple

$$\mathsf{BB} \Leftarrow (C, \mathsf{sig}, \pi_2)$$

Tallying Phase:

- To prevent double casting if more than one lines with correct proofs contains C the EA keeps only the last submitted.
- For each submitted ballot with valid proofs the EA calls

$$\mathsf{EncVerify}_{\text{CBS}}(\text{params}_{\text{CBS}}, \text{sk}_{\text{CBS}}, C, \mathsf{sig})$$

and publishes the result tuples $\mathsf{R} = (M, V, R, \pi_1, \pi_2, \pi_3)$ from Figure 2.
- The EA appends $L \Leftarrow (C, \mathsf{R})$ where L is a designated section of the BB
- Then it executes $L' := \{(C', \mathsf{R}')\} := \mathsf{Shuffle}(L)$.
- The EA verifiably decrypts all pairs. A vote is counted iff $\mathsf{D}_z(R') = 1$

Fig. 4. The voting protocol

such as Benaloh challenges and code-voting as in [18,33,37], it cannot be completely disregarded. This is easier said than done, but it is a common practice in the vast majority of proposed voting protocols at our level of abstraction.

We assume two types of adversaries, one computationally bounded that acts during or shortly after the election and one that is computationally unbounded and acts in the future. The former models the security requirements which are vital during the election such as integrity, verifiability and coercion resistance while the latter models our requirement for everlasting privacy.

As far as present adversaries are concerned, we assume that they can perform only probabilistic polynomial time computations and for which our computational assumptions hold. To prove verifiability we assume that the adversary fully controls the election authorities and corrupts voters of his choice [33].

As far as coercion resistance is concerned, the adversary can fully control a subset of the voters by impersonating them, but there exists another subset with uncertain behavior. As in [12] each uncontrolled voter has a moment of privacy. The adversary can corrupt a subset of the voting authorities, which consist of mutually distrusting agents. Moreover he is capable of controlling the Bulletin Board and all other public channels, but there exist anonymous channels, where the identity of the sender of a message cannot be discovered. Finally there are honest participants, maybe nonprofit organizations, that cast invalid votes with valid voter IDs in order to thwart a forced abstention attack.

The future adversary is computationally unbounded and so can break any cryptographic assumption. Her goal is to gain information about the votes of a subset of the voters. We make the assumption that she can gain no information about the identity of the voter by the anonymous channel.

Verifiability. We follow the end-to-end verifiability definition proposed by Kiayias *et al.* [33], which can be viewed as a computational variant of the KTV framework as summarized in [35]. The adversarial goal against system's integrity is to cause deviation from the intended tally of all the honest voters while election auditing remains successful without complains. We consider an adversary that controls the EA and a subset of the voters. All the voters who did not participate in the election are considered to be compromised. This is because a malicious (registration) authority can always impersonate absent voters without the PKI assumption.

Our scheme achieves end-to-end verifiability against a fully corrupted EA under the random oracle model. As a standard requirement, we assume the existence of a trusted BB. Although the voters' clients are assumed to be honest for current protocol description, it is easy to add the Benaloh challenge mechanism [14] to prevent the malicious clients from tampering the ballot as the patch for Helios [18]. The voter needs to verify that her submitted ballot was recorded correctly on the BB and was taken as an input of the shuffle/mix-net.

During registration (Fig. 3 - step 2), the consistency between the voter's credential σ and the published $E_h(\sigma)$ is guaranteed by the DVP, which is intentionally not universally verifiable to enable coercion resistance. In the authorization phase, the signatures for the validity of the credential (Fig. 3 - step 10) are verifiable due to the design of PACBS Sign and the proof published for each unprocessed request. More specifically, the *EA* shows that the produced signature is valid if and only if the submitted credential matches the recorded one. In the tallying phase, the public auditability property of the PACBS Verify protocol, the verifiable shuffle and the proof of correct decryption prevent the authority from deviating in any way from the protocol specification. Finally, everyone can check if the total number of valid signatures are less than or equal to the number of voters, n. This would prevent the malicious *EA* from inserting additional valid signatures. Since the honest voters' signatures are all cast, recorded, and tallied correctly, the rest valid signatures can be viewed as the adversarial ones. Hence, the malicious *EA* cannot add more votes even if she has the signing key.

Eligibility. The eligibility property is based on the resistance to Strong One More Forgery property of the signature scheme, since a valid signature is required for the vote to be counted. This implies the strong assumption that the adversary is restricted to a polylogarithmic number of honest authorizations.

Privacy. Our protocol satisfies vote privacy. In the authorization phase the encrypted vote is blinded when posted to the BB. As a result there is no way to recover the selection of the voter even if the *EA* is fully corrupted. In the voting phase the privacy of the vote depends on the privacy of the actions performed by the *EA* (Decryption, Shuffle). Without the assumption of an anonymous channel our system offers Helios [18] level privacy under similar trust assumptions. However, assuming an anonymous channel privacy protection becomes complete.

Everlasting Privacy. Our scheme easily meets the requirements for practical everlasting privacy set in [28], despite the fact that there are no private channels between the participants. A future adversary with access to the data in the BB, but without access to the untappable channels and to network related information will not be able to associate authorization requests and votes because of the blindness of the signatures. Moreover, the tallying phase where there are neither voter identities nor credentials present, matches the Helios without identities case of [28] which is proved to satisfy practical everlasting privacy. However if we assume an anonymous channel as in [4, 36] our scheme has complete everlasting privacy. In the authorization phase, the perfect blindness of the signature scheme ensures that no information regarding the vote is leaked. Furthermore, when the ballots are posted in the BB, despite being only computationally protected, they are cast through an anonymous channel and contain no information about the identity of the voter. Finally, the encrypted vote and signatures cannot be associated with any particular execution of the signing protocol that validated it. As a result a semi-honest unbounded adversary, watching all the public interactions cannot associate any voter with his vote.

Coercion Resistance. Our scheme is Coercion Resistant. In particular if a coercer requests a credential σ from a voter, its validity cannot be proved. As a result the validity of the signature issued for this credential is unknown to the coercer, due to the properties of PACBS. Moreover multiple votes cast with the same ID in the authorization phase, protect from a forced abstention attack. The reasoning is similar to [23, 27]. In the tallying phase, shuffling and PACBS Verify ensure the coercer loses track of his submitted vote and the only information he gets is the final tally. A detailed analysis is given in Appendix A.

6   Conclusion

In this paper we presented a new approach to provide coercion resistance in an efficient manner and combine it with everlasting privacy. Our protocol is based on minimal assumptions: a single use of an untappable channel and the existence of an anonymous channel. We utilized Conditional Blind Signatures [41], a recent primitive that allows a signer to inject a bit of secret information to a blind signature that controls if it should validate or not, which we improved for our purposes. Our scheme is proved secure under the JCJ [12] coercion resistance framework. The perfect blindness provided by CBS allows for stronger privacy guarantees; combined with a perfectly anonymous channel it provides the everlasting privacy property. In a future version of this work we plan to augment the intuitive security analysis presented here, using rigorous definitions and proofs.

Acknowledgements. The authors would like to thank Peter Browne Roenne and the anonymous reviewers for their helpful comments and suggestions.

A   Analysis of Coercion Resistance

We prove the coercion resistance property of the proposed voting scheme by closely following the JCJ techniques. We slightly modify the games c-resist and c-resist-ideal of JCJ to account for the extra authorization phase. We treat the auth functionality as a function that provides a valid or invalid ballot in relation to its private input.

Firstly, we examine the options of a coerced voter. Such a voter, can simply supply the adversary with a fake random element of $\mathbb{G}$. Having a fake credential, the signature she receives will be invalid, a fact undetectable by $\mathcal{A}$ due to the design of the PACBS protocol. The voter can authenticate and cast her real vote during her moment of privacy. The coercer cannot decrypt the corresponding entry in the voter roll and find out if he was presented with the real one or not. If he tries to vote, when he receives the signature he will not be able to validate it himself. In the tallying phase the shuffle will make him lose track of the vote.

The Games c-resist and c-resist-ideal. The only change in the c-resist game of JCJ is the extra authorization phase. During this phase voters supply the essential information, based on their secret credential, and they get a ballot which can be either valid or invalid. We assume that all messages are exchanged via the bulletin board and thus are available to the adversary.

In the c-resist-ideal game an extra ideal functionality is needed, which we call idauth and its purpose is to authenticate and cast the ballots to the BB. This functionality gets the inputs of the players and computes the ballots as follows:

- It gives only one valid ballot for each valid credential.
- For honest voters it extracts the underlying credential and responds with a valid/invalid ballot based on it.
- Adversarial requests with credentials of corrupted players are answered normally. For the credential of the coerced voter the validity of the ballot computed is determined by the coin toss.
- The outputs are written directly to the BB.

In both games, λ is the security parameter, n is the number of voters and n_V is the number of voters the adversary can corrupt. Further inputs include the candidate slate $\mathbf{C}$ and the distribution D that governs the behaviour of the uncontrolled voters. In c-resist-game, the adversary corrupts a subset V of the voters and obtains their credentials after registration. We denote by U the rest of the voters. They perform the registration process and receive their credential. Subsequently the coercer chooses the voter j to coerce and her uncoerced vote β. Of course the voter should not be already corrupted and the vote should be a valid choice. A coin is flipped and if it is 0, the coerced voter fools $\mathcal{A}$ by invoking the functionality fakekey and generating a fake credential while voting with her real one. If it is 1 she obeys and gives her real credential sk_j to $\mathcal{A}$. Honest voters perform the authorization phase and cast their votes, while $\mathcal{A}$ invokes the auth functionality with any input of his choice using the information gathered so far.

The tallying phase is then performed and $\mathcal{A}$ tries to guess the result of the coin, using the data on the BB, the final tally $\mathbf{X}$ and the proofs provided. In c-resist-ideal-game the same things happen with minor differences. The keys obtained by $\mathcal{A}$ do not assist him with the choice of the voter to coerce. He is always given the real credential and auth is replaced with idauth. Finally, the only data $\mathcal{A}$ can use to guess the coin flip is the final tally $\mathbf{X}$ and the number of invalid votes Γ.

We now present the simulation for the proof that our scheme is coercion resistant.

1. **Input:** The simulator $\mathcal{S}$ takes as input the elements g_1, g_2, h_1, h_2 of a group $\mathbb{G}$ of order q and a vector w from a distribution D, which mirrors $\mathcal{A}$'s uncertainty. Each element of w is a set of valid and invalid votes, taking into account that each voter casts more than one ballot. $\mathcal{S}$ tries to answer whether (g_1, g_2, h_1, h_2) is a DH quadruple or not.

2. **Parameter generation:** Initially the S creates the M-El Gamal encryption key by randomly choosing $x_1, x_2 \in \mathbb{Z}_q$ and computing $h = g_1^{x_1} g_2^{x_2}$. The public key is (g_1, g_2, h). He then creates a signing key pair for the CBS scheme by choosing $g_3, g_4, y \leftarrow_R \mathbb{G}$, $s \in \mathbb{Z}_q$ and $k = g_3^s$. The secret key is s and the public key is (g_3, g_4, y, k).

3. **Registration:** Each voter is assigned a random $\sigma_i \leftarrow_R \mathbb{G}$. Using the public key, S publishes the voter roll. Finally, the candidate slate $\mathbf{C}$ is published.

4. **Corruption:** $\mathcal{A}$ corrupts voters.

5. **Coercion:** $\mathcal{A}$ chooses the player to coerce and her honest vote (j, β). The appropriate tests are performed in (j, β) according to the games' definitions.

6. **Coin Flip:** S chooses $b \leftarrow_R \{0, 1\}$. If $b = 0$, $\mathcal{A}$ is given a random group element $\sigma^* \leftarrow_R \mathbb{G}$, else she is given the real credential $\sigma^* \leftarrow \sigma_j$.

7. **Authorization Requests:** S issues the signature requests for the honest voters according to w. For each element of w she issues $(\mathbf{E}_h(\sigma_i), ID_i, \mathrm{PoK}_1)$ where $\mathbf{E}_h(\sigma_i) = (h_1^{u_i}, h_2^{u_i}, h_1^{u_i x_1} h_2^{u_i x_2} \sigma_i)$ for random u_i and the proof PoK_1 is simulated by the programmability of the random oracle by using standard techniques. $\mathcal{A}$ issues his authorization requests.

8. **Double requests elimination:** Using the secret key x_1, x_2, S decrypts and eliminates double requests with the same credential.

9. **Authorization:** S simulates this phase using her PACBS signing key. The messages are encrypted votes according to w. Encryptions are done in the same way as before. $\mathcal{A}$ is given signatures in a straightforward manner.

10. **Vote Casting:** S submits ballots for the honest voters. $\mathcal{A}$ submits ballots for the corrupt and the coerced voters.

11. **Tallying:** Using his secret keys and standard techniques for proofs, S simulates tallying in a straightforward manner.

12. **Guess:** $\mathcal{A}$ decides b'.

13. **Output:** S outputs 1 iff $b = b'$.

Let's examine the view of $\mathcal{A}$. Apart from the data he produces, in the authorization phase he sees the encrypted credentials with the proofs that accompany them, and the signatures given. These include a message x uniformly distributed in $\mathbb{G}$, an encrypted first part of a signature and the second part of the signature which is a uniformly distributed element in $\mathbb{Z}_q$. In the tallying phase he sees the encrypted ballots, their proofs and the signatures. The signatures include two random elements x^*, sig_2 and an encrypted first part. Finally he gets the intermediate results and the tally with the proof. Apart from the encrypted messages and the proofs, all other data are random and do not assist him in deciding b.

Suppose that the input of S is a Diffie-Hellman (DH) tuple. Then all the encryptions done by S are valid and the view of $\mathcal{A}$ is the same as the c-resist experiment. If the input is not a DH tuple then every encryption S did results in uniformly distributed elements in $\mathbb{G}^3$. $\mathcal{A}$'s view is the same as in the c-resist-ideal experiment.

These imply that

$$\mathbf{Adv}^{\text{c-resist}}_{ES,\mathcal{A}} = |\Pr[\mathcal{S} = 1|\text{DH}(g_1, g_2, h_1, h_2)] - \Pr[\mathcal{S} = 1|\neg\text{DH}(g_1, g_2, h_1, h_2)]|$$

which is equal to $\mathbf{Adv}^{DDH}_{\mathcal{S}}$ and so it is negligible if the DDH assumption holds.

Algorithm 1. c-resist	Algorithm 2. c-resist-ideal
Input : $n, n_V, \mathbf{C}, D, \lambda$	Input : $n, n_V, \mathbf{C}, D, \lambda$
Output: $result \in \{0, 1\}$	Output: $result \in \{0, 1\}$
$(V, U) \leftarrow \mathcal{A}(\mathbf{corrupt})$	$(V, U) \leftarrow \mathcal{A}(\mathbf{corrupt})$
$\{(sk_i, pk_i) \leftarrow \text{reg}(sk_R, ID_i, \lambda)\}_{i \in [n]}$	$\{(sk_i, pk_i) \leftarrow \text{reg}(sk_R, ID_i, \lambda)\}_{i \in [n]}$
$(j, \beta) \leftarrow \mathcal{A}(\{sk_i\}_{i \in V}, \mathbf{Coerce})$	$(j, \beta) \leftarrow \mathcal{A}(\mathbf{Coerce})$
if $\beta \notin \mathbf{C}$ or $j \notin U$ then	if $\beta \notin \mathbf{C}$ or $j \notin U$ then
| output 0	| output 0
end	end
$b \leftarrow_R \{0, 1\}$	$b \leftarrow_R \{0, 1\}$
if $b = 0$ then	$sk^* \leftarrow sk_j$
| $sk^* \leftarrow \text{fakekey}(pk_T, sk_j, pk_j)$	if $b = 0$ then
| BB $\Leftarrow$	| BB $\Leftarrow$
| $\text{auth}(sk_j, pk_j, sk_T, pk_T, \mathbf{C}, \beta, \lambda)$	| $\text{idauth}(sk_j, pk_j, sk_T, pk_T, \mathbf{C}, \beta, \lambda)$
else	end
| $sk^* \leftarrow sk_j$	
end	
	$\{$BB $\Leftarrow$
BB $\Leftarrow$	$\text{idauth}(sk_i, pk_i, sk_T, pk_T, \mathbf{C}, D, \lambda)\}_{i \in U \setminus \{j\}}$
$\text{auth}(sk_i, pk_i, sk_T, pk_T, \mathbf{C}, D, \lambda)\}_{i \in U \setminus \{j\}}$	BB $\Leftarrow$
BB $\Leftarrow$	$\mathcal{A}^{\text{idauth}(\cdot)}(\{sk_i\}_{i \in V}, sk^*, pk_T, \mathbf{C})$
$\mathcal{A}^{\text{auth}(\cdot)}(\{sk_i\}_{i \in V}, sk^*, pk_T, \mathbf{C}, \text{BB})$	$(\mathbf{X}, P) \leftarrow$
$(\mathbf{X}, P) \leftarrow$	
$\text{tally}(sk_T, \text{BB}, \mathbf{C}, \{pk_i\}_{i \in V \cup U}, \lambda)$	$\text{tally}(sk_T, \text{BB}, \mathbf{C}, \{pk_i\}_{i \in V \cup U}, \lambda)$
$b' \leftarrow \mathcal{A}(\mathbf{X}, P, \text{BB}, \mathbf{Guess})$	$b' \leftarrow \mathcal{A}(\mathbf{X}, P, \Gamma, \mathbf{Guess})$
output $b == b'$	output $b == b'$

Finally, we must note that the exact level of protection each voter receives depends on the size of the anonymity set, i.e. the number of decoy votes cast with their ID by other honest voters or organizations. We plan to incorporate this analysis in future versions of our work.

B   Plain Okamoto-Schnorr CBS Scheme

We briefly present the simple Okamoto Shnorr CBS Scheme from [41]. The secret signing key consists of the values $s_1, s_2 \in \mathbb{Z}_q$ as in [5] with corresponding public verification key $v = g_1^{-s_1} g_2^{-s_2}$. During the signing and unblinding phases the public key k of the verifier is used. For the verification algorithm, the verifier checks the verification equation using the hash of the message and the commitment using the secret key $s \in \mathbb{Z}_q$. If the secret signer bit is 1, then the signature will be valid, otherwise the verification equation will not hold. Thus the verifier will learn the secret bit of the signer. We also assume the existence of a random oracle $\mathcal{H}$.

Common input: $\mathbb{G}, g_1, g_2, v, k \in \mathbb{G}, \mathcal{H} : \mathcal{M} \times \mathbb{G} \to \mathbb{Z}_q$
Signers's private input: $s_1, s_2 \in \mathbb{Z}_q : v = g_1^{-s_1} g_2^{-s_2}$ and $b \in \{0, 1\}$
Verifier's private input: $s \in \mathbb{Z}_q : k = g_1^s$
Recipient's private input: m

Commitment Phase. The Signer:

- Picks random $r_1, r_2 \leftarrow_R \mathbb{Z}_q$;
- Computes $x := g_1^{r_1} g_2^{r_2}$;
- Sends x to the recipient.

Blinding Phase. The Recipient:

- Selects blinding factors $u_1, u_2, d \leftarrow_R \mathbb{Z}_q$;
- Computes $x^* := x g_1^{u_1} g_2^{u_2} v^d, e^* := \mathcal{H}(m, x^*), e := e^* - d$;
- Sends e to the signer.

Signing Phase. The Signer:

- Computes $y_1 := r_1 + e s_1, y_2 := r_2 + e s_2$;
- If $b = 1$ then computes $(bsig_1, bsig_2) := (k^{y_1}, y_2)$;
- If $b = 0$ then selects randomly $(bsig_1, bsig_2) \leftarrow_R \mathbb{G} \times \mathbb{Z}_q$;
- Outputs $(x, e, bsig_1, bsig_2)$.

Unblinding Phase. The Recipient:

- Unblinds by computing $sig_1 := bsig_1 \cdot k^{u_1}$ and $sig_2 := bsig_2 + u_2$;
- Outputs $(m, x^*, e^*, sig_1, sig_2)$.

Verification Phase. The Verifier:

- Computes $e^{*'} := \mathcal{H}(m, x^*)$
- Computes $y_1' := sig_1$ and $y_2' := sig_2$;
- Checks if $x^{*s} = y_1' g_2^{y_2' \cdot s} v^{e^* \cdot s}$ and $e^{*'} = e^*$.

Fig. 5. The original CBS Scheme based on Okamoto Schnorr signatures

C Modified Okamoto-Schnorr CBS Scheme

The protocol in Fig. 5 can be combined with a multiplicatively homomorphic encryption scheme. It can also be made more practical if the parties agree in a common method to randomly generate the commitment message x. Moreover, we can let the signer play the role of the verifier, as a way to send the secret bit to oneself in the future.

We present this modified version in Fig. 6. Note that the unblinding of the first part of the signature, still occurs on the exponent, but this time in encrypted form.

Common input: $\mathbb{G}, g_1, g_2, h_1, v, x \in \mathbb{G}$, public keys k, h, $\mathcal{H} : \mathcal{M} \times \mathbb{G} \rightarrow \mathbb{Z}_q$
Signers's private input: $s \in \mathbb{Z}_q : k = g_1^s$, $z \in \mathbb{Z}_q : h = h_1^z$ and $b \in \{0, 1\}$
Recipient's private input: m

Blinding:

- $\mathcal{U}$ chooses random $u_1, u_2, d \leftarrow_R \mathbb{Z}_q$
- $\mathcal{U}$ computes $x^* := xg_1^{u_1} g_2^{u_2} v^d$, $e^* := \mathcal{H}(m, x^*)$ and $e := e^* - d$;
- $\mathcal{U}$ sends e to $\mathcal{S}$

Signing:

- $\mathcal{S}$ randomly selects $bsig_2 \leftarrow_R \mathbb{Z}_q$;
- If $b = 1$ then compute $bsig_1 := \mathrm{E}_h((x \cdot g_2^{-bsig_2} \cdot v^{-e})^s)$;
- If $b = 0$ then select randomly $bsig_1 \leftarrow \mathbb{G}^2$;
- Output $(x, e, bsig_1, bsig_2)$.

Unblinding:

- $\mathcal{U}$ computes $sig_1 := bsig_1 \cdot \mathrm{E}_h(k^{u_1})$ and $sig_2 := bsig_2 + u_2$;
- Output $(m, x^*, e^*, sig_1, sig_2)$.

Verification:

- $\mathcal{V}$ recomputes e^* as $\mathcal{H}(m, x^*)$. If $e^* \neq \mathcal{H}(m, x^*)$ $\mathcal{V}$ outputs 0.
- $\mathcal{V}$ decrypts the first part of the signature to receive $y_1' := \mathrm{D}_z(sig_1)$
- $\mathcal{V}$ sets $y_2' := sig_2$
- $\mathcal{V}$ checks if $x^{*s} = y_1' g_2^{y_2' \cdot s} v^{e^* \cdot s}$ and outputs 1 iff it holds

Fig. 6. Modified conditional blind signatures

References

1. Chaum, D.: Blind signatures for untraceable payments. In: Chaum, D., Rivest, R.L., Sherman, A.T. (eds.) Advances in Cryptology, pp. 199–203. Springer, Boston (1983). https://doi.org/10.1007/978-1-4757-0602-4_18

2. Fiat, A., Shamir, A.: How to prove yourself: practical solutions to identification and signature problems. In: Odlyzko, A.M. (ed.) CRYPTO 1986. LNCS, vol. 263, pp. 186–194. Springer, Heidelberg (1987). https://doi.org/10.1007/3-540-47721-7_12

3. Schnorr, C.P.: Efficient identification and signatures for smart cards. In: Brassard, G. (ed.) CRYPTO 1989. LNCS, vol. 435, pp. 239–252. Springer, New York (1990). https://doi.org/10.1007/0-387-34805-0_22

4. Fujioka, A., Okamoto, T., Ohta, K.: A practical secret voting scheme for large scale elections. In: Seberry, J., Zheng, Y. (eds.) AUSCRYPT 1992. LNCS, vol. 718, pp. 244–251. Springer, Heidelberg (1993). https://doi.org/10.1007/3-540-57220-1_66

5. Okamoto, T.: Provably secure and practical identification schemes and corresponding signature schemes. In: Brickell, E.F. (ed.) CRYPTO 1992. LNCS, vol. 740, pp. 31–53. Springer, Heidelberg (1993). https://doi.org/10.1007/3-540-48071-4_3

6. Chaum, D., Pedersen, T.P.: Wallet databases with observers. In: Brickell, E.F. (ed.) CRYPTO 1992. LNCS, vol. 740, pp. 89–105. Springer, Heidelberg (1993). https://doi.org/10.1007/3-540-48071-4_7

7. Cramer, R., Damgård, I., Schoenmakers, B.: Proofs of partial knowledge and simplified design of witness hiding protocols. In: Desmedt, Y.G. (ed.) CRYPTO 1994. LNCS, vol. 839, pp. 174–187. Springer, Heidelberg (1994). https://doi.org/10.1007/3-540-48658-5_19

8. Jakobsson, M., Sako, K., Impagliazzo, R.: Designated verifier proofs and their applications. In: Maurer, U. (ed.) EUROCRYPT 1996. LNCS, vol. 1070, pp. 143–154. Springer, Heidelberg (1996). https://doi.org/10.1007/3-540-68339-9_13

9. Juels, A., Luby, M., Ostrovsky, R.: Security of blind digital signatures. In: Kaliski, B.S. (ed.) CRYPTO 1997. LNCS, vol. 1294, pp. 150–164. Springer, Heidelberg (1997). https://doi.org/10.1007/BFb0052233

10. Ohkubo, M., Miura, F., Abe, M., Fujioka, A., Okamoto, T.: An improvement on a practical secret voting scheme. ISW 1999. LNCS, vol. 1729, pp. 225–234. Springer, Heidelberg (1999). https://doi.org/10.1007/3-540-47790-X_19

11. Jakobsson, M., Juels, A.: Mix and match: secure function evaluation via ciphertexts. In: Okamoto, T. (ed.) ASIACRYPT 2000. LNCS, vol. 1976, pp. 162–177. Springer, Heidelberg (2000). https://doi.org/10.1007/3-540-44448-3_13

12. Juels, A., Catalano, D., Jakobsson, M.: Coercion-resistant electronic elections. In: Proceedings of the 2005 ACM Workshop on Privacy in the Electronic Society, pp. 61–70. ACM (2005)

13. Smith, W.D.: New cryptographic voting scheme with best-known theoretical properties. In: Frontiers in Electronic Elections (FEE 2005), June 2005

14. Benaloh, J.: Simple verifiable elections. In: EVT 2006 (2006)

15. Moran, T., Naor, M.: Receipt-free universally-verifiable voting with everlasting privacy. In: Dwork, C. (ed.) CRYPTO 2006. LNCS, vol. 4117, pp. 373–392. Springer, Heidelberg (2006). https://doi.org/10.1007/11818175_22

16. Araújo, R., Foulle, S., Traoré, J.: A practical and secure coercion resistant scheme for remote elections. In: Frontiers of Electronic Voting (2007)

17. Weber, S.G., Araujo, R., Buchmann, J.: On coercion-resistant electronic elections with linear work. In: ARES, pp. 908–916. IEEE (2007)

18. Adida, B.: Helios: web-based open-audit voting. In: Proceedings of the 17th Conference on Security Symposium, pp. 335–348. USENIX Association (2008)

19. Clarkson, M.R., Chong, S., Myers, A.C.: Civitas: toward a secure voting system. In: IEEE Security and Privacy Symposium (2008)

20. Araújo, R., Ben Rajeb, N., Robbana, R., Traoré, J., Youssfi, S.: Towards practical and secure coercion-resistant electronic elections. In: Heng, S.-H., Wright, R.N., Goi, B.-M. (eds.) CANS 2010. LNCS, vol. 6467, pp. 278–297. Springer, Heidelberg (2010). https://doi.org/10.1007/978-3-642-17619-7_20

21. Moran, T., Naor, M.: Split-ballot voting: everlasting privacy with distributed trust. ACM Trans. Inf. Syst. Secur. **13**(2), 16 (2010)

22. Koenig, R., Haenni, R., Fischli, S.: Preventing board flooding attacks in coercion-resistant electronic voting schemes. In: Camenisch, J., Fischer-Hübner, S., Murayama, Y., Portmann, A., Rieder, C. (eds.) SEC 2011. IAICT, vol. 354, pp. 116–127. Springer, Heidelberg (2011). https://doi.org/10.1007/978-3-642-21424-0_10

23. Schläpfer, M., Haenni, R., Koenig, R., Spycher, O.: Efficient vote authorization in coercion-resistant internet voting. In: Kiayias, A., Lipmaa, H. (eds.) Vote-ID 2011. LNCS, vol. 7187, pp. 71–88. Springer, Heidelberg (2012). https://doi.org/10.1007/978-3-642-32747-6_5

24. Schröder, D., Unruh, D.: Security of blind signatures revisited. IACR Cryptology ePrint Archive, p. 316 (2011)

25. Bayer, S., Groth, J.: Efficient zero-knowledge argument for correctness of a shuffle. In: Pointcheval, D., Johansson, T. (eds.) EUROCRYPT 2012. LNCS, vol. 7237, pp. 263–280. Springer, Heidelberg (2012). https://doi.org/10.1007/978-3-642-29011-4_17

26. Spycher, O., Koenig, R., Haenni, R., Schläpfer, M.: A new approach towards coercion-resistant remote E-voting in linear time. In: Danezis, G. (ed.) FC 2011. LNCS, vol. 7035, pp. 182–189. Springer, Heidelberg (2012). https://doi.org/10.1007/978-3-642-27576-0_15

27. Clark, J., Hengartner, U.: Selections: internet voting with over-the-shoulder coercion-resistance. In: Danezis, G. (ed.) FC 2011. LNCS, vol. 7035, pp. 47–61. Springer, Heidelberg (2012). https://doi.org/10.1007/978-3-642-27576-0_4

28. Arapinis, M., Cortier, V., Kremer, S., Ryan, M.: Practical everlasting privacy. In: Basin, D., Mitchell, J.C. (eds.) POST 2013. LNCS, vol. 7796, pp. 21–40. Springer, Heidelberg (2013). https://doi.org/10.1007/978-3-642-36830-1_2

29. Araújo, R., Traoré, J.: A practical coercion resistant voting scheme revisited. In: Heather, J., Schneider, S., Teague, V. (eds.) Vote-ID 2013. LNCS, vol. 7985, pp. 193–209. Springer, Heidelberg (2013). https://doi.org/10.1007/978-3-642-39185-9_12

30. Buchmann, J., Demirel, D., van de Graaf, J.: Towards a publicly-verifiable mixnet providing everlasting privacy. In: Sadeghi, A.-R. (ed.) FC 2013. LNCS, vol. 7859, pp. 197–204. Springer, Heidelberg (2013). https://doi.org/10.1007/978-3-642-39884-1_16

31. Cuvelier, É., Pereira, O., Peters, T.: Election verifiability or ballot privacy: do we need to choose? In: Crampton, J., Jajodia, S., Mayes, K. (eds.) ESORICS 2013. LNCS, vol. 8134, pp. 481–498. Springer, Heidelberg (2013). https://doi.org/10.1007/978-3-642-40203-6_27

32. Grewal, G.S., Ryan, M.D., Bursuc, S., Ryan, P.Y.A.: Caveat coercitor: coercion-evidence in electronic voting. In: IEEE Security and Privacy Symposium. IEEE (2013)

33. Kiayias, A., Zacharias, T., Zhang, B.: End-to-end verifiable elections in the standard model. In: Oswald, E., Fischlin, M. (eds.) EUROCRYPT 2015. LNCS, vol. 9057, pp. 468–498. Springer, Heidelberg (2015). https://doi.org/10.1007/978-3-662-46803-6_16

34. Araújo, R., Barki, A., Brunet, S., Traoré, J.: Remote electronic voting can be efficient, verifiable and coercion-resistant. In: Clark, J., Meiklejohn, S., Ryan, P.Y.A., Wallach, D., Brenner, M., Rohloff, K. (eds.) FC 2016. LNCS, vol. 9604, pp. 224–232. Springer, Heidelberg (2016). https://doi.org/10.1007/978-3-662-53357-4_15

35. Cortier, V., Galindo, D., Kuesters, R., Mueller, J., Truderung, T.: SoK: verifiability notions for e-voting protocols. In: IEEE Security and Privacy Symposium, pp. 779–798 (2016)

36. Locher, P., Haenni, R., Koenig, R.E.: Coercion-resistant internet voting with everlasting privacy. In: Clark, J., Meiklejohn, S., Ryan, P.Y.A., Wallach, D., Brenner, M., Rohloff, K. (eds.) FC 2016. LNCS, vol. 9604, pp. 161–175. Springer, Heidelberg (2016). https://doi.org/10.1007/978-3-662-53357-4_11

37. Ryan, P.Y.A., Rønne, P.B., Iovino, V.: Selene: voting with transparent verifiability and coercion-mitigation. In: Clark, J., Meiklejohn, S., Ryan, P.Y.A., Wallach, D., Brenner, M., Rohloff, K. (eds.) FC 2016. LNCS, vol. 9604, pp. 176–192. Springer, Heidelberg (2016). https://doi.org/10.1007/978-3-662-53357-4_12

38. Grontas, P., Pagourtzis, A., Zacharakis, A.: Coercion resistance in a practical secret voting scheme for large scale elections. In: ISPAN-FCST-ISCC 2017, pp. 514–519 (2017)

39. Iovino, V., Rial, A., Rønne, P.B., Ryan, P.Y.A.: Using selene to verify your vote in JCJ. In: Brenner, M., et al. (eds.) FC 2017. LNCS, vol. 10323, pp. 385–403. Springer, Cham (2017). https://doi.org/10.1007/978-3-319-70278-0_24
40. Yang, N., Clark, J.: Practical governmental voting with unconditional integrity and privacy. In: Brenner, M., et al. (eds.) FC 2017. LNCS, vol. 10323, pp. 434–449. Springer, Cham (2017). https://doi.org/10.1007/978-3-319-70278-0_27
41. Zacharakis, A., Grontas, P., Pagourtzis, A.: Conditional blind signatures. In: 7th International Conference on Algebraic Informatics (Short Version) (2017). http://eprint.iacr.org/2017/682

Modeling a Bulletin Board Service Based on Broadcast Channels with Memory

Severin Hauser[1,2] and Rolf Haenni[1(✉)]

[1] Bern University of Applied Sciences, 2501 Biel, Switzerland
{severin.hauser,rolf.haenni}@bfh.ch
[2] University of Fribourg, 1700 Fribourg, Switzerland
severin.hauser@unifr.ch

Abstract. The publication of the election data is fundamental for making electronic voting systems universally verifiable. For this, voting protocols usually rely on a secure bulletin board, which keeps track of the data produced during the protocol execution. This paper presents a general model for implementing such a bulletin board service. The design of the model is based on the concept of an ideal broadcast channel with memory, which transmits messages without loss of information to a present or future receiver. The challenge of implementing a bulletin board service is to approximate the properties of such an ideal channel to the best possible degree. Our model contributes to a better understanding of these properties and may help in designing future bulletin board implementations.

1 Introduction

To achieve universal verifiability, all parties involved in a cryptographic voting protocol must achieve an agreement on the public data created during the protocol execution. This problem can be seen as a *Byzantine agreement problem* [17]. For some voting contexts like boardroom voting, state-of-the-art Byzantine agreement (or *reliable broadcast*) protocols are reasonable solutions. Unfortunately, for many voting contexts these protocols are not well fitted for two reasons. First, these protocols are not sufficiently efficient on a large scale with many computationally limited parties. Secondly, the model for these protocols assumes that all honest parties are available at the moment of the protocol execution. For parties such as voters in real-world political elections, this is not a realistic assumption. Their limited connectivity could even lead to the point where no agreement can be achieved at all. Cryptographic voting is not the only application with this kind of problems. Other applications that have to deal with similar problems are online auctions or cryptographic currencies. From a more general viewpoint, these applications can be regarded as secure multi-party computation problems with a public audit, in which external auditors can check whether the protocol output was computed correctly or not [2].

© International Financial Cryptography Association 2019
A. Zohar et al. (Eds.): FC 2018 Workshops, LNCS 10958, pp. 232–246, 2019.
https://doi.org/10.1007/978-3-662-58820-8_16

So instead of applying Byzantine agreement protocols, papers from the cryptographic voting literature often refer to a *broadcast channel with memory* (BCM) for making the public election data available to everyone. The existence of a BCM is often assumed without providing a detailed definition of what a BCM is and without specifying its properties [6,20]. The lack of proper definitions is a problem for the general understanding of the cryptographic protocols and for analyzing their security properties. To the best of our knowledge, the first proposal for a formal BCM model has been published recently in [14]. According to this model, which defines a BCM as an idealized theoretical construct, messages can be transmitted instantaneously and without loss to a present or future receiver.

In a real-world implementation of a given cryptographic protocol, the theoretical model of a BCM can at best be approximated. A common approach is to substitute the BCM with a service provided by one or more additional protocol parties. The job of these parties is to receive and memorize the messages transmitted over the broadcast channel during the protocol execution. A group of parties providing this service is what we call *bulletin board service* (BBS). Its goal is to guarantee that all submitted messages are recorded, that messages are never deleted or modified, and that the order in which the messages appeared is tracked. Bulletin board implementations with this property are called *append-only*. In addition, some voting protocols require designated board sections for all involved parties [6], while other protocols require that the board rejects messages that are not well-formed [13]. When implementing a BBS, appropriate solutions for such protocol-specific requirements need to be provided in addition to the append-only property. Since a large amount of the available BBS literature focuses on providing solutions for a specific cryptographic protocol, distinguishing the properties derived from the BCM and the ones introduced by the cryptographic protocol is sometimes difficult.

1.1 Contribution and Paper Overview

In Sect. 2, we introduce formal definitions for various types of channels, including a definition for a broadcast channel with memory. We summarize the model presented in [14] and expand it with the concept of return-link channels. Our definitions describe how such channels behave under ideal circumstances. As such, they serve as a guideline for the design of a bulletin board service, which mimics the ideal behaviour of a broadcast channel with memory under real-world circumstances.

The main contribution of this paper is a proposal for a general BBS model, which we introduce in Sect. 3. This model is derived from the BCM definition with the goal of providing an analogous functionality and similar guarantees. Based on the necessary communication channels to the rest of the system, we identify several communication roles and describe the tasks and responsibilities of parties fulfilling these roles. We illustrate the generality of the model with some real-world examples.

1.2   Related Work

The idea of publishing the election data on a public bulletin board has a long tradition in the literature of verifiable electronic voting. While almost every existing
cryptographic voting protocol uses a BBS as a central communication platform
between the parties involved, almost no paper describing such a protocol gives
a precise specification of the properties expected from the board. Usually, the
existence of an appropriate BBS is just taken for granted, but the BBS itself
remains a black box.

Given the importance of the bulletin board concept in electronic voting, only
a remarkably small number of specific papers is devoted to the problem of specifying and implementing a BBS. Peters was one of the first to suggest such a
specification and solution [20]. His main focus was on making the bulletin board
robust against failures or attacks, using multiple peers and protocols from the
multi-party computation literature. In [15,18], Heather and Lundin made some
proposals to ensure the append-only property and to solve the resulting conflicts
with the robustness property. Some reports on corresponding implementations
have been published later [3,16]. Another description of a practical BBS implementation is included in the report about the voting system used in the state
of Victoria, Australia [4]. In a follow-up paper [9], Culnane and Schneider proposed a robust algorithm for a peered bulletin board and verified its correctness
formally. Recently Dold and Grothoff presented a Byzantine consensus protocol
that allows to synchronize a set of elements [10]. They use it to implement the
bulletin board for an e-voting system that is based on the protocol proposed by
Cramer et al. [7].

2   Broadcast Channel with Memory

Many cryptographic voting protocols in the literature assume the existence of a
broadcast channel with memory to achieve universal verifiability. The BCM is
used by the involved parties to exchange public data during the execution of the
protocol. Unfortunately, a proper formal definitions of the core functionalities
and properties of a BCM is often entirely missing. This lack of proper definitions
leads to problems in the understanding of the cryptographic protocols and their
security properties. In this section, based on the notion of a distributed system,
we give formal definitions of broadcast channels and broadcast channels with
memory. Our model is both a summary and an extension of the BCM model
proposed in [14].

2.1   Distributed Systems and Channels

A *distributed system* (Ω, Γ) consists of a finite set of *parties* $\Omega = \{p_1, \ldots, p_n\}$
and a finite set of *channels* $\Gamma = \{c_1, \ldots, c_m\}$. The parties in this system exchange
messages over the available channels to achieve some security (and other) objectives in the context of a given problem domain. It is usually assumed that the

channels provide some properties such as authenticity or confidentiality. In our model of a distributed system, we assume—as a general rule—that all channels are *ideal*. This means that they are *noiseless*, possess *unlimited capacity*, and provide a *total message order*. This implies that no message can be lost or modified during transmission, that messages of arbitrary size are transmitted instantaneously, and that no two messages can be sent at the exact same point in time.

Definition 1. A *(ideal) channel* $c \in \Gamma$ of a distributed system (Ω, Γ) is defined by a *sender domain* $S_c \subseteq \Omega$ (the parties that can send messages over c), a *receiver domain* $R_c \subseteq \Omega$ (the parties that can receive messages over c), and a *message space* $\mathcal{M}_c \subseteq \mathcal{M}$ (the messages that can be transmitted over c). If $s \in S_c$ transmits $m \in \mathcal{M}_c$ over c to R_c, then every $r \in R_c$ receives m instantaneously when m is sent. Parties $p \in \Omega \setminus R_c$ not from the receiver domain can observe the transmission of m over c, but can not learn any information about m itself (except its length). On the other hand, parties $p \notin \Omega$ not belonging to the distributed system do not have access to the channels and can therefore not even observe the transmission of m.

The general definition of an ideal channel includes a number of useful limiting cases, which are important in cryptographic protocols. We call $c \in \Gamma$ a *public channel*, if $S_c = \Omega$. This means that every party in the system is able to send messages over c. Similarly, c is called *broadcast channel*, if $R_c = \Omega$.[1] In this case, every message transmitted is received by all parties in the system. If $S_c = \{s\}$ consists of a single sender $s \in \Omega$, then c is an *authentic channel*. Receiving m over such an authentic channel guarantees that s is the author of m. Similarly, if $R_c = \{r\}$ consists of a single receiver $r \in \Omega$, then c is a *confidential channel*. In this case, the channel guarantees that no party other that r learns anything about m (beyond its length). If the sender and receiver domains are identical, i.e., if $S_c = R_c$, we speak of a *closed group channel*. In this case, every member of the closed group can send and receive messages over c.

Some of the above properties are mutually exclusive. For instance, a broadcast channel can not be confidential and a public channel can not be authentic (except for $|\Omega| = 1$). On the other hand, there are a number of useful combinations that are very common in cryptographic protocols. Most importantly, if c is authentic and confidential at the same time, i.e., if both $S_c = \{s\}$ and $R_c = \{r\}$ consist of a single party only, it is called a *secure channel*. A secure channel is called *untappable* in the special case of $\Omega = \{s, r\}$. This implies that no other party can observe the transmission of messages between s and r.

---

[1] In the literature, broadcast channels are defined in many different ways, for example as a $(m, \lambda, \ldots, \lambda) \mapsto (m, m, \ldots, m)$, where λ denotes an empty message. Such a *broadcast functionality* is an important building block for designing secure multi-party computation protocols in the presence of active adversaries. Assuming a public-key infrastructure, such broadcast channels can be implemented for any number of malicious parties using a signature scheme [12].

Definition 2. A *return-link channel* is a channel $c \in \Gamma$ of a distributed system (Ω, Γ) that creates temporary *return-links* from every receiver $r \in R_c$ of a transmitted message $m \in \mathcal{M}_c$ to the sender $s \in S_c$ of the message. Return-links can be used by a receiver for sending a response $\ell \in \mathcal{L}_c$ to the (possibly unknown) sender s, where $\mathcal{L}_c$ denotes the message domain of the return-links created by c. By submitting ℓ over the return-link, r does not learn more about s other than $s \in S_c$. The transmission of ℓ from r to s is instantaneous and noiseless. Parties other than s and r can observe the transmission, but they do not learn anything about ℓ.

Return links are expected to be available only for a short time after the transmission of a message. The exact purpose of sending back a response is not further specified, but in most cases it will be something like an acknowledgement, receipt, status report, error message, etc. In protocols relying on such responses, return-link channels are useful to reduce the total amount of necessary channels between the parties. They are also useful to return the response directly to the actual sender $s \in S_c$, even if S_c contains multiple parties and therefore s is unknown to r. Return-links with such properties are widely available in the real world, for example in the case of TCP connections. An example of a distributed system with 10 parties and 3 channels is shown in Fig. 1. Regular channels are depicted as single-headed arrows and return-link channels as double-headed arrows.

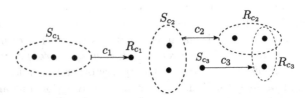

Fig. 1. Example of a distributed system with a confidential channel c_1, a return-link channel c_2, and an authentic channel c_3.

2.2   Broadcast Channel with Memory

In our ideal model of noiseless channels with unlimited capacities, we assume that every submitted message reaches every receiver from the receiver domain instantaneously, independently of the receiver's actual availability and capacity to process the incoming message. In a non-ideal setting, receivers might not always be capable of processing the messages the moment they arrive. They might even miss some incoming messages entirely. In cryptographic protocols, in which broadcast channels are used to spread information to everyone, this imperfection can cause complicated coordination problems.

To allow a receiver to recover from messages lost during the protocol execution, we introduce the concept of a channel with memory. The idea is that the transmission of a message $m \in \mathcal{M}_c$ over a channel $c \in \Gamma$ is performed by two operations s : $\mathsf{Send}_c(m)$ and r : $\mathbf{M}_c \leftarrow \mathsf{Receive}_c()$. The former is invoked by the sender $s \in S_c$ and the latter by the receiver $r \in R_c$. A channel with memory guarantees that the messages and the order in which they have been sent are stored and never lost. For this, the channel maintains an internal state, called *channel history* $\mathbf{M}_c$, which is initialized by $\mathbf{M}_c \leftarrow \langle\rangle$ and updated by $\mathbf{M}_c \leftarrow \mathbf{M}_c \| \langle m \rangle$ each time a new message $m \in \mathcal{M}_c$ is sent. This idea is further formalized in the following definition.

Definition 3. A channel $c \in \Gamma$ of a distributed system (Ω, Γ) with sender domain $S_c \subseteq \Omega$ and receiver domain $R_c \subseteq \Omega$ is called *channel with memory*, if every $s \in S_c$ can perform the operation s : $\mathsf{Send}_c(m)$ to send a message $m \in \mathcal{M}_c$ over the channel and every $r \in R_c$ can perform r : $\mathbf{M}_c \leftarrow \mathsf{Receive}_c()$ to receive the current channel history $\mathbf{M}_c \in \mathcal{M}_c^*$ of all messages sent so far. An ideal channel with memory has unlimited capacity, i.e., $\mathbf{M}_c$ can get arbitrarily large.

The concept of a channel with memory applies to all particular channel types described before. For example, a *broadcast channel with memory* (BCM) gives every party permanent access to all the messages sent over this channel. In an authentic BCM, it is guaranteed that every message included in the channel history has been sent by the same single sender. In a public BCM, the senders of the messages are unknown within Ω (except for $|\Omega| = 1$). Authentic and public broadcast channels with memory are the most useful instances in cryptographic voting protocols, for example to provide authentic broadcasting to the election authorities and public broadcasting to the voters. If a protocol provides multiple authentic broadcast channels with different senders, it may be necessary to augment Definition 3 to support a common history over multiple channels. For this, we refer to the definition of a *bundled broadcast channel with memory* (BBCM), which additionally keeps track of the sender of every transmitted message [14].

3   Bulletin Board Service

The concept of a BCM as described in the previous section is an idealized theoretical construct, for which no one-to-one practical implementation exists in the real world. For this reason, cryptographic protocols that require such a channel need a substitution that provides an equivalent functionality and similar guarantees. Knowing that the exact same properties of an ideal broadcast channel with memory can at best be approximated by a practical implementation, designing such a substitution is a very delicate problem on its own. A common approach in the literature is to add one or multiple additional parties offering the service of a *bulletin board* to the other parties of the distributed system. In this section, we introduce a general model for such a *bulletin board service* (BBS). We first describe the desired properties of a BBS and the basic functionality. Then we introduce various roles for the parties involved and show how several examples from the real world fit into the general model.

3.1   Guarantees

In Sect. 2, we introduced the concept of a BCM as a channel with ideal properties. For a BBS to offer similar properties, we identified a number of guarantees that seem to be crucial for a BBS to provide. Knowing that the ideal BCM properties can at best be approximated, it is important to have at least a clear understanding of some realistic goals and an overview of the possibilities for reaching them. For each guarantee introduced below, we refer to the corresponding BCM property, from which it is derived.

Authentication. This addresses the fact, that an ideal BCM c only allows parties from its sender domain S_c to submit messages. For the BBS, this means that the sender of a message must be authenticated to ensure that only messages from parties belonging to the sender domain are accepted. If the authentication evidence provided by the sender is transferable to third parties, it can be recorded together with the message and forwarded to third parties on request. Digital signatures are examples of such transferable authentication evidence, which ensures sender authenticity without relying on trust in the BBS.

Non-discrimination. When a message is transmitted over an ideal BCM, parties are discriminated only with respect to the channel's sender domain. Therefore, the BBS needs to ensure that no party from the sender domain is excluded from accessing the interface provided by the service for submitting a message. Similarly, it must be ensured that no party is discriminated against retrieving the set of all submitted messages. Known solutions for this are based on the assumption that at least some of the parties responsible for accepting the incoming messages and disseminating the recorded messages behave correctly.

Message Ordering. An ideal channel with memory records and returns the transmitted messages in perfect chronological order. Therefore, the BBS has to provide an equivalent mechanism which ensures a unique message ordering even if a large amount of messages is submitted almost simultaneously. This message ordering has to be immutable and everyone must be able to verify its correctness. Since submitting messages over real-world channels always implies some delay and the BBS might need time for processing them, implementing a perfect chronological order is very difficult. Therefore, the goal of a BBS implementation is to provide an order that approximates the perfect chronological ordering as close as possible.

Message Well-Formedness. The message space $\mathcal{M}_c$ of a BCM c restricts the type and format of the transmitted messages. This restriction can be transferred easily to a BBS by performing corresponding checks for each incoming message. Valid messages $m \in \mathcal{M}_c$ are accepted and recorded, whereas invalid messages $m \notin \mathcal{M}_c$ are rejected.

Uniqueness. An ideal BCM c has a unique and unchangeable channel history $\mathbf{M}_c$ consisting of all previously submitted messages in chronological order. Therefore, the BBS also has to ensure that set of recorded messages is unique and can not be altered, i.e., all parties retrieving the board content will receive compatible views. More precisely, if two parties request the board content at two different points in time $t_1 < t_2$, then the list of messages retrieved at t_1 must be a prefix of the list retrieved at t_2.

Completeness. With an ideal BCM c, submitted messages are recorded instantaneously and added to the channel history without any delay. This implies that the BCM always returns the complete channel history $\mathbf{M}_c$ of all messages submitted so far. Therefore, a BBS also needs to ensure that submitted messages are processed as quickly as possible and that requests are always responded with the complete board content of all recorded messages. The maximal necessary time for a message to be processed by the BBS is denoted by Δ. This value is an important characteristics of a given BBS implementation.

3.2 Basic Model and Functionality

Let (Ω, Γ) be a distributed system with a single broadcast channel with memory $c_{\mathsf{BCM}} \in \Gamma$. Replacing c_{BCM} by a BBS means to introduce an extended distributed system (Ω', Γ'), where $\Omega' = \Omega \cup \Phi$ denotes the extended set of parties and $\Gamma' = (\Gamma \setminus \{c_{\mathsf{BCM}}\}) \cup \Psi$ the updated set of channels. The elements of Φ and Ψ are called *bulletin board parties* and *bulletin board channels*, respectively. The BBS must be designed in a way that all parties from $S_{c_{\mathsf{BCM}}}$ have access to a channel in Ψ that connects them with the bulletin board parties for submitting a message to the BBS. Similarly, all parties from Ω must have access to a channel for receiving the channel history $\mathbf{M}_{\mathsf{BCM}}$ from the bulletin board parties. The bulletin board parties themselves may be mutually connected over additional (possibly authentic or confidential) channels to coordinate their current state of memory. To accomplish the substitution of c_{BCM}, it is crucial that Ψ introduces no new channel with memory, i.e., that all channels in Γ' can be realized using standard communication and network technology.

For a BBS to provide the same functionality as c_{BCM}, it needs to provide operations similar to $\mathsf{Send}_{c_{\mathsf{BCM}}}(m)$ and $\mathsf{Receive}_{c_{\mathsf{BCM}}}()$. To avoid confusion between channel and service, we call them $\mathsf{Post}_{\mathsf{BBS}}(p)$ and $\mathsf{Get}_{\mathsf{BBS}}()$, where $p = (m, \alpha)$ contains the broadcast message $m \in \mathcal{M}_{\mathsf{BCM}}$ and some meta-data $\alpha \in \mathcal{A}$. The purpose and format of α depends on the concrete realization of the BBS, but it often contains some *authentication evidence* such as a digital signature, that can be verified by third parties. The pair p itself is called *post* and the process of submitting p to the BBS is called *posting*. If a party posts p to the BBS, it sends it over one of the available bulletin board channels to one or multiple bulletin board parties, which are responsible for the further processing of p.

To be as general as possible, we assume that posts are processed in blocks $b = (\{p_1, \ldots, p_s\}, \beta)$, where $\beta \in \mathcal{B}$ denotes some meta-data added to the block by the bulletin board parties. The main purpose of β is to provide some *publishing evidence* such as a signed hash chain, which again can be verified by third parties. Note that the posts included in a block are unordered. The internal processing of a block b by the bulletin board parties is called *publication* of b.

Depending on the block size, there are different publication modes. If the block size s is a fixed value for all blocks, it means that the incoming posts are buffered until the block size is reached. If the blocks are created periodically, for example one block every minute, we obtain blocks of different sizes. Corresponding publication modes are called *buffered publication* and *periodical publication*, respectively. A fixed block size $s = 1$ is an important special case of buffered publication, in which individual posts are published immediately. This particular mode is called *immediate publication*. The selected publication mode is an important characteristics of a concrete BBS implementation.

The bulletin board parties are responsible for keeping track of all the processed blocks of posts. This internal state of the BBS consisting of all blocks is called *board history*. One can think of it as an initially empty list $\mathbf{B} \leftarrow \langle \rangle$, which is updated to $\mathbf{B} \leftarrow \mathbf{B} \| \langle b \rangle$ each time a new block b has been formed. This means that $\mathbf{B}$ contains the list of all blocks published by the BBS so far. Therefore, $\mathbf{B}$ is also the expected return value of $\mathsf{Get_{BBS}}()$, which then enables the derivation of the channel history $\mathbf{M_{BCM}}$ by extracting the messages from the individual posts in the blocks. Note that immediate publication is the only mode that implies a unique message ordering. This is because the order over the blocks is fixed and in this case each block contains only one message.

3.3   Basic Roles

Every party involved in a BBS has a certain role with corresponding tasks. As the specific roles and tasks depend greatly of the protocol used to run the BBS, we can not introduce the roles and tasks in a general way. However, given the general goal of providing two basic operations $\mathsf{Post_{BBS}}(p)$ and $\mathsf{Get_{BBS}}()$, we identified four basic *communication roles*, which depend on how a given bulletin board party is involved in communicating with the main protocol parties. To provide the basic functionality, the BBS must provide at least two channels, one for collecting the posts submitted by parties from the sender domain S_{CBCM} and one for disseminating the board history to Ω. Without loss of generality, we assume that both channels have a return-link (see explanations given below). An auxiliary channel for broadcasting additional information about the current board state may be necessary to achieve some of the guarantees. The receiver and sender domains of these three channels define three different communication roles, which we call *collector*, *disseminator*, and *broadcaster*. The channels are denoted by $c_C, c_D, c_B \in \Psi$, respectively.

Figure 2 shows the communication roles of the bulletin board parties and illustrates how the parties interact with the rest of the system over the associated channels. The figure also shows how these roles could overlap depending on the protocol. Bulletin board parties not involved in the communication to the rest of the system define an additional role. We call them *associates* and the set of associates is denoted by Φ_A. Below, we give a more detailed description of each communication role, the interface they provide to the rest of the system, and the attributed tasks.

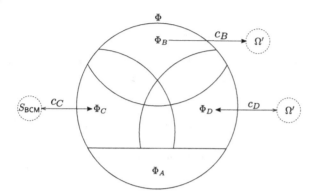

Fig. 2. Illustration of the communication roles and channels of a BBS. Corresponding sets of parties are denoted by Φ_A, Φ_B, Φ_C, and Φ_D. The channels c_C and c_D each have a return-link. The channel c_D is a public channel and the channel c_B is a broadcast channel.

Collector. The collectors are responsible for providing the $\mathsf{Post}_{\mathsf{BBS}}(p)$ operation to the sender domain S_{CBCM} of the BCM c_{BCM}. Upon receiving a new post $p = (m, \alpha)$ from a party of the sender domain S_{CBCM} over the channel c_C, the collectors have to check the authenticity and conformity of the message $m \in \mathcal{M}_{\mathsf{BCM}}$ and the meta-data $\alpha \in \mathcal{A}$. In case some check fails, an error message is returned over the return-link of c_C to the sender and the procedure aborts. Otherwise, p is added to the current block for further processing and some response $\gamma \in \mathcal{C}$ (acknowledgment, receipt, status report, etc.) is sent back to the sender. Returning such a response over the return-link extends the signature of the Post-operation as follows:

$$\gamma \leftarrow \mathsf{Post}_{\mathsf{BBS}}(p).$$

Disseminator. The disseminators are responsible for providing the $\mathsf{Get}_{\mathsf{BBS}}()$ operation to the main protocol parties. To avoid unnecessary restrictions, we extend the sender domain of c_D from Ω to $\Omega' = \Omega \cup \Phi$, which implies that c_D becomes a public channel in (Ω', Γ'). It can be used by every involved party to submit a request for the current board history to the disseminators. The return-link of c_D is required for returning the current board history $\mathbf{B}$ to the party requesting it. In addition to returning $\mathbf{B}$, the BBS may also produce and return some meta-data $\delta \in \mathcal{D}$ concerning the request. The following extended signature summarizes the Get-operation:

$$\mathbf{B}, \delta \leftarrow \mathsf{Get}_{\mathsf{BBS}}().$$

Invoking this operation will always return the complete set of blocks of the current board history, even if only some particular blocks or posts are of interest. In a productive environment, where $\mathbf{B}$ could grow into a very large set, this solution might not be very practical. Therefore, we propose an extended Get-operation,

$$\mathbf{B}_q, \delta \leftarrow \mathsf{Get}_{\mathsf{BBS}}(q),$$

which accepts a *query* $q \in \mathcal{Q}$ as input parameter. The query is applied to the board history and only the subset $\mathbf{B}_q \subseteq \mathbf{B}$ of blocks satisfying the query is returned.

Broadcaster. As the disseminators act only on request, the spreading of the board history $\mathbf{B}$ is somewhat limited. Since responding with $\mathbf{B}$ to a request is like a commitment to the current board state, not getting requests over a long period means that no commitments are made for a long time. Under such circumstances, guaranteeing completeness is more difficult. Therefore, we propose an additional broadcast channel c_B for spreading information about the board history to a larger group. The broadcasters are responsible for using this channel, for example each time a new block is added to the board history, or periodically, to broadcast some information $\phi = f(\mathbf{B})$ derived from $\mathbf{B}$ to everyone (for example the current header of a hash chain).

Associate. The group of associates in a BBS only communicates internally with the other bulletin board parties. They support the BBS in achieving its guarantees, for example by issuing signatures for each newly added block. They can also be in charge of maintaining the database, in which the current board state is stored, or of replicating this database for backup purposes.

Some particular bulletin board parties may fulfill the additional role of a *bulletin board trustee*. The set of all trustees is denoted by $\Phi_T \subseteq \Phi$. They are responsible for establishing the trust assumptions of the service, which are necessary for providing the desired guarantees. We assume that each trustee is in possession of a private signature key and that corresponding public keys are publicly known. An important tasks of a trustee is to sign every change made to the board history, i.e., each time a new block is added. In this case, signatures issued by the trustees may be added to the block's meta-data β, possibly together with a digital time-stamp, or they may be returned to the sender as part of the acknowledgment γ. In a similar way, signatures may be created and added to the response δ whenever a party requests the current board history $\mathbf{B}$. Figure 3 shows an example of a BBS with three collectors $\Phi_C = \{p_1, t_1, t_3\}$, three disseminators $\Phi_D = \{p_2, t_2, t_3\}$, three associates $\Phi_A = \{p_3, t_4, t_5\}$, and one broadcaster $\Phi_B = \{p_4\}$. There are five trustees $\Phi_T = \{t_1, t_2, t_3, t_4, t_5\}$.

3.4   BBS Examples

To show that the roles and guarantees introduced in this section can be applied to existing BBS implementations and that they are useful for a better understanding, we sketch here three examples and highlight their properties. An illustrative overview of these examples and the parties involved is given in Fig. 4.

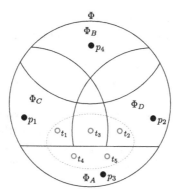

Fig. 3. Example of a BBS with parties $\Phi = \{p_1, p_2, p_3, p_4, t_1, t_2, t_3, t_4, t_5\}$ and trustees $\Phi_T = \{t_1, t_2, t_3, t_4, t_5\}$. We use red circles to represent trustees and black dots for ordinary bulletin board parties. (Color figure online)

Single-Party BBS. The setup as shown in Fig. 4a is the simplest possible one. It consists of a single trusted bulletin board party, which is responsible for everything. This setting is comparable to a classical central database, which stores the application data and responds to queries. Variations of this simple setup can be found in many implementations of verifiable voting systems [1,5,11]. To guarantee important properties such as completeness, non-discrimination, message-ordering, and uniqueness, this type of BBS relies completely on its single party to be honest. In most practical systems, the decision to adopt such a simple BBS design was due to lack of time or resources.

In most single-party implementations of this kind, posts are published immediately, i.e., the block size is equal to 1. The maximal publication time Δ is therefore relatively low. In a proposal by Heather and Lundin [15], in order to guarantee a unique message-ordering, the party submitting a post $p = (m, \alpha)$ first retrieves the current hash chain header from the board and incorporates it into α. The problem is that this may create race condition between multiple parties trying to submit a post simultaneously.

Multi-Party BBS. A setup with multiple trusted bulletin board parties of the same type often emerges from protocols that provide solutions to the *Byzantine Agreement Problem* [17]. All parties are assumed to act identically, and as a group, they are responsible for the proper functioning of the BBS. In the setup shown in Fig. 4b, all bulletin board parties act as collectors and disseminators. To guarantee important properties such as completeness, message-ordering, non-discrimination, and uniqueness, agreement protocols between the parties usually require more than 2/3 of the involved parties to be honest. Such agreement protocols are relatively complex and thus limit the throughput of the system. Peters proposed a design of such a setup based on a protocol by Reiter [20,21], and Beuchat presented an implementation of Peter's approach [3]. An other implementation is shown by Dold and Grothoff in [10]. They take a different approach as they use a protocol that allows for agreement on sets of messages. This way they only need to reach agreement between all bulletin board parties at the end of the voting period.

Into this category also belong most of the blockchain implementations presented until today, for example the blockchain used in the digital currency *Bit-Coin* [19]. There, so-called *miners* create a blockchain based on the *proof of work* concept and with an average block size of approximately 1800 transactions every ten minutes. This ensures uniqueness as long as the honest miners control more than half of the computation power. Because BitCoin integrates the miners into the protocol they also cover authentication and message well-formedness as honest miners will only accept blocks containing valid transactions. The other guarantees are addressed by different mechanics of the BitCoin protocol.

vVote System Bulletin Board. Culnane and Schneider presented in [9] a BBS proposal for the *vVote Verifiable Voting System* [8]. As shown in Fig. 4c, they introduce parties of different types and for different roles. There is a group of parties, called the *peers*, which act as collectors and trustees. Another party, called the *web bulletin board* (WBB), acts as disseminator and is therefore responsible for spreading the board history. Finally, a party called *publisher* uses a traditional printed newspaper for broadcasting daily the current hash chain header. By creating a new block only once a day, the protocol works with periodic publication. Completeness is ensured by the fixed schedule of the block creation and by the information printed in the newspaper. Uniqueness, non-discrimination and message ordering are guaranteed as long as more than 2/3 of the peers are honest.

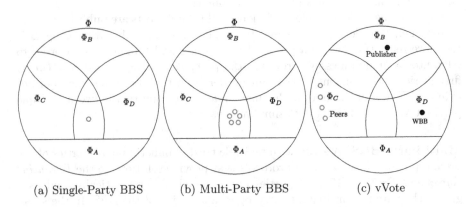

(a) Single-Party BBS   (b) Multi-Party BBS   (c) vVote

Fig. 4. Examples of existing BBS implementations.

4   Conclusion

In this paper, we presented and extended formal definitions for various types of channels. This also includes a broadcast channel with memory, which is often required in cryptographic voting protocols. Since a broadcast channel with memory has no direct implementation in the real world, it needs to be substituted by something that is often called bulletin board. Based on our definitions, we introduced a model for a bulletin board service. This model describes the guarantees this service must provide and what kind of roles exists inside the service. We showed that the model helps to understand existing bulletin board implementations by discussing some examples.

Acknowledgments. This research has been supported by the Hasler Foundation (project no. 14028). We thank the anonymous reviewers for their reviews and appreciate their valuable comments and suggestions.

References

1. Adida, B.: Helios: web-based open-audit voting. In: Van Oorschot, P. (ed.) SS 2008, 17th USENIX Security Symposium, pp. 335–348. San Jose, USA (2008)
2. Baum, C., Damgård, I., Orlandi, C.: Publicly auditable secure multi-party computation. In: Abdalla, M., De Prisco, R. (eds.) SCN 2014. LNCS, vol. 8642, pp. 175–196. Springer, Cham (2014). https://doi.org/10.1007/978-3-319-10879-7_11
3. Beuchat, J.: Append-Only Web Bulletin Board. Master's thesis, Bern University of Applied Sciences, Biel, Switzerland (2012)
4. Burton, C., et al.: A supervised verifiable voting protocol for the Victorian electoral commission. In: Kripp, M., Volkamer, M., Grimm, R. (eds.) EVOTE 2012, 5th International Workshop on Electronic Voting, no. P-205 in Lecture Notes in Informatics, Bregenz, Austria, pp. 81–94 (2012)
5. Clarkson, M.R., Chong, S., Myers, A.C.: Civitas: toward a secure voting system. In: SP 2008, 29th IEEE Symposium on Security and Privacy, pp. 354–368. Oakland, USA (2008)
6. Cramer, R., Gennaro, R., Schoenmakers, B.: A secure and optimally efficient multi-authority election scheme. In: Fumy, W. (ed.) EUROCRYPT 1997. LNCS, vol. 1233, pp. 103–118. Springer, Heidelberg (1997). https://doi.org/10.1007/3-540-69053-0_9
7. Cramer, R., Gennaro, R., Schoenmakers, B.: A secure and optimally efficient multi-authority election scheme. Eur. Trans. Telecommun. **8**(5), 481–490 (1997)
8. Culnane, C., Ryan, P.Y.A., Schneider, S., Teague, V.: vVote: a verifiable voting system. ACM Trans. Inf. Syst. Secur. **18**(1), 3:1–3:30 (2015)
9. Culnane, C., Schneider, S.: A peered bulletin board for robust use in verifiable voting systems. In: CSF 2014, 27th Computer Security Foundations Symposium, pp. 169–183. Vienna, Austria (2014)
10. Dold, F., Grothoff, C.: Byzantine set-union consensus using efficient set reconciliation. In: Wicker, S.B., Engel, D. (eds.) ARES 2016, 11th International Conference on Availability, Reliability and Security, pp. 29–38. Salzburg, Austria (2016)
11. Dubuis, E., et al.: Verifizierbare Internet-Wahlen an Schweizer Hochschulen mit UniVote. In: Horbach, M. (ed.) INFORMATIK 2013, 43. Jahrestagung der Gesellschaft für Informatik. LNI P-220, Koblenz, Germany, pp. 767–788 (2013)
12. Goldreich, O.: The Foundations of Cryptography - Volume II: Basic Applications. Cambridge University Press, New York (2004)
13. Haenni, R., Koenig, R.E.: A generic approach to prevent board flooding attacks in coercion-resistant electronic voting schemes. Comput. Secur. **33**, 59–69 (2013)
14. Hauser, S., Haenni, R.: Implementing broadcast channels with memory for electronic voting systems. JeDEM eJournal eDemocracy Open Gov. **8**(3), 61–79 (2016)

15. Heather, J., Lundin, D.: The append-only web bulletin board. In: Degano, P., Guttman, J., Martinelli, F. (eds.) FAST 2008. LNCS, vol. 5491, pp. 242–256. Springer, Heidelberg (2009). https://doi.org/10.1007/978-3-642-01465-9_16
16. Krummenacher, R.: Implementation of a Web Bulletin Board for E-Voting Applications. Project report, Hochschule für Technik Rapperswil (HSR), Switzerland (2010)
17. Lamport, L., Shostak, R., Pease, M.: The Byzantine generals problem. ACM Trans. Programm. Lang. Syst. **4**, 382–401 (1982)
18. Lundin, D., Heather, J.: The robust append-only web bulletin board. Technical report, University of Surrey, Guildford, U.K. (2008)
19. Nakamoto, S.: Bitcoin: A Peer-to-Peer Electronic Cash System. Anonymous Publication (2009)
20. Peters, R.A.: A Secure Bulletin Board. Master's thesis, Department of Mathematics and Computing Science, Technische Universiteit Eindhoven, The Netherlands (2005)
21. Reiter, M.K.: Secure agreement protocols: reliable and atomic group multicast in Rampart. In: CCS 1994, 2nd ACM Conference on Computer and Communications Security, pp. 68–80. Fairfax, USA (1994)

Verifiability of Helios Mixnet

Ben Smyth[(✉)]

Interdisciplinary Centre for Security, Reliability and Trust,
University of Luxembourg, Esch-sur-Alzette, Luxembourg
research@bensmyth.com

Abstract. We study game-based definitions of individual and universal verifiability by Smyth, Frink and Clarkson. We prove that building voting systems from El Gamal coupled with proofs of correct key generation suffices for individual verifiability. We also prove that it suffices for an aspect of universal verifiability. Thereby eliminating the expense of individual-verifiability proofs and simplifying universal-verifiability proofs for a class of encryption-based voting systems. We use the definitions of individual and universal verifiability to analyse the mixnet variant of Helios. Our analysis reveals that universal verifiability is not satisfied by implementations using the weak Fiat-Shamir transformation. Moreover, we prove that individual and universal verifiability are satisfied when statements are included in hashes (i.e., when using the Fiat-Shamir transformation, rather than the weak Fiat-Shamir transformation).

1 Introduction

An election is a decision-making procedure to choose representatives [3,13,24,31]. Choices should be made by voters with equal influence, and this must be ensured by voting systems [26,27,41]. Many electronic voting systems build upon creativity and skill, rather than scientific foundations, and are routinely broken in ways that permit adversaries to unduly influence the selection of representatives, e.g., [5,7,14,18,40]. Breaks can be avoided by carefully formulating rigorous and precise security definitions that capture notions of voters voting with equal influence, and proving that systems satisfy these definitions. Applicable definitions include [9,10,15,17,19,20,37,38] and we build upon work by Smyth, Frink and Clarkson [37]. (The relative merits of definitions are considered in Sect. 2.) They present game-based security definitions in the computational model of cryptography [16], whereby a benign challenger, a malicious adversary and a voting system engage in a series of interactions which task the adversary to complete a challenge. Successful completion of the task corresponds to an execution of the voting system in which security is broken. Thus, the task captures what the adversary should not be able to achieve.

Universal verifiability formalises a notion of checking whether voters voted with equal influence.

– Universal verifiability. Anyone can check whether an outcome corresponds to votes expressed in recorded ballots.

© International Financial Cryptography Association 2019
A. Zohar et al. (Eds.): FC 2018 Workshops, LNCS 10958, pp. 247–261, 2019.
https://doi.org/10.1007/978-3-662-58820-8_17

Smyth, Frink and Clarkson formalise a game-based definition of universal verifiability [37]. That game tasks the adversary to compute inputs to the tallying procedure, including an election outcome and some ballots, that cause checks to succeed when the outcome does not correspond to the votes expressed by those ballots, or that cause checks to fail when the outcome does correspond to the votes expressed.

Merely casting a ballot is insufficient to ensure it is recorded, because an adversary may discard ballots. Individual verifiability formalises the notion of voters convincing themselves that their ballot is amongst those recorded.

– Individual verifiability. A voter can check whether their ballot is recorded.

Smyth, Frink and Clarkson formalise individual verifiability as a game that tasks the adversary to cause a collision between ballots [37]. That game proceeds as follows: First, the adversary provides any inputs necessary to construct a ballot, including a vote v_0. Secondly, the challenger constructs a ballot using those inputs. Finally, the adversary and the challenger repeat the process to construct a second ballot for vote v_1. The adversary wins if the two independently constructed ballots are equal. Hence, winning signifies the existence of a scenario in which two voters cannot uniquely identify their ballot, thus a voter cannot be convinced that their ballot is recorded.

Equipped with definitions of individual and universal verifiability, we can analyse existing voting systems to determine whether they are secure. As is exemplified by the following two voting systems. The first (Enc2Vote) instructs each voter to encrypt their vote using an asymmetric encryption scheme and instructs the tallier to decrypt the encrypted votes and publish the number of votes for each candidate. The second (Enc2Vote*) extends the former to include proofs of correct computation, in particular, the tallier computes proofs of correct key generation and decryption. The former system achieves neither individual nor universal verifiability. Indeed, a public key can be maliciously constructed such that ciphertexts collide and spurious outcomes need not correspond to the encrypted votes. By comparison, the latter system achieves both individual and universal verifiability, because well-formed ciphertexts are unique (individual verifiability) and anyone can check proofs to determine whether the election outcome corresponds to votes expressed in recorded ballots (universal verifiability). Voting systems Enc2Vote and Enc2Vote* leak the ballot-vote relation during tallying; more advanced voting systems, such as Helios, do not.

Helios is intended to satisfy verifiability and ballot secrecy. For ballot secrecy, each voter encrypts their vote using a homomorphic encryption scheme. Those encrypted votes are homomorphically combined and the homomorphic combination is decrypted to reveal the outcome [2]. Alternatively, a mixnet is applied to the encrypted votes and the mixed encrypted votes are decrypted to reveal the outcome [1,6]. We refer to the former voting system as *Helios* and the latter as *Helios Mixnet*. For universal verifiability, the encryption and decryption steps are accompanied by non-interactive proofs demonstrating correct computation.

Contribution and Structure. Section 3 proves that individual verifiability and an aspect of universal verifiability are satisfied by voting systems built from El Gamal coupled with proofs of correct key generation, thereby eliminating the expense of individual-verifiability proofs and simplifying universal-verifiability proofs for a class of encryption-based voting systems. Section 4 presents an analysis of Helios Mixnet that uncovers a vulnerability in implementations, discusses a fix, and proves that individual and universal verifiability are satisfied when the fix is applied. The remaining sections present syntax and definitions of individual and universal verifiability (Sect. 2) and a brief conclusion (Sect. 5). Definitions of cryptographic primitives, security definitions and proofs are deferred to an accompanying technical report [36].

2   Election Scheme Syntax and Verifiability Definitions

We recall syntax for *election schemes* (Definition 1) from Smyth, Frink and Clarkson [37]. Election schemes capture a class of voting systems that consist of the following four steps. First, a tallier generates a key pair. Secondly, each voter constructs and casts a ballot for their vote. These ballots are recorded on a bulletin board. Thirdly, the tallier tallies the recorded ballots and announces an outcome, i.e., a frequency distribution of votes. Finally, voters and other interested parties check that the outcome corresponds to votes expressed in recorded ballots.[1]

Definition 1 (Election scheme [37]). An *election scheme* is a tuple of probabilistic polynomial-time algorithms (Setup, Vote, TallyVerify) such that:

Setup, denoted $(pk, sk, mb, mc) \leftarrow$ Setup(κ),[2] is run by the tallier. It takes a security parameter κ as input and outputs a key pair pk, sk, a maximum number of ballots mb, and a maximum number of candidates mc.

Vote, denoted $b \leftarrow$ Vote(pk, v, nc, κ), is run by voters. It takes as input a public key pk, a voter's vote v, some number of candidates nc, and a security parameter κ. The vote should be selected from a sequence $1, \ldots, nc$ of candidates. The algorithm outputs a ballot b or error symbol $\perp$.

---

[1] Smyth, Frink and Clarkson use the syntax to model first-past-the-post voting systems and Smyth shows the syntax is sufficiently versatile to capture ranked-choice voting systems [33]. Moreover, Smyth, Frink and Clarkson extend the syntax to voting systems with eligibility verifiability, which enables anyone to check whether counted votes were cast by voters. (Quaglia and Smyth [29] define a transformation from election schemes to the extended syntax which ensures secrecy and verifiability.) Eligibility verifiability seems to require expensive infrastructures for voter credentials and some systems – including Helios and Helios Mixnet – forgo eligibility verifiability in favour of cheaper, non-verifiable ballot authentication mechanisms. Hence, we do not pursue eligibility verifiability further.

[2] Let $A(x_1, \ldots, x_n; r)$ denote the output of probabilistic algorithm A on inputs $x_1, \ldots, x_n$ and random coins r. Let $A(x_1, \ldots, x_n)$ denote $A(x_1, \ldots, x_n; r)$, where r is chosen uniformly at random. And let $\leftarrow$ denote assignment.

Tally, denoted $(\mathfrak{v}, pf) \leftarrow \mathsf{Tally}(sk, \mathfrak{bb}, nc, \kappa)$, is run by the tallier. It takes as input a private key sk, a bulletin board $\mathfrak{bb}$, some number of candidates nc, and a security parameter κ, where $\mathfrak{bb}$ is a set. And outputs an election outcome $\mathfrak{v}$ and a non-interactive tallying proof pf demonstrating that the outcome corresponds to votes expressed in ballots on the bulletin board. The election outcome $\mathfrak{v}$ should be a vector of length nc such that $\mathfrak{v}[v]$ indicates the number of votes for candidate v.

Verify, denoted $s \leftarrow \mathsf{Verify}(pk, \mathfrak{bb}, nc, \mathfrak{v}, pf, \kappa)$, is run to audit an election. It takes as input a public key pk, a bulletin board $\mathfrak{bb}$, some number of candidates nc, an election outcome $\mathfrak{v}$, a tallying proof pf, and a security parameter κ. And outputs a bit s, where 1 signifies success and 0 signifies failure.

Election schemes must satisfy *correctness*: there exists a negligible function negl, such that for all security parameters κ, integers nb and nc, and votes $v_1, \dots, v_{nb} \in \{1, \dots, nc\}$, it holds that, given a zero-filled vector $\mathfrak{v}$ of length nc, we have:

$$\Pr[(pk, sk, mb, mc) \leftarrow \mathsf{Setup}(\kappa);$$

$$\textbf{for } 1 \leq i \leq nb \textbf{ do}$$
$$\quad \left\lfloor \begin{array}{l} b_i \leftarrow \mathsf{Vote}(pk, v_i, nc, \kappa); \\ \mathfrak{v}[v_i] \leftarrow \mathfrak{v}[v_i] + 1; \end{array} \right.$$
$$(\mathfrak{v}', pf) \leftarrow \mathsf{Tally}(sk, \{b_1, \dots, b_{nb}\}, nc, \kappa) :$$
$$nb \leq mb \wedge nc \leq mc \Rightarrow \mathfrak{v} = \mathfrak{v}'] > 1 - \mathsf{negl}(\kappa).$$

For individual verifiability, voters must be able to check whether their ballot is recorded. Smyth, Frink and Clarkson capture this notion using a game that challenges the adversary to provide inputs to algorithm Vote that cause ballots to collide.

Definition 2 (Individual verifiability [37]**).** An election scheme (Setup, Vote, Tally, Verify) satisfies *individual verifiability*, if for all probabilistic polynomial-time adversaries $\mathcal{A}$, there exists a negligible function negl, such that for all security parameters κ, we have $\Pr[(pk, nc, v, v') \leftarrow \mathcal{A}(\kappa); b \leftarrow \mathsf{Vote}(pk, nc, v, \kappa); b' \leftarrow \mathsf{Vote}(pk, nc, v', \kappa) : b = b' \wedge b \neq \perp \wedge b' \neq \perp] \leq \mathsf{negl}(\kappa)$.

For universal verifiability, anyone must be able to check whether the election outcome represents the votes used to construct ballots on the bulletin board. The formal definition of universal verifiability by Smyth, Frink and Clarkson requires algorithm Verify to accept if and only if the election outcome is correct.[3] The *if* requirement is captured by completeness (Definition 3), which stipulates that election outcomes produced by algorithm Tally will actually be accepted by algorithm Verify. And the *only if* requirement is captured by soundness (Definition 5), which challenges an adversary to concoct a scenario in which algorithm Verify accepts, but the election outcome is not correct.

---

[3] Quaglia and Smyth [28] provide a tutorial-style introduction to the individual and universal verifiability definitions by Smyth, Frink and Clarkson and Smyth [35] provides a detailed technical introduction.

Definition 3 (Completeness [37]**).** An election scheme (Setup, Vote, Tally, Verify) satisfies *completeness*, if for all probabilistic polynomial-time adversaries $\mathcal{A}$, there exists a negligible function negl, such that for all security parameters κ, we have $\Pr[(pk, sk, mb, mc) \leftarrow \mathsf{Setup}(\kappa); (\mathfrak{bb}, nc) \leftarrow \mathcal{A}(pk, \kappa); (\mathfrak{v}, pf) \leftarrow \mathsf{Tally}(sk, \mathfrak{bb}, nc, \kappa) : |\mathfrak{bb}| \leq mb \wedge nc \leq mc \Rightarrow \mathsf{Verify}(pk, \mathfrak{bb}, nc, \mathfrak{v}, pf, \kappa) = 1] > 1 - \mathsf{negl}(\kappa)$.

Smyth, Frink and Clarkson capture correct election outcomes using function *correct-outcome*, which is defined such that *correct-outcome*$(pk, nc, \mathfrak{bb}, \kappa)[v] = \ell$ iff $\exists^{=\ell} b \in \mathfrak{bb} \setminus \{\bot\} : \exists r : b = \mathsf{Vote}(pk, v, nc, \kappa; r)$,[4] where *correct-outcome*$(pk, nc, \mathfrak{bb}, \kappa)$ is a vector of length nc and $1 \leq v \leq nc$. Hence, component v of vector *correct-outcome*$(pk, nc, \mathfrak{bb}, \kappa)$ equals ℓ iff there exist ℓ ballots on the bulletin board that are votes for candidate v. The function requires ballots to be interpreted for only one candidate, which can be ensured by injectivity.

Definition 4 (Injectivity). An election scheme (Setup, Vote, Tally, Verify) satisfies *injectivity*,[5] if for all probabilistic polynomial-time adversaries $\mathcal{A}$, security parameters κ and computations $(pk, nc, v, v') \leftarrow \mathcal{A}(\kappa); b \leftarrow \mathsf{Vote}(pk, v, nc, \kappa); b' \leftarrow \mathsf{Vote}(pk, v', nc, \kappa)$ such that $v \neq v' \wedge b \neq \bot \wedge b' \neq \bot$, we have $b \neq b'$.

Definition 5 (Soundness [37]**).** An election scheme $\Gamma = $ (Setup, Vote, Tally, Verify) satisfies *soundness*, if Γ satisfies injectivity and for all probabilistic polynomial-time adversaries $\mathcal{A}$, there exists a negligible function negl, such that for all security parameters κ, we have $\Pr[(pk, nc, \mathfrak{bb}, \mathfrak{v}, pf) \leftarrow \mathcal{A}(\kappa) : \mathfrak{v} \neq$ *correct-outcome*$(pk, nc, \mathfrak{bb}, \kappa) \wedge \mathsf{Verify}(pk, \mathfrak{bb}, nc, \mathfrak{v}, pf, \kappa) = 1] \leq \mathsf{negl}(\kappa)$.

Definition 6 (Universal verifiability). An election scheme Γ satisfies *universal verifiability*, if completeness, injectivity and soundness are satisfied.

Comparison with Other Verifiability Definitions. Other definitions of verifiability exist. In particular, definitions have been proposed by Juels, Catalano and Jakobsson [15], Cortier *et al.* [9] and Kiayias, Zacharias and Zhang [17]. Smyth, Frink and Clarkson [37, §7] show that definitions by Juels, Catalano and Jakobsson and Cortier *et al.* do not detect attacks that arise when tallying and verification procedures are corrupt nor when verification procedures reject legitimate outcomes. Moreover, they show that the definition by Kiayias, Zacharias and Zhang does not detect the latter class of attacks. By comparison, Definition 6 detects these attacks, thereby motivating its adoption.

---

[4] Function *correct-outcome* uses a *counting quantifier* [32] denoted $\exists^=$. Predicate $(\exists^{=\ell} x : P(x))$ holds exactly when there are ℓ distinct values for x such that $P(x)$ is satisfied. Variable x is bound by the quantifier, whereas ℓ is free.

[5] Smyth, Frink and Clarkson [37] consider a definition of injectivity which quantifies over all public keys, rather than public keys constructed by an adversary. That definition is stronger than necessary.

Küsters *et al.* [20–22] propose an alternative, holistic notion of verifiability called *global verifiability*, which must be instantiated with a goal. Smyth, Frink and Clarkson [37, §8] show that goals proposed by Küsters *et al.* [23, §5.2] and by Cortier et al. [10, §10.2] are too strong (in the sense that they cannot be satisfied by some verifiable voting systems, including Helios). Moreover, Smyth, Frink and Clarkson propose a slight weakening of the goal by Küsters *et al.* and proved that their notion of verifiability is strictly stronger than global verifiability with that goal (the "gap" is due to an uninteresting technical detail), which further motivates the adoption of Definition 6.[6]

3 Encryption Ensures Individual Verifiability and Injectivity

Definitions of individual verifiability and injectivity only focus on properties of algorithm Vote, hence, to prove these properties for election scheme (Setup, Vote, Tally, Verify), it suffices to prove the existence of an election scheme (Setup′, Vote, Tally′, Verify′) satisfying both properties. We demonstrate the existence of such schemes by coupling election scheme Enc2Vote with proofs of correct key generation.[7,8]

Definition 7 (Enc2Vote$^+$). Suppose $\Pi = (\mathsf{Gen}, \mathsf{Enc}, \mathsf{Dec})$ is an asymmetric encryption scheme, Σ is a sigma protocol that proves correct key generation, and $\mathcal{H}$ is a hash function. Let $\mathsf{FS}(\Sigma, \mathcal{H}) = (\mathsf{ProveKey}, \mathsf{VerKey})$.[9] We define $\mathsf{Enc2Vote}^+(\Pi, \Sigma, \mathcal{H}) = (\mathsf{Setup}, \mathsf{Vote}, \mathsf{Tally}, \mathsf{Verify})$ such that:

- Setup(κ) selects coins s uniformly at random, computes $(pk, sk, \mathfrak{m}) \leftarrow \mathsf{Gen}(\kappa; s); \rho \leftarrow \mathsf{ProveKey}((\kappa, pk, \mathfrak{m}), (sk, s), \kappa); pk' \leftarrow (pk, \mathfrak{m}, \rho); sk' \leftarrow (pk, sk)$, derives mc as the largest integer such that $\{0, \ldots, mc\} \subseteq \{0\} \cup \mathfrak{m}$ and for all $m_0, m_1 \in \{1, \ldots, mc\}$ we have $|m_0| = |m_1|$, and outputs $(pk', sk', p(\kappa), mc)$, where p is a polynomial function.
- Vote(pk', v, nc, κ) parses pk' as vector $(pk, \mathfrak{m}, \rho)$, outputting $\bot$ if parsing fails or $\mathsf{VerKey}((\kappa, pk, \mathfrak{m}), \rho, \kappa) \neq 1 \vee v \notin \{1, \ldots, nc\} \vee \{1, \ldots, nc\} \nsubseteq \mathfrak{m}$, computes $b \leftarrow \mathsf{Enc}(pk, v)$, and outputs b.

---

[6] Cortier *et al.* [10, §8.5 & §10.1] claim that definitions by Smyth, Frink and Clarkson are flawed. Those claims were discussed with Cortier *et al.* (email communication, April'16) and are believed to be false [37, §9]. Moreover, Smyth, Frink and Clarkson prove that any flaw in their definitions implies flaws in the context of global verifiability, which should increase confidence in their definitions.

[7] Election scheme Enc2Vote* (Sect. 1) couples Enc2Vote with proofs of correct key generation *and* proofs of correct decryption, hence, it is distinguished from schemes produced by Enc2Vote$^+$. This distinction enables Enc2Vote* to satisfy individual and universal verifiability, whereas Enc2Vote$^+$ cannot produce schemes satisfying universal verifiability.

[8] Election scheme Enc2Vote$^+(\Pi, \Sigma, \mathcal{H})$ adopts the setup algorithm formalised by Smyth, Frink and Clarkson for Helios [37, Appendix C].

[9] Let $\mathsf{FS}(\Sigma, \mathcal{H})$ denote the non-interactive proof system derived by application of the Fiat-Shamir transformation to sigma protocol Σ and hash function $\mathcal{H}$.

- Tally(sk', $\mathfrak{bb}$, nc, κ) initialises vector $\mathfrak{v}$ of length nc, parses sk' as vector (pk, sk), outputting $(\mathfrak{v}, \perp)$ if parsing fails, computes **for** $b \in \mathfrak{bb}$ **do** $v \leftarrow$ Dec(sk, b); **if** $1 \le v \le nc$ **then** $\mathbf{v}[v] \leftarrow \mathbf{v}[v] + 1$, and outputs $(\mathfrak{v}, \epsilon)$, where ϵ is a constant symbol.
- Verify(pk, $\mathfrak{bb}$, nc, $\mathfrak{v}$, pf, κ) outputs 1.

To ensure $\mathsf{Enc2Vote}^+(\Pi, \Sigma, \mathcal{H})$ is an election scheme, we require asymmetric encryption scheme Π to produce distinct ciphertexts with overwhelming probability. Hence, we restrict the class of asymmetric encryption schemes used to instantiate $\mathsf{Enc2Vote}^+$.

Lemma 1. *Let $\Pi = (\mathsf{Gen}, \mathsf{Enc}, \mathsf{Dec})$ be an asymmetric encryption scheme, Σ be a sigma protocol that proves correct key generation, and $\mathcal{H}$ be a hash function. We have $\mathsf{Enc2Vote}^+(\Pi, \Sigma, \mathcal{H})$ is an election scheme if for all security parameters κ and messages m and m', we have $\Pr[(pk, sk, \mathfrak{m}) \leftarrow \mathsf{Gen}(\kappa); c \leftarrow \mathsf{Enc}(pk, m); c' \leftarrow \mathsf{Enc}(pk, m') : m, m' \in \mathfrak{m} \Rightarrow c \ne c'] > 1 - \mathsf{negl}(\kappa)$.*

Our correctness proof (Lemma 1) and all further proofs appear in [36, Appendix B].

Security properties of asymmetric encryption schemes ensure ciphertexts do not collide. Indeed, IND-CPA demands that no adversary can construct a ciphertext that collides with the challenge ciphertext.[10] But, such security properties assume public keys are generated (by key generation algorithms) using coins chosen uniformly at random. By comparison, individual verifiability and injectivity assume public keys are constructed by the adversary. Thus, security properties are insufficient to ensure election scheme $\mathsf{Enc2Vote}^+(\Pi, \Sigma, \mathcal{H})$ satisfies individual verifiability and injectivity. Nonetheless, given that the scheme's Vote algorithm checks correct key generation, it suffices that ciphertexts do not collide for correctly generated keys.

Proposition 2. *Let $\Pi = (\mathsf{Gen}, \mathsf{Enc}, \mathsf{Dec})$ be an asymmetric encryption scheme, Σ be a sigma protocol that proves correct key generated, and $\mathcal{H}$ be a hash function. We have $\mathsf{Enc2Vote}^+(\Pi, \Sigma, \mathcal{H})$ satisfies individual verifiability if for all probabilistic polynomial-time adversaries $\mathcal{A}$ and security parameters κ we have*

$$\Pr[(pk, \mathfrak{m}, \rho, m, m') \leftarrow \mathcal{A}(\kappa); c \leftarrow \mathsf{Enc}(pk, m); c' \leftarrow \mathsf{Enc}(pk, m')$$
$$: \mathsf{VerKey}((\kappa, pk, \mathfrak{m}), \rho, \kappa) = 1 \wedge m, m' \in \mathfrak{m} \Rightarrow c \ne c'] > 1 - \mathsf{negl}(\kappa),$$

where $\mathsf{FS}(\Sigma, \mathcal{H}) = (\mathsf{ProveKey}, \mathsf{VerKey})$. Moreover, the election scheme satisfies injectivity if the probability is 1 when plaintexts m and m' are distinct.

Our proof of Proposition 2 [36, Appendix B.2] follows immediately from our preconditions. It is nevertheless useful, because the preconditions are defined over encryption scheme Π and proof system $\mathsf{FS}(\Sigma, \mathcal{H})$, rather than election scheme $\mathsf{Enc2Vote}^+(\Pi, \Sigma, \mathcal{H})$, which makes the preconditions easier to reason with. For El Gamal [12], the preconditions are ensured if the proof system checks parameters:

---

[10] Correctness of asymmetric encryption schemes only ensures ciphertexts do not collide for distinct plaintexts.

Definition 8. Let (ProveKey, VerKey) be a non-interactive proof system that proves correct key generation. The proof system *checks El Gamal parameters*, if for all security parameters κ, public keys pk, messages spaces $\mathfrak{m}$, and proofs ρ, we have $\mathsf{VerKey}((\kappa, pk, \mathfrak{m}), \rho, \kappa) = 1$ implies pk is a vector (p, q, g, h) such that $p = 2 \cdot q + 1$, $|q| = \kappa$, g is a generator of $\mathbb{Z}_p^*$ of order q, $h \in \mathbb{Z}_p^*$, and $\mathfrak{m} = \{1, \ldots, p - 1\}$.

Theorem 3. *Let Π be El Gamal, Σ be a sigma protocol that proves correct key generation, and $\mathcal{H}$ be a hash function. Suppose proof system $\mathsf{FS}(\Sigma, \mathcal{H})$ checks El Gamal parameters. We have $\mathsf{Enc2Vote}^+(\Pi, \Sigma, \mathcal{H})$ satisfies individual verifiability and injectivity.*

We exploit Theorem 3 in the following section to derive a proof of individual verifiability for free and to simplify a proof of universal verifiability.

4   Case Study: Helios Mixnet

Helios Mixnet can be informally modelled as an election scheme such that:

Setup generates a key pair for an asymmetric homomorphic encryption scheme, proves correct key generation in zero-knowledge, and outputs the public key coupled with the proof.

Vote enciphers the vote to a ciphertext, proves correct ciphertext construction in zero-knowledge, and outputs the ciphertext coupled with the proof.

Tally selects the ballots on the bulletin board for which proofs hold, mixes the ciphertexts in those ballots, decrypts the ciphertexts output by the mix to reveal the frequency distribution of candidate preferences, and announces that distribution, along with zero-knowledge proofs demonstrating correct decryption and mixing.

Verify checks the proofs and accepts the frequency distribution if these checks succeed.

Neither Adida [1] nor Bulens, Giry and Pereira [6] have released an implementation of Helios Mixnet.[11] Tsoukalas *et al.* [39] released *Zeus* as a fork of Helios 3.1.4 spliced with mixnet code to derive an implementation, and Yingtong Li released *helios-server-mixnet* as an extension of Zeus with threshold asymmetric encryption. Both implementations use multiplicatively-homomorphic asymmetric encryption, rather than additively-homomorphic encryption.

  Chang-Fong and Essex [8] show that Helios 2.0 does not satisfy completeness (because cryptographic parameters were not checked for suitability), hence, implementations of Helios Mixnet did not satisfy completeness until Helios was

---

[11] The planned implementation of Helios Mixnet (http://documentation.heliosvoting. org/verification-specs/mixnet-support, published c. 2010, accessed 19 Dec 2017, and https://web.archive.org/web/20110119223848/http://documentation.heliosvoting. org/verification-specs/helios-v3-1, published Dec 2010, accessed 15 Sep 2017) has not been released.

patched (because the implementations fork Helios and do not add code to check parameters).[12] Moreover, Bernhard, Pereira and Warinschi [4] show that Helios 3.1.4 does not satisfy soundness.[13,14] They also demonstrate a denial of service attack. We exploit their denial of service attack to show that implementations of Helios Mixnet do not satisfy soundness: A malicious tallier can decrypt the ciphertexts output by the mix to reveal the distribution of candidate preferences, select the ciphertexts that decrypt to the tallier's preferred subdistribution, prove correct decryption of those ciphertexts, and exploit the attack by Bernhard, Pereira and Warinschi to falsify proofs that the remaining ciphertexts decrypt to arbitrary elements of the message space, thereby enabling the malicious tallier to exclude votes from the election outcome.

Remark 4. Zeus does not satisfy soundness.

Similarly, helios-server-mixnet does not satisfy soundness when a (n, n)-threshold is used. An informal proof of these claims follows from our discussion and a formal proof is omitted.

Helios 3.1.4 uses additively-homomorphic El Gamal, hence, an adversary can falsify that ciphertexts decrypt to arbitrary elements of the group, but cannot recover the corresponding messages, because solving discrete logarithms for arbitrary group elements is hard. Thus, the attack by Bernhard, Pereira and Warinschi leads to a denial of service attack against Helios 3.1.4, whereby the election outcome is not recovered, rather than an attack that violates soundness. By comparison, our attack against implementations of Helios Mixnet violates soundness, because a malicious tallier can exclude votes from the election outcome.

Bernhard, Pereira and Warinschi attribute vulnerabilities of Helios 3.1.4 to use of the Fiat-Shamir transformation without including statements in hashes (i.e., the weak Fiat-Shamir transformation), and recommend including statements in hashes (i.e., using the Fiat-Shamir transformation) as a defence. Implementations of Helios Mixnet can be extended to use the Fiat-Shamir transformation and we derive a formalisation of that extension from $\mathsf{Enc2Vote}^+(\Pi, \Sigma, \mathcal{H})$ by replacing its tallying and verification algorithms,[15] and by using a suitable asymmetric encryption algorithm. Using the Fiat-Shamir transformation (rather than the weak Fiat-Shamir transformation) ensures that proofs of correct decryption cannot be falsified, hence, the formalisation is not vulnerable to the aforementioned attack.

---

[12] https://github.com/benadida/helios-server/pull/133, published 31 May 2016, accessed 21 Sep 2017.

[13] Bernhard, Pereira and Warinschi show that a malicious tallier can add votes for their preferred candidate and remove votes for other candidates. Smyth, Frink and Clarkson formalise that attack and prove that soundness is not satisfied [37].

[14] A further soundness vulnerability is known [37], as are secrecy [11] and eligibility [25] vulnerabilities.

[15] The tallying and verification algorithms in Definition 9 adapt (unpublished) algorithms prepared by Quaglia and Smyth in the context of [30]. Quaglia and Smyth have since incorporated these adaptations into their work to take advantage of the results presented in this manuscript.

Definition 9. Suppose Π = (Gen, Enc, Dec) is a homomorphic asymmetric encryption algorithm, Σ_1 is a sigma protocol that proves correct key construction, Σ_2 is a sigma protocol that proves plaintext knowledge, and $\mathcal{H}$ is a hash function. Let $\mathsf{FS}(\Sigma_1, \mathcal{H})$ = (ProveKey, VerKey) and $\mathsf{FS}(\Sigma_2, \mathcal{H})$ = (ProveCiph, VerCiph). Moreover, let $\pi(\Pi, \Sigma_2, \mathcal{H})$ = (Gen, Enc', Dec') be an asymmetric encryption scheme such that:

- Enc'(pk, v) selects coins r uniformly at random, computes $c \leftarrow$ Enc$(pk, v; r)$; $\sigma \leftarrow$ ProveCiph$((pk, c), (v, r), \kappa)$, and outputs (c, σ).

Suppose Σ_3 is a sigma protocol that proves correct decryption and Σ_4 is a sigma protocol that proves mixing. Let $\mathsf{FS}(\Sigma_3, \mathcal{H})$ = (ProveDec, VerDec) and $\mathsf{FS}(\Sigma_4, \mathcal{H})$ = (ProveMix, VerMix). We define $\mathsf{HeliosM}(\Pi, \Sigma_1, \Sigma_2, \Sigma_3, \Sigma_4, \mathcal{H})$ = (Setup, Vote, Tally, Verify), where $\mathsf{Enc2Vote}^+(\pi(\Pi, \Sigma_2, \mathcal{H}), \Sigma_1, \mathcal{H})$ = (Setup, Vote, Tally', Verify') and algorithms Tally and Verify are defined below.

Tally$(sk', nc, \mathfrak{bb}, \kappa)$ initialises $\mathfrak{v}$ as a zero-filled vector of length nc, parses sk' as a vector (pk, sk), outputting $(\mathfrak{v}, \bot)$ if parsing fails, and proceeds as follows:

1. *Remove invalid ballots.* Let $\{b_1, \ldots, b_\ell\}$ be the largest subset of $\mathfrak{bb}$ such that for all $1 \leq i \leq \ell$ we have b_i is a pair and VerCiph$((pk, b_i[1]), b_i[2], \kappa) = 1$. If $\{b_1, \ldots, b_\ell\} = \emptyset$, then output $(\mathfrak{v}, \bot)$.
2. *Mix.* Select a permutation χ on $\{1, \ldots, \ell\}$ uniformly at random, initialise $\mathbf{bb}$ and $\mathbf{r}$ as vectors of length ℓ, fill $\mathbf{r}$ with coins chosen uniformly at random, and compute

   for $1 \leq i \leq \ell$ **do**
   $\quad \lfloor \ \mathbf{bb}[i] \leftarrow b_{\chi(i)}[1] \otimes \mathsf{Enc}(pk, \mathfrak{e}; \mathbf{r}[i]);$
   $pf_1 \leftarrow \mathsf{ProveMix}((pk, (b_1[1], \ldots, b_\ell[1]), \mathbf{bb}), (\mathbf{r}, \chi), \kappa);$
   where $\mathfrak{e}$ is an identity element of Π's message space with respect to $\odot$.
3. *Decrypt.* Initialise $\mathbf{W}$ and pf_2 as vectors of length ℓ and compute:

   for $1 \leq i \leq \ell$ **do**
   $\quad \mathbf{W}[i] \leftarrow \mathsf{Dec}(sk, \mathbf{bb}[i]);$
   $\quad pf_2[i] \leftarrow \mathsf{ProveDec}((pk, \mathbf{bb}[i], \mathbf{W}[i]), sk, \kappa);$
   $\quad$ **if** $1 \leq \mathbf{W}[i] \leq nc$ **then**
   $\quad \quad \lfloor \ \mathfrak{v}[\mathbf{W}[i]] \leftarrow \mathfrak{v}[\mathbf{W}[i]] + 1;$

Output $(\mathfrak{v}, (\mathbf{bb}, pf_1, \mathbf{W}, pf_2))$.

Verify$(pk', nc, \mathfrak{bb}, \mathfrak{v}, pf, \kappa)$ derives the largest integer mc such that $\{0, \ldots, mc\} \subseteq \{0\} \cup \mathfrak{m}$; parses pk' as a vector $(pk, \mathfrak{m}, \rho)$ and $\mathfrak{v}$ parses as a vector of length nc, outputting 0 if parsing fails, VerKey$((\kappa, pk, \mathfrak{m}), \rho, \kappa) \neq 1$, $|\mathfrak{bb}| \not\leq p(\kappa)$, or $nc \not\leq mc$, where p is the polynomial function used by algorithm Setup to bound the maximum number of ballots; and proceeds as follows:

1. *Remove invalid ballots.* Compute $\{b_1, \ldots, b_\ell\}$ as per Step 1 of algorithm Tally. If $\{b_1, \ldots, b_\ell\} = \emptyset$ and $\mathfrak{v}$ is a zero-filled vector, then output 1. Otherwise, perform the following checks.

2. *Check mixing.* Parse pf as a vector $(\mathbf{bb}, pf_1, \mathbf{W}, pf_2)$, outputting 0 if parsing fails, and check $\mathsf{VerMix}((pk, (b_1[1], \ldots, b_\ell[1]), \mathbf{bb}), pf_1, \kappa) = 1$.
3. *Check decryption.* Check $\mathbf{W}$ and pf_2 are vectors of length ℓ, $\bigwedge_{i=1}^{\ell} \mathsf{VerDec}((pk, \mathbf{bb}[i], \mathbf{W}[i]), pf_2[i], \kappa) = 1$, and $\bigwedge_{v=1}^{nc} \exists^{=\mathfrak{v}[v]} i \in \{1, \ldots, \ell\} : v = \mathbf{W}[i]$.

If the above checks hold, then output 1, otherwise, output 0.

Lemma 5. *Suppose Π, Σ_1, Σ_2, Σ_3, Σ_4 and $\mathcal{H}$ satisfy the preconditions of Definition 9 and Π satisfies the condition in Lemma 1. We have $\mathsf{HeliosM}(\Pi, \Sigma_1, \Sigma_2, \Sigma_3, \Sigma_4, \mathcal{H})$ is an election scheme.*

Our formalisation of Helios Mixnet is similar to the formalisation of Helios by Smyth, Frink and Clarkson [37]. The main distinctions are as follows: First, given a vote v from a sequence of candidates $1, \ldots, nc$, a Helios-Mixnet ballot contains an encryption of v, whereas a Helios ballot contains ciphertexts $c_1, \ldots, c_{nc-1}$ such that if $v < nc$, then c_v encrypts plaintext one and the remaining ciphertexts all encrypt zero, otherwise, all ciphertexts encrypt zero. (Both Helios Mixnet and Helios ballots prove correct ciphertext construction, only Helios ballots prove the vote is selected from the sequence of candidates.) Secondly, Helios Mixnet decrypts individual ciphertexts after mixing, whereas Helios homomorphically combines ciphertexts and decrypts the resulting homomorphic combination. (Both Helios Mixnet and Helios prove correct decryption. For Helios Mixnet, decryption of individual votes is proved correct. Whereas Helios proves correct decryption of the election outcome.) Finally, the aforementioned distinctions lead to slight differences in the verification algorithms.

Since election schemes $\mathsf{HeliosM}(\Pi, \Sigma_1, \Sigma_2, \Sigma_3, \Sigma_4, \mathcal{H})$ and $\mathsf{Enc2Vote}^+(\pi(\Pi, \Sigma_2, \mathcal{H}), \Sigma_1, \mathcal{H})$ share the same voting algorithm, both schemes satisfy individual verifiability and injectivity by Proposition 2, assuming the proposition's preconditions are satisfied. Moreover, since the preconditions hold for El Gamal when parameters are checked (Corollary 2), we have:

Corollary 6. *Suppose Π, Σ_1, Σ_2, Σ_3, Σ_4 and $\mathcal{H}$ satisfy the preconditions of Definition 9. Further suppose Π is El Gamal and Σ_1 checks El Gamal parameters. Election scheme $\mathsf{HeliosM}(\Pi, \Sigma_1, \Sigma_2, \Sigma_3, \Sigma_4, \mathcal{H})$ satisfies individual verifiability and injectivity.*

To evaluate whether universal verifiability is satisfied, it remains to consider completeness and soundness.[16]

---

[16] Our proof of Theorem 7 uses a result by Bernhard *et al.* [4] that shows non-interactive proof systems derived by application of the Fiat-Shamir transformation satisfy zero-knowledge, assuming the underlying sigma protocols satisfy *special soundness* and *special honest-verifier zero-knowledge*. We will not need the details of those properties, so we omit formal definitions; see Bernhard *et al.* for formalisations.

Theorem 7. *Suppose* Π, Σ_1, Σ_2, Σ_3, Σ_4 *and* $\mathcal{H}$ *satisfy the preconditions of Definition 9. Moreover, suppose* Σ_2 *satisfies special soundness and special honest verifier zero-knowledge and* $\mathcal{H}$ *is a random oracle. Election scheme* HeliosM$(\Pi, \Sigma_1, \Sigma_2, \Sigma_3, \Sigma_4, \mathcal{H})$ *satisfies completeness. Further suppose,* Π *is perfectly correct and perfectly homomorphic,* Σ_1, Σ_3 *and* Σ_4 *satisfy special soundness and special honest verifier zero-knowledge, and* HeliosM$(\Pi, \Sigma_1, \Sigma_2, \Sigma_3, \Sigma_4, \mathcal{H})$ *satisfies injectivity. The election scheme satisfies soundness.*

Theorem 7 requires perfect correctness, rather than computational correctness,[17] because soundness quantifies over public keys constructed by an adversary and such an adversary might not construct the public key using coins chosen uniformly at random. (We can, nonetheless, verify whether public keys are constructed using the correct algorithm.) Thus, perfect correctness is required, because it quantifies over all coins. Moreover, perfect homomorphisms are similarly required.

These findings were reported to the Zeus developers, who conducted an investigation of their code and confirmed Zeus does not satisfy soundness. They promptly adopted and deployed the proposed fix,[18] this was straightforward, because they had already written code for the Fiat-Shamir transformation. These findings were also reported to the developer of helios-server-mixnet, who confirmed soundness is not satisfied with a (n, n)-threshold, but is for other thresholds because code from the PloneVote cryptographic library is used rather than code from Helios, and has since adopted and deployed the proposed fix.[19]

Beyond verifiability, Smyth has shown that HeliosM produces election schemes that satisfy ballot secrecy [34].

5   Conclusion

We have introduced a construction that serves as a foundation for verifiable voting systems, and we have shown that it produces systems satisfying individual verifiability and the injectivity aspect of universal verifiability, when instantiated with El Gamal. Moreover, we have analysed verifiability of two implementations of Helios Mixnet and shown that the soundness aspect of universal verifiability is not satisfied, due to vulnerabilities in Helios. Finally, we propose a fix and exploit our construction to prove that the fix suffices for individual and universal verifiability.

---

[17] Properties such as correctness are typically required to hold with overwhelming probability. A property is perfect if the probability is 1.

[18] See commitments `d2653d4` (9 Oct 2017), `4fddcd3` (11 Oct 2017), and `aab1b6f` (9 Oct 2017), accessed 20 Dec 2017.

[19] See commitment `9af7674` (25 Dec 2017).

Acknowledgements. I am grateful to Steve Kremer and the anonymous reviewers for useful feedback that helped improve this paper. I am also grateful to Yingtong Li (developer of helios-server-mixnet) and to Georgios Tsoukalas and Panos Louridas (developers of Zeus) for discussions about their voting systems.

References

1. Adida, B.: Helios: web-based open-audit voting. In: USENIX Security 2008: 17th USENIX Security Symposium, pp. 335–348. USENIX Association (2008)
2. Adida, B., Marneffe, O., Pereira, O., Quisquater, J.: Electing a university president using open-audit voting: analysis of real-world use of Helios. In: EVT/WOTE 2009: Electronic Voting Technology Workshop/Workshop on Trustworthy Elections. USENIX Association (2009)
3. Alvarez, R.M., Hall, T.E.: Electronic Elections: The Perils and Promises of Digital Democracy. Princeton University Press, Princeton (2010)
4. Bernhard, D., Pereira, O., Warinschi, B.: How not to prove yourself: pitfalls of the fiat-shamir heuristic and applications to Helios. In: Wang, X., Sako, K. (eds.) ASIACRYPT 2012. LNCS, vol. 7658, pp. 626–643. Springer, Heidelberg (2012). https://doi.org/10.1007/978-3-642-34961-4_38
5. Bowen, D.: Secretary of State Debra Bowen Moves to Strengthen Voter Confidence in Election Security Following Top-to-Bottom Review of Voting Systems. California Secretary of State, press release DB07:042, August 2007
6. Bulens, P., Giry, D., Pereira, O.: Running Mixnet-based elections with Helios. In: EVT/WOTE 2011: Electronic Voting Technology Workshop/Workshop on Trustworthy Elections. USENIX Association (2011)
7. Bundesverfassungsgericht: Use of voting computers in 2005 Bundestag election unconstitutional, press release 19 March 2009
8. Chang-Fong, N., Essex, A.: The cloudier side of cryptographic end-to-end verifiable voting: a security analysis of Helios. In: ACSAC 2016: 32nd Annual Conference on Computer Security Applications, pp. 324–335. ACM Press (2016)
9. Cortier, V., Galindo, D., Glondu, S., Izabachène, M.: Election verifiability for Helios under weaker trust assumptions. In: Kutyłowski, M., Vaidya, J. (eds.) ESORICS 2014, Part II. LNCS, vol. 8713, pp. 327–344. Springer, Cham (2014). https://doi.org/10.1007/978-3-319-11212-1_19
10. Cortier, V., Galindo, D., Küsters, R., Mueller, J., Truderung, T.: SoK: verifiability notions for E-voting protocols. In: S&P 2016: 37th IEEE Symposium on Security and Privacy, pp. 779–798. IEEE Computer Society (2016)
11. Cortier, V., Smyth, B.: Attacking and fixing Helios: an analysis of ballot secrecy. J. Comput. Secur. **21**(1), 89–148 (2013)
12. ElGamal, T.: A public key cryptosystem and a signature scheme based on discrete logarithms. IEEE Trans. Inf. Theory **31**(4), 469–472 (1985)
13. Gumbel, A.: Steal This Vote: Dirty Elections and the Rotten History of Democracy in America. Nation Books, New York (2005)
14. Jones, D.W., Simons, B.: Broken Ballots: Will Your Vote Count?, CSLI Lecture Notes, vol. 204. Center for the Study of Language and Information, Stanford University (2012)
15. Juels, A., Catalano, D., Jakobsson, M.: Coercion-resistant electronic elections. In: Chaum, D., et al. (eds.) Towards Trustworthy Elections. LNCS, vol. 6000, pp. 37–63. Springer, Heidelberg (2010). https://doi.org/10.1007/978-3-642-12980-3_2

16. Katz, J., Lindell, Y.: Introduction to Modern Cryptography. Chapman & Hall/CRC, Boca Raton (2007)
17. Kiayias, A., Zacharias, T., Zhang, B.: End-to-end verifiable elections in the standard model. In: Oswald, E., Fischlin, M. (eds.) EUROCRYPT 2015, Part II. LNCS, vol. 9057, pp. 468–498. Springer, Heidelberg (2015). https://doi.org/10.1007/978-3-662-46803-6_16
18. Kohno, T., Stubblefield, A., Rubin, A.D., Wallach, D.S.: Analysis of an electronic voting system. In: S&P 2004: 25th Security and Privacy Symposium, pp. 27–40. IEEE Computer Society (2004)
19. Kremer, S., Ryan, M., Smyth, B.: Election verifiability in electronic voting protocols. In: Gritzalis, D., Preneel, B., Theoharidou, M. (eds.) ESORICS 2010. LNCS, vol. 6345, pp. 389–404. Springer, Heidelberg (2010). https://doi.org/10.1007/978-3-642-15497-3_24
20. Küsters, R., Truderung, T., Vogt, A.: Accountability: definition and relationship to verifiability. In: CCS 2010: 17th ACM Conference on Computer and Communications Security, pp. 526–535. ACM Press (2010)
21. Küsters, R., Truderung, T., Vogt, A.: Verifiability, privacy, and coercion-resistance: new insights from a case study. In: S&P 2011: 32nd IEEE Symposium on Security and Privacy, pp. 538–553. IEEE Computer Society (2011)
22. Küsters, R., Truderung, T., Vogt, A.: Clash attacks on the verifiability of e-voting systems. In: S&P 2012: 33rd IEEE Symposium on Security and Privacy, pp. 395–409. IEEE Computer Society (2012)
23. Küsters, R., Truderung, T., Vogt, A.: Accountability: Definition and relationship to verifiability. Cryptology ePrint Archive, Report 2010/236 (version 20150202:163211) (2015)
24. Lijphart, A., Grofman, B.: Choosing an Electoral System: Issues and Alternatives. Praeger, New York (1984)
25. Meyer, M., Smyth, B.: An attack against the Helios election system that exploits re-voting. arXiv, Report 1612.04099 (2017)
26. Organization for Security and Co-operation in Europe: Document of the Copenhagen Meeting of the Conference on the Human Dimension of the CSCE (1990)
27. Organization of American States: American Convention on Human Rights, "Pact of San Jose, Costa Rica" (1969)
28. Quaglia, E.A., Smyth, B.: A short introduction to secrecy and verifiability for elections. arXiv, Report 1702.03168 (2017)
29. Quaglia, E.A., Smyth, B.: Authentication with weaker trust assumptions for voting systems. In: Joux, A., Nitaj, A., Rachidi, T. (eds.) AFRICACRYPT 2018. LNCS, vol. 10831, pp. 322–343. Springer, Cham (2018). https://doi.org/10.1007/978-3-319-89339-6_18
30. Quaglia, E.A., Smyth, B.: Secret, verifiable auctions from elections. Theor. Comput. Sci. **730**, 44–92 (2018)
31. Saalfeld, T.: On Dogs and Whips: Recorded Votes. In: Döring, H. (ed.) Parliaments and Majority Rule in Western Europe, chap. 16. St. Martin's Press (1995)
32. Schweikardt, N.: Arithmetic, first-order logic, and counting quantifiers. ACM Trans. Comput. Logic **6**(3), 634–671 (2005)
33. Smyth, B.: First-past-the-post suffices for ranked voting (2017). https://bensmyth.com/publications/2017-FPTP-suffices-for-ranked-voting/
34. Smyth, B.: Ballot secrecy: Security definition, sufficient conditions, and analysis of Helios. Cryptology ePrint Archive, Report 2015/942 (2018)
35. Smyth, B.: A foundation for secret, verifiable elections. Cryptology ePrint Archive, Report 2018/225 (2018)

36. Smyth, B.: Verifiability of Helios Mixnet. Cryptology ePrint Archive, Report 2018/017 (2018)
37. Smyth, B., Frink, S., Clarkson, M.R.: Election Verifiability: Cryptographic Definitions and an Analysis of Helios and JCJ. Cryptology ePrint Archive, Report 2015/233 (version 20170111:122701) (2017)
38. Smyth, B., Ryan, M., Kremer, S., Kourjieh, M.: Towards automatic analysis of election verifiability properties. In: Armando, A., Lowe, G. (eds.) ARSPA-WITS 2010. LNCS, vol. 6186, pp. 146–163. Springer, Heidelberg (2010). https://doi.org/10.1007/978-3-642-16074-5_11
39. Tsoukalas, G., Papadimitriou, K., Louridas, P., Tsanakas, P.: From Helios to Zeus. J. Election Technol. Syst. 1(1) (2013). https://urldefense.proofpoint.com/v2/url?u=https-3A__www.usenix.org_jets_issues_0101_tsoukalas&_0101_tsoukalas&d=DwIFaQ&c=vh6FgFnduejNhPPD0fl_yRaSfZy8CWbWnIf4XJhSqx8&r=UyK1_569d50MjVlUSODJYRW2epEY0RveVNq0YCmePcDz4DQHW-CkWcttrwneZ0md&m=6EAFPmFSNE5qoSAwI-hDvmdi5W1Y-7BmKHjhYQo8nTNU&s=IXGRxucaGDKopsMW-my9O271R16qfbDPYE2rcbjui-yI&e=--
40. UK Electoral Commission: Key issues and conclusions: May 2007 electoral pilot schemes, May 2007
41. United Nations: Universal Declaration of Human Rights (1948)

Trusted Smart Contracts

Verifiable Sealed-Bid Auction
on the Ethereum Blockchain

Hisham S. Galal[(⊠)] and Amr M. Youssef

Concordia Institute for Information Systems Engineering,
Concordia University, Montréal, QC, Canada
{h_galal,youssef}@ciise.concordia.ca

Abstract. The success of the Ethereum blockchain as a decentralized
application platform with a distributed consensus protocol has made
many organizations start to invest into running their business on top of it.
Technically, the most impressive feature behind the success of Ethereum
is its support for a Turing complete language. On the other hand, the
inherent transparency and, consequently, the lack of privacy poses a great
challenge for many financial applications. In this paper, we tackle this
challenge and present a smart contract for a verifiable sealed-bid auction
on the Ethereum blockchain. In a nutshell, initially, the bidders submit
homomorphic commitments to their sealed-bids on the contract. Subsequently, they reveal their commitments secretly to the auctioneer via
a public key encryption scheme. Then, according to the auction rules,
the auctioneer determines and claims the winner of the auction. Finally,
we utilize interactive zero-knowledge proof protocols between the smart
contract and the auctioneer to verify the correctness of such a claim. The
underlying protocol of the proposed smart contract is partially privacy-
preserving. To be precise, no information about the losing bids is leaked
to the bidders. We provide an analysis of the proposed protocol and the
smart contract design, in addition to the estimated gas costs associated
with the different transactions.

Keywords: Ethereum · Smart contract · Sealed-bid auction

1 Introduction

Online auctions have played an important role in the world economy by transferring trillions of dollars in exchange for goods and services in the recent decades.
An auction is a platform for sellers to advertise the sale of arbitrary assets where
buyers place competitive bids as the highest prices they are willing to pay. Practically, auctions promote many economic advantages for the efficient trade of
goods and services. Traditionally, there are four main types of auctions [7]:

1. First-price sealed-bid auctions (FPSBA). Bidders submit their bids in sealed
   envelopes and hand them to the auctioneer. Subsequently, the auctioneer
   opens the envelopes to determine the bidder with the highest bid.

© International Financial Cryptography Association 2019
A. Zohar et al. (Eds.): FC 2018 Workshops, LNCS 10958, pp. 265–278, 2019.
https://doi.org/10.1007/978-3-662-58820-8_18

2. Second-price sealed-bid auctions (Vickrey auctions). It is similar to FPSBA with the exception that the winner pays the second highest bid instead.
3. Open ascending-bid auctions (English auctions). Bidders increasingly submit higher bids and stop bidding when they are not willing to pay more than the current highest bid.
4. Open descending-bid auctions (Dutch auctions). Auctioneer initially sets a high price, which is gradually decreased until a bidder decides to pay at the current price.

Arguably, the main advantage behind the sealed-bid auctions lies in the fact that no bidder learns any information about the other bids. Hence, the bidders are encouraged to bid according to their monetary valuation of the asset. However, a collusion between the auctioneer and a malicious bidder can break this advantage. In other words, there is a conflict between preserving the privacy of the bids and trusting the auctioneer to individually determine the winner. Hence, in online sealed-bid auctions, cryptographic protocols can be utilized to accomplish the publicly verifiable correctness without sacrificing the privacy of the bids.

According to a recent Reuters report [10], as part of the efforts to improve the transparency in government transactions, the Ukraine's justice ministry carried out trial auctions on top of the blockchain. The main goal is to make the auction system more transparent and secure such that the information is accessible to everyone to check if there is any manipulation or corruption.

Recently, cryptocurrencies have gained high popularity as evidenced by the surge in Bitcoin exchange rate. The foundation of cryptocurrencies is based on a decentralized public ledger on a peer-to-peer network that maintains the history of all transactions in an append-only fashion. Peers agree on the state of the ledger through an incentive-based consensus protocol. Additionally, cryptocurrencies also use cryptography to secure transactions as well as to control the creation of new currency units. Furthermore, many cryptocurrencies blockchains go beyond the simple means of payments. In fact, they provide a support for building and executing contracts on top of them. Simply, a smart contract is a piece of code that is stored and run on the blockchain. The smart contract resides passive until its execution is triggered by transactions. With the help of the consensus protocol, the contract is also guaranteed to be executed as its code dictates.

The Ethereum blockchain [17] presumably provides the highest support for smart contracts creation. Smart contracts are executed by a simple stack-based Turing complete 256-bit virtual machine known as the Ethereum Virtual Machine (EVM). Solidity is the common scripting language for writing smart contracts with a growing community. Ether represents the unit of currency in Ethereum and there are two types of accounts: externally owned accounts and contract accounts. An externally owned account is typically associated with a user, it consists of a unique public-private key pair. On the other hand, a contract account is controlled by the contract instead of a single private key. Transactions are created and signed by externally owned accounts. The receiver of the transaction can be an externally owned account or a contract account. In the former case, the transaction's purpose is to transfer ethers between users. Whereas in the latter case, the transaction triggers the execution of a function on the smart contract. Transactions also include a gas limit and a gas price; the amount of gas consumed to execute the transaction is converted into ethers using the gas price. These ethers are charged to the sender's account as transaction fees.

The Ethereum project has been planned in four locksteps [16]: Frontier, Homestead, Metropolis, and Serenity. Each update brings a set of approved Ethereum Improvement Proposals (EIP). Recently, the Ethereum blockchain has been upgraded to the first phase of Metropolis which is named Byzantium. The fork has been announced by the Ethereum team at the block number 4,370,000 [14]. Byzantium includes EIP-196 to efficiently perform elliptic curve point addition and scalar multiplication operations on alt_bn128 curve [15]. Simply, it is a pre-compiled contract with a special address that is intercepted by the client software which provides an efficient native implementation for elliptic curve operations, rather than the inefficient EVM implementation. EIP-196 along with EIP-197 proposals prepare Ethereum for untraceable transactions by incorporating zk-SNARK as it is the case Zcash [12] blockchain.

Despite the flexibility and power of the smart contracts, the present form of the blockchain technologies lacks transactional privacy. Typically, every sequence of actions executed in the smart contract is propagated across the network and ends up being recorded on the blockchain. As a result, the lack of privacy is considered a major challenge towards the adoption of smart contracts as alternatives to many financial applications. Many individuals are not willing to reveal their financial transactions to the public. In this paper, we tackle this challenge and present an auction smart contract that utilizes a set of cryptographic primitives to guarantee the following attributes:

1. Bid privacy. All bidders cannot know the bids submitted by the others before committing to their own. This property is also guaranteed even in a collusion with a malicious auctioneer.
2. Posterior privacy. Given a semi-honest auctioneer, all committed bids are maintained private from the bidders and public users.
3. Bid Binding. Once the bid interval is closed, bidders cannot change their commitments.
4. Public verifiable correctness. The auction contract verifies the correctness of the auctioneer's work to determine the auctioneer winner.
5. Financial fairness. Bidders or auctioneer may attempt to deviate from the protocol and prematurely abort to affect the behavior of the auction protocol. The aborting parties are financially penalized while honest parties are refunded after a specific timeout.
6. Non-Interactivity. Bidders do not participate in complex interactions with the underlying protocol of the auction contract. In fact, no extra communications between the bidders and the auction contract are required aside from the submission of the bid commitments and the associated opening values.

We have also made our implementation prototype available on Git-hub[1] for researchers and community to review it.

---

[1] https://github.com/HSG88/AuctionContract.

The rest of this paper is organized as follows. Section 2 provides a review of state-of-the-art research on auction solutions on the blockchain. The cryptographic primitives and the protocol for comparing the bids and verifying the correctness of the auction winner are presented in Sect. 3. In Sect. 4, we provide an analysis of the auction contract design and the estimated gas cost of the relevant transactions. Finally, we present our conclusions and future work in Sect. 5.

2 Related Work

Many of the previous research have focused on combining cryptocurrencies with secure multiparty computation protocols (MPC) and/or zero-knowledge proofs (ZKP). Typically, the cryptocurrency is used to incentive fairness and correctness, and avoid deviations from the MPC or ZKP protocol [1,2,8,9]. Initially, each participant deposits an amount of cryptocurrency in a smart contract. These funds are reserved while the protocol is still running. Subsequently, once the protocol reaches a final state after an arbitrary timeout, the deposits get refunded only to the honest players. This in effect encourages parties to strictly follow the protocols to avoid the financial penalty.

Kosba et al. [6] presented Hawk, a framework for creating Ethereum smart contract that does not store financial transactions in the clear on the blockchain. One can easily write a Hawk program without having to implement any cryptography. The associated compiler utilizes different cryptographic primitives such as ZKP to automatically generate privacy-preserving smart contracts. A Hawk program contains public and private parts. The public part consists of the logic that does not deal with the data or the currency. Conversely, the private part is responsible for hiding the information about data and input currency units. The compiler translates the Hawk program into three pieces that define the cryptographic protocol between users, manager, and the blockchain nodes. The security of a Hawk program is guaranteed to satisfy *on-chain privacy* that protects the flow of money and data from the public view, and *contractual security* that protects the parties in the agreement of the contract from each other. Up to our knowledge, the Hawk framework has not been released yet on the project homepage http://oblivm.com/hawk/download.html.

Blass and Kerschbaum [3] presented *Strain*, a protocol to implement sealed-bid auctions on top of blockchains that protects the bid privacy against fully-malicious parties. To achieve efficiency and low latency cost, the authors avoided the use of highly interactive MPC primitives such as garbled circuits. Instead, they designed a two-party comparison mechanism executed between any pair of bidders in parallel. The outcome of the comparison is broadcasted to all bidders such that each one can verify it using ZKP. An additional ZKP protocol is used to verify that the comparisons only involved the committed bids. Moreover, to achieve fairness against prematurely aborting malicious parties, the protocol uses a reversible commitment scheme such that a group of bidders can jointly open the bid commitment. The authors mentioned that the proposed protocol leaks the order of bids similar to Order Preserving Encryption (OPE) schemes.

Sánchez [13] proposed *Raziel*, a system that combines MPC and ZKP to guarantee the privacy, correctness and verifiability of smart contracts. The associated proofs of the smart contracts can effectively prove the functional correctness of a computation, besides to additional properties such as termination, security, pre-conditions and post-conditions. Furthermore, the author presented how a smart contract owner can prove its validity to third parties without revealing any information about the source code by using Zero-Knowledge Proofs to create Proof-Carrying Code certificates. Moreover, the author also proposed an incentive-based scheme for miners to generate preprocessed data of MPC.

3   Preliminaries

In this section, we briefly explain the cryptographic primitives that are utilized in the design of our proposed protocol:

1. Homomorphic commitment scheme that supports the addition operation on the underlying values
2. Zero-knowledge proof of interval membership $x \in [0, B]$.

3.1   Homomorphic Commitment Scheme

Our protocol makes an extensive use of Pedersen commitment scheme [11]. Let G and H be fixed public generators of the elliptic curve *alt_bn128* which is supported in EIP-196 and EIP-197 with the group order q [15]. The value of H is chosen such that neither the bidders nor the auctioneer know its discrete log. To commit a bid $x \in Z_q$, the bidder chooses a random $r \in Z_q$, then computes the commitment as $C = xG + rH$. Later, to open the commitment C, the bidder simply reveals the values of x and r. The Pedersen commitment scheme also possesses the homomorphic addition property on the underlying committed values by simply computing the point addition operation on the commitments. In other words, given two commitments $C_1 = x_1 G + r_1 H$ and $C_2 = x_2 G + r_2 H$, then $C_1 + C_2 = (x_1 + x_2)G + (r_1 + r_2)H$ which is essentially the outcome commitment to $x_1 + x_2$.

3.2   Zero-Knowledge Proof of Interval Membership

We adapt the interval membership ZKP protocol proposed in [4]. Given an arbitrary number x which belongs to an interval $[0, B)$, the prover is able to convince the verifier that $x \in [-B, 2B)$. Since the financial values of bids cannot be negative numbers, the proved interval membership becomes $x \in [0, 2B)$. The protocol runs as follows:

1. **Commit.** The prover picks a number $w_1 \in [0, B]$ and sets $w_2 = w_1 - B$. Then, the prover sends the commitments $X = xG + uH, W_1 = w_1 G + r_1 H$, and $W_2 = w_2 G + r_2 H$ to the verifier.

2. **Challenge.** The verifier picks a random variable $b \in \{0, 1\}$.
3. **Response.** The prover sends one of the following responses to the verifier based on the value of b:
   - Case $b = 0$, the prover sends $w_1, r_1, w_2,$ and r_2. The verifier checks $|w_1 - w_2| = B$, and the successful opening of the commitments W_1 and W_2.
   - Case $b = 1$, the prover sends $m = x + w_z$ and $n = u + r_z$, where $m \in [0, B)$ and $z \in \{0, 1\}$. The verifier checks $XW_z = (x + w_z)G + (u + r_z)H$.

In this protocol, the probability of cheating is $\frac{1}{2}$ which is non-negligible. However, with multiple k rounds of the protocol, the cheat probability becomes $\frac{1}{2^k}$.

3.3 Proving Claimed Inequality $x_1 > x_2$

Based on the primitives outlined above, we can prove that one bid is greater than another as follows. Suppose that $x_1, x_2 \in Z_q$, where q is a 256-bit prime number representing the order of alt_bn128 elliptic curve as specified in EIP-197 and EIP-198 [15]. Then it is relatively easy to prove that $x_1 > x_2$ if and only if the following three interval membership hold (i) $x_1 \in [0, \frac{q}{2})$, (ii) $x_2 \in [0, \frac{q}{2})$, and (iii) $\Delta x_{1,2} \in [0, \frac{q}{2})$ where $\Delta x_{1,2} = (x_1 - x_2) \bmod q$.

In our work, the auctioneer acts as a prover and the auction contract acts as a verifier. Recall that in the interval membership ZKP, the prover is able to convince the verifier that $x \in [0, 2B)$ given that $x \in [0, B)$. As a result, we set an upper bound $V = \frac{q}{4}$ on the range of possible bids. Additionally, the auctioneer is not allowed to create any commitments for the bids, instead, the auctioneer only uses the commitments submitted by the bidders on the smart contract. The auction contract utilizes the additive homomorphic feature of Pedersen commitment scheme to compute the commitment to the differences between each pair of bids $\Delta X_{i,j} = X_i + (-1)X_j$.

4   Auction Smart Contract

In this section, we illustrate all the interactions between the bidders, the auctioneer, and the auction contract. Although our work applies to both types of sealed-bid auctions, we demonstrate the interactions in the case of FPSBA.

There are five sequential phases from the initial deployment of the auction contract to the collection of the highest bid from the winner given a successful verification of correctness. There are two methods to define phases of a smart contract: time interval and block interval. In time interval, the smart contract checks the time of the mined block (*block.timestamp or now*) which is specified by the block's miner. Ethereum developers discourage this method since it can be easily manipulated by the miners. On the other hand, in block interval, the smart contract loses the notion of time.

4.1   Phase 1: Contract Deployment and Parameters Setup

As shown in Fig. 1, the auctioneer initially deploys the auction contract on the Ethereum blockchain with the following set of parameters:

1. T_1, T_2, T_3, T_4 define the time intervals for the following four phases: commitments of bids, opening the commitments, verification of the winner, and finalizing the auction, respectively.
2. F defines the amount of initial deposit of ethers received from the bidders and the auctioneer to achieve financial fairness against malicious parties.
3. N is the maximum number of bidders.
4. A_{pk} is the auctioneer's public key of an asymmetric encryption scheme.

Create:	upon receiving from auctioneer A $(T_1, T_2, T_3, T_4, N, F, A_{pk})$: Set state := INIT, bidders := {}, zkpCommits := {} Set highestBid := 0, winner := 0 Set challengeBlockNumber := 0, challengedBidder := 0 Assert $T < T_1 < T_2 < T_3 < T_4$ Assert ledger[A] >= F Set ledger[A] := ledger[A] - F Set deposit := deposit + F

Fig. 1. Pseudocode for the deployment of the auction contract

4.2   Phase 2: Commitment of Bids

This phase starts immediately after the deployment of the auction contract. Each bidder submits a bid commitment using Pedersen commitment scheme along with the initial deposit F in ethers to the function Bid as shown in Fig. 2.

Bid:	upon receiving from a bidder B (com_B): Assert $T < T_1$ Assert ledger[B] > F Set ledger[B] := ledger[B] - F Set deposit := deposit + F Set bidders[B].Commit := com_B

Fig. 2. Pseudocode for the Bid function

Suppose that an arbitrary bidder Bob is known to be very rich and is really interested in winning the auctioned item, i.e., Bob is very likely to be the one who submits the highest bid. Then, a collusion between a malicious bidder Alice and the auctioneer can eliminate Bob's winning chance by abusing the homomorphic property of the Pedersen commitment. The attack can be carried out as follows:

1. Bob submits the commitment $C_B = (xG + rH)$.
2. Subsequently, Alice submits the commitment $C_A = C_B + (G + H)$.
3. Bob reveals (x, r) to the auctioneer.
4. The auctioneer forwards (x, r) to Alice.
5. Alice reveals $(x + 1, r + 1)$.

To avoid this attack, we utilize Chaum-Pedersen non-interactive ZKP [5], which is not shown in Fig. 2. for the sake of simplicity. In this case, the above attack is not applicable because Bob sends commitments to random numbers rather than the actual bid which are subsequently challenged to verify the knowledge of values (x, r). As a result, Alice cannot succeed to imitate Bob's commitment since she will receive different challenges to verify the knowledge of $(x+1, r+1)$.

4.3   Phase 3: Opening the Commitments

Each bidder B_i sends the outcome ciphertext of encrypting (x_i, r_i) by the public key of the auctioneer A_{pk} to the function Reveal on the auction contract as shown in Fig. 3.

Reveal:	upon receiving from a bidder B (*ciphertext*):
	Assert $T_1 < T < T_2$
	Assert B ∈ bidders
	Set bidders[B].Ciphertext := ciphertext

Fig. 3. Pseudocode for the Reveal function

The ciphertext are stored on the auction contract instead of being sent directly to the auctioneer in order to avoid the following attack scenario. Suppose a malicious auctioneer pretends that an arbitrary bidder Bob has not revealed the opening values of the associated commitment. In this case, Bob has no chance of denying this false claim. However, if the ciphertext are to be stored on the auction contract, then their mere existence successfully prevents this attack.

We have also taken into our account the possibility of the following attack as well. Suppose a malicious auctioneer intends to penalize an arbitrary bidder Bob by claiming that the decryption outcome of Bob's ciphertext CT_B does not successfully open Bob's commitment C_B. We prevent this attack by requiring the auctioneer to verify the opening correctness of the commitments once they are submitted by the bidders. In the case of unsuccessful opening, the auctioneer declares on the auction contract that the ciphertext associated with the bidder

B is invalid. The honest bidder can deny this claim by revealing (x_B, r_B) to the auction contract. Subsequently, the auction contract encrypts the revealed values by the public key A_{pk}. If the outcome ciphertext is found to be equivalent to the previously submitted ciphertext, then the auction contract penalizes the auctioneer and terminates the auction after refunding the bidders. Otherwise, the bidder is penalized and the associated commitment is removed, such that only the valid commitments exist on the auction contract.

To guard against *forward search* attack on the submitted ciphertext, the parameter r in the opening values is a 256-bit random number that has no restriction on its value compared to the parameter x. Additionally, the opening values are combined to form one message which is passed to the encryption scheme.

4.4   Phase 4: Verification of Comparison Proofs

The auctioneer orders the bids to determine the wining bid x_w, the associated account address B_w and commitment C_w. Then, the auctioneer has to prove that $x_w > x_i$ for all $i \neq w$ and $0 < i < N$. The auction contract has a set of states to impose an order on the functions being invoked by the auctioneer for verification. Initially, the auctioneer calls the function ClaimWinner to claim that a winner is found by specifying the account address and opening values of the bid commitment as shown in Fig. 4.

```
ClaimWinner: upon receiving from auctioneer A (B_w, x_w, r_w):
             Assert state = INIT
             Assert T_2 < T < T_3
             Assert x_w < V
             Assert B_w ∈ bidders
             Assert bidders[B_w].commit = Pedersen.Commit(x_w, r_w)
             Set winner := B_w
             Set highestBid := x_w
             Set state := Challenge
```

Fig. 4. Pseudocode for the ClaimWinner function

Recall that the interval membership ZKP has a probability of cheating $\frac{1}{2}$ which is non-negligible; however, this probability can be further reduced to $(\frac{1}{2})^k$ by running the protocol k times. Moreover, in the *challenge* step, the verifier sends to the prover a random value $b \in \{0, 1\}$ which has to be non-predictable. However, smart contracts cannot send data to externally owned accounts, (i.e., the auction contract cannot send a challenge value to the auctioneer). Hence, we utilize a non-interactive interval membership ZKP to prove $x_i \in [0, \frac{q}{2})$ as follows:

1. **Commit:** The auctioneer chooses k-pairs of $(w_{1,j}, w_{2,j})$ where $w_{1,j} \in [-V, V)$ and $w_{2,j} = w_{1,j} - V$ such that $|w_{1,j} - w_{2,j}| = V$ for $1 \leq j \leq k$. Then, the auctioneer invokes the function ZKPCommit with the account address of the challenged bidder and the commitments to w_1 and w_2 as shown in Fig. 5.

```
ZKPCommit: upon receiving from auctioneer A (B_i, commits):
            Assert state = Challenge
            Assert T_2 < T < T_3
            Assert B_i ∈ bidders
            Set zkpCommits :=commits
            Set challengeBidder := B_i
            Set challengeBlockNumber := QueryBlockNumber()
            Set State := Verify
```

Fig. 5. Pseudocode for the ZKPCommit function

2. Challenge and Response:

- The auctioneer receives a transaction receipt which includes the hash of the block containing the transaction after it has been confirmed. The ZKPCommit function has no access to this hash while it is being executed; therefore it stores the current block number in **challengeBlockNumber**.
- The least significant k-bits of the hash are chosen as the challenge b_j.
- The auctioneer creates k responses R_j based on the values of b_j.
- Case $b_j = 0$, then $R_j = \{w_{1,j}, r_{1,j}, w_{2,j}, r_{2,j}\}$.
- Case $b_j = 1$, then $R_j = \{m_j, n_j, z\}$ where $m_j = x_j + w_{z,j}$, $n_j = u_j + r_{z,j}$ such that $m_j \in [0, V)$ and $z \in \{1, 2\}$.
- The auctioneer invokes the function ZKPVerify with input parameter *responses* which is an array of R_j as shown in Fig. 6.

```
ZKPVerify:    upon receiving from auctioneer A (responses)
              Assert State = Verify
              Assert T_2 < T < T_3
              Set hash := QueryBlockHash(challengeBlockNumber)
              for j ∈ [1, k], R_j ∈ responses, C_j ∈ zkpCommits
                  Set b_j := Bit(hash, j)
                  if b_j = 0
                      Assert VerifyFirstCase(C_j, R_j)
                  else
                      Assert VerfiySecondCase(C_j, R_j)
              Set bidders[challengeBidder].ValidBid := true
              Set state := Challenge
```

Fig. 6. Pseudocode for the ZKPVerify function

As explained in Sect. 3, three interval membership ZKP are required to prove that $x_w > x_i$. However, since the bid of the winner B_w is revealed, then the number of proofs is reduced to two. In other words, the auctioneer has to prove the interval membership for all bids x_i other than the winning bid and their associated differences Δ_{wi}. The function ZKPCommit and ZKPVerify contain extra logic to also verify the correctness of $\Delta_{wi} \in [0, \frac{q}{4})$.

4.5   Phase 5: Finalizing the Auction

After the successful verification of correctness, the auctioneer invokes the function VerifyAll as shown in Fig. 7 to change the state of the auction contract so that the winner can pay the winning bid.

VerifyAll	upon receiving from auctioneer A ()
	Assert state = Challenge
	Assert $T_2 < T < T_3$
	For all b $\in$ bidders - $\{winner\}$
	Assert b.ValidBid = true and b.ValidDelta = true
	Set State := ValidWinner

Fig. 7. Pseudocode for the VerifyAll function

Subsequently, The winner invokes the function WinnerPay to deposit the difference between the winning bid and the initial deposit F as shown in Fig. 8.

WinnerPay	upon receiving from a bidder B ($"winnerPay"$)
	Assert State = ValidWinner
	Assert $T_3 < T < T_4$
	Assert B = winner
	Assert ledger[B] > highestBid - F
	Set ledger[B] := ledger[B] - highestBid +F
	Set deposit := deposit + highestBid - F
	Set state := WinnerPaid

Fig. 8. Pseudocode for the WinnerPay function

The auction contract guarantees to refund the initial deposit to all honest players after the time T_3 as shown in Fig. 9. In the case of invalid proofs, it penalizes the auctioneer and refunds all bidders. Otherwise, it refunds the losing bidders and the auctioneer as well. It is also clear that the only way for the winner to refund the initial deposit is by invoking WinnerPay function.

```
Timer
        if T > T₃ then
                if state ≠ ValidProof then
                        refund(F) for all b ∈ bidders
                else
                        refund(F) to auctioneer A
                        refund(F) for all b ∈ bidders - {winner}
```

Fig. 9. Pseudocode for the Timer function

4.6 Gas Cost

We have created a local private Ethereum blockchain to test our prototype using the *Geth* client version 1.7.2. To support the Byzantium EIP-196 and EIP-197, the *genesis.json* file has to contain the attribute {*"byzantiumBlock"*: 0}. Additionally, since Ethereum does not support timer triggered functions, we have implemented a *Withdraw* function that is invoked by an explicit request from the honest players to refund their initial fairness deposit. We have tested the auction contract with ten bidders, and we have set $k = 10$ as the number of multiple rounds to verify interval membership NiZKP which results in a probability of cheat less than 0.001. The upper bound on bid values is up to 250-bit length which is very adequate for financial values. The Pedersen commitment size is 512-bits that represent two points on the elliptic curve. The ciphertext submitted to the Reveal function is 1024-bits. Table 1 shows the consumed gas and the equivalent monetary cost in *US* dollars for invoking different functions on the auction contract. As of November 30, 2017, the ether exchange rate is 1 ether = 450\$ and the gas price is approximately 20 *Gwei* = 20×10^{-9} ether. Furthermore, the execution of "heavy" functions in Ethereum is not only costly in dollar terms, but may be even impossible, if the function's gas requirements exceed the block gas limit. The block gas limit at time of writing is 8 m gas, whereas the most expensive protocol function consumes 2 m gas, which seems feasible.

Table 1. Consumed gas cost for different functions of the Auction contract

Function	Gas units	Gas cost (USD)
Deployment	3131261	28.18
Bid	130084	1.17
Reveal	132849	1.19
ClaimWinner	166288	1.49
ZKPCommit	656689	5.91
ZKPVerify	2002490	18.02
VerifyAll	46580	0.42
Withdraw	47112	0.42

5   Conclusion and Future Work

In this paper, we presented a smart contract for a verifiable sealed-bid auction on the Ethereum blockchain. We utilized Pedersen commitment scheme along with ZKP of interval membership to create the underlying protocol. The auction contract maintains the privacy of bids such that bidders do not learn any information about the other bids when they commit. Additionally, the auction contract also exhibits the public verifiable correctness as it is designed to verify the proofs claimed by the auctioneer to determine the winner. Moreover, no complex interaction is required from the bidders other than submitting and revealing the commitments to their bids. The proposed protocol can be easily modified to support the full privacy of all bids including the winner's bid if there is a desire to receive the payment of winning bid aside from the blockchain. For future work, we will investigate other approaches applicable to the Ethereum blockchain where we can also protect the privacy of bids from all parties including the auctioneer.

References

1. Andrychowicz, M., Dziembowski, S., Malinowski, D., Mazurek, L.: Secure multiparty computations on bitcoin. In: 2014 IEEE Symposium on Security and Privacy (SP), pp. 443–458. IEEE (2014)
2. Bentov, I., Kumaresan, R.: How to use bitcoin to design fair protocols. In: Garay, J.A., Gennaro, R. (eds.) CRYPTO 2014, Part II. LNCS, vol. 8617, pp. 421–439. Springer, Heidelberg (2014). https://doi.org/10.1007/978-3-662-44381-1_24
3. Blass, E.-O., Kerschbaum, F.: Strain: A secure auction for blockchains. Cryptology ePrint Archive, Report 2017/1044 (2017). https://eprint.iacr.org/2017/1044
4. Brickell, E.F., Chaum, D., Damgård, I.B., van de Graaf, J.: Gradual and verifiable release of a secret (Extended Abstract). In: Pomerance, C. (ed.) CRYPTO 1987. LNCS, vol. 293, pp. 156–166. Springer, Heidelberg (1988). https://doi.org/10.1007/3-540-48184-2_11
5. Chaum, D., Pedersen, T.P.: Wallet databases with observers. In: Brickell, E.F. (ed.) CRYPTO 1992. LNCS, vol. 740, pp. 89–105. Springer, Heidelberg (1993). https://doi.org/10.1007/3-540-48071-4_7
6. Kosba, A., Miller, A., Shi, E., Wen, Z., Papamanthou, C.: Hawk: the blockchain model of cryptography and privacy-preserving smart contracts. In: 2016 IEEE Symposium on Security and Privacy (SP), pp. 839–858. IEEE (2016)
7. Krishna, V.: Auction Theory. Academic Press, San Diego (2009)
8. Kumaresan, R., Bentov, I.: Amortizing secure computation with penalties. In: Proceedings of the 2016 ACM SIGSAC Conference on Computer and Communications Security, pp. 418–429. ACM (2016)
9. Kumaresan, R., Vaikuntanathan, V., Vasudevan, P.N.: Improvements to secure computation with penalties. In: Proceedings of the 2016 ACM SIGSAC Conference on Computer and Communications Security, pp. 406–417. ACM (2016)
10. Prentice, A., Vasina, O.: Ukrainian ministry carries out first blockchain transactions. Reuters Technology News. https://goo.gl/J8X1up
11. Pedersen, T., Petersen, B.: Explaining gradually increasing resource commitment to a Foreign market. Int. Bus. Rev. **7**(5), 483–501 (1998)

12. Ben Sasson, E., et al.: Zerocash: decentralized anonymous payments from bitcoin. In: 2014 IEEE Symposium on Security and Privacy (SP), pp. 459–474. IEEE (2014)

13. Cerezo Sánchez, D.: Raziel: Private and verifiable smart contracts on blockchains. Cryptology ePrint Archive, Report 2017/878 (2017). https://eprint.iacr.org/2017/878

14. Ethereum Project Team. Byzantium HF announcement (2017). https://blog.ethereum.org/2017/10/12/byzantium-hf-announcement/

15. Ethereum Project Team. Ethereum improvement proposals (2017). https://github.com/ethereum/EIPs

16. Ethereum Project Team. The ethereum launch process (2017). https://blog.ethereum.org/2015/03/03/ethereum-launch-process/

17. Wood, G.: Ethereum: a secure decentralised generalised transaction ledger. Ethereum Project Yellow Paper, 151 (2014)

The Scalability of Trustless Trust

Dominik Harz[1](✉) and Magnus Boman[2,3]

[1] IC3RE, Imperial College London, London SW7 2RH, UK
d.harz@imperial.ac.uk
[2] RISE, Box 1263, 16429 Kista, Sweden
[3] KTH/ICT/SCS, Electrum 229, 16440 Kista, Sweden

Abstract. Permission-less blockchains can realise trustless trust, albeit at the cost of limiting the complexity of computation tasks. To explain the implications for scalability, we have implemented a trust model for smart contracts, described as agents in an open multi-agent system. Agent intentions are not necessarily known and autonomous agents have to be able to make decisions under risk. The ramifications of these general conditions for scalability are analysed for Ethereum and then generalised to other current and future platforms. Finally, mechanisms from the trust model are applied to a verifiable computation algorithm and implemented in the Ethereum blockchain. We show in experiments that the algorithm needs at most six semi-honest verifiers to detect false submission.

Keywords: Trustless trust · Smart contract · Agent · Ethereum · Blockchain · Scalability · Multi-agent system · Distributed ledger

1 Introduction

Turing-complete programming languages allow creating a generic programmable blockchain by means of smart contracts [30]. A smart contract can be defined as a decentralised application executed on the distributed P2P network that constitutes the blockchain. The smart contract captures the formalisation of electronic commerce in code, to execute the terms of a contract. However, a smart contract is, in fact, neither smart nor a contract. In practice, it codes an agreement about what will come to pass, in the form of a production rule. Since there cannot be a breach of contract—which would happen only if one or more parties would not honour the agreement—thanks to how this production rule is coded, a smart contract is not a contract. Since there is no opportunity for learning on the contract's behalf, it is also not smart.

Smart contracts do code the preferences of their owners, and their negotiating partners as appropriate, with respect to the decision under risk or uncertainty. They react on events, have a specific state, are executed on a distributed ledger, and are able to interact with assets stored on the ledger [28]. Ethereum offers smart contracts through its blockchain. The Ethereum Virtual Machine (EVM) handles the states and computations of the protocol and can theoretically execute code of

© International Financial Cryptography Association 2019
A. Zohar et al. (Eds.): FC 2018 Workshops, LNCS 10958, pp. 279–293, 2019.
https://doi.org/10.1007/978-3-662-58820-8_19

arbitrary algorithmic complexity [3]. Using Ethereum, developers can implement smart contracts as lines of code in an account that execute automatically when transactions or function calls are sent to that account. The outcome is final and agreed on by all participants and blockchains can thus enable a system of trust.

In Ethereum, smart contracts can interact through function calls via their Application Binary Interface (ABI). Single smart contracts or multiple smart contracts together can act as decentralised autonomous organisations by encoding the rules of interaction for the organisation's inner and outer relationships (e.g., The DAO, MakerDAO). *Full nodes* store the distributed ledger and validate new blocks in the chain *pro bono*. Permission-less blockchains limit the complexity of computation tasks and thus, the scalability of these blockchains. When utilising smart contracts, external services can be required to circumvent these computational limitations to code the preferences of their owners. The result of computations performed by external parties are not subject to the consensus protocol of the underlying blockchain, and their provided solution or correct execution cannot be formally verified. Hence, the oft-cited benefit of blockchains allowing for transparency over every transaction and enforced trust through a consensus mechanism cannot be guaranteed with external entities [17]. A trust model for smart contracts in permission-less blockchains is thus missing, a fact that limits their adaptability. Earlier trust models used in related applications, such as those devised for quantitative trading or speculative agent trading (see the patent text [14] for a good indication of this range), need to be adjusted for the inherent transparency and particular trust implications of blockchain systems. We propose a model that incorporate all these aspects.

2   Method

We answer the following research questions:

1. Which models of trust can be applied to smart contracts to reflect public permission-less blockchains?
2. What can be done to clarify the link between, on the one hand, the preferences and intentions of authors of smart contracts and, on the other hand, the runtime properties of those smart contracts?
3. How can properties of trust models be applied to verify computations in permission-less blockchains?

Question 1 is analysed in two steps. First, the applicability of agent-based trust models for smart contracts is evaluated by deducing their strong and weak notions based on agent theory. Second, a trust model suitable for smart contracts in permission-less blockchains is developed, based on a review of existing multi-agent system trust models [23]. Question 2 is analysed deductively, based on literature on decision theory and decision analysis, and on limitations of formal representations of preference, and their logical closure, e.g., what can be derived from them. Question 3 is investigated instrumentally, by developing an algorithm for verifiable computations. The development of the algorithm followed a deductive method of merging verifiable computation concepts using blockchains

[29,34] with cloud and distributed systems research [6,7]. This revolves around preserving privacy of user data, whereby aspects of the blockchain are used to enforce the algorithm [34], and on verifiable computation for Ethereum using computation services inside the blockchain [29]. In the latter, a verification algorithm with dispute resolution and an incentive layer were suggested, and the relevant assumptions critically assessed to develop a new algorithm, since their proposal had two practical issues: First, the verification game includes a 'jackpot' to reward solvers and verifiers for their work. This introduces an incentive to steal the jackpot by solvers and verifiers colluding to receive the jackpot without providing a correct solution. Second, they propose to implement the computation tasks in C, C++, or Rust code using the Lanai interpreter implemented as a smart contract on Ethereum. This limits the flexibility of computation services by forcing them to use one of the three programming languages. The objective of the here presented algorithm is to achieve:

1. execution of arbitrary computations requested from a smart contract in Ethereum, and executed outside the blockchain;
2. verification of the computation result achievable within reasonable time, i.e., $\mathcal{O}(n)$;
3. guarantees that the result of the computation is correct without having to trust the providing service.

Our development was experimental and explorative. Different parameters and the agents they pertain to were first considered in a pen and paper exercise, then validated via qualitative assessment as well as quantitative analysis. The quantitative experiments constitute an evaluation basis for the last two algorithm objectives.

3   Explicating Smart Contracts

Consensus protocols are used to decide upon the state of the distributed ledger [21]. This ledger is in permission-less blockchains accessible to anyone participating in the network and through blockchain explorers even to entities outside of the network. This means everyone is able to see for example which public key owns the most Ether. Also, each transaction can be inspected, making it possible for participating parties to monitor the progress of their transaction. To provide an incentive to the miner and prevent unnecessary changes to the ledger, blockchains introduce fees on executing transactions [21]. In Ethereum, the blockchain stores transactions and the code of smart contracts as well as their state. Hence, the state of a smart contract needs to be updated in the same fashion as executing a transaction including fees, consensus, and mining time.

Smart contracts on Ethereum are executed by each node participating in the P2P network and hence operations are restricted to protect the network [31]. To circumvent operational issues (e.g., someone executing a denial of service attack on the network), Ethereum introduces a concept to make users pay for execution of a smart contract functions, and the EVM supports only certain defined operations [31], with each operation coming with a certain cost referred to as *gas*. Before executing a state-changing function or a transaction, the user has to send a certain amount of gas to the function or the transaction. Only if the provided amount of gas is sufficient for the function or transaction to execute, it will successfully terminate. Otherwise, the transaction or function will terminate prematurely, with results contingent on the handling of the smart contract function.

We now look at two ways of explicating the roles that smart contracts may take on. First, the agent metaphor is employed to provide an informal understanding in terms of a widely accepted and understood terminology. Second, the concept of utility is employed to provide a formal understanding of how the preferences and intentions of smart contract owners may be encoded in the contract itself.

3.1   Smart Contracts as Agent Systems

Agents have certain properties separable in weak and strong notions [32]. Weak notions include *autonomy, pro-activeness, reactivity*, and *social ability*. *Autonomy* refers to the smart contract ability to operate without a direct intervention of others and include control over their actions and state. In Ethereum, the state of smart contracts is maintained on the blockchain, while the actions are coded into the smart contract itself. These actions can depend on the state, thus providing a weak form of autonomy. *Pro-activeness* describes goal-directed behaviour by agents taking initiative. This is somewhat limited in Ethereum, as smart contracts currently act on incoming transactions or calls to their functions. However, if one perceives an agent as a collection of multiple different parts, smart contracts might well be extended by external programs triggering such initiatives. Thereby, the limitations set by Ethereum can be circumvented and an agent with pro-active notions can be created. The result is in effect a multi-agent system and can be analyzed as such. *Reactivity* is based on perception of an agent's environment and a timely response to those changes. By design, smart contracts only have access to the state of the blockchain they are operating in. Reactivity for state changes in Ethereum is reached via event, transaction, or function implementation. To react to environment changes outside of the blockchain (e.g. executing a function based on changes in stock market prices) requires importing this information to the blockchain via e.g. Oracles [4]. *Social ability* enables the potential interaction with other agents or humans through a communication language. In Ethereum, users and contracts are identifiable by their public key [31] and interaction is possible through transactions or function calls on smart contracts.

Strong notions include properties such as *beliefs and intentions, veracity, benevolence, rationality*, and *mobility*. As mentioned in the introduction above, pro-activeness is somewhat limited in Ethereum smart contracts, and so these properties are present only to a limited extent. The two properties *veracity*, which refers to not knowingly communicating false information, and *rationality*, describing the alignment of the agent's actions to its preferences, both pertain to the incentives an author of a smart contract might have to develop an agent which is rational but not truthful, in order to maximise profits. This can be deliberate so that the agent correctly encodes the true preferences of the smart contract owner, or non-deliberate, in which case the owner preferences might be inadequately coded. To deal with the uncertainty of agent intentions, three approaches have emerged. First, security approaches utilise cryptographic measures to guarantee basic properties such as authenticity, integrity, identities, and privacy [23]. Within blockchains, this is mainly achieved through cryptographic measures, which do not provide trust in the content of the messages. Second, institutional approaches enforce behaviour through a centralised authority. This entity controls agents' actions and can penalise undesired behaviour. Governance functions enforcing behaviour not defined in the core protocol do not exist. Third, social approaches utilise reputation and trust mechanisms to e.g. select partners, punish undesired behaviour, or evaluate different strategies. In blockchains, there is no system of trust implemented in the core protocol, which would rate behaviour according to certain standards. These three approaches are complementary and can be used to create a system of trust [23]. Trust research and current implementations are primarily focused on the first two approaches. This allows creating agents on a platform that enforces these defined trust measurements [1, 20, 24, 26].

3.2 Utility and Risk

Some researchers believe that all game-theoretical aspects of making decisions can be pinned down by logical axiomatizations: it is only a matter of finding the right axioms. Game-theoretical studies often concentrate on two-person games, one reason being that many conflicts involve only two protagonists. In any game, the players may or may not be allowed to cooperate to mutual advantage. If cooperation is allowed, the generalized theory of n-person games can sometimes be reduced to the one for two-person games, since any group of cooperating players may be seen as opposing the coalition of the other players. In the case of smart contracts, this would allow for an owner of multiple contracts (in effect, a multi-agent system) to maximize the utility of interplaying contracts by employing game theory, at least on paper. For a given set of smart contracts, the problem is how to determine a rule that specifies what actions would have been optimal for the smart contract owner. Actions could here pertain to details of a particular contract, or to the order of their execution, for instance. Comparing different rules measures the risk involved in consistently applying a particular rule, e.g., a chain of smart contract employment. Formally, we wish to determine a decision function that minimizes this risk. The simpler case of handling risk is in decisions under certainty. This means that the owner of one or more smart contracts can predict the consequences of employing them. This represents the ideal case in which all smart contracts execute as intended. Thus, the owner simply chooses the alternative whose one and only possible consequence has a value not less than the value of any other alternative. This seems simple enough, but it is necessary to investigate a bit further what the value of a consequence denotes. The preferences of the owner should be compatible with the following axioms (A is not preferred to B is henceforth denoted by $A \leq B$).

$\leq$ is a weak ordering on the set of preferences P:

A1. (i) Transitivity: If $A \leq B$ and $B \leq C$, then $A \leq C$, for all A, B, and C in P.

A1. (ii) Comparability: $A \leq B$ or $B \leq A$, for all A and B in P.

From this, we may derive the relation of indifference and strict preference, and we state the consistency criteria for these:

A2. (i) $A = B$ is equivalent to $A \leq B$ and $B \leq A$, for all A and B in P.

A2. (ii) $A < B$ is equivalent to $A \leq B$ and not $B \leq A$, for all A and B in P.

However, A1 implies that the owner has to admit to all consequences being comparable. This is typically not the case in smart contracts, and it becomes necessary to replace Comparability with Reflexivity, yielding a partial ordering instead:

A1. (iii) Reflexivity: $A \leq A$, for all A in P.

There is much to be gained by representing the preference ordering as a real-valued order-preserving function. If we cannot find such a function there is not much sense in speaking of the numerical value of a sequence of employed smart contracts, and we might as well throw a coin for deciding. Assuming axioms A1 and A2 hold, we must find a function $f(X)$ with the property $f(A) \leq f(B)$ iff $A \leq B$, which we can always do fairly easily for decisions under certainty [13], but we now turn to decisions under risk, which is the class of decisions that normally pertain to owners of smart contracts. In the Bayesian case, with subjective probabilities, we can think of a smart contract employment S as consisting of a matrix of probabilities $p_1, ..., p_n$ and their corresponding consequences $c_1, ..., c_n$. Then the real-valued function $f(X)$ we seek lets us compute the value of S as $\Sigma p_i f(c_i)$. This fixes one possible definition of an agent as rational, by making it maximize its own utility (in accordance with its preferences, i.e. with the preferences it codes). Formally, an agent accepts the utility principle iff it assigns the value $\Sigma p_i v_i$ to S, given that it has assigned the value v_i to c_i. Any ordering Ω of the alternatives is compatible to the principle of maximizing the expected utility iff $a\Omega b$ implies that the expected value of a is higher than the expected value of b. In other words, we are now free to start experimenting with various axiom systems for governing the owners, or at least recommending them actions based on the smart contracts they have at hand. While game-theoretic axiom systems have been favoured among agent researchers, a wide variety of axiomatizations are surveyed in the more formal literature [12,19].

4   A Trust Model for Smart Contracts

From the 25 models covered in [23], five consider global visibility and nine consider cheaters. The overlap of those models leaves one model focusing on reputation of actors in electronic markets [25]. The core idea is to use incentives to encourage truthful behaviour of agents in the system by social control. Social control implies that actors in the network are responsible for enforcing secure interactions instead of using an external or global authority.

Assuming a rational agent, there is a possible motivation to break protocol if this maximizes utility. Speculation-free protocols have been recommended for some agent applications, but the Ethereum smart contract environment is much too complex to allow for such control features, which require equilibrium markets [27]. To provide a certain level of trust, new agents have to deposit a certain cryptocurrency value for participation, and this deposit is returned when an agent decides to stop participating. However, dishonest or corrupt agents can be penalised by either destroying their deposit or distributing it to honest agents. This is in line with norm-regulation of agent systems [2] and does not make any other strong requirements on models. Norm-regulation has been formalized for multi-agent systems, e.g., in the form of algebra [22].

Gossiping can be used to communicate experiences with other agents in a P2P fashion and thereby establish trust or reputation. In the protocol of Bitcoin or Ethereum gossiping is the basis for propagating new transactions and subsequently validating blocks [10]. A similar approach can be taken for smart contracts, whereby agents could exchange knowledge or experiences of other agents [8]. Reputation of an agent is based on its interaction with other agents, whereby agents mutually need to sign a transaction if they are satisfied with the interaction. Over time, an agent collects these signed transactions to build up its reputation. However, this model is prone to colluding agents boosting their reputation [5]. Trust can also be implemented by relying on independent review agents [9,15,16]. However, both gossiping and review agents are subject to detection rate issues.

5   Applying Trust Measures to Verifiable Computation

Due to the restrictions set by the EVM (i.e. gas cost of operations), implementing functions in Ethereum with a complexity greater than $\mathcal{O}(n)$ is not feasible. To circumvent these limitations, computations can be executed outside of Ethereum and results stored on the blockchain. We present an algorithm to achieve verifiable computations outside of Ethereum through measures presented in the trust model. Agents' rational behaviour can be aligned to the overall objective of the algorithm. The actors involved in the verifying computation algorithm are presented in Fig. 1. *Users* request solving a specific computation problem. They provide an incentive for solving and verifying the problem. *Computation services* provide computation power in exchange for receiving a compensation. For participation, they are providing a deposit. One of the computation services acts as a *solver* and at least one other computation service acts as a *verifier*. *Judges* decide whether basic mathematical operations are correct or not. They are neutral parties and are not receiving any incentives. An *arbiter* enforces the verifiable computation algorithm when users request a new computation.

Users are assumed as agents with the objective to receive a correct computation. They are required to send a fee to reward solvers and verifiers for executing the computation. This fee depends on the complexity of the computation to be performed, the complexity of the input data, and the number

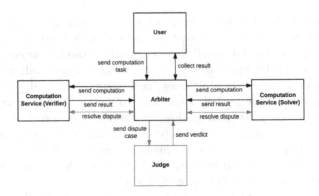

Fig. 1. Overview of actors in the verification algorithm.

of verifiers. Computation services are assumed to optimise their incentive. They might purposely communicate false information to maximise their incentive. Further, enough computation services are available (i.e. a minimum of 2) to execute the computation with at least one verifier. The probability of detecting a false computation depends on the number of verifiers in the algorithm. The arbiter and judge are trusted by participating parties, respectively enforcing the algorithm and reaching a verdict. This is a strong assumption in a trustless system and needs to be justified. To limit their incentive for undesired behaviour (i.e. cheating) in the algorithm, these two agents are not rewarded for taking part in the computations. Thus, their work is *pro bono* and only the operational cost in gas are covered.

Alternatively and not further covered in this paper, other approaches limit or eliminate trust in arbiter and judge. First, following the trust is risk approach [18], a network of trusted entities with a fixed amount of deposited value could be created to find arbiters and judges trusted commonly between computation services and users. Second, a user might create their own arbiter and judge, while storing the fee in an escrow contract between user and computation services. The computation services store an encrypted hash of the result in the escrow contract. Upon completion of the protocol, the user issues the payment and receives the result in full. Third, the protocol could be executed with different test cases while results would be publicly stored on the blockchain. Thus, a user and computation service could verify correct execution of the protocol, if arbiter and judge remain unchanged.

5.1   Algorithm

The algorithm is initiated when a user requests a computation by sending the input data, the operation to be performed, and the desired number of verifiers to the arbiter. One computation service is randomly determined as a solver, and the other(s) are randomly assigned as verifiers by the arbiter. The user instructs the arbiter to forward the input data and operation to the computation services smart contracts, triggering the off-chain computation by sending a request through an oracle. This requires sending a fee for the computation as well as providing the fee for using the oracle. Verifiers and the solver report their result back to the arbiter. If all results are reported back, then the user can trigger the arbiter to compare the available results. If the solver and all participating verifiers agree on one solution, the algorithm is finished and the user can collect the result. However, if at least one verifier disagrees with the solver the user can initiate a dispute resolution algorithm. The dispute resolution is inspired by a technique introduced in [6,7,29] to split up the operation into simple parts with intermediary results until the computation is simple enough for the judge to solve it. Overall and intermediary results are stored in a Merkle tree for the solver, and each verifier challenging the solver. The comparison is achieved through a binary search on the trees. The root of the tree encodes the overall result, while the leaves in the lowest layer encode the input data. Leaves in between represent intermediary results.

5.2   Interactions

Under the assumption that arbiter, judge, and user behave rational and follow the algorithm, computation services have a combination of four different behaviours with respect to their role as solver S or verifier V. The behaviours are summarised in Table 1 with either verifiers accepting the solution (i.e. V_A) or challenging the solution (i.e. V_C). S profits the most if it provides a correct solution, which is challenged by V, while V profits the most when S provides a false solution and V is able to challenge it. The problematic case is that the incentives for accepting a false or correct solution are the same. To prevent this from happening we will consider the behaviour of V and S in detail.

Case 1: S provides a correct solution and no V challenges the solution. Agents behave as intended by the algorithm. As no V challenges the solution, the judge is not triggered and the fee is equally split between S and the involved V.

Case 2: S provides a correct solution and at least one V challenges the solution. This is an undesired behaviour since the solution provided is actually correct.

Table 1. Possible behaviours of computation services as solver S and verifier V, whereby all verifiers behave the same.

		S	
		Correct solution	False solution
V	Challenge	S receives S fee share	S receives nothing
		S receives V_C fee share	V_C receives V_C fee share
		V_C receives nothing	V_C receives S fee share
	Accept	S receives S fee share	S receives S fee share
		V_A receives V_A fee share	V_A receives V_A fee share

This triggers the dispute resolution with a verdict by the judge determining S as correct. In this case S profits from the extra work due to the additional dispute steps by receiving the fee share of V_C. V_A receive their part of the fee since their amount of work remained the same.

Case 3: S provides a false solution and no V challenges the solution. S and all V would receive their share of the fee. This is an undesired behaviour in the algorithm as it would flag a false result as correct. To prevent this from happening two measures are used. First, computation services do not know their role in advance as they are randomly assigned by the arbiter. If several services collude to provide false solutions, all of them would need to work together to provide the "same wrong" result. However, if just one V_C exists, it profits by gaining the fee shares of itself, S, and all V_A. Thus, second, the user is able to determine the number of V for each computation. The probability of having at least one V_C depends on the prior probability p of V providing correct or false solutions and the number n of V in the computation.

Case 4: S provides a false solution and at least one V_C challenges the solution. Hereby, S and V_A are not receiving their share of the fee, which goes to all V_C. This is based on the verdict by the judge. However, this is also an undesired case since the user does not receive a solution to his computation.

Considering the four scenarios, rational S is trying to receive its share of the incentive and get a chance to receive fees of any V challenging a correct solution. The strategy for S considering V is to provide a correct solution to the problem. V profits the most form challenging a false solution. A rational V provides the correct solution to a computation to receive its fee share or to have the chance of becoming a challenger to a false solution. Arguably, S and V could try to deliver a false solution to save up on computation cost or trick the user. In this case, the probability of discovering the false solution relies on the number of Vs and the prior probability of cheating Vs. If a V delivers a false solution, it must be the same solution as S' to not trigger the dispute resolution. Moreover, by destroying the services' deposits and excluding them from the algorithm after detected cheating, the prior probability of having such a service can be reduced.

5.3   Implementation and Experiments

The algorithm was implemented using Solidity smart contracts and AWS Lambda external computation services. The quantitative analysis is conducted by executing experiments with one exemplary type of computation. The computation is a multiplication of two integers to simplify the verification steps in the algorithm. The results depend on external and internal parameters of the algorithm. Externally, the prior probability of computation services providing false solutions is considered. Internally, the number of verifiers the user requests for each computation are examined. Experiments are executed for each different configuration of parameters to determine gas consumption and outcome of the computation. Assuming a potentially large number of computation services

(>10,000), this gives a confidence level of 95% and a maximum confidence interval of 3.1 for the three different prior probabilities. Before each iteration of the experiment, the environment is initialised with a new set of smart contracts. Experiments are executed within *TestRPC* [11].

Reporting the amount of gas used equals the time and space complexity of the algorithm, as gas consumption is determined by the type and number of operations in the EVM. It further excludes the time used for sending transactions or calls. Independent of the prior probability of false solutions, the μ gas consumption increases linearly as presented in Fig. 2. Further, σ decreases with an increasing number of verifiers. At a low number of verifiers, the dispute resolution is less likely triggered, leading to a higher σ in gas consumption. With an increasing number of verifiers, the probability of triggering the dispute resolution increases. As the dispute resolution is almost always triggered, σ is reduced.

The algorithm is tested for three different cases of verification: First, the algorithm can accept a correct solution. Second, each verifier agrees with the solver although the solution is not correct. The dispute resolution is not triggered and the user receives a false solution marked as correct. Third, at least one

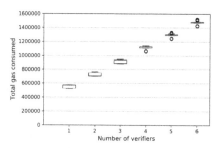

(a) 30% of computation services providing incorrect solutions.

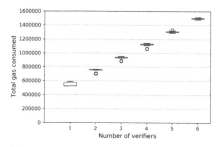

(b) 50% of computation services providing incorrect solutions.

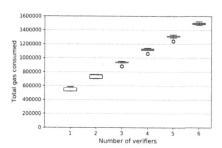

(c) 70% of computation services providing incorrect solutions.

Fig. 2. Total amount of gas used by algorithm with different number of verifiers and percentage of computation services providing incorrect solutions. Each combination of specific number of verifier(s) and percentage of computation services with incorrect solutions with $N = 1000$.

Table 2. Comparison of expected and actual probabilities of accepting a false solution in the algorithm.

Prior p	Verifiers n	Expected false [%]	Actual false [%]
0.3	1	9.0	2.7
0.3	2	2.7	0.0
0.3	3	0.81	0.0
0.3	4	0.243	0.0
0.3	5	0.0729	0.0
0.3	6	0.02187	0.0
0.5	1	25.0	28.6
0.5	2	12.5	12.2
0.5	3	6.25	4.6
0.5	4	3.125	1.2
0.5	5	1.5625	0.0
0.5	6	0.78125	0.0
0.7	1	49.0	41.2
0.7	2	34.3	24.4
0.7	3	24.01	12.1
0.7	4	16.807	4.9
0.7	5	11.7649	2.9
0.7	6	8.23543	0.0

verifier disagrees with the solver providing a false solution and the judge rules that the solver's solution is false. For the second case, invoking the dispute resolution depends on the prior probability of computation services providing false solutions described by $P(V_C) = 1 - p^n$. The experiments as shown in Table 2 indicate that the expected and actual value are similar for $p = 0.5$. However, for $p = 0.3$ and $p = 0.7$ the actual values are below the expected ones. Since the experiment is executed with a confidence level of 95% and interval of 3.1, those changes are accounted towards sampling size not being a perfect representative of the actual distribution. Also, the random assignment of false and correct computation services could be a cause for having a higher detection rate.

6   Discussion

Within the presented trust model, deposits are simple to implement in permission-less blockchains that already have a cryptocurrency. However, the deposit value can be volatile. This poses two risks: Either the escrow or independent entity maintaining the deposit may be motivated to steal the deposits, or the deposit value might be so little that its trust-building attribute vanishes.

To prevent this, the deposit value could be bound to a fiat currency or a stable asset. The deposit can also be dynamically adjusted and deposits only kept a short time or one iteration of interactions. Gossiping could be used as a basis to communicate experiences with other agents. In permission-less blockchains, the agents can use a common protocol to exchange this information and use a rating approach [33]. Yet, gossiping can be misused by agents to boost their own reputations by executing Sybil attacks. Review agents can be used that reach a verdict on a specific issue or problem. Their implementation is simple and potential scenarios to manipulate agents' reputations are prevented. However, the judge or review agent needs to be trusted by other agents. The algorithm is based on its actors and their interaction. The idea of arbiter, judge, user, and computation services is strongly influenced by [29,34]. The main differences are in the idea of using a jackpot to reward verifiers as well as the implementation either entirely on Ethereum or using external computation services. Moreover, the algorithm defers from [34] as its goal is to deliver verifiable computations for entities (i.e. users or smart contracts) on the blockchain, while [34] primarily delivers privacy-preserving computations, where blockchain enables the algorithm.

The algorithm cannot guarantee to detect false solutions. It is based on the assumption that solvers and verifiers behave as desired (i.e. delivering correct solutions), as their strategy is aligned with the incentives provided by the algorithm. This assumption is based on game-theoretic properties. The algorithm leaves no dominant strategy considering the interactions in Table 1. S can choose either to provide a correct or false solution and V can challenge or accept. Only when considering both agents, a Nash equilibrium exists. If there is a (high) probability that a V_C exists, the only valid strategy for S is to provide a correct solution. Consequently, V in turn has to provide a correct solution, which accepts correct S and challenges false S. In the algorithm, both S and V providing correct solutions gives a Pareto efficient result. If they change their strategy under the assumption that no V_C exists, their utility remains the same. However, a V has an incentive to challenge a false solution, which would increase his utility and reduce the utility of the others. Social welfare considers the sum of all agent's utilities depending on their strategy which can be disregarded in permission-less blockchains since overall the agent wants to optimise his utility independent of the overall utility. Specifically, the overall utility is potentially unknown to an individual agent, since he is unable to determine with certainty the utility of other agents.

7 Conclusion

On permission-less blockchains like Ethereum, rational agents through smart contracts code the preferences of their owners. This could motivate maximizing their utility by dishonest behaviour, and hence, further social control mechanisms are required. We have presented a trust model for smart contracts in permission-less blockchains that incorporate state-of-the-art research into deposits, reputation, and review agents for social control. Trust can be extended to entities outside of permission-less blockchains through applying the trust measures presented in our model. An example application is an algorithm implementing verifiable computation. The model includes users requesting computational tasks, computational services providing solutions and acting either as solver or verifier, arbiters enforcing the algorithm, and judges resolving disputes. Due to the incentive structure and the potential penalty cause by cheating, providing correct solutions to the computation task is a Nash equilibrium. Under the assumption that arbiter and judge are trusted, the algorithm detects false solutions provided based on a probability distribution. The algorithm is realised as Solidity smart contracts and AWS Lambda functions, implementing verification of multiplying two integers. Experiments show that with six verifiers the algorithm detects cheaters with prior probabilities of 30%, 50%, and 70% dishonest computation services. Experiments show that the algorithm performs overall with a linear time and space complexity depending on the number of verifiers.

As future work, we leave eliminating trust requirements regarding arbiter and judge by a fully decentralised algorithm.

Acknowledgement. The authors thank Babak Sadighi and Erik Rissanen for comments and discussions, and Daniel Gillblad for important support for Magnus Boman's part of the project. Also, the authors thank Outlier Ventures Ltd. for partly funding Dominik Harz' share of the project.

References

1. Balakrishnan, V., Majd, E.: A comparative analysis of trust models for multi-agent systems. Lect. Notes Softw. Eng. **1**(2), 183–185 (2013)
2. Boman, M.: Norms in artificial decision making. Artif. Intell. Law **7**(1), 17–35 (1999)
3. Buterin, V.: A Next-Generation Smart Contract and Decentralized Application Platform (2013). https://github.com/ethereum/wiki/wiki/White-Paper
4. Buterin, V.: Chain Interoperability. Technical report 1, R3CEV (2016)
5. Can, A.B., Bhargava, B.: SORT: a self-organizing trust model for peer-to-peer systems. IEEE Trans. Dependable Secure Comput. **10**(1), 14–27 (2013)
6. Canetti, R., Riva, B., Rothblum, G.N.: Practical delegation of computation using multiple servers. In: Proceedings of the 18th ACM Conference on Computer and Communications Security - CCS 2011, p. 445. ACM Press, New York (2011)
7. Canetti, R., Riva, B., Rothblum, G.N.: Refereed delegation of computation. Inf. Comput. **226**, 16–36 (2013)
8. Carboni, D.: Feedback based Reputation on top of the Bitcoin Blockchain (2015)
9. Cerutti, F., Toniolo, A., Oren, N., Norman, T.J.: Context-dependent Trust Decisions with Subjective Logic (2013)
10. Decker, C., Wattenhofer, R.: A fast and scalable payment network with bitcoin duplex micropayment channels. In: Pelc, A., Schwarzmann, A.A. (eds.) SSS 2015. LNCS, vol. 9212, pp. 3–18. Springer, Cham (2015). https://doi.org/10.1007/978-3-319-21741-3_1
11. Ethereum: Ethereum TestRPC (2017). https://github.com/ethereumjs/testrpc
12. Fishburn, P.: Foundations of decision analysis: along the way. Manag. Sci. **35**, 387–405 (1989)

13. French, S. (ed.): Decision Theory: An Introduction to the Mathematics of Rationality. Halsted Press, New York (1986)
14. Hoffberg, S.: Multifactorial optimization system and method, 19 April 2007. https://www.google.com/patents/US20070087756. uS Patent App. 11/467,931
15. Huynh, T.D., Jennings, N.R., Shadbolt, N.R.: An integrated trust and reputation model for open multi-agent systems. Auton. Agents Multi-Agent Syst. **13**(2), 119–154 (2006)
16. Jakubowski, M., Venkatesan, R., Yacobi, Y.: Quantifying Trust (2010)
17. Kosba, A., Miller, A., Shi, E., Wen, Z., Papamanthou, C.: Hawk: the Blockchain model of cryptography and privacy-preserving smart contracts. In: 2016 IEEE Symposium on Security and Privacy (SP), vol. 2015, pp. 839–858. IEEE (2016)
18. Litos, O.S.T., Zindros, D.: Trust is risk: a decentralized financial trust platform. IACR Cryptol. ePrint Archive **2017**, 156 (2017)
19. Malmnäs, P.E.: Axiomatic justifications of the utility principle. Synthese **99**(2), 233–249 (1994)
20. Mui, L., Mohtashemi, M., Halberstadt, A.: A computational model of trust and reputation. In: HICSS Proceedings of the 35th Annual Hawaii International Conference on System Sciences, vol. 5, pp. 2431–2439. IEEE (2002)
21. Narayanan, A., Bonneau, J., Felten, E., Miller, A., Goldfeder, S.: Bitcoin and Cryptocurrency Technologies - Draft. Princeton University Press, Princeton (2016)
22. Odelstad, J., Boman, M.: Algebras for agent norm-regulation. Annals Math. Artif. Intell. **42**(1), 141–166 (2004)
23. Pinyol, I., Sabater-Mir, J.: Computational trust and reputation models for open multi-agent systems: a review. Artif. Intell. Rev. **40**(1), 1–25 (2013)
24. Ramchurn, S.D., Huynh, D., Jennings, N.R.: Trust in multi-agent systems. Knowl. Eng. Rev. **19**(01), 1–25 (2004)
25. Rasmusson, L., Jansson, S.: Simulated social control for secure Internet commerce. In: Proceedings of the 1996 Workshop on New Security Paradigms - NSPW 1996, pp. 18–25 (1996)
26. Sabater, J., Sierra, C.: Review on computational trust and reputation models. Artif. Intell. Rev. **24**(1), 33–60 (2005)
27. Sandholm, T., Ygge, F.: On the gains and losses of speculation in equilibrium markets. In: Proceedings IJCAI 1997, pp. 632–638. AAAI Press (1997)
28. Szabo, N.: Formalizing and Securing Relationships on Public Networks (1997). http://ojphi.org/ojs/index.php/fm/article/view/548/469
29. Teutsch, J., Reitwießner, C.: A scalable verification solution for blockchains (2017)
30. Vukolić, M.: Hyperledger fabric: towards scalable blockchain for business. Technical report. Trust in Digital Life 2016, IBM Research (2016). https://www.zurich.ibm.com/dccl/papers/cachin_dccl.pdf
31. Wood, G.: Ethereum: a secure decentralised generalised transaction ledger. Ethereum Project Yellow Paper, pp. 1–32 (2014)
32. Wooldridge, M.: An Introduction to MultiAgent Systems, 2nd edn. Wiley Publishing, Chichester (2009)
33. Zhou, R., Hwang, K., Cai, M.: GossipTrust for fast reputation aggregation in peer-to-peer networks. IEEE Trans. Knowl. Data Eng. **20**(9), 1282–1295 (2008)
34. Zyskind, G.: Efficient Secure Computation Enabled by Blockchain Technology. Master thesis, Massachusetts Institute of Technology (2016)

The Game Among Bribers in a Smart Contract System

Lin Chen$^{(\boxtimes)}$, Lei Xu$^{(\boxtimes)}$, Zhimin Gao$^{(\boxtimes)}$, Nolan Shah$^{(\boxtimes)}$, Ton Chanh Le$^{(\boxtimes)}$, Yang Lu$^{(\boxtimes)}$, and Weidong Shi$^{(\boxtimes)}$

Department of Computer Science, University of Houston, Houston, TX 77054, USA
chenlin198662@gmail.com, xuleimath@gmail.com, mtion@hotmail.com,
nolanshah212@gmail.com, letonchanh@gmail.com, ylu17@central.uh.edu,
wshi3@uh.edu

Abstract. Blockchain has been used to build various applications, and the introduction of smart contracts further extends its impacts. Most of existing works consider the positive usage of smart contracts but ignore the other side of it: smart contracts can be used in a destructive way, particularly, they can be utilized to carry out bribery. The hardness of tracing a briber in a blockchain system may even motivate bribers. Furthermore, an adversary can utilize bribery smart contracts to influence the execution results of other smart contracts in the same system. To better understand this threat, we propose a formal framework to analyze bribery in the smart contract system using game theory. We give a full characterization on how the bribery budget of a briber may influence the execution of a smart contract if the briber tries to manipulate its execution result by bribing users in the system.

1 Introduction

Various applications are developed on top of blockchain technology [31–33]. However, most of these works assume that the blockchain is a perfect system, e.g., all records stored in the system are correct, and ignore the complexity of the way that the decentralized system achieves consensus. For purely cryptocurrency systems, both static model [24] and game theory model [21,27] have been used to analyze their security features. The introduction of the smart contract makes the situation trickier while extending the applicability of blockchain technology. A smart contract can involve multiple users/participants and have a high value stake. Thus, it has the potential to be more critical than mining in pure cryptocurrency systems (e.g., Bitcoin), in which only a fixed reward is paid to successful miners. The amount of cryptocurrency involved in a contract may be many times and significantly higher than the cost of running the contract itself. Therefore, users involved in a smart contract have the incentive to push through a certain outcome. In particular, they may achieve such a goal through bribery, i.e., offering cryptocurrencies to other users in the system. Interestingly, bribery itself can also be carried out using smart contracts. A recent work discussed this

© International Financial Cryptography Association 2019
A. Zohar et al. (Eds.): FC 2018 Workshops, LNCS 10958, pp. 294–307, 2019.
https://doi.org/10.1007/978-3-662-58820-8_20

concept and proposed a straightforward framework to implement bribery on blockchain [20] where the briber offers incentive to the bribee through a smart contract.

Bribery is a serious problem as it may help to compromise the fundamental assumption of smart contract execution model based on consensus or majority accepted outcome. Note that a user is honest in mining does not necessarily means that he/she will remain honest when offered with monetary reward in making decisions. Their honesty is even more questionable when taking into consideration the unlinkability of users' identities to real persons, and the fact that there is no punishment for reporting a wrong execution result in many smart contract systems like Ethereum. Therefore, it is important to investigate the problem whether a briber can succeed in manipulating a smart contract execution result.

It is remarkable that the execution of a smart contract can be cast as an election and we may leverage the research on elections to understand the bribery problem in a smart contract system. Specifically, we can view users in the system as voters, and all the possible outcome of a smart contract as candidates. Each voter (user) will vote for a specific candidate (outcome), and a briber will bribe voters to alter the election result (smart contract execution outcome). We remark that by using an election model we are actually simplifying the consensus protocol implemented in a smart contract system without considering, e.g., the Byzantine behavior of a user who tries to send different messages to different other users. However, note that such kind of behaviors typically influence users who are following the protocol. In this paper, we take a game theoretical point of view by treating all users as rational people who are trying to maximize their own profit, and will therefore stick to the choice which is the best for their own interest regardless of the choices of others. Hence, it is reasonable to adopt an election model.

There exist a series of papers focusing on the bribery problem in an election model, see, .e.g., [1–3,9,10,12,15,18,19,23,26,34,35]. Specifically, researchers have studied extensively the computational complexity of the bribery problem and show that in many settings it is NP-hard for a briber to decide which subset of voters should he/she bribe (see, e.g., [17] for a nice survey). Such hardness results can also be viewed as a way to discourage people from carrying out bribery, if computational complexity is of concern.

Classical hardness results for the election model apply readily to the bribery problem in a blockchain system by viewing a smart contract execution as an election. However, we observe that a briber needs to overcome more difficulties if he/she really wants to carry out bribery in a blockchain system. Indeed, a briber not only needs to handle the computational complexity in determining a suitable subset of voters to be bribed, but he/she may also have to compete with other bribers in the system. Note that in most real-world elections, bribery is carried out in secrecy. A person, once offered a bribe, may either take it and cast his/her vote shortly afterwards, or reject it. The "incorrectness" in the nature of bribery prevents it from becoming a free market where bribers "sell" their bribes to people. However, things change completely in a blockchain system.

As we will provide details in the following section, a briber is able to establish a smart contract with a bribee. The smart contract will be executed by users in the system and a transfer of cryptocurrencies will be carried out once the contract is fulfilled, i.e., once the bribee casts his/her vote accordingly. In this case, a bribee may establish smart contracts with multiple bribers and strategically chooses the best. The unlinkability from a user identity in a blockchain system to a real person behind and the fact that a smart contract may not necessarily be executed immediately allow a user to easily involve in multiple smart contracts. Such a situation poses a severe task to bribers and they end up in competing with each other unavoidably without even knowing their opponents. Under such a competition in a blockchain system, how difficult it is for a specific briber to win? This paper is targeting at such a problem.

Our Contributions. There are two major contributions of this paper. First, we study the bribery problem in a blockchain system from a game theoretical point of view and model it as a smart contract bribery game. This is a first step towards a better understanding of the bribery problem in a blockchain system; and may also be of separate interest to the studies of elections. In this model, every briber is a player and has a bribing budget which can be allocated to voters. Every voter has a bribing price p_j. The voter will only take smart contracts that offer a price no less than p_j. Once he/she is offered multiple smart contracts, he/she will fulfill the one with the highest price (ties are broken arbitrarily). The strategy set of a briber is all possible allocations of the budget to voters.

Second, given a smart contract bribery game, we consider its Nash equilibrium. We are particularly interested in the following problem: if a briber is very lucky, can he/she compromise the smart contract execution by getting the majority of votes through a small amount of budget? The answer is no. We show that, a briber cannot win more than 50% of the votes unless he/she controls more than 20% of the total bribing budgets in *any* Nash equilibrium. That is, even if the briber is lucky enough to end up in a Nash equilibrium that is the best for him/her, he/she still needs to have a significantly large bribery budget, more than 20% of the sum of all the budgets, in order to manipulate the execution result arbitrarily.

Organization of the Paper. The remainder of the paper is organized as follows: In Sect. 2 we give a short review of smart contract and describe the problem we address in this paper. In Sect. 3 we present our main result by studying the Nash equilibria of the smart contract bribery game. In Sect. 4 we give further discussion on our results. Section 5 discusses related work, and we conclude the paper in Sect. 6.

2 Preliminaries and Problem Statement

Smart Contract. We begin by defining smart contracts. The definition provided by Szabo in 1997 is [28]:

Definition 1. *A smart contract is a set of promises, specified in a digital form, including protocols within which the parties perform on these promises.*

A blockchain system, equipped with smart contracts, is a powerful tool that allows users to build various applications on top. In particular, a voting system can be implemented on blockchain. We first briefly describe the election model for a voting system studied in the literature.

Election Model. In an election, given are a set of n candidates $C = \{C_1, C_2, \ldots, C_n\}$ and a set of m voters $V = \{V_1, V_2, \ldots, V_m\}$. Each voter V_j has a preference list of candidates, which is essentially a permutation of candidates, denoted as τ_j. The preference of v_j is denoted by $(C_{\tau_j(1)}, C_{\tau_j(2)}, \ldots, C_{\tau_j(m)})$, meaning that v_j prefers candidate $C_{\tau_j(z)}$ to $C_{\tau_j(z+1)}$, where $z = 1, 2, \ldots, m-1$.

An *election rule* is implemented, which takes as input the set of candidates and voters together with their preference lists, and outputs a set of winner(s). There are various election rules studied in the literature. In this paper, we focus on one of the most fundamental rules called *plurality*. In plurality, every voter votes for exactly one candidate which is on top of his/her preference list. The candidate(s) with the highest number of votes then become the winner(s).

The abstract election model is general enough to incorporate a lot of real-world elections as well as other applications that involve voting in their execution. In particular, it is very much relevant to a blockchain system since almost all decisions made in such a system, e.g., block construction and verification [30], are based on the consensus among users. A consensus protocol can be modeled as an election where every user votes for his/her decisions, and eventually one decision is elected by the system.

Bribery in an Election. In recent years, the problem of bribery in an election has received much attention in the literature [1–3,9,10,12,15,18,19,23,26,34,35]. On a high level, bribery in an election is defined as a way to manipulate the election by giving monetary reward to voters so as to change their preference lists. Researchers have proposed different bribery models. In this paper, we focus on the *constructive bribery model*, that is, the briber tries to make one specific candidate become the winner by bribing a subset of voters. This is particularly the case when bribery happens in a blockchain based system – a briber tries to make the system to reach a specific consensus.

Bribery through Smart Contract. In most real-world elections, briberies are carried out in secrecy. It is, however, interesting that briberies can be carried out "publicly" using smart contracts. Roughly speaking, the briber and the user to be bribed (or bribee) can create a special smart contract that claims a transfer of cryptocurrency upon the condition that the user votes for a specific candidate (decision). Users of the system will execute this smart contract. Once the condition is satisfied, the transfer of the cryptocurrency will be enforced by the system. The anonymous feature of a blockchain system, especially the unlinkability of a user account from the real person behind, allows part of the information of the bribery to be transparent, e.g., the transfer of cryptocurrency from one account to another, while preserves the privacy of the persons involved.

The concept of carrying out bribery through smart contract naturally follows from many real-world contracts that are created to facilitate bribery. However, there is a lack of a systematic study on the creation and execution of such smart contracts for bribery, and its influence on the whole blockchain system. A very recent paper by Kothapalli and Cordi [20] gave the first detailed study on the creation and execution of the smart contracts for bribery and presented pseudo codes. Briefly speaking, the whole bribery procedure, via smart contracts, is divided into three phases: (i) Propose stage. The briber creates a briber contract indicates the incentive that the bribee will receive upon fulfilling the bribe and/or the punishment if the bribee fails to fulfill that. The contract is submitted to the blockchain. (ii) Commit stage. A bribee who decides to participate creates a claim on the blockchain. (iii) Verify stage. After a time period, if the bribe condition is reached, the bribee can get the incentive. Otherwise, the bribee pays the penalty.

Given their research [20], it becomes crucial to understand the impact of such smart contracts for bribery to the whole blockchain system. Although we may leverage the research on bribery in elections, the problem of bribery via smart contracts has its own unique characteristics. Particularly, when there are multiple bribers in the system, the bribee is free to participate in any smart contract for bribery and he/she can thus strategically maximize his/her own profit. In this paper, we try to understand the behavior of bribers and bribees through game theory. Towards this, we first introduce some basic concepts.

Definition 2 ([25]). *A normal form game Γ consists of:*

- A finite set N of players (agents).
- A nonempty set Q_i of strategies available for each player $i \in N$.
- A preference relation $\preceq_i$ on $Q = \times_{j \in N} Q_j$ for each player i.

We restrict our attention to normal form games in this paper. For simplicity, when we say a game, we mean a normal form game. We consider Nash equilibrium in this paper. A Nash equilibrium is a solution concept of a game involving two or more players in which each player is assumed to know the equilibrium strategies of the other players, and no player has anything to gain by unilaterally changing his/her own strategy [25].

Taking a game theoretical point of view, we are able to model the bribery problem in a blockchain system with multiple bribers as follows.

Smart Contract Bribery Game. We first describe the basic setting for the smart contract bribery game. Given are a set of n candidates $\mathcal{C} = \{C_1, C_2, \ldots, C_n\}$, a set of m voters $\mathcal{V} = \{V_1, V_2, \ldots, V_m\}$ and a set of k bribers $\mathcal{B} = \{B_1, B_2, \ldots, B_k\}$. Each briber B_h has a budget b_h for bribing and prefers one specific candidate. Each voter v_j has a preference list τ_j and a bribing price p_j. Each briber can sign a smart contract with a voter, which offers a certain amount of reward in cryptocurrency if the voter changes his/her preference list and votes for the candidate preferred by the briber. A voter v_j can sign a smart contract with every briber and then do the following:

- he/she will discard all smart contracts that offer a price lower than p_j;
- if there are multiple smart contracts offering a price larger than p_j, he/she will pick the one with the highest price and vote for the candidate preferred by this briber;
- ties are broken arbitrarily, i.e., the voter will randomly choose one smart contract if there are several smart contracts offering the same highest price (larger than or equal to p_j).

Note that if all the smart contracts are offering a price lower than p_j, the voter will vote honestly.

Bribers and the candidates need not be the same, however, as each briber prefers a distinct candidate, we assume for simplicity that the briber is *the same as* the candidate he/she prefers, i.e., $\mathcal{B}$ is a subset of the candidates. By re-indexing the candidates, we may assume without loss of generality that $B_h = C_h$ for $1 \leq h \leq k$, i.e., the first k candidates are trying to bribe voters.

Let the bribers be players in the game. The strategy set of a briber is the set of possible smart contracts he/she can make with voters, i.e., every strategy of a briber b_h is an allocation of the budget b_h among all the voters, which can be represented as an m-vector $(b_h^1, b_h^2, \ldots, b_h^m)$ where b_h^j is the price the briber offers to voter V_j and $\sum_j b_h^j \leq b_h$. The goal of each briber, as a player, is to maximize the (expected) number of votes he/she received.

Nash Equilibrium in Smart Contract Bribery Game. A pure Nash equilibrium for the smart contract bribery game, if it exists, is a solution where every briber B_h specifies some strategy $(b_h^1, b_h^2, \ldots, b_h^m)$ such that if B_h changes his/her strategy unilaterally to some $(\bar{b}_h^1, \bar{b}_h^2, \ldots, \bar{b}_h^m)$, the expected number of votes he/she can get will not increase.

3   The Smart Contract Bribery Game

If there is only one briber, then obviously the briber is able to increase the number of his/her votes if his/her bribing budget is at least as large as the cheapest bribing price of some voter who votes for another candidate. When there are multiple bribers, things become much more complicated. Considering an arbitrary briber, say, B_1, can he/she really benefit from bribery in the presence of other bribers? Of course the answer is no if there exists another briber with an infinite or sufficiently larger budget, who is able to bribe every voter with a price larger than b_1 and B_1 will get no votes at all. If, however, B_1 is more powerful, say $b_1 \geq b_i$ for every $2 \leq i \leq k$, is it possible for B_1 to get additional votes? Unfortunately, this may not necessarily be the case and is highly dependent on the strategies of other bribers. In this section, we focus on Nash equilibrium in the smart contract bribery game. We consider the following problem: In a Nash equilibrium, how many votes can B_1 get when competing against bribers who are weaker than him/her? Furthermore, can B_1 get more votes than he/she gets in the absence of bribery in the system?

Theorem 1. *There may exist a pure Nash equilibrium for the smart contract bribery game where the briber B_1 can get at most $\lfloor 1/\epsilon \rfloor$ votes even if $b_1 \geq 1/\epsilon \cdot b_i$ for every $2 \leq i \leq k$, where $\epsilon \in (0,1)$ is an arbitrary number.*

We remark that a pure Nash equilibrium may not always exist.

Proof. Consider the following smart contract bribery game in which there are $m = k - 1 + \lfloor 1/\epsilon \rfloor$ voters and exactly k candidates (i.e., $\mathcal{C} = \mathcal{B}$). Let $p_j = 1$ for $1 \leq j \leq k - 1$, $p_j = 1/\epsilon$ for $k \leq j \leq m$. Let b_1 be an arbitrary integer larger than $1/\epsilon$, and $b_i = \epsilon b_1$ for every $2 \leq i \leq k$.

Consider the following feasible solution: each briber B_i, $2 \leq i \leq k$, bribes V_{i-1} at the price of ϵb_1. The briber B_1 then bribes V_k to V_m, each at the price of ϵb_1.

It is easy to verify that B_1 gets $\lfloor 1/\epsilon \rfloor$ votes. It suffices to argue that the feasible solution above is a Nash equilibrium. First, we claim that every briber B_i, $2 \leq i \leq k$, will not deviate from the current solution. Note that if B_i aims to bribe some other voter instead of V_{i-1}, then he/she needs to pay at least ϵb_1, for otherwise that voter will simply ignore his/her offer. Therefore, B_i has to take away all the money ϵb_1 from V_{i-1} and bribes some V_h for $h \neq i - 1$. However, since V_h already receives ϵb_1 amount of money from another briber, thus in expectation B_i only gets $1/2$ votes, which is worse than the current solution. Hence, B_i will not unilaterally change his/her strategy. Next, we claim that B_1 will not deviate from the current solution. Note that currently B_1 gets one vote at the cost of ϵb_1. If he/she aims at getting votes from any V_h, $1 \leq h \leq k - 1$, he/she has two choices. Either he/she pays the price of ϵb_1 and gets $1/2$ votes in expectation, or he/she pays a price strictly larger than ϵb_1 and gets one vote. In both cases, B_1 will lose one vote from the set of voters in $\{V_h : k \leq h \leq m\}$ and get at most one vote from the set of voters $\{V_h : 1 \leq h \leq k - 1\}$.   □

Note that k is a parameter that can be significantly larger than $1/\epsilon$, Theorem 1 thus implies that a briber may only get a small number of votes even if the bribing budget of any other briber is at most ϵ fraction of his/her budget.

It is worth mentioning that in the proof of Theorem 1 we do not specify which candidate does a voter votes in the absence of bribery. We may assume that without bribery V_h, $1 \leq h \leq k - 1$, all vote for B_1, while V_h, $k \leq h \leq m$, all vote for B_2. Therefore, B_1 actually loses an arbitrary amount of votes when bribery happens. More precisely, we have the following corollary.

Corollary 1. *In a smart contract bribery game, a briber may lose an arbitrary number of votes even if he/she is only competing against other bribers whose budget is significantly smaller.*

Theorem 1 implies that the worst Nash equilibrium for a briber can be very bad. However, what if a briber is lucky and ends up in a Nash equilibrium which is the best for him/her? In this case, can the briber win significantly more votes with a very small budget? Unfortunately, even in the best Nash equilibrium, the fraction of the votes a briber can win may not exceed the portion of the bribing budget he/she owns by $O(1)$ times, as is implied by the following theorem.

Theorem 2. *Let $\epsilon < 1/3$ be an arbitrary small constant and suppose $b_i \geq \epsilon b_1$ for $2 \leq i \leq k$. In any Nash equilibrium, B_1 gets at most $1/\epsilon$ votes or a $\frac{4(1+2\epsilon)b_1}{4(1+2\epsilon)b_1+\sum_{i=2}^{k} b_i}$ fraction of the votes, whichever is larger.*

Proof. Consider an arbitrary Nash equilibrium. If B_1 only gets $1/\epsilon$ votes in expectation, then the theorem is proved. From now on we assume that B_1 receives more than $1/\epsilon$ votes in expectation. In this case, B_1 must have paid less than $b_1\epsilon$ to some voter, say, V_j, who votes for him/her with a positive probability. Since $b_i \geq \epsilon b_1$, the briber B_i must have received a positive number of votes, for otherwise this briber can devote all the budget to V_j and gets one vote, contradicting the fact that the solution is a Nash equilibrium.

Let $\phi_i > 0$ be the expected number of votes received by each briber B_i. We make the following two assumptions.

- Each B_i pays out a total price of exactly b_i to voters;
- If B_i gets 0 vote from a voter in expectation, B_i pays 0 to this voter.

The two assumptions are without loss of generality since each B_i gets a positive number of votes from at least one voter, and we can simply let B_i pays all the remaining money in his/her budget to this voter if he/she does not use up the budget. By doing so, B_i cannot get fewer votes. The fact that the original solution is a Nash equilibrium ensures that B_i will not get more votes. Thus, the modified solution is still a Nash equilibrium.

We define the average cost per vote for B_i as $a_i = b_i/\phi_i$. Let S_j be the set of bribers who offers the same highest price for V_j, then every briber $B_i \in S_j$ gets in expectation $1/|S_j|$ votes from V_j. For simplicity we remove all the voters where $S_j = \emptyset$ from now on. We define $x_{ij} \in \{0, 1\}$ as an indicating variable such that $x_{ij} = 1$ if $B_i \in S_j$ and $x_{ij} = 0$ otherwise. Recall that a briber B_i pays b_i^j to V_j, thus we have

$$\sum_{j=1}^{m} x_{ij}/|S_j| = \phi_i, \qquad \forall i \qquad (1a)$$

$$\sum_{j=1}^{m} b_i^j x_{ij} = b_i, \qquad \forall i \qquad (1b)$$

There are two possibilities with respect to a_1. If $a_1 \geq \epsilon b_1$, then $\phi_1 \leq 1/\epsilon$, which means B_1 gets at most $1/\epsilon$ votes and Theorem 2 is proved. Otherwise $a_1 < \epsilon b_1$ and there are two possibilities.

Case 1. $|\{j : 0 < b_1^j < (1 + 2\epsilon)a_1\}| \leq 1$. Note that a_1 is the average cost. We claim that $\phi_1 < 1/\epsilon$. Otherwise $\sum_{j=1}^m x_{1j} \geq 1/\epsilon$ and it follows that $\sum_{j=1}^m b_1^j x_{1j} \geq (1+2\epsilon)a_1(\sum_{j=1}^m x_{1j} - 1) = (1+2\epsilon)b_1 - (1+2\epsilon)a_1 > b_1$, where the last inequality follows from the fact that $b_1 \geq (1 + 2\epsilon)(1/\epsilon - 1)a_1 = (1 + 1/\epsilon - 2\epsilon)a_1$, whereas $2\epsilon b_1 > (1 + 2\epsilon)a_1$. This, however, is a contradiction to Eq (1b). Therefore, B_1 gets in expectation at most $1/\epsilon$ votes and Theorem 2 is proved.

Case 2. $|\{j : 0 < b_1^j < (1 + 2\epsilon)a_1\}| \geq 2$. In this case, we have the following lemma.

Lemma 1. *If* $|\{j : b_1^j < (1 + 2\epsilon)a_1\}| \geq 2$, *then for any* $2 \leq i \leq k$, $a_1 \geq \frac{a_i}{4(1+2\epsilon)}$.

Proof (Proof of Lemma 1). Towards the proof, we need the following claims.

Claim. For every i, there exists some set of voters Γ_i such that $\sum_{j \in \Gamma_i} x_{ij}/|S_j| \leq 1$ and $\sum_{j \in \Gamma_i} b_i^j x_{ij} \geq a_i/2$.

To see the claim, we suppose on the contrary that for every set of voters Γ_i satisfying that $\sum_{j \in \Gamma_i} x_{ij}/|S_j| \leq 1$, it holds that $\sum_{j \in \Gamma_i} b_i^j x_{ij} < a_i/2$. We list all the variables $x_{i1}, x_{i2}, \ldots, x_{im}$ and divide them into q subsets where the h-th subset consists of $x_{i,\ell_{h-1}}, x_{i,\ell_{h-1}+1}, \ldots, x_{i,\ell_h-1}$ for $1 = \ell_0 < \ell_1 < \ldots < \ell_q = m + 1$, such that the followings hold for every h:

$$\frac{x_{i,\ell_{h-1}}}{|S_{\ell_{h-1}}|} + \frac{x_{i,\ell_{h-1}+1}}{|S_{\ell_{h-1}+1}|} + \ldots + \frac{x_{i,\ell_h-1}}{|S_{\ell_h-1}|} \leq 1 \tag{2a}$$

$$\frac{x_{i,\ell_{h-1}}}{|S_{\ell_{h-1}}|} + \frac{x_{i,\ell_{h-1}+1}}{|S_{\ell_{h-1}+1}|} + \ldots + \frac{x_{i,\ell_h-1}}{|S_{\ell_h-1}|} + \frac{x_{i,\ell_h}}{|S_{\ell_h}|} > 1 \tag{2b}$$

By Eq (2a) we have

$$\sum_{s=\ell_{h-1}}^{\ell_h-1} b_i^s x_{is} < a_i/2.$$

Taking the summation over $1 \leq h \leq q$, we have

$$\sum_{s=\ell_{h-1}}^{\ell_h-1} b_i^s x_{is} < a_i q/2.$$

We show in the following that $q \leq 2\phi_i$, whereas

$$\sum_{h=1}^q \sum_{s=\ell_{h-1}}^{\ell_h-1} b_i^s x_{is} < a_i q/2 \leq a_i \phi_i = b_i,$$

contradicting Eq (1b) and the claim is proved. To see $q \leq 2\phi_1$, we can view each $x_{ij}/|S_j|$ as an item of size $x_{ij}/|S_j|$. We pack these items into bins of size 1 one by one using the *Next-fit* algorithm in Bin packing [29], i.e., as long as the item fits in the same bin as the previous item, put it there; otherwise, open a new bin and put it in there. It is easy to see that the Next-fit algorithm returns a solution using q bins with the h-th bin containing exactly $x_{i,\ell_h-1}/|S_{\ell_h-1}|$ to $x_{i,\ell_h-1}/|S_{\ell_h-1}|$. Note that $\phi_i = \sum_{j=1}^m x_{ij}/|S_j|$ is exactly the total size of all items. It is a classical result [29] that the Next-fit algorithm for bin packing returns a solution that uses the number of bins at most twice the total item size (to see this, simply observe that any two consecutive bins have a total size larger than 1), hence $q \le 2\phi_i$.

We are able to prove Lemma 1 now using the above claim. Suppose on the contrary that for some i it holds that $a_1 < a_i/(4+8\epsilon)$. According to the claim, there exists some Γ_i such that $\sum_j \in \Gamma_i x_{ij}/|S_j| \le 1$ and $\sum_{j \in \Gamma_i} b_i^j x_{ij} \ge a_i/2 > 2(1+2\epsilon)a_1$. Hence, the briber B_i pays in total more than $2(1+2\epsilon)a_1$ and only receive in expectation 1 vote. As $|\{j : 0 < b_1^j < (1+2\epsilon)a_1\}| \ge 2$, there exist at least two voters V_{j_1} and V_{j_2} to whom B_1 pays less than $(1+2\epsilon)a_1$. Since B_1 have received a positive number of votes from each of them (otherwise B_1 would have paid 0), V_{j_1} and V_{j_2} receive offers from bribers with a price less than $(1+2\epsilon)a_1$. Hence, if B_i changes his/her solution unilaterally by paying $(1+2\epsilon)a_1$ to V_{j_1} and V_{j_2}, and meanwhile 0 to voters in Γ_i, he/she gets 2 votes instead, contracting the fact that the solution is a Nash equilibrium. Thus, Lemma 1 is true.   □

By Lemma 1, we know that in Case 2 every briber B_i gets at least $\frac{b_i}{4(1+2\epsilon)a_1}$ votes. Therefore, B_1 can get at most $\frac{4(1+2\epsilon)b_1}{4(1+2\epsilon)b_1+\sum_{i=2}^k b_i}$ fraction of the total votes.   □

Theorem 2 implies that, even if a briber is very lucky and ends up in a Nash equilibrium which is the best for him/her, he/she cannot get more than $\frac{4(1+2\epsilon)b_1}{4(1+2\epsilon)b_1+\sum_{i=2}^k b_i}$ fraction of the total votes if there are significantly many voters (larger than $1/\epsilon$ which is a constant). By taking $\frac{b_1}{\sum_{i=1}^k b_i} = 1/5$, this fractional value becomes $1/2 + O(\epsilon)$, therefore we have the following corollary.

Corollary 2. *Even in a best Nash equilibrium, a briber needs to control more than 20% of the total bribing budgets in order to get more than 50% of the votes.*

4   Further Discussion

We have shown that, although smart contracts can be used to carry out bribery in a blockchain system, it is, however, much more difficult for a briber to do so than in an ordinary real-world election. The major challenge comes from the fact that a voter is free to establish multiple smart contracts with different bribers and can strategically pick the best one.

A natural question is whether a briber can prevent a bribee from establishing smart contracts with other bribers. One potential approach is to introduce a penalty for a bribee if he/she fails to fulfill the smart contract. Indeed, a recent paper by Abhiram and Christopher [20] presents a pseudocode for such kind of smart contracts. It is questionable whether such smart contracts can change our results substantially. Obviously, if the briber can charge an infinite amount of penalty, then surely the bribee has no choice but to follow the smart contract.

However, this is usually unreasonable. A penalty is usually achieved via a deposit from the bribee to the briber, a sufficiently high penalty may exceed the wallet balance of a voter, which means the briber is losing these potential bribees. More critically, the decision whether a smart contract is fulfilled or not is also achieved through consensus. Once the bribee pays a high deposit, even if he/she fulfills the smart contract, the briber may also bribe others to alter the decision and take away the deposit. Hence, even if penalty may be introduced, it should be reasonably low. A low penalty, however, only prevents a voter from making smart contracts with a lot of bribers. It does not prevent a voter from making smart contracts with only a few bribers, which is already enough to yield a non-cooperative game among bribers and our results readily apply.

5   Related Work

In this section, we briefly review related works.

Smart Contract Systems. Ethereum is by far the most popular smart contract system [4] and many works have been done to detect potential vulnerabilities in smart contracts, see, e.g., [22]. Although game theory has been extensively used to analyze mining activities [5,6,13,27], users' behavior in a smart contract system is not well understood.

Bribery in Elections. There are various researches studying the bribery issue in elections. Faliszewski et al. [15] gave the first systematic characterization on the complexity of the bribery problem where the briber can pay a fixed, but voter-dependent, price to arbitrarily manipulate the preference list of a bribed voter. Different bribery models were addressed subsequently in, e.g., [1,7,8,11, 14,16,18]. We refer the readers to [17] for a nice survey on this topic and the references therein.

6   Conclusion and Future Work

Bribery is an important issue in real-world elections. Recent studies have shown that smart contracts can be utilized to conduct bribery in a blockchain system; and it is crucial to understand how smart contract based bribery can influence the whole blockchain system. In this paper, we make the first improvement towards this direction. We cast the bribery problem in a blockchain system as an election and leverage the research in voting systems. We observe that, bribery via smart contracts in a blockchain system is likely to end up in a game situation where different bribers compete with each other in bribing users. We model this problem as a smart contract bribery game and study the behavior of bribers under Nash equilibrium. Interestingly, we show that in *any* Nash equilibrium, a briber cannot win the majority of the votes unless he/she controls more than 20% of the total bribing budgets. Therefore, the phenomenon of "anarchy" in game theory actually helps in discouraging people from carrying out bribery in a blockchain system.

There are several interesting open problems along this line of research. In this paper, we assume every voter has the same weight, i.e., each voter can only cast one vote. However, it is common that voters do have weights. It is not clear whether a constant threshold like 20% also exists when voters/users have weights. Another important problem is to study how to protect the blockchain system through other methods, particularly by deploying resources. It is true that the 20% threshold can discourage people from bribing, but it does not fully defend the system from bribery, especially when some briber owns a large amount of cryptocurrencies. There are several works in the research of voting systems which study the problem of protecting an election by awarding honesty or punishing bribery [36]. It is not clear how to implement a similar scheme in a blockchain system.

References

1. Bredereck, R., Chen, J., Faliszewski, P., Nichterlein, A., Niedermeier, R.: Prices matter for the parameterized complexity of shift bribery. Inf. Comput. **251**, 140–164 (2016)
2. Bredereck, R., Faliszewski, P., Niedermeier, R., Talmon, N.: Complexity of shift bribery in committee elections. In: AAAI, pp. 2452–2458 (2016)
3. Bredereck, R., Faliszewski, P., Niedermeier, R., Talmon, N.: Large-scale election campaigns: combinatorial shift bribery. J. Artif. Intell. Res. **55**, 603–652 (2016)
4. Buterin, V.: A next-generation smart contract and decentralized application platform. white paper (2014)
5. Chen, L., Xu, L., Gao, Z., Shah, N., Lu, Y., Shi, W.: Smart contract execution-the (+-)-biased ballot problem. In: LIPIcs-Leibniz International Proceedings in Informatics. vol. 92. Schloss Dagstuhl-Leibniz-Zentrum fuer Informatik (2017)
6. Chen, L., Xu, L., Shah, N., Gao, Z., Lu, Y., Shi, W.: Decentralized execution of smart contracts: agent model perspective and its implications. In: Brenner, M., et al. (eds.) FC 2017. LNCS, vol. 10323, pp. 468–477. Springer, Cham (2017). https://doi.org/10.1007/978-3-319-70278-0_29
7. Chen, L., et al.: Protecting election from bribery: new approach and computational complexity characterization (extended abstract). In: Proceedings of the 2018 International Conference on Autonomous Agents and Multiagent Systems, vol. 1. International Foundation for Autonomous Agents and Multiagent Systems (2018)
8. Dey, P., Misra, N., Narahari, Y.: Frugal bribery in voting. In: Proceedings of the Thirtieth AAAI Conference on Artificial Intelligence, pp. 2466–2472. AAAI Press (2016)
9. Dorn, B., Krüger, D.: On the hardness of bribery variants in voting with CP-nets. Ann. Math. Artif. Intell. **77**(3–4), 251–279 (2016)
10. Dorn, B., Krüger, D., Scharpfenecker, P.: Often harder than in the constructive case: destructive bribery in CP-nets. In: Markakis, E., Schäfer, G. (eds.) WINE 2015. LNCS, vol. 9470, pp. 314–327. Springer, Heidelberg (2015). https://doi.org/10.1007/978-3-662-48995-6_23
11. Elkind, E., Faliszewski, P., Slinko, A.: Swap bribery. In: Mavronicolas, M., Papadopoulou, V.G. (eds.) SAGT 2009. LNCS, vol. 5814, pp. 299–310. Springer, Heidelberg (2009). https://doi.org/10.1007/978-3-642-04645-2_27

12. Erdélyi, G., Reger, C., Yang, Y.: The complexity of bribery and control in group identification. In: Proceedings of the 16th Conference on Autonomous Agents and MultiAgent Systems, pp. 1142–1150. International Foundation for Autonomous Agents and Multiagent Systems (2017)

13. Eyal, I., Sirer, E.G.: Majority is not enough: bitcoin mining is vulnerable. In: Christin, N., Safavi-Naini, R. (eds.) FC 2014. LNCS, vol. 8437, pp. 436–454. Springer, Heidelberg (2014). https://doi.org/10.1007/978-3-662-45472-5_28

14. Faliszewski, P.: Nonuniform bribery. In: Proceedings of the 7th International Joint Conference on Autonomous Agents and Multiagent Systems, vol. 3, pp. 1569–1572. International Foundation for Autonomous Agents and Multiagent Systems (2008)

15. Faliszewski, P., Hemaspaandra, E., Hemaspaandra, L.A.: How hard is bribery in elections? J. Artif. Intell. Res. **35**, 485–532 (2009)

16. Faliszewski, P., Hemaspaandra, E., Hemaspaandra, L.A., Rothe, J.: Llull and copeland voting computationally resist bribery and constructive control. J. Artif. Intell. Res. **35**, 275–341 (2009)

17. Faliszewski, P., Rothe, J.: Control and Bribery in Voting. Cambridge University Press, Cambridge (2016)

18. Kaczmarczyk, A., Faliszewski, P.: Algorithms for destructive shift bribery. In: Proceedings of the 2016 International Conference on Autonomous Agents & Multiagent Systems, pp. 305–313. International Foundation for Autonomous Agents and Multiagent Systems (2016)

19. Knop, D., Koutecký, M., Mnich, M.: Voting and bribing in single-exponential time. In: LIPIcs-Leibniz International Proceedings in Informatics, vol. 66. Schloss Dagstuhl-Leibniz-Zentrum fuer Informatik (2017)

20. Kothapalli, A., Cordi, C.: A bribery framework using smartcontracts (2017)

21. Lewenberg, Y., Bachrach, Y., Sompolinsky, Y., Zohar, A., Rosenschein, J.S.: Bitcoin mining pools: a cooperative game theoretic analysis. In: Proceedings of the 2015 International Conference on Autonomous Agents and Multiagent Systems, pp. 919–927. International Foundation for Autonomous Agents and Multiagent Systems (2015)

22. Luu, L., Chu, D.H., Olickel, H., Saxena, P., Hobor, A.: Making smart contracts smarter. In: Proceedings of the 2016 ACM SIGSAC Conference on Computer and Communications Security, pp. 254–269. ACM (2016)

23. Mattei, N., Pini, M.S., Venable, K.B., Rossi, F.: Bribery in voting over combinatorial domains is easy. In: Proceedings of the 11th International Conference on Autonomous Agents and Multiagent Systems, vol. 3, pp. 1407–1408. International Foundation for Autonomous Agents and Multiagent Systems (2012)

24. Nakamoto, S.: Bitcoin: A peer-to-peer electronic cash system (2008)

25. Osborne, M.J., Rubinstein, A.: A Course in Game Theory. MIT Press, Cambridge (1994)

26. Pini, M.S., Rossi, F., Venable, K.B.: Bribery in voting with soft constraints. In: AAAI (2013)

27. Sapirshtein, A., Sompolinsky, Y., Zohar, A.: Optimal selfish mining strategies in bitcoin. arXiv preprint arXiv:1507.06183 (2015)

28. Szabo, N.: Formalizing and securing relationships on public networks. First Monday **2**(9) (1997)

29. Vazirani, V.V.: Approximation Algorithms. Springer, Heidelberg (2013). https://doi.org/10.1007/978-3-662-04565-7

30. Vukolić, M.: The quest for scalable blockchain fabric: proof-of-work vs. BFT replication. In: Camenisch, J., Kesdoğan, D. (eds.) iNetSec 2015. LNCS, vol. 9591, pp. 112–125. Springer, Cham (2016). https://doi.org/10.1007/978-3-319-39028-4_9

31. Xu, L., Chen, L., Gao, Z., Lu, Y., Shi, W.: CoC: secure supply chain management system based on public ledger. In: 2017 26th International Conference on Computer Communication and Networks (ICCCN), pp. 1–6. IEEE (2017)
32. Xu, L., Chen, L., Shah, N., Gao, Z., Lu, Y., Shi, W.: DL-BAC: distributed ledger based access control for web applications. In: Proceedings of the 26th International Conference on World Wide Web Companion, pp. 1445–1450. International World Wide Web Conferences Steering Committee (2017)
33. Xu, L., et al.: Enabling the sharing economy: privacy respecting contract based on public blockchain. In: Proceedings of the ACM Workshop on Blockchain, Cryptocurrencies and Contracts, pp. 15–21. ACM (2017)
34. Yang, Y., Shrestha, Y.R., Guo, J.: How hard is bribery in party based elections? In: Proceedings of the 2015 International Conference on Autonomous Agents and Multiagent Systems, pp. 1725–1726. International Foundation for Autonomous Agents and Multiagent Systems (2015)
35. Yang, Y., Shrestha, Y.R., Guo, J.: How hard is bribery with distance restrictions? In: ECAI, pp. 363–371 (2016)
36. Yin, Y., Vorobeychik, Y., An, B., Hazon, N.: Optimally protecting elections. In: IJCAI, pp. 538–545 (2016)

Lightweight Blockchain Logging
for Data-Intensive Applications

Yuzhe (Richard) Tang[1]([✉]), Zihao Xing[1], Cheng Xu[2], Ju Chen[1],
and Jianliang Xu[2]

[1] Syracuse University, Syracuse, NY, USA
{ytang100,zixing,jchen133}@syr.edu
[2] Hong Kong Baptist University, Kowloon Tong, Hong Kong
{chengxu,xujl}@comp.hkbu.edu.hk

Abstract. With the recent success of cryptocurrency, Blockchain's
design opens the door of building trustworthy distributed systems. A
common paradigm is to repurpose the Blockchain as an append-only log
that logs the application events in time order for subsequent auditing
and query verification. While this paradigm reaps the security benefit, it
faces technical challenges especially when being used for data-intensive
applications.

Instead of treating Blockchain as a time-ordered log, we propose to lay
the log-structured merge tree (LSM tree) over the Blockchain for efficient
and lightweight logging. Comparing other data structures, the LSM tree
is advantageous in supporting efficient writes while enabling random-
access reads. In our system design, only a small digest of an LSM tree is
persisted in the Blockchain and minimal store operations are carried out
by smart contracts. With the implementation in Ethereum/Solidity, we
evaluate the proposed logging scheme and demonstrate its performance
efficiency and effectiveness in cost saving.

1 Introduction

Recent years witnessed the advent and wide adoption of the first cryptocurrency,
BitCoin [3], followed by many others including Ethereum [4], Litecoin [8], Namecoin [19], etc. The initial success of cryptocurrency demonstrates the trustworthiness of Blockchain, the underlying platform of cryptocurrency. The Blockchain
supports the storage and processing of cryptocurrency transactions. In abstraction, it is a trust-decentralized network storing transparent state designed with
incentives to enable open membership at scale. A line of the latest research and
engineering aims at applying the trustworthy design of Blockchain for applications beyond cryptocurrency.

A common paradigm of repurposing Blockchain is to treat the Blockchain
as a public append-only log [23], where application-level events are logged
into the Blockchain in the order of time, and the log is used later for
verification and auditing. While this public-log paradigm reaps the security
benefit of Blockchain, it is limited to the applications handling small data

© International Financial Cryptography Association 2019
A. Zohar et al. (Eds.): FC 2018 Workshops, LNCS 10958, pp. 308–324, 2019.
https://doi.org/10.1007/978-3-662-58820-8_21

(due to high Blockchain storage cost) and tolerating long verification delay (linear scanning the entire chain for verification).

In this work, we tackle the research of repurposing Blockchains for hardening the security of data-intensive applications hosted in a third-party platform (e.g., cloud). A motivating scenario is to secure the cloud-based Internet-of-things (IoT) data storage where the IoT data producers continuously generate an intensive stream of data writes to the third-party cloud storage which serves data consumers through queries. Including Blockchain could enhance the trustworthiness of the third-party cloud storage.

A baseline approach is to log the sequence of data writes in the time order into the Blockchain, in a similar way to log-structured file systems [27]. This approach causes a high read latency (linear to the data size). Another baseline is to digest the latest data snapshot, e.g., using Merkle tree, and place the digest inside the Blockchain. In the presence of dynamic data, the digest scheme usually follows classic B-tree alike data structures [17,28] that perform "in-place" updates. These schemes incur high write amplification as writing a record involves a read-modify-write sequence on the tree and has $O(logN)$ complexity per write. On Blockchain, this high write amplification causes high cost, as writing a data unit in Blockchain is costly (which involves duplicated writes on miners and expensive proof-of-work alike computation). The problem compounds especially in the write-intensive applications as IoT streams.

To log write-intensive applications using write-expensive Blockchain, we propose to place the log-structured merge tree (LSM tree) [24] over the Blockchain for efficient and lightweight logging. An LSM tree is a write-optimized data structure which supports random-access reads; comparing the above two baselines (append-only log as in log-structured file system and update-in-place structures in database indices), an LSM tree strikes a better balance between read and write performance and is adopted in many modern storage systems, including Google BigTable [15]/LevelDB [7], Apache HBase [2], Apache Cassandra [1], Facebook RocksDB [5], etc.

At a high level, an LSM tree lays out its storage into several "levels" and supports, in addition to reads/writes, a compaction operation that reorganizes the leveled storage for future read/write efficiency. We propose a scheme to log the LSM tree in Blockchain: (1) individual levels are digested using Merkle trees with the 128-bit root hashes stored in Blockchain. (2) The compaction that needs to be carried out in a trustworthy way is executed in smart-contracts, which allow for computations on modern Blockchain, such as Ethereum [4]. Concretely, we propose compaction mechanisms that realize several primitives inside the smart contract. We propose a duplicated compaction paradigm amenable for implementation on the asynchronous Smart-Contract execution model in Ethereum. Based on the primitives and paradigm, we realize both sized and leveled compaction mechanisms in the smart contract.

We have implemented the design on Ethereum leveraging its Smart-contract language, Solidity [10], and programming support in the Truffle framework [11]. In particular, invoking a Solidity smart-contract is asynchronous and our system addresses this property by asynchronously compacting the LSM storage. Based on the implementation, we evaluate the cost of our proposed scheme with the comparison to alternative designs. The results show the effectiveness of cost-reducing approaches used in our work.

The contributions of this work are the following:

1. We propose TPAD, a novel architecture to secure outsourced data storage over the Blockchain. The TPAD architecture considers an LSM-tree-based storage protocol and maps security-essential state and operations to the Blockchain. The architecture includes a minimal state in Blockchain storage and offline compaction operations in the asynchronous smart-contract.
2. We implement a prototype on Ethereum/Solidity that realizes the proposed design. Through evaluation, we demonstrate the effective cost saving of the TPAD design with the comparison to state-of-the-art approaches.

The rest of the paper is organized as following: Section 2 formulates the research problem. The proposed technique, LSM-tree based storage over the Blockchain, is presented in Sect. 3. The system implementation is described in Sect. 4. Evaluation is presented next in Sects. 5 and 7 surveys the related work. Section 8 concludes the paper.

2   Problem Formulation

2.1   Target Applications

This work targets the application of secure data outsourcing in a third-party host (e.g., Amazon S3). A particular scenario of interest is to outsource the data generated by the Internet of things (IoT) devices to the cloud storage, which serves read requests from data consuming applications. The IoT data is usually personal and could be security sensitive; for instance, in the smart home, the IoT devices such as smart TV controller capture residents' daily activities which could reveal personal secrets such as TV view habits. The IoT data, on the other hand, can be used to improve the life quality and enable novel applications. For instance, analyzing patient's activities at home can improve out-patient care and predict possible disease. In practice, various IoT data is widely collected and outsourced [16]. A noteworthy characteristic of our target application is that data is generated continuously and intensively. The workload is more write intensive than the static workload (e.g., in classic database systems).

2.2   System Model

The data-outsourcing system consists of data producers, a cloud host, and several data consumers. A data producer submits data write requests to the cloud and a data consumer submits data read requests to the cloud. The cloud exposes a

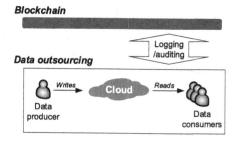

Fig. 1. Logging data outsourcing in Blockchain

standard key-value store interface for reads and writes. Formally, given key k, value v, timestamp ts, a data write and data read are described below:

$$ts := \mathsf{Put}(k, v)$$
$$\langle k, v, ts \rangle := \mathsf{Get}(k, ts_q) \tag{1}$$

In our system, we assume the data producers and consumers are trusted. The third-party cloud is untrusted and it can launch various attacks to forge an answer to the consumer which will be elaborated on in Sect. 2.3.

Our data-outsourcing system has a companion of Blockchain, as illustrated in Fig. 1. The Blockchain logs certain events in the workflow of data outsource for the purpose of securing it.

2.3   Security Goals

In the presence of the untrusted host, there are threats that could compromise data security. An adversary, be it the cloud host or man-in-the-middle adversary in networks, could forge a fake answer to a data consumer and violate the data integrity, membership authenticity, etc. The data integrity can be protected by simply attaching a message-authentication code (MAC) to each key-value record. This work considers the more advanced attacks — membership attacks that manifest in many forms: It could be the untrusted host deliberately skips query results and presents an incomplete answer (violating query completeness). It could be the host presents a stale version of the answer (violating query freshness). It could have the host to return different answers to different consumers regarding the same query (violating the fork consistency). On the write path, a man-in-the-middle adversary could replay a write request to result in incorrectly duplicated data versions. The formal definition of membership data authenticity is described in the existing protocols of authenticated data structures (ADS) [21,26,29,32].

While this work mainly focuses authenticity, we consider a weak security goal w.r.t. the data confidentiality that deterministic encryption suffices. The extension for data confidentiality will be discussed in Sect. 6.

2.4 Existing Techniques and Applicability

Existing works on **ADS construction**, while ensuring the security of membership authentication, are mostly designed based on read-optimized database structures such as B trees and R trees [17,28] that perform data updates in place. These update-in-place structures translate an update operation from applications to a read-modify-write sequence on the underlying storage medium, and they are unfriendly to the write performance. The only ADS work we are aware of on address write efficiency is [25], which is however constructed using expensive lattice-based cryptography.

Without security, there are various write-optimized **log-structured data structures** that do not perform in-place updates but conduct append-only writes instead. A primary form of these data structures is to organize the primary data storage into a time-ordered log of records where an update is an append to the log end and a read may have to scan the entire log. The pure-log design is widely used in the log-structured journaling file systems [27].

A log-structured merge tree [24] represents a middle ground between the read-optimized update-in-place structure and the write-optimized log. An LSM tree serves a write in an append-only fashion and also supports random-access read without scanning the entire dataset. The LSM design has been adopted in many real-world cloud storage systems, including Google BigTable [15]/LevelDB [7], Apache HBase [2], Apache Cassandra [1], Facebook RocksDB [5], etc. The read-write characteristic of an LSM tree renders it well suited for the applications of IoT data outsourcing.

2.5 Motivation

Our target applications such as IoT data outsourcing feature a high-throughput stream of data updates and random-access read queries. As aforementioned, a Log-Structured Merge Tree is a good fit for this workload, assuming some offline hours for data compaction.

To map the LSM-tree workflow in an outsourcing scenario, it is essential to find a trusted third-party to conduct the data-compaction work. Relying on one of data owners to do the compaction is unfeasible due to availability, data owner's limited power (e.g., a low-end IoT device), etc.

We propose to leverage the Blockchain for the secure compaction in LSM storage. The decentralized design and large-scale deployment of existing Blockchain render it a trustworthy platform. The new smart-contract interface of the latest Blockchain makes it friendly to run general-purpose trustworthy computation on the platform.

Despite the advantages, designing a system for Blockchain-based LSM-storage outsourcing is non-trivial. Notably, Blockchain's innate limitation (in low storage capacity, high cost, low write throughput) presents technical challenges when being adapted to the high-throughput data-outsourcing workflow. We address these challenges by limiting Blockchain's involvement in the online path of data outsourcing, such that the state on Blockchain can be "updated" infrequently.

2.6 Preliminary: LSM Trees

The mechanism of an LSM tree is the following: It represents a dataset by multiple sorted runs (or files) and organized in several so-called "levels". The first level stores the most recent data writes and is "mutable". Other levels are immutable and are updated only in an offline manner. Concretely, a data write synchronously updates the first level. The first level may periodically persist data to an external place, called write-ahead log (WAL). When the first level becomes full, it is flushed to the next level. A read iterates over levels, and for each level, it is served by an indexed lookup. In the worst case, a read has to scan all levels and in practice, the total number of levels is bounded. In addition, if the application exhibits some data locality (i.e., reads tend to access recently updated data), a read can stop in the first couple of levels. An LSM tree supports a compaction[1] operation that merges multiple sorted runs into one and helps reorganizes the storage layout from a write-optimized one to a read-optimized one. The compaction is a batched job that usually runs asynchronously and during offline hours. There are two flavors in compaction, namely, flush and merge. A flush operation takes as input multiple sorted runs at level i and produces a sorted run as output at level $i + 1$. A merge operation takes as input one selected file at level i and multiple files at level $i + 1$ that overlap the selected file in key ranges. It produces sorted runs that replace these input files at level $i + 1$.

An LSM mechanism supports different policies to trigger the execution of a compaction. These policies include sized configuration and leveled configuration: (1) In a sized configuration, each tree level has the capacity of storing a fixed number of sorted files, say K. The file size at level i is K^i (the first level has i to be 0). A flush-based compaction is triggered when there are K files filled in a level, say i. The compaction merges all K files at level i into one file at level $i+1$. With the sized-compaction policy, files at the same level may have their content overlap in key ranges, and a read has to scan all files in a level. (2) In a leveled configuration, any tree level is a sorted run where different files do not overlay in their key ranges. Data at level 0 is flushed to level 1 and data at level i, $\forall i \geq 1$, is merged to level $i+1$ [7]. A compaction can be triggered by application-specific conditions. A read within a level can be served by an indexed lookup without scanning.

3 LSM Data Storage over Blockchain

3.1 Baseline and Design Choices

Baseline: Our general design goal is to leverage Blockchain for securing data outsourcing. A baseline approach is to replace the cloud host by Blockchain. In the baseline, the Blockchain stores the entire dataset and directly interacts with the trusted clients of data producers and consumers through three smart

---

[1] In this work, the words of "compaction" and "merge" are interchangeably used.

contracts. On the write path, a "writer" contract accepts the data-write requests from the producers (encoded in the form of transactions) and sends them to the Blockchain. On the read path, a "reader" contract reads the Blockchain content to find the LSM tree level that contains the result. The Blockchain runs an offline "compaction" contract that is triggered by the same conditions of original LSM stores and that merges multiple sorted runs to reorganize the layout.

Design Space: The above baseline design raises two issues as below:

First, the baseline approach uses the Blockchain as the primary data storage, which is cost inefficient. Concretely, storing a bit in Blockchain is much more expensive and costly than storing it off-chain (e.g., in the cloud). A promising solution is to partition the LSM workflow and to result in a minimal and security-essential partition in Blockchain. This way, the primary data storage which is cumbersome is mapped off-chain to the cloud host.

Second, the baseline approach enforces a strong consistency semantic over the Blockchain which is weakly consistent; this mismatch across layers may present issues and incur unnecessary cost. More specifically, the current system of Blockchain promises only eventual consistency (or timed consistency [30]) in the sense that it allows an arbitrary delay between the transaction-submission time and the final settlement time (i.e., when the transaction is confirmed in the blockchain). The eventual consistency limits the use of Blockchain for real-time data serving and renders the baseline approach that aggressively checks the Blockchain digests to be ineffective.

3.2   Blockchain-Based TPAD Protocol

TPAD Overview: Our proposed TPAD protocol addresses the partitioning problem of an LSM tree for the minimal involvement with the Blockchain. The TPAD design separates the "data plane" (the primary data storage) and the "control plane" (e.g., digest management), and maps the former to the off-chain cloud and only loads the latter in Blockchain. Recall that an LSM tree supports three major operations (i.e., data write, read and compaction). For online data reads/writes, TPAD places only in Blockchain/smart-contract the access of the digests, while leaving data access and proof construction off-chain. To address the consistency limits, TPAD embeds the weak-consistency semantics in the application layer; for instance, it does not access the Blockchain if the results are too recent to be reflected in the Blockchain. The data-intensive computation of compaction is however materialized inside the Blockchain, which simulates a multi-client verifiable computation protocol [18]. This subsection presents the details of the TPAD protocol.

Recall that our overall system includes data producers, the cloud, the blockchain, and data consumers. The data producers generate data records and upload them to the third-party cloud-blockchain platform. Data consumers query the cloud by data keys to retrieve relevant records. For the ease of presentation, we use a concrete setting w.l.o.g. that involves two data producers, say Alice (A) and Bob (B), and one data consumer, say Charlie (C).

Initially, each data producer has a pubic-private key pair and uses the public key as her pseudonymous identity. In other words, the system is open membership that anyone can join, which is consistent with the design of open Blockchain. We assume the identities of data producer and Blockchain are established in a trusted manner, which in practice could be enforced by external mechanisms for user authentication and attestation. Conceptually, there are two virtual chains registered in the Blockchain to materialize the two states of an LSM tree, that is, the WAL and digests of data levels. These two virtual chains can be materialized in the same physical Blockchain.

On the write path, Alice, the producer, generates a record (R_A) and submits it to the Blockchain through the logger contract that logs the record as a transaction in the WAL Blockchain. The logger contract is called asynchronously in that it returns immediately and does not wait for the final inclusion of the transaction in WAL Blockchain. Simultaneously, Alice also sends the record to the untrusted cloud, which stores it in Level 0 of its local LSM system. Bob sends another record R_B to the Blockchain and cloud, which is processed in a similar fashion. The logger contract is responsible for serializing multiple records received and sending transactions in order. The total order between R_A and R_B is not resolved until the transactions are finally settled in the WAL Blockchain, which could occur as late as up to 40 min (e.g., in BitCoin) after the submission time. We maintain the consistency semantics that there is no time ordering among records in Level 0 on the cloud. Upon flush, it only flushes the records whose transactions are fully settled in the Blockchain.

On the read path, Charlie submits a query to the cloud, which returns the result as well as query proof. In addition, Charlie obtains the relevant digests from the Blockchain. Specifically, the proof consists of the Merkle authentication paths of all relevant levels, that is, the level that has the answer (i.e., membership level) and all the levels (i.e., non-membership levels) that do not have the answer but are more recent than the membership level. The digests, namely Merkle root hashes, are obtained from Digest Blockchain. As aforementioned, the system does not provide membership authentication for data in Level 0.

On the compaction path, TPAD supports two relevant contracts for data flush and merge. For the flush, the flush contract is triggered every time there is a new block found in the WAL Blockchain. It flushes all the files/records at level i to a single sorted file at Level $i + 1$. Inside the flush, the contract sorts the records at level i (which are originally organized in the time order), builds a digest of the sorted run, and sends it to the Digest Blockchain. At the same time, the off-chain cloud runs the flush computation that builds the sorted run locally.

For the merge, a separate contract merges multiple sorted runs into one run and places it at a certain level of the LSM tree. When a compaction contract runs, it validates all the input runs fed from the cloud using the digests stored in the Blockchain. It then performs the merge computation, builds a Merkle root hash on the merged run, and sends a transaction encoding the hash to update the Digest Blockchain. In the last step, the Digest Blockchain stores the digests of different LSM levels and the contract replaces the digests by those of the merged run. At the same time, the off-chain cloud runs the merge computation that builds the sorted run locally.

The two compaction contracts update the Blockchain state and have a companion computation going on the off-chain side. Given the delay to finally settle a transaction, we defer the time the updated state in Blockchain becomes available. For instance, even though the merge contract finishes the execution and sends the transaction, the off-chain data store will wait until the transaction is settled to activate the use of merged runs. The above two compaction contracts involve data-intensive computation and are executed at off-line hours. The specific triggering conditions are described next.

The algorithms in TPAD are illustrated in Listing 2.

Compaction-Triggering Policies: In TPAD, the policy that determines when and how to run a compaction is executed by the cloud host. As aforementioned, the off-chain cloud can opt for the sized LSM tree policy where the number of files per level is fixed and an overflowing file triggers the execution of flush operation. The off-chain cloud can also take the leveled LSM tree policy where application-specific condition triggers the execution of merge operations. In practice, the sized policy lends itself to serving time-series workloads where newer data does not replace older data.

In our implementation, an LSM level in the Smart Contract program is represented by an array in memory. The output is the digest of merged data which is stored persistently on Blockchain. Note that we do not store or send the merge data in Smart Contract to save the Gas cost.

Security Analysis. We consider a data-freshness attack where an adversary, e.g., the untrusted host, presents a valid but stale key-value pair as the result. That is, given a query $\mathsf{Get}(k, ts_q)$, it returns $\langle k', v', ts' \rangle$ that belongs to the data store, while there exists another more fresh key-value record $\langle k, v, ts \rangle$ such that $ts' < ts < ts_q$.

The LPAD scheme can authenticate the following two properties that establish the data freshness: (1) Result membership: Given a result record from a specific level (called result level), the LPAD scheme can prove the membership of the record in the level using the corresponding Merkle tree. That is, given query result $\langle k', v, ts \rangle := \mathsf{Get}(k, ts_q)$, LPAD can authenticate the membership of $\langle k', v, ts \rangle$ in the level it resides in (using the per-level Merkle tree) and hence the membership in the data store. (2) Non-membership of any fresher result. That is, the LPAD scheme can prove the non-membership of any record of the same queried key in levels fresher than the result level. Note that for a given key, levels are ordered by time.

In a query-completeness attack, valid result records are deliberately omitted. The completeness security is similarly provided by the LPAD scheme with the freshness security: In LPAD, the result completeness (i.e., no valid result is missed) in each query level can be deduced from that the leaf nodes in each per-level Merkle tree is sorted by data keys.

In a forking attack, different views are presented to different querying clients (presenting "X" to Alice and "Y" to Bob). The forking-attack security (or fork consistency) can be guaranteed by LPAD by that the Blockchain can provide a single source of truth for the dataset state, and any violation (by forking) can be detected by checking the result against the Blockchain state.

4   Implementation on Ethereum

We have implemented the TPAD protocol over the Ethereum Blockchain which keeps two states: WAL and digests. The other players in the protocol, including the data producers, consumers, and the cloud, are implemented in JavaScript.

A data producer writing a record to the cloud triggers the execution of logger contract on Ethereum that computes the hash digest and sends a transaction wrapping the digest.

A data consumer submits a query by key to the cloud which returns the answer and proof. The data consumer inquires about the digests stored in the Blockchain by triggering the execution of a reader contract on Blockchain. The answer proof consists of authentication paths of Merkle trees from the cloud and is used to compare against the digests for answer verification. Note that we implement the reading of digests in a smart contract for the ease of engineering.

A compaction operation is implemented on both the cloud and Blockchain. Consider the compaction of two files (or sorted runs). First, the compaction smart-contract on the Blockchain takes as input the data stored in JSON on the cloud side and the digest hashes stored in the Blockchain. As mentioned, the compaction code validates the inputs based on the digests, conducts the merge computation by heap sort, computes the new digest of the merged run, and sends the transaction encoding the digest to the Blockchain. Second, the JavaScript program on the cloud side also runs the merge computation locally on the input files. It then replaces the input files in the local JSON store by the merged file. We choose this implementation (merge computation done on both cloud and smart contract), because the JavaScript runs the smart contract asynchronously (i.e., the call returns in JavaScript without waiting for the smart contract finishes the execution) and it saves bandwidth.

A compaction operation is implemented as a distributed process running on the both sides of cloud and Blockchain. When the cloud (or a cloud administrator) decides to merge the LSM storage, it first uploads the data to be merged to the Blockchain using a batch of transactions. Then, the cloud starts to run a local merge operation. Concurrently, the transactions sent by the cloud triggers the execution of a smart-contract that does the merge computation on the Blockchain based on the data sent earlier. The cloud and Blockchain is synchronized when the merge computations on both sides end. Concretely, the cloud, once it finishes the local merge computation, will wait until being notified by the completion event of the remote merge on the Blockchain. On implementation, the cloud merge program is written in Javascript and the synchronization is realized using Promise [9], which is a multithreading support in Javascript. After the synchronization, the cloud proceed to replace the data by the merged data.

On the blockchain, the verifiable-merge smart contract is implemented as below: The compaction code validates the input data based on the digest on Blockchain, carries out the merge computation based on heap sort, computes the new digest of the merged run, and persists it into the Blockchain by sending a transaction.

The logger contract is triggered when a data producer uploads a record and its digest. The flush contract is triggered by a block in the Blockchain is found. The compaction contract is triggered by LSM compaction policies elaborated in the next section.

Implementation Notes: The current version of Solidity (i.e., 0.4.17) does not support multi-dimensional nested array in a public function. We have to implement the array of digests as a one-dimensional array and interpret it as a two-dimensional array (by levels and files) manually in the program. To collect the Gas consumption in a view function (i.e., the function that does not change state), we call `estimateGas()` function. In our implementation, the JavaScript code runs smart contract functions through JSON ABI files generated by the truffle compiler [11]. The state overwrites in Ethereum/Solidity program has to be explicit and is realized by delete and "push" operations (Fig. 2).

```
1  TPADContract{
2    uint[] WAL;
3    unit[] digests;
4    flush(){
5      while(block_found()!=true);
6        list l0=get_6th_block();
7      validate(l0);
8      ll0=sort(l0);
9      digests.send_tx(digest(ll0));
10   }
11   compact(list l1, list l2){
12     while(l1,l2=compact_policy());
13     validate(l1,l2);
14     ll2=merge(l1,l2);
15     digests.send_tx(digest(ll2));
16   }
17 }
18 class Client {
19   write(record r){
20     cloud.write(r);
21     WAL.send_tx(r);
22   }
23   read(key k){
24     result a, proof p=cloud.read(r);
25     d=digests.read_tx(a);
26     if(verify(a,p,d)) return a;
27   }
28 }
```

Fig. 2. Implementing TPAD

5   Evaluation

This section presents the evaluation of TPAD. The goal is to understand the cost saving of TPAD comparing alternative designs including on-chain storage (Sect. 5.1) and other data structures (Sect. 5.2). We first present our evaluation platform.

Setup: Our smart-contracts written in Solidity are compiled in the Truffle programming suit. They run on a personal Blockchain network set up by Ganache [6]. This local Blockchain network is sufficient for our evaluation purpose which only evaluates the cost consumption. For comparison, we implement the baseline approach of storing data in Blockchain. Here, the blockchain keeps a state of the LSM tree stored in a multi-dimensional storage array. In the implementation, no in-memory index is maintained and finding a record in a file is materialized by binary search. We also implement the other two baselines, namely append-only log and update-in-place structures. For the latter, we implement a binary-search tree and build a Merkle tree based on it with the root node stored in Blockchain.

5.1   Cost Saving of Off-Chain Storage

The TPAD is firstly a Blockchain logging scheme with the data stored off-chain. A relevant baseline is to treat the Blockchain as the primary storage, namely on-chain store. We implement the baseline by placing an entire LSM tree, including leaf-level data nodes, inside the Blockchain.

On our platform, we conduct experiments by driving $20,000$ records into the data store. We varied the "shape" of the LSM tree in terms of the size of a level (number of files allowed in a level, K) and the number of levels. We measure the cost in terms of Gas consumption of the two approaches respectively with on-chain and off-chain storage.

The results are presented in Fig. 3. Figure 3a is the write cost when the LSM tree has two levels. With different values of K (recall K is the number of files in a level), the cost is relatively stable. Comparing the on-chain storage, the off-chain storage saves a significant amount of cost, which is about $5X$ saving. When fixing K at 3, varying the number of levels from 1 to 5, the cost of on-chain store increase which is consistent with the fact that write amplification increases

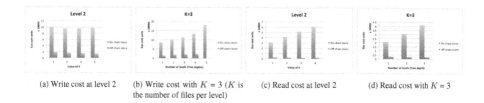

(a) Write cost at level 2   (b) Write cost with $K = 3$ (K is   (c) Read cost at level 2   (d) Read cost with $K = 3$
the number of files per level)

Fig. 3. On-chain storage cost versus off-chain cost

along with the number of compaction jobs. Comparing on-chain and off-chain storage, the cost saving also increases along with the number of levels. In both Figs. 3c and d, the read cost increases along with the value of K. The off-chain storage saves the Gas cost up to $60X$ and $20X$ respectively for the settings of two levels and K equal to 3.

5.2 Efficiency of LSM-Based Storage on Blockchain

The TPAD is an authenticated key-value store that supports random-access reads/writes. In this regard, relevant baselines that implement the key-value store abstraction include an append-only log where records are ordered by time and an update-in-place structure, namely a single Merkle tree where leaf nodes are ordered by keys. We implement the first baseline by simply sending the hash digest of every data write to the Blockchain. The second baseline is implemented by maintaining the root hash of the key-ordered Merkle tree in Blockchain and by translating every data read/write to a leaf-to-root path traversal on the Merkle tree. In more details, a data read to the cloud store would present as a proof the authentication path of the leaf node to the root hash of the Merkle tree and a data write consists of a data read followed by a local modification and a remote update to the authentication path.

We conduct small-scale experiments by loading a thousand records into the storage system; the keys and values in the records are randomly distributed. We measure the average costs of read and write. The cost consists of the Gas cost for running smart contract that retrieves the digests stored in the Blockchain and the costs of preparing and verifying query proof (e.g., the authentication paths in Merkle trees). We use a heuristic to combine the two costs by multiplying the Gas cost by 100 times before adding it and the proof-related cost. The proof-related cost is measured by the number of cycles spent locally for proof verification.

The results are presented in Fig. 4. The results show that the TPAD can result in cost efficiency on both reads and writes. Concretely, for the write results in Fig. 4a, the online part of TPAD has a similar cost with the other two baselines, as each write results in a single transaction in all three approaches. The

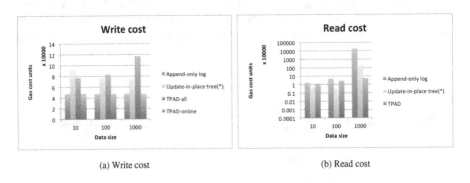

(a) Write cost   (b) Read cost

Fig. 4. LSM tree-based TPAD compared against other structures in cost

overall TPAD approach that includes both online and offline operations (i.e. compaction) would incur write amplification as shown in Fig. 4a. For the data read results in Fig. 4b, the cost saving of TPAD is significant, provided that the y-axis is plotted in log scale. The TPAD incurs even lower cost than update-in-place trees partly because of the locality in our query workloads where recently updated data is more likely being queried.

6   Discussion: Data Confidentiality and Key Management

Data producers concerned about data confidentiality can upload the records in an encrypted form. Specifically, a data producer sends the ciphertext of the record, instead of plaintext, to the third-party host. The decryption key is shared through an offline key-distribution channel between the data producer and the data consumers who are permissioned to access the record. Those consumers can obtain the ciphertext of the record from the host and use the key to decrypt. To enable the query over ciphertext, we consider the use of deterministic encryption which supports exact-match query in the encrypted form, that is, the consumer could submit the encrypted query key to the host who will conduct exact-match query between the query ciphertext and data ciphertext. The integration with more secure encryption primitives is complementary to this scope of this work.

The data-encryption layer is laid over the membership-/data- authentication layer of TPAD (as described above). This is similar to the classic encryption-then-authentication scheme [20]. With deterministic encryption, the merge operation of TPAD occurs in the domain of ciphertext.

7   Related Work

7.1   Blockchain Applications

A common paradigm of supporting applications over Blockchain is that the application-level workflow is partitioned and mapped to the on-/off-chain parts. Decentralizing privacy [34] supports access-control oriented data-sharing applications over Blockchain. It publishes the access control list onto the Blockchain and enforces the access control by smart contract. A similar approach is used in MedRec [13] to enforce access control for medical data sharing. MedRec runs a proprietary Blockchain network where miners are computers in an academic environment and are rewarded by an anonymized medical dataset.

Namecoin [19] and Blockstack [12] support general-purpose key-value storage in the decentralized fashion. They allow open-membership and accept any users to upload their data signed with their secret keys. They support the storage of name-value binding, with a canonical application to be DNS servers. Namecoin is a special-purpose Blockchain system and Blockstack is realized as a middleware on top of any Blockchain substrates. The VirtualChain in Blockstack supports a (single) state-machine abstraction. Re-purposing original Blockchain for storage, its system design tackles the challenges of limited storage capacity, long write latency, and low transactional throughput.

Catena [31] is probably the closest related work to TPAD. Catena is a non-equivocation scheme over the Blockchain that repurposes its no-double-spending security for non-equivocation in logging and auditing. In essence, it aligns the application-specific log (for auditing) with the underlying linear Blockchain and reuses the non-fork property of Blockchain for the non-fork application log. Briefly, Catena's mechanism is to build a virtual chain on BitCoin blockchain by (ab)using OP_RETURN transaction interface. Logging sends a BitCoin transaction and auditing performs an ordered sequence of statement-verification calls in the log history. The statement verification does not scan full history but simply runs the Bitcoin-validation logic (e.g., Simplified Payment Validation), which ensures no BitCoin double-spending. Importantly, it enforces the rule that a Catena transaction spends the output of its immediate predecessor for efficient valida-tion. The genesis transaction is served as the ground truth of validation and it assumes a broadcast channel to establish the consistent view of the Genesis transaction.

Our TPAD is different from Catena in the following senses: (1) Catena is built on Bitcoin or the first-generation blockchain, and TPAD leverages the smart-contract capabilities widely existing in the latest Blockchain systems, such as Ethereum [4]. (2) More importantly, Catena only supports auditing which is essentially sequential reads. TPAD supports verifiable random-reads. (3) While Catena claims to be low cost, the increasing rate of BitCoin ($700 per BitCoin at the time of Catena paper writing versus $17000 per BitCoin at early 2018) makes the Catena more expensive. TPAD address the cost minimization of these repurposed Blockchains.

7.2 Outsourced Storage and ADS

Outsourcing data storage to a third-party host such as public cloud is a popular application paradigm. In the presence of an untrusted host, it is important to ensure the data security, especially membership authenticity. An authenticated data structure (ADS) is a protocol that formally the security property. Depend-ing on the operations supported (queries and updates), an ADS protocol can be constructed by different cryptographic primitives such as secure hash and Merkle trees [22], SNARK [14], bilinear pairings [32,33], etc.

8   Conclusion

This work proposes the TPAD system for securely outsourcing data storage on third-party hosts by leveraging the Blockchain. Instead of using Blockchain as a time-ordered log, TPAD lays the log-structured merge tree (LSM tree) over the Blockchain for efficient and lightweight logging. Realizing the design, a small state is persisted in the Blockchain and computation-oriented compaction operations are carried out by smart contracts. With the implementation in Ethereum/-Solidity, we evaluate the proposed logging scheme and demonstrate its performance efficiency and effectiveness in cost saving.

References

1. Apache Cassandra. http://cassandra.apache.org/
2. Apache HBase. http://hbase.apache.org/
3. Bitcoin. https://bitcoin.org/en/
4. Ethereum project. https://www.ethereum.org/
5. Facebook RocksDB. http://rocksdb.org/
6. Ganache. http://truffleframework.com/ganache/
7. Google LevelDB. http://code.google.com/p/leveldb/
8. Litecoin. https://litecoin.org/
9. Promise. https://developer.mozilla.org/en-us/docs/web/javascript/reference/global_objects/promise
10. Solidity. https://solidity.readthedocs.io/en/develop/
11. Truffle. http://truffleframework.com/
12. Ali, M., Nelson, J.C., Shea, R., Freedman, M.J.: Blockstack: a global naming and storage system secured by blockchains. In: Gulati, A., Weatherspoon, H. (eds.) 2016 USENIX Annual Technical Conference, USENIX ATC 2016, Denver, CO, USA, 22–24 June 2016, pp. 181–194. USENIX Association (2016)
13. Azaria, A., Ekblaw, A., Vieira, T., Lippman, A.: MedRec: using blockchain for medical data access and permission management. In: Awan, I., Younas, M. (eds.) 2nd International Conference on Open and Big Data, OBD 2016, Vienna, Austria, 22–24 August 2016, pp. 25–30. IEEE Computer Society (2016)
14. Ben-Sasson, E., Chiesa, A., Genkin, D., Tromer, E., Virza, M.: SNARKs for C: verifying program executions succinctly and in zero knowledge. In: Canetti, R., Garay, J.A. (eds.) CRYPTO 2013. LNCS, vol. 8043, pp. 90–108. Springer, Heidelberg (2013). https://doi.org/10.1007/978-3-642-40084-1_6
15. Chang, F., et al.: Bigtable: a distributed storage system for structured data (awarded best paper!). In: OSDI, pp. 205–218 (2006)
16. Chung, H., Iorga, M., Voas, J.M., Lee, S.: Alexa, can I trust you? IEEE Comput. 50(9), 100–104 (2017)
17. Elmasri, R., Navathe, S.B.: Fundamentals of Database Systems, 2nd edn. Benjamin/Cummings, Redwood City (1994)
18. Gordon, S.D., Katz, J., Liu, F.-H., Shi, E., Zhou, H.-S.: Multi-client verifiable computation with stronger security guarantees. In: Dodis, Y., Nielsen, J.B. (eds.) TCC 2015. LNCS, vol. 9015, pp. 144–168. Springer, Heidelberg (2015). https://doi.org/10.1007/978-3-662-46497-7_6
19. Kalodner, H.A., Carlsten, M., Ellenbogen, P., Bonneau, J., Narayanan, A.: An empirical study of namecoin and lessons for decentralized namespace design. In: 14th Annual Workshop on the Economics of Information Security, WEIS 2015, Delft, The Netherlands, 22–23 June 2015 (2015)
20. Katz, J., Lindell, Y.: Introduction to Modern Cryptography. Chapman and Hall/CRC Press (2007)
21. Li, F., Hadjieleftheriou, M., Kollios, G., Reyzin, L.: Dynamic authenticated index structures for outsourced databases. In: SIGMOD Conference, pp. 121–132 (2006)

22. Merkle, R.C.: Protocols for public key cryptosystems. In: IEEE Symposium on Security and Privacy, pp. 122–134 (1980)

23. Narayanan, A., Bonneau, J., Felten, E.W., Miller, A., Goldfeder, S.: Bitcoin and Cryptocurrency Technologies - A Comprehensive Introduction. Princeton University Press, Princeton (2016)

24. O'Neil, P.E., Cheng, E., Gawlick, D., O'Neil, E.J.: The log-structured merge-tree (LSM-tree). Acta Inf. **33**(4), 351–385 (1996)

25. Papamanthou, C., Shi, E., Tamassia, R., Yi, K.: Streaming authenticated data structures. In: Johansson, T., Nguyen, P.Q. (eds.) EUROCRYPT 2013. LNCS, vol. 7881, pp. 353–370. Springer, Heidelberg (2013). https://doi.org/10.1007/978-3-642-38348-9_22

26. Papamanthou, C., Tamassia, R., Triandopoulos, N.: Authenticated hash tables based on cryptographic accumulators. Algorithmica **74**(2), 664–712 (2016)

27. Rosenblum, M.: The Design and Implementation of a Log-Structured File-System. Kluwer, Norwell (1995)

28. Silberschatz, A., Korth, H.F., Sudarshan, S.: Database System Concepts, 5th edn. McGraw-Hill Book Company, Boston (2005)

29. Tamassia, R.: Authenticated data structures. In: Di Battista, G., Zwick, U. (eds.) ESA 2003. LNCS, vol. 2832, pp. 2–5. Springer, Heidelberg (2003). https://doi.org/10.1007/978-3-540-39658-1_2

30. Terry, D.: Replicated data consistency explained through baseball. Commun. ACM **56**(12), 82–89 (2013)

31. Tomescu, A., Devadas, S.: Catena: efficient non-equivocation via bitcoin. In: 2017 IEEE Symposium on Security and Privacy, SP 2017, San Jose, CA, USA, 22–26 May 2017, pp. 393–409. IEEE Computer Society (2017)

32. Zhang, Y., Katz, J., Papamanthou, C.: IntegriDB: verifiable SQL for outsourced databases. In: Proceedings of the 22nd ACM SIGSAC Conference on Computer and Communications Security, Denver, CO, USA, 12–16 October 2015, pp. 1480–1491 (2015)

33. Zhang, Y., Katz, J., Papamanthou, C.: An expressive (zero-knowledge) set accumulator. In: 2017 IEEE European Symposium on Security and Privacy, EuroS&P 2017, Paris, France, 26–28 April 2017, pp. 158–173. IEEE (2017)

34. Zyskind, G., Nathan, O., Pentland, A.: Decentralizing privacy: using blockchain to protect personal data. In: 2015 IEEE Symposium on Security and Privacy Workshops, SPW 2015, San Jose, CA, USA, 21–22 May 2015, pp. 180–184. IEEE Computer Society (2015)

Proof-Carrying Smart Contracts

Thomas Dickerson[1], Paul Gazzillo[2(✉)], Maurice Herlihy[1], Vikram Saraph[1],
and Eric Koskinen[2]

[1] Brown University, Providence, USA
[2] Stevens Institute of Technology, Hoboken, USA
paul@pgazz.com

Abstract. We propose a way to reconcile the apparent contradiction between the immutability of idealized smart contracts and the real-world need to update contracts to fix bugs and oversights. Our proposal is to raise the contract's level of abstraction to guarantee a specification φ instead of a particular implementation of that specification. A combination of proof-carrying code and proof-aware consensus allows contract implementations to be updated as needed, but so as to guarantee that φ cannot be violated by any future upgrade.

We propose proof-carrying smart contracts (PCSCs), aiming to put formal correctness proofs of smart contracts *on the chain*. Proofs of correctness for a contract can be checked by validators, who can enforce the restriction that no update can violate φ. We discuss some architectural and formal challenges, and include an example of how our approach could address the well-known vulnerabilities in the ERC20 token standard.

1 Introduction

Motivation. The promise of smart contracts seems impossible to fulfill. In theory, a smart contract is a transparent agreement, freely agreed upon by informed parties. Irrevocable and immutable, it enforces itself without need for help from humans and their civic institutions. In reality, an unhappy history of exploits, theft, and fraud has established that people are bad at writing correct contracts, and no better at detecting flaws in the contracts they agree to [5,6,17,18].

The Solidity language and EVM bytecode permit contracts to call code at a dynamic address. While intended to support legitimate functions such as sending a payment to a user or contract, it allows the contract to implement the *pointer to implementation* (or *PIMPL*) idiom. This idiom has one benefit: it provides a path through which a buggy contract implementation might be patched. Even though the *code* is immutable, the *state* managed by the code, including the implementation pointer, is not. The danger, of course, is that a dishonest party could use such dynamic control flow to make substantial changes to the contract's terms after it has been agreed upon.

We believe this dilemma can be avoided, or at least mitigated, by including formal correctness proofs in the blockchain itself. Suppose we identify a property φ critical to the contract's integrity. If a flawed implementation C that formally

A. Zohar et al. (Eds.): FC 2018 Workshops, LNCS 10958, pp. 325–338, 2019.
https://doi.org/10.1007/978-3-662-58820-8_22

satisfies φ can only be replaced by an improved implementation C' such that $C' \vDash \varphi$, then all parties to the contract can be confident that φ will continue to hold even as bugs (not covered by φ) are detected and patched.

The idea of mixing code and proofs goes back to Necula's proof-carrying code (PCC) [16]. The blockchain context, however, brings new challenges: What format is needed for contracts' specifications, and where are these specifications stored? Which code needs to be verified? Who generates the proofs? How do miners repeatedly validate the proofs? Here we sketch preliminary work on the architectural and formal aspects of these challenges, illustrated by a running example based on the ERC20 token standard [21].

Overview. We believe that one may be able to adapt Necula's PCC into a variation that we call *proof-carrying smart contracts* (PCSC). The idea is that a contract's API and specification φ are published to the blockchain. Any subsequent updates to the implementation C must be accompanied by a valid proof that the specification is maintained: $C \vDash \varphi$. Smart contracts are well-suited to PCC, because a proof only needs to generated once by the contract owner, before the implementation pointer is updated. Publishing the proof to the blockchain makes it immutable, and the participants in the network only need check the proof's validity, a task that is far less computationally expensive than generating the proof.

Blockchains and blockchain consensus require some changes to standard PCC. In the original formulation, a code *consumer* specifies the specification, and the code *producer* generates a proof that the policy is preserved by the remote code. In the blockchain context, the smart contract owner is the code producer. All validators and clients in the blockchain network are code consumers, since smart contracts are replicated and rerun by all.

We exploit the immutability of blockchain to enable the producer to provide the specification. Because this specification is published before any updates to the contract implementation, code consumers can inspect it before transacting with the contract. Immutability of blockchain data guarantees the policy can never be weakened by the producer. The producer updates the implementation pointer with a special setter that must be accompanied by a valid proof. Blockchain consensus ensures that updates by the contract writer preserve the specification, as long as a majority of participants validate the proof.

Running Example. The ERC20 specification [21] defines a number of operations intended to provide a standardized API for managing tradeable tokens on the Ethereum platform [7]. Using ERC20, Alice may `approve` up to some number n tokens, the `allowance`, to be transferred to Bob, and Bob may then execute multiple `transfer` calls until all n have been transferred (or Alice reduces Bob's `allowance`). Here is an example, based on a simplified version of the ERC20 operations, how one might use PCSC. In our simplified ERC20 specification, there are only two accounts, `from` and `to`. Token transfers happen only unilaterally, flowing from `from` to `to`.

There are several invariants linking operations i and $i + 1$. First, we enforce conservation of tokens, by defining

$$\texttt{total\_supply}_i = \texttt{from\_balance}_i + \texttt{to\_balance}_i \tag{1}$$

and requiring

$$\texttt{total\_supply}_{i+1} = \texttt{total\_supply}_i \tag{2}$$

Second, we enforce the allowance limit:

$$\Delta_i \leq \texttt{allowance}_i \tag{3}$$

$$\texttt{from\_balance}_{i+1} = \texttt{from\_balance}_i + \Delta_i \tag{4}$$

$$\texttt{allowance}_{i+1} = \texttt{allowance}_i - \Delta_i \tag{5}$$

The naïve implementation in Fig. 1a appears to respect both invariants. Unfortunately, these conditions, while necessary, are not sufficient to guarantee the expected behavior. Alice, having initially **approved** an allowance of 100 tokens, may later wish to decrease Bob's allowance by calling **approve(50)**. But if Bob has already executed **transfer(n)** (for $n > 50$), Alice's call has the unexpected effect of *increasing* Bob's total withdrawal.

This is essentially a data race: even though the EVM execution is single-threaded, transactions are submitted in parallel, and miners may reorder and interleave those transactions arbitrarily.

Figure 1b is a version of **approve** that is safe from the data race. It forces the sender to first set the allowance to 0 before updating[1], effectively clearing the allowance before setting a new one.

Contributions. This paper makes make the following contributions:

– We propose proof-carrying smart contracts (PCSC), a way to allow contracts to be upgraded while ensuring that critical properties such as φ are preserved.
– We describe an architecture for PCSC, along with a discussion of needed changes to the blockchain protocol and virtual machine (Sect. 2).
– A treatment of PCSC with specifications and proofs (Sect. 3).

This paper describes the ideas and insights motivating this work, which is still in progress.

2   Realizing Proof-Carrying Smart Contracts

Adopting the language of PCC, the code *producer* is the contract writer, while the *consumers* are all other participants in the blockchain network, miners, validators, and the clients who issue transactions. The producer's role is to create

---

[1] This unfortunately restricts the possible valid semantics of the ERC20 implementation, later in the paper we will propose yet a 3rd implementation that is thread safe without being subject to this restriction.

```
1 bool transfer(uint256 value) {        1 bool transfer(uint256 value) {
2   if (value <= allowed) {              2   if (value <= allowed) {
3     from_balance -= value;             3     from_balance -= value;
4     to_balance += value;               4     to_balance += value;
5     allowed -= value;                  5     allowed -= value;
6     return true;                       6     allowed_known = false;
7   } else { return false; }             7     return true;
8 }                                      8   } else { return false; }
9 uint256 allowance() {                  9 }
10   return allowed;                     10 uint256 allowance() {
11 }                                     11   if(caller == sender) {
12 // vulnerable to a data race          12     allowed_known = true;
13 bool approve(uint256 value) {          13   }
14   allowed = value;                    14   return allowed;
15   return true;                        15 }
16 }                                     16 bool approve(uint256 value) {
                                         17   // sender must have observed
                                                  allowance
                 (a)                     18   if(allowed_known){
                                         19     allowed = value;
─────────────────────────────────       20     return true;
1 bool approve(uint256 value) {          21   } else { return false; }
2   // sender sets allowed to 0          22 }
3   // first to avoid data race
4   if (allowed == 0 && value > 0                         (c)
5     ||allowed > 0 && value==0) {
6     allowed = value;
7     return true;
8   } else { return false; }
9 }

                 (b)
```

Fig. 1. (a) First version. (b) Altered version of `approve`. (c) A safe version of `approve`, emulating LL/SC for `allowed`. *A simplified example of an implementation of the ERC20 token standard where tokens are sent with a two-step `approve`/`transfer` process.*

the contract specification, consisting of an API and persistent contract state. Unlike the original formulation of PCC, the specification is provided by the producer, rather than the code consumer, along with the contract code. The specification is provided as invariants on contract state as well as pre- and post-conditions on the API interface methods. The *parent* part of a PCSC includes the smart contract's internal state, API methods, and formal specification. A (successfully deployed) *child* part of the PCSC includes the source code for all API methods, and a proof that the implementation satisfies the specification (found in the corresponding parent).

We exploit the immutability of the blockchain to put executive control of specification in the hands of consumers. In order to run smart contract transactions, the contract is first appended to the chain. By requiring producers to include the specification with the contract, it becomes part of the immutable history of the chain, and can't be modified, even if, for example, the contract uses PIMPL and the implementation pointer changes to a new child contract. Even though the consumers do not directly create the specification, a consumer can inspect the specification and choose not to issue transactions on the contract (though they must still process any transactions issued by other consumers, as long as those transactions obey the specification).

We use the consensus mechanism of the blockchain to ensure that all updates to the implementation of the smart contract preserve the original specification. The producer specifies the fields of any child contract addresses. Any updates to these fields must be accompanied by a proof that the new child contract satisfies the original specification[2]. Participants trust that miners and validators check the validity of proofs, just as they trust them not to zero out someone's token balance or put the contract in some other incorrect state. As with Bitcoin, Ethereum, and other cryptocurrencies, as long as the majority of miners are well-behaved, the contract updates will obey the specification.

Being a manifestation of PCC, the producer generates this proof off-the-chain before making the update. The special setter function, allowing the child address to be updated, uses a new bytecode operation, SAFEUPDATE, to check the provided proof preserves the specification. This ensures that miners and validators can guarantee the new child contract is safe. The code for the child contract must be available before the call to update the child address, so the parent must publish the initial contract before issuing the update or prove an existing contract satisfied the specification[3]. This is safe because contract addresses are not reassigned or unassigned due to the immutability of the blockchain.

As with other violations (out-of-gas, exceeded stack depth), an update to the child address without a proof or with an invalid one is rejected with an exception. The validation of the proof is far less computationally expensive than generating the proof, enabling higher throughput for miners. But due to the added computational expense of validation, this new update operation will require more gas than a typical store operation, perhaps proportional to the size of the proof.

Figure 2 illustrates the operation of proof-carrying smart contracts (PCSC). This diagram assumes the producer has already published the parent contract (containing the API and specification) as well as the candidate child contract's code, because these operations require no verification[4]. The producer first generates a proof that the proposed child contract satisfied the invariants of the specification (Step 1). This proof is packaged in an update transaction. The producer

---

[2] For the purposes of this paper, we assume that the compiler is able to translate proofs & invariants for the source language (e.g. Solidity) into proofs & invariants for the host language (e.g. EVM bytecode).

[3] A dummy contract which always terminates with an exception should vacuously satisfy the specification, since, for example, under the Ethereum model of execution, a contract could run out of gas and terminate at any point anyway.

[4] Generally-speaking, a parent contract can include arbitrary computation as long as it is accompanied by its own proof.

Fig. 2. The proof-carrying smart contract update operation.

issues the transaction to the blockchain network as usual for mining (Step 2). The miner validates the proof against the code of the proposed child contract and produces a new block containing the safe update (Step 3). If the proof is invalid, the block will still record the attempted update as a transaction, but the safe update will fail with an exception (and consume gas to disincentivize spurious update requests). Finally, the rest of the blockchain network participants rerun and validate the SAFEUPDATE (Step 4), as they would any other transaction.

2.1   Proof-Carrying Smart Contracts in Detail

Here we describe the details that a realization of the PCSC architecture entails as well as discussion of generalizations to the architecture.

For many use cases, the parent contract will be nothing more than a thin wrapper for calls to the child contract, and perform no computation other than delegating its method calls. This means that proofs about the behavior of the parent should typically be compact, and in this way the parent contract resembles a formal specification for an API more than it does a fully-fledged smart contract in its own right. Similarly, in the PIMPL pattern, the child contract will typically have no persistent state of its own, operating instead on the state of the parent. If some persistent state is present, e.g., caching of expensive math operations, in the child, it must be guaranteed to not affect the global state invariants of the parent. This organization provides a clean separation of specification and implementation. In the Ethereum virtual machine, the parent contract would use a DELEGATECALL to the child contract, to ensure the contract operates on the parent contract state.

In addition to declaring the API specification and persistent state, the parent contract must declare the fields holding the addresses to the child contracts. At the source-code level, this is achieved with a specially declared setter that modifies the addresses. There are several options for ensuring the smart contract cannot subvert proof validation by modifying a child contract address without using the setter. For instance, runtime instrumentation of store operations can ensure nothing touches a child address field. Additionally, the specification itself can describe invariants about updates to the child address field. This latter option is more amenable to source code analysis, rather than byte code analysis, since we can prohibit arbitrary address computation.

We assume that the contract is not valid until provided an initial child contract. Exception handling can be encoded in the specification to ensure correct behavior if a client calls the parent contract before the initial update. As previously noted, the specification must always be robust to exceptions on platforms where computations (of potentially unpredictable length) must be paid for in advance (e.g. Ethereum). For our PIMPL-based examples, the parent has only one child contract, but it is straightforward to extend this to multiple contracts. The producer identifies the fields of each child contract and must provide proofs when updating each. Again, in our examples, the parent makes no other calls to contracts in our current formulation of simplified ERC20, but there is nothing fundamental preventing multiple child contracts, so long as each child address must be modified only with the safe update command that ensures a proof is provided with the update. Similarly, the child contract may also call yet more contracts, so long as proofs can be generated for their behavior.

As for altering the specification, a more flexible architecture can permit updates to the specification by the contract writer. This would be possible as long as the new specification implies the previous one, i.e., the specification can only become more strict.

Lastly, it is not necessary that the smart contract specification be decided by an individual. A common type of proposal and voting contract can be used to distribute decision-making. Participants can propose and vote on the specification, which is automatically installed by the voting contract. Furthermore, in cases where a specification is for standard behavior that might be incorporated into many contracts, we might imagine this proposal voting system be used to produce standardized APIs. In this way, all blockchain participants are both producers and consumers. Modifications to the specification, under the previously stated implication rule, could be decided in a similar way.

There are two sorts of upgrades that our proof-carrying code scheme permits. *Minor upgrades* can install a new child contract as long as the parent contract's safety policy is preserved. This is enforced by the proof verification performed by SAFEUPDATE. This permits safe upgrades without involving the slower consensus process required to decide on the safety policy. The proof verification makes this possible without having to trust the developer to maintain the safety policy. This enables upgrades due to minor bugs not covered by the safety policy or performance upgrades for instance. *Major upgrades* can alter the safety policy itself and require consensus among contract participants, e.g., via a proposal and voting system. Like the minor upgrade, the child contract implementation is replaced, but the new safety policy itself is also provided. The SAFEUPDATE verifies the new child contract against the new policy. This requires the new child contract author to generate a proof against the new safety policy.

The tradeoffs here are that maintainers can easily perform minor upgrades whose safety is ensured by the original safety policy of the contract, lowering obstacles to development. But the discovery of limitations of the safety policy itself or a desire for organizational changes may warrant an upgrade to the policy itself.

Let us assume the token contract Fig. 1a has been initially installed with only the invariants specified in Eqs. 1–5, i.e., the safety policy only guarantees the results of balance transfers, but does not account for the approve/transfer data race A minor upgrade, such as eliminating a superfluous call to a safe math library, can be performed, since it provably does not violate the safety policy. At a later point, the organization discovers the data race and agrees to update the safety policy to ensure future versions of the contract avoid it. This major update is accompanied with a revised implementation of the contract that satisfies the new invariants. Future contracts can then perform minor maintenance or performance upgrades, like removing safe math calls, that continue to satisfy the safety policy.

3   A Proposal for Specifications and Proofs

In recent years there has been substantial progress on formal verification of smart contracts at both the high-level Solidity language [15, 19] as well as low-level EVM bytecode [11, 12]. We aim to exploit this progress to enrich the blockchain so that (i) smart contract APIs come with formal specifications of how they should operate and (ii) proposed smart contract implementations can include proofs that they satisfy those specifications. In this section, we discuss sketch formal aspects, building on specification formats for objects [2, 3, 8, 13] and Necula's proof-carrying code [16].

As discussed in the prior section, our PCSCs involve two components. The *parent* part of a PCSC includes the smart contract's internal state, API methods, and formal specification. A (successfully deployed) *child* part of the PCSC includes the source code for all API methods, and a proof that the implementation satisfies the specification (found in the corresponding parent). We now provide more detail on each of these, using the running example.

3.1   Parent: APIs and Specifications

State and Methods. The parent in a PCSC includes the *state* in the form of object fields. It could include any of the smart contract language's data-types (integers, strings, Booleans, mappings, arrays, etc.). In the ERC20 running example, the state of the PCSC includes:

`balance` :	$Addr \mapsto \mathbb{N}$	Relate addresses to balances
`allowed` :	$Addr \mapsto (Addr \mapsto \mathbb{N})$	How much others can transfer
`child_ptr` :	$Addr$	Pointer to implementation

We have already discussed the purpose of `balance` (a mapping from addresses to tokens, represented as natural numbers) and `allowed` (a mapping from addresses to address-token mappings). The final element of the state above is a critical component of the PCSC parent. It is a pointer to the *child* part of the PCSC which will contain the implementation (discussed below).

The parent in a PCSC also includes the interface, in the form of methods that can be called by participants in the network. The bodies of these methods simply relay the call, following the `child_ptr` to the corresponding method in the child in the PCSC. Here is an example:

```
1  api_transfer(uint256 value, addr from) : bool {
2     return child_ptr.transfer(value, from);
3  }
```

This PIMPL paradigm means that the correctness of the parent contract follows immediately from that of the child (discussed below), modulo initialization concerns. In general, PCSCs needn't necessarily follow the PIMPL paradigm and it is easy to imagine other arrangements. For example, a contract may wish to specialize dispatch, in which case all child contracts would need to be proved correct. For simplicity, we focus on the common PIMPL case in the remainder of this paper.

$\{I\}$
`api_transfer(uint256 value, addr from) : bool`
$$\left\{ \begin{array}{l} I \wedge \Sigma_a \text{ `balance}(a) = \Sigma_a \text{ balance}(a) \\ \quad \wedge \text{ `allowed(from)}(me) \geq \text{value} \\ \qquad \Rightarrow \text{allowed} = \text{`allowed[from,} me \mapsto \text{`allowed(from)}(me) - \text{value]} \wedge \text{rv} = \text{true} \\ \quad \wedge \text{ `allowed(from)}(me) \leq \text{value} \Rightarrow \text{allowed} = \text{`allowed} \wedge \text{rv} = \text{false} \end{array} \right\}$$

$\{I\}$
`api_allowance(addr whom) : uint256`
$\{I \wedge \Sigma_a \text{ `balance}(a) = \Sigma_a \text{ balance}(a) \wedge \rho_{me}(\text{whom}) = \text{allowed}(me)(\text{whom})\}$

$\{I\}$
`api_approve(uint256 value, addr whom) : bool`
$$\left\{ \begin{array}{l} I \wedge \Sigma_a \text{ `balance}(a) = \Sigma_a \text{ balance}(a) \\ \quad \wedge (\text{`allowed}(me)(\text{whom}) = \rho_{me}(\text{whom}) \\ \qquad \Rightarrow \text{allowed} = \text{`allowed[}me, \text{whom} \mapsto \text{value]} \wedge \text{rv} = \text{true}) \\ \quad \wedge (\text{`allowed}(me)(\text{whom}) \neq \rho_{me}(\text{whom}) \Rightarrow \text{allowed} = \text{`allowed} \wedge \text{rv} = \text{false}) \end{array} \right\}$$

where I is the global invariant, defined to be:

$$\forall a.\text{balance}(a) \geq 0 \wedge \forall a \, b.\text{allowed}(a)(b) \geq 0 \wedge \forall a.\text{balance}(a) \geq \Sigma_b \text{ allowed}(a)(b)$$

Fig. 3. Formal specification φ (in blue) for some of the ERC20 token standard (Color figure online).

Formal Specifications. The parent in the PCSC also contains the specification φ of how the overall PCSC is intended to behave. As we will discuss later, a candidate child implementation C is required to include a proof that $C \vDash \varphi$.

Figure 3 provides an example specification φ for a portion of the (simplified) ERC20 token standard that we are using as a running example. Each method API includes standard Floyd-Hoare style *pre*-conditions as well as *post*-conditions, depicted in blue. For a given method, say, `api_transfer`, the meaning is that, if we assume that the associated pre-condition holds before `api_transfer` executes, then a correct implementation will ensure that the corresponding post-condition must hold upon completion. (We assume that every method will terminate, because the smart contract architecture enforces termination through "gas.") Each pre/post-condition includes I which is a global invariant on the state of the PCSC. I is defined at the bottom of Fig. 3. There are three conditions given by I: that all balances are non-negative, all allowances are non-negative, and that, for a given address a the sum of all outstanding allowances is bounded by a's balance (respectively). The latter condition corresponds to Eqs. 3–5 in Sect. 1.

In the specification for `api_transfer`, *me* is used to denote the caller's address and notation '`allowed` indicates the value of `allowed` before the method executed. The post-condition for `api_transfer` includes a stipulation that the sum of all participants' `balances` is unchanged (corresponding to Eqs. 1 and 2 in Sect. 1). We use a as a quantifier variable over each participant's address. The post-condition includes two further cases, depending on whether the transfer request is permitted by `allowed`. If it is permitted, then the value of `allowed` is the same as '`allowed`, except that the appropriate slot is decremented. Otherwise, `allowed` is unchanged. `rv` indicates the return value of the method.

Specification for `approve`. The published ERC20 standard has a well-publicized flaw, demonstrated by the naïve implementation in Fig. 1a, which is that calls to `approve` a new allowance do not impose any particular semantic requirements on the previous value. Thus an account holder may inspect the blockchain, and see a current allowance value and attempt to reduce it at the same time that another transaction is issued to transfer some of it. Since pending transactions are subject to arbitrary reordering by the miner, the transfer may execute first, and altered allowance may have the net effect of raising the total that can be transferred.

Conceptually, we wish to add another invariant: the allowance may not be altered unless the allowance is known *when the transaction executes* (this may be different than the value it had when the transaction was issued). The implementation shown in Fig. 1b patches this vulnerability by requiring that a new positive allowance can only be set if the allowance is currently being set to 0 (either by `transfers` or by `approves`). This blocks the data race, but also forces the account holder to pay for unnecessary transactions when a competing transaction is *not pending*.

Multiprocessor architectures address similar data race problems with atomic instructions such as *compare-and-swap*. To fix the ERC20 API, however, it is more convenient to mimic the functionality of *load-linked* (LL) and *store-conditional* (SC) instructions. LL loads a value from memory, and SC writes a new value to the same location, if and only if it has not been written since the matching LL.

Our specification in Fig. 3 includes the requirement that `allowance` is known at the time of approval, using a ghost variable. The specification for `api_-allowance` uses ghost variable ρ in the post-condition. This variable tracks the fact that the caller (me) has checked how much recipient `whom` is currently permitted to transfer. ρ_{me} can become out-of-date if the recipient makes a call to `transfer`, and this will be the saving grace in the specification of `api_approve`. In the specification for `api_approve`, `allowed` is updated, approving a pending recipient `whom` to receive `value`. The two cases depend on whether ghost variable $\rho_{me}(\text{whom})$ is up-to-date, indicating that me is aware of how much has been approved.

In the next subsection, we will discuss how the implementation using strategy employed in Fig. 1c can be proved to satisfy this specification.

3.2 Child: Proposed Implementations and Proofs

Miners propose the child portion of a PCSC: an implementation C, coupled with a proof that the implementation satisfies the specification φ housed in the parent. We now discuss what the child portion of the PCSC entails.

Implementation C. The implementation C of each API method (`transfer`, `allowance`, etc.) is housed in the child PCSC such that, if C can be shown to satisfy φ, then the child will be installed and these implementations will be accessed via `child_ptr.transfer()`, etc.

Proof that $C \vDash \varphi$. How can we be 100% sure that this proposed implementation in Fig. 1c operates correctly? The child portion of a PCSC includes a proof that code C satisfies the corresponding parent's specification φ.

The Floyd-Hoare style pre/post specifications shown above can be verified to hold of an implementation using verification conditions as seen in tools such as Spec# [3], Boogie [2], Dafny [13], Why3 [8], etc. Intuitively, the format of the proofs are, for each line of each method, invariants that must hold at that line (more precisely: the invariant comes just before or just after the line). Finding these invariants is difficult (searching for a proof). Checking these invariants, however, is much faster: a symbolic analysis can traverse the method, starting by ensuring that the first invariant holds from the pre-condition and effect of the first line of code. When the analysis reaches the end of the method, it checks that the post-condition is entailed by the penultimate invariant and last line of code.

PCSCs allow us to prevent buggy implementations like `approve` in Fig. 1a from being accepted onto the blockchain, but permit correct implementations like Fig. 1c. There is no proof that Fig. 1a satisfies the specification in Fig. 3. On the other hand, a proof can easily be given for Fig. 1c, which is a simplified case where there are only two participants and variable `allowed_known` is used to ensure the correct behavior of `approve`.

3.3 Verification Tool Development

In our ongoing work, we are developing verification tools for PCSC, building on recent works for verification of solidity [15,19] and EVM [11,12].

Ultimately, the proofs published to the blockchain need to be expressed in terms of the bytecode, to avoid dependencies on a specific verified compiler. Fortunately, others have developed formal semantics for EVM bytecode [11,12]. Down the road, we plan to extend work on certified compilation [14] to translate source-level correctness guarantees to bytecode guarantees. However, there are already verification challenges at the source code level, being tackled by us and others [15,19].

4   Related Work

Ethereum's [7] *ERC20* token standard [21] is widely used as the basis for many recent *initial coin offerings*. Vladimirov and Khovratovich [20] give a clear description of the ERC20 design flaw discussed here.

The notion that proofs should be included with code first appears in Necula's seminal proof-carrying code paper [16]. As mentioned, we make use of the functionality of the Why3 platform [4]. Hicks and Nettles [10] pioneered the idea of using PCC for dynamic software updates.

There is other work that investigates vulnerabilities in smart contracts. For example, Luu *et al.* [15] develop a software tool called Oyente, which detects security bugs in Ethereum contracts. Atzei *et al.* [1] describe common pitfalls that lead to security vulnerabilities, and demonstrate how they can be exploited. Sergey and Hobor [17] analyze smart contract vulnerabilities by drawing comparisons between contract execution and concurrent shared-memory computing. Grossman *et al.* [9] discuss a dynamic approach.

5   Conclusion and Future Work

This paper describes preliminary work attempting to reconcile the apparent contradiction between the immutability of idealized smart contracts and the real-world need to update contracts to fix bugs and oversights. Our proposed solution is to raise the contract's level of abstraction to guarantee an invariant φ instead of a particular implementation of that invariant. A combination of proof-carrying code and proof-aware consensus allows contract implementations to be updated as needed, but so as to guarantee that φ cannot be violated by any future upgrade.

Much remains to be done on proof-carrying smart contracts. The work reported here is still in an early stage, and we are not yet far enough along to report on progress or difficulties.

Future goals include formally modeling proof-carrying smart contracts and creating an implementation as an extension of the Ethereum blockchain and virtual machine. A formal specification will permit proofs of guarantees that proof-carrying smart contracts provide. Additionally, we intend to investigate how consensus integrates with these proofs and perhaps extend the model consensus to include them. Extending smart contracts with specifications requires defining extensions to the smart contract implementation language and the bytecode to represent the specifications as well as mappings from source code to bytecode specifications. For generating and validating proofs, we plan to use off-the-shelf tools, such as Why3. Our language extensions and the proof tools need to be integrated with the smart contract toolchain and virtual machine itself.

For implementation, we intend to extend the contract virtual machine with new opcodes to add new contracts with specifications as well as update them given a new proof. To enable this, we will extend the binary format of smart contract to encode specifications and proofs. Using these changes in an existing chain would require a hard fork to extend the binary format and virtual machine. With proof-carrying smart contracts in hand, we will use them to improve the ERC20 token standard, demonstrated with example implementations, and show how contract writers can take advantage of these.

Proof-carrying smart contracts open up new research questions. For instance, how do we integrate proofs into blockchain consensus and how do mining and consensus mechanisms, such as proof-of-work and proof-of-stake, interact with formal proofs? Formal verification enables trust for updates, but consensus mechanisms are still needed to agree on what the right specifications are. For instance, contract participants can vote on changes to the specifications, but allow formal verification to eliminate the need for voting on implementation changes.

The ability of formal verification to support trusted computing has the potential to improve how consensus is achieved, and proof-carrying smart contracts are an important step in integrating proofs with blockchain.

References

1. Atzei, N., Bartoletti, M., Cimoli, T.: A survey of attacks on ethereum smart contracts (SoK). In: Maffei, M., Ryan, M. (eds.) POST 2017. LNCS, vol. 10204, pp. 164–186. Springer, Heidelberg (2017). https://doi.org/10.1007/978-3-662-54455-6_8
2. Barnett, M., Chang, B.-Y.E., DeLine, R., Jacobs, B., Leino, K.R.M.: Boogie: a modular reusable verifier for object-oriented programs. In: de Boer, F.S., Bonsangue, M.M., Graf, S., de Roever, W.-P. (eds.) FMCO 2005. LNCS, vol. 4111, pp. 364–387. Springer, Heidelberg (2006). https://doi.org/10.1007/11804192_17
3. Barnett, M., Leino, K.R.M., Schulte, W.: The spec# programming system: an overview. In: Barthe, G., Burdy, L., Huisman, M., Lanet, J.-L., Muntean, T. (eds.) CASSIS 2004. LNCS, vol. 3362, pp. 49–69. Springer, Heidelberg (2005). https://doi.org/10.1007/978-3-540-30569-9_3
4. Bobot, F., Filliâtre, J.C., Marché, C., Melquiond, G., Paskevich, A.: The Why3 platform. http://why3.lri.fr/manual.pdf. Accessed 14 Jan 2018
5. Daian, P., Breidenbach, L.: Parity proposals' potential problems. http://hackingdistributed.com/2017/12/13/ether-resurrection/. Accessed 14 Jan 2018
6. DAO: the DAO smart contract. Accessed 8 Feb 2017
7. Ethereum. https://github.com/ethereum/. Accessed 14 Jan 2018
8. Filliâtre, J.-C., Paskevich, A.: Why3—where programs meet provers. In: Felleisen, M., Gardner, P. (eds.) ESOP 2013. LNCS, vol. 7792, pp. 125–128. Springer, Heidelberg (2013). https://doi.org/10.1007/978-3-642-37036-6_8

9. Grossman, S., et al.: Online detection of effectively callback free objects with applications to smart contracts. In: ACM SIGPLAN Symposium on Principles of Programming Languages (POPL) (2018)
10. Hicks, M., Nettles, S.: Dynamic software updating. ACM Trans. Program. Lang. Syst. **27**(6), 1049–1096 (2005). https://doi.org/10.1145/1108970.1108971
11. Hildenbrandt, E., et al.: KEVM: a complete semantics of the ethereum virtual machine. Technical report (2017)
12. Hirai, Y.: Defining the ethereum virtual machine for interactive theorem provers. In: Brenner, M., et al. (eds.) FC 2017. LNCS, vol. 10323, pp. 520–535. Springer, Cham (2017). https://doi.org/10.1007/978-3-319-70278-0_33
13. Leino, K.R.M.: Dafny: an automatic program verifier for functional correctness. In: Clarke, E.M., Voronkov, A. (eds.) LPAR 2010. LNCS (LNAI), vol. 6355, pp. 348–370. Springer, Heidelberg (2010). https://doi.org/10.1007/978-3-642-17511-4_20
14. Leroy, X., et al.: The CompCert verified compiler. Documentation and user's manual, INRIA Paris-Rocquencourt (2012)
15. Luu, L., Chu, D.H., Olickel, H., Saxena, P., Hobor, A.: Making smart contracts smarter. In: Proceedings of the 2016 ACM SIGSAC Conference on Computer and Communications Security. CCS 2016, pp. 254–269. ACM, New York (2016). https://doi.org/10.1145/2976749.2978309
16. Necula, G.C.: Proof-carrying code. In: Proceedings of the 24th ACM SIGPLAN-SIGACT Symposium on Principles of Programming Languages. POPL 1997, pp. 106–119. ACM, New York (1997). https://doi.org/10.1145/263699.263712
17. Sergey, I., Hobor, A.: A concurrent perspective on smart contracts. CoRR abs/1702.05511 (2017). http://arxiv.org/abs/1702.05511
18. Sirer, E.G.: Parity's Wallet Bug is not Alone (2017). https://blogs.apache.org/foundation/entry/apache-struts-statement-on-equifax. Accessed 05 Nov 2017
19. Various: formal verification for solidity contracts. https://forum.ethereum.org/discussion/3779/formal-verification-for-solidity-contracts. Accessed 14 Jul 2018
20. Vladimirov, M., Khovratovich, D.: ERC20 API: an attack vector on approve/transferfrom methods. https://docs.google.com/document/d/1YLPtQxZu1UAvO9cZ1O2RPXBbT0mooh4DYKjA_jp-RLM/edit#heading=h.m9fhqynw2xvt. Accessed: 14 Jan 2018
21. The Ethereum Wiki: ERC20 token standard. https://theethereum.wiki/w/index.php/ERC20_Token_Standard. Accessed 14 Jan 2018

Comparative Analysis of the Legal Concept of Title Rights in Real Estate and the Technology of Tokens: How Can Titles Become Tokens?

Oleksii Konashevych[(✉)]

Obolonskij Avenue, 2a, apt. 69, Kiev 04210, Ukraine

Abstract. This paper discusses how to use blockchain tokens to represent real estate titles. Tokens on the blockchain as a technological concept is the closest solution to the legal concept of titles, because it provides for evidence of ownership and can be transferred from one address to another, while giving exclusive access to such an address to the owner. This paper contains the analysis of the concept of tokens in the context of its applicability to title rights on real estate. There is also a discussion of the outcomes of conducted interviews with professionals in the field of Computer Science, technologies, blockchain and smart contracts. Some critical mismatches were found: tokens are not able to satisfy current demand to manage title rights online. To develop a mature and sustainable electronic system, there are certain issues that need to be addressed: inheritance procedures, litigation, guardianship, delegation of rights and rights of third parties (liens and encumbrances) as well as the legal concept of bundle of rights (possession, disposition, enjoyment, etc.), which requires a strong mathematical model. During the abovementioned interviews, some weaknesses were found in the existing ideas of the use of the blockchain for real estate, mostly related to the undesirable centralization and issues with security. As the result of this research, it is obvious what needs to be developed is the concept of a high-level design of the technology, capable of managing title rights on the blockchain, which includes a three-level mechanism of (1) e-voting, which provides for a democratic implementation of governing algorithms; (2) Smart Laws, as the concept of high level "smart" algorithms that implement (by e-voting) existing laws related to property rights in a form of the program/protocol; and (3) smart contract templates which are based on the smart laws, that allow people to manage their title rights online.

Keywords: Blockchain · Smart contracts · Titles · Real estate · Tokens · E-Governance · E-Voting · E-Democracy

O. Konashevych—Erasmus Mundus Joint International Doctoral Fellow in Law, Science and Technology.
Supervisors: Prof. Marta Poblet Balcell and Prof. Pompeu Casanovas.

A. Zohar et al. (Eds.): FC 2018 Workshops, LNCS 10958, pp. 339–351, 2019.
https://doi.org/10.1007/978-3-662-58820-8_23

1   Introduction

A [crypto] token is a record of a number which is kept by a specific address on the blockchain and can be divided (usually up to 8 decimals) and transferred to another address within the ledger of the blockchain system [1, 2]. For the purposes of this paper, we do not distinguish between tokens and cryptocurrency. However, tokens have more features and may be considered as a technological evolution of the cryptocurrency, presented by someone who called himself Satoshi Nakamoto [1].

A few principal features make tokens ideal for the management of property rights:

1. The blockchain protocol is designed to make transactions – the transfer of tokens from one address to another, while not allowing double spending [1, 3].
2. Such address provides for exclusive access, because only a person who has a cryptographic private key may manage the token.
3. The blockchain ledger is a complete, transparent history of records, which allows a person to track each token from the moment of creation, including fractional transactions (decimals and less than 1) and transactions between any number of addresses.

The three next features make tokens principally different and more developed compared to a traditional, centralized way of making ledgers that is typical for banks and public registries:

1. The technology offers a decentralized way of keeping records; no one keeps all of the power in his hand, and that prevents usurpation of power and corruption.
2. The immutability and the non-returnability of transactions, which means that it is practically unfeasible to delete or alter a record or in any other way to corrupt it.
3. The next generation of blockchains (after Bitcoin) offers algorithms to introduce a high level of automation and security for the management of tokens and at the same time, excludes the necessity of a human to operate it manually (See all critical features in a diagram on Fig. 1).

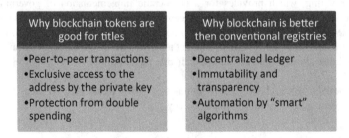

Fig. 1. Critical features of the blockchain for the managing of titles

Ethereum [4] and NXT [5] are examples of blockchain-based platforms that develop such automated systems. However, they stand on different ideological grounds. Ethereum is a Turing-complete programming language platform [6] for the developing of so-called "smart contracts" [7], and NXT suggests ready-to-use user services implemented into the core of the blockchain protocol with no need to develop applications.

The mentioned features of the blockchain technology with smart contracts can be considered as an alternative technology to existing centralized land (real estate/cadastral) registries and a way to protect and manage title rights.

However, technological concepts appeared to be non-synchronized with legal concepts. In the following sections, it is shown why titles are not tokens, and what should be developed to introduce the world to a sustainable electronic system, able to improve the way how relations on real estate ownership is organized now.

2   Comparative Analysis of the Legal Concept of Title Rights and the Technology Tokens

The legal concept of titles and the technology of tokens have much in common, along with differences.

A "title" is an evidence of ownership. The title represents the property rights of an estate; this is an equivalent of estate (land, for example), but on paper, which is legally recognized. The crypto-token is a technology that has the same purposes – the token can represent values and prove ownership. The only difference is that titles of real estate have a long tradition and legacy of regulation, and there is no place for tokens in the existing laws. That is why transactions that are made with real estate tokens will not have any legal consequences.

Title deeds must be *acknowledged* in some countries before a notary, in some - before other authorized persons, and *recorded* in the public registry. Thus, the use of tokens for real estate requires legislative changes that legitimize new procedures of acknowledgement and recording on the blockchain.

The title can be divisible, that is, what in the language of law means co-ownership, joint ownership, community property (also known as marital property) and some other concepts that exist in different jurisdictions. There are two main aspects of property rights: the type of ownership, and a set of specific rules which co-owners must follow to respect the rights of other co-owners.

In the theory of law, there are two basic types of co-property: it may belong to persons on the right of common share, or on the right of common joint ownership. In common share, there are no fractions; the property belongs to all co-owners equally (spouses, condominium owners, etc.). In joint ownership, owners have shares (1/2, 1/3 etc.).

As to a set of rules, the law and the agreement may establish some specific rules which co-owners must follow. For, example, there is a typical rule that one co-owner cannot convey his share in the title without the consent of the other owners. The other owners have the right to buy the share for the same price as the owner wants to sell it.

The common property may become joint ownership. In the case, for example, that spouses divorce in some jurisdictions, they become 50/50 co-owners.

Different jurisdictions may have some specifics in co-ownership law, as well as individual may have agreements between co-owners to establish specific rules. All these rules in general can be represented in the theory of "property rights," which is further discussed.

That is why when we are talking about tokens, it is clear that at least two layers of technology solutions must be applied to tokens: the first is a set of algorithms that establish general rules (laws) specific for certain jurisdictions, and the second, individual rules based on contracts, that do not contradict general rules.

However, co-owners are not the only category of third parties that can influence the property rights of an owner. There are two other categories of third parties:

- third parties which are not owners but have interests in the property (the property rights of third parties) as per the law or agreement; and
- third parties that have no interests but have legal access to the property and may influence it (judge, notary, parents, custodian, town's clerk (registrar) etc.).

The concept of property rights includes a bundle of rights: the right to dispose, the right to possess and the right to use (enjoy)[1]. The owner is free to manage these rights and deeds that he concludes influence this bundle (See Fig. 2 "Components of ownership: bundle of rights").

Fig. 2. Components of ownership: bundle of rights

For example, when an owner rents out his property, he transfers his right to possess and own the property to the third party – the tenant. At the same time, he as a landlord is restricted in these rights (to possess and to use) while the contract is valid. He is also restricted in his right to dispose of the property in the sense of allowing the use of the property by others. However, he keeps the right to convey the title (for example, to sell it). So, if he sells the property, the tenant keeps the rights to possess and to use the estate (unless otherwise provided by the contract), and a new title owner is granted with the same restrictions. There also can be other limits to dispose: in a mortgage, the owner is not able to convey the title without the agreement of the creditor.

---

[1] There are a couple of main theories about property rights, and they vary from 3 to 5 main rights: possession, disposition, enjoyment (use), control, exclusion etc. However, they do not have principal differences for this stage of research, and so it is not critical to make a choice now which theory fits best to design the technology. Our aim here is just to argue that these kinds of legal concepts create the necessity to find a solution to develop the technology.

As we see, the concept of property rights is complex, and the situation is more complicated by the existence of different jurisdictions and traditions of law. We see an essential need to present a mathematical model of property rights that matches the concept of tokens driven by smart contracts, taking into account all specifics the comes from the blockchain technology, i.e. immutability of records and smart contracts, so all necessary high-level features must be developed by design not on the run. So, the mathematical model will become a metamodel for designing systems oriented on certain legal systems and jurisdictions.

There is also another category that has no interests in property, but acts in the interest of owners and other persons and may change property rights.

The judicial system allows interested parties to contest rights in court, so judges and then bailiffs are those who can change the title and property rights and enforce these things.

Another important group of third parties is a notary public. Notaries execute wills and apply inheritance laws.

Another case of the disposition of estate without the will of an owner are parents' rights, guardianship, and custodianship in respect of the rights of minors and disabled persons.

Parents, guardians, and custodians have the rights to act in the name of minors and disabled persons, including the right to dispose of estates and acquire property rights. Their rights may be unlimited or regulated by law and revised by a public body (custodian committees/boards, etc.).

The delegation of rights by contract is another case when the title is operated by the third party. In contrast to parents/custodians this delegation is not by law but by an agreement. The exact volume of rights is defined by law and by a contract and usually is confirmed by the power of attorney.

The last case when a title is under the influence of third parties, is when it is under the obligation to obtain permission from the public body to convey the property. There can be variety of reasons to do so. In this way, a government can:

- prevent illegal construction on the land;
- enforce owners to pay taxes before selling the property;
- oblige an appraisal of real estate (for some categories of owners, like state enterprises); or a
- local community may protect its right to not let unwanted people live in their territory.

Therefore, the approval and certain legal actions must be performed before a deed.

Another case which requires further development is the separation and merging of titles. That happens when adjoined plots of land are united into one title or a plot is divided. So, the mechanism to separate and merge the tokens by linking them to a new survey[2] is also required for a prospective electronic system.

---

[2] Surveying or land surveying is the technique of determining the terrestrial or three-dimensional positions of points and the distances and angles between embodied on the plan of the plot.

None of this is implemented in the existing electronic solutions, and yet needs to be designed in the system that aims to provide a full range of legal instruments to manage property rights by smart contracts.

3   The High-Level Design of the System

In preparation for this paper, 4 interviews were conducted and an analysis was made of existing projects related to the blockchain and real estate, and some typical cases of ICOs.

Those interviewed were: (1) Vassilis Vutsadakis, Ph.D. in Science and Technology, Researcher at Propy[3] (Blockchain Supermarket for Real Estate); (2) Matt McKibbin, Masters of Science in Industrial Hygiene, Co-founder and Business Development Director of "Ubitquity, LLC."[4] (the blockchain-secured platform for real estate recordkeeping), Founder and Chief Decentralization Officer of "DecentraNet" (blockchain consulting); (3) Mykhailo Tiutin, Masters in Information Security, Co-Founder/CTO of "Vareger" (Blockchain Developer, Ukraine)[5], smart contracts and blockchain developer, cryptographer and IT security expert; (4) Vadim Sukhomlinov, Masters in Computer Science, Software Engineer/Architect at Intel Corporation.

The research includes the analysis of projects that develop different solutions in blockchain and real estate domain.

- Velox.re[6] (USA, since 2016) is ongoing startup that aims to digitize the process of purchase in Cook County on Illinois state by creating a Bitcoin based platform that unites professionals (intermediaries) of real estate industry around the world [8–10].
- Ubitquity.io[7] (USA, since 2015) develops services on e-recording companies, title companies, municipalities, and custom clients to record of ownership [11].
- Bitland[8] (Ghana, since 2016) is a partner of Ubitquity.io and currently is developing solutions for Real Estate Land Registration services to citizens of Ghana as well as companies and farm unions [12, 13].
- Chromaway[9] (Sweden, since 2016) is piloting the first project to model a property purchase using the blockchain and smart contract technology [14].
- Flip[10] (USA, since 2016) is a peer-to-peer leasing marketplace in New York city [15];

---

[3] http://propy.com/.

[4] https://www.ubitquity.io/web/index.html.

[5] https://vareger.com/.

[6] https://www.velox.re/.

[7] https://www.ubitquity.io/web/index.html.

[8] http://bitlandglobal.com/.

[9] https://chromaway.com.

[10] https://flip.lease/.

- REX[11] (USA, since 2016) is a peer to peer MLS[12] built on Ethereum. REX aims to connect vendors, buyers and agents over an open network by using the blockchain cryptocurrencies [16].
- Bitfury[13] (Republic of Georgia, since 2016; Ukraine, since 2017) proposed a solution to protect records of the central cadastral registry by casting hashes of such records to the blockchain, mixing by fact two blockchain technologies: private DLT[14] EXONUM and Bitcoin [17, 18].
- Xinyuan Real Estate Co.[15] (China, since 2016), a company that declared its interest in the blockchain in the cooperation with IBM to develop a smart city in China [19].
- Propy, Inc.[16] (USA, since 2016), a company that develops the supermarket for real estate and platform for deeds based on Ethereum smart contracts.

Now let us summarize the aforesaid and the first section and discuss how to design the system in the best way. While doing interviews and researching, we distinguished some solutions which are not acceptable from our point of view. So, let us discuss first what we should not do and why.

The first is to use the blockchain as a database of records that reflects acts made offline. The blockchain in this case in not a primary source of evidence, but collects everything that is happening offline (on papers) or in the central database. Each new record is not necessary valid, but it helps to find the truth in a court while considering all possible paper evidences. We don't see much benefit in using the blockchain in this way because the central public registry does the same. The only thing the blockchain does is it protects against altering records, while a well-designed and protected central database can do the same. What is more important here, is that it does not require changes in the existing bureaucratic systems. But our aim is to find a better system that can reduce regulations and manual work.

Another sub-option of this approach is just to store hashes on the blockchain of records made in the central database, which is almost the same, but does give more protection to the database against corruption, and adds a new bureaucratic procedure [20].

In this concept, a private company or a public body keeps copies of private keys, and/or use multi signatures (escrow mechanism) [21]. In case the token is stolen, the company will announce it invalid and reissue a new token (we remember that we cannot alter the transaction, so if it is stolen we cannot do anything), so the company

---

[11] http://rexmls.com/.

[12] MLS is a standard of listing real estate and services of brokers, http://www.mls.com/.

[13] http://bitfury.com/.

[14] DLT is a Distributed Ledger Technology which means shared ledger technologies similar but not equal to the blockchain.

[15] http://www.prnewswire.com/news-releases/xinyuan-real-estate-co-ltd-announces-blockchain-powe-red-real-estate-finance-technology-platform-300299818.html.

[16] www.propy.com.

needs to manually track the list of tokens[17] and its validity. We see that this concept does not bring much value compared to the existing approaches because it is still centralized. There are too many examples of even large and well secured companies being hacked and losing personal data. A private company can lose not only the private keys of users, but also their own keys; they can also be corrupted or even become bankrupt, which is especially an undesirable risk for people whose real estate is the only wealth they have.

In the case that we use the public body instead of a private entity, we will have more trust and more authority, but at the same time, we will create the same high-level regulations and bureaucracy.

Another arguable solution found was a creation of an electronic compliance system. For each transaction of a token, the owner uses a specific smart contract. As we remember, the smart contract is not a contract in the common sense, but just an electronic algorithm. For example, for a purchase: the program holds the transaction of the token until the buyer pays.

In real life, the contract is not a self-sufficient and closed legal act. The contract reflects the agreement of parties as to essential conditions, but laws at the same time provide for norms that are not necessarily included in the agreement, and are followed as if they were in the contract.

Sometimes it is almost impossible to include all of the provisions in the contract. So, the contract may only refer to the law, or even just presume that a law or a general practice will be applied to a missing part of the contract. A smart contract, which is a sort of a closed system, in this sense is flawed because cannot be influenced by external factors (like the law).

One solution is to use electronic compliance systems. Before a transaction, the compliance system will verify the token and the parties. In this case, we must ensure that such a system is good enough to protect the rights of parties according to the local jurisdiction and is not corrupted, which bring us similar issues to that of the previous example with the private company that manages keys and records.

Considering these items, we see that the best way to proceed is to develop the system so that the government will adopt it, is to implement by design existing specifics of jurisdictions according to the concept "code is law."[18] The code implements required provisions from the legislation, and in case something goes wrong, parties will use mechanisms of litigation and arbitration.

Algorithms adopted by the government will be a higher layer for smart contracts and will work as obligatory standards. Let us call these "smart laws." Smart laws will establish rules and mechanism of access of third parties to tokens and some basics principles of work (that reflect existing "paper" regulations).

---

[17] During the research we also found some ideas not to use tokens, but only to make deed records on the blockchain. However, the same as with tokens it requires a third party manually to track all legal facts which are occurred with the title and reflect its validity in case it has been recognized as invalid.

[18] The expression "code is law" was proposed by Lawrence Lessig in his Book "Code and Other Laws of Cyberspace" (1999).

Combining this system with the concept of oracles[19], which is proposed by Buterin [22], we will be able to keep track of authorized persons: the list of addresses of public notaries, judges, bailiffs, custodians, etc., that may perform transactions.

Any smart contract designed based on these smart laws will be able to provide the whole range of legal instruments, and if the situation with ownership and property rights is stuck, parties will be able to settle it in a court.

For example, the smart contract does not "know" when the owner dies; that is why we need an oracle that tracks records on a public demographic registry, and will trigger inheritance mechanisms of the smart contract. In this case a "smart will" would be executed.

If the person did not leave a will, general rules "smart laws" will be applied. The smart contract also does not "know" which notary will manage the distribution of the inheritance. That is why the oracle will provide the valid list of addresses of notaries, and only a transaction that comes from the address on the trusted list will be executed by the system.

Smart laws will provide necessary rules to run public oracles. Oracles require manual management: someone must add records in the demographic registry, update the notaries list, the custodians list, etc. But now this is performed by the government anyway; the only question is how well enough it is digitized and protected from corruption and fraud.

Oracles assume a certain degree of centralization or at least we cannot think of it as a pure distributed system (as the blockchain is) because it requires actions of third parties. The fact is that it is merely possible with reasonable efforts on this stage of development of science and technology to automate and digitalize everything. For, example, how to digitize the fact of human's death and make it a system event that triggers smart contract execution? Someone must certify plenty of facts that occur in real world that have legal meaning for property rights.

The centralization is not a threat it is only an environment where risks of corruption and excessive regulations arise from. Therefore, the question is how such oracles are well designed to protect from these risks.

To protect smart laws that run oracles from the corruption, they must not allow any backdoor access of someone specific to change them. The code, once deployed, must remain unchanged. And here the blockchain plays a significant role, because as we see with the example of a "smart contract," we can deploy completely transparent and verifiable applications protected from someone's manual control.

These closed, decentralized applications can work permanently secured from an alteration, and this is a benefit and a limit at the same time. The only way to change something here is to change the code of the blockchain protocol, which as we know requires a large consensus (usually 50+1% of nodes must support a "hard fork").

---

[19] i.e. special servers, from which a smart contract receives reliable information from outside the smart contract.

However, we still must have access to update the system. That is why at the upper level will be algorithms of electronic voting on the blockchain. Voting will be a public democratic mechanism of the control over smart laws systems and protect them from the corruption.

If someone's token is stolen, an authorized third party from the public oracles list will bring back access. But in case any of the public oracles are compromised, i.e. hacked, or keys are lost, or similar threats when oracles become technically uncontrolled or controlled and corrupted by unauthorized persons, the general public and/or specially governed body (committee) by the voting mechanism will recall and reissue private keys to the operator of the oracle.

Finally, we have the mechanism of 4 layers of a democratic electronic governance (see Fig. 3):

- **Blockchain.** On the top we have a public blockchain which protocol remains unchanged by the consensus of node owners. It is important to have as many as possible of the active citizens that share their resources to the network. Good Samaritans will give a critical mass of consensus that will not allow changing of the protocol. The software and the consensus mechanism must be affordable to allow as many as possible "good Samaritans" to have their nodes. In this sense Proof-of-Work is not good, since the mining rush leads to high costs of entrance into the business. And of course, the blockchain must be public, so anyone can become a part of the network and receive crypto currency for its work.
- **E-Voting** is an irrevocable mechanism for voting on implementing smart laws, as nobody can change this mechanism, except to change the blockchain protocol (which requires consensus). Ballots are recorded on the blockchain, and the result of the voting automatically triggers mechanism of implementation of a smart law.

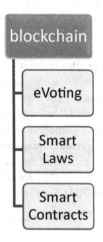

Fig. 3. The layers of the blockchain governing

- **Smart laws** – the mechanism that controls public oracles and other basic mechanisms of the operating of tokens. Oracles keep lists of addresses that are authorized to change the status of smart contracts (judicial system, public notary, social system of custodian and guardianship).
- **Smart contracts** (templates of smart contracts) – owners will be able to use specific templates for their tokens (smart will, purchase, rent, mortgage). Each jurisdiction can use specific rules to introduce smart contracts. One of the possible scenarios is that in each state, local professionals (lawyer, notaries etc.) and IT developers will develop necessary templates of smart contracts in accordance with local jurisdiction. However, another way is when the government takes this process in its hands and introduces smart contract templates as model solutions (similar to "Model Company Charter"[20].

4 Conclusion

Tokens on the blockchain as a technological concept is the closest solution to the issues of the legal concept of real estate titles. This paper distinguished the principal features that make the blockchain suitable for title rights and transactions: tokens can represent property rights, the technology protects from double spending while allowing for conveyance, addresses that store records of tokens are designed in a way to provide for exclusive access to such addresses to the owner and immutably of records which protect from corruption and fraud. The blockchain technology addresses the inherent issues of conventional governing since it works in a decentralized manner. With the second generation of blockchains that integrate smart contracts and similar algorithms, one can automate tokens/titles management, which reduces the participation of third parties (brokers, notaries, agents) or even governments to manually control the relations in the real estate domain. All these features make the technology applicable to significantly improve relations in real estate and governance.

This paper presented analysis of the concept of tokens in the context of its applicability to the legal concept of title rights on real estate, there is also a discussion of the outcomes of the conducted interviews with professionals in the field of Computer Science, technologies, blockchain and smart contracts. It was found some critical mismatches: tokens are not able to satisfy current demand to manage title rights online. To develop mature and sustainable electronic system there are certain issues to be addressed: inheritance procedures, litigation, guardianship, delegation of rights and rights of third parties (liens and encumbrances) as well as the legal concept of bundle of rights (possession, disposition, enjoyment, etc.), which requires strong mathematical

---

[20] In many countries, governments adopt a "Model Company Charter" which people may use when they list a new company, so they do not need to write articles of incorporation (statute, charter) from scratch, but just to refer to this model paper which they submit as the official application to a registrar.

model. During interviews it was found some weaknesses in existing ideas of the use of the blockchain for real estate: mostly related to the undesirable centralization and issues with security. It is clear that some standalone private companies cannot manually manage tokens, that does not bring any value, or even threaten title rights. In this sense the public authorities have more trust, however at the same time generate regulatory constraints and bureaucracy. We also found that such solution like hashing of title (deed) records in the cadastral/land registries will not significantly improve relations in the domain.

As the result of this research it is developed the concept of a high-level design of the technology, capable to manage title rights on the blockchain which includes three-level mechanism of (1) e-voting, which provides for a democratic implementation of governing algorithms; (2) Smart Laws, as the concept of high level "smart" algorithms that implement (by e-voting) existing laws related to property rights in a form of the program/protocol; and (3) smart contract templates which are based on the smart laws, that allows people to manage their title rights online.

Acknowledgments. This paper is an outcome of the PhD research performed inside of the Joint International Doctoral (Ph.D.) Degree in Law, Science and Technology, coordinated by the University of Bologna, CIRSFID in cooperation with University of Turin, Universitat Autònoma de Barcelona, Tilburg University, Mykolas Romeris University, The University of Luxembourg. Thanks to my supervisor Prof. Marta Poblet Balcell, RMIT University (Melbourne, Australia), and Pompeu Casanovas, Universitat Autònoma de Barcelona (Barcelona, Spain).

References

1. Nakamoto, S.: Bitcoin: A Peer-to-Peer Electronic Cash System. https://bitcoin.org/bitcoin.pdf
2. Nachiappan Pattanayak, P., Crosby, M., Verma, S., Kalyanaraman, V.: BlockChain technology: beyond bitcoin. Appl. Innov. Rev. **2**, 6–19 (2016)
3. Distributed Ledger Technology & Cybersecurity: Improving information security in the financial sector (2016)
4. Ethereum Project. https://www.ethereum.org
5. Nxt - The Blockchain Application Platform. https://nxt.org
6. Ethereum Wiki. https://github.com/ethereum/wiki/wiki/Glossary
7. Szabo, B.N., et al.: Formalizing and Securing Relationships on Public Networks
8. Velox.re. https://www.velox.re/
9. Surda, P.: Economics of Bitcoin: is Bitcoin an alternative to at currencies and gold? (2012). http://nakamotoinstitute.org/static/docs/economics-of-bitcoin.pdf
10. Mirkovic, J.: Blockchain Pilot Program. Final Report (2017)
11. UBITQUITY - The First Blockchain-Secured Platform for Real Estate Recordkeeping
12. Bitland. Land Title Protection Ghana. http://www.bitland.world/about/
13. Real Estate Land Title Registration in Ghana Bitland. http://bitlandglobal.com/
14. Blockchain and Future House Purchases. https://chromaway.com/landregistry/
15. Flip Blog. https://blog.flip.lease/
16. REX. The Global Real Estate Data Marketplace. http://rexmls.com/
17. Chavez-Dreyfuss, G.: Ukraine launches big blockchain deal with tech firm Bitfury. http://www.reuters.com/article/us-ukraine-bitfury-blockchain-idUSKBN17F0N2

18. Vavilov, V.: The Bitfury Group. http://bitfury.com/
19. Xinyuan Real Estate Co., Ltd. Announces Blockchain-Powered Real Estate Finance Technology Platform. https://www.prnewswire.com/news-releases/xinyuan-real-estate-co-ltd-announces-blockchain-powered-real-estate-finance-technology-platform-300299818.html
20. Antadze, L.: Bits of "Blockchain" is pointless in Govtech. https://medium.com/@lashaantadze/bits-of-blockchain-is-pointless-in-govtech-5b8044fd2d9c
21. Sharma, T.: How Blockchain Can Be Used In Escrow & How It Works? https://www.blockchain-council.org/bitcoin/blockchain-can-used-escrow-works/
22. Buterin, V.: Ethereum and Oracles. https://blog.ethereum.org/2014/07/22/ethereum-and-oracles/

Ghazal: Toward Truly Authoritative Web Certificates Using Ethereum

Seyedehmahsa Moosavi and Jeremy Clark$^{(\boxtimes)}$

Concordia University, Montreal, Canada
j.clark@concordia.ca

Abstract. Recently, a number of projects (both from academia and industry) have examined decentralized public key infrastructures (PKI) based on blockchain technology. These projects vary in scope from full-fledged domain name systems accompanied by a PKI to simpler transparency systems that augment the current HTTPS PKI. In this paper, we start by articulating, in a way we have not seen before, why this approach is more than a complementary composition of technologies, but actually a new and useful paradigm for thinking about who is actually authoritative over PKI information in the web certificate model. We then consider what smart contracts could add to the web certificate model, if we move beyond using a blockchain as passive, immutable (subject to consensus) store of data—as is the approach taken by projects like Blockstack. To illustrate the potential, we develop and experiment with an Ethereum-based web certificate model we call Ghazal, discuss different design decisions, and analyze deployment costs.

1 Introductory Remarks

The blockchain data structure and consensus mechanism has received significant interest since being introduced as the underlying technology of the cryptocurrency Bitcoin in Satoshi Nakamoto's (pseudonymous) 2008 whitepaper [25]. In 2014, Buterin presented a new blockchain based application known as Ethereum [10]. As a blockchain-based distributed public network, Ethereum implements a decentralized virtual machine, known as the Ethereum Virtual Machine (EVM), which allows network nodes to execute deployed programmable smart contracts on the Ethereum blockchain [31]. This platform enables developers to create and execute blockchain applications called *decentralized applications (dapps)* that are executed correctly according to the consensus of the network. A Dapp's code and data is stored in a decentralized manner on the blockchain. Dapps or smart contracts are now often written in a high level programming language such as *Solidity* which is syntactically similar to Java [1]. Digital smart contracts were first described Nick Szabo in 1993 [28], however they reached a high level of adoption through blockchain technology.

One application of blockchain technology that has received some research and commercial interest is the idea of replacing (or augmenting) the web certificate

© International Financial Cryptography Association 2019
A. Zohar et al. (Eds.): FC 2018 Workshops, LNCS 10958, pp. 352–366, 2019.
https://doi.org/10.1007/978-3-662-58820-8_24

model used by clients (OS and browsers) to form secure communication channels with web-servers (described in more detail below). This model has been plagued with issues from fraudulent certificates used to impersonate servers to ineffective revocation mechanisms; see Clark and van Oorschot for a survey [12]. We argue that the application of blockchains to this model is more than an interesting experiment; it is actually a new uni-authoritative paradigm that resolves some of the fundamental issues with the current model—authority and indirection. We also argue that adding programmability to a dapp-based PKI provides benefits beyond using the blockchain as an append-only broadcast channel. Finally, we instantiate our ideas in a novel system called Ghazal implemented in Solidity and deployed on Ethereum. At the time of writing, the overall system costs under $100 to deploy. Basic actions like domain registration costs under $5.

2 Related Work

The HTTPS (HTTP over SSL/TLS) protocol enables secure connections to websites with confidentiality, message integrity, and server authentication. Server authentication relies on a client being able to determine the correct public key for a server. The current web certificate model uses a system of certificate authorities (CAs); businesses that provide this binding in the form of a certificate. Client devices, through the browser and/or the operating system, are pre-installed with a set of known CAs who can delegate authority to intermediary CAs through a protocol involving certificates. When a CA issues a certificate to a web-server, there are generally three types: domain validated (DV) certificates bind a public key only to a domain (e.g., example.com), while organization validated (OV) and extended validated (EV) certificates validate additional information about the organization that operates the server (Example, Inc.).

Namecoin is an altcoin (software based on Bitcoin with a distinct blockchain) that implements a decentralized namespace for domain names [17]. The main feature of Namecoin is that for a fee, users can register a .bit address and map it to an IP address of their choice. CertCoin [14], and PB-PKI [7] are extensions to Namecoin that add the ability to specify an HTTPS public key certificate for the domain (as well as other PKI operations like expiration and revocation, which we discuss in Sect. 4.1). Blockstack [6] achieves the same goal by embedding data into a root blockchain, a process called virtualchains that could be instantiated with OP_RETURN on Bitcoin's blockchain. These approaches are closest to our own system Ghazal. These systems disintermediate CAs from the web certificate model. The main difference is that we use Ethereum to provide full programmability (motivated below in Sect. 3.2). In addition, we provide some minor improvements such as allowing multiple keys to be bound to the same domain, as is common for load balancing and CDNs.

Some research has looked at adding transparency, effectively through an efficient log of CA-issued certificates, to augment the current web certificate model. This is a very active area of research that includes certificate transparency (CT) [18], sovereign keys (SKs) [2], and ARPKI [8]. IKP [22] provides an

Ethereum-based system for servers to advertise policies about their certificates (akin to a more verbose CAA on a blockchain instead via DNS). Research a bit further removed from web certificates concerns decentralized PKIs and broader identities. While not decentralized, CONIKS provides a distributed transparency log similar to CT but for public keys (while they could be for anything, email and IM are the primary motivations) [23]. Bonneau provides an Ethereum smart contract for monitoring CONIKS [9]. ClaimChain is similar to CONIKS but finds a middle-ground between a small set of distributed servers (CONIKS) and a fully decentralized but global state (blockchain) by having fully decentralized, local states that can be cross-validated. CONIKS and ClaimChain do not use CAs but rather rely on users validating the logs, which are carefully designed to be non-equivocating. ChainAnchor provides identity and access management for private blockchains [15], while CoSi is a distributed signing authority generic logging [27]. Each of these systems is concerned with logging data (a generic umbrella that encapsulates many of these is Transparency Overlays [11]). As logging systems, they do not provide programmability which is the primary motivation for our system.

Finally, some research has explored having public validated by external parties but replacing the role of CAs with a PGP-style web of trust. SCPKI is an implementation of this idea on Ethereum [5]. Our observation is that for domain validation, a blockchain with a built-in naming system is already authoritative over the namespace and does not require additional validation.

3   Motivation

3.1   Are Blockchains a New Paradigm for PKI?

In the related work, most blockchain-approaches to identity (or specifically PKI) motivate their approach with Zooko's triangle; an articulation of three natural properties one might want from an identity system: memorable names, secure (as in hard to impersonate), and a distributed authority for issuing names. His assertion is that two of the three properties can be achieved effortlessly but adding the third is difficult or impossible. Blockchains, starting with Namecoin for domain names and extensions to PKI, are often claimed to resolve this trilemma enabling all three properties in one system. A blockchain is distributed, short human-friendly names can be claimed by anyone, and ownership over a name is secured with a strong cryptographic key.

We approach thinking about this issue a little differently. In the current web certificate model, certificate authorities are meant to be *authorities*: that is, they are authoritative over the namespace they bind keys to. The reality is that the web still runs largely on domain validated certificates [13,16] and for domain validation, certificate authorities are not any more or less authoritative over who owns what domain than you or I. Certificate authorities instead rely on indirection. For example, a certificate authority might validate a request by Alice for a certificate for `alice.com` by sending an email to `admin@alice.com` with a secret nonce that Alice must type into a webform. This involves 2 levels of indirection: (1) CAs appeal to DNS to establish the MX record of the domain (*i.e.*, the subscriber's mail server's IP address); (2) CAs appeal to SMTP to establish a communication channel to the subscriber. For each level of indirection, there are a set of vulnerabilities which might allow a malicious party to break the verification process and obtain a fraudulent certificate for a domain they do not own. For example, consider the attack surface of email-based validation:

1. **Reserved Emails:** A CA specifies a list of email addresses to receive the challenge. The underlying assumption is that only the domain owner controls this address. However the domain owner might not reserve that email address or even be aware that a certain email address is being used by one of the CAs for this purpose. And recall that just a single CA needs to use a single non-standard email address (*e.g.*, a translation of administrator into their local language) to open up this vulnerability. For example, Microsoft's public webmail service `login.live.com` saw an attacker successfully validate his ownership of the domain using an email address `sslcertificates@live.com` which was open to public registration [32].

2. **Whois Emails:** A CA also optionally draws the email address from the Whois record for the domain. A domain's whois record is generally protected by the username/password set by the domain owner with their registrar. Any attack on this password (*e.g.*, guessing or resetting) or directly on the account (*e.g.*, social engineering [3]) would allow the adversary to specify an email address that they control.

3. **MX Record:** A CA establishes the IP address of the mailserver from the MX record for the domain. As above, all domain records including the MX record is managed through the owner's account with her domain registrar. Any method for obtaining unauthorized access to this account would enable an adversary to list their own server in the MX record and receive the email from the CA.

4. **DNS Records:** If an adversary cannot directly change a DNS record, they might conduct other attacks on the CA's view of DNS. For example, they might employ DNS cache poisoning which can result in invalid DNS resolution [26]. They might also exploit an available dangling DNS record (Dare) [19]. Dares occur when data in a DNS record (such as CNAME, A, or MX) becomes invalid but is not removed by the domain owner. For example, if the domain owner forgets to remove the MX record (the IP address of the server) from DNS, the associated DNS MX record is said to be dangling. If an adversary can acquire this IP address at some future point, he is able to redirect all traffic intended for the original domain to his server, including information sufficient for a CA's domain validation process. Thus a malicious party can use a Dare to obtain a fraudulent certificate. In a uni-authoritative system, Dares are still possible (old data that has not been purged from the system) but the public keys dangle with the IP address, which resolves the security issue for mis-issued certificates.

5. **SMTP:** Once the CA establishes the mailserver's record, it will send the email to the mailserver with SMTP (the standard protocol for transfer of email). Since the email contains a secret nonce, confidentiality of this email is crucial. SMTP uses opportunistic encryption that is not secure against an active adversary. Thus a man-in-the-middle between the CA's mailserver and the ultimate destination (including an forwarding mailservers) could request a fraudulent certificate, intercept the ensuing email, reply with the correct nonce, and be issued the fraudulent certificate.

6. **Email Accounts:** Email accounts are generally protected with a username and password (over IMAP or POP3) to prevent unauthorized access. In some cases, they might be protected with a client certificate. An adversary who can gain access to any one of the accounts that should be reserved by the domain owner (*e.g.,* textttadmin, `hostmaster`, `webmaster`, *etc.*) could obtain a fraudulent certificate for that site. This could include guessing or resetting the password, using social engineering, or obtaining access to the server hosting the email for the account.

Blockchains are actually a new paradigm; they collapse the indirection for domain validation. If a PKI were added to a blockchain, who would be authoritative over the namespace of domain names? When domain names themselves are issued through the blockchain (*e.g.,* Namecoin), then the blockchain is actually the authoritative entity. Arguably, this indirection can be collapsed in the traditional web certificate model as well. There DNS (in conjunction with ICANN) is authoritative over the namespace and if ICANN/DNS held key bindings, there would be no indirection or CAs needed—indeed, this is exactly the proposal of DANE. Thus blockchains and DANE are both examples of what we might call a uni-authoritative paradigm. A deployment issue with DANE is that DNS records do not generally have message integrity (except via the under-deployed DNSSEC) whereas blockchain transactions do.

3.2   Does Programmability Add Anything?

In the related work, some systems take a uni-authoritative approach while others rely on third party authorities (generally, CAs or web of trust). Most systems that use a blockchain (or similar transparency log) do it in a passive way—as an append-only broadcast channel; a few systems actually use smart contracts or the programmability that a blockchain provides. Of all these systems, to the best of our knowledge, none are both uni-authoritative and use programmability. We have argued the merits of uni-authoritative above, what about programmability? What does it provide?

Programmability, or PKI bindings within a smart contract, can enable features that seem desirable. A few examples include: external contracts that can easily obtain information about a domain in making decisions; atomicity within domain name transfers where payments and transfers are inputs to the same transaction (*e.g.,* even Namecoin relies on a third party tool called ANTPY to perform atomic name ownership transfer transactions); and fancier options for transferring domain names: we implement an auction where any domain owner can auction off their domain within the smart contract itself. The reader might think of other features that programmability could add.

In defence of non-programmable blockchain-based PKIs, such as Blockstack, it is not clear how well a system like ours scales and what demands it puts on user clients to quickly fetch information on domains. We return to this in the next section, however we note here that we are not claiming programmability necessarily wins out in the end, only that it is worth exploring from a research perspective to better understand the trade-offs.

4   The Ghazal System

Our proposed scheme is entitled Ghazal, a smart contract-based naming and PKI uni-authoritative system.[1] It enables entities, whether they are people or organizations, to fully manage and maintain control of their domain name without relying on trusted third parties. In Ghazal, a user can register an unclaimed domain name as a globally readable identifier on the Ethereum blockchain. Subsequently, she is able to assign arbitrary data, such as TLS certificates to her domain. These values are globally readable, non-equivocating, and not vulnerable to the indirection attacks outlined above. The penalty paid for a uni-authoritative approach is that Ghazal has to carve out its own namespace that is not already in use (e.g., names ending in .ghazal like Namecoin's .bit or Blockstack's .id). OS and browsers would have to be modified before any system like this can be used. Anyone can claim a domain on a first-come, first-serve basis. Because it is decentralized, names cannot be re-assigned without the cooperation of the owner (whereas an ICANN address like davidduchovny.com can be re-assigned through administrative mediation).

The design of Ghazal consists of two essential elements. First, the smart contract that resides on the Ethereum blockchain and serves as an interface between entities and the underlying blockchain. The second primary component of the system are the clients, including people or organizations that interact with Ghazal smart contract in order to manage their domain names. Figure 1 represents the primary states a domain name can be in and how state transitions work. These states are enforced within the code itself to help mitigate software security issues related to unintended execution paths.

4.1   Exploring Ghazal Design Choices

Beyond simply presenting our design, we think it is useful to explore the landscape of possible designs. To this end, we discuss some deployment issues that we faced where there was no obvious "one right answer." These are likely to be faced by others working in this space (whether working narrowly on PKI or broad identity on blockchain solutions).

---

[1] https://github.com/mahsamoosavi/Ghazal.

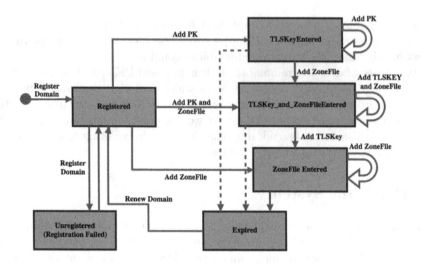

Fig. 1. Primary states and transitions for a domain name in Ghazal.

Design Decision #1: Domain Name Expiration

Typically domain name ownership eventually *expires*. Once a domain expires, it is returned to the primary market, except if the users renews it. However, expiration does not necessarily have to mean a disclaimer of ownership; there are other options.

1. **Domain names never expire and last forever.** Designing a system with no domain name expiration would be highly vulnerable to domain squatting. Domain squatting is registering domain names in speculation that the will increase in value. These domain names generally do not point to any relevant IP address (except to earn revenue on accidental visits). If domain names never expire, squatting may be significantly problematic as squatted names would be locked forever while legitimate users will end up choosing unusual names from the remaining namespace. To be clear, even without expiration, if domains are cheap, squatting is problematic (*e.g.,* Namecoin [17]).

2. **Domain names get deleted once they expire, except being renewed by the user.** The most restrictive system design is where a domain name effectively gets deleted and is returned to the registry of unclaimed names once it expires, unless the user renews it. This model has the following two issues. First, if a browser tries to resolve an expired domain, because the blockchain has a complete, immutable history of that domain, we would expect users to want it resolved according to the previous owner. Rolling back expirations is possible in a way not supported by DNS and it resolves simple human errors of forgetting to renew domains, so we do not expect browsers to necessarily fail when it could make a sensible guess as to which server their users are looking for. The second reason to drop the deletion model of expiration is that Ethereum contracts can only run when a function is called. If no one

calls a function at expiration time, the contract cannot self-execute to modify itself. The fact that it is expired can be inferred from contract if it includes a time but the contract itself will not transition states until someone calls a function that touches that particular contract. An alternative is to rely on a third party like Ethereum Alarm Clock [4] for scheduling future function calls. This is suitable only if the threat model permits relying on a trusted third party and a single point of failure (for this one feature).

3. **Control over domain names is lost once they expire, except being renewed by user.** In Ghazal, expired domains continue to function although the owner (i) looses the sole claim to that domain and cannot preserve it if someone else purchases it, and (ii) she cannot modify the domain in anyway (*e.g.,* add certificates or change zone information) unless if she first renews it. Essentially, purchasing a domain name does not entitle an entity to own it forever; expired domain names are returned back to the primary market and are available for all the users within the system. However since a full history of a domain is present, the system's best effort at resolving the domain will be to preserve the last known state. Expiration in conjunction to the amount of the fee will influence the degree of domain squatting, and having expiration at all will allow abandoned domains to churn if they are under demand.

Design Decision #2: Registration Fees

In Ghazal, new registrations and renewals require a fee. This fee is a deterrent against domain squatting. The fee amount is difficult to set and no fee will be perfectly priced to be exactly too high for squatters but low enough for all 'legitimate' users. Rather it will trade-off the number of squatters with the number of would-be legitimate users who cannot pay the fee. Namecoin is evidently too cheap and ICAAN rates seem reasonable. We leave this as a free parameter of the system. The important decisions are: (1) in what currency are they paid and (2) to whom. Every Ethereum-based system, even without a fee, will at least require gas costs. Additional fees could be paid in Ether or in some system-specific token. Since it is a decentralized system and the fee is not subsidizing the efforts of any entity involved, there is no one in particular to pay. The fee could be paid to an arbitrary entity (the system designer or a charity), burned (made unrecoverable), or to the miners. In Ghazal, fees are paid in Ether and are released to the miner that includes the transaction in the blockchain.

Design Decision #3: Domain Name Renewal

We design Ghazal in such a way that the domain owners can renew their domains before their validity period comes to an end, however they cannot renew an arbitrary number of times. Specifically, a renewal period becomes active after the domain is past 3/4 of its validity period. Renewal pushes the expiration time forward by one addition of the validity period (thus renewing at the start or end of the renewal period is inconsequential and results in the domain having the same expiration time). Requiring renewal keeps users returning regularly to maintain domains, and unused domains naturally churn within the system.

```
1   //Possible states of every auction.
2   enum Stages {Opened, Locked, Ended}
3
4       struct AuctionStruct
5       { uint CreationTime;
6           address Owner;
7           uint highestBid;
8           address highestBidder;
9           address Winner;
10          Stages stage;
11          //To return the bids that were overbid.
12          mapping(address => uint) pendingReturns;
13              //To return the deposits the bidders made.
14          mapping(address => uint) deposits;
15          //Once an address bids in the auction, its associated boolean
                    value will be set to true within the "already_bid" mapping.
16          mapping(address => bool) already_bid;
17          bool AuctionisValue;
18          }
19  //AuctionLists mappings store AuctionStructs.
20  mapping (bytes32 => AuctionStruct) internal AuctionLists;
```

Code 1.1. Implementation of AuctionStruct and AuctionLists mapping in Ghazal* smart contract.

Domain name redemption period can take different values. We experiment with a validity period of 1 year; thus, the renewal period would start after 9 months and last 3 months.

Design Decision #4: Domain Name Ownership Transfer

In Ghazal, domain owners can transfer the ownership of their unexpired domains to new entities within the system. Basically, transferring a domain name at the Ethereum level means changing the address of the Ethereum account that controls the domain. Our system offers two ways of transferring the ownership of a domain:

1. **Auctioning off the domain name.** A domain owner can voluntarily auction off an unexpired domain. Once an auction is over, the domain is transferred to the highest bidder, the payment goes to the previous owner of the domain, and the validity period is unaffected by the transfer (to prevent people from shortcutting renewal fees by selling to themselves for less than the fee). If there are no bidders or if the bids do not reach a reserve value, the domain is returned to the original owner. While under auction, a domain can be modified as normal but transfers and auctions are not permitted. To implement the auction feature, we use the fact that Solidity is object-oriented. We first deploy a basic Ghazal function without advanced features like auctions, and then use *inheritance* to create a child contract Ghazal* that adds the auction process. Using Ghazal*, a user can run any number of auctions on any number of domains he owns. This is implemented through a mapping data structure called *AuctionLists* to store every auctions along with its attributes.

AuctionLists accepts *Domain names* as its keys, and the *AuctionStructs* as the values (see Code 1.1). Using the mapping and Ethereum state machine, we enforce rules to prevent malicious behaviours *e.g.,* domain owners can auction off a domain only if there is no other auction running on the same domain. To encourage winners to pay, all bidders must deposit a bounty in Ether the first time they bid in an auction (amount set by the seller). This is refunded to the losers after bidding closes, and to the winner after paying for the domain. Without this, users might disrupt an auction by submitting high bids with no intention of paying.

```
1   modifier CheckDomainExpiry(bytes32 _DomainName) {
2           if (Domains[_DomainName].isValue == false)
3               {Domains[_DomainName].state=States.Unregistered;}
4           if (now>=Domains[_DomainName].RegistrationTime+10 minutes)
5               {Domains[_DomainName].state = States.Expired;}
6           _;
7   }
8   modifier Not_AtStage(bytes32 _DomainName, States stage_1, States stage_2)
        {
9           require (Domains[_DomainName].state != stage_1 && Domains[
                _DomainName].state != stage_2);
10          _;
11      }
12  modifier OnlyOwner(bytes32 _DomainName) {
13          require(Domains[_DomainName].DomainOwner == msg.sender);
14          _;
15      }
16  function Transfer_Domain(string _DomainName,address _Reciever,bytes32
        _TLSKey,bytes32 _Zone) public
17  CheckDomainExpiry(stringToBytes32(_DomainName))
18  Not_AtStage(stringToBytes32(_DomainName),States.Unregistered,States.
        Expired)
19  OnlyOwner(stringToBytes32(_DomainName))
20      {
21          DomainName = stringToBytes32(_DomainName);
22          Domains[DomainName].DomainOwner = _Reciever;
23          if (_TLSKey == 0 && _Zone != 0) { Wipe_TLSKeys(DomainName); }
24          if (_Zone  == 0 && _TLSKey != 0 ) { Wipe_Zone(DomainName); }
25          if (_Zone  == 0 && _TLSKey == 0 ) { Wipe_TLSKeys_and_Zone(
                DomainName); }
26      }
```

Code 1.2. Transfer_Domain function of Ghazal smart contract.

2. **Transfer the ownership of a domain name.** A domain owner can also transfer an unexpired domain to the new Ethereum account by calling the *Transfer_Domain* function which simply changes the Ethereum address that controls the domain name. The owners can also decide to either transfer domain's associated attributes (*e.g.,* TLS certificates) or not, when they transfer the domain. This is possibe with either supplying these attributes with zero or other desired values when calling the **Transfer_Domain** function (see Code 1.2).

To prevent from MITM attacks, TLS certificates should be revoked once a domain name is transferred. However, security incidents reveal that this is not commonly enforced in the current PKI. For instance, Facebook acquired the domain fb.com for $8.5M in 2010, yet no one can be assured if that the previous owner does not have a valid unexpired certificate bound to this domain [12]. This has been successfully enforced in our system as the new owner of the domain is capable of modifying the domain's associated TLS keys, which results in protecting communications between the clients and his server from eavesdropping.

Design Decision #5: Toward Lightweight Certificate Revocation
In the broader PKI literature, there are four traditional approaches to revocation [24]: certificate revocation lists, online certificate status checking, trusted directories, and short-lived certificates. Revocation in the web certificate model is not effective. It was built initially with revocation lists and status checking, but the difficulty of routinely obtaining lists and the frequent unavailability of responders led to browsers failing open when revocation could not be checked. Some browsers build in revocation lists, but are limited in scope; EV certificates have stricter requirements; and some research has suggested deploying short-lived certificates (e.g., four days) that requires the certificate holders to frequently renew them [29] (in this case, certificates are not explicitly revoked, they are just not renewed). Which model does a blockchain implement? At first glance, most blockchain implementations would implement a trusted directory: that is, a public key binding is valid as long as it is present and revocation simply removes it. The issue with this approach on a blockchain is how users establish they have the most recent state. With the most recent state in hand, revocation status can be checked. This check is potentially more efficient than downloading the entire blockchain (this functionality exists for Bitcoin where it is called SPV and is a work in progress for Ethereum where it is called LES). However a malicious LES server can always forward the state immediately preceding a revocation action and the client cannot easily validate it is being deceived.

At a foundational level, most revocation uses a `permit-override` approach where the default state is permissive and an explicit action (revocation) is required. Short-lived certificates (and a closely related approach of stapling a CA-signed certificate status to a certificate) are `deny-override` meaning the default position is to assume a certificate is revoked unless if there is positive proof it is not. This latter approach is better for lightweight blockchain clients as LES servers can always lie through omitting data, but cannot lie by including fraudulent data (without expending considerable computational work). As an alternative or compliment, clients could also take the consensus of several LES servers, although this 'multi-path probing' approach has some performance penalties (it has been suggested within the web certificate model as Perspectives [30] and Convergence [21]).

In Ghazal, public keys that are added to a domain name expire after a maximum lifetime, e.g., four days. Expiration is not an explicit change of state but is inferred from the most recent renewal time. Owners need to rerun the key binding function every several days to renew this. If an owner wants to revoke a key, she simply fails to renew. To verify the validity of a certificate, one is now able

Table 1. Gas used for operations in the Ghazal* smart contract.

Operation	Gas	Gas cost in Ether	Gas cost in USD
Register	169 990	3.56×10^{-3}	$3.15
Renew	54 545	1.14×10^{-3}	$1.01
Transfer_Domain	53 160	1.11×10^{-3}	$0.98
Add_TLSKey	77 625	1.63×10^{-3}	$1.43
Add_ZoneFile	57 141	1.19×10^{-3}	$1.05
Add_TLSKey_AND_ZoneFile	68 196	1.43×10^{-3}	$1.26
Revoke_TLSkey	37 672	7.91×10^{-4}	$0.69
StartAuction	119 310	2.50×10^{-3}	$2.21
Bid	112 491	2.36×10^{-3}	$2.08
Withdraw_bids	46 307	9.72×10^{-4}	$0.85
Withdraw_deposits	47 037	9.87×10^{-4}	$0.87
Settle	77 709	1.63×10^{-3}	$1.44
Ghazal* Contract Creation	2 402 563	0.05	$44.54

to use a LES-esque protocol. Once a user queries a semi-trusted LES node for a corresponding record of a domain, the node can either return a public key that is four days old, which user will assume is revoked, or a record that newer that the user will assume is not revoked. Although this approach requires the frequent renewal of public keys, it is a cost that scales in the number of domains as opposed to revocation checks which scale in the number of users accesses a domain.

5   Evaluation

The aim of this section is to provide the technical implementation details of our system on the Ethereum blockchain. We specifically discuss the costs related to the deployment of Ghazal* smart contract on the Ethereum blockchain in addition to executing its functions on the Ethereum virtual machine. Moreover, a smart contract analysis tool is used to analyze the security of our system against a several number of security threats to which smart contracts are often vulnerable.

5.1   Costs

Ghazal smart contract is implemented in 370 lines of Solidity language, a high level programming language resembles to JavaScript, and tested on the Ethereum test network. We use the Solidity compiler to evaluate the rough cost for publishing the Ghazal* smart contract on the Ethereum blockchain as well as the cost for the various operations to be executed on the Ethereum virtual machine. As of January 2018, 1 gas = 21×10^{-9} ether[2], and 1 ether = $882.92[3].

---

[2] https://ethstats.net/.
[3] https://coinmarketcap.com/.

Table 1 represents the estimated costs for Ghazal* (and its inherited Ghazal functionality) smart contract deployment and function invocation in both gas and USD. As it can be seen from both Table 1, the most considerable cost is the one-time cost paid to deploy the system on Ethereum. There are then relatively small costs associated with executing the functions, *i.e.*, users could easily register a domain by paying $3.15 or they could bind a key to the domain they own for a cost of $1.43, which is relatively cheap when compared with the real world costs associated with these operations.

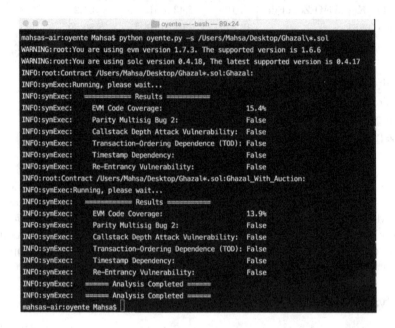

Fig. 2. Results of Ghazal* security analysis using Oyente [20].

5.2   Security Analysis

Ethereum smart contracts, in particular the ones implemented in Solidity, are notorious for programming pitfalls. As they generally transfer and handle assets of considerable value, bugs in Solidity code could result in serious vulnerabilities which can be exploited by adversaries. We use standard defensive programming approaches, in particular around functions that transfer money (such as the auction function that refunds the security deposits), by using explicitly coded state machines and locks, and by not making state-changes after transfers. We also analyze Ghazal and Ghazal* against Oyente, a symbolic execution tool proposed by Luu *et al.* [20] which looks for potential security bugs like the re-entry attack (infamously). The results of the security analysis represent that both of the smart contracts are not vulnerable to any known critical security issue (see Fig. 2).

6   Concluding Remarks

We hope that uni-authoritative systems with programmability continue to be explored in the literature. There are many open problems to work on. First and foremost is understanding the scalability issues and how to minimize the amount of data a client browser needs to fetch for each domain lookup. Blockstack has done an excellent job on this issue for non-programmable contracts. Future work could also look at the layer above the smart contract: building web tools with user interfaces to enable interaction with the underlying functions. Finally, while auctions are one illustrative example of why programmability might be added to a PKI, we are sure there are many others. The modular design of Ghazal using object-oriented programming should allow easy additions to our base contract, which we will provide as open source. Indeed, the auction itself in Ghazal* was added via inheritance and one function override (to enforce that ownership transfers, part of the parent class, could not be called during a live auction).

Acknowledgements. J. Clark thanks NSERC, FRQNT, and the Office of the Privacy Commissioner of Canada for funding that supported this research.

References

1. Ethereum development tutorial ethereum/wiki wiki. https://github.com/ethereum/wiki/wiki/Ethereum-Development-Tutorial. Accessed 12 July 2017
2. git.eff.org git - sovereign-keys.git/blob - sovereign-key-design.txt. https://git.eff.org/?p=sovereign-keys.git;a=blob;f=sovereign-key-design.txt;hb=HEAD. Accessed 10 Jan 2018
3. Godaddy owns up to role in epic twitter account hijacking—pcworld. https://www.pcworld.com/article/2093100/godaddy-owns-up-to-role-in-twitter-account-hijacking-incident.html. Accessed 13 Feb 2018
4. Home. http://www.ethereum-alarm-clock.com/. Accessed 29 Dec 2017
5. Al-Bassam, M.: SCPKI: a smart contract-based PKI and identity system. In: Proceedings of the ACM Workshop on Blockchain, Cryptocurrencies and Contracts, pp. 35–40. ACM (2017)
6. Ali, M., Nelson, J.C., Shea, R., Freedman, M.J.: Blockstack: a global naming and storage system secured by blockchains. In: USENIX Annual Technical Conference, pp. 181–194 (2016)
7. Axon, L., Goldsmith, M.: PB-PKI: a privacy-aware blockchain-based PKI (2016)
8. Basin, D., Cremers, C., Kim, T.H.-J., Perrig, A., Sasse, R., Szalachowski, P.: ARPKI: attack resilient public-key infrastructure. In: Proceedings of the 2014 ACM SIGSAC Conference on Computer and Communications Security, pp. 382–393. ACM (2014)
9. Bonneau, J.: EthIKS: using ethereum to audit a CONIKS key transparency log. In: Clark, J., Meiklejohn, S., Ryan, P.Y.A., Wallach, D., Brenner, M., Rohloff, K. (eds.) FC 2016. LNCS, vol. 9604, pp. 95–105. Springer, Heidelberg (2016). https://doi.org/10.1007/978-3-662-53357-4_7
10. Buterin, V., et al.: A next-generation smart contract and decentralized application platform. White paper (2014)

11. Chase, M., Meiklejohn, S.: Transparency overlays and applications. In: Proceedings of the 2016 ACM SIGSAC Conference on Computer and Communications Security, pp. 168–179. ACM (2016)
12. Clark, J., van Oorschot, P.: SSL and HTTPS: revisiting past challenges and evaluating certificate trust model enhancements. In: IEEE S&P (2013)
13. Durumeric, Z., Kasten, J., Bailey, M., Halderman, J.A.: Analysis of the https certificate ecosystem. In: IMC (2013)
14. Fromknecht, C., Velicanu, D., Yakoubov, S.: Certcoin: a namecoin based decentralized authentication system 6.857 class project (2014)
15. Hardjono, T., Pentland, A.S.: Verifiable anonymous identities and access control in permissioned blockchains (2016)
16. Holz, R., Braun, L., Kammenhuber, N., Carle, G.: The SSL landscape: a thorough analysis of the X.509 PKI using active and passive measurements. In: IMC (2011)
17. Kalodner, H.A., Carlsten, M., Ellenbogen, P., Bonneau, J., Narayanan, A.: An empirical study of namecoin and lessons for decentralized namespace design. In: WEIS (2015)
18. Laurie, B.: Certificate transparency. Queue **12**(8), 10 (2014)
19. Liu, D., Hao, S., Wang, H.: All your DNS records point to us: understanding the security threats of dangling DNS records. In: Proceedings of the 2016 ACM SIGSAC Conference on Computer and Communications Security, pp. 1414–1425. ACM (2016)
20. Luu, L., Chu, D.-H., Olickel, H., Saxena, P., Hobor, A.: Making smart contracts smarter. In: Proceedings of the 2016 ACM SIGSAC Conference on Computer and Communications Security, pp. 254–269. ACM (2016)
21. Marlinspike, M.: SSL and the future of authenticity. In: Black Hat, USA (2011)
22. Matsumoto, S., Reischuk, R.M.: IKP: Turning a PKI around with blockchains. IACR Cryptology ePrint Archive, 2016:1018 (2016)
23. Melara, M.S., Blankstein, A., Bonneau, J., Felten, E.W., Freedman, M.J.: Coniks: bringing key transparency to end users. In: USENIX Security Symposium, pp. 383–398 (2015)
24. Myers, M.: Revocatoin: options and challenges. In: Hirchfeld, R. (ed.) FC 1998. LNCS, vol. 1465, pp. 165–171. Springer, Heidelberg (1998). https://doi.org/10.1007/BFb0055480
25. Nakamoto, S.: Bitcoin: a peer-to-peer electronic cash system (2008)
26. Son, S., Shmatikov, V.: The Hitchhiker's guide to DNS cache poisoning. In: Jajodia, S., Zhou, J. (eds.) SecureComm 2010. LNICST, vol. 50, pp. 466–483. Springer, Heidelberg (2010). https://doi.org/10.1007/978-3-642-16161-2_27
27. Syta, E., et al.: Keeping authorities "honest or bust" with decentralized witness cosigning. In: 2016 IEEE Symposium on Security and Privacy (SP), pp. 526–545. IEEE (2016)
28. Szabo, N.: Formalizing and securing relationships on public networks. First Monday **2**(9) (1997)
29. Topalovic, E., Saeta, B., Huang, L.-S., Jackson, C., Boneh, D.: Towards short-lived certificates. In: Web 2.0 Security and Privacy (2012)
30. Wendlandt, D., Andersen, D.G., Perrig, A.: Perspectives: improving SSH-style host authentication with multi-path probing. In: USENIX Annual Tech (2008)
31. Wood, G.: Ethereum: a secure decentralised generalised transaction ledger. Ethereum Project Yellow Paper, 151 (2014)
32. Zusman, M.: Criminal charges are not pursued: hacking PKI. DEFCON 17 (2009)

Toward Cryptocurrency Lending

Mildred Chidinma Okoye[1,2] and Jeremy Clark[1(✉)]

[1] Concordia University, Montreal, Canada
j.clark@concordia.ca
[2] Deloitte, London, UK

Abstract. Lending has been posited as an application of blockchain technology but it has seen little real deployment. In this paper, we discuss the roadblocks preventing the effortless lending of cryptocurrencies, and we survey a number of possible paths forward. We then provide a novel system, Ụgwo, consisting of experimental smart contracts written in Solidity and deployed on Ethereum to demonstrate how a decentralized lending infrastructure might be constructed.

1 Introductory Remarks

Lending has been posited as an application of blockchain technology but we have seen little real deployment of lending. In Sect. 2, we discuss roadblocks and possible paths forward. We do this in service of other researchers who might want to look at this issue—we view our own contributions as an initial look and not the final word in this complex area. We outline our agenda in a few steps: (1) we review the role of lending in a modern economy, (2) we identify the key tensions between cryptocurrencies like Bitcoin and Ethereum and lending, (3) we review proposals for lending, and (4) we suggest how to move forward. In Sect. 3, we present our lending infrastructure Ụgwo which incorporates the points we discuss. Ụgwo is designed to be flexible and extensible; traditional fiat-based lending is not one-size-fits-all and consists of a patchwork of loan structures, instruments, and intermediaries. We show some basic types of loans and basic types of risk mitigation as examples of what could be added to Ụgwo to support an infrastructure for lending.

2 A Research Agenda for Cryptocurrency Lending

2.1 The Role of Lending in a Modern Economy

It is difficult to overstate the role of lending in a modern economy. Take, as an illustrative example, the role of a central bank; one of the main national institutes (along with the treasury) that cryptocurrencies aim to displace. First and foremost, a central bank is an actual bank, providing accounts for its member banks to deposit money and earn interest. Member banks provide interest-earning accounts to the public. Interest is paid to the public because banks use

© International Financial Cryptography Association 2019
A. Zohar et al. (Eds.): FC 2018 Workshops, LNCS 10958, pp. 367–380, 2019.
https://doi.org/10.1007/978-3-662-58820-8_25

the deposited money to form loans. Because central bank interest rates are low, banks prefer to lend to other banks any excess cash they hold at day's end instead of depositing them (other banks borrow to meet liquidity requirements). These loans earn interest, and central banks target this specific lending rate when they intervene in the economy. The most common intervention is the buying (circulating new money) or selling (removing circulating money) of government bonds, which are interest-earning loans from investors to the government. Central banks will also provide loans (of 'last resort') to banks unable to secure loans from other banks, typically during some sort of liquidity crisis. An economy without loans would have no interest rates, no bonds, and essentially nothing for a modern central bank to do.

2.2   Two Critical Issues for Lending with Cryptocurrencies

The crypto-economy is effectively an economy without loans. We identify two primary roadblocks:

- **Monetary instability.** While a loan might be in anything of value, it is typically done with money. Cash loans work best when the value of the money is relatively stable. By contrast, cryptocurrencies have historically appreciated in value over time (as of the time of writing). In a lending situation, this means the cash taker will end up owing far more than he borrowed. If the scenario were reversed and the currency depreciated rapidly, the cash provider would prefer to spend the money rather than locking it up in a loan where it will shed value over time. Even without long-term upward or downward drifts in value, short-term volatility adds risk to a loan for both the cash taker and the cash provider.
- **Counter-party risk.** While the hype surrounding blockchain technology centers on how it can enable trustless financial systems, there is no way to blockchain your way out of counter-party risk. If Alice truly lends money to Bob—truly in the sense that Bob fully owns it and can do with it as he pleases—then Bob can abscond with the money.

2.3   Existing Proposals

A number of companies have launched loan products or systems based on cryptocurrencies. In the most common architecture, a central company arranges loans and the loans are simply denominated in cryptocurrencies like Bitcoin. These services vary from at interest bearing accounts to peer-to-peer lending for investment purposes to social justice orientations like mirco-lending for the unbanked or the subprime market. As opposed to our system Ugwo, these do use smart contracts to structure the actual loans.

2.4   Dealing with Monetary Instability

We summarize a few suggestions for adding stability to cryptocurrencies.

- The rate of release of new currency into the system could be modified to enable new currency to be introduced at (i) a more insightful rate or (ii) based on some internal metrics of the system like number of transactions. [*Remark:* an insightful rate has been elusive despite many alt-coins customizing the schedule and it is difficult to see how metrics could not be gamed].
- A cryptocurrency can also use explicit pegging but it is no better suited to this system than standard currencies.
- A central bank could manage currency circulation while allowing other aspects to be decentralized [4]. [*Remark:* Central banks have been historically unsuccessful at using money circulation as a target [7]].
- The loan could be use the cryptocurrency as the medium of exchange but use a stable (*e.g.*, government) currency as the unit of account.

Fig. 1. Standard approaches to dealing with counter-party risk.

In Ugwo, we use the last approach. In other words, a loan could be $100 USD paid in Ether at the exchange rate at loan time and repaid 3 months later at $110 USD paid in Ether at the new exchange rate. This approach requires the smart contract to be aware of the exchange rate which introduces a trusted third party, called an oracle [11] and is discussed further in the next section.

2.5   Dealing with Counter-Party Risk

In Fig. 1, we outline the basic approaches from finance for dealing with counter-party risk.

- *Full Collateral:* It is common for Bitcoin-based solutions, *e.g.*, for fair exchange [1,3,10] or payment channels [5,9], to deal with counter-party risk by requiring full collateral. This is a simple approach but one unlikely to scale to an entire economy: economic actors are chagrinned to leave money where it earns no interest and economic benefit.

- *Repurchase Agreement:* A loan collateralized fully with same currency as the loan is not a loan therefore collateral only works if it is something different of the same value. If this something is on-blockchain (say a token representing something of value), the cash provider can have the collateral sit locked up in escrow (where it benefits neither the cash provider or taker) or could take full ownership of the collateral with the promise of returning it when the loan is repaid. This is a repurchase agreement and is common when the cash provider is perceived to be at less risk of absconding than the cash taker.
- *Partial Collateral:* The cash taker might stake something of lesser value than the loan in collateral, a third party to a loan might use partial collateral to insure a loan (see below), or sometimes loans are internal to a system such as leveraged positions in financial markets where the manager can liquidate the loan if the partial collateral (margin) dissipates due to market conditions.
- *Reputation:* A more abstract form of collateral is one's reputation and lending history. The difficulty with reputation is that it requires strong identities, something missing from decentralized currencies, as rogue entities can regenerate a new identity if the reputation of their old identity suffers and they can generate fake histories by lending to themselves with fake identities. These are not impossible to address but are difficulties.
- *Insurance:* Consider the case where Alice lends to Bob and does not trust him. If Alice trusts Carol and Carol trusts Bob, then Carol could insure the loan. Of course, Carol in this case could also just lend the money to Bob but there are a few scenarios where she might let Alice lend the money. One is if Carol's assets are not liquid. A second is that Carol might employ partial collateral: she could insure 100 loans of similar value but only stake 10% of the lent money as a margin against defaults. This costs her less than making the loans herself, and provides the cash providers insurance assuming the default rate is less than 10%. One standard financial instrument to implement this type of insurance, with some additional complexities discussed later, is a credit default swap (CDS).

3   The Ụgwọ Lending Infrastructure

Ụgwọ is an extensible system of smart contracts to enable different types of lending on Ethereum.[1] It is centred around recording credit events—when a party fails to fulfill the terms written in a loan contract—in a common ledger called a Credit Event object. We considered two implementation approaches:

- *Internal Variable.* In one approach, a loan has a credit event object within itself where the credit event is a variable contained within the loan contract. The issue with this approach is one of encapsulation: any external contract protecting the loan (via insurance or collateral) would have to reach inside the loan object when all it needs to know to function is whether a credit event occurred or not.

---

[1] https://github.com/MildredOkoye/Ugwo.

- *Object Oriented Approach.* It would be interesting if the Credit Event object sat at its own address such that protection contracts could be externally deployed and would not have to be worried about each loan that they insure individually. Protection would be external contracts and would just have a global view of all credit events from a single address given specific loan identifier (such as the loan address). To ensure compatibility, we can use interfaces which in object oriented programming specify the functions that must exist. Interfaces are similar to abstract classes in that they do not have any definition of functions contained within. An interface provides developers a guide as to how to implement the contract. Thus the Credit Event object is the core of extendable system where new loan types can be added and new protection types.

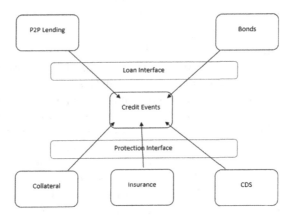

Fig. 2. The Ugwo lending infrastructure showing how the various loan and protection objects interface with the Credit Event object.

In Ugwo, we implement two interfaces: a Loan interface and Protection Interface. The Loan interface forces any loan object that would like to interact with the Credit Event object to implement certain functions that would enable the interaction. This same concept applies for the Protection Interface. These interfaces and their links to the loan objects are shown in Fig. 2.

3.1   Overview of Loan Objects

Peer to Peer Lending. We start with a basic loan contract constructed by the cash provider. The loan has parameters such as the address of the cash provider and cash taker, the principal amount to be lent, the start and end dates of the loan, the repay value and repay schedule. The cash provider runs the constructor and funds the contract. The cash taker runs a function in the loan contract to retrieve the principal in the contract. At maturity, the borrower calls a function to pay back the principal with the corresponding interest. As with all of our objects, modifiers ensure that only the stated party can run each a function in a contract, and an internal state machine governs at which phase of the contract each function can be called. If the borrower does not show up to retrieve the principal from the contract, the lender's money would remain the loan contract forever. To combat this, a kill function was implemented such that the lender can retrieve the money from the contract if the borrower does not retrieved the money after a timeout.

If the cash taker fails to pay back the loan within the timeframe, the loan object itself cannot transition states without someone calling a function. In Ụgwọ, a default function can be triggered by any person watching or monitoring the loan if the borrower fails to pay after the due term. This default function when run, updates the Credit Event object discussed below. This is how a loan moves into a default state and it relies one someone having an incentive to transition the loan (otherwise it is likely inconsequential if it sits dormant).

Bonds and Commercial Paper. We implement a simple 'zero coupon' bond. The contract uses an external library implementing EIP20 tokens.[2] The cash taker, generally an organization or corporation in this case, creates a set of tokens that represent units of cash it will accept (and later repay) from individual cash providers. The cash taker runs the constructor (with variables for start date, end date, bond value, repay value, *etc.*) and funds the contract with tokens. A function is used to accept payment from investors where tokens representing the amount borrowed is sent to the investors. The token is calculated as the value deposited over the price of the bond. An event is created that informs watchers of the contract of all bonds sold. The bond is a bearer bond in the sense that the bond contract does not track the addresses of who owns each bond. The token can be transferred from one person to another without interacting with the bond contract (however, the interaction is performed with the standard token contract). To get paid at maturity, only the token needs to be submitted irrespective of the bearer of the token. Defaults are implemented the same as in the P2P lending contract. The default function can be triggered by any person watching or monitoring the bond if the organization defaults on its payment after the due term.

3.2   Overview of Protection Objects

Collateral. Two types of collateral are defined in Ụgwọ—a token collateral and an ether collateral. A token collateral contract accepts a EIP20 token which might represent a token from a ICO, DAO-style contract, loan contract or anything else with value that the cash provider is willing to accept. The constructor function of the contract states the amount of tokens the cash taker is willing to put up as collateral. A separate function allows the cash taker to instantiate all agreements with the cash provider; they were not included in the constructor

---

[2] https://github.com/ConsenSys/Tokens.

function to allow the collateral function to be run by any investor. If at the end of the term the cash taker defaults, a function to get the token out of escrow can be run by the cash provider. The function first checks for a credit event, or triggers a credit event if the conditions for a default are met. An ether collateral accepts ether as collateral—since the loan itself is in Ether, this is useful for partial collateral functions or when the collateral is backing insurance rather than a loan.

Credit Default Swaps. A credit default swap (CDS) is an agreement between two parties (a seller and a buyer) where the CDS seller fulfils the debt of a loan to the CDS buyer if a credit event occurs on the loan. The CDS seller then takes ownership of the loan. If more there is more than one seller of a CDS per loan (as is permitted and common in financial markets for speculation), the loan is auctioned and the market clearing price is used to settle the swaps.[3] A CDS seller subsumes the same risk position as the actual cash provider in the loan but the benefit to the CDS seller is not having to liquidate any assets (she can have effectively no cash on hand if an event never happens). The benefit to the cash provider is that a loan with a CDS only defaults if both the cash taker and the CDS seller default.

CDSs have a bad reputation after the 2008 financial crisis in the United States, where the CDS market was unlit and considered by many to be under-regulated. In Ugwo, the CDS market is transparent and CDS buyers can have enforced reserves that automatically settle with CDS buyers when a credit event occurs on an insured loan. CDS sellers themselves an be given a Credit Event object. Our implementation is rudimentary (without naked CDSes, auctions, or other features) and we expect that a full-fledged, decentralized CDS market would constitute an entire research paper by itself.

3.3   Overview of the CreditEvent Object

It would be simpler to implement a CreditEvent object within each loan (P2P or Bond) contract. One reason to pull it out and make it an object of its own is to prevent redundancy in the use of code. This is a basic principle of object oriented programming. Another reason is to create a somewhat central place where all the loans can be monitored.

The simplest model of a CreditEvent object begins with a contract that holds all default variables such as defaulter's address, the lender's address and the defaulted amount. It implements a struct variable that is used to hold all the values pertaining to each loan. The contract implements the zero coupon payment model and hence has only one value for defaults. The value of the defaults could either be a string (yes or no) or a number (the amount defaulted). This contract has a constructor that is triggered by a loan contract. The major task of the constructor is to allocate memory for the loan that triggered it and set the necessary parameters (defaulter's address, the lender's address). An update

---

[3] http://www2.isda.org/.

function within the CreditEvent contract is triggered by loans to insert default value into the struct variable. A defaultlist function acts as a getter function and returns all the values within the contract. This contract by itself performs no specific action beside receiving information from loans linked to it and acting as a global table visible to different protection objects and users.

In Ugwo, each loan's constructor triggers the CreditEvent function to insert arguments such as the lender's and debtor's address. A payback function contained within the loan is triggered by the debtor in other to pay back the principal and interest. It takes into factor the state of the contract as well as the maturity date of the loan. If the amount being paid by the debtor is less than the total amount (principal and interest), the amount is paid to the cash provider and a default written to the CreditEvent contract. A value of zero is written if the amount being paid covers the total amount or is in excess (in this case, the surplus is returned to the cash taker). A report function can be triggered by anyone watching the contract if the borrower defaults on its loan. This would set the loan to a default state such that anyone watching the loan can tell that the borrower defaulted on the loan.

4   Discussion

4.1   Exploring the Use of Oracles for Exchange Rates

It is not uncommon to encounter use cases that require a smart contract to trigger or change state in response to an event external to the blockchain. For example, an insurance contract might pay farmers based on the temperature and sunlight for a given period. A hypothetical smart contract might listen for any change in the weather, parse this information from an external source such as a URL, and then trigger payments or other events based on this information. As simple as this contract might sound, it is not possible to run contracts on Ethereum this way. This is because the blockchain follows a consensus-based model that ensures all inputs can be validated. Externally fetched data might differ between nodes, some nodes may not be able to access the data due to networking issues, and the amount of gas that should be consumed by the miner for spending time fetching the data is difficult to determine objectively.

In the case of our lending infrastructure, we want to implement a loan where the unit of account for the loan is based on the value of a fiat currency. The actual loan will be in Ether but the amount owed will be based on its current exchange rate with the underlying currency. This is side-step the monetary instability of Ether which makes it unattractive for lending. Thus in nominal terms, the amount of ether being paid back might be more or less than the amount borrowed depending on whether it's value increased or decreased relative to the fiat dollar. Bonds do not only offer an investment opportunity, but they allow investors to speculate or hedge on rates of inflation.

Since contracts cannot fetch external data, a service has emerged, called an oracle, which is trusted external entity that puts data onto the blockchain where it can be accessed by other contracts. In Ụgwo, we use Oraclize[4] to feed the exchange rate of Ether with USD into our contracts. Using an oracle is not foolproof and we note a few challenges in using an oracle. The first challenge is that the price is needed at each execution of the contract. Another challenge is that in order to feed the current exchange value into the blockchain, a link to any exchange has to be manually inserted into the oracle's code; if the link goes down, the oracle will not be able to provide the appropriate data into the blockchain to be used by the miners. Finally oracles are trusted parties that can lie about the exchange rate and collude with cash takers to steal from cash providers. We remark that oracles do have a reputation and in most countries, stealing is still subject to legal recourse even if it is on a blockchain.

4.2 Automatic Actions

Many Ethereum beginners have to adjust their mental model of smart contracts to the fact that a contract will not run unless if one of its functions is called. It cannot automatically perform actions, say, after some period of time has passed. In Ụgwo, loans like bonds have a default function that checks if there has been a default by the cash taker. This default function has to be triggered by someone in order to default the loan and update the CreditEvent object. An option is to use the Ethereum Alarm Clock[5] to trigger the function monthly. It is a trusted third party service that supports scheduling of transactions such that they can be executed at a later time on the Ethereum blockchain. This is done by providing all of the details for the transaction to be sent, an up-front payment for gas costs, which would allow your transaction to be executed on ones' behalf at a later time. The drawback is its heavy integration with the loan contract, as well as arranging payments to the service. Would it be possible for an actor in the loan contract to run the function monthly in other to avoid the heavy integration and cost of using the Ethereum alarm clock? Which actor in the loan contract would have a higher incentive to run the default function? All answers point towards the cash provider. Due to the fact that the insurance or collateral can only be claimed after a default occurs, the cash provider in the contract would have more incentive to run the function every month. Hence, we did not deploy the alarm clock.

4.3 Implementing the Monthly Array Object

To implement a monthly payment, we could reference either time (*e.g.,* now or block.timestamp) or block interval (*e.g.,* block.number). Timestamps are not reliable and be manipulated by miners. This is due to the decentralization of the system; there is no wall clock for reference and node's local clocks can never be

---

[4] https://github.com/oraclize.

[5] http://www.ethereum-alarm-clock.com/.

perfectly synchronized (*i.e.*, to the millisecond). Ethereum permits a 900 ms lead or lag in time. When using block numbers, there is also a lack of precision. One could estimate that a 31 day month would be something like 179 759 blocks.[6] While this is a challenge for applications that need near real-time fidelity but for loan payments, we would argue that time slippage is not critical for loans. We utilize time not blocks. If a loan lies dormant for longer than a month, with Ethereum's model of function-initiated state changes, the loan's state will not change. However the next function to be called, whether a payment or default check, will update the previously skipped months in CreditEvent while writing the current result of the called function.

4.4   Implementing the CreditEvent Contract

Choosing an appropriate data structure for CreditEvent presented some challenges. We want loans to be individually encapsulated with the addresses of the cash provider and cash taker, and some data structure to hold a credit score for the loan (such as an array of values that indicate for each month whether the payment was repaid, late, defaulted, *etc.*). Note that it is not up to the CreditEvent object to penalize credit events. It passively records them and then protection objects can chose how to act. CreditEvent should be agnostic of what type of loan it is representing (*e.g.*, peer-to-peer, bond, *etc.*). In Ugwo, each bond is an individual loan. Protection objects, like credit default swaps, are generally written to monitor credit events across the entire issue of bonds, not just one individual bond. We leave for future work improvements to how sets of loans can be insured.

This credit history could be a struct, mapping or array. According to solidity documentation, in order to restrict the size of a struct, a struct is prevented from containing a member of its own type. However, the struct can itself be the value type of a mapping member. Following that, another way is to have a mapping to another struct outside of itself that contains the monthly defaults. In Solidity, mappings are like hash tables that are initialized dynamically with key/value pairs. Unmapped keys return an all zero byte-representation. However, it is not possible to iterate through the contents of a mapping and therefore, the best implementation was to have an array contained within a struct. In all cases, the inner container cannot be visible within the interface of the Ethereum wallet even if the outside container is made public. For example, if you implement a struct inside another struct and on, eventually the interface would give up trying to display all the subviews within it. To make the contract more developer friendly, we use getter functions to reach inside structs and expose the contents to the wallet interface.

In other to uniquely identify loans in the CreditEvent contract, when a loan calls the CreditEvent contract to pass in the initial parameters, a loan id number is created by the CreditEvent contract. This loan id number can be used by a protection object to monitor a loan. Using a loan id number creates an extra

---

[6] Blocks 4652926 to 4832685 were mined in December 2017.

variable that floats around the contract that might not necessarily be needed. A better approach is to use the loan address as a unique identifier. This way the protection object do not need to keep the loan id number of every loan they monitor as the address of the loan by itself serves as a unique identifier. This however, is not a hard rule as either a loan ID number or address can be used to uniquely identify a loan without causing any mishap in general. Even in situations where two loans are created at the same time, the id of the loans is set by the miner in the order in which they are place within the block. The interface of the Ethereum wallet for the CreditEvent object contains the parameters for identifying each loan on the CreditEvent object. The loan address is used to retrieve this information. The months which have no default are represented with zero and 300000000000000000 wei (0.3 ether) is the default amount for the second month. To pay out this default, any protection object would just need to fetch the value from the CreditEvent object.

4.5   Implementing a Credit Default Swap

A way to address counter party risk, without solving it, is to have a third party provide insurance on a loan. Such a contract is both a protection object and also introduces a new counter-party risk: that the insurer will default on paying the insurance if a credit event occurs. We implement a very simple CDS contract. The basic CDS contract is drawn up by the insurance seller who initializes agreed upon facts such as the CDS buyer, amount to be insured, premium, among others. During the payment by the CDS buyer, the function allocates space in the CreditEvent object to hold information regarding the standings of payments made to the CDS buyer.

If a default occurs on a loan that has been insured with a CDS, the default function would be run by the CDS buyer (the buyer has a higher stake and more incentive to run the function). This function would update the CreditEvent object with the balance of the loan to be paid. This is because when a default occurs, the rest of the debt is paid to the CDS buyer and the CDS seller takes over the loan (this is where the swap occurs). The idea behind this is that we wanted the CDS contract to fetch the balance of the debt directly from the CreditEvent object just as the Collateral object gets the default for the month from the CreditEvent object and pays out to the cash provider. This way the amount to be paid cannot be manipulated by either the CDS seller or anyone and the payment can be made automatically when triggered.

When the payment is made to the CDS buyer, a change of ownership occurs. This could be implemented in two ways. One way is to have a new contract created for the change of ownership where the CDS seller becomes the Lender in the loan contract. This would create a new contract which might be hard to track as it would have a new address with no relation to the old address. The other way, which we implemented, is to have the same loan contract implemented for the CDS change the owner name. This way the new owner (CDS seller) is tied to the loan contract and anyone who had the address for watching the CDS loan would be aware that a credit swap occurred. The change of ownership is also reflected in the CreditEvent object.

5   Evaluation

Our contracts were developed in Remix and tested on Ethereum's test network.

Table 1. Cost of running the basic and loan contracts

Contract	Gas	Ether	USD
Base System			
Tokens	857,106	0.018	$5.00
Token Transfer	51,501	0.001	$0.30
Oraclized	154,711	0.003	$0.90
Credit Score	462,453	0.010	$2.70
Peer to Peer Lending			
P2P Lending	2,198,423	0.046	$12.82
Receive Money	474,112	0.009	$2.77
Payback	105,827	0.002	$0.62
Report Default	60,605	0.001	$0.35
Kill	25,098	0.001	$0.12
Bond			
Bond	2,229,084	0.047	$13.00
Purchase Bond	231,397	0.005	$1.35
Withdraw	292,787	0.006	$1.71
Repay	415,213	0.009	$2.42
Report Default	55,798	0.001	$0.33

5.1   Security

Solidity (and Serpent) is notorious for security issues [2,6,8]. We made our contract resilient to the re-entrancy bug by ensuring that all checks are performed before transfers (such as, does the sender have enough ether?) and also ensuring that state variables are changed before transfers. Mishandled exceptions have the potential to allow unauthorized access to functions or result in denial of service attacks on individual smart contracts. We handle this in our contracts with the use of modifier functions that act as an access control mechanism. This allows only authorized users to access functions and also sanitizes inputs to reduce the likelihood of exceptions. Transaction-ordering dependence and timestamp dependence attacks do not break our contract due to the nature of our project. Although timestamps (as opposed to block numbers) are used in our project, our contract is not time dependent and any modification of the time by factor of 900 s by the miner will not break the contract. Last, the price for a bond in our system is fixed by the bond issuer and cannot be changed after deployment. Therefore, the contracts are not susceptible to a transaction ordering attacks.

Table 2. Cost of running the protection contracts

Contract	Gas	Ether	USD
Collateral			
Collateral	442,035	0.009	$2.58
Serve	204,509	0.004	$1.20
Get Ownership	312,667	0.007	$1.82
Cancel	27,664	0.001	$0.16
Credit Default Swap			
CDS Contract	452,035	0.009	$2.58
Monthly Premium	204,509	0.004	$1.20
Report Default	61,709	0.001	$0.16
Kill	27,664	0.001	$0.16

In order to test our system for known security bugs, we use a symbolic execution tool called Oyente [8].[7] The tool has been proved in successfully identifying critical security vulnerability, such as a famous incident called the DAO vulnerability. The various APIs used by both contracts were analyzed together simulating the exact same way it would be deployed. None are vulnerable to any of the tests.

5.2   Cost

In this section we would analyze the gas cost of using our contracts. As of this writing, the current price per gas is 21 gwei (0.000000021 Ether) while the current price of 1 ether = $277.78. For any contract, the gas cost = gas * gas price. As of this writing, it is useful to note that any transfer of ether from one account to another has a gas of 21,000, a gas cost of 0.00044 Ether resulting to $0.12 USD. Tables 1 and 2 represent the cost of running each smart contract and its functions contained therein on the Ethereum Virtual Machine. The cost of deploying the P2P lending contract and the Bond contract is roughly about $13.00 respectively. This is due to the API's called by those contracts, the more API's a contract import the more the code needed to be executed by the miners and the higher the gas consumption. In particular, the high gas consumption is attributed to the Oraclized API. However, once deployed, the cost of running the rest of the function inside the contract is less than $3.00.

5.3   Concluding Remarks

We have present Ụgwọ, an Ethereum implementation of a lending infrastructure. We use the term infrastructure because Ụgwọ is not a single system, but rather a central component (CreditEvent) with two interfaces for an extensible system,

---

[7] https://github.com/ethereum/oyente.

where new loan and loan protection techniques can be added. Future work might deploy more exotic bonds or commercial paper arrangements, or other types of protection techniques like reputation systems and repurchase agreements.

Acknowledgements. J. Clark acknowledges funding for this work from NSERC and FQRNT.

References

1. Andrychowicz, M., Dziembowski, S., Malinowski, D., Mazurek, L.: Secure multiparty computations on Bitcoin. In: IEEE Symposium on Security and Privacy (2014)
2. Atzei, N., Bartoletti, M., Cimoli, T.: A survey of attacks on Ethereum smart contracts (SoK). In: Maffei, M., Ryan, M. (eds.) POST 2017. LNCS, vol. 10204, pp. 164–186. Springer, Heidelberg (2017). https://doi.org/10.1007/978-3-662-54455-6_8
3. Bentov, I., Kumaresan, R.: How to use Bitcoin to design fair protocols. In: Garay, J.A., Gennaro, R. (eds.) CRYPTO 2014. LNCS, vol. 8617, pp. 421–439. Springer, Heidelberg (2014). https://doi.org/10.1007/978-3-662-44381-1_24
4. Danezis, G., Meiklejohn, S.: Centrally banked cryptocurrencies. In: NDSS (2015)
5. Decker, C., Wattenhofer, R.: A fast and scalable payment network with bitcoin duplex micropayment channels. In: Pelc, A., Schwarzmann, A.A. (eds.) SSS 2015. LNCS, vol. 9212, pp. 3–18. Springer, Cham (2015). https://doi.org/10.1007/978-3-319-21741-3_1
6. Delmolino, K., Arnett, M., Kosba, A., Miller, A., Shi, E.: Step by step towards creating a safe smart contract: lessons and insights from a cryptocurrency lab. In: Clark, J., Meiklejohn, S., Ryan, P.Y.A., Wallach, D., Brenner, M., Rohloff, K. (eds.) FC 2016. LNCS, vol. 9604, pp. 79–94. Springer, Heidelberg (2016). https://doi.org/10.1007/978-3-662-53357-4_6
7. Latter, T.: The choice of exchange rate regime. In: Centre for Central Banking Studies, vol. 2. Bank of England (1996)
8. Luu, L., Chu, D.-H., Olickel, H., Saxena, P., Hobor, A.: Making smart contracts smarter. In: CCS (2016)
9. Poon, J., Dryja, T.: The bitcoin lightning network: scalable off-chain instant payments. Technical report (draft) (2015). https://lightning.network
10. Ruffing, T., Kate, A., Schröder, D.: Liar, liar, coins on fire!: Penalizing equivocation by loss of Bitcoins. In: CCS (2015)
11. Zhang, F., Cecchetti, E., Croman, K., Juels, A., Shi, E.: Town crier: an authenticated data feed for smart contracts. In: CCS (2016)

Author Index

Printed in the United States
By Bookmasters